Prayer
Touching Heaven in Prayer

Cal Bodeutsch

Grace Publications, Inc.
1011 Aldon SW
PO Box 9432
Grand Rapids, MI 49509-0432
Phone: (616) 247-1999

Published by Grace Publications, Inc. PO Box 9432, Grand Rapids, MI 49509.

Scripture quotations marked ASV are taken from the *The Holy Bible*, the American Standard Version. Public domain.

Scripture quotations marked KJV are taken from *The Holy Bible*, the King James Version. Public domain.

Scripture quotations marked NKJV are taken from *The Holy Bible*, the New King James Version. Copyright© 1982 by Thomas Nelson, Inc. Used by permission. All rights reserved.

Scripture quotations marked NIV are taken from *The Holy Bible*, the New International Version. Copyright© 1973, 1978, 1984 by the International Bible Society. Used by permission of Zondervan Publishing House. All rights reserved.

Scripture quotations marked NSAB are taken from the New American Standard Bible®. Copyright © 1960, 1962, 1963, 1968, 1971, 1972, 1973, 1975, 1977, 1995 by the Lockman Foundation. Used by permission. (www.Lockman.org)

ISBN 978-0-89814-067-5

dedication

I would like to dedicate this book to those hungry souls who are seeking a greater prayer life. Your passion for prayer is really a passion for God. God will reward your earnest search for Him!

acknowledgments

Although my name is on this book as it's author, I know and you know, no one person could ever write a book on his or her own. I have read over a hundred books on prayer and I am indebted to every one of those authors. I am also deeply grateful to those who have encouraged me and supported me in the process of writing this book. Many of them have attended my "Passion for Prayer" seminars and pressed me to write down that material for future reference.

I can never thank enough those individuals who have joined with me in prayer times, putting into practice the ideas I share in this book. They prove that everything I wrote is not just theory, but actually works.

Above all, I thank God for wanting to have a deep, personal relationship with me and drawing me to himself. I am also thankful to him for allowing me, by his grace, to learn these principles, many through trial and error.

Cal

table of contents

foreword

While no book can ever be considered the all-encompassing work on any subject, this book seeks to lay a foundation that will strengthen all of its readers' prayer life. The journey of the author is obvious from his own admissions regarding his lack of adequate prayer life in the past.

On page eleven there is a quote that should disturb everyone. Philip Yancey expresses the thought that many see prayer as a burden instead of a pleasure. When Moses stood before the burning bush, God spoke to him and required Moses to remove his sandals because the ground he was standing on was holy. It was holy because it was in the presence of God. As we approach the throne of Grace in prayer, we are also standing on holy ground that was purchased for us through Jesus Christ. God instructs us to come and bring our burdens and requests, our praises and our heartaches. This is a wonderful privilege we have in Christ and should never be seen as a burden. *Touching Heaven in Prayer* is a simple, yet thought-provoking introduction to a joyful prayer life.

Scripture tells us that we do not know how to pray or what we should be praying for as we approach God. This book will begin to teach you how to pray Scripture. Prayer is not a self-centered thing. Too many people view prayer as a means to acquire perceived needs from God as though He was a large vending machine in Heaven simply waiting to hear from us. As we pray in accordance with His Word, we realize the blessings from God are real and that He does provide our needs.

Sections of this book will evoke thoughtful retrospection and tears as it drives you to your knees in search of the ability to touch Heaven and the heart of God with your prayers. A well researched book, *Touching Heaven in Prayer* is a book that needs to be read over time. The journal portions of each chapter should not be rushed through. They are a great means to self-evaluation.

Those who have read this book already have expressed their enthusiasm and desire to see it published. To that end, we offer *Touching Heaven in Prayer* for you spiritual growth and enrichment.

Pastor Timothy McGarvey
Coopersville Bible Church
Director, Grace Publications

> *Prayer is the Christian's vital breath,*
> *The Christian's native air.*
>
> James Montgomery

I was a *prayer phony* most of my Christian life and much of my ministry! It's my own fault. My mother prayed. I heard many sermons on the importance of prayer, and even preached some myself. Yes, I knew the theology of prayer, yet still I lied to people, telling them I prayed for them when, in fact, I didn't. It's not that I didn't want to pray or never tried to pray, but, to be brutally honest, prayer was boring. Though I never admitted it, I considered prayer a waste of time. (There, I got that off my chest and I'm glad I did.) He could have been referring to me when Michael M. Smith wrote, "Over and over Christians confess that the spiritual discipline they struggle with most is prayer" (Smith. 5).

Philip Yancey interviewed ordinary people with questions about prayer before writing his book, *Prayer, Does it Make any Difference?*

"Typically, the results went like this: Is prayer important to you? *Oh, yes.* How often do you pray? *Every day.* Approximately how long? *Five minutes—well, maybe seven.* Do you find prayer satisfying? *Not really.* Do you sense the presence of God when you pray? *Occasionally, but not often.*"

"Many I talked to experienced prayer more as a burden than as a pleasure. They regarded it as important, even paramount, and felt guilty about their failure, blaming themselves" (Yancey. 14).

It's not just the ordinary people in the pew who aren't praying though.

"Many leaders in the church today are not, by biblical stands, praying leaders. Two thousand pastors who attended a pastor's conference in Dallas, Texas, were surveyed regarding their prayer habits. Ninety-five percent admitted that they spent five minutes or less each day in prayer. Another survey of 572 pastors conducted by Peter Wagner revealed that pastors spend an average of eighteen minutes a day in prayer. The same survey revealed no noticeable difference between leaders' and church members' prayer habits" (Vander Griend and Bajema. 14).

In this book, my desire is to share how I journeyed from thinking prayer was a waste of time to experiencing a passion for prayer. Today, I can honestly say, prayer is the highlight of my day. I

can't wait to get together with God and talk about what's going on. I love prayer more than preaching or teaching (and that's saying a lot!). I want to share with you what I have learned that turned my prayer life completely around. My prayer is the same happens to you.

In meeting various pastors and missionaries at conferences, I found many did not pray either. They were too busy "doing the ministry" to pray. I must admit I identified with them completely. I too, was so busy doing things *for* God I had no time to be *with* God. Too often, if we don't see prayer as an action that "does something" then we pass it over for more "practical" activities.

The change in me began in the mid 1980's. Discouraged and depressed while pastoring a small church in Palm Bay, Florida, I considered getting out of the ministry again. I quit the ministry once before after doing youth work for five years in the 1970's. As far as I could see, the ministry was like preaching to a brick wall. As hard as I tried, the wall never seemed to respond. After serious evaluation I concluded I lacked the desire and the power to do anything for God. Overwhelmed with guilt and shame, I wondered, "why would anyone want me for a pastor?" But I stuffed my thoughts and feelings and continued going through the motions of serving Christ. Still, I knew something was wrong.

At the same time I met an itinerant pastor who talked about prayer like it was something exciting. He shared with me some solid biblical truths concerning prayer (many of which are in this book). God broke through my "self-sufficiency" wall and placed a desire in me to know all I could about prayer, so I too could become a man of prayer.

From then on, I bought every book on prayer I could find, not looking for more information on prayer to preach to others, but instead, personally wanting to learn how to pray. I vowed to put everything I learned into practice. Some things I discarded, for there is much misinformation about prayer. But I can say, I learned something from every book I read.

Slowly, I began to develop a prayer life. Prayer went from a *should* to a *discipline*. Then, eventually from a *discipline* to a *desire* and finally it has become a *passion*. I cannot express how much I hope my passion for prayer becomes yours, too.

Every book I have read on prayer has been incomplete. This book will be no exception. It has to be incomplete because my prayer knowledge and experience is incomplete. In the future, I would like nothing better than to write a "part two" to this book with all the new things I will learn and experience about prayer in the years to come.

If you ask me "what makes you qualified to write a book on prayer?" I would have to say, "I do not feel qualified." Perhaps that is why God has laid it on my heart to write it. I am on a journey, a journey to know God more and become like my Savior. Along the way, I have learned a few things about prayer. It is those things I want to share with you.

One of my favorite Christian writers is A.W. Tozer. He was known as the "Prophet for Today" because of his books on the deeper spiritual life. In his book *Keys to the Deeper Life,* there is a chapter entitled, "Touching Heaven in Prayer." I freely confess borrowing it for the title of this book as it precisely describes what occurs when we bow our knee in prayer.

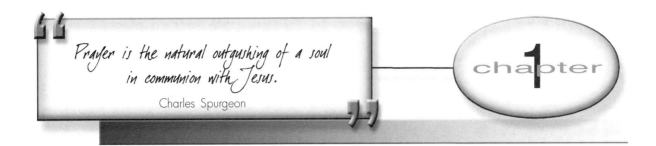

> *Prayer is the natural outgushing of a soul in communion with Jesus.*
>
> Charles Spurgeon

Building Intimacy with God

"One night recently my infant daughter fell asleep as I held her. With her head on my chest she seemed to listen to my heart beating. Gradually her squirming movements calmed until she lay quiet and relaxed. Her little body sleeping on my chest reminded me of a definition of prayer I had once heard 'Listening to the heart of God.'" (Hamma 1)

What is Prayer?

Let's start at the beginning. What is prayer? Think about it for a minute. Perhaps even jot some thoughts down on paper. In response to this question, the most common answer I hear is "Prayer is talking to God." It certainly sounds good and to a great extent is theologically accurate. In fact, for many years, this would have been my answer. That was when I considered prayer boring. Over the years, though, I think I have developed a deeper definition in my heart and life.

Some who have listened to sermons or read books on prayer might say, "Prayer is talking *with* God." Certainly this is a little better answer since it implies a two-way communication with God. My talking to God may be

boring, but God talking to me is always exciting.

But talking isn't always communicating (just ask my wife, Karen). One evening we were having a conversation where we both felt we were communicating well. Karen began. "*Tiersa,* [our oldest daughter] *is flying home tomorrow. Do you think you could pick her up?*"

"*Sure. What time does her flight get in?*"

"*It should arrive at nine o'clock.*"

Mentally I check my calendar and concluded that I had nothing scheduled at nine o'clock that evening. "*Sure. I'd be glad to pick her up.*"

The next <u>morning</u>, at ten o'clock, I received at call from Tiersa.

"*Dad, where are you? I thought you were picking me up at the airport.*"

When Karen and I discussed picking up Tiersa the night before I thought we were talking about nine o'clock at night and Karen thought we were talking about nine o'clock in the morning. We were talking but we were not communicating.

Also, not all communication leads to intimacy. Karen and I can talk about the weather, the Mariners baseball team, the price of gas and a whole number of things but never share ourselves, our feelings. Prayer is more than just "talking with God."

My favorite definition of prayer is "prayer is the talking part of the most important love relationship we can ever have, our love relationship with God." Prayer is the means whereby we enter into the presence of Almighty God and discuss what's on our minds and deep within our hearts. In her book, *Two-Way Prayer*, Priscilla Brandt wrote,

"The highest form [of prayer] that I have found is 'Two-Way' prayer—sitting comfortably in quiet meditation, taking time to come into the presence of God, and actually having God communicate with me. It is a fascinating, rewarding, and beautiful experience."

Moses had this kind of a relationship with God. *"The LORD would speak to Moses face to face, as a man speaks with his friend"* (Exodus 33:11 NIV). Who wouldn't want to know God like that?

Prayer's ultimate goal (with our heavenly Father) is to deepen our relationship —just as this is ultimately the goal in our conversations with close friends and family members. Prayer is not just an exchange of information. People have asked me, "If God knows everything, why pray?" We might as well ask, "why should I talk with my spouse" or "why should I talk with my children?" It took me a while to discover that talking to Karen, was not for the purpose of exchanging information. The goal is relationships building. With this then in mind, prayer cannot be done as a Christian obligation.

"Why have a devotional life? Why take time every single day to read the Word, worship God and pray? Let's get one thing clear from the start: We don't do it only because it is an obligation, but because it is an opportunity. Once you make your daily quiet time only an obligation, you have robbed it of being a blessing and have turned it into a potential burden. More Christians go on guilt trips over their undisciplined prayer life than

perhaps any other personal problem"
(Wiersbe 38-39).

If it is an obligation then it is something I "have to do." Where's the excitement there?

Prayer is not just asking God for things either, or even telling God what he should or should not do (contrary to a lot of prayers I have heard and a more than a few of my own).

"True prayer then is not asking in itself, but the relationship of friendship with God, in which asking and receiving is simply part of the outcome. True friendship means shared love and, therefore, shared resources, shared life, shared time and shared confidence regarding one another and regarding others…. Prayer must be real, must allow dialogue with God, not a monologue on our part. One-sided friendship is not friendship; one sided prayer is not prayer" (Hamma 30).

The purpose of prayer is to build intimacy with God. All other aspects of prayer are a by-product of that love relationship. Prayer can be as exciting and satisfying as any quality human relationship. So let's begin by looking at some of the basics of prayer.

Prayer is to be dynamic

Prayer is something so simple any child can participate in it; yet, prayer is also something so complex we could spend the rest of our lives developing it and never fully understand it. Perhaps this is true because God designed prayer to be dynamic, not static. Let me explain what I mean.

Through the course of my life, I have designed three website. In designing a website, the first question I ask myself is, "Will this be a dynamic or static website?" Static means it always stays the same. Here new people come once to get the information they need. Businesses might want a static website to introduce themselves to potential customers. They might also create a static website to advertise a product as it will always provide the description of the product.

A dynamic website, on the other hand, is designed for people to return to it again and again. To accomplish this, the information on the website must constantly change. The web pages must be updated continuously with new information or pictures, continuously changing to attract people to come back again and again.

God wants our prayer life to be "dynamic" not static. My prayer life has changed dramatically in the last twenty years. Still, I want to know more about prayer and pray more wisely five years from now than I do today. It is acceptable for a child to pray like a child, but as children mature so should their prayers.

Prayer as communication suggests that as we develop our ability to communicate more clearly, more deeply, and more honestly, our prayer life will ever be changing and growing as well. For example, Karen directs our Awana Cubbies Club in the church. I've seen her kneel down on the floor and talk eye-to-eye with those little four and five year olds. She can communicate on their level. But when she talks with me she talks on a completely different level (unless I have been acting like a four year old). Likewise, our prayers change as we grow older.

_____

_____

_____

_____

_____

_____

_____

_____

_____

_____

_____

_____

_____

_____

_____

_____

_____

I don't want to pray the same way I did as a child. I want my prayers to grow up with me.

Why pray?

There are as many reasons for praying as there are days in our lives. Each new challenge, each trial or tribulation is a new reason for prayer. Let me categorize some briefly.

1. God knows we constantly need direction as we journey through life. We make countless decisions every day. Many decisions are minor and some decisions we make without even thinking. Others will have major ramifications for years to come. How do I make those decisions? Do I write all the pros in one column and the cons in another, and then follow whichever list is longest? Does God have a will or a plan for my life? I need to pray because as I trust the Lord is all-knowing and all-wise I need God's direction for every decision I make.

2. God knows we need comfort and assurance in order to get through all of the world's trials and tribulations. I am so insecure! My name, "Calvin," literally means "bald." Figuratively, it means, "to be uncovered or unprotected." A bald man, obviously, has no natural covering on his head and therefore is unprotected from the sun's heat. I am also told, by those who know this sort of thing, 50% of heat loss comes from our head. So a bald man is unprotected in the winter too. Even my name reminds me I need God's protection, assurance, comfort and encouragement in life's trials and therefore I need to pray.

3. *God wants us to get to know him, not just know about him, but also know him.* The Christian's goal is not to just know about God intellectually. The Devil knows about God. Our goal is to know him intimately and personally. Knowing God is experiential and subjective. Knowing God is unique and special for each person. My parents know me intimately and personally from their experiences with me as their child. My wife knows me intimately and personally from her experiences with me as her husband. My friends all have different experiences with me and therefore their knowledge of me differs. The same is true with God. Your experiences with God are going to differ from mine. God and I have gone through different problems than you. God wants us to know him in relationship to our own unique lives.

4. *God desires to have fellowship with us.* This constantly boggles my mind. The very same God who created the whole universe wants to have fellowship with me? Like King David, the question often runs through my mind, *"What is man that You are mindful of him, and the son of man that You visit him?"* (Psalm 8:4 NKJV). Yet the truth is we are God's most precious creation. He loves us and desires fellowship with us. The only way we experience this fellowship with God is in prayer.

5. *Prayer is how we build our intimate relationship with God.* "Once we have been born again into the family of God, the Holy Spirit is then able to give us the understanding of how we can progressively find fulfillment in the most exciting relationship of our lives—

friendship with God" (Dawson 12). We know *about* God by reading his Word. We *know* God by praying! Intimacy and depth of prayer are related. The believer who never prays does not have an intimate relationship with God! For many years, I could speak of God intellectually, but not of him intimately. I studied my Bible *religiously*, but because I hardly ever prayed, I was missing the entire point, an intimate, personal and experiential relationship with God. Before we can discuss things like praying Scripture or becoming an intercessory prayer warrior, we must understand how intimacy with God takes place.

Building Intimacy with God

How do we build intimacy with God in our prayer life? First, since intimacy must be learned, it is a process, so there is no such thing as instant intimacy. The Apostle Paul's greatest desire was to experience the richness of this process in his life. *"That I may know Him, and the power of His resurrection and the fellowship of His sufferings, being conformed to His death"* (Philippians 3:10 NASB). Paul considered this a process on which he was still working. *"Not that I have already obtained it or have already become perfect, but I press on in order that I may lay hold of that for which also I was laid hold of by Christ Jesus"* (Philippians 3:12 NASB).

When Karen and I first met there was no intimacy, we were mere acquaintances. But as we got to know each other, we began to build a friendship. Then we spent time together. We walked and talked together. Often we would hold hands or just sit talking with each other.

Intimacy takes time. We must spend time with God in order to get to know him. Then we can build a friendship with him. Many Christians aren't friends with God, let alone intimate with him. Not everyone will take the time to become friends with God. But for those who do there is the rich reward of truly knowing God. There are some great side benefits too. *"...but the people who know their God will display strength and take action"* (Daniel 11:2b NASB). Those who know God experience God's power in their life and enjoy fruitful service for him.

Take Time to be Still

It is hard to be still! Yet intimacy with God must begin with stillness. Often people associate being still with doing nothing. And doing "nothing" is the unpardonable sin in "multi-tasking" America today. People try to cram as much into a day as possible. Have you ever noticed; the more important someone is the longer it takes to schedule an appointment with him or her. I think some people stay busy just so others will think they are important.

Busyness is the biggest enemy of godliness! We are too busy for God. We are too busy to pray and we are too busy to spend time becoming intimate with God. Pastors and church boards unwittingly add to the problem by getting people "active" in church work. If some pastor went to his board and said, "I want to do less this year so I can be more intimate with God" the board is likely to say, "then we would like to pay you less." Somehow *doing* has replaced *being* in our spiritual priorities.

God calls us to stillness. *"Be still, and*

know that I am God; I will be exalted among the nations, I will be exalted in the earth" (Psalm 46:10 NIV). King David exclaimed, *"Meditate in your heart upon your bed, and be still. Selah."* (Psalm 4:4b NASB). "True intimacy with God cannot be realized without total *quietness* of body, mind, and spirit. And that requires scheduling adequate time to be alone in His presence. An atmosphere of quietness is absolutely essential for listening prayer" (Swope 40).

Have you ever noticed how even in times of relaxation we refuse to be quiet and still? When home alone, we often turn on the TV or radio just to have noise in the background. When driving, we listen to a CD or our favorite radio station. Why do we do that? Are we afraid of being still? Are we afraid of what we might hear?

When Elijah threw a big pity party in the desert after defeating the prophets of Baal, an angel came to him. *"Then He said, 'Go out, and stand on the mountain before the LORD.' And behold, the LORD passed by, and a great and strong wind tore into the mountains and broke the rocks in pieces before the LORD, but the LORD was not in the wind; and after the wind an earthquake, but the LORD was not in the earthquake; and after the earthquake a fire, but the LORD was not in the fire; and after the fire a still small voice"* (1 Kings 19:11-12 NKJV). That's how God speaks, in a still small voice. God is not going to out-shout the other sounds that fill our life. We need the stillness so we can hear God's voice. We need to turn off the TV (probably a good idea anyway) and the radio, even the Christian station, to be still. We need periods of total quietness where we can listen to God's voice. (I'm not talking about an audible voice. We'll look at how God speaks to us today in the next chapter.)

Find Solitude

Solitude is the twin sister to silence. Often, without the one, you can't find the other. Solitude refers to a place. It is a place where you can be all alone with God. Jesus knew the value of solitude. "*That evening after sunset the people brought to Jesus all the sick and demon-possessed. The whole town gathered at the door, and Jesus healed many who had various diseases. He also drove out many demons, but he would not let the demons speak because they knew who he was. Very early in the morning, while it was still dark, Jesus got up, left the house and went off to a solitary place, where he prayed*" (Mark 1:32-35 NIV).

On the previous day, Jesus healed the sick and cast out demons. He then went to the home of Peter's mother-in-law where he healed her. Then the throngs of people started knocking on the door for Jesus to heal more people. Jesus had a busy day. The next day, he began by going to a solitary place to pray. Why not pray in the house or while walking down the road? After all, we can pray anywhere and anytime, right?

Some prayers we can pray anytime. I've prayed that simple little prayer, "Lord, help me!" when confronted with an immediate need. But this wasn't the kind of prayer Jesus needed. He sought solitude because he wanted to spend some quality and intimate time with the Father. Quick little words here and there do not build or maintain our relationship with God. Just as it doesn't in a marriage, niether does it with God.

For me, solitude means a place without a TV or telephones. It means turning the cell phone off too. Solitude must be a place without distractions. Right now, I am writing at a cousin's summer home by the ocean. Bob and Nancy have often ministered to me by allowing me free use of their "ocean home." I have used this place before for personal prayer retreats. It is the perfect place to write or pray because only a very few people know where I am or how to reach me. It's truly a solitary place and it's quite a bit bigger and nicer than a prayer closet. A prayer closet isn't good for everyone. One woman said her closet was not good for prayer because, "I look at my clothes and think of all the shoes I need to buy to go with them."

Not only did Jesus need solitude, but he also insisted his disciples have times of solitude. There was a time when Jesus sent his disciples out to minister in groups of two. *"Calling the Twelve to him, he sent them out two by two and gave them authority over evil spirits"* (Mark 6:7 NIV). Returning from this mission, the disciples were all excited about what they did and saw. But, instead of capitalizing on their momentum and starting a major campaign in the area, Jesus led the disciples into solitude. *"And He said to them, 'Come aside by your-selves to a deserted place and rest a while.' For there were many coming and going, and they did not even have time to eat"* (Mark 6:31 NKJV). A deserted place makes for a nice solitary place.

Scott Myers pastors a church in the Puget Sound area. Besides pastoring the church, he also works a full-time job. He doesn't have an office in the church, so he prepares his sermons at home. There is no solitary place at his home, nor is there one at the church, so Scott jumps into his car and drives. He just drives until he has had his intimate time with God. Sometimes he drives all the way to the Pacific Ocean, about a three-hour drive from his house.

I have several solitary places. Where we live in, the Pacific Northwest, we are one and a half hours from the mountains and two hours from the ocean. There are many wonderful spots, less than half an hour from our house that are deserted and quiet. The easiest place for me is my office, but only before the rest of the staff arrives. If I am going to my office for prayer, it is well-worth getting up a couple hours earlier for the silence and solitude.

But to be honest with you, it is not the TV, radio or other voices that distract me the most. It is the voice in my head! It is my own mind that often keeps me from experiencing silence. It took me a long time to learn to silence my mind enough to listen to God. I would day-dream a lot. (Daydreaming is a skill I learned early in school and perfected in church on Sundays.) When I tried to be quiet before God, all sorts of thoughts flooded my mind.

Just when I was ready to give it all up as a hopeless cause, I read an article on how to silence my mind, learning some very practical techniques I still use today. The first is to have my time with God first thing in the morning. I don't read the paper or listen to the radio. My mind is just getting started for the day so there are fewer things in my mind then, fewer thoughts to distract me.

Another technique which keeps me from daydreaming is journaling my times with God. During my prayer times, I have two pads of

_____

_____

_____

_____

_____

_____

_____

_____

_____

_____

_____

_____

_____

_____

_____

paper on the table before me. One pad is for writing my questions to God and recording what he says to me. The other pad is for recording distractions, like people I should call and things I need to do for the day. Once I have written them down on paper, I know I will remember them later and am then freed from thinking about them during my time with God.

"It can be a struggle to detach from the world in order to attach to God. But it's worth it to learn how to be still and know God is God…You many wish to jot down the things that distract you—errands, to run, people to call—so that you can release them for a few moments. The more you practice quieting yourself, the easier it becomes each time. It takes some discipline at first, but once you begin adjusting to God's wavelength, expect to enjoy abiding there. The quiet will renew you, not bore you" (Jan Johnson Introduction).

Quieting my mind takes patience, but I can now do it more quickly and not waste as much of my special time with God.

Surrender Everything

Nothing hinders my intimate relationship with God quicker than failing to yield some area of my life. In Hebrews 12:1-3, the writer tells us to *"lay aside every encumbrance."* I must lay aside everything weighing me down, like my will, my wants and my desires. I need to surrender things I think I need but, in fact, will only slow me down.

We all have "no-go" areas with God. These are areas of our life we are not willing to

surrender to God. It might be our *possessions*. Karen and I live in a very nice house, custom built for us by a man in the church for a lot less than market value. It has a great view. From almost any room in the house, we can look out and see ocean-going freighters and cruise ships sailing by on the Puget Sound. Beyond them is a spectacular view of the skyline of downtown Seattle with its signature Space Needle and beyond that, the Cascade Mountain range with it snow-capped peaks. On the other side of the house is a tree-filled ravine with a salmon stream trickling through its center. This is the nicest place I've ever lived, a prized possession. But failure to surrender my house—and view—to God's will, slows down my growing relationship with God. I cannot allow it to become a "no-go" area with God.

Another "no-go" area can be our *plans*. "Lord, I'll listen to you and we can have wonderful fellowship, but just don't interfere with my plans." I am amazed how many people have planned out their whole lives. They know what kind of job they want to have and how long they will have to work before they can retire. Then they know what they want to do after retirement. Some people even claim to know how much money they will have in savings when they retire. Surrendering our plans to God may mean not knowing where we will be next year. By not surrendering our plans to God, we create a big area where God can't talk to us. Our intimacy with him is blocked and our relationship is strained.

Then there is our *position*. This is a harder one for me. I started off doing youth work in Altoona, PA. It was an entry level for a young pastor. Then I worked up to Minister of Christian Education in South Gate, CA. It was a

step up in the church staff pecking order. I was the Sr. Pastor in two small churches after that. That all took over twenty years. Now I pastor one of the more prestigious churches in our fellowship. There are many pastors who would love to pastor this church. (But it's mine, all mine!!) Sorry.

A day came when I had to decide what was more important to me, my position here at the church or my relationship with God? I love this church and I love the people here (well, most of them), and I would like to stay here for the rest of my ministry. But as long as my position here was a "no-go" area with God, I could not progress in my relationship with him. It was a weight encumbering me while running the race.

Next, there are the *people*. Most of my ministry years have taken me away from being close to my parents. Now, they live within three miles of me. The kids are grown up and have moved away. But, now for the first time ever, we all live within twenty miles of each other. (Update: My youngest daughter just married and is now living half way around the world in New Zealand, thus almost ruining this illustration.) It is good to be around family. Now that I'm older, I appreciate them more than ever.

To leave this area now would mean leaving them behind. Karen and I have talked in depth about what it would mean to have God say, "I have a new ministry for you...far, far away." The view from our house is next-to-none, but we could leave it. My position in this church is comfortable and pleasing, but I do like new and exciting challenges. My plans for my career seem reasonable to me, but they're not set in concrete. All these areas, although difficult to surrender, I could leave. But what about my family? For my relationship with God to be intimate and deep, I must not hold anything back from him.

Pray According to God's Will

We cannot build intimacy in prayer with God if we are praying outside God's will. But how can I pray according to God's will, if I can't accept his will in an area of my life I am withholding from him? Christ told his disciples *"If you abide in Me, and My words abide in you, ask whatever you wish, and it shall be done for you"* (John 15:7 NASB). This is not a blanket promise saying God would give the disciples anything they prayed for—there was a condition. They had to abide in him and his words had to abide in them. It is just another way of saying they must pray according to God's will. We can't abide in Christ and desire what is contrary to his will. Our communication with God will fail if we are on different wavelengths. Thus, it is most important to know the will of God.

Pray in Faith

God says *"...and whatever is not from faith is sin"* (Romans 14:23b NASB). Faith believes God, it is an assurance of the heart and mind that God can and will do what he has promised (Romans 4:20-21). Faith is not telling God what we want him to do and then believing he will do it. That is presumption, not faith. Faith is total assurance that God has a plan and a purpose for each part of our lives and trusting that he will work out each detail for our good and his glory.   The certainty of faith is

always based upon God's faithfulness to do what he has promised, not just what we want. Faith must be a part of our prayers. If we pray but don't believe God will keep his promises to us, then we can sin even in our prayers.

Pray Patiently

My prayer life is nothing like it was fifteen years ago, but the changes have been slow in coming. I have had to learn to be patient allowing myself time to grow in my prayer life. But I am not a patient man. I want everything and I want it right now! I have had to learn to "put on" a prayer principle and tried it for a while. See if it worked. Sometimes I didn't see any change right way, but as time passed, God used it in my life. I also have had to learn God has his own schedule. I wanted a great prayer life right now, but God knew I couldn't handle it if he gave me everything at once. Allow God time to change your prayer life and take it one step at a time.

1. For the next half hour, find a solitary and quiet spot.

2. Begin by telling God honestly where you are in your prayer life and where you would like to be.

3. Tell God your expectations and ask for God's strength to accomplish them.

4. Read through the main points of this chapter and discuss them with God.

5. Leave times of quietness between the different points for God to direct your heart and mind.

6. Write down any thoughts, questions and ideas that come to you during this time.

7. Is there anything you feel God is asking you to do?

8. Are there any decisions you need to make?

9. If you find yourself daydreaming or your mind wandering, write down what it was you found yourself thinking about.

Discussion questions for this chapter.

1. What would be a better definition of prayer than just "talking to God" or "talking with God?"

2. What does it mean to have a *dynamic* prayer life?

3. How has prayer helped you discern God's will in a particular decision you needed to make?

4. How has God shown you that you need his protection and comfort?

5. How has God used life's trials and tribulations to encourage you to know him better?

6. When have you had real fellowship with God?

7. What does intimacy with God look like?

8. How much "still time" do you have in your life now? Why?

9. Where can you go to find solitude?

10. Do you have any practical ways to quiet you mind?

11. Do you have any "no-go" areas with God? Why?

12. How do you know if you are praying against God's will?

13. What is your definition of faith? How does it apply to your prayer life?

14. How long are you willing to work on developing a better prayer life?

chapter 2

> *Speak LORD, for your servant hears.*
>
> 1 Samuel 3:9

Does God Still Speak?

I don't like to talk. That may seem strange coming from one who has taught and preached an average of five times a week for over 30 years. All the same, I would rather listen to an intelligent conversation than talk. When I listen, I learn. The same is true in prayer.

The exciting part of prayer is not me talking to God, but God talking to me. I *need* to listen to God for his wisdom and power. I also *enjoy* listening to God. Nothing compares to hearing God's clear voice. No, I don't hear audible voices, but the inaudible voice of God is just as clear as anyone else's audible voice. I never tire of going to God with a question or problem and knowing his thoughts by the end of my prayer time.

So how does God speak today? Put a (1) for "Absolutely," a (2) for "Maybe" or a (3) for never next to each way you think God speaks to us today.

____ From His Word
____ His Spirit to our spirit (inaudible voice)
____ Audible voice of God
____ Music
____ Other Christians
____ Sermons, Bible studies, Christian teaching

____ Visions and dreams

____ Word of wisdom

____ Word of knowledge

____ Mediums, Spiritualists, Horoscopes, Tarot Cards

Most Christians give the first, "From His Word" a "1" and the last, "Mediums, Spiritualists, Tarot Cards and Horoscopes" a "3." There is a great deal of disagreement on the others. My purpose is not to agree or disagree on the questionable methods but to show how God speaks to us today in the one way on which we all agree, "From His Word."

In this chapter, we will examine one of the three major Scripture passages addressing the topic of God speaking to us today. It is found in 1 Corinthians 2:9-16. Let's begin by considering what this passage teaches. *Attention! This study is the basis for everything else in the book; so don't go on until you have mastered this chapter.*

THE PROBLEM

A universal problem is presented first. "*But as it is written: 'Eye has not seen, nor ear heard, nor have entered into the heart of man the things which God has prepared for those who love Him'*" (1 Corinthians 2:9 NKJV). We are unable to see or understand "something" through our visual senses. We cannot perceive the "something" through our physical ears. Also, our heart, the seat of all our desires and imaginations cannot comprehend this "thing" either. The eyes and ears represent our physical sensors. The heart represents our emotional sensors.

Most people process information and make

sense of their surroundings by analyzing what their physical sensors pick up. When meeting someone, we make initial judgments based on what our eyes, ears and sometimes noses indicate to us. We rely heavily on our physical sensors.

On the other hand, my wife, Karen, relies on her emotional sensors. She has "intuition." Once we entertained a person in our home who, according to my physical sensors, seemed to be a godly Christian. After this person left our house, my wife said to me, "I don't trust that man! I don't know what it is but something isn't right with him." Her evaluation was not based on her physical sensors, but her emotional sensors. As it turned out, her emotional sensors were more accurate than my physical ones.

But neither my physical sensors nor Karen's emotional sensors are able to comprehend something very important, *"the things which God has prepared for those who love Him."* What is it God has prepared for us? These are God's plans, purposes and will for us. They include the good works mentioned in Ephesians 2:10. *"For we are His workmanship, created in Christ Jesus for good works, which God prepared beforehand that we should walk in them"* (NKJV). These are the things God has already planned and prepared for us.

"The things which God has prepared for those who love Him" is more than just the big picture. It is more than being saved by grace through faith and having an eternal inheritance awaiting us in heaven some day. It also includes the day-by-day plans, purposes and will of God for us, the hundreds, if not thousands, of decisions we must make every day.

If God did not speak to us, then we could never know God's will in these matters.

THE SOLUTION

Having introduced the problem, God now reveals the solution. *"But God has revealed them to us through His Spirit. For the Spirit searches all things, yes, the deep things of God"* (1 Corinthians 2:10 NKJV). These things, which we cannot know through our physical and emotional sensors, God chooses to reveal to us utilizing the indwelling Holy Spirit.

Have you ever wondered why the Holy Spirit indwells us? It wasn't because heaven got too crowded and the Holy Spirit had to find somewhere else to live. God gave us the Holy Spirit for important purposes and one is so he can reveal to us the day by day plans, purposes and will of God.

The Holy Spirit knows the deep things of God. It is his responsibility to seek out the depths of the Father's wisdom and then share them with us. The Holy Spirit has to do this because we can't. *"Oh, the depth of the riches both of the wisdom and knowledge of God! How unsearchable are His judgments and His ways past finding out!"* (Romans 11:33 NKJV). Were it not for the Holy Spirit's ministry within the believer, we could never know God's will. But because the Holy Spirit is God, he knows the complete and perfect will of God, and reveals it to us.

We cannot know, through our natural senses, what God wants us to know and therefore, cannot feel what God wants us to feel nor do what God wants us to do. But God has revealed them to us by his Holy Spirit, who searches out and utters to us the depths of God's wisdom and knowledge. Therefore, we must live our lives in response to what the Holy Spirit reveals to us and not by our visible circumstances. *"For we walk by faith, not by sight"* (2 Corinthians 5:7 NKJV). The word "sight" in 1 Corinthians 2:9 is the same word used in 1 Corinthians 2:9, translated "eye has not *seen*." We must live the Christian life by faith's insight, not natural physical sight.

I think one of the biggest secrets within Christianity today deals with the Holy Spirit's working. While we all acknowledge the Holy Spirit's work within the believer, few can give accurate details on *how* the Holy Spirit does it. Many are like my doctor who tells me I need to lose weight, but fails to come through on the how. Preachers tend to be long on the "what" and short on the "how" also. Every Christian needs to know about and experience the Holy Spirit's working within them. *"For it is God who works in you both to will and to do for His good pleasure"* (Philippians 2:13 NKJV). We cannot know, desire or do God's good pleasure apart from the Holy Spirit. We are totally dependent on the Holy Spirit to reveal it to us.

Having stated this important truth, the Apostle Paul now seeks to prove his point. To do this he begins submitting evidence. Each piece of evidence is a logical point that builds upon the previous. Each point when taken alone isn't conclusive, but put them all together and Paul proves his case.

POINT ONE - THE SPIRIT OF MAN AND THE SPIRIT OF GOD

To make sure we understand how the Holy Spirit is able to perform this ministry, God goes

into details. *"For what man knows the things of a man except the spirit of the man which is in him? Even so no one knows the things of God except the Spirit of God"* (1 Corinthians 2:11 NKJV). There is only one who knows, really knows, a person and it is that man himself. We can fool those around us. I have heard it said, "We are all three people." The person we pretend to be, the person we want to be and the person we are. We can get good at pretending to be a "spiritual" Christian when in fact we are harboring secret sins. Others may not know the real me, but I am faced with the real me everyday. No one knows me as well as I know myself.

In the same way, we cannot know God's thoughts because we are not God. Only God can really know himself. Because the Holy Spirit is God, he knows God completely. (One side note here: This is a great proof text on the trinity: the Holy Spirit is God because the Holy Spirit knows God.)

POINT TWO - THE SPIRIT OF THE WORLD AND THE SPIRIT OF GOD

The next verse speaks of the world's wisdom. *"Now we have received, not the spirit of the world, but the Spirit who is from God, that we might know the things that have been freely given to us by God"* (1 Corinthians 2:12 NKJV). The "spirit of the world" is the way the world perceives and understands things. The world's spirit is not from God and it cannot enable us to understand his wisdom and knowledge. It is the "Spirit who is from God," the Holy Spirit, whom the Father gave to us to reveal his wisdom.

Notice the words, "might know" in verse

12.   They imply a choice. This wisdom does not come automatically. We must do something to make it happen, and that is to make a choice.   In the Greek, "might know" also means to continue to know, and the word "freely" comes from the same root word meaning "grace."   If we put it all together we get, "God has given us the Holy Spirit so we can see and keep on seeing, the things God wants to give us by his grace."

Did you know God has secrets? These are truths we cannot know unless God reveals them to us. The Apostle Paul called the truths concerning the church, the body of Christ, "a secret" (Ephesians 3:1-6). God kept these truths secret until he chose to reveal them to Paul. In the same way, God has secrets he wants to reveal to us. Once revealed, we can act upon that knowledge. Moses told the children of Israel, just prior to their entering the Promised Land, *The secret things belong to the LORD our God, but those things which are revealed belong to us and to our children forever, that we may do all the words of this law"* (Deuteronomy 29:29 NKJV). The context is Israel's but the principle is universal. Some truths God has not revealed to us. These are the secret things. But some truths God does reveal. These belong to us. These have to do with the purposes, plans and will of God for us. When God reveals his will to us then we are to do all he asks. But first, God must reveal truth.

Some people think God has to be coaxed into revealing his will. Only after long hours of prayer and fasting will God grudgingly reveal his will to us. Nothing could be further from the truth. *"Thus says the LORD who made it, the LORD who formed it to establish it (the LORD is*

His name): 'Call to Me, and I will answer you, and show you great and mighty things, which you do not know'" (Jeremiah 33:2-3 NKJV). God desires to answer our questions. God wants to reveal to us the things we could not know unless he showed them to us.

POINT THREE - THE HOLY SPIRIT AND THE MINISTRY OF THE WORD

I have a favorite saying. "The Holy Spirit of God, uses the Holy Word of God, to create the holy child of God." When God speaks to us, through the Holy Spirit, he uses the Word of God. *"These things we also speak, not in words which man's wisdom teaches but which the Holy Spirit teaches, comparing spiritual things with spiritual"* (1 Corinthians 2:13 NKJV). When Paul refers to "these things we also speak" he is bringing to their attention the things he told the Corinthians either in person or in a letter. These words were the "thing freely given by God," the result of his grace.

Paul's words weren't *"taught by human wisdom."* Paul didn't come up with these words on his own. They were not a part of Paul's natural wisdom and knowledge but rather were revealed to him by the Holy Spirit. Even though Paul was now writing these truths to the Corinthians, the Holy Spirit was the source. Paul is illustrating the fact that spiritual truth must come from the Holy Spirit.

The Holy Spirit reveals *"spiritual thoughts with spiritual words"* (NIV). The Holy Spirit first gave the thought to Paul and then Paul taught it with his words. Paul gives credit to the Holy Spirit's ministry for knowing God's mind.

_____

_____

_____

_____

_____

_____

_____

_____

_____

_____

_____

_____

_____

_____

_____

_____

_____

_____

POINT FOUR - THE NATURAL MAN

"But the natural man does not receive the things of the Spirit of God, for they are foolishness to him; nor can he know them, because they are spiritually discerned" (1 Corinthians 2:14 NKJV). I would think many of you readers are very knowledgeable in the Scriptures. So I feel I need to clear up a few misconceptions before getting to the point. First, the natural man is not synonymous with being unsaved. Nowhere, in the passage's context has God addressed the unsaved individual. The contrast is between the natural mind (the mind without the Holy Spirit's input) and the mind enlightened by the Holy Spirit of God. The natural mind would include the unsaved but is not limited only to them. It would also include the believer who lives his or her liFe apart from the Holy Spirit's leading.

Second, the "things of the Spirit" may be revealed to me through other means, not directly from God's Word. The Apostle Paul has just stated "the things of the Spirit" are the wisdom and knowledge given by the Holy Spirit to the believer. God speaks to me through sermons, Christian music, books written by Christians and the wise counsel of godly believers. It doesn't have to be just when I have my Bible open and am one-on-one with God. The Spirit can speak thought a wide spectrum. But, eventually it goes back to God's Word as the source of truth.

The "natural man" corresponds to the "eyes and ears" in verse nine. Once again Paul states God is not revealing his will, purposes and plans to us through the things we can perceive with our eyes and ears. This includes any person, male or female, saved or unsaved, apart from the Holy Spirit's working. It is not saying the unsaved cannot know doctrine or theology. But rather, no one, saved or unsaved, can understand or receive the things the Holy Spirit wishes to reveal to him or her, unless the Holy Spirit reveals them.

The reason we cannot receive them is "*they are spiritually discerned*." This word "discerned" means to investigate and make a determination. For us to understand *"the things of the Spirit of God"* we must allow the Holy Spirit to lead us. The Holy Spirit investigates the Father's mind, makes the determination as to what his specific will for our situation is and then reveals it to us. He knows the Father's mind, knows what is right and best and reveals it to us.

POINT FIVE - WE CAN HAVE THE MIND OF CHRIST

Paul is now beginning to wrap up his argument. *"But he that is spiritual judgeth all things, and he himself is judged of no man"* (1 Corinthians 2:15 ASV). The word "judgeth" here is the same word "discerned" in verse 14. The Spirit-led believer investigates and discovers the "Holy Spirit given" determination in every situation or problem in life. This is how we know God's mind and will.

No one else can investigate God's mind and determine what is right for us. Only the Holy Spirit, within the believer, can reveal God's will for them. No person or organization can control us by claiming to know God's specific will and plan for us. This must come personally from the Holy Spirit.

Then we can know the mind of Christ. *"For who has known the mind of the LORD that he may instruct Him? But we have the mind of Christ"* (1 Corinthians 2:16 NKJV). Who can know the mind of Christ? This is not a rhetorical question with a "no one" answer. The answer is the one Paul has been giving all along. The answer is, only those to whom the Holy Spirit reveals the mind of God.

Can we instruct God? This part of the verse puzzled me for years. The Greek word for "instruct," means, "to drive together." So the question really is, *"For who has known the mind of the Lord the he may drive together with him?"* Who can take a drive with God? It is really a question of unity. *"Who has known the mind of the Lord that he may walk in unity with him?"* We can't teach God, but we can walk in unity with him as the Holy Spirit leads us.

"But we have the mind of Christ." This is the end result of the Holy Spirit revealing to us God's plans and purposes in every situation of life. We do not have to guess what God's will is; he wants us to know. Paul told the Philippians, *"Therefore let us, as many as are mature, have this mind; and if in anything you think otherwise, God will reveal even this to you"* (Philippians 3:15 NKJV). This is a promise made to believers who are allowing the Holy Spirit to reveal God's will. God will reveal his mind to those who seek it.

The Holy Spirit of God uses the Holy Word of God to produce the holy child of God! When the Holy Spirit is free to reveal the Father's mind, then God's Word accomplishes its intended purposes. *"All Scripture is given by inspiration of God, and is profitable for doctrine, for reproof, for correction, for instruction in righteousness, that the man of God may be complete, thoroughly equipped for every good work"* (2 Timothy 3:16-17 NKJV).

FINALLY - THE BIG POINT!

What does this have to do with prayer? Everything! If all our prayer time is spent talking, then we won't hear the Holy Spirit's voice revealing God's will. We need to listen for the Holy Spirit's voice! *"For as many as are led by the Spirit of God, they are the sons of God"* (Romans 8:14 KJV). Who exhibits God's character? Only those who allow the Holy Spirit to lead them! Who maintains an ongoing, intimate relationship with the Father? Those who listen to the Holy Spirit!

Like Samuel of old, God sought time after time to speak with me, but I did not hear his voice (1 Samuel 3:1-10). I never said, "Speak, for thy servant is listening." I was too busy talking. I didn't hear God's voice because I never expected God to speak to me. So I never listened.

HOW TO LISTEN TO GOD

1. Ask God questions

Often I begin my prayer time by asking God a question. It might be, "What is the next step you want me to take in my ministry or in my relationship with Karen?" Or it might be, "What do you want me to do today?" Some- times it is "Lord, is there anything in my life not pleasing you?" Quite often it is, "What do you want me to do about this problem I'm facing?" There are endless possibilities of questions to ask God.

2. Ask God to lead the prayer time

Sometimes I think everything is about me. I come to God with my agenda, the things I want to talk about with God. But I am sure God has an agenda too. There are some very specific things he wants to discuss with me. Things like my sins! So I start off my prayer times by saying, "Father, you lead my prayer time. You bring up the topics you want us to discuss." God never fails to get to the real issues in my life. Often the topic is one I never would have chosen. Sometimes it deals with issues I am not even aware of yet. I have learned it is always better to follow the Holy Spirit's leading in prayer rather than try to force him to follow my leading.

3. Pray with open eyes and an open Bible

God speaks, primarily or secondarily, through his Word, the Bible. I usually ask God to lead me to the passage of Scripture he has for me that day. Don't limit God here! Sometimes a verse comes to mind. Those who have memorized Scripture have a distinct advantage. Sometimes a Scripture reference will come to mind. You may not know what 1 Chronicles 26:18 says, but that particular reference comes to your mind. Look it up. It may be the Holy Spirit's leading. I have had God place a desire in my heart to read a certain book in the Bible. It might be a gospel or a minor prophet but God has always had something there to say to me. Finally, if nothing else is coming, just open your Bible up at random and start reading. My God is big enough to have my Bible open to just the right spot!

4. Write down what God says to you

Write down what God says to you so you won't forget it. Write it down so you can refer back to it later. God always has a reason for speaking to us. It may have to do with a problem in your life. You may not see the connection right away so write it down. I keep notebooks, recording what God says to me. I have quite a stack of them now. It is always interesting to go back and see how God has led me in the past. Not only does it bring confidence in God, but it also encourages me to keep praying. I have a short memory, so writing down what God says helps me remember it later.

5. Pray back what God has revealed

Think of a conversation with a friend. They say something about a particular subject. What do you do? You don't change subjects without responding to what they've said! You say something back to them about that subject. When God says something to us, he expects us to respond back to him about that subject, not just quickly change the subject. Perhaps he wants us to agree with him. Maybe he wants us to look into our hearts and see if we see the same thing he sees. How we respond back to God will be the subject in future chapters.

OBSTACLES TO LISTENING TO GOD

As I have taught this material in seminars and retreats around the country, I have heard people express doubts about "hearing God's inaudible voice." Let me respond with four

misunderstandings and get them out of the way.

1. "The Holy Spirit won't speak to me."

The problem here is a lack of faith. Often, because one has never heard God's voice in the past, they conclude it can't happen now. But the truth is, God wants to reveal his will and plans for you. This is why we have taken so much time in this chapter to lay the biblical foundation. As you have just read, God says his Spirit wants to talk to our spirit. It is biblical and God will do it if you let him.

2. "How can I determine if it is God's voice or Satan's?"

This problem is as old as the Garden of Eden. The first words Satan spoke to Eve were to cast doubt on what God said. "Now the serpent was more cunning than any beast of the field which the LORD God had made. And he said to the woman, "Has God indeed said, 'You shall not eat of every tree of the garden'?" (Genesis 3:1 NKJV). An individual in Florida told me Satan tried to deceive her by saying it would be his voice she heard, not God's. Jesus said, "The watchman opens the gate for him, and the sheep listen to his voice. He calls his own sheep by name and leads them out. When he has brought out all his own, he goes on ahead of them, and <u>his sheep follow him because they know his voice</u>" (John 10:3-4 NIV). We can discern Satan's voice from God's because God's voice is always consistent with his Word. God never contradicts himself.

3. "Am I just projecting my wants and desires upon God?"

I must confess this is true for me sometimes. This is why my relationship with God must be kept up to date. If I am quenching the Holy Spirit's working, then the only voice I am going to hear is my own. Again I go back to Jesus' words. "Then Jesus said to those Jews who believed Him, 'If you abide in My word, you are My disciples indeed. And you shall know the truth, and the truth shall make you free'" (John 8:31-32 NKJV). God's own promise is if we abide in the Word, we will know the truth.

Only God's Word can distinguish between my "soulish" thoughts and God's "spiritual" thoughts. "For the word of God is living and powerful, and sharper than any two-edged sword, piercing even to the division of soul and spirit, and of joints and marrow, and is a discerner of the thoughts and intents of the heart" (Hebrews 4:12 NKJV). The Word cuts through, distinguishes between, what I want and what God wants. It can reveal the source of the "thoughts and intents of the heart."

4. "This is too 'mystical' for me."

Men and women of God, who have sought to know God in deeper and more intimate ways are usually branded as "mystics." Within the general group called "mystics," there are some whose views of the Holy Spirit's leading and guidance are very distorted. J.I Packer describes them this way.

"Their basic mistake is to think of guidance as essentially *inward prompting by the Holy Spirit, apart from the written Word*. This idea, which is as old as the false prophets of the Old Testament...is a seed-bed in

which all forms of fanaticism and folly can grow" (*Knowing God* 212).

There are mystics who seek the Holy Spirit's leading apart from the anchor of God's Word, and then there are mystics who seek the Holy Spirit's leading through God's Word. When we allow God's Word (which is Holy Spirit inspired) to be the means through which the Holy Spirit speaks, then we are always on solid ground. If that makes one a mystic, then count me in.

The most exciting time of the day is my time spent with God. I talk; He talks; I respond to him; and He responds to me. There is nothing like it! Does this sound exciting to you? Prayer is no longer boring for me. My prayer is that you will "try it out." Take a test drive and see if God won't take you places you have never been before.

1. For the next half an hour, quiet your mind and listen for God's voice from His Word.

2. Pray, "God, I can't do this but you can. I desire to listen to you. Direct me in your Word where you want to speak to me. Help me identify your voice."

3. If a Scripture passage comes to your mind, start reading there. Otherwise, just start reading in the Bible until there is a verse or statement you can't seem to get past. Focus on that statement or verse.

4. Write down what you feel God is saying to you from the passage.

5. Thank God for meeting with you today.

chapter 2

1. How has sin affected our prayer life?

2. What can't we know from our natural senses? Why?

3. What is the spirit of the world? What can't it do?

4. What does it mean to "have the mind of Christ?"

5. Jot down a list of questions to ask God. Do you expect God to answer them? Why?

6. How would the type of prayer mentioned in this chapter differ from your usual experiences in prayer?

7. Which of the four obstacles mentioned in this chapter expresses a concern of yours? Why?

He appointed some of the Levites to minister before the ark of the LORD, to make petition, to give thanks, and to praise the LORD, the God of Israel.   1 Samuel 3:9

chapter 3

The Purpose of Personal Praise

Think of the word "worship." What images come to your mind? Most people immediately picture singing in church on Sunday. Certainly this can be worship. But have you ever thought about worship as an everyday activity? "If in public a person really does worship, how can he content himself with only a weekly experience when such a glorious and satisfying God can be experienced in private worship all throughout the week?" (Whitney 98). What we do in worship on Sunday should be an extension of what we do all week long on our own. But how can we worship without a hymnal or PowerPoint® presentations? Don't we need someone to lead us in worship? Well, we do have someone to lead us in worship all week long. His name is the Holy Spirit.

The word "worship" literally means "to ascribe worth." Anything which ascribes worth to God is considered worship. The Old Testament word for worship means to bow down, like one would in front of royalty. So worship does not have to be something we say, it can be an action too. The definition I've settled upon is, "Worship is a lifestyle which declares God's glory both in private and public life." Worship is more than just singing songs.

God has called us to a lifestyle of worship. Anyone who worships only on Sunday morning is missing the boat!

Living a godly life is worship. The Apostle Paul wrote, "I beseech you therefore, brethren, by the mercies of God, that ye present your bodies a living sacrifice, holy, acceptable unto God, which is your reasonable service" (Romans 12:1 KJV). The New American Standard Translation of the Bible translates "your reasonable service" as "your spiritual service of worship." Therefore, anything we do, public or private, which declares God's glory is worship. So what does it mean, "to declare God's glory?"

"God's glory consists of his attributes and power" (Vine's Expository Dictionary of New Testament Words). So if we are declaring anything about who God is or what he has or is doing, we are declaring his glory. We have a good example of verbal worship in the book of Revelation. "The twenty-four elders fall down before him who sits on the throne, and worship him who lives forever and ever. They lay their crowns before the throne and say: 'You are worthy, our Lord and God, to receive glory and honor and power, for you created all things, and by your will they were created and have their being'" (Revelation 4:10-11 NIV). Here, the elders declare the glory of God in his creative acts and power to sustain all life. They declare he is worthy of worship and speak of his glory, honor and power.

But worship can be more than a verbal expression on our part. Because God is the Almighty God and therefore is worthy of our service, acts of Christian service can be worship. I say "can be" because service one does for personal gain or recognition does not reflect the glory of God and therefore would not be worship. If we are doing them for self, then we are not doing them for God.

Because God is holy and has called us to live a holy life (Romans 12:1), living a holy life can be worship. Again, I say, "can be" because if we are trying to live a holy life in our own strength, then we are not reflecting the holiness of God. Only Holy Spirit empowered holiness reflects the holiness of God and therefore is worship.

Singing songs which focus on an attribute of God or on God's power can be worship as well. Why only "can be?" If the song expresses a personal awareness of that attribute of God then it is worship. But, as is so often the case, we can sing a worshipful song without even thinking about the words, or with no personal experience of what the words express. Sometimes the words are light years away from our personal experience. I have sung songs like "More Love to Thee O God" when loving God was the last thing on my mind. That is not worship.

Worship focuses on God, not me. For our private worship to truly be worship, it has to focus on God. Focusing on our needs or the needs of others is not worship. Often we get caught up on the everyday tasks and they become our focus. We pray for comfort and convenience and forget to worship God for his provision. If our everyday focus were on God instead of us, we would worship a lot more.

Worship is an exciting part of prayer. Some days I spend my whole prayer time in worship. I never fail to leave those times of prayer feeling uplifted and excited about my relationship with God.

An important part of worship is praise. Praise, when directed toward God, declares his glory. There are several Old Testament words that are translated "praise" in our English Bibles. One word means to "hold out the hand" as in worshiping God with extended hands. Another word means, "to speak or sing," another "to boast about God." Praise can mean, "bowing down, giving thanks or "touching strings, as on a musical instrument." One word for praise means, "to celebrate." Have you ever thought of praise as resembling a celebration? Think of a victory celebration when a team wins the Super Bowl or World Series. Would such an image describe your praise? Writing on prayers of praise, Earl F. Palmer states,

> "Prayers of praise are called the Hallel prayers. The most famous prayer word that is used in the Old Testament is the Hebrew word *hallal*, which means 'magnify, boast, shout.' This is a word of excitement and joyous urgency. When 'hallal' is combined with the holy name for God—'Yahweh'—it becomes the Hebrew word Hallelujah. We find 'Hallelujah' frequently in the Psalms and it is translated in our Bibles as 'Praise the Lord'" (Palmer 32).

The New Testament words for praise have the ideas of speaking well of someone and celebrating in song. Again, there is that idea of celebrating. King David is my idea of a man who knew how to praise God. He danced before the Lord. "David, wearing a linen ephod, danced before the LORD with all his might" (2 Samuel 6:14 NIV). He even took

off his outer garment (their equivalent of a suit coat and tie) so to be unrestricted in his praise. David loved to praise God and called on others to praise him too. Listen to the words of the Psalms.

"I will give thanks to the LORD because of his righteousness and will sing praise to the name of the LORD Most High" (Psalm 7:17 NIV).

"I will be glad and rejoice in you; I will sing praise to your name, O Most High" (Psalm 9:2 NIV).

"Sing praises to the LORD, enthroned in Zion; proclaim among the nations what he has done" (Psalm 9:11 NIV).

"I call to the LORD, who is worthy of praise, and I am saved from my enemies" (Psalm 18:3 NIV).

Notice how closely praise fits our definition of worship, "A lifestyle which declares God's glory both in private and public life." Praise, directed toward God, declares the glory of God. When we praise God, we are talking to him, not just about him. We say things like, "You are faithful" or "You are full of love." Songs we sing directly to God are "praise songs," i.e. "I worship you, Almighty God." Songs we sing that are about God are affirmations of faith and belief, i.e. "Holy is the Lord." Both are worship.

What is the purpose of worship and praise? Is it something we do for our benefit? No, we praise him because he is worthy to be praised. Yet, how many times do we look at a worship service for what we can get out of it?

_____

_____

_____

_____

_____

_____

_____

_____

_____

_____

_____

_____

_____

_____

_____

_____

_____

_____

If we got nothing out of a service, but offered up our sincere praise to God, then we have worshiped and God is pleased. Paul Billheimer stresses this point.

"Here is one of the greatest values of praise: it decentralizes self. The worship and praise of God demands a shift of center from self to God. One cannot praise God without relinquishing occupation with self. Praise produces forgetfulness of self—and forgetfulness of self is health" (Billheimer 118).

"We should praise the Lord because God loves praise and He seeks worshipers…Praise is important to God; every time you praise Him, you are fulfilling one of the deepest desires of his heart…We should praise the Lord because we were made to bring him pleasure, and praise pleases him"(DeMoss 211-212).

God desires our praise so we praise him and not just on Sunday mornings. "Through Jesus, therefore, let us continually offer to God a sacrifice of praise — the fruit of lips that confess his name" (Hebrews 13:15 NIV). We are to praise him all the time, not just when we gather together on Sunday. Sunday mornings we do corporately what God desires we do individually all week long.

Some of the best guidance we could ever discover is found right in God's Word. Let's just consider Psalm 9:1-2. "I will praise you, O LORD, with all my heart; I will tell of all your wonders. I will be glad and rejoice in you; I will sing praise to your name, O Most High." (NIV). What do we learn about praise from these two verses?

1. "I will praise you, O Lord with *all my heart.*" God wants wholehearted worship. Our focus is to be on him alone. This is easier said than done in a culture that teaches us to put our needs and ourselves at the very center of everything we do. It takes a great amount of diligence to make worship 100% about God. When we take time to praise and worship God, we need to turn off the cell phone and beeper, close our eyes if necessary, so all of our focus is on him. When we praise God it is to be with all our heart not just our lips. God is not pleased with halfhearted worship. There are times when I halfheartedly listened to Karen. She knows it and she is not pleased. The same is true with God.

2. *"I will tell* of *all* your wonders." First, worship is not passive; it is participatory. Just listening to Christian music is not worship. To listen is passive; to worship is active. There are times in a church service when I stop singing and start praying the words of a song to God because singing can be passive when my mind isn't focused on what we are singing. Second, our worship and praise tell of all God's wonders. In order for us to participate in this we have to consciously be looking around to see what God is doing in our own lives, in the lives of those around us, in our church body and in our world. If life is all about me, I won't even know what to praise the Lord for, because I won't know what he's doing. Again, the focus is on God, his attributes and his actions. This is true praise and worship.

3. "I will be *glad* and *rejoice.*" I don't see how we can praise God without being joyful. I come from a Christian heritage where worship

is slow and more on the quiet side. I'm not advocating chaos in the worship service, but I've encouraged my congregation to express gladness and joy more often. Celebrations are marked with joy and gladness. When did you last celebrate something? When your team won the Super Bowl? The birth of a child? The 1980 winter games where the USA hockey team took the gold metal? Chances are, unless you are extremely emotionally damaged, you were loud and your body language expressed happiness. When we worship and praise God, it should be done joyfully with body language that naturally reflects the state of our heart and what we are expressing with our mouths.

4. "*I will* sing praises." "I will," means making a conscious decision. It is making a choice to do something. I am amazed at how many Christians do not sing in church. They excuse themselves by saying they "don't like the song" or they are "not good singers." I would be willing to bet they don't do much praising God during the week either. A joyful heart wants to sing. When I am full of joy, I can't help but sing (or at least hum). I think the real reason some people don't sing is there is no joy in their life and there is no joy because they have focused their thoughts and attention on their own problems rather than on God's attributes and actions. Real praise and worship produces joy which in turn causes us to want to praise and worship God more. It's so cyclical. We are to sing praise because God delights in our praise. We do it for him, not for us!

Praise and worship must be an important part of our prayer life. It is another area where we can receive the Holy Spirit's aid. We can ask the Holy Spirit to reveal to us specific things for which we can praise God. The Holy Spirit might lead us to a portion of Scripture that illustrates one of God's attributes. We can use that Scripture then as a catalyst for praising God for how that attribute of God has been evidenced in our own life. The Holy Spirit can also remind us of things God has done for us. As a place to begin, we can praise the Lord for the gift of our salvation. But God didn't stop blessing us when we got saved.   The Holy Spirit might lead us to think about a victory we have had over temptation. That's a reason to praise God! Or perhaps the Holy Spirit will bring to mind a difficult time when he was your strength.

When I want to praise God, I often pray through a Psalm. I do this for several reasons. First, I am reminded to pray for things that I would otherwise skip. David praised God for everything. As I pray through a Psalm, I see the things for which David praises God and then I praise God for them, too. Second, praying through a Psalm helps me to pray according to God's will. This, of course, can be true for praying through other Scriptures as well. We will study this further in another chapter. Third, praying through a Psalm helps me greatly to personalize Scripture.

David talked with God about everything. Just as he shared his fears with God, so can I. As David journeyed to the point where he could say, "But I will trust you God," I can be brought to that same point as I pray through a Psalm. Fourth, praying the Word of God brings me closer to the One who wrote it.

"Learning to pray Scripture—communicating with God in His own words—has revolutionized the way I pray. It leads me into

intimate worship and communion with God. It gives me a fresh, new, and exciting vocabulary to express my heart to the Lord" (Butts 53).

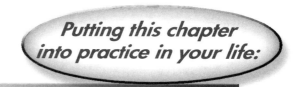

1. For this assignment, pick a Psalm, any Psalm. Go ahead pick one now. (I bet you didn't pick Psalm 119.)

2. Read through the Psalm slowly. Spend time on each praise, meditate on it and pray it back, out loud, to God in praise.

3. Focus on praising God for who he is (his attributes) and what he has done (his works).

4. Don't ask for anything for yourself or anyone else.

Here is a second assignment to help you turn listening to Christian music (which is passive) into praise and worship (which is active).

1. Pick a tape or CD with Christian music that is primarily praise oriented.

2. As you listen to the music, start praying back to God, out loud, the words of the song. Don't worry about missing some lines while you are praising God. Just go on to the next line you hear.

3. Focus on praising God for who he is (his attributes) and what he has done (his works).

4. Don't ask for anything for yourself or anyone else. Keep the focus and attention on <u>God</u>, not yourself and what you can get out of it.

1. Define worship. How do you worship during the week?

2. In what way does our attitude affect worship?

3. It what way does culture influence our concept of prayer?

4. What is the purpose of worship and praise?

5. Why is God not pleased with "halfhearted" praise?

6. What are some of the benefits of praying Scripture?

Praying Scripture

When I was a child, I saw the Bible as a book of stories. Throughout Sunday School and Vacation Bible School I learned about Noah, David and Goliath, Jonah, Jesus and the feeding of the 5,000, etc. When I went to Bible college, the Bible became a book of doctrines about bibliology, soteriology, ecclesiology and eschatology, etc. It was a book I had to study out of necessity in order to pass a quiz or exam. When I graduated from Bible college, I thought I knew the stories and doctrines pretty well. Then, as a Pastor, the Bible became a source of sermons and Bible lessons. I had to study it for applicable lessons to pass on to my congregation. It was many years later; I discovered God gave me the Bible for a much greater purpose. God wanted a relationship with me and the Bible is his means of communication with me.

Adam and Eve had no Bible. They "walked with God in the cool of the day" enjoying direct communication and communion with God. But by willful disobedience, they forfeited that relationship with God. So God gave us his Word, both in written and living form, to bring us back into a personal relationship with him. But a relationship necessarily

requires communication. Without it, a relationship cannot grow. Prayer and God's Word are critical in that communication process. <u>Prayer</u> is a portal into heaven so that we might touch God. <u>The Bible</u> is the living and active Word that speaks to my needs. "For the word of God is living, and active, and sharper than any two-edged sword, and piercing even to the dividing of soul and spirit, of both joints and marrow, and quick to discern the thoughts and intents of the heart" (Hebrews 4:12 ASV). The Word is living because of the ongoing ministry of the Holy Spirit speaking through it.

In the previous chapter, we used Scripture to give direction to our praise and worship. Now, we want to focus on using Scripture to direct our petitions to God. By praying Scripture, we are using God's own promises as the basis for our prayers. There is much less of a chance that we will pray selfishly when we pray God's Word. There is a much better chance we will pray according to God's will.

Prayer Power

Could this describe your prayer life?

"I used to have dazzling quiet times. I sat on my bed, holding my four-part prayer notebook as if it were a cherished artifact. Pulling back the tab marked 'adoration,' I peered at a list of forty words that described God and picked three to praise God for. Moving on to the tab marked 'confession' I mulled over another forty-word list of faults, especially those I'd underlined in red: laziness and grouchiness. Racing on to 'thanksgiving,' I skimmed a list of

twenty items I felt thankful for including friends, relatives, books, and—to be especially spiritual—God Himself. I remember the day my quiet time died. After gathering all my devotional props, I settled into a terrible emptiness. I needed God as I had never needed Him before, but my regimented prayers were puny containers for my anguish" (Johnson 7-8).

God never intended for prayer to be a religious formality without power. To the early Jewish church, James wrote, "Therefore confess your sins to each other and pray for each other so that you may be healed. The prayer of a righteous man is powerful and effective" (James 5:16 NIV). This passage seems to imply some prayers are "powerful and effective" thus others would have to be "powerless and ineffective." So the question arises: Why are some prayers more powerful and effective than others and how can my prayers be more powerful and effective?

I love Tony Evans! If you aren't familiar with him, he has a ministry called "The Urban Alternative." He has some great videos and whenever they come out with a new one, I buy it and show it to my adult Sunday School classes. In a couple of his videos he makes this statement, "The physical and visible world is controlled by that which is invisible and spiritual. If you want to change that which is visible and material you must first deal with that which is invisible and spiritual." That is what prayer does. When we make petitions for ourselves and others, we are dealing with the invisible and spiritual world. Therefore, we need to know what we are doing. How do we pray

correctly? How can our prayers be powerful and effective?

The Prerequisite

Before we can do battle with the invisible forces of evil, we must be strong. "Finally, be strong in the Lord and in his mighty power" (Ephesians 6:10 NIV). We need spiritual strength, not the energy of the flesh, which is limited and temporary at best. We need the power that only God can provide. We need supernatural power if we are going to take on the principalities and power of the Wicked One. Our prayers must have supernatural power behind them. That means the Holy Spirit must be involved in our prayers. He is "the Spirit of power" (2 Timothy 1:7).

We have already seen that we need the power of the Holy Spirit to reveal to us God's plans, purposes and will, because we cannot discern those through our natural senses. The same principle applies to our prayer life as well. God's power always comes to us through our personal weakness. "But he said to me, 'My grace is sufficient for you, for my power is made perfect in weakness.' Therefore, I will boast all the more gladly about my weaknesses, so that Christ's power may rest on me. That is why, for Christ's sake, I delight in weaknesses, in insults, in hardships, in persecutions, in difficulties. For when I am weak, then I am strong" (2 Corinthians 12:9-10 NIV). As long as I think I can pray in my flesh, I will have no need to go to God for his strength. The power to pray according to the will of God must come from humility and honesty that says, "I need the power of God in my prayer life."

Only then can God give the grace of his power. "But he gives us more grace. That is why Scripture says: 'God opposes the proud but gives grace to the humble'" (James 4:6 NIV).

Many Christians never get past the prerequisite state in their prayer life. They never admit they don't know how to pray. Therefore, they do not seek God's strength to overcome this weakness. The result is a powerless and unexciting prayer life—and they stop praying. If prayer has no power, then it is a waste of time. That is a conclusion I came to at one time in my life. It is the conclusion many Christians have come to as well and, as a result, we stopped praying.

The Preparation

Ephesians 6:11-17 commands us to put on the whole armor of God. Each piece is listed and explained in spiritual terms. I have heard many sermons on the "armor of God" and preached some of my own. Many of them miss the point completely. I've heard some preachers say the way we put on the armor is to pray, "Lord, I'm putting on the breastplate of righteousness, etc." Others teach we put on the armor by asking God to put the armor on us. The whole armor terminology is just a human illustration that would have helped Christians of the first century understand better how we prepare for battle with Satan and his hosts.

The point is, if we are going to do battle with the invisible and spiritual forces of life, we need to be living a surrendered and holy life. Truth and righteousness must be ever present in our lives. We must live out the gospel of

peace. We must believe God's truth, not Satan's lies and that the Holy Spirit is going to use the Word of God to defeat the Devil. Until these truths are present in our daily lives, we are not prepared to go to battle. You don't go into battle when you are still putting on the armor. Powerful prayer must be preceded by spiritual preparation.

The Battle

If putting on the armor is the preparation for battle, then what is the battle? Paul sets forth our part in spiritual warfare next. "And pray in the Spirit on all occasions with all kinds of prayers and requests. With this in mind, be alert and always keep on praying for all the saints" (Ephesians 6:18 NIV). First of all, we are to pray in the Spirit. This is important. If we are to have powerful prayers, we must pray in the Spirit. But what does it mean to "pray in the Spirit?" We are going to examine this in detail in the next chapter. But for now, we know a couple things. First, it will involve the Word of God because Paul has just said the sword of the Spirit is the Word of God. Second, it will involve the Holy Spirit's work within us. We saw in chapter two that God gave the Holy Spirit to us to reveal to us the plans, purposes and will of God.

This doesn't sound to me like we can go to God and pray any old thing we want. God never condones careless praying. There is a right way to pray and a wrong way to pray. People don't like to hear that. I get more people upset with that statement than just about anything else I can say. People don't want to believe it because then they will have to work at praying instead of rattling off meaningless phrases to God in their prayers. But if "praying in the Spirit" is the right way to pray, then not "praying in the Spirit" is the wrong way. This is all I'm going to say about "praying in the Spirit" right now, or I'll ruin the surprise in the next chapter.

The Apostle Paul gives us more details on the battle in 2 Corinthians. "For though we live in the world, we do not wage war as the world does. The weapons we fight with are not the weapons of the world. On the contrary, they have divine power to demolish strongholds. We demolish arguments and every pretension that sets itself up against the knowledge of God, and we take captive every thought to make it obedient to Christ" (2 Corinthians 10:3-5 NIV). Prayer is the warfare where we seek to change the physical and visible world by affecting the spiritual and invisible world. Again prayer is cloaked in "battlefield" terminology.

How do we seek to make real change in situations or people? Verse five lays out two different strategies. First is the world's way. By "the world's way" Paul is referring to the way the unsaved, and Christians who walk according to the world, seek to make change. Their way has no spiritual dynamic. They argue and dispute (2 Timothy 2:4; Philippians 2:14). The result is strife, division, jealousy, wrath and factions (1 Corinthians 3:3; Galatians 5:20). This wisdom of the world (James 3:14-16) is powerless. It cannot destroy strongholds, which are the root problems.

In verse 5 Paul explains strongholds. Strongholds are "arguments and every pretension that sets itself up against the knowledge of

God." The King James version of the Bible uses the word "imaginations." I like that. What are imaginations? They are something that can seem real but have no actual substance. Imaginations exist only in our minds. In this context, they are incorrect reasons or thoughts. They are thoughts contrary to God's truth, thoughts which oppose God's truth. They are lies of Satan. The mind is the battlefield where God's truth and Satan's lies vie for our acceptance. The one that wins will control our thoughts and attitudes and ultimately our actions.

Everybody makes decisions according to some thought process. We have reasons for every decision we make. But sometimes people make decisions based on wrong information. Those decisions cause behavioral problems. To change the behavior problem they must go back and change the false information. This is the foundation of counseling. Some counselors make big bucks helping people find out where their thinking went wrong, leading to a life of addiction of some sort. But they had better have the right information to give their patients if they want them to be truly free.

Where does this incorrect reasoning that "sets itself up against the knowledge of God" come from? It comes from "The Liar." Jesus spoke of him when condemning those that opposed him in his earthly ministry saying, "You belong to your father, the devil, and you want to carry out your father's desire. He was a murderer from the beginning, not holding to the truth, for there is no truth in him. When he lies, he speaks his native language, for he is a liar and the father of lies" (John 8:44 NIV). God is the author of truth; Satan is the author of lies.

When Satan appeared to Eve in the Garden of Eden, it was to cast doubt about what God had said was true. And he continues even today to cast doubt on what God says is true. When God says we can trust him, Satan tells us we can't. Satan is the ultimate source of every "argument and every pretension that sets itself up against the knowledge of God." Spiritual warfare is a battle for truth.

Over a period of time, the individual believing the lies of Satan will develop a stronghold or fortress of lies. Lie upon lie believed by Christian and non-Christian alike, become like bricks of a wall, until they become an almost impenetrable stronghold. Spirit led prayer is the only thing that can tear down these strongholds.

The Desired Result

The ultimate goal in tearing down strongholds is found in 2 Corinthians 10:5; "we take captive every thought to make it obedient to Christ." Instead of imaginations that are against the knowledge that comes from God, we are to have thoughts that are in conformity to and in submission to Christ. In prayer, we attack the lies of Satan by replacing it with the truth. Now, where can we find "truth" to pray that will contrast Satan's lies? How about in the Word of God? When interceding for others who are being held captive by the lies of Satan, I have found nothing more powerful than praying Scripture on their behalf. Praying the Word of God is powerful!

How many weapons do we have against Satan? For many years I thought I only had one weapon, that mentioned in Ephesians.

Prayer
Touching Heaven in Prayer

Personal Thoughts

73

"Take the helmet of salvation and the *sword of the Spirit*, which is the word of God" (Ephesians 6:16 NIV). Our one offensive weapon is "the Word of God." But one day, I read about "weapons" (plural). "The <u>weapons</u> we fight with are not the weapons of the world. On the contrary, they have divine power to demolish strongholds" (2 Corinthians 10:4 NIV). We have more than one weapon in our battle against Satan. What is the other weapon? It is prayer! If we put these two weapons together by praying the Word of God, we are the strongest in our fight against Satan. Then we are utilizing both of our weapons at the same time.

In the early Jewish church, there arose a problem about the care of certain women. The Apostle's solution was to pick certain men to make sure the physical needs of the believers were being taken care of correctly. Then of themselves they said, "and we will give our attention to prayer and the ministry of the word" (Acts 6:4 NIV). Often this is thought of as two ministries, preaching and praying. But the word for preaching is not used here. It is the "ministry of the Word." The Word "ministers" in prayer as it attacks the lies of Satan. When we pray the Word of God, as led by the Spirit, we are using the "Sword of the Spirit." It is the truth of the Word of God that tears down the lies of Satan. Since "praying in the Spirit" is the way we do battle, it only makes sense to pray the Word of God. Many times my prayers are almost exclusively praying back to God his Word. Again, I have never found a more powerful way to demolish strongholds in my mind than praying Scripture as it reinforces in prayer the truths that contradict the lies I am believing.

I believe God looks for, and the church needs more, men and women like Epaphras. He, too, was an intercessor. *"Epaphras, who is one of you and a servant of Christ Jesus, sends greetings. He is always <u>wrestling</u> in prayer for you, that you may stand firm in all the will of God, mature and fully assured"* (Colossians 4:12 NIV). Did you notice he "wrestled" in prayer? That certainly seems to fit with, *"For we do not <u>wrestle</u> against flesh and blood, but against principalities, against powers, against the rulers of the darkness of this age, against spiritual hosts of wickedness in the heavenly places"* (Ephesians 6:12 NKJV). Epaphras was a prayer warrior. Interceding on behalf of others, He prayed against the lies of the Devil. The purpose was so that other believers might *"stand firm in all the will of God, mature and fully assured."*

Since Spirit led intercessory praying is the way we defeat Satan, then we can understand why Satan would want to make sure our prayer life and the prayer life of the church is ineffective. "Satan would not be a good general, he would not be a good strategist unless the prayer life could be destroyed. A church is as powerful as its prayer life. The men and women who learn the secret of reaching the throne, getting the ear of God, become dangerous to the hosts of darkness" (Kenyon 140). I never said it would be easy, but it is worth the battle.

A Call to Prayer

Max Lucado, in his book *In the Grip of Grace*, wrote, "God has enlisted us in his

navy and placed us on his ship. The boat has one purpose—to carry us safely to the other shore. This is no cruise ship; it's a battleship. We aren't called to a life of leisure; we are called to a life of service. Each of us has a different task. Some…are occupied with the enemy, so they man the cannons of prayer and worship."

The Enemy is having a field day, because very few are manning the cannons of prayer anymore. Christians believe the lies of Satan and continuously build strongholds of vain imaginations.

How do we pray Scripture?

There are many books dealing solely with praying Scripture. Beth Moore's book, *Praying God's Word, Breaking Free from Spiritual Strongholds,* is one of the best. (The introduction to her book confirmed for me the truth of what I believe about praying Scripture and wrote in this chapter.) If you want more details, I recommend her book and books like hers. But briefly let me tell you how I pray Scripture. I ask God to take me to the Scriptures that speaks the truth about a situation with which I am dealing. I confess I need the Holy Spirit's aid in knowing what to pray. What I am looking for is a verse or passage of Scripture that will expose a lie of Satan I have believed. I follow the same format you used in the "putting this chapter into practice in your life" in Chapter two. God may bring a passage of Scripture to my mind. Or he might impress on me a reference in the Bible. A lady, who attended one of my "Passion for prayer Semi-

nars," said, "It's like I can see a Bible reference written on a chalk board in my mind." God is not limited to just one way of leading us to the truth he has for us. Just ask God to show you how to pray for a situation and then go the Word of God and let the Holy Spirit do his work.

To help us pray Scripture individuals have written books placing Scripture in topical order. Then going one step further, some have changed the wording of the verses into a prayer format. In her chapter on "Overcoming Despair," Beth Moore takes Jeremiah 29:11 and turns it into the prayer, "For you know the plans you have for me, Lord. Plans to prosper me and not to harm me, plans to give me a hope and a future." By personalizing the verse, she has made it into a verse to be prayed back to God. *Prayers that Avail Much*, volumes 1, 2 and 3 do the same. (Although some of the prayers completely twist the original meaning of the passage, which can lead to praying against God's will.) If the Holy Spirit reveals a root problem about a situation such as unbelief, pride, insecurity, depression, etc. then these books can take you directly to the Scriptures that deal with that particular subject. They are already in a prayer format, which makes praying them really easy.

Here is a sample from *Prayers That Avail Much* on praying against pride in yourself or someone else. This is a good example of how to pray Scripture.

"Father, I pray for _____, that they might choose to be clothed with humility. May they choose to renounce pride and arrogance. Father, You give

_____

_____

_____

_____

_____

_____

_____

_____

_____

_____

_____

_____

_____

_____

_____

grace to the humble. Therefore, may they allow themselves to be humbled under Your mighty hand, that in due time You may exalt them.

Father, in the name of Jesus, may _____ choose to refuse to be wise in their own eyes, but may they choose to fear You and shun evil. May they humble themselves and submit themselves to your Word that speaks . . . exposes, sifts, analyzes, and judges the very thoughts and purposes of their heart. May they choose to test their own actions, so that they might have appropriate self-esteem, without comparing themselves to anyone else.

Father, may they choose to listen carefully and hear what You are saying to them. May they incline their ear to wisdom and apply their heart to understanding and insight. Humility and fear of You bring honor and life.

Father, may they choose to hide Your Word in their heart that they might not sin against You. As one of your chosen people, holy and dearly loved, clothe them with compassion, kindness, humility, gentleness and patience that they might bear with others and forgive whatever grievances they may have against anyone. May they desire the peace of Christ to rule in their heart, and be thankful for Your grace and the power of the Holy Spirit."

This whole prayer is taken directly from the Word of God. If you want to check it out, go to 1 Peter 5:5-7; Proverbs 3:3-8; 22:4; 2:2; Psalm 119:11; Hebrews 4:12; Colossians

3:12-15; Galatians 6:4-5; and Matthew 6:10.

When I come across a verse of Scripture that deals with an issue in my life (like humility), I will stop and pray that truth for myself. This tears down the stronghold of pride in my life (or at least removes one of the bricks). Then I will ask the Lord, "for whom else can I pray this truth?" As names come to my mind, I pray the same truth for them that I prayed have for myself.

Other times a person comes to my mind for whom I believe God wants me to pray. But I don't know what to pray for them so I ask God to take me to a verse or passage of Scripture that would be appropriate to pray for them. Sometimes God leads me to more than one passage. This, of course, takes time. I might pray an hour and only pray for one or two people. The next chapter will deal more with intercessory prayer. So let's stop now and do the practical application section to this chapter.

1. For the next half an hour, longer if you want, pray Scripture passages.

2. Ask God to reveal the truth that is contrary to a lie in some situation. Perhaps it is a problem in your life or the life of a friend or family member.

3. Ask God a question about a given situation and then allow him to lead you to a portion of Scripture that contains the truth he wants you to pray to tear down a stronghold.

4. There is no one "right way" of doing this, so allow the Holy Spirit to lead you by listening to the "still small voice of God."

Discussion questions for this chapter:

1. What is the highest purpose for which God gave us the Bible? Has that been your purpose for reading it?

2. What makes the Bible "living and powerful?"

3. What makes prayer powerful and effective?

4. What is the prerequisite for spiritual warfare?

5. How do we prepare ourselves for spiritual warfare?

6. How do we fight the battle against Satan?

7. What are spiritual strongholds? How are they built?

8. How are spiritual strongholds destroyed?

9. How does praying Scripture destroy strongholds?

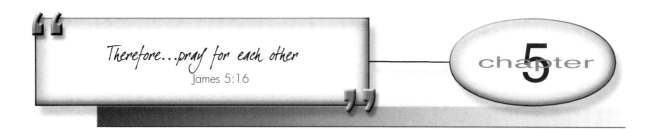

> *Therefore...pray for each other*
> James 5:16

Praying in the Spirit

What is an intercessor? *When* does one need an intercessor? Why would someone be an intercessor? These are all important questions! How we answer them is equally important, so let's start with the first one. An intercessor is a go-between. It is one who consults with someone on behalf of someone else. So then, what is intercessory prayer?

"Intercession is, by nature, the exercise by which an individual positions himself between two parties—one with a need and the other with the answer—and seeks to bring the two together. It is a matter of reaching out to take the hand of the one with the problem and reaching up to take the hand of the One with the provision...so that they meet." (Elliff 124)

Spiritually speaking, intercession is talking to God on behalf of somebody else. It is praying for other people. But how do we do that? How do I know *when* I should pray for someone? How do I know *what* I am to pray for them that will be the will of God? How do I know for *whom* I should pray? Can we know with certainty, answers to these questions? The answer to this question is a resounding "yes!"

And it is found solidly in Scripture. But first we must overcome a prayer problem we all have.

Our Weakness

I have a problem and you have the same problem. It's a prayer problem caused by sin. Listen to what Paul says. "We know that the whole creation has been groaning as in the pains of childbirth right up to the present time" (Romans 8:22 NIV). All of God's creation suffers in some way because of sin. Sin has messed up everything and its not just a little messed up either. Paul says sin has caused us pain, like labor pains and having watched my wife give birth to our children, I can tell you this is not a small amount of pain.

As Christians, we are not exempt from this pain. "Not only so, but we ourselves, who have the first fruits of the Spirit, groan inwardly as we wait eagerly for our adoption as sons, the redemption of our bodies" (Romans 8:23 NIV). Until the day when we are delivered from the presence of sin, we will suffer. We are in a constant fight against the world, our flesh and the Devil. We are weak, and we sin even though we abhor the very sin we commit. All this pain is the result of Adam and Eve's original sin in the Garden of Eden.

Because of sin we experience great weakness in our ability to pray. "In the same way, the Spirit helps us in our weakness. We do not know what we ought to pray for, but the Spirit himself intercedes for us with groans that words cannot express" (Romans 8:26 NIV). The reality is, we don't know how to pray. We don't know for whom to pray, nor do we know when to pray for them, or what to pray. As a result, it can be very discouraging to pray. It can cause us to question, "why bother praying?" And that is exactly what some Christians have done. They think, "Since we don't know how to pray, then why bother." I know, at one time this thought found its way into my head. Because of my personality, I like to do things I am good at. Things I'm not good at, I avoid. Since I couldn't be good at praying because of sin's consequences, I avoided it.

But there is exciting news. God does not leave us in our weakness. He wants us to be strong (Ephesians 6:10). So he has given us the permanently indwelling Holy Spirit to take away the weakness. The Holy Spirit is God's answer to our weakness, "the Spirit helps us in our weakness." The word "help" here means, "to come together, to participate together." The Holy Spirit promises to participate in our prayers thus eliminating our prayer weakness. God is not going to leave us weak. God has a solution to our weakness and that solution is the Holy Spirit.

Sometimes I think we don't realize just how weak we are when it comes to prayer. The word "weakness" ("infirmity" in some translations) means "feebleness, frailty or total lack of ability to produce results". It's not that we have some ability and God makes up for what we lack. No, we have *no* strength at all. In trying to picture what this might look like, I am reminded of a time when I was young and a Cub Scout. Each week at our Den meeting, we had to report a good deed we had done during the previous week. Consistently, mine was always, "I helped an old lady cross the street." (It didn't matter that I really didn't; that was my stock answer.) This would <u>not</u> be the

idea of the word "help" here. A better illustration of the word "help" would be if I picked up a completely paralyzed man and carried him across the street. He would be totally helpless, and without any strength to cross the street on his own. Similarly, we are totally helpless and without strength to know how to pray. It is not that we can pray 60% right and need help with the other 40%. No, we are at 0% right and need the Holy Spirit for the 100%.

God never leaves us weak. For every weakness, he becomes our strength. The Apostle Paul discovered this truth when he complained to God about some physical infirmity. Scripture records Paul praying three times, pleading God to take it away. I can identify with Paul completely. Whether it was a kidney stone, an asthma attack or Polycythemia Vera, I have prayed for God to take away my suffering. I don't like to suffer. Pain hurts! But God had a greater plan for the Apostle Paul. "But he said to me, 'My grace is sufficient for you, for my power is made perfect in weakness.' Therefore I will boast all the more gladly about my weaknesses, so that Christ's power may rest on me. That is why, for Christ's sake, I delight in weaknesses, in insults, in hardships, in persecutions, in difficulties. For when I am weak, then I am strong" (2 Corinthians 12:9-10 NIV). Basically, what God said was, "I will leave you physically weak, but I will give you great spiritual strength which will enable you to handle the physical weakness."

God is not going to leave us not knowing how to pray. He will not leave us weak. His desire is to make us strong with his strength. He most certainly does not say, "You don't know how to pray and you never will." Rather, he is saying to us, "Yes, you don't know how to pray, but I will show you how."

A Seriousness Weakness

Let's look at Romans 8:26 again. "In the same way, the Spirit helps us in our weakness. We do not know what we ought to pray for, but the Spirit himself intercedes for us with groans that words cannot express" (Romans 8:26 NIV). The word "know" means "to see, or to perceive by our sense of sight." In many other verses throughout the Bible, the Greek word translated here as "know" is translated in some form of the word "see." For example:

"After Jesus was born in Bethlehem in Judea, during the time of King Herod, Magi from the east came to Jerusalem and asked, 'Where is the one who has been born king of the Jews? We saw his star in the east and have come to worship him'" (Matthew 2:1-2 NIV).

"As soon as Jesus was baptized, he went up out of the water. At that moment heaven was opened, and he saw the Spirit of God descending like a dove and lighting on him" (Matthew 3:16 NIV).

"For we walk by faith, not by sight" (2 Corinthians 5:7 NKJV).

In Chapter two, we looked at the truth concerning what we cannot perceive with our senses. "As it is written: 'No eye has seen, no ear has heard, no mind has conceived what God has prepared for those who love him'—but God has revealed it to us by his Spirit. The

_____

_____

_____

_____

_____

_____

_____

_____

_____

_____

_____

_____

_____

_____

_____

_____

_____

Spirit searches all things, even the deep things of God'" (1 Corinthians 2:9-10 NIV). The things the "eye" cannot see, the Holy Spirit reveals. Therefore, that for which we pray is not to be based upon what we can see, but rather upon that which the Holy Spirit reveals.

Our prayer problem grows even bigger when we consider the meaning of the word "what" in "_we do not know what we ought to pray for._" The Greek word translated "what" here can mean "who, what, which, why, whether, and wherewith." It can mean any of these words or a combination of them. In the Greek, there is the definite article "the" used before this word indicating Paul is not speaking generally about prayer but specifically about the object of our prayer in a given hour of need. So our passage could mean, "We do not know for whom to pray, what to pray, and why to pray. This would go right along with "_The man without the Spirit does not accept the things that come from the Spirit of God, for they are foolishness to him, and he cannot under- stand them, because they are spiritually dis- cerned_" (1 Corinthians 2:14 NIV). We need the Holy Spirit to reveal to us the who, what and why to pray. Even knowing how to pray needs spiritual discernment.

If that wasn't bad enough, consider the word "ought" in "_we do not know what we ought to pray for._" Ought is one of those "should" words. "I ought to mow my lawn." Does that mean I have to mow the lawn? No, I should, but if I don't I can always do it tomorrow. The Greek word for "ought" in Romans 8:26 really means "must" or "neces- sary." Let's look at a few other verses that use the same Greek word.

"And He said to them, 'Why did you seek Me? Did you not know that I <u>must</u> be about My Father's business?'" (Luke 2:49 NKJV).

"For the perishable <u>must</u> clothe itself with the imperishable, and the mortal with immortality" (1 Corinthians 15:53 NIV).

"For we <u>must</u> all appear before the judgment seat of Christ, that each one may receive what is due him for the things done while in the body, whether good or bad." (2 Corinthians 5:10 NIV).

"You should not be surprised at my saying, 'You <u>must</u> be born again'" (John 3:7 NIV).

Can you take the word "must" out of any of those verses and replace it with the word "should?" To do so would create a great injustice to the verses. So, it is not a matter of not knowing how to pray as we <u>should</u>, but not knowing how to pray as we <u>must</u>. This is the great prayer weakness we must overcome. "The deepest need of the Church today is not for any material or external thing, but the deepest need is spiritual. Prayerless work will never bring in the kingdom. We neglect to pray *in the prescribed way*." (Italics mine) (E.M Bounds quoting Dr. A.J. Gordon in *Purpose in Prayer*, p. 97)

If there is a way we "must" pray, then definitely implied is there is a right way to pray and a wrong way. Because of the effects of sin, we do not know the right way to pray. This is where the Holy Spirit steps in and exchanges our weakness for God's strength.

The Intercessory Work of the Holy Spirit

What did Paul mean when he wrote, *"the Spirit himself intercedes for us?"* Is this the same as Christ's intercessory work? *"Who is he that condemns? Christ Jesus, who died — more than that, who was raised to life — is at the right hand of God and is also interceding for us"* (Romans 8:34 NIV). It is true that all three persons of the Trinity are God. Yet, there are distinctive works of each person of the Trinity. The Father and the Holy Spirit did not die on the cross. It was the Son of God, Jesus Christ who hung there that day. Likewise, it is neither the Father nor the Son who indwells the believer today. It is the Holy Spirit. All three are equal, yet they have separate and unique workings. It is not the Holy Spirit who sits at the right hand of the Father interceding for us. It is Christ Jesus.

It is Christ Jesus who intercedes between the believer and God, the Father. "But because Jesus lives forever, he has a permanent priest-hood. Therefore he is able to save completely those who come to God through him, because he always lives to intercede for them" (Hebrews 7:24-25 NIV). Our salvation is complete. Because it is complete nothing can change it, not even our sins. When the Evil One brings up our sins to the Father, the Son of God intercedes on our behalf, saying, "No, he or she is completely saved, finished completely forever." That is his intercessory work.

Christ Jesus is the one and only mediator between man and God. "For there is one God and one mediator between God and men, the man Christ Jesus" (1 Timothy 2:5 NIV). Christ Jesus is the go-between from man to God. The

Holy Spirit, on the other hand, is the go-between from <u>God to man</u>.

I hope you understand the significance of what you have just read. This is contrary to what most people believe the Bible teaches. Most of us were taught the Holy Spirit intercedes from man to God, not God to man, and therefore, duplicates Christ's intercessory ministry. We were taught Romans 8:26 says the believer cannot ever know the who, how or why to pray as we must. Therefore, believers pray the best they can and then the Holy Spirit cleans it up to make our prayer presentable to God. The Holy Spirit intercedes from man to God.

I have a problem with this interpretation of Romans 8:26. The result of this view is believers do not seek to know the who, what and why of prayer. They do not exchange their prayer weakness for God's strength. They pray what their natural senses perceive instead of through the insight of faith given by the Holy Spirit. This encourages sloppy, careless, unthinking prayer. They can pray things like "God be with all the missionaries around the world" believing the Holy Spirit will make it a better prayer.

If the Holy Spirit is going to "clean up" our prayers then it is impossible to pray incorrectly. Yet, God's word says we can. "When you ask, you do not receive, because you ask with wrong motives, that you may spend what you get on your pleasures" (James 4:3 NIV). What do we mean when we pray, "Lord, give us a safe journey?" Are we saying a safe journey is the only answer we will accept? What if God wanted us to have an accident so we would meet someone and share the gospel with him or her? Are we saying our comfort

and pleasure is more important? Those would be wrong the motives.   Does adding the tag line "if it be your will" make it any better? If the Holy Spirit take our bad prayer, cleans it up before passing it on the Father, then it is impossible to pray with wrong motives and James 4:3 makes no sense.

This is what I think is a much better interpretation of Romans 8:26. Instead of the Holy Spirit interceding from a believer to the Father, which would be a duplication of Christ's ministry, the Holy Spirit intercedes from the Father to the believer. We have already seen that the Holy Spirit knows the mind of the Father, so he can reveal the Father's will to us. And, not only does the Holy Spirit know the mind of the Father, he also knows what is going on inside you and me. So it would be really easy for the Holy Spirit to reveal to other believers who to pray for, when to pray for them and why to pray, all in accordance with the will of the Father. Now we no longer have a prayer weakness. We have divine power to direct our intercessory prayers.

How does the Holy Spirit reveal to us the who, what and why to pray as we must. Do we hear an audible voice? Romans 8:26 says he does it "with groans that words cannot express." The NAS says with groans "too deep for words." The word "groans" means "sighs." We are not seeking an auditory sound. It clearly states, "that words cannot express." What we have here is a non-verbal form of communication. There is no sound, but rather a feeling, a "prayer burden." It's not objective like seeing writing on the wall. It's not something others can hear or see and confirm its existence. Rather it is very subjective. It is a personal call to prayer from God to you. I have awakened in the middle of the night with a strong burden to pray for someone. I take that to be the ministry of the Holy Spirit revealing to me who I must pray for right then.

The Apostle Paul talks about this type of experience. "For though I be absent in the flesh, yet am I with you in the spirit, joying and beholding your order, and the stedfastness of your faith in Christ" (Colossians 2:5 KJV). Paul does not say, "I am with you in spirit." That would be like saying' "I can't be there with you but I will be thinking about you." Kind of a "wish I was there too" sentiment. No, Paul says he is with them "in the Spirit." By the insight of faith, through the ministry of the Holy Spirit, Paul could "see" their order and steadfastness of faith in Christ. Paul knew how to pray for them. He knew how to pray for them, as he must. It was not because of what his physical senses told him, but because of the ministry of the Holy Spirit within him.

We must be careful to not think of intercessory prayers as just problem solving. Lee Brase correctly observed, "Most Christians today seem to view prayer as a problem-solver, therefore they wait until they hear of difficulties or a crisis before praying for a person or a group. However, Paul did not see problem solving as the primary purpose of prayer" (Brase 19). Look at Paul's intercessory prayers in Ephesians chapters one and three. Sometimes the Holy Spirit will reveal a truth for us to pray for someone that has no connection to any problem they are currently experiencing. A greater need and, therefore, a subject of intercessory prayer is for them to be conformed to the image of Christ Jesus. So, when the Holy Spirit leads you to pray a specific passage of

_____

_____

_____

_____

_____

_____

_____

_____

_____

_____

_____

_____

_____

_____

_____

_____

_____

Scripture for someone, don't try to figure out their problem.

I believe this view of the intercessory work of the Holy Spirit is what Paul meant when he told us to pray "in the spirit" (Ephesians 6:17,18). We are to pray as the Holy Spirit reveals to us the who, what and why to pray as we must. We are commanded to pray in the Spirit. No sloppy, careless prayers hoping the Holy Spirit will clean them up. No prayers with selfish motives. No doing the best we can in the energy of the flesh. Divine prayers have divine power. "We have come to a critical breaking point when we admit that we can't pray effectively on our own and that we need to rely on the leadership of the Holy Spirit. This is a line of demarcation. In a sense, it is both a finish line and a starting point" (Hartley III 69).

Who else believes this?

Since this view of Romans 8:26 is not the most common interpretation taught, I thought it would be good to see if I was way out in left field on this. I started reading other commentaries on Romans 6:26. Here are some other individuals who share this interpretation.

John Bunyan in an article titled, *Praying in the Spirit*.

"It is only the Spirit that can teach us what to ask; only the Spirit is able to search everything out, even the deep things of God. Without the Holy Spirit, though we pray a thousand different prayers, yet we would be unable to know what to pray for, because we have a built-in weakness that makes us absolutely incapable of praying correctly."

Charles H. Spurgeon from a sermon titled *The Holy Spirit's Intercession*, preached April 11, 1880 at the Metropolitan Tabernacle, in Newington.

"In a measure, through our ignorance, we never know what we should pray for until we are taught of the Spirit of God ...Even when ignorance and perplexity are removed, we know not what we should pray for 'as we ought'...Coming to our aid in our bewilderment he instructs us. This is one of his frequent operations upon the mind of the believer...But the blessed Spirit does more than this, he will often direct the mind to the special subject of prayer...We do not know why it is so, but we sometimes find our minds carried as by a strong under current into a particular line of prayer for some one definite object...Nor is this all, for the spirit of God is not sent merely to guide and help our devotion, but he himself 'maketh intercession for us' according to the will of God. By this expression it cannot be meant that the Holy Spirit ever groans or personally prays; but that he excites intense desire...in us...Notice, our difficulty is that we know not what we should pray for; but the Holy Spirit does know, and therefore he helps us by enabling us to pray intelligently."

Alvin VanderGriend in *Love to Pray*, page 10.

"I want to share a radical thought. It has transformed my way of praying and my way of thinking about prayer. For years I believed that my prayers started with me. I had to think them up. I had to get God's attention. Not surprisingly, with this frame of mind, prayer was often a chore."

"I learned that I was wrong. Prayer doesn't start with us. Prayer starts with God. That's the radical idea that changed my prayer life. God is the initiator. He moves us to pray. He gives us prayer ideas."

"God is at work in all our praying. He makes his will known to us so that we will ask for the very things he longs to give us. Out of love he burdens us to pray for others so that, in response to our intercession, he can pour out blessings on them."

"And it's the Spirit, says Paul, that makes our prayer possible. We don't know what to pray, but we don't have to. The Spirit is there revealing God's will to us in the Scriptures and bringing God's prayer concerns to life within us."

"If prayer starts with God, then the first order of business as we learn to pray is to learn to listen to God's whispers, to tune our hearts to him to respond to his promptings."

E.M Bounds quoting Rev. J. Stuart Holden in *Purpose in Prayer*, pages 97-98

"Here is the secret of prevailing prayer, to pray under a direct inspiration of the Holy Spirit, whose petitions for us and

through us are always according to the Divine Purpose..."

C. Sumner Wemp in *How on Earth Can I Be Spiritual?*, p. 32-33

"Likewise the Spirit also helpeth our infirmities...It is a common admission that most persons have a weak prayer life. Too often Christians are in a dilemma as to how to pray and for what to pray.

"God has the answer by telling us that this is the ministry of the Holy Spirit. While the Lord was here, the disciples prayed, 'Lord, teach us to pray' (Luke 11:1). Doesn't it follow, then, that Christians should seek and depend on the Holy Spirit to help and direct them in prayer. Go to the proper authority in this area as well. It could transform your prayer life."

Testimonials

When I feel the Holy Spirit's prompting to pray for someone and I have allowed the Holy Spirit to take me to a Bible passage, I send them a note telling them I prayed and list the Scriptures I used. Here are some of the responses I have received in return.

From a missionary
"The Lord is good and greatly to be praised! Only He knew the discouragements that were thrown my way the past 48 hours. He comforted me along the way in knowing that the trials we endure are for His glory and to conform us into the likeness of His Son, but the ache continued to gnaw at me. I took a nap this afternoon feeling not so much physically tired but emotionally and spiritually."

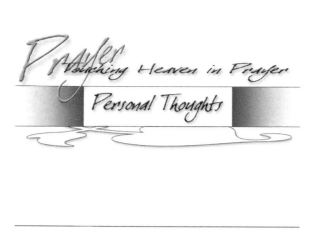

Prayer
Touching Heaven in Prayer
Personal Thoughts

_____

_____

_____

_____

_____

_____

_____

_____

_____

_____

_____

_____

_____

_____

_____

_____

_____

"To get up and find your email waiting for me was an affirmation from the Lord of His presence and care. Thanks for allowing him to prompt your heart to send me those verses and words of encouragement."

From a missionary

"I can't express to you how much I love and appreciate you. The half hour of prayer was a wonderful gift, and the following note about the Lord's leading in that prayer time was a tremendous gift of grace. I thank Him for leading you to pray those things, to share those verses, and to express your love for us in that way. I thank you for your submissive heart to follow His leading in prayer."

From a pastor

"I thank our Lord for bringing me to your mind and heart. I took up your word of encouragement and looked up the verses from Deuteronomy that you prayed on my behalf. Thanks!!!!!! I am going to share these verses tonight at our prayer meeting."

From a pastor

"I wanted to let you know how much your notes mean to me as a man and as a fellow minister of the gospel. Thank you for *'praying the scriptures'* on my behalf."

From a missionary

"Thanks for the prayers and sharing the Scripture passages. I looked them up this morning and found them very encouraging. It's quite amazing watching God use his body to strengthen each other."

From a missionary

"I want to thank you so much for your prayers and for the great encouragement in your email. You were definitely led by the Spirit in your prayers because you are right on target about everything. I was so moved by God's care that I decided to concentrate on these passages this week for my fellowship time with God. As a direct result of your prayers my wife and I are planning a 3-day getaway, just two of us this month. Thank you for your care and loving concern."

You can well imagine how excited I get when I receive these notes. To know the Holy Spirit has replaced my prayer weakness with his power is amazing. Did you also notice how God set it up so we can't take the credit? It is all a work of God so he gets the glory. All we are is a vessel, used of God to express love and encouragement to others through prayer. You too can be a vessel, used of God, to pray in the Spirit. Jesus is our role model. He is our example of intercessory prayer.

"How did Jesus relate to Peter, who was one of his closest friends when He was on earth? The ultimate Friend, Jesus prayed for Peter during his time of severe testing. 'Simon, Simon, Satan has asked to sift you as wheat. But I have prayed for you, Simon, that your faith may not fail' (Luke 22:31-32a). I believe that Jesus interceded to the Father on Peter's behalf so that Peter's faith in the character of God would not fail under the pressure of satanic buffeting." (Dawson 29)

I have a good pastor friend, Sam Whittaker. Sam interned at our church during his final year at Grace Bible College. One of the first things I did with Sam was to teach him how to be an intercessor. I knew that if he was to enter the ministry, he had to know how to follow the leading of the Holy Spirit in his prayer life. He quickly learned how to pray the Word of God. I hadn't thought of it at the time but I have received an unexpected benefit. Now he sends me emails sharing his prayers for me, including the Scripture passages he has prayed.

1. In previous chapters, you have already asked God to show you truths from his Word to pray. Now we add asking God for whom to pray and what to pray for them.

2. Take time to quiet yourself.

3. Acknowledge to God you cannot know the who, what or why to pray, as you must. You need the Holy Spirit's help.

4. Ask God to give you a prayer burden of someone for whom you can pray right now.

5. Ask God to lead you to a portion of Scripture to pray for them.

6. Ask God if he wants you to send a note to that person, telling them what you prayed for them.

chapter **5**

1. What is an intercessor and when is one needed?

2. In what way has sin affected our prayer life?

3. How does the Holy Spirit eliminate our prayer weakness?

4. How does the Holy Spirit's intercessory ministry differ from Christ's?

5. How do we pray "amiss?" Why doesn't the Holy Spirit just "clean-up" those prayers?

6. How many of your prayers are "problem solving" prayers? How many are "problem preventing" prayers? Why?

7. What are the benefits of praying Scripture?

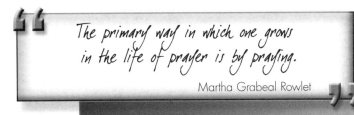

The primary way in which one grows in the life of prayer is by praying.

Martha Grabeal Rowlet

Changing Our Prayers

At the beginning of this book I confessed my opinion about my own previous personal prayer times. Boring. Unproductive. Multiply these feelings by about ten and you can imagine how I felt about most prayer meetings! Prayer meetings use what I call the "shotgun" approach to prayer. In the typical prayer meetings I have attended there have usually been about a half dozen or so people gathered together sitting in rows or in a circle. After a 45-minute bible study, the leader takes some prayer requests (including a couple "unspoken requests.") Usually two or three people pray about Grandma Betty's gout or Uncle Chester's trick knee. Almost everything prayed for deals with some physical need. On a good night, everyone might pray and throw in a couple requests from missionary letters. When all the prayer requests have been prayed for, the leader closes in a summary prayer. They covered all the prayer requests, but have they prayed about anything "in the Spirit?"

Another common experience in prayer meetings is the great lengths of time taken in sharing the details of our prayer requests then very little time is left to actually pray. Richard L. Pratt, Jr. recalls such a prayer meeting in his

Prayer Touching Heaven in Prayer

Personal Thoughts

book *Pray with Your Eyes Open.*
"A young pastor asked for prayer requests…Much to his surprise the members of the congregation made one request after another. 'This is wonderful' the pastor thought. Then he looked down at his watch and realized he had only two minutes left to pray for all of these requests. In a panic, he simply read quickly through his list: 'Lord, take care of…and bless… and take care … and bless…'" (136-137).

No time is spent seeking the Holy Spirit's leading in regard to these requests. We just rush through our list. As A.W. Tozer acknowledged in his day, "Many prayer meetings are being called these days. And no wonder, for the need is great. But if my observation is correct much effort is wasted; very little comes of them" (59).

The question must then be asked, "Can we pray in the Spirit in a corporate prayer gathering?" Yes, but perhaps it will require that we change the way we pray together. First, we will need to grow up in our prayer understanding. We must know how to pray in the Spirit and how to pray Scripture. In our church I regularly teach a "Passion for Prayer" seminar, using the materials in this book. Perhaps it's worth gathering a group of people together and to use this book as a study guide. Discuss together the questions at the end of each chapter. Have each person do the "Putting this chapter into practice" several times during the week. When you finish with the book, perhaps each person could take a few friends through it as well. Our goals must be to build up a small army of individuals who can go to battle against the lies of the Devil!

Another change we must make is to rethink silence during a prayer meeting. If there is thirty seconds of silence in a regular prayer meeting, people usually get uncomfortable. People who have already prayed begin to wonder, "Who hasn't prayed yet and what are they waiting for?" The leader begins silently counting to twenty-five, which, if he makes it, it's his cue to close the prayer time. If the silence is at the beginning of the prayer time, the person who feels the most uncomfortable will finally start rattling off his or her requests. The problem here is we think we have to do all the talking during the prayer time. This is such a deception. Silence is one of God's greatest tools.

Silence is what allows time for the Holy Spirit to impress a prayer burden upon our hearts. Only then can we know for whom to pray. It takes even more time to allow the Holy Spirit to lead us to the correct Scripture to pray for them. In a small prayer group there can be long periods of silence as each person seeks the leading of the Holy Spirit. We must learn to be comfortable during the periods of silence.

Praying around a circle and praying from a prayer list keep things going, but can be guilty of stifling the Holy Spirit. Praying around a circle often pressures people to have a prayer ready when it's their turn to pray. But what happens if the Holy Spirit hasn't revealed the who, what or why to pray "as we must" yet? Few people will risk the embarrassment of skipping their turn because the Holy Spirit hasn't prepared them to pray.

As a personal conclusion, prayer lists can be good or bad, depending on how they are used. Here is how Jan Johnson described praying from her lists.

"I used to have dazzling quiet times. I sat on my bed, holding my four-part prayer notebook as if it were a cherished artifact. Pulling back the tab marked 'adoration,' I peered at a list of forty words the described God and picked three to praise God for. Moving on to the tab marked 'confession' I mulled over another forty-word list of faults, especially those I'd underlined in red: laziness and grouchiness. Racing on to 'thanksgiving,' I skimmed a list of twenty items I felt thankful for including friends, relatives, books, and—to be especially spiritual—God Himself"

"I remember the day my quiet time died. After gathering all my devotional props, I settled into a terrible emptiness. I needed God as I had never needed Him before, but my regimented prayers were puny containers for my anguish" (Johnson 7-8).

I have several lists. I have a list for the people in my church, another for family members, one for missionaries and one for pastors and Christian leaders. But I don't pick one from list A and two from list B to pray for each day (sounds like ordering Chinese food, doesn't it). Rather, as I sit quietly before the Lord, I allow the Holy Spirit to guide me as to which list to go to and who to pray for in that list. Instead of trying to pray through the lists in order every month, I ask God to show me who needs prayer each day. Also, during my prayer times, when I look down my lists, some names just seem to jump out at me. I believe this is one way the Holy Spirit directs my prayer times. In times of great prayer needs, it is beneficial to gather with others who truly know God. "But the people who know their God shall be strong, and carry out great exploits" (Daniel 11:32b NKJV). Intimacy must come before intercession, or in other words, before the asking must come the basking! We must spend time in worship before we start rattling off our prayer requests. "There is a profound difference between request-based prayers and worship-based prayers. I've watched as this distinction transformed the way thousands of people pray, privately and in groups gathers. Broken down, it really is the difference between seeking God's hand and His face" (Henderson & Saylar 85). Knowing prayer techniques will never replace loving God. When we love God, we want to come before Him in prayer. A passion for prayer is really a passion for God.

My ideal prayer meeting

Here is how I would like to conduct a prayer meeting. First we would gather with no predetermined idea of how long the prayer meeting would last. We would stay to pray until the Holy Spirit released us. My experience has shown such a prayer meeting might last two or three hours.

We would begin our prayer time by humbling ourselves before God, remembering, "God opposes the proud but gives grace to the humble" (James 4:6b NIV). Here everyone would be encouraged to acknowledge in some way, "Lord, we do not know how to pray as we must. But we are asking you to direct our time of prayer." People are free to pray when they want and as often as the want. There is

no restriction on how long or short the prayer has to be. Each person prays as they are led. But, our goal is to humble ourselves before our Lord.

Next we might join our hearts together in praise and worship of our Lord, focusing on his attributes and actions. Again, with open Bibles and open eyes we might pray through a Psalm, allowing the Psalm to direct our prayers of thanksgiving and praise. This might be all the further we get, just spending time in worship and praise of God.

But, assuming we want to continue in our prayer time, next we could introduce a subject for prayer. It might be a person or a situation for which they personally have felt a prayer burden. Everyone would then focus on just that one subject. Rather than praying out loud right way, each person would privately seek God's guidance for the who, what and why to pray, as we must regarding the situation. With open eyes and open Bibles we would begin to pray the Scriptures that we felt led by the Spirit to pray. There would be quiet times between our prayers as each sought the leading of God. It has never failed, in this type of prayer meeting, that after awhile we find a common thread in our prayers. God is leading us to understand the "real" or "root" need. From the real need, God reveals the real solution. Often it is a truth to be believed that tears down a stronghold of Satan's lies.

When it becomes clear God is giving no more direction for prayer, then someone else can introduce a new topic for prayer and we go through the process over again. I have never been in this type of prayer meeting where we could pray for more than two or three people. It takes a great deal of time to go through the intercessory prayer process.

I have been a part of prayer gatherings that were called to pray for just one topic. Sometimes it is for a person, other times for a church problem. The first one was in Palm Bay, Florida. The prayer meeting was called for one person, a lady in the church. She was one of the key ladies in our church and she was going through a difficult time. We prayed the Scriptures for her for about three hours. By the end of that time, we knew where the stronghold of Satan was in her life and the truth God wanted her to believe. None of this was visible to us before as we watched her struggle in this one area of her life. It was just a short time later God answered our prayers as she, without a word from us, saw the same thing God had revealed to us. She was delivered from that situation almost overnight.

Each fall we have a group of missionaries who come to our church for a fall missionary conference. For the past several years, I have invited them to join me for prayer each morning. Most of them come. On the first morning, I tell them we are going to pray a little differently than they may have prayed before. That morning we allow a Psalm to direct our time of prayer. The time always goes by quickly as missionaries are quick to adapt to the changes. The next morning, we pray through another Psalm. Then the third and fourth days we pray about one topic or need each day. I tell the missionaries to just open their Bibles and allow God to lead them to pray Scripture concerning the need that was brought up that morning. It has never failed, that at the end of the week as we debrief the missionaries, they say the prayer time in the morning was one of the highlights of the conference. Some of those missionaries confessed they prayed very little if at all

_____

_____

_____

_____

_____

_____

_____

_____

_____

_____

_____

_____

_____

_____

before but now they want to continue on their own doing what we did during those morning meetings.

If you start a prayer group based upon "praying in the Spirit" don't expect a lot of people to show up. One summer I started a prayer group like this and only two other couples joined Karen and me. It wasn't a big group but boy did we have great times praying. We laughed together and we cried together. But more importantly, we prayed according to the will of God together. As a side benefit, we became closer to those two couples than we were before. They have become some of our best friends.

How to get started

When you have some people who understand Spirit led intercessory prayer (it might only be a couple), start a prayer group. Start by praying for just one person each time or start by praying for a special need in your church. After a week or two, start sharing with others what you are doing. Tell them how exciting your prayer life has become. Be prepared to see God answer prayer as you pray according to the will of God. When he does, share that too. Send "prayer notes" to those for whom you pray. One missionary told me, in response to a prayer note I sent him, "I have never before received a note from anyone saying they prayed for me and what it was they prayed." Share with others the notes you get back from people, telling you how God used your prayers (make sure you do it anonymously or with their permission).

Another idea would be to start an intercessory prayer group that meets during the morning worship service. There is real power in Spirit-led praying. People come to Christ for salvation. Christians become excited and on

fire for God. Spirit led praying before, during and after the service can lead to a major breakthrough by the Spirit in our churches. Charles Spurgeon wrote,

"There is always a connection, even if we do not see it, between that great crowd on Sunday and the pleading of the saints. There is always a most intimate connection between the flocking converts of the ministry and those secret prayers that follow and precede them. There is such a connection that the two cannot be parted. God will not send great blessings in the way of open conversions if secret prayer is neglected. Let the preacher or the church forbear to pray, and God will forbear to bless." (Spurgeon 26)

At our church we are currently working on wiring a room so people can see and hear the service from there. A couple people a week can sit in that room, observing the service and praying over each part of it. During the music, they can take the words of the songs and pray them back to God. During the sermon, they can take the scriptures and pray them for the people in the church service. This is a ministry we are just beginning (as I write this book). I am excited to see what God is going to do with it.

I have a special burden to pray for Christian leaders. I'm not talking about the Colson and Dobson level of a ministry. No, I pray for the Christian leaders, the pastors and missionaries I know. I want to encourage you to pray for them too. Spend one prayer time a week praying for Christian leaders. Write them; tell them you are praying for them and what you

_____

_____

_____

_____

_____

_____

_____

_____

_____

_____

_____

_____

_____

_____

_____

_____

_____

_____

are praying. Ask God to lead you to which one to pray for each week. Christian leaders are continuously under attack by Satan. Just as the Apostle Paul was under attack "from without and from within" so are Christian leaders. As I have prayed for pastors and missionaries and have heard back from them in response to a prayer card I sent them, I am more and more impressed with the need for Spirit-led prayer warriors who will hold these leaders up in prayer.

Every month, I seek to take a day devoted just to prayer. Sometimes, I go away for the day. Some days, I stay in my office with the doors closed. I do not schedule any appointments for that day, for I have an appointment with God. No lunch meetings, no phone calls, and no visits. This day is given completely to prayer. For me, the first Friday of the month works well. It is on these days I can spend long periods of time praying for family, friends and church issues. I always look forward to the first Friday of each month. As news of this time of prayer spread out, people started sending me notes with specific prayer needs. They knew I would be praying and they wanted to be on the receiving end of those prayers.

One final idea for a prayer ministry, once or twice a year, consider going on a prayer retreat. You can go alone or go with a small group of friends who know how to pray in the Spirit. If you go with others, spend some time praying separately and then gather together to pray. For a Friday night and Saturday prayer retreat, you could spend Friday night in separate prayer, asking God to reveal sins in your life, confessing that sin and thanking God for his forgiveness. Then gather together and share what God did during that time. Saturday could begin with a time of corporate praise, worship and thanksgiving. Separate again for a time of intercessory prayer and then gather together again for a corporate time of intercessory prayer.

In the introduction, I told you this book would be incomplete. I wrote very little about confession, adoration or thanksgiving. These are all important parts of prayer. Not all of our prayer times should be in intercession and petition. But this book was not meant to be about all forms of prayer. My purpose in writing this is to show you how you can touch God with your prayers. When God's Word and the Holy Spirit come together in our prayers, God is touched and moved to answer them.

"Let us not become weary in doing good,
for at the proper time
we will reap a harvest
if we do not give up."
Galatians 6:9 NIV

bibliography

Anson, Elva. *How to Keep the Family That Prays Together From Falling Apart*.
    Chicago, IL: Moody Press, 1975.

Bonar, Horatius. *God's Way of Holiness*. Chicago, IL: Moody Press, no date.

Bounds, E.M. *Power Through Prayer*. Westwood, NJ: The Christian Library, 1984.

Bounds, E.M. *Purpose In Prayer*. Westwood, NJ: The Christian Library, 1984.

Brandt, Priscilla. *Two-Way Prayer*. Waco, TX: Word Books, 1979.

Brase, Lee. *Approaching God*. Colorado Springs, CO: NavPress, 2003.

Bryant, David. *Concerts of Prayer*. Ventura, CA: Regal Books, 1984.

Butts, Kim. *The Praying Family*. Chicago, IL: Moody publishers, 2003.

Chambers, Oswald. *If You Will Ask*. Grand Rapids, MI: Discovery House Publishers, 1937.

Christenson, Evelyn. *What Happens When Women Pray*. Wheaton, IL: Victor Books, 1975.

Compolo, Anthony. *The Power Delusion*. Wheaton, IL: Victor Books, 1983.

Dawson, Joy. *Intercession, Thrilling and Fulfilling*. Seattle, WA: YWAM Publishing, 1997.

Dawson, Joy. *Intimate Friendship with God*. Grand Rapids, MI: Chosen Books, 1986.

Demarest, Bruce. *Satisfy Your Soul*. Colorado Springs, CO: NavPress, 1999.

DeMoss, Nancy Leigh. *A Place of Quiet Rest*. Chicago, IL: Moody Press, 2000.

Duke, Dee. *Prayer Quest*. Colorado Springs, CO: NavPress, 2004.

Elliff, Tom. *A Passion for Prayer*. Wheaton, IL: Crossway Books, 1998.

Frizzell, Gregory R. *How to Develop a Powerful Prayer Life*. Memphis, TN: The Master's
    Design, 1999.

Fromke, DeVern F. *The Ultimate Intention*. Cloverdale, IN: The Sure Foundation, 1963.

George, Bob. *A Scriptural Journey to Discover the Grace of God*. Dallas, TX: People to
    People Ministries, 1999.

Getz, Gene A. *Praying For One Another*. Wheaton, IL: Victor Books, 1960.

Graf, Jonathan. *The Power of Personal Prayer*. Colorado Springs, CO: NavPress, 2002.

Hall, Terry. *Getting More From Your Bible*. Wheaton, IL: Victory Books, 1978.

Hamma, Robert M. *Letting the Bible Inspire Your Prayer*. St. Meinrad, IN: Abbey Press, 1988.

Hanegraaff, Hank. *The Prayer of Jesus, Secret's to Real Intimacy with God*. Nashville,
    TN: Word Publishing, 2001.

Hanne, John Anthony. *Prayer or Pretense?* Grand Rapids, MI: Zondervan Publishing House,
    1974.

Hartley, Fred A. *Lord, Teach Us To Pray.* Colorado Springs, CO: NavPress, 2003.

Hartley, Fred A. *Prayer On Fire.* Colorado Springs, CO: NavPress, 2006.

Henderson, Daniel. *Fresh Encounters.* Colorado Springs, CO: NavPress, 2004.

Hunt, Art. *Praying with the One You Love.* Sisters, OR: Questar Publishers, 1996.

Johnson, Jan. *Enjoying the Presence of God.* Colorado Springs, CO: NavPress, 1996.

Johnson, Jan. *Listening To God.* Colorado Springs, CO: NavPress, 1998.

Kenyon, E.W. *In His Presence.* Old Tappan, NJ: Fleming H. Revell Company, 1969.

Krutza, William J. *How Much Prayer Should a Hamburger Get?* Grand Rapids, MI: Baker Book
     House, 1975.

Lucado, Max. *God's Open Arms.* Nashville, TN: Word Publishing, 1999.

Martin, Catherine. *Revive My Heart!.* Colorado Springs, CO: NavPress, 2003.

Miller, Kathy Collard. *Through His Eyes.* Colorado Springs, CO: NavPress, 1999.

Moore, Beth. *Praying God's Word.* Nashville, TN: Broadman & Holman Publishers, 2000.

Murray, Andrew, *The Ministry of Intercessory Prayer.* Minneapolis, MN: Bethany House
     Publishers, 1981.

Packer, J.I. *Knowing God.* Downers Grove, IL: InterVarsity Press, 1973.

Palmer, Earl F. *Prayer Between Friends.* Tarrytown, NY: Fleming H. Revell Company, 1991.

Peace, Richard. *Meditative Prayer.* Colorado Springs, CO: NavPress, 1998.

Peace, Richard. *Spiritual Journaling.* Colorado Springs, CO: NavPress, 1998.

Pratt, Richard L. *Pray With Your Eyes Open.* Phililipsburg, NJ: Presbyterian and Reformed
     Publishing Company, 1987.

Rinker, Rosalind. *How to Have Family Prayers.* Grand Rapids, MI: Zondervan Publishing
     House, 1977.

Rowlett, Martha Graybeal. *In Spirit and in Truth*, A Guide to Praying. Nashville, TN: The
     Upper Room, 1982.

Sanders, J. Oswald. *Every Life is a Plan of God.* Grand Rapids, MI: Discovery House
     Publishers, 1992.

Sherman, Dean. *Spiritual Warfare For Every Christian.* Seattle, WA: YWAM Publishing,
     1990.

Smith, Michael M. *Nurturing A Passion For Prayer.* Colorado Springs, CO: NavPress, 1999.

Spurgeon, Charles. *The Power of Christ's Prayer Life.* Lynwood, WA: Emerald Books, 1995.

Spurgeon, Charles. *The Power of Prayer in a Believer's Life.* Lynwood, WA: Emerald
     Books, 1993.

Swope, Mary Ruth. *Listening Prayer.* Melbourne, FL: Whitaker Publishing, 1987.

Tozer, A.W. *Keys to the Deeper Life.* Grand Rapids, MI: Zondervan Pulishing House, 1957.

Tozer, A.W. *The Pursuit of God/The Pursuit of Man Pocket Devotional.* Camp Hill, PA:
     Christian Publications, Inc., 2002.

Tyre, Jacquie. *The Jabez Prayer Guide*. Colorado Springs, CO: NavPress, 2001.

VanderGriend, Alvin J. *Love to Pray*. Terre Haute, IN: Harvest Prayer Ministries, 2003.

VanderGriend, Alvin J. *The Praying Church Sourcebook*. Grand Rapids, MI: CRC
        Publications, 1990.

Wemp, C. Sumner. *How on Earth Can I Be Spiritual?* New York, NY: Thomas Nelson
        Publishers, 1978.

White, Ellen. *The Desire of Ages*. Nampa, ID: Pacific Press Publishing Association, 2006.

Whitney, Donald S. *Ten Questions to Diagnose our Spiritual Health*. Colorado Springs, CO:
        NavPress, 2001.

Wiersbe, Warren. *God Isn't In a Hurry*. Grand Rapids, MI: Baker Books, 1994.

Yancey, Philip. *Prayer: Does it Make a Difference?* Grand Rapids, MI: Zondervan, 2006.

_____ . *Prayers That Avail Much - Volume One*. Tulsa, OK: Harrison House, 1989.

_____ . *Prayers That Avail Much - Volume Two*. Tulsa, OK: Harrison House, 1989.

_____ . *Prayers That Avail Much - Volume Three*. Tulsa, OK: Harrison House, 1989.

Other writings by this author

From the back cover...

This publication is for all those Christians who have been trying to live the Christian life and have been failing. It is also for those who believe there is more to the Christian life but don't know what it is or how to get it. Reading this book won't make you more spiritual but it will show you how God can. Starting with a solid and practical biblical foundation, *THE GRACE WAY* distinguishes God's responsibility from ours in the process of spiritual maturity. *THE GRACE WAY* is a workbook. *THE GRACE WAY* is a journal. *THE GRACE WAY* is God's path to successful Christian living.

Grace Publications, Inc.
PO Box 9432
1011 Aldon SW
Grand Rapids, MI 49509
(616) 247-1999

The
Learning Equation®

INTERMEDIATE ALGEBRA

Instructor's Resource Manual

BROOKS/COLE

™

THOMSON LEARNING

Australia • Canada • Mexico • Singapore • Spain • United Kingdom • United States

Sponsoring Editor: Jennifer Huber

Marketing Manager: Kevin Connors

Advertising: Samantha Cabaluna

Project Manager: Carolyn Richards

Production Coordinator: Stephanie Andersen

Cover Design: Denise Davidson

Print Buyers: Nancy Panziera and
Kristine Waller

Typesetting: First Folio

Printing and Binding: Webcom Ltd.

For more information about this or any other Brooks/Cole product, contact:

BROOKS/COLE
511 Forest Lodge Road
Pacific Grove, CA 93950 USA
www.brookscole.com
1-800-423-0563 (Thomson Learning Academic Resource Center)

For permission to use material from this work, contact us by
www.thomsonrights.com
fax: 1-800-730-2215
phone: 1-800-730-2214

Printed in Canada.

10   9   8   7   6   5   4   3   2   1

Content Review Panel

Mark D. Clark
Associate Professor of Mathematics,
Palomar College,
San Marcos, CA

John E. Daggett
Math Lab Coordinator,
DeAnza College,
Cupertino, CA

Beth Hempleman
Math Learning Center Coordinator,
Mira Costa College,
Mira Costa, CA

Tim Hempleman
Adjunct Faculty,
Palomar College and California
StateUniversity,
San Marcos, CA

Harris S. Shultz
Professor of Mathematics,
California State University,
Fullerton, CA

Authors

Karen Auch	*Ted Keating*	*Grant L. Plett*
Leo Boissy	*Chris Kirkpatrick*	*Caleb Reppenhagen*
Mark Bredin	*Jean MacEachern*	*Kevin Rowan*
Lana Chow	*Melani McCasin*	*Rod Rysen*
Gloria Conzon	*Greg McInulty*	*Selina Samji*
Brent Corrigan	*Roxane Menssa*	*Rick Sept*
Colin Garnham	*Lee Mitchell*	*Joe Shenher*
Mike Gmell	*Keith Molyneux*	*Brenda Stewart*
Connie Goodwin	*Loretta Morhart*	*Katharine D. Tetlock*
Barry Gruntman	*Rob Muscoby*	*Colleen Tong*
Christine Henzel	*Kanwal I.S. Neel*	*Terry Wallace*
Joe Hirschegger	*David Nutbean*	*Dale Weimer*
Carol Besteck Hope	*Robert Payne*	*Ketri Wilkes*
Terry Imhoff	*Brent Pfeil*	

Product Development

Garry Popowich	*Barry Mitschke*	*Peggy Hill*
Ron Blond	*Larry Markowski*	*Carol Besteck Hope*
Milt Petruc	*Eleanor Milne*	*Ted Keating*
Sharon Tappe	*Maxine Stinka*	*Chris Kirkpatrick*
Dale Weimer	*Joanne Adomeit*	*Ralph Lee*
Lisa Wright	*Steven Daniels*	*Bob Robinson*
Angus McBeath	*Lee Kubica*	*Brenda Stewart*
Tom Winkelmans	*Barb Morrison*	*Frances I. Tallon*
Paula Allison	*Connie Goodwin*	*Stella Tossell*
Duncan McCaig	*Theresa Gross*	*Susan Woollam*
Katharine D. Tetlock	*Terri Hammond*	

Math Explorers

Design and Programming
Ron Blond

Windows Versions
Grant Arnold
Vladislav Hala

Editorial Development

First Folio Resource Group, Inc.

Project Manager
David Hamilton

Senior Editor
Eileen Jung

Print Materials
Fran Cohen, Project Manager   *Robert Templeton*, Supervising Editor   *Brenda McLoughlin*, Editor
Tom Dart, Bruce Krever, Design and Layout

Storyboard Editors
Shirley Barrett   *Mark Bryant*   *Angel Carter*   *Jackie Lacoursiere*   *Anna Marsh*
Darren McDonald   *Don Rowsell*   *Robert Templeton*   *Jackie Williams*   *Susan Woollam*

Picture Research and Copy Editing
Robyn Craig   *Bruce Krever*   *Jonathan Lampert*   *Catherine Oh*   *Mike Waters*

Multimedia Development

Calian eLearning

Vice-President – eLearning
Justin Ferrabee

Project Manager
Kevin Kernohan

Technical Manager
Collin Chenier

Director, Delivery
Lenka Jordanov

Project Administration
Sylvia Panaligan

Testing Manager
Geoffrey Heaton

Graphic Design
Mike Martel, Creative Lead

Illustration, Photo Adaptation
Mike Martel   *Catherine Fitzpatrick*

Authoring
Bill Currie, Senior Author   *Collin Chenier*   *Geoffrey Heaton*   *Jo-anne Landriault*
Kevin Kernohan   *Lianne Zitzelsberger*   *Madelyn Hambly*   *Mike Cherun*
Catherine Fitzpatrick   *Mike Martel*

Programming
Andrée Descoteaux, Main Engine Programmer
Collin Chenier   *Kevin Kernohan*   *Reed Carriere*

Testing
Diana Guy   *Geoffrey Heaton*

Audio Production
Kevin Kernohan

Narration Voices
June Dewetering   *Patrick Fry*   *Ron Purvis*   *Genevieve Spicer*

Contents

PREFACE

The Learning Equation® (TLE) is interactive multimedia courseware and student workbooks for developmental mathematics, from basic math/arithmetic through intermediate algebra. Developed in Macromedia Director®, TLE is attractive with a professional look and feel, and runs fast and reliably on all Windows and Macintosh platforms. Delivered on CD-ROMs, it can run on a stand-alone computer, over a LAN, and over the internet. The Learning Equation ships with a sophisticated, browser-based course management system and assessment package.

TLE uses interactive, activity-directed learning to involve the student in their own education. Each TLE lesson is designed to build skills in algebra and problem solving. The entire series of lessons has a sound, curriculum-based foundation. As students progress through the lessons, they will learn the vocabulary of mathematics, practice key concepts, and develop their skills in reasoning, modeling, and analysis.

Each TLE lesson contains a wealth of application problems. Numerous applications are included from disciplines such as business, entertainment, science and technology, and history.

Components

The Learning Equation® *Intermediate Algebra* consists of 64 lessons that cover the college intermediate algebra curriculum. Lessons are designed to take about 90 minutes but learners can progress at their own pace.

Every lesson consists of the following seven components.

Introduction

The opening screen briefly outlines the lesson and its objectives. Prerequisites for the lesson and instructions are available from an on-screen tabbed notebook.

To start the lesson, select the NEXT button on the opening screen.

The **Introduction** opens the lesson with a problem set in the context of a career, a real world or consumer experience, or a game. Students use knowledge they already have to solve the proposed problem. The **Introduction** is short, motivating, and highly interactive.

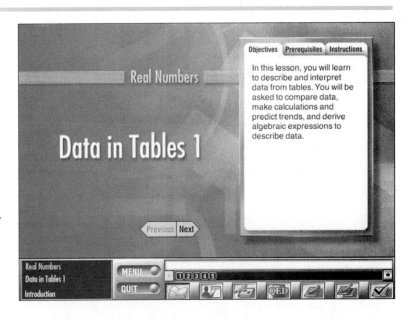

![Tutorial icon] Tutorial

The *TLE* **Tutorial** offers the main instruction for the topic of the lesson. This section includes simple examples that help students understand the concepts. The **Tutorial** is intended to encourage students to learn by doing.

By providing different solutions or different routes through the same problem, *TLE* is designed to help students realize that there can be many ways to solve a problem.

TLE uses **Hints** to remind students when they can use strategies they've already learned. **Success Tips** offer ways to build student confidence or to support independent study and learning.

> ### Feedback Boxes
> You can move any feedback box by selecting the green bar at the top of the box, and dragging it to the desired location. You can hide, and then reveal, the content of the feedback box by double clicking on the green bar. To close the feedback box, select the button in the upper left corner of the green bar.

![Examples icon] Examples

The *TLE* **Examples expand** on what students learned in the Tutorial. The Examples are highly interactive and include feedback to student responses, hints, or alternative solutions.

Up to 12 examples may be presented in each lesson. A **hidden picture** is progressively revealed as students complete each example. Once the picture has been completely revealed, students may select a **Picture Information** button to learn more about it.

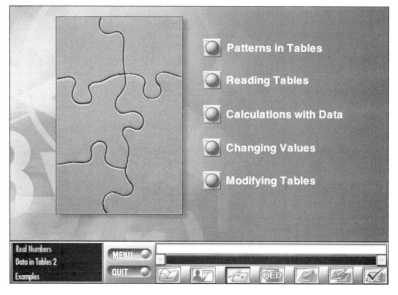

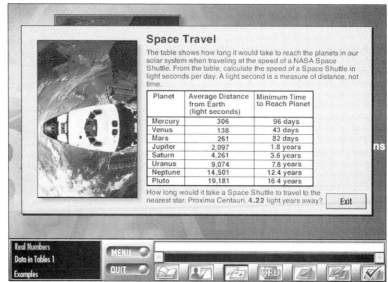

Summary

The *TLE* **Summary revisits the Introduction** and encourages students to **apply the mathematics learned** in the Tutorial and Examples to the problem in the Introduction.

Practice and Problems

The *TLE* **Practice and Problems** presents up to 25 questions. They are organized in **four or five categories** with five questions in each category. You can click on any box to try a question.

As in the **Examples,** another **hidden picture** is revealed when questions are completed correctly.

Extra Practice

The *TLE* **Extra Practice** presents **questions** like the ones in the Examples. After each question, students have the option of seeing a sample solution, **retrying** the question, or seeing the correct answer if they were incorrect.

Questions for each type of exercise are dynamically generated from a **mini-data bank** of up to 60 questions.

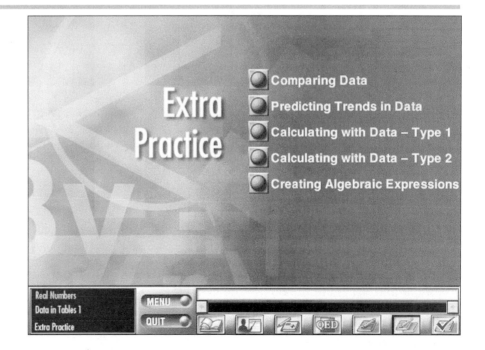

✓ Self-Check

The *TLE* **Self-Check** presents up to **10 questions** like those in the **Extra Practice**. There are **three unique Self-Checks** for each lesson.

After students see their scores, they can **review the questions** and their **answers** one at a time, **try again**, or **see** the **correct answer** or a **sample solution**.

On achieving a minimum standard (usually about 70%), the lesson is considered to be completed. Completed lessons are indicated by a check mark that appears beside the lesson on the main menu.

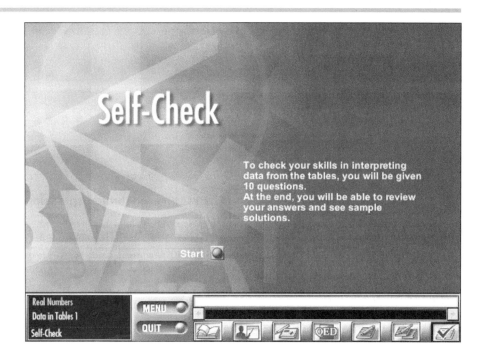

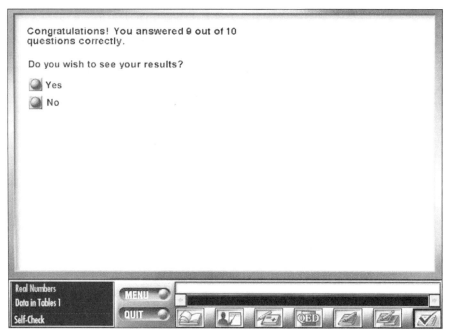

NOTES

Feedback Boxes

Please note that the Feedback Boxes can be moved by clicking on the green bar and dragging the box to the desired location on the screen. You can hide, and then reveal, the content of the Feedback Box by double-clicking on the green bar. To close the Feedback Box, click on the button in the upper left corner of the green bar.

Features

Interacting with *TLE* Courseware

Students interact with *TLE* in a variety of ways.

Interaction 1

They may input **simple text** and press RETURN after each input.

Every effort has been made to anticipate all reasonable forms in which students might enter answers. Text answers usually consist of numbers, and sometimes variables. Other alphabetic entries are rarely required, in order to avoid entering mis-spelled but mathematically correct answers.

Different numerical forms of answers may be allowed, such as 1/2, 0.5, 0.50, and so on. However, if all the information in a problem is expressed in one form, like whole numbers, the answers are usually expected to be in the same form.

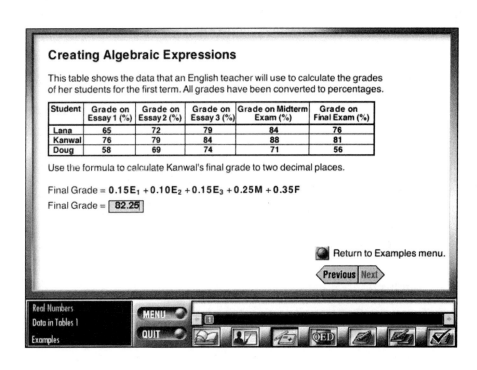

Creating Algebraic Expressions

This table shows the data that an English teacher will use to calculate the grades of her students for the first term. All grades have been converted to percentages.

Student	Grade on Essay 1 (%)	Grade on Essay 2 (%)	Grade on Essay 3 (%)	Grade on Midterm Exam (%)	Grade on Final Exam (%)
Lana	65	72	79	84	76
Kanwal	76	79	84	88	81
Doug	58	69	74	71	56

Use the formula to calculate Kanwal's final grade to two decimal places.

Final Grade $= 0.15E_1 + 0.10E_2 + 0.15E_3 + 0.25M + 0.35F$

Final Grade $=$ 82.25

Return to Examples menu.

Previous Next

Real Numbers
Data in Tables 1
Examples

MENU
QUIT

Interaction 2

They may click a button for a multiple choice response.

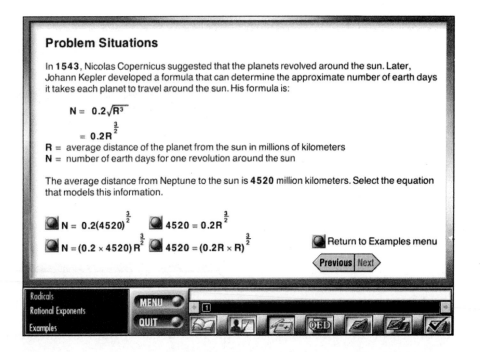

Problem Situations

In **1543**, Nicolas Copernicus suggested that the planets revolved around the sun. Later, Johann Kepler developed a formula that can determine the approximate number of earth days it takes each planet to travel around the sun. His formula is:

$$N = 0.2\sqrt{R^3}$$
$$= 0.2R^{\frac{3}{2}}$$

$R =$ average distance of the planet from the sun in millions of kilometers
$N =$ number of earth days for one revolution around the sun

The average distance from Neptune to the sun is **4520** million kilometers. Select the equation that models this information.

$N = 0.2(4520)^{\frac{3}{2}}$ $4520 = 0.2R^{\frac{3}{2}}$

$N = (0.2 \times 4520)R^{\frac{3}{2}}$ $4520 = (0.2R \times R)^{\frac{3}{2}}$

Return to Examples menu

Previous Next

Radicals
Rational Exponents
Examples

MENU
QUIT

In some multiple choice questions, students may select more than one response, and then press a DONE button. Students can then reflect on their choice(s).

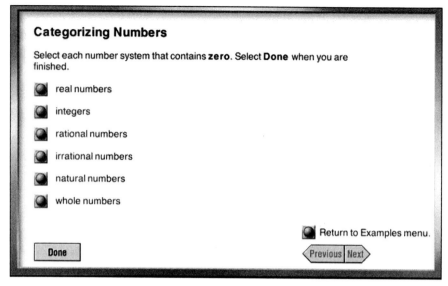

Interaction 3

They may drag one or more items to the appropriate location(s).

Click on the item and drag it with the mouse. Correctly placed items stick; incorrectly placed items bounce back.

Students should drag and place the items carefully with the mouse. If they are careless about the position of an item in a box, a correct item may bounce back and appear to be incorrect.

For some "drag-and-drop" questions, students may drag more than one item to the appropriate location and then press a DONE button.

After any of the above interactions, they select NEXT to continue.

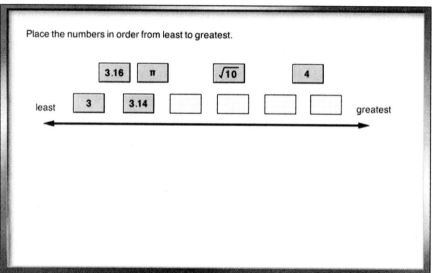

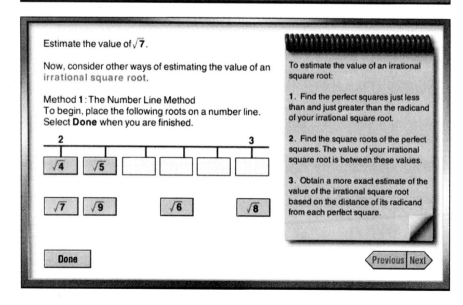

Sound

A soundtrack accompanies parts of *TLE* with a **sound control (Off or 1 to 7)**, which is available to students. Narration accompanies the Introduction, Tutorial, and Summary components.

Explorers

In several *TLE* lessons, students can use supplementary software called **Explorers**. They are designed to **encourage** students **to explore** mathematics concepts, skills, and procedures, **test** their ideas, and **reflect** on their actions.

The **Explorers** use simulations of activities using materials like tiles or spinners, as well as programs to create graphs and geometric diagrams.

The *TLE Explorers* are available from a pull-down menu and cover the following topics:

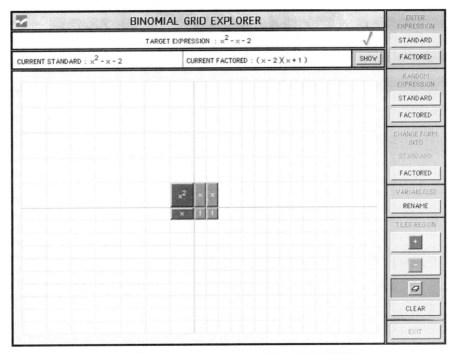

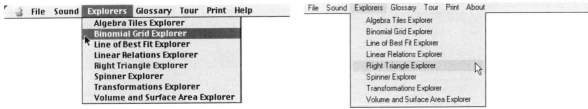

Glossary

TLE allows students to **access** an **on-screen** Glossary using **hot text** or a pull-down **menu**. Hot text is highlighted on screen and can be clicked for direct access to the Glossary.

The Glossary provides complete definitions and examples. It helps students understand **the language of mathematics** and is just one of the many features that promote math connections within mathematics and to other disciplines.

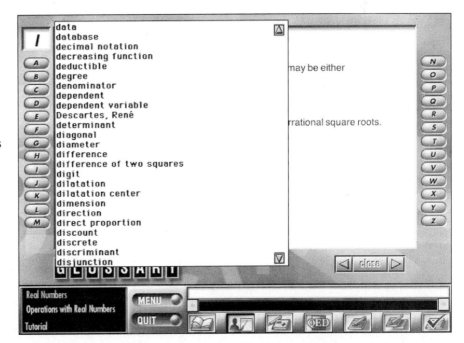

Student Workbooks

Every *TLE* lesson has a four-page refresher in the *Student Workbook* – a brief, printed review of the lesson, with examples, solutions, and some new exercises and problems. Answers to every odd-numbered exercise are found in the back of the book.

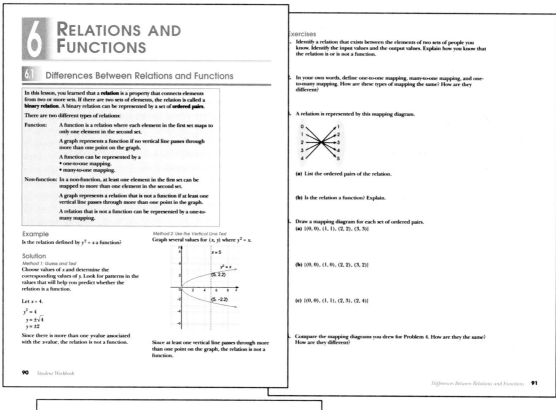

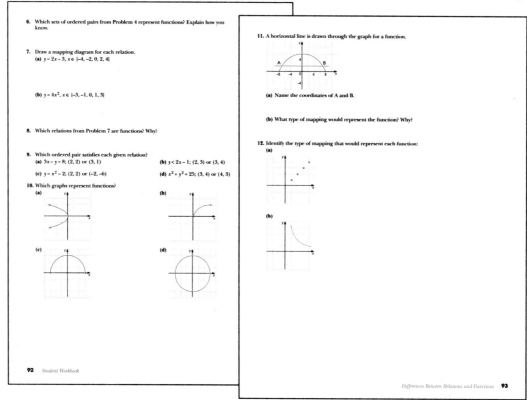

Getting Started and Moving Around

Installation Instructions

Welcome to The Learning Equation® (TLE) multimedia courseware for developmental mathematics. This courseware is designed to be used in two ways:
- By you and your students in a college or university lab setting
- Independently, on your home or office computer

Installing TLE in a College or University Lab Setting
This installation should be performed by the system administrator at your college/university lab. Complete instructions are available with the The Learning Equation Implementation Kit. Instructions are also available on Disk 1 of the enclosed CDs. Look for the README file on the CD. For updates, see our website at www.thelearningequation.com.

Installing TLE On Your Home or Office Computer
You can install The Learning Equation courseware on your home or office computer to view the program content and determine which lessons you want to assign to your class. To use the Brooks/Cole course management components (Activity Page, Assignments, Gradebook, Testing, and Courseware) you will use the Brooks/Cole web site dedicated to your institution on the Brooks/Cole servers.

PC Minimum Requirements
- 100 MHz Pentium processor or better
- 32 MB RAM
- 75 MB free hard disk space
- Monitor supporting 256 colors, 800x600 resolution or better
- Sound card
- Double-speed CD-ROM drive
- Microsoft® Windows® 95/98/NT/2000
- Browser (Microsoft® Internet Explorer 5.0 or later, Netscape® Navigator 4.5 or later)

Macintosh® Minimum Requirements
- Macintosh® PowerPC, Power Macintosh®, G3 or better
- 32 MB RAM free memory
- 75 MB free hard disk space
- 14" RGB monitor (256 colors) with 800x600 resolution or better
- Sound card
- Double-speed CD-ROM drive
- System 8.0 or higher
- Browser (Microsoft® Internet Explorer 4.5 or later, Netscape® Navigator 4.5 or later)

PC Installation
To install TLE on your home computer, insert Disk 1 in your CD-ROM drive. Use "My Computer" or "Windows Explorer" to locate your CD-ROM drive. Double-click to display the contents of the CD. Locate the README file, open it, and print it. Follow the installation instructions in the README file.

Macintosh Installation
To install TLE on your home computer, insert Disk 1 in your CD-ROM drive. Click on the TLE/BCA icon to display the contents of the CD. Locate the README file, open it and print it. Follow the installation instructions in the README file.

Lesson Title

The objectives and prerequisites for the lesson and basic navigation instructions are presented in the on-screen tabbed notebook. Click on individual heading tabs.

Select the NEXT button to start the **Introduction.**

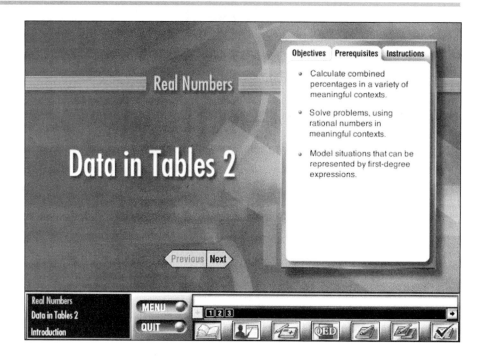

Menu Bar

The MENU bar has seven pull-down options.

Under **File**, you can **Open** your personal record file or create a **New** one. You can **Save** your current results, return to the main TLE MENU, or **Quit.** Students are advised to save their work as they go.

The sound can be adjusted to individual needs. Use the pull-down **Sound** menu from the menu bar to turn the sound off or to set the level from 1 to 7. Headsets may also be used with the sound feature.

Under **Explorers**, you'll find a number of programs for solving problems involving numbers, algebra, geometry, and statistics.

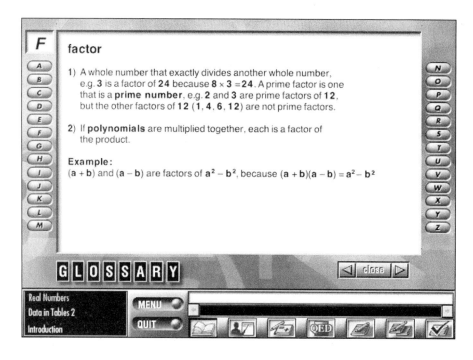

You can also access the **Glossary**. Within each lesson, the **Glossary** is available by double clicking words highlighted in blue ("hot text"). Once in the **Glossary,** select the word of your choice from the alphabetic menu. Return to the lesson by selecting **Close.**

Navigation Bar

You always know where you are in a lesson by looking at the bottom left corner of the TLE Navigation Bar.

Chapter
Lesson
Component

The TLE Navigation Bar is designed to be easy to use, with seven icons to reference the lesson components.

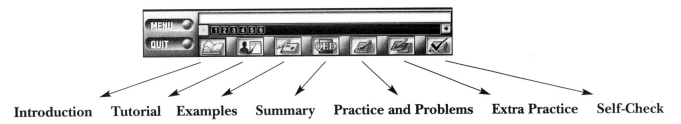

Introduction   Tutorial   Examples   Summary   Practice and Problems   Extra Practice   Self-Check

Click the appropriate icon to go to the lesson component of your choice.

Pages

The number of "pages" in each lesson component is also displayed in the Navigation Bar. Several screens of material may be included in a "page," which represents a "complete thought."

A yellow border highlights the current page of the lesson component. Once a page is completed, it is highlighted in red.

A user can jump to individual pages by clicking the page number on the Navigation Bar.

Previous and Next

Navigate through the lesson by selecting the NEXT button.

The PREVIOUS button allows you to go back to review earlier screens.

Success Tips for Users

Students learn by doing. The following suggestions will facilitate this process:

1. **Take notes:** Have students write down an example or two that they worked out in the **Tutorial** to keep as a model for other problems throughout the lesson. Also have them write down any steps they find in the **Summary** or rules provided in the **Tutorial**.

2. **Use the Glossary:** Key terms are highlighted in blue throughout the lesson. Students can find the meaning of these terms in the **Glossary**. To access the **Glossary** they can either click on the term itself or use the pull-down menu on the MENU bar.

   Have students keep a list of the highlighted terms, along with an example. Such a list is helpful while working through a lesson and also aids in review at the end of a lesson.

3. **Discuss:** Whenever possible, have students discuss what they have learned or what they do not understand with a partner.

4. **Review the Examples:** The **Examples** section usually provides different information from that covered in the **Tutorial**. Review each category in the **Examples** section.

5. **Use the calculators and other tools:** Though students can complete some examples and problems using mental math skills, they should also, where appropriate, use other tools such as pencil and paper, diagrams, and calculators, to figure out a problem.

6. **Be aware of levels of difficulty in Practice and Problems:** Recognize that the categories of questions in the **Practice and Problems** section tend to increase in difficulty from left to right across the columns, and from top to bottom within each column or category.

   It is wise to suggest that weaker students attempt the first two categories (columns) and the questions at the top of the other columns. Advanced students may wish to try the last questions in each category.

   It may turn out that a student may choose to do all questions – this enthusiasm is to be applauded! But, when suggesting to students which questions to try, bear in mind that one would never assign every question in a textbook to a student.

7. **Provide enrichment:** Further enrichment can be addressed by following up on the Picture Information provided for each completed Hidden Screen in the **Examples** and **Practice and Problems** components.

8. **Use pencil and paper:** Having students use pencil and paper when completing the **Extra Practice** and **Self-Check** components allows practice with the transfer of information from screen to paper. In addition, when answers are reviewed, student work can be compared with sample answers for completeness and accuracy.

9. **Use the Self-Check:** The **Self-Check** component can be used in different ways:
   (a) as a placement tool – it can be attempted before the start of a lesson to determine whether the lesson material is new to the student.
   (b) to check for understanding – it can be attempted at the end of a lesson to check that the student has understood the lesson material.

   A poor mark on **Self-Check** indicates that the student should be directed back to the **Tutorial** and **Examples** components of the lesson, or alternatively, to the **Extra Practice** section.

   Achievement of at least 70% on **Self-Check** produces a check mark indicator in the box to the left of the lesson, on the MENU.

10. **Create an instruction manual:** Students may wish to create their own guide on how to use different functions and features of this program.

11. ***Explorer* screen dumps:** On Macintosh computers, it is possible to take a "screen dump" (a picture of what is on the screen) by pressing the keys "shift-command-3" simultaneously. In Windows, press alt-shift-print screen. When using the *Explorers*, students may wish to take screen dumps for later reference as well as note any observations they made about features not mentioned in the software.

Note: When following any of these suggestions, keep in mind that the strengths of the courseware lie in the fact that it is student-driven and flexible in addressing student needs. Allow students the opportunity to explore.

Instructor's Preview Version

The **Instructor's Preview Version** is not meant for use by students. It allows you to progress through the lessons without having to perform every student interaction. Simply use the Next button or the arrow keys to proceed to a new screen display without answering any question currently displayed.

Windows 95/98/NT:

To launch TLE-Teacher Preview Mode, hold the shift key down and click the "OK" button when you are launching TLE from the BCA server. Keep holding the shift key down until TLE has started. You will see a second window labeled "Floater". The default setting of floater is normal mode, indicated by the green button. Click the green button. When it is red, then TLE is running in Teacher Preview Mode. You can switch between the two modes at any time.

To completely disable the Teacher Preview Mode, go to the TLE-coursware folder (default location is C:\Program Files\BrooksCole\TLEIA). Open the Main folder and delete the file Floater.dxr. This will not affect the normal running of TLE products. To re-enable the Teacher Preview Mode, copy the Floater.dxr file from the Instructors CD (disc 1) Main folder to the Main folder on the your computer (default location is C:\Program Files\BrooksCole\TLEIA).

The Learning Equation®

INTERMEDIATE ALGEBRA

1 REAL NUMBERS

1.1 Data in Tables 1

Cross-References
Real Numbers

Student Workbook: pages 2–5

Key Objectives
The student will:
- use words and algebraic expressions to describe the data and the inter-relationships in a table with rows that are not related recursively (not calculated from previous data).

Key Terms
data, expression, algebraic formula, equation

Prerequisite Skills
- Calculate combined percentages in a variety of meaningful contexts.
- Solve problems, using rational numbers in meaningful contexts.
- Model situations that can be represented by first-degree equations.

Lesson Description

In this lesson, students interpret data shown in table form. Most problems involve everyday data that will be familiar to most students, such as pay rates, clothing prices, and test grades.

In the **Introduction**, students use tables to calculate wages for three types of employees – office staff who are paid an hourly wage, sales staff who are paid a 7% commission, and delivery staff who are paid an hourly wage plus a flat fee for each delivery. In the **Summary**, students derive algebraic formulas for calculating each type of wage. With these formulas, the employer can write a computer program to generate tables showing gross pay for all his staff.

The **Tutorial** uses a price list from a clothing store as a context for work with data. Students compare taxes on different items in order to calculate and compare the state and city sales tax rates. Then they develop an algebraic formula for calculating the total cost, including tax, of a garment purchased at the store. Finally, they test the expression by substituting data from the table.

The **Examples** focus on four skills: comparing, predicting, calculating, and creating algebraic expressions. A percent theme runs through the **Examples** that may help students review percent skills developed in previous years.

Instructor Intervention

- Encourage students to use estimation and mental arithmetic as they make predictions and calculations. Demonstrate some techniques, such as:
  - **(a)** If you are calculating a percent of a number, multiply as with a whole number, then divide the result by 100. For example, 7% of $16 = 7 \times 16 \div 100$.
  - **(b)** If you are calculating a percent of a number, you can interchange the terms. For example, 7% of 50 = 50% of 7.
  - **(c)** You can calculate percents mentally by thinking of 10% and 1%. For example, 9% of 30 is 10% of 30 – 1% of 30 or 3 – 0.3 or 2.7.

- Since the emphasis in this lesson is on thinking skills rather than computation, permit the use of calculators as necessary. Take this opportunity to assess basic calculator skills, especially with regard to percent.

  If students are equipped with new calculators, invite them to store their manuals at school for reference as needed. You may wish to establish a classroom library of manuals for different types of calculators.

- Some problems require students to create algebraic expressions. Review these conventions for recording algebraic sentences:
  - **(a)** In an algebraic sentence, you can replace a multiplication sign with a dot or a pair of parentheses. In a term with a variable and a coefficient, you can leave it out entirely.
  - **(b)** When a term has a variable and a coefficient, write the coefficient first.

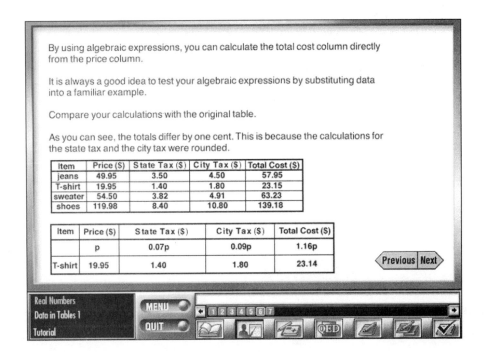

By using algebraic expressions, you can calculate the total cost column directly from the price column.

It is always a good idea to test your algebraic expressions by substituting data into a familiar example.

Compare your calculations with the original table.

As you can see, the totals differ by one cent. This is because the calculations for the state tax and the city tax were rounded.

Item	Price ($)	State Tax ($)	City Tax ($)	Total Cost ($)
jeans	49.95	3.50	4.50	57.95
T-shirt	19.95	1.40	1.80	23.15
sweater	54.50	3.82	4.91	63.23
shoes	119.98	8.40	10.80	139.18

Item	Price ($)	State Tax ($)	City Tax ($)	Total Cost ($)
	p	0.07p	0.09p	1.16p
T-shirt	19.95	1.40	1.80	23.14

⟨Previous│Next⟩

Real Numbers
Data in Tables 1
Tutorial

MENU
QUIT
1 2 3 4 5 6 7

Evaluation

- Give small groups several cylindrical containers. Ask them to order the containers according to the capacity written on the outside of each one, then complete a table such as the following.

Contents	Radius of Base	Circum- ference	Capacity

When the table is finished, pose these problems:
(a) What trends can you find in the data?
(b) Which container holds the most? the least?
(c) List six different percent relationships you can find in the data.
(d) Write an algebraic expression you could use to find the circumference of a cylinder if you knew the base radius.

(e) Add three rows to the table. List a different base radius in each row. Calculate each matching circumference.
(f) Why can't you use the base radius alone to estimate the capacity?
(g) Create a problem based on the data in your table.

- Observe how students identify trends in data. Do they simply look for patterns of increase or decrease or do they also consider whether these increases and decreases are mathematically related?

- Students can work in pairs or small groups to create a table of data with the following characteristics:
(a) at least one visible trend
(b) at least one visible mathematical relationship between columns

The groups can exchange tables, identify trends, and create algebraic expressions to describe the data.

Remediation

- Review these processes:
(a) converting between decimals and percents
(b) evaluating algebraic expressions by substituting values for variables
(c) calculating means

- For practice, invite students to bring in tables of sports statistics gathered from newspapers, magazines, almanacs, or the Internet.

Ask why the table was arranged as it was, and what trends or mathematical relationships students can see in the data. Discuss these processes:
(a) comparing data
(b) making percent calculations
(c) considering factors that may have influenced the data
(d) generating algebraic expressions
(e) making predictions based on the data

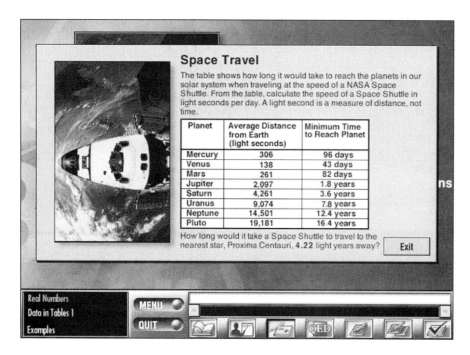

Space Travel

The table shows how long it would take to reach the planets in our solar system when traveling at the speed of a NASA Space Shuttle. From the table, calculate the speed of a Space Shuttle in light seconds per day. A light second is a measure of distance, not time.

Planet	Average Distance from Earth (light seconds)	Minimum Time to Reach Planet
Mercury	306	96 days
Venus	138	43 days
Mars	261	82 days
Jupiter	2,097	1.8 years
Saturn	4,261	3.6 years
Uranus	9,074	7.8 years
Neptune	14,501	12.4 years
Pluto	19,181	16.4 years

How long would it take a Space Shuttle to travel to the nearest star, Proxima Centauri, 4.22 light years away?   Exit

Real Numbers
Data in Tables 1
Examples   MENU   QUIT

Extension

A

Invite pairs to choose two calculator operations, such as +3 and × 4. Limit the operations to +, −, ×, and ÷, and the numbers to integers from −9 to 9.

Students can enter 0 in the calculator, perform the two operations, then record the results in a table.

Have them repeat with other starting numbers to complete the table, then exchange with another pair, identify the pattern, and record the algebraic expression.

Once students have identified the pattern, they can extend the list of starting numbers forward or back and use the algebraic expression to find each related ending number.

Starting Number	Ending Number
0	3
1	16
2	
3	
3	

B

Students could use spreadsheet programs to duplicate and extend tables from the lesson or tables based on data they've collected. More experienced students could act as mentors to help others learn more about how to use these programs. Most programs also have graphing components.

Enrichment

A

Students who have graphing calculators could consult their manuals to find out how to create spreadsheets for non-recursive data.

For example, with a TI-83 calculator, students can access a blank spreadsheet by pressing STAT, then choosing 1:Edit. To name columns, they can press the keys that show letters above and to the right. To enter a formula for a particular column, they will need to position the cursor in the column heading and enclose the formula in quotation marks (ALPHA +). They will also need to use 2nd STAT to incorporate elements from previous columns into their formulas.

When finished, students can press 2nd + , choose 2:Delete, and then choose 4:List to erase the spreadsheet from memory. (They will need to be careful not to press 1:All on the delete list, or they will erase all the programs they have entered into the calculator memory.)

B

Once students know how to create spreadsheets using graphing software and graphing calculators, they could choose a topic of interest – such as a sport, an area of scientific inquiry, or a particular business – look for related tables, and incorporate the data into a spreadsheet.

Students with access to the Internet could share their knowledge of websites that might prove useful.

C

Have students collect statistics about the performance of school sports teams over several years, then display the information in graphs and tables. Individuals or pairs might present their information for the class and pose related math problems.

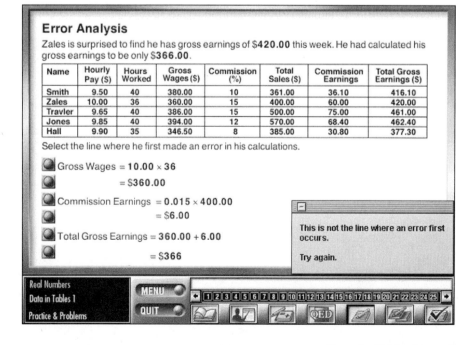

Data in Tables 2

Cross-References
Real Numbers

Student Workbook: pages 6–9

Key Objectives
The student will:

- use words and algebraic expressions to describe the data and the inter-relationships in a table with rows that are related recursively (calculated from previous data).

Key Terms
recursive, principal, interest, loan period, balance

Prerequisite Skills
- Calculate combined percentages in a variety of meaningful contexts.
- Solve problems using rational numbers in meaningful contexts.
- Model situations that can be represented by first-degree equations.

Lesson Description

This lesson deals with tables where rows of data are related recursively (calculated from previous data). Students interpret the data, make calculations and predictions, and use words and algebraic expressions to describe the data and the recursive relationship.

In the **Introduction,** a nonrecursive table is used to illustrate the year-by-year interest earned on a $500 Regular Interest Savings Bond. A second table shows the changes in yearly earnings when the same amount of principal earns compound interest. This table is recursive, since interest is compounded based on the amount of principal and interest for the previous year. The **Summary** invites students to use what they have learned to project the value of the Compound Interest Bond through years 4 and 5.

The **Tutorial** begins with two models dealing with cat-breeding that establish the difference between nonrecursive and recursive relationships. Next, students use a recursive table to examine a time-payment plan for the purchase of a mountain bike. From the table, students develop verbal and algebraic expressions they can use to calculate the data. They also predict how the data would change if the down payment were increased.

In the **Examples**, students work with three recursive tables that illustrate payment plans. In the first and second examples, students interpret and describe data and identify the recursive relationships. In the third, they perform calculations with given data. The final two sections deal with the effects of modified data.

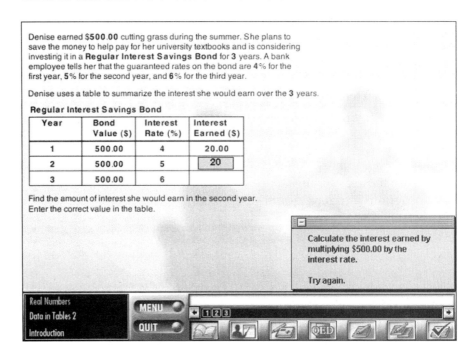

Denise earned **$500.00** cutting grass during the summer. She plans to save the money to help pay for her university textbooks and is considering investing it in a **Regular Interest Savings Bond** for 3 years. A bank employee tells her that the guaranteed rates on the bond are **4**% for the first year, **5**% for the second year, and **6**% for the third year.

Denise uses a table to summarize the interest she would earn over the **3** years.

Regular Interest Savings Bond

Year	Bond Value ($)	Interest Rate (%)	Interest Earned ($)
1	500.00	4	20.00
2	500.00	5	20
3	500.00	6	

Find the amount of interest she would earn in the second year.
Enter the correct value in the table.

Calculate the interest earned by multiplying $500.00 by the interest rate.

Try again.

Real Numbers
Data in Tables 2
Introduction

MENU
QUIT
1 2 3

Instructor Intervention

- Review percent concepts to prepare students for problems they will encounter in the lesson. They should be able to:
  - **(a)** express a rate as a percent.
  - **(b)** express decimals as percents and percents as decimals.
  - **(c)** find a percent of a number.
  - **(d)** find one number as a percent of another.
  - **(e)** recognize that if a value is reduced by 25%, the resulting value is 75% of the original, but the original value is *not* 125% of the reduced value.

- Review how to calculate interest earned on an investment or charged on a loan. Most problems use an annual rate, but some involve calculating monthly interest. For example, to calculate the monthly interest charged on a $2000 loan at 10%, find $\dfrac{0.1 \times 2000}{12}$.

Lesson Components

 Examples

Patterns in Tables (1)
Reading Tables (1)
Calculations with Data (1)
Changing Values (1)
Modifying Tables (1)

Practice and Problems

Reading Tables
Recursive Relations
Calculating Values
Equations
Modifying Tables

Extra Practice

Reading Tables
Recursive Relationships
Equations
Calculating Values
Calculations with Data
Modifying Tables

 Self-Check

Reading Tables (2)
Recursive Relationships (1)
Equations (2)
Calculating Values (1)
Calculations with Data (2)
Modifying Tables (1)

Minimum score: 7 out of 9

Reading Tables

Tables are an effective way of organizing data. It is important to be able to read data from tables. Consider this example.

Rakia is planning to buy a mountain bike on a payment plan. She will make a down payment of **$100**, and then she will make monthly payments of **$150** from November to April. In May, she will make a final payment of the balance owing on the bike.

The store provides her with this table of the payment plan.

Which column shows the monthly payment? Select the correct heading on the table.

$1300.00 tax incl.

Month	Opening Balance ($)	Interest Rate(%)	Interest Charged($)	Regular Payment ($)	Closing Balance ($)
November	1200.00	10	10.00	150.00	1060.00
December	1060.00	10	8.83	150.00	918.83
January	918.83	10	7.66	150.00	776.49
February	776.49	10	6.47	150.00	632.96
March	632.96	10	5.27	150.00	488.23
April	488.23	10	4.07	150.00	342.30
May	342.30	10	2.85	345.15	0.00

Mountain Bike Price:
$1300.00

Down Payment:
$100.00

⟨Previous | Next⟩

Real Numbers
Data in Tables 2
Tutorial

MENU

QUIT

1 2 3 4 5 6 7

Evaluation

- Gather or create tables that show recursive data. Pose problems similar to those in the **Examples** and **Practice and Problems** sections. For example:

Justin used a credit card to buy $250 worth of clothes. The credit card company charges an interest rate of 20% per year. Each month, the company sends a bill for that month's interest plus a given percent of the principal.

The table shows Justin's payments for the first six months.

Month	Opening Balance	Interest	Monthly Bill	Payment Toward Principal
Jan.	250.00	4.18	29.17	25.00
Feb.	225.00	3.76	26.26	22.50
Mar.	202.5	3.38	23.63	20.25
Apr.	182.25	3.04	21.27	18.73
May	164.02	2.74	19.14	16.40
June	147.62	2.47	17.23	14.76

(a) Is the table recursive or nonrecursive? Why?

(b) What was Justin's monthly bill in April?

(c) Why does Justin's monthly bill decrease each month?

(d) In all, how much did Justin pay the credit card company from January until June?

(e) How much money will Justin still owe at the beginning of July?

(f) What percent of the principal does the monthly interest represent? [20% ÷ 12 or 1.67%]

(g) What percent of the principal does the company require Justin to pay each month? [10%]

(h) Why is the opening balance each month not equal to (previous balance – monthly bill)? [Only part of the monthly bill payment is applied to the principal. The rest goes to interest.]

(i) Write an equation to show how the opening balance is actually calculated.

(j) Complete the table to show data for July and August.

(k) Redo the table to show how the data would change if Justin paid an extra $10 each month. Assume that this money will be applied directly to the principal.

- Observe how students analyze data in tables. Can they explain how to recognize recursive data? How well do they read data directly from a table? Can they express relationships between pieces of data in words and in algebraic form? Do they know how to express a rate as a percent? express percents in different forms? find a percent of a number? find one number as a percent of another?

Remediation

- Remind students to read given information carefully and to examine row and column headings. Encourage them to ask questions if they do not understand problem information or information presented in table form. It may be helpful to have students work in pairs.

- Some students may need reinforcement of percent concepts. Review the types of calculations listed in the **Instructor Intervention** section of this lesson.

- Students sometimes have difficulty expressing mathematical relationships using algebraic terms. It frequently helps to describe each relationship in words before writ-

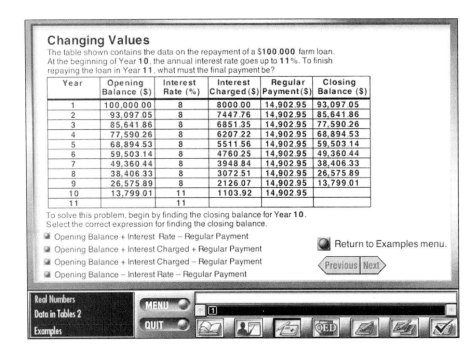

Changing Values

The table shown contains the data on the repayment of a $100,000 farm loan. At the beginning of Year 10, the annual interest rate goes up to 11%. To finish repaying the loan in Year 11, what must the final payment be?

Year	Opening Balance ($)	Interest Rate (%)	Interest Charged ($)	Regular Payment ($)	Closing Balance ($)
1	100,000.00	8	8000.00	14,902.95	93,097.05
2	93,097.05	8	7447.76	14,902.95	85,641.86
3	85,641.86	8	6851.35	14,902.95	77,590.26
4	77,590.26	8	6207.22	14,902.95	68,894.53
5	68,894.53	8	5511.56	14,902.95	59,503.14
6	59,503.14	8	4760.25	14,902.95	49,360.44
7	49,360.44	8	3948.84	14,902.95	38,406.33
8	38,406.33	8	3072.51	14,902.95	26,575.89
9	26,575.89	8	2126.07	14,902.95	13,799.01
10	13,799.01	11	1103.92	14,902.95	
11		11			

To solve this problem, begin by finding the closing balance for Year 10. Select the correct expression for finding the closing balance.

☑ Opening Balance + Interest Rate – Regular Payment
☑ Opening Balance + Interest Charged + Regular Payment
☑ Opening Balance + Interest Charged – Regular Payment
☑ Opening Balance – Interest Rate – Regular Payment

☑ Return to Examples menu.
◁ Previous | Next ▷

Real Numbers
Data in Tables 2
Examples

MENU
QUIT
[1]

ing the algebraic sentence. Review especially the relationship between the word "of" and multiplication, and how to express percents in decimal form. For example:

The interest is 7% of the opening balance.

$I = 7\% \times O$
$I = 0.07 \times O$

• You may wish to create transparencies showing tables from the lesson for use in class discussion.

Extension

A

Problem 6 in the *Student Workbook* and the "Modifying Tables" problem in the **Examples** section involve similar situations, but are solved in different ways. Have students interchange the solution methods to solve each problem in a different way.

B

Students could gather information about interest rates, then set up loan tables that illustrate loan repayment plans at different rates over different loan periods. Have them create problems based on their tables that involve:

(a) interpreting information shown in a table.
(b) identifying missing information.
(c) determining the effect of changes to the principal, interest rate, or loan period.

C

Invite students to look for tables that show recursive data, for example, in magazines or newspapers. The students could present their tables for the class and create a series of problems to go with each one.

Enrichment

A

Have students create a spreadsheet based on one of the situations described in the lesson. Demonstrate how to use formulas to enter and change spreadsheet data. Encourage students to explore what happens when they change parameters such as the interest rate or the amount of the regular payment.

B

Students could develop a spreadsheet to calculate the data shown in the problem in the **Evaluation** section of this lesson. Ask them to predict how long they think it will take Justin to pay off his bill if he makes only the required payment each month. Then have them use the spreadsheet to check. [about 90 months]

Have students sum the monthly payments and compare the total amount paid with the initial cost of the clothes.

C

Students might contact a bank to find out how loan and mortgage payments are determined.

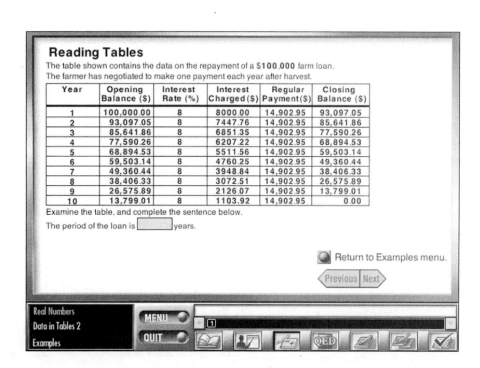

Reading Tables

The table shown contains the data on the repayment of a $100,000 farm loan. The farmer has negotiated to make one payment each year after harvest.

Year	Opening Balance ($)	Interest Rate (%)	Interest Charged ($)	Regular Payment ($)	Closing Balance ($)
1	100,000.00	8	8000.00	14,902.95	93,097.05
2	93,097.05	8	7447.76	14,902.95	85,641.86
3	85,641.86	8	6851.35	14,902.95	77,590.26
4	77,590.26	8	6207.22	14,902.95	68,894.53
5	68,894.53	8	5511.56	14,902.95	59,503.14
6	59,503.14	8	4760.25	14,902.95	49,360.44
7	49,360.44	8	3948.84	14,902.95	38,406.33
8	38,406.33	8	3072.51	14,902.95	26,575.89
9	26,575.89	8	2126.07	14,902.95	13,799.01
10	13,799.01	8	1103.92	14,902.95	0.00

Examine the table, and complete the sentence below.

The period of the loan is [   ] years.

Return to Examples menu.

‹ Previous | Next ›

Real Numbers
Data in Tables 2
Examples

MENU
QUIT

Cross-References

Real Numbers

Student Workbook: pages 10–13

Key Objectives

The student will:

- classify numbers as natural, whole, integer, rational, or irrational, and show that these number sets are nested within the real number system.

Key Terms

natural number, whole number, integer, rational number, irrational number

Prerequisite Skills

- Give examples of numbers that satisfy the conditions of natural, whole, integral, and rational numbers, and show that these numbers comprise the rational number system.
- Describe, orally and in writing, whether or not a number is rational.
- Give examples of situations where answers would involve only the positive square root, or both positive and negative square roots of a number.
- Solve problems, using rational numbers in meaningful contexts.

Lesson Description

This lesson reviews the natural, whole, integer, and rational number systems, and introduces irrational numbers as decimals that neither terminate nor repeat.

In the **Introduction**, a management trainee at a bank charts fluctuating interest rates. First, she decides to express each rate in both fraction and decimal forms. Students build the chart by converting fractional rates to decimals, then decimal rates to fractions. In the process, they discover that some decimals cannot be expressed in fraction form. In the **Summary**, students return to the list of interest rates to identify those with nonterminating, repeating periods as irrational numbers.

The **Tutorial** reviews each number system, beginning with natural numbers, and gradually builds a visual representation to show how the number sets are nested within the real number system.

In the **Examples**, students classify decimals as rational or irrational, order numbers in different forms, examine nested systems in more detail, and select the number system(s) to which a given number belongs. Problems deal with all six number systems, but their primary focus is on rational, irrational, and real numbers.

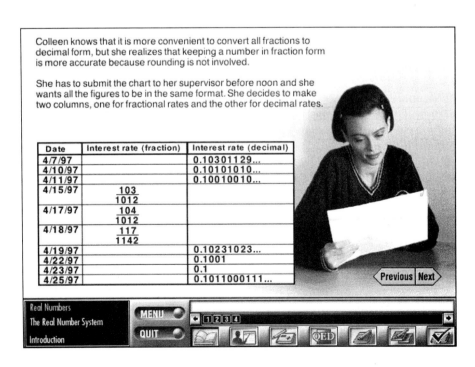

Colleen knows that it is more convenient to convert all fractions to decimal form, but she realizes that keeping a number in fraction form is more accurate because rounding is not involved.

She has to submit the chart to her supervisor before noon and she wants all the figures to be in the same format. She decides to make two columns, one for fractional rates and the other for decimal rates.

Date	Interest rate (fraction)	Interest rate (decimal)
4/7/97		0.10301129...
4/10/97		0.10101010...
4/11/97		0.10010010...
4/15/97	$\frac{103}{1012}$	
4/17/97	$\frac{104}{1012}$	
4/18/97	$\frac{117}{1142}$	
4/19/97		0.10231023...
4/22/97		0.1001
4/23/97		0.1
4/25/97		0.1011000111...

Real Numbers
The Real Number System
Introduction

MENU

QUIT

1 2 3 4

Previous | Next

Instructor Intervention

- Before you begin this lesson, review the natural, whole, integer, and rational number systems. Some students may need a diagram to help them see why some numbers belong to more than one system. For example, a number such as 7 belongs to all four systems, while a number such as $-\frac{2}{3}$ belongs to the rational system alone.

- In the **Examples** section called "Ordering Numbers," students discover that $\sqrt{2}$ is an irrational number. Ask whether all square roots are irrational, and invite students to give examples to support their answers.

- To demonstrate that some rational numbers can appear to be irrational if you see a limited number of decimal places, invite students to use a calculator to find $\frac{1}{103}$. The calculator will show the decimal form as 0.009708737, but the number must by definition be rational because $\frac{1}{103}$ is a fraction. Explain that numbers with long periods will not appear in this lesson, in order to make it easier to distinguish between rational and irrational numbers.

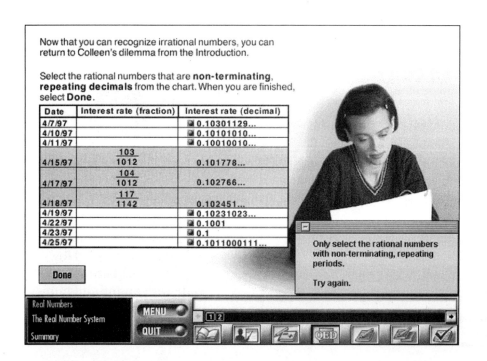

Now that you can recognize irrational numbers, you can return to Colleen's dilemma from the Introduction.

Select the rational numbers that are **non-terminating, repeating decimals** from the chart. When you are finished, select **Done**.

Date	Interest rate (fraction)	Interest rate (decimal)
4/7/97		☑ 0.10301129...
4/10/97		☑ 0.10101010...
4/11/97		☑ 0.10010010...
4/15/97	$\frac{103}{1012}$	0.101778...
4/17/97	$\frac{104}{1012}$	0.102766...
4/18/97	$\frac{117}{1142}$	0.102451...
4/19/97		☑ 0.10231023...
4/22/97		☑ 0.1001
4/23/97		☑ 0.1
4/25/97		☑ 0.1011000111...

Done

Only select the rational numbers with non-terminating, repeating periods.

Try again.

Real Numbers
The Real Number System
Summary

MENU
QUIT
[1] [2]
QBD

Evaluation

- List examples of different types of numbers on the board. Ask students to classify each number and to locate it on a Venn diagram like the one illustrated in the **Tutorial**. You might use numbers such as:
  - **(a)** −4
  - **(b)** $\frac{8}{4}$
  - **(c)** 0
  - **(d)** .2
  - **(e)** 1.2345
  - **(f)** $\sqrt{5}$
  - **(g)** $\sqrt{9}$
  - **(h)** $0.\overline{6}$

- Observe how students classify numbers. Do they understand how a number can belong to more than one system? Do they recognize all terminating or repeating decimals as rational? Can they define an irrational number? a real number?

Remediation

- Have students define the natural number system, then explain what must be added to this system to get whole numbers. Continue this process through integers, rational numbers, and irrational numbers to build up to the real number system. Emphasize that irrational numbers form a separate system that does not include rational, integer, whole, or natural numbers.

- List examples of different types of numbers. Have students:
  - **(a)** identify the smallest number system to which each number belongs.
  - **(b)** identify all the number systems to which each number belongs.

- Have students work in pairs. Each partner draws a number line from −5 to 5, then selects six numbers, both rational and irrational, between −5 and 5. Partners trade pages and locate the numbers along the lines, then identify each number as rational or irrational.

- Ask students to create and solve matching problems similar to Problem 4 in the *Student Workbook*, where the task involves matching a mathematical expression, such as $-4 \leq x < 1$, where x is a real number, to a number line representation.

Extension

A

In this lesson, many irrational numbers were generated by taking the square roots of positive rational numbers. Students could look for other ways of generating irrational numbers, such as finding multiples of π, or using calculators to find roots other than square roots.

B

Students may be interested in doing some research to find out how calculators and computers cope with irrational numbers. Calculator manuals are a good place to start, although it may also be necessary to look for additional information or to contact a calculator manufacturer. For example, students might ask questions such as:
- **(a)** On many calculators, if you press $\sqrt{\ }$ 5 $=$, then square the result, the answer is exactly 5, rather than the square of the decimal approximation. How does the calculator store a value with an infinite number of decimal places in its memory?

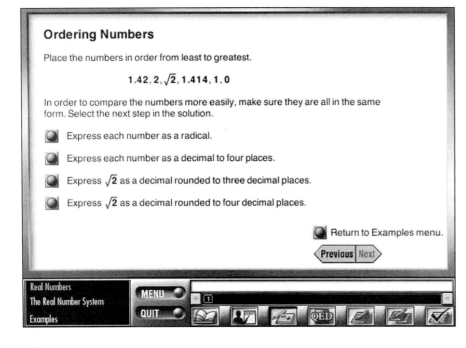

Ordering Numbers

Place the numbers in order from least to greatest.

$$1.42, 2, \sqrt{2}, 1.414, 1, 0$$

In order to compare the numbers more easily, make sure they are all in the same form. Select the next step in the solution.

- Express each number as a radical.
- Express each number as a decimal to four places.
- Express $\sqrt{2}$ as a decimal rounded to three decimal places.
- Express $\sqrt{2}$ as a decimal rounded to four decimal places.

Return to Examples menu.

Previous | Next

Real Numbers
The Real Number System
Examples

MENU
QUIT

(b) What value do calculators use for π? Is the value in the computer's memory different from the one shown in the display?

(c) Does a calculator truncate or round values for the display?

(d) If a calculator display shows a decimal value that appears to repeat at the end, how can you find more digits in order to determine for sure whether the number is rational or irrational?

C

Students may be interested in knowing that it is possible to change the rounding protocol on many graphing calculators. For example, on a TI-83 calculator, students can press MODE, then move the cursor down to Float. From here, they can cursor to the right and press Enter to specify the number of digits that are to be displayed in a rounded number.

Enrichment

A

Pose this problem:
Is the distance around a circle a rational or an irrational number? Give reasons for your answer.

Some students will argue that the distance is measurable, and so it is rational. Others will maintain that since the circumference of a circle is equal to πd, it must be an irrational number. Through discussion, bring out the point that the answer depends on the length of d. For example, a circle can have a rational circumference of 3 units, if d is the irrational number $\dfrac{3}{\pi}$.

B

Students can create a series of radicals by using right triangles.

(a) Draw a right triangle where both legs are 1 unit long. The first number in the series is equal to the length of the hypotenuse.

(b) Now draw a new right triangle so one leg is on the hypotenuse of the first triangle, and the other leg is 1 unit long. The hypotenuse of the new triangle is the second number in the series.

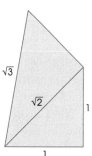

(c) Continue the series for a total of ten triangles, so each new triangle builds on the hypotenuse of the old one. The other leg of each triangle is always 1 unit long. Record the numbers in the series.

(d) Which numbers in the series are rational? irrational?

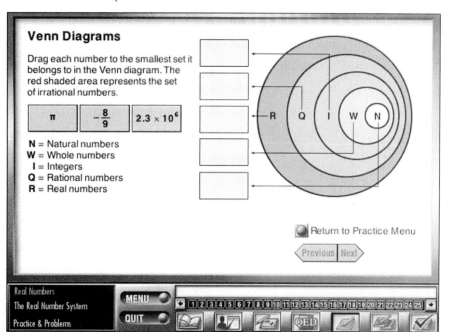

Venn Diagrams

Drag each number to the smallest set it belongs to in the Venn diagram. The red shaded area represents the set of irrational numbers.

π $-\dfrac{8}{9}$ 2.3×10^6

N = Natural numbers
W = Whole numbers
I = Integers
Q = Rational numbers
R = Real numbers

R   Q   I   W   N

Return to Practice Menu

Previous | Next

Real Numbers
The Real Number System
Practice & Problems

MENU
QUIT

1 2 3 4 5 6 7 8 9 10 11 12 13 14 15 16 17 18 19 20 21 22 23 24 25

1.4 Solving Problems

Cross-References
Real Numbers

Student Workbook: pages 14–17

Key Objectives
The student will:
- communicate a set of instructions used to solve an arithmetic problem.

Key Terms
arithmetic, operator, equivalent, sum, difference, product, quotient, squared, cubed, square root, cube root, reciprocal, negative, deduct, increase, average, radical, radicand, root index, base, exponent, spreadsheet

Prerequisite Skills
- Describe, orally and in writing, whether or not a number is rational.
- Document and explain the calculator keystroke sequences used to perform calculations involving rational numbers.
- Design, conduct, and report on an experiment to investigate a relationship between two variables.

Lesson Description

As students advance to more complex problems, difficulties can arise because of misinterpretations of problem information. The lesson focuses on how to interpret problem information in words and in arithmetic sentences, and how to translate from one form to the other.

The **Introduction** deals with two students who are trying to create a spreadsheet. One has already successfully completed the task and is trying to communicate information to the other, who is having difficulty. Through analyzing a series of verbal instructions, students see that it is sometimes easier to interpret information when it is expressed algebraically. In the **Summary**, students recreate the spreadsheet, this time using mathematical formulas.

The **Tutorial** begins with several arithmetic statements. Students interpret each one by choosing the appropriate words from a given list. In the second part of the **Tutorial**, students select mathematical expressions to match a verbal statement. In the process, they revisit concepts such as percent, reciprocals, and roots. In the final section of the **Tutorial**, students solve a problem by constructing an arithmetic sentence from a series of verbal clues.

The **Examples** component begins by inviting students to express verbal statements in a form that can be understood by their calculator. Feedback comments provide help with using the $\sqrt{}$, $\sqrt[x]{y}$, and x^2 functions. (Procedures will vary somewhat for different types of calculators.)

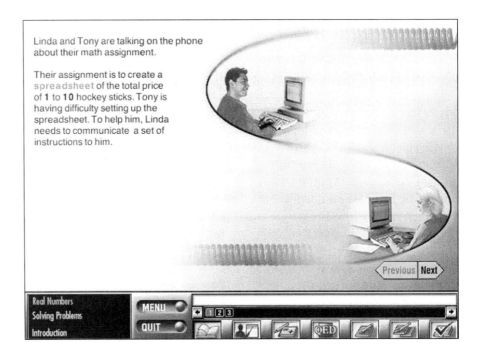

Linda and Tony are talking on the phone about their math assignment.

Their assignment is to create a spreadsheet of the total price of 1 to 10 hockey sticks. Tony is having difficulty setting up the spreadsheet. To help him, Linda needs to communicate a set of instructions to him.

Previous | Next

Real Numbers
Solving Problems
Introduction

MENU
QUIT

In the remaining **Examples**, students examine how slight changes to a verbal statement can affect its mathematical meaning, compare arithmetic approaches to identify the most efficient way to solve a problem, and then apply what they have learned to solve a different problem.

Instructor Intervention

- Success with this lesson depends on a broad understanding of mathematical vocabulary. Review the key terms listed at the beginning of this section. As students proceed through the lesson, ask them to record any terms they do not clearly understand. Make a list of these terms and discuss them with the class.

- Students who find this lesson easy could move directly from the **Introduction** to the **Examples**, then check their skills with **Practice and Problems**, **Extra Practice**, and the *Student Workbook*.

- Since calculator functions vary somewhat from brand to brand, you may need to assist students in finding keystroke sequences that work with their calculators.

- One of the **Examples** deals with averages. Review the three types of averages and ask which type is being used here.
  - (a) The **mean** tells you what one piece of data would be if all the pieces were the same.
  - (b) The **mode** is the piece of data that is used most often.
  - (c) The **median** is the middle piece of data in a set when the pieces are listed in order from least to greatest.

Lesson Components

 Examples

Translating for the
  Calculator (2)
Matching Expressions (2)
Words to Symbols (2)
Problem Situations (2)

 Practice and Problems

Matching Expressions
Translating for the Calculator
Symbols to Words
Words to Symbols
Problem Situations

 Extra Practice

Words to Symbols
Matching Expressions
Translating for the Calculator
Symbols to Words
Problem Situations

 Self-Check

Words to Symbols (2)
Matching Expressions (2)
Translating for the
  Calculator (2)
Symbols to Words (2)
Problem Situations (2)

Minimum score: 7 out of 10

This is Tony's screen. See if you can follow Linda's instructions to obtain what she has on her screen.

	A	B	C	D	E
1	Number of Sticks	Price of Sticks ($)	City Tax ($)	State Tax ($)	Total Price ($)
2	1	14.99			
3	2	28.98			
4	3	44.97			
5	4	59.96			
6	5	74.95			
7	6	89.94			
8	7	104.93			
9	8	119.92			
10	9				
11	10				

To fill in the next column, Linda wrote a formula on her computer. The computer calculated the values and entered them into the spreadsheet for her. Linda is not sure she can explain to Tony how to enter the formula, so she tells him what numbers to enter, one cell at a time.

Complete the column by entering **134.91** into cell **B10** and **149.90** into cell **B11**.

⟨Previous | Next⟩

Real Numbers
Solving Problems
Introduction

MENU
QUIT
◀ 1 2 3 ▶

Evaluation

- Have each student prepare a mathematical statement in words, then express the same statement in a number sentence. Invite volunteers to write one form of their statement on the board for the rest of the class to express in the other form.

  Discuss any differences in the results. Focus on the importance of expressing the mathematical idea clearly and unambiguously in both forms.

- Problem 1 in the *Student Workbook* deals with words that are associated with each of the four mathematical operators, +, −, ×, and ÷. Students could consolidate and expand on their ideas to create a master list for classroom reference.

- Pose several problems similar to those in the "Problem Situations" in **Practice** and **Extra Practice**. Include some where an important piece of information is missing, and some where there are extraneous pieces of information.

  Ask students to identify the key points in each problem and to decide whether they would need any additional information to solve the problem.

- Students who have completed the previous activity could go on to create similar problems of their own, which could then be exchanged and solved.

Remediation

- Review these processes:
  (a) apply the rules for order of operations, including using parentheses to give priority to an operation
  (b) simplify powers with whole-number exponents
  (c) find a given percent of a number
  (d) find the reciprocal of a number
  (e) find the mean of a given set of numbers

- A short quiz based on vocabulary terms might help you identify not only students in need of assistance, but also more proficient students who could offer this assistance.

- Make sure students have calculators that can work with exponents, square roots, and higher roots. Students will need to know how to use the $\sqrt{x}$, y^x, and $\sqrt[x]{y}$ keys (or equivalent).

If students have graphing calculators, they may be able to perform these operations more easily. For example, to find $\sqrt{5^3 \times 3^4}$ with a TI-83 calculator, press 2ndF MODE, then enter $\sqrt{5 \wedge 3 \times 3 \wedge 4}$. For higher roots, students will need to access the math menu by pressing MATH.

Extension

A

Have students create as many English phrases as they can for a basic mathematical operation, such as $2 \times 6 + 8$. Emphasize that recording mathematical ideas with symbols rather than words helps to eliminate vagueness and ambiguity.

B

Ask students to write arithmetic expressions on individual cards. Gather the cards and place them in a paper bag.

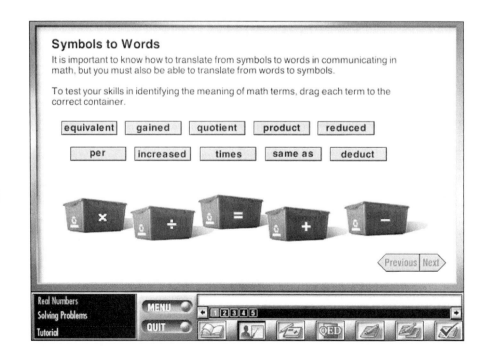

Invite a student to reach into the bag, draw out a card, and give a verbal description of the operation. Record this description, then have the rest of the class try to reproduce the arithmetic expression. Compare the results with the original and invite explanations for any differences.

C

Although many words and phrases are often associated with certain operations, these connections are not always reliable. If students have made a list of words and phrases associated with certain operations, as in Problem 1 in the *Student Workbook*, they might look for ways to use the same words to describe other operations.

For example, the phrase "more than" is usually associated with addition. However, students might also suggest uses such as:
(a) Five is two more than a number. (subtraction)
(b) A number is 50% more than another number. (multiplication)

Enrichment

A

Students could look through magazines or newspapers to find examples of imprecise mathematical language. For example, they might find references to an "average" person or a "very frequent" occurrence.

Students might do some additional research about the topics they identify in order to rewrite these statements more precisely.

B

Students could read a book or magazine article about mathematics and analyze the language. Ask:
(a) How accessible is the text?
(b) What examples can you find of places where it is important to state things precisely?
(c) What new vocabulary and ideas did you learn from your reading?
(d) Choose an information book or article about another topic and compare it with the one you read.

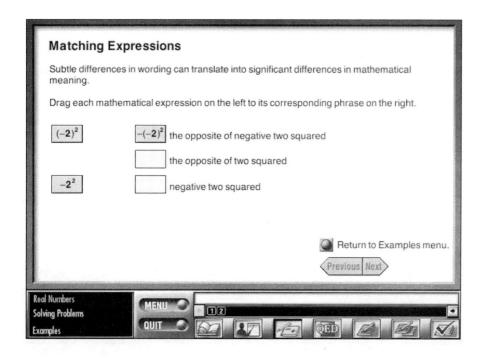

Matching Expressions

Subtle differences in wording can translate into significant differences in mathematical meaning.

Drag each mathematical expression on the left to its corresponding phrase on the right.

$(-2)^2$

$-(-2)^2$ the opposite of negative two squared

the opposite of two squared

-2^2 negative two squared

Return to Examples menu.

Previous | Next

Real Numbers
Solving Problems
Examples

MENU
QUIT

1 2

Cross-References

Real Numbers

Student Workbook: pages 18–21

Key Objectives

The student will:

- perform arithmetic operations on irrational numbers, using appropriate decimal approximations.

Key Terms

approximate, estimate, calculate, evaluate, rational, irrational, terminating, nonterminating, square root, cube root

Prerequisite Skills

- Document and explain the calculator keystroke sequences used to perform calculations involving rational numbers.
- Solve problems, using rational numbers in meaningful contexts.
- Use approximate representations of irrational numbers.

Lesson Description

In this lesson, students approximate irrational numbers in order to solve problems involving multiple operations.

In the **Introduction**, a student uses the Pythagorean relationship to develop a formula she can use to calculate the length of cable used to suspend the Golden Gate Bridge. In the **Summary**, students substitute known bridge measurements into the formula in order to approximate the length of one section of cable, and then they multiply to find the total length.

The **Tutorial** begins by reviewing how to estimate an irrational square root by using the neighboring perfect squares. Here, students learn to make more accurate estimates by dividing the amount between the perfect squares into equal increments. For example, $\sqrt{7}$ is $\frac{3}{5}$ of the way between $\sqrt{4}$ and $\sqrt{9}$, so it is $\frac{3}{5}$ or 0.6 more than $\sqrt{4}$.

The last part of the **Tutorial** develops two methods for doing calculations – one using the fraction estimation method and the other using calculator keystroke sequences.

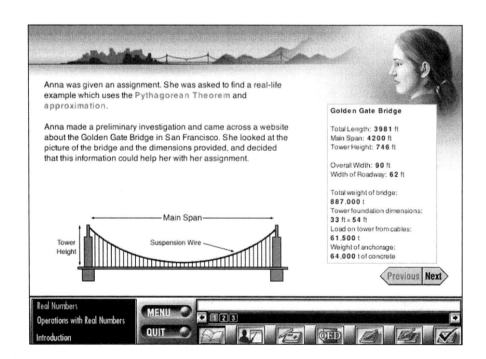

Anna was given an assignment. She was asked to find a real-life example which uses the Pythagorean Theorem and approximation.

Anna made a preliminary investigation and came across a website about the Golden Gate Bridge in San Francisco. She looked at the picture of the bridge and the dimensions provided, and decided that this information could help her with her assignment.

Golden Gate Bridge

Total Length: **3981** ft
Main Span: **4200** ft
Tower Height: **746** ft

Overall Width: **90** ft
Width of Roadway: **62** ft

Total weight of bridge:
887,000 t
Tower foundation dimensions:
33 ft × 54 ft
Load on tower from cables:
61,500 t
Weight of anchorage:
64,000 t of concrete

Previous | Next

Main Span

Tower Height

Suspension Wire

Real Numbers
Operations with Real Numbers
Introduction

MENU

QUIT

1 2 3

The **Examples** focus on calculator skills – using the $\boxed{y^x}$ and $\boxed{\sqrt[x]{y}}$

functions, calculating with the π key, entering calculations with multiple operations and higher roots, and specifying answers to a given degree of approximation. In the last section, students apply what they have learned to problem situations.

Instructor Intervention

- Many of the problems in this lesson involve multiple operations. Review the rules for order of operations:
  1. Brackets/Parentheses
  2. Exponents/Roots
  3. Division/Multiplication
  4. Addition/Subtraction

- Write several examples of rational and irrational numbers, including fractions, terminating decimals, repeating decimals, roots, and irrational decimals. Ask students to identify the irrational numbers. Review the definition of an irrational number as a number that cannot be written in fraction form, and that neither terminates nor repeats in decimal form.

- Students will need calculators that have a π key and that can work with cube roots as well as square roots. Explain that keystroke sequences for some calculator types will differ from those illustrated in the lesson.

  It may be useful to group students who have the same type of calculator so they can help one another learn the appropriate sequences.

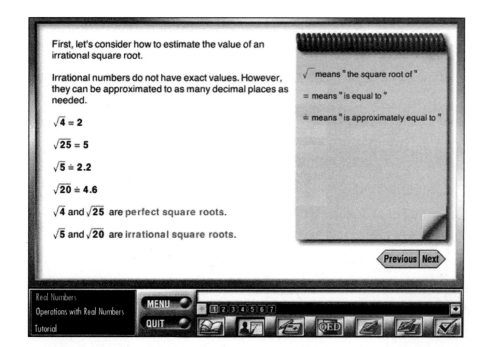

First, let's consider how to estimate the value of an irrational square root.

Irrational numbers do not have exact values. However, they can be approximated to as many decimal places as needed.

$\sqrt{4} = 2$

$\sqrt{25} = 5$

$\sqrt{5} \doteq 2.2$

$\sqrt{20} \doteq 4.6$

$\sqrt{4}$ and $\sqrt{25}$ are perfect square roots.

$\sqrt{5}$ and $\sqrt{20}$ are irrational square roots.

$\sqrt{}$ means "the square root of "

$=$ means "is equal to "

$\doteq$ means "is approximately equal to "

Previous | Next

Real Numbers
Operations with Real Numbers
Tutorial

MENU
QUIT

1 2 3 4 5 6 7

Evaluation

- Have students work in pairs. Each student writes an irrational number in square root form on a card and approximates the decimal form on a sheet of paper. Then the students switch cards, approximate each root again, and compare results. In cases where the results differ, students could use a calculator to check.

  Have students exchange root cards with another pair and repeat.

- Use the root cards generated from the previous activity. Choose three or four of the cards and ask pairs of students to use the numbers to generate an expression with several operations. For example, if the cards show $2\sqrt{3}$, $\sqrt{26}$, and $\sqrt{35}$, the pair might create the expression $(2\sqrt{3} - \sqrt{35})(\sqrt{26})$.

  Ask the students to simplify the expression and write a full solution, showing the result to three decimal places. Then repeat with other sets of root cards.

- Choose several of the expressions created for the previous activity to use for additional assessment. Write the expressions on the chalkboard and ask the students to simplify them and express the results to two decimal places. Check by comparing with the original solutions.

- Observe how students perform multiple operations with calculators. Do they apply the rules for order of operations? Can they sometimes adapt the order of operations to perform the calculations more efficiently? Do they use estimation to check the reasonableness of their results?

Remediation

- Review these terms:
  (a) rational/irrational number
  (b) terminating/ nonterminating decimal
  (c) repeating period

- Some students may have difficulty if their calculators operate differently from those illustrated in the lesson. Help these students identify the keystroke sequences they need to make the necessary calculations. Ask them to record these keystroke sequences for reference.

- Review how to round a number to a given number of decimal places. Remind students that it is the digit after the one in the specified decimal place that determines whether or not the number will be rounded up.

Extension

A

The **Introduction** featured a problem about the Golden Gate Bridge in San Francisco. The measurements used in the problem were found on a website about suspension bridges.

Students might search the Internet to find out more about the Golden Gate Bridge or other famous bridges. Ask them to choose a different bridge and create a problem that involves calculations made with approximations of irrational numbers.

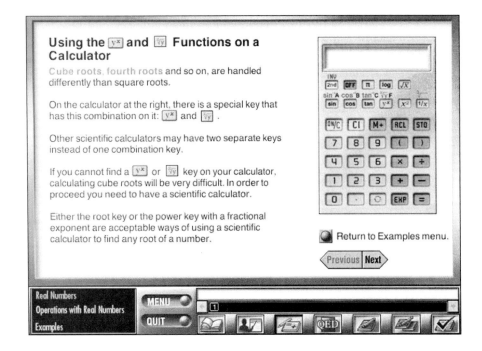

Using the $\boxed{y^x}$ and $\boxed{\sqrt[x]{y}}$ Functions on a Calculator

Cube roots, fourth roots and so on, are handled differently than square roots.

On the calculator at the right, there is a special key that has this combination on it: $\boxed{y^x}$ and $\boxed{\sqrt[x]{y}}$.

Other scientific calculators may have two separate keys instead of one combination key.

If you cannot find a $\boxed{y^x}$ or $\boxed{\sqrt[x]{y}}$ key on your calculator, calculating cube roots will be very difficult. In order to proceed you need to have a scientific calculator.

Either the root key or the power key with a fractional exponent are acceptable ways of using a scientific calculator to find any root of a number.

Return to Examples menu.

‹ Previous │ Next ›

Real Numbers
Operations with Real Numbers
Examples

MENU
QUIT

B

Give students the assignment that was used as the context for the **Introduction**. Have them find another real-life problem they can solve using the Pythagorean relationship.

C

Have students research π. Questions such as the following could be used to frame their research:

(a) Why is π irrational?

(b) Who discovered π?

(c) How did π get its name?

(d) What are some of the uses for π?

(e) To how many decimal places has π been approximated?

Enrichment

A

Ask: Is the set of irrational numbers finite or infinite?

Encourage students to present evidence for their conclusions.

B

Ask the students to find the surface area of a conical paper drinking cup. (Have some drinking cups on hand for this activity.)

One way to accomplish this task is to have students position the cup with the pointed end up, then tape sections of centimeter grid paper to the outside of the cup, with no overlapping, until the outside surface of the cup is covered. The students can then count the squares.

Another method students can use is to make one cut in from the edge of the cup to its center. Then they spread the cup flat,

forming a section of a circle. Ask them to find the area of the whole circle, then subtract the area of the section that is missing.

C

Have students formalize the method used in this lesson to calculate square roots using a number line and fractions. Could a formula be developed to estimate all roots between perfect roots?

D

Students could investigate and experiment with Newton's method of obtaining square roots, which is outlined in the hidden picture at the beginning of the **Practice and Problems** section of the lesson.

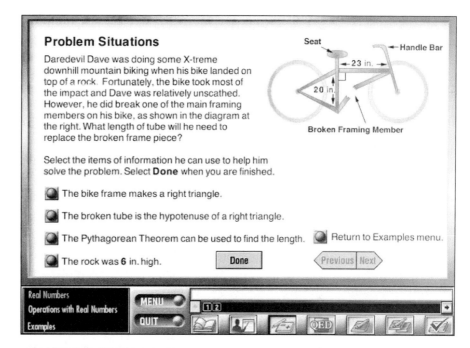

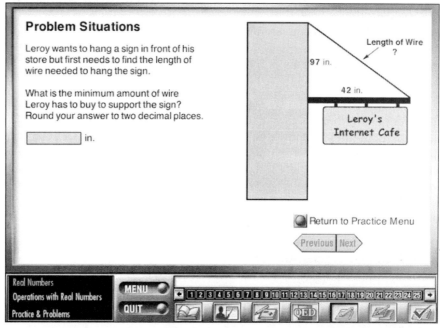

2 RADICALS

2.1 Rational Exponents

Cross-References
Radicals

Student Workbook: pages 22–25

Key Objectives
The student will:
- interpret powers with rational exponents.
- convert between radical notation and exponential notation.
- explain and apply the exponent laws for powers of numbers and for variables with rational exponents.
- solve problems involving rational exponents.

Key Terms
power, variable, rational number, exponent, extrapolate, radical, radicand, root index, numerator, denominator

Prerequisite Skills
- Interpret integral exponents.
- Use exponent laws to simplify expressions with variable and numerical bases.
- Use a calculator to calculate with scientific notation and apply exponent laws.

Lesson Description

In this lesson, students learn to interpret powers with rational exponents and to use exponent laws to evaluate these powers. The **Introduction** presents data about population growth and asks students to use a graph to predict when Earth's population will reach 50 billion. Students are then given an equation (involving a rational exponent) that they can use to confirm their prediction. In the **Summary**, students return to the population problem, this time using the equation to make the prediction. In the second part of the **Summary**, students work backward to determine the approximate world population in 1900. This results in a power with a negative rational exponent.

The **Tutorial** uses patterns to develop the idea of rational values in exponents. Students begin by exploring the meaning of $3^{\frac{1}{2}} = \sqrt{3}$ and then extend to the general case: $x^{\frac{1}{n}} = \sqrt[n]{x}$

Students also examine rational exponents with numerators other than 1 to conclude that $x^{\frac{m}{n}} = \left(\sqrt[n]{x}\right)^{m}$.

The **Examples** guide students through four different problem types. In Example 1, students discover that numbers in radical form can be written two ways: $\sqrt[4]{16^5}$ or $\left(\sqrt[4]{16}\right)^5$. As students progress to Examples 2 and 3, they should be able to complete most of the work without calculators.

Examples 4 and 5 involve Kepler's Third Law of Planetary Motion. Students will need to use a calculator. Emphasize that students check that the number shown in the calculator display is reasonable.

Instructor Intervention

- Rational exponents and root indices other than 2 are abstract concepts that can pose difficulties for students. You may wish to choose some students to act as mentors for others.

- Some problems in this lesson deal with expressing numbers with negative rational exponents in radical form. Review how to change an exponent from negative to positive by taking the reciprocal of the base. For example, $\left(\dfrac{8}{27}\right)^{-\frac{2}{3}} = \left(\dfrac{27}{8}\right)^{\frac{2}{3}}$.

- The **Tutorial** deals with logical restrictions on the values of x, m, and n. It might be helpful to review these with the class. Students should recall that the set of real numbers is comprised of the combined sets of rational and irrational numbers.

- The first problem in the **Examples** section states that numbers in radical form can be written in two ways: $\sqrt[4]{16^5}$ or $\left(\sqrt[4]{16}\right)^5$.
  You can use the following proof to help students see why these expressions are equal.
  $$\left(\sqrt[4]{16}\right)^5 = \sqrt[4]{16} \times \sqrt[4]{16} \times \sqrt[4]{16} \times \sqrt[4]{16} \times \sqrt[4]{16}$$
  If $\left(\sqrt[4]{16}\right)^5 = x$, then
  $$x^4 = \left(\sqrt[4]{16} \times \sqrt[4]{16} \times \sqrt[4]{16} \times \sqrt[4]{16} \times \sqrt[4]{16}\right)^4$$
  $$= 16 \times 16 \times 16 \times 16 \times 16 \text{ (power of a power law)}$$
  $$= 16^5$$
  $$x = \sqrt[4]{16^5}$$

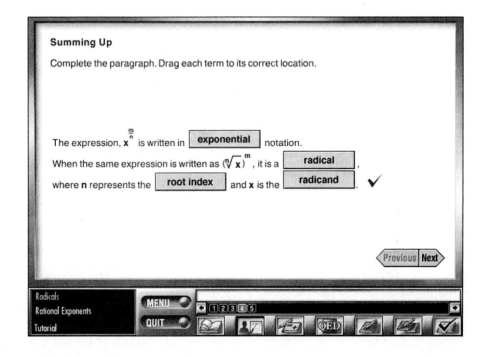

Summing Up

Complete the paragraph. Drag each term to its correct location.

The expression, $x^{\frac{m}{n}}$ is written in [exponential] notation.

When the same expression is written as $\left(\sqrt[n]{x}\right)^m$, it is a [radical],

where **n** represents the [root index] and **x** is the [radicand]. ✓

‹Previous | Next›

Radicals
Rational Exponents
Tutorial

MENU
QUIT

Evaluation

- Observe how students evaluate expressions with rational exponents. Make sure they have a thorough understanding of integral exponents. Review their written work to determine if their knowledge of the terminology is adequate. Do they know the difference between radical and exponential form? Can they simplify correctly? Do they understand the difference between exact values and decimal approximations? Are they correctly applying the exponent laws? Can they use the root and exponent keys on a scientific calculator?

- Choose several problems generated by students during their work with the *Student Workbook*. Students can solve the problems and then compare solutions within their groups. Invite volunteers to use overhead transparencies to demonstrate solutions.

- Brainstorm a list of key terms in this lesson and assign students to define each term in their own words. Compare students' definitions with the definition from the glossary and other definitions from math textbooks or math dictionaries.

- Have small groups design posters that convey the key ideas from this lesson, along with sample problems. Mount the posters around the room and let the class use them as a resource as they study for quizzes and tests. Make each group of students responsible for the accuracy of the math on their poster rather than correcting errors yourself before you display their work.

Remediation

- Although students have been working with exponent laws in recent lessons, some may still need review. Prepare a worksheet with questions that illustrate errors people often make when applying the laws.

Have the students analyze the mistakes and correct the errors. It may be helpful to do this before students begin work on this lesson.

If students continue to have difficulty applying the exponent laws with rational exponents, it may be because they need to review how to add, subtract, and multiply fractions.

- It is very important to provide practice with integral exponents before students begin the **Practice** section. For example, show $5^3 > 5^2 > 5^1 > 5^0 > 5^{-1}$, … Without this understanding, students will have more difficulty interpreting negative rational exponents.

- Provide a set of problems that have exact value solutions so pairs of students can work them out on paper, then verify the solutions with a calculator. Include problems that may produce calculator error messages, such as:
$$(-32)^{\frac{2}{5}}$$

- When students are converting exponential powers to radical form, they may find it difficult to remember which part of the fraction to use as the root index and which part to use as the exponent. Remind them to think of unit fractions. For example, $2^{\frac{1}{2}} = \sqrt{2}$ or $\sqrt[2]{2^1}$, so the denominator of the exponent must be the root index.

Extension

A

Extend the bases and exponents to irrational values such as $\sqrt{3}$

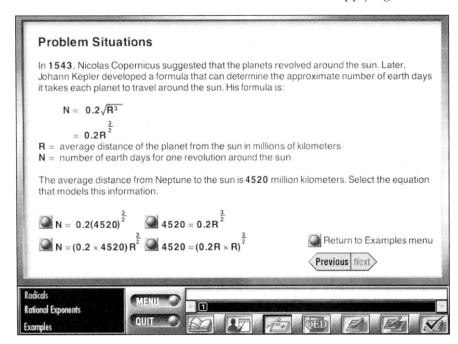

Problem Situations

In **1543**, Nicolas Copernicus suggested that the planets revolved around the sun. Later, Johann Kepler developed a formula that can determine the approximate number of earth days it takes each planet to travel around the sun. His formula is:

$$N = 0.2\sqrt{R^3}$$
$$= 0.2R^{\frac{3}{2}}$$

R = average distance of the planet from the sun in millions of kilometers
N = number of earth days for one revolution around the sun

The average distance from Neptune to the sun is **4520** million kilometers. Select the equation that models this information.

- $N = 0.2(4520)^{\frac{3}{2}}$
- $4520 = 0.2R^{\frac{3}{2}}$
- $N = (0.2 \times 4520)R^{\frac{3}{2}}$
- $4520 = (0.2R \times R)^{\frac{3}{2}}$
- Return to Examples menu

Previous | Next

Radicals
Rational Exponents
Examples

MENU
QUIT

and π. Why are graphs of exponential functions continuous? Ask how mathematicians might have calculated values such as 2^{π} before the invention of calculators.

B

Challenge students to prove that $\sqrt{2}$ is irrational. They can start by trying to show that $\sqrt{2}$ is rational, meaning that it can be written as a simplified fraction.

C

In this lesson, students were given the equations they needed to solve problems. Encourage them to explore other situations where they can develop equations directly from numerical data. Start with some number patterns similar to those shown in the **Tutorial**.

D

Discuss the meaning of more difficult expressions, such as:

(a) $0^{-\frac{1}{2}}$ (b) 0^0 (c) 2^{22}

(d) $\sqrt{\sqrt{\sqrt{\sqrt{256}}}}$ (e) $\sqrt{-9}$

E

Invite pairs or small groups to look through science materials to locate various examples of formulas that use radicals or rational exponents. They can present their findings to the class and create a class list, perhaps displayed as a poster. Encourage the students to talk with science instructors or with professional scientists. You may also wish to help them structure an Internet

search. Useful Internet search terms might include:
- acceleration
- air pressure
- algebra
- decibel scale
- force
- radioactivity
- Richter scale

Enrichment

A

Students can use graphing calculators or computer software to graph the following equations, then try to generalize from the results. Encourage students to explore related graphs with powers greater than 2 or 3.

The key to understanding these graphs is to examine the restrictions placed on radicals. Compare pencil-and-paper interpretations with the graphs to help students gain some understanding of why calculators behave as they do. Extend the problem by using powers greater than 2 or 3.

(a) $y = \sqrt{x^2}$ (b) $y = \left(\sqrt{x}\right)^2$

(c) $y = \left(\sqrt[3]{x}\right)^3$ (d) $y = x^{\frac{2}{3}}$

B

After students have completed the final exercise in the **Practice and Problems** section, they may be interested in researching the basis for carbon dating. (The ratio of C-14 to C-12 changes after an organism dies because the C-14 decays and the C-12 does not. The half-life of C-14 is about 5730 years. Estimates using this technique are accurate for objects up to about 10,000 years old.)

Ask why there are limits on the ages of objects that can be dated using this method. Some students may wish to explore the alternative method scientists use to date moon rocks, which are billions of years old.

This investigation may lead some students to ask questions about logarithms, which could be answered through additional research.

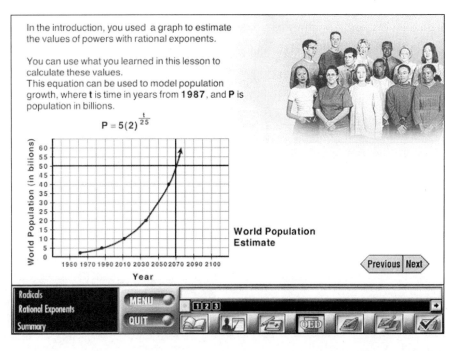

In the introduction, you used a graph to estimate the values of powers with rational exponents.

You can use what you learned in this lesson to calculate these values.
This equation can be used to model population growth, where **t** is time in years from **1987**, and **P** is population in billions.

$$P = 5(2)^{\frac{t}{25}}$$

World Population Estimate

Radicals
Rational Exponents
Summary

Previous | Next

Simplifying Radical Expressions

Cross-References
Radicals

Student Workbook: pages 26–29

Key Objectives
The student will:
- simplify radical expressions using the quotient and product properties of radicals.
- simplify radical expressions by combining like radicals.

Key Terms
radical, Pythagorean theorem, square root, product property of radicals, quotient property of radicals, radical, radicand, index, prime-factored form, mixed radical, entire radical, perfect square, perfect cube

Prerequisite Skills
- Apply the laws of exponents to expressions involving numbers and variables.
- Use the rules for the order of operations to simplify expressions involving numbers and variables.

Lesson Description

In this lesson, students learn to simplify radical expressions by applying the product and quotient properties of radicals. They also learn to add and subtract radical expressions.

The **Introduction** presents a problem involving two different routes between two places: one L-shaped and the other a straight line. Students need to determine how much shorter one route is than the other. The different routes create a right triangle, so students use the Pythagorean theorem and calculators to arrive at an approximate answer. In the **Summary**, students solve the problem again, by calculating directly with radicals.

In the **Tutorial**, students learn about the product and quotient properties of radicals, and use these properties to simplify radical expressions. Students learn that they can simplify radical expressions by rewriting the radicands as products of prime factors, or as products of perfect squares and other numbers. They also learn to recognize, form, and combine like radicals.

The **Examples** section reinforces learning developed in the **Tutorial**. Students:
- simplify radical expressions with numerical radicands and variable radicands.
- use the product and quotient properties of radicals.
- add and subtract radical expressions.
- practice recognizing and simplifying perfect cubes, fourths, and so on.

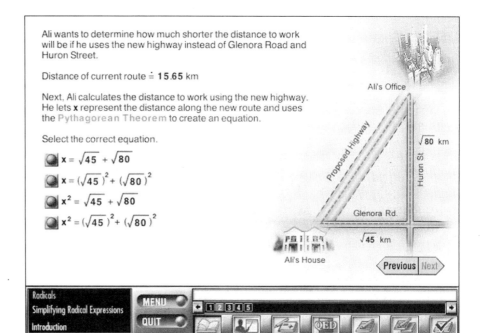

Instructor Intervention

- Before students begin the lesson, they may need to review the Pythagorean theorem and prime factorization.

- Review how to read radical expressions. For example, $\sqrt[4]{3}$ is read as "the fourth root of 3" and $\sqrt{20}$ is read as "the square root of 20," or, more simply, "root 20." The computer-guided lesson uses both words and symbols in feedback.

- Discuss the different skills involved in finding an exact answer and finding an approximate answer to problems involving radicals. For example, to find an approximate answer, you must know how, and at what stages, to round numbers; to find an exact answer, you must know how to simplify radicals. Also ask students to give examples of when you would want each type of answer.

- Encourage students to estimate the values of radical expressions before simplifying. They could then practice their calculator skills by checking their estimates.

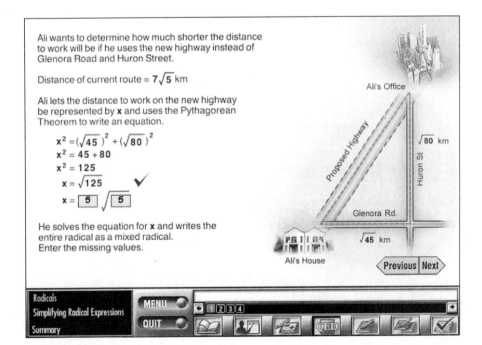

Ali wants to determine how much shorter the distance to work will be if he uses the new highway instead of Glenora Road and Huron Street.

Distance of current route = $7\sqrt{5}$ km

Ali lets the distance to work on the new highway be represented by **x** and uses the Pythagorean Theorem to write an equation.

$$x^2 = (\sqrt{45})^2 + (\sqrt{80})^2$$
$$x^2 = 45 + 80$$
$$x^2 = 125$$
$$x = \sqrt{125} \quad \checkmark$$
$$x = \boxed{5}\sqrt{\boxed{5}}$$

He solves the equation for **x** and writes the entire radical as a mixed radical. Enter the missing values.

Ali's Office

$\sqrt{80}$ km — Huron St

Proposed Highway

Glenora Rd.

$\sqrt{45}$ km

Ali's House

Previous | Next

Radicals
Simplifying Radical Expressions
Summary

MENU
QUIT

Evaluation

- In groups, have students create a ten-question quiz, including one question from each category:
  - **(a)** product of 2 radicals with numerical radicands
  - **(b)** product of 2 radicals with variable radicands
  - **(c)** quotient of 2 radicals with numerical radicands
  - **(d)** quotient of 2 radicals with variable radicands
  - **(e)** simplify a radical expression with a numerical radicand using the product property
  - **(f)** simplify a radical expression with a variable radicand using the product property
  - **(g)** simplify a radical expression with a numerical radicand using the quotient property
  - **(h)** simplify a radical expression with a variable radicand using the quotient property
  - **(i)** add or subtract radicals with numerical radicands in which like radicals can be formed
  - **(j)** add or subtract radicals with variable radicands in which like radicals can be formed

Each group should create an answer key. Have the groups trade questions, write complete solutions, and then compare their answers to the answer key. Encourage students to create questions which require them to find roots other than square roots.

- Observe students as they complete the activities. Do they use the notation correctly? Do they understand how to use the product and quotient properties? Do they use the vocabulary correctly?

Remediation

- Review prime factorization using factor trees.

- Students may have difficulty simplifying radical expressions because they cannot quickly identify perfect squares and cubes. They should be able to recognize that 4, 9, 16, 25, 36, 49, 64, 81, and 100 are all perfect squares, and they should begin to recognize perfect cubes.

- Some students may have difficulty identifying like radicals. Connect like and unlike radicals to like and unlike terms in algebra. Students should find it very easy to identify like terms in $2a + 8b + 2b - 8a$. Show how in the expression $2\sqrt{5} + 8\sqrt[3]{12} + 2\sqrt[3]{12} - 8\sqrt{5}$, a could represent $\sqrt{5}$ and b could represent $\sqrt[3]{12}$. The rewritten expression would be $2a + 8b + 2b - 8a$.

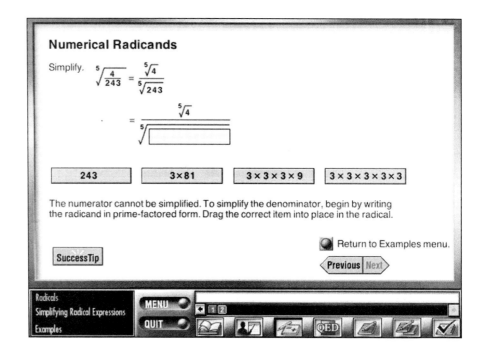

Extension

A

There are many everyday situations that require the use of radicals; for example, problems where the side length of a square must be found given its area. Encourage students to think of other situations which commonly involve radicals (e.g., any area or volume problem, any problem involving the Pythagorean theorem, etc.), and then make up and solve problems about these situations.

B

Present Heron's formula for the area of a triangle:

$$A = \sqrt{s(s-a)(s-b)(s-c)}$$

where a, b, and c are the side lengths of the triangle and s is one-half of the perimeter. Encourage students to use the formula to find the areas of different triangles.

Enrichment

A

Ask students to solve the following problem:

An aerospace engineer designing a satellite communications system wants to find the distance between a satellite at an altitude of h and its home base. Find the distance, d, in terms of h and r (the radius of Earth).

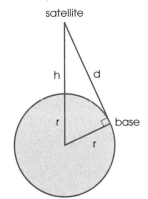

B

Students could investigate the dimensions of different shapes with a given area. For example, present the following problem:

Suzy has enough money to buy 50 mi^2 of land. What would be the length of each side if the land were in the shape of a square? in the shape of an equilateral triangle? What would be the radius if the land were in the shape of a circle? If she needs to put a fence around the land, which option would require the least amount of fencing?

C

Some students may question how to determine the square root of a negative number. Introduce imaginary and complex numbers, and direct students to the lesson "Complex Numbers."

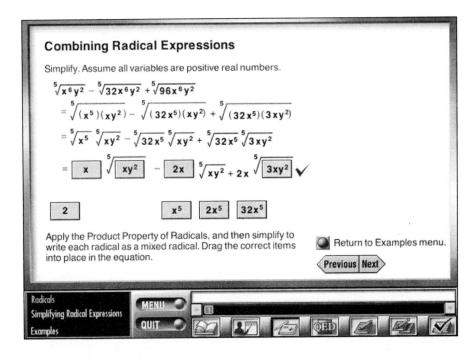

Multiplying and Dividing Radical Expressions

Cross-References
Radicals

Student Workbook: pages 30–33

Key Objectives
The student will:
- multiply radical expressions.
- divide radical expressions.
- rationalize denominators of radical expressions.

Key Terms
radical, root, root index, variable, monomial, polynomial, binomial, product, factor, quotient, numerator, denominator, distributive property, product property, quotient property, FOIL method, rationalization, conjugate

Prerequisite Skills
- Simplify radical expressions using addition and subtraction.
- Apply the exponent laws for powers of numbers and for variables with rational exponents.
- Multiply polynomials using the distributive property and the FOIL method for binomials.
- Factor a difference of squares.
- Use a calculator to evaluate radical expressions and solve problems involving radicals.

Lesson Description

This lesson deals with multiplying and dividing radical expressions and rationalizing the denominator in a division expression. Students find products of two monomials, a monomial and a polynomial, and two binomials. In division situations, they rationalize both monomial and binomial denominators.

The **Introduction** presents a problem about settings on a 35 mm camera. The relationship between the variables is described by the equation $f\text{-}number = \dfrac{food\ length}{aperture\ diameter}$. When the focal length is 12 cm and the *f*-number is 2, the aperture diameter is 6 cm. Students develop a table of values for different *f*-numbers at this focal length and use a guess-and-test strategy to approximate the *f*-number that will reduce the aperture area by 50%, allowing half as much light into the lens. In the **Summary**, students revisit the problem. This time, they solve it more efficiently by substituting values into the equation and simplifying the resulting radical expression by rationalizing the denominator.

In the **Tutorial**, students work through four problems. They:
- find the product of two monomials by multiplying the coefficients, applying the product property to the radicals, and simplifying the result.
- use the distributive property to find the product of a monomial and a binomial.
- rationalize a cube-root denominator in order to divide one monomial by another.
- use the quotient property to express the quotient of two algebraic terms as a single radical, simplify the radicand, and then divide by rationalizing the denominator.

The **Examples** expose students to various approaches to multiplying and dividing radicals and radical expressions. Multiplication problems illustrate that some radicals can be simplified and that this can be done at any stage in the solution of a problem. Division problems focus attention on the conditions that must be fulfilled before a radical expression is considered to be in simplified form. (These conditions are summarized in **Instructor Intervention**.)

Instructor Intervention

- Prior to the **Tutorial**, review the distributive property and the FOIL method using examples that do not involve radicals.

- Review the exponent laws, since students will require an understanding of these rules in order to complete some of the problems in the lesson—especially those involving algebraic terms.

- Many students will be comfortable finding many simple roots by inspection. Encourage them to try doing so if they wish and then to check the results by multiplying.

- Review how to express a number as a product of prime factors.

- Students should recognize that a radical expression is in simplified form when the following conditions are true:
  - **(a)** No radicals appear in the denominator of a fraction.
  - **(b)** The radicand contains no fractions or negative numbers.
  - **(c)** Each factor in the radicand is a power that is less than the index of the radical.
  - **(d)** The numerator and denominator have no common factors.

- Students may need help rationalizing higher powers. Initially, some students may not recognize that the cube root of a perfect cube is a whole number. Help students see that to rationalize a denominator of $\sqrt[3]{5}$, they must recreate a perfect cube in the denominator by multiplying the fraction by $\dfrac{\sqrt[3]{5}}{\sqrt[3]{5}} \times \dfrac{\sqrt[3]{5}}{\sqrt[3]{5}}$.

Lesson Components

Examples

Multiplying Radical Expressions 1 (1)
Multiplying Radical Expressions II (1)
Multiplying Radical Expressions III (1)
Rationalizing a Denominator I (1)
Rationalizing a Denominator II (1)

Practice and Problems

Working with Radical Expressions
Multiplying Radical Expressions
Dividing Radical Expressions
Error Analysis
Problem Situations

Extra Practice

Multiplying Radical Expressions I
Multiplying Radical Expressions II
Multiplying Radical Expressions III
Rationalizing a Denominator I
Rationalizing a Denominator II

Self-Check

Multiplying Radical Expressions I (2)
Multiplying Radical Expressions II (2)
Multiplying Radical Expressions III (2)
Rationalizing a Denominator I (2)
Rationalizing a Denominator II (2)

Minimum score: 7 out of 10

Denise bought a new **35**-mm camera. The camera has an adjustable circular opening, called the **aperture**, that controls the amount of light that passes through the lens. According to the camera's manual, the **f-number** of a lens is its **focal length** divided by the diameter of the aperture.

$$\text{f-number} = \frac{\text{focal length}}{\text{diameter}}$$

Denise mounted a lens, adjusted the focal length to **12** cm (**120** mm), and set the f-number to **2** (written as **f/2**). This setting resulted in an aperture diameter of **6** cm. What should the f-number be to reduce the area of the aperture to let in **50%** as much light?

Previous | Next

Radicals
Multiplying and
Dividing Radical Expressions
Introduction

MENU

QUIT

Evaluation

- Pose problems similar to those in the **Extra Practice** section. Invite small groups to solve each problem and compare solutions. Select a student from each group to present one solution to the class.

- Observe the groups as they work through problems. Can they explain the steps in each solution? Do they use appropriate vocabulary? Can they verify their answers?

- Have students create and solve a problem of each type:
  (a) simplifying a radical
  (b) multiplying radicals
  (c) dividing radicals by rationalizing the denominator

- Give examples of radical operations and ask students to explain the meaning of each of these terms: **simplified radical**, **root index**, **multiply coefficients**, **multiply radicals**, **distributive property**, **FOIL method**, **simplest terms**, **rationalize**

- Observe students as they work through the **Extra Practice** exercises. Which types of problems do they feel are most difficult? Why?

Remediation

- Have students explain these terms in their own words: **product**, **quotient**, **numerator**, **denominator**, **radical**, **root**, **root index**, **factor**, **variable**

- Review the process for simplifying radicals. Create a bulletin board display for easy

reference. Include examples with both variables and numbers.

- Review these concepts:
  (a) Product Property
  For real numbers a and b and integer $n > 1$,
  $$\sqrt[n]{a} \times \sqrt[n]{a} = \sqrt[n]{ab}$$
  If n is even, a and b must be ≥ 0.

  (b) Distributive Property
  $$\sqrt{a} \times \left(\sqrt{b} + \sqrt{c} \right)$$
  $$= \sqrt{a} \times \sqrt{b} + \sqrt{a} \times \sqrt{c}$$

  (c) FOIL Method
  $$\left(\sqrt{a} + \sqrt{b} \right)\left(\sqrt{c} + \sqrt{d} \right)$$
  $$= \sqrt{a}\sqrt{c} + \sqrt{a}\sqrt{d} + \sqrt{b}\sqrt{c}$$
  $$+ \sqrt{b}\sqrt{d}$$

  (d) Quotient Property
  For real numbers a and b, $b \neq 0$, and integer $n > 1$,
  $$\frac{\sqrt[n]{a}}{\sqrt[n]{b}} = \sqrt[n]{\frac{a}{b}}$$
  If n is even, a must be ≥ 0 and b must be > 0.

Extension

A

Have students find the following product and explain how they know the result is in simplest form.

$$\sqrt[5]{\frac{3}{4}} \times \sqrt[5]{\frac{5}{8}} = \sqrt[5]{\frac{3}{4} \times \frac{5}{8}}$$
$$= \sqrt[5]{\frac{15}{32}}$$
$$= \frac{\sqrt[5]{15}}{\sqrt[5]{32}}$$
$$= \frac{\sqrt[5]{15}}{2}$$

B

Review how to add and subtract like radicals before posing this problem:

A volleyball has a volume of 864π cm^3. A tennis ball has a volume of 32π cm^3. By how much does the radius of the volleyball exceed that of the tennis ball?

(Hint: The formula for finding the volume of a sphere is $V = \frac{4}{3}\pi r^3$.)

Solution
Volleyball
$$\frac{4}{3}\pi r^3 = 864\pi$$
$$\frac{4}{3}r^3 = 864$$
$$r^3 = \frac{3 \times 864}{4}$$
$$r = \sqrt[3]{\frac{3 \times 864}{4}}$$
$$r = \sqrt[3]{\frac{3 \times 4 \times 6 \times 6 \times 6}{4}}$$
$$r = 6\sqrt[3]{3}$$

Tennis Ball
$$\frac{4}{3}\pi r^3 = 32\pi$$
$$\frac{4}{3}r^3 = 32$$
$$r^3 = \frac{3 \times 32}{4}$$
$$r^3 = \frac{3 \times 32}{4}$$
$$r = \sqrt[3]{\frac{3 \times 2 \times 2 \times 2 \times 2 \times 2}{2 \times 2}}$$
$$r = 2\sqrt[3]{3}$$

$6\sqrt[3]{3} - 2\sqrt[3]{3} = 4\sqrt[3]{3}$, so the radius of the volleyball is $4\sqrt[3]{3}$ cm longer.

C

Review the exponent laws and especially the link between rational exponents and radicals:

$$x^{\frac{3}{4}} = \sqrt[4]{x^3} \text{ or } \left(\sqrt[4]{x}\right)^3$$

To provide additional practice with exponents, have students simplify $\left(\dfrac{x^{-2}y^6}{9}\right)^{-\frac{1}{2}}$.

Solution

$$\left(\frac{x^{-2}y^6}{9}\right)^{-\frac{1}{2}} = \left(\frac{9x^2}{y^6}\right)^{\frac{1}{2}}$$

$$= \sqrt{\frac{9x^2}{y^6}}$$

$$= \frac{\sqrt{9x^2}}{\sqrt{y^6}}$$

$$= \frac{3x}{y^3}$$

Enrichment

A

Have students determine the hypotenuse and area of this triangle.

Solution

Use the Pythagorean relationship to find the hypotenuse length.

$$H^2 = \left(\frac{1}{\sqrt{3}-1}\right)^2 + \left(\frac{1}{\sqrt{3}+1}\right)^2$$

Rationalize each term.

$$\frac{1}{\sqrt{3}-1} \times \frac{\sqrt{3}+1}{\sqrt{3}+1} = \frac{\sqrt{3}+1}{2}$$

$$\frac{1}{\sqrt{3}+1} \times \frac{\sqrt{3}-1}{\sqrt{3}-1} = \frac{\sqrt{3}-1}{2}$$

Solve for H.

$$H^2 = \left(\frac{\sqrt{3}+1}{2}\right)^2 + \left(\frac{\sqrt{3}-1}{2}\right)^2$$

$$H^2 = 2$$

$$H = \sqrt{2}$$

Use $A = \dfrac{b \times h}{2}$ to find the area.

$$A = \frac{\dfrac{1}{\sqrt{3}-1} \times \dfrac{1}{\sqrt{3}+1}}{2}$$

$$= \frac{1}{4}$$

B

The hidden picture in the **Examples** menu gives the formula for finding the orbital radius in meters of an Earth satellite.

$$r = \sqrt[3]{\frac{GMt^2}{4\pi^2}}$$

where G is the universal gravitational constant, 6.67×10^{-11} N•m^2/kg^2, M is Earth's mass, 5.98×10^{24} kg, and t is the orbital period in seconds. (In the gravitational constant, N•m^2 is the unit "Newton meters squared.")

Invite students to research the universal gravitational constant. Then pose this problem: A satellite is in orbit 22,260 mi above Earth's surface. What is the period of the orbit? (Hint: To express the orbital radius in meters, use 1 mi = 1609 m.)

Solution

Reorganize the formula to isolate t.

$$\frac{GMt^2}{4\pi^2} = r^3$$

$$GMt^2 = 4\pi^2 r^3$$

$$t^2 = \frac{4\pi^2 r^3}{GM}$$

$$t = \sqrt{\frac{4\pi^2 r^3}{GM}}$$

Simplify the other side by substituting known values for variables.

$$t = \sqrt{\frac{4\pi^2 r^3}{(6.67 \times 10^{-11})(5.98 \times 10^{24})}}$$

To find the orbital radius, r, add Earth's radius, 3963 mi, to the given distance above Earth's surface and convert to meters.

$$r = 3963 + 22{,}260$$
$$= 26{,}223 \text{ mi}$$
$$= 4.22 \times 10^7 \text{ m}$$

Substitute 4.22×10^7 for r.

$$t = \sqrt{\frac{4\pi^2 (4.22 \times 10^7)^3}{(6.67 \times 10^{-11})(5.98 \times 10^{24})}}$$

$$= \sqrt{\frac{2.97 \times 10^{24}}{3.99 \times 10^{14}}}$$

$$= \sqrt{0.744 \times 10^{10}}$$

$$= 0.863 \times 10^5$$

$$= 86{,}300 \text{ s} \div 3600 \text{ s}/\text{h}$$

$$= 24.0 \text{ h}$$

Since Earth's rotational period is also 24 h, the satellite moves at the same speed as Earth's rotation and therefore remains stationary in relation to Earth.

3 LINEAR EQUATIONS

3.1 Simplifying Algebraic Expressions

Key Objectives
The student will:
- review basic properties of real numbers.
- simplify algebraic expressions by grouping like terms and by using the distributive property.

Key Terms
additive identity, multiplicative identity, additive inverse, reciprocal, algebraic term, variable, coefficient, algebraic expression, like terms, commutative property, associative property, distributive property

Prerequisite Skills
- Differentiate between natural, integral, and rational numbers.
- Write and evaluate algebraic expressions.
- Solve and verify one- and two-step equations.
- Create and solve problems using first-degree equations.

Lesson Description

In this lesson, students review properties of real numbers and learn to simplify algebraic expressions by grouping like terms and using the distributive property. The **Introduction** asks students to find the length of fencing needed to enclose the Self-Parking section of this lot:

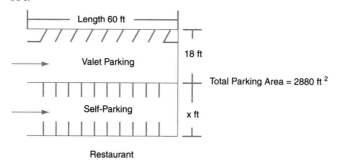

In the **Summary**, students solve the area equation for the problem, $2880 = 60(x + 18)$, and then determine the necessary fence length.

The **Tutorial** defines algebraic terms and introduces the following properties of real numbers.
- The **additive identity** is 0 because $0 + a = a + 0 = a$.
- The **multiplicative identity** is 1 because $1(a) = a(1) = a$.
- The product of 0 and any number is 0.
- If the sum of two numbers is 0, they are **additive inverses**: $a + (-a) = (-a) + a = 0$
- If the product of two numbers is 1, they are **reciprocals**: $a\left(\dfrac{1}{a}\right) = \left(\dfrac{1}{a}\right)a = 1$
- The basic division properties are:
  $\dfrac{a}{1} = a \qquad \dfrac{0}{a} = 0$, if $a \neq 0 \qquad \dfrac{a}{a} = 1$, if $a \neq 0 \qquad \dfrac{a}{0}$ is undefined
- These properties can be shown in the following formulas:
  - **commutative property**: $a + b = b + a$ and $ab = ba$
  - **associative property**: $(a + b) + c = a + (b + c)$ and $(ab)c = a(bc)$
  - **distributive property**: $a(b + c) = ab + ac$ and $a(b - c) = ab - ac$

In the **Examples**, students use various properties of real numbers to simplify algebraic expressions. By the end of this section, students should be able to:

- calculate simple products with variables.
- apply the distributive property.
- distribute a negative sign across parentheses.
- group or combine like terms.

Instructor Intervention

- For the **Introduction** and some of the problems in the **Practice** section, students will need to determine the areas and perimeters of rectangles and composite figures. Some students may need to review the relevant formulas.

- When students are entering algebraic terms, remind them that the coefficient should precede the variable. For polynomials, the constant should be the last term.

- Encourage students to discuss the purpose of using algebraic expressions. Students should understand that although variables represent numbers, they are more flexible than numbers because they can represent different quantities.

- When applying the distributive property, students sometimes forget to distribute the number outside the parentheses to each term inside. Use arrows to demonstrate the correct procedure. For example:

$$5(4a + 3) = (5 \times 4a) + (5 \times 3)$$
$$= 20a + 15$$

- Some students will have difficulty distinguishing between like and unlike terms when the terms contain the same variable. Remind them that B and b are not like terms, nor are a, a^2, and a^3.

- Have algebra tiles on hand so that students can practice applying the distributive property and combining like terms. Provide sample expressions that can be modeled and simplified using number tiles and tiles for x and x^2.

Evaluation

- Provide pairs of students with a list of the number properties described in this lesson. These properties are summarized in the **Lesson Description** at the beginning of these teaching notes.

  Have students review the **Tutorial** in order to:
  (a) define each property in words.
  (b) define each property in algebraic terms.
  (c) write a numerical example to show how each property is applied.

  Choose one pair to present each property for the class. In each case, students can use a poster or overhead to show how and why the property works.

- Have students create algebraic expressions to match these three categories:
  (a) finding a simple product
  (b) applying the distributive property
  (c) combining like terms

  Choose ten expressions to use for a class quiz. Give the quiz. Then give the answer for the first example and invite a volunteer who got that answer to present his or her solution for the class. Repeat with the remaining examples.

  After each solution has been presented, draw attention to any features that might have led to errors for some students. For example:
  (a) For a simple product, did the students multiply both constants and variables?
  (b) Were there negative signs that might have led to sign errors?
  (c) Were there like terms that needed to be combined?
  (d) Were there terms that were similar, but not alike (e.g., terms with a common variable but a different exponent)?

Remediation

- Encourage students who are having difficulties to try modeling some simple examples with algebra tiles. Doing so will be especially useful for tactile learners. For example, students could use tiles to combine like terms in $5x^2 + 3x + 4x + 4$, or to multiply $5(x + 4)$.

- Some students may need help applying the associative, commutative, and distributive properties. Have them try simplifying many numerical expressions before they proceed to algebraic examples.

- Some students may need additional practice with these processes:
  (a) applying the distributive property with negative signs
  (b) applying the distributive property with more complex expressions involving fractions and decimals
  (c) combining like terms that contain similar variables but different exponents
  (d) simplifying complex multi-step expressions

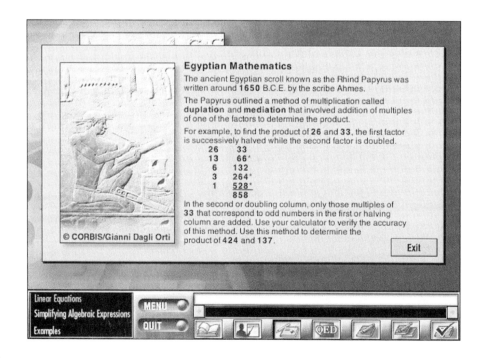

Egyptian Mathematics

The ancient Egyptian scroll known as the Rhind Papyrus was written around **1650** B.C.E. by the scribe Ahmes.

The Papyrus outlined a method of multiplication called **duplation** and **mediation** that involved addition of multiples of one of the factors to determine the product.

For example, to find the product of **26** and **33**, the first factor is successively halved while the second factor is doubled.

26	33
13	66*
6	132
3	264*
1	528*
	858

In the second or doubling column, only those multiples of **33** that correspond to odd numbers in the first or halving column are added. Use your calculator to verify the accuracy of this method. Use this method to determine the product of **424** and **137**.

© CORBIS/Gianni Dagli Orti

Exit

Linear Equations
Simplifying Algebraic Expressions
Examples

MENU

QUIT

Extension

A

Have students find the perimeters, areas, and volumes of shapes and solids where some side lengths are variables. Once students have solved several problems of this type, they can create similar problems of their own. Encourage them to structure the problems so solvers need to calculate simple products, use the distributive property, and group like terms.

Have students exchange and solve the problems they created.

B

Invite students to find and record the dictionary meanings of these terms and then explain how these meanings relate to the mathematical properties in the lesson: **identity**, **inverse**, **reciprocate**, **commute**, **associate**, **distribute**

Enrichment

A

Present students with the following problem:

Shanta is collecting money for a food bank. She collects $5 from friends and then asks the manager at a food store if she would like to donate. The manager says that instead of donating now, she will wait until Shanta has finished collecting money, and then will double whatever amount Shanta has collected.

Shanta sets up a computer spreadsheet to find out how much money she can collect in total. To calculate the Total Donation, she uses the expression $2(x + 5)$, where x represents the additional money Shanta collects before the doubling occurs.

(a) Simplify the expression using the distributive property.

(b) Complete the spreadsheet to determine how much Shanta could donate to the food bank for each collected amount.

Additional Amount Collected Before Doubling ($)	Total Donation ($)
0	
1	
2	
4	
6	
10	

(c) Graph the data from the table. Describe the graph. Is it a line or a curve?

B

This activity builds on the one described in part A:

(a) Simplify $2(x^2 + 5)$.

(b) Make a table of values for $y = 2(x^2 + 5)$.

(c) Graph the points on a coordinate plane. Describe the shape of the graph.

Students can research the terms **parabola** and **quadratic equation** to find out more about graphs that have this shape.

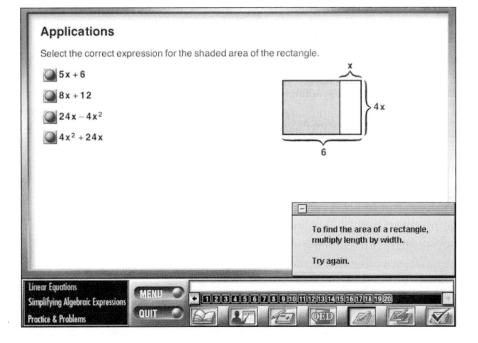

Applications

Select the correct expression for the shaded area of the rectangle.

- $5x + 6$
- $8x + 12$
- $24x - 4x^2$
- $4x^2 + 24x$

To find the area of a rectangle, multiply length by width.

Try again.

Linear Equations
Simplifying Algebraic Expressions
Practice & Problems

MENU
QUIT

3.2 Solving Linear Equations and Formulas

Cross-References

Linear Equations

Student Workbook: pages 38–41

Key Objectives

The student will:
- solve linear equations and formulas in one variable written in any form.
- determine if an equation has a real solution.

Key Terms

linear equation, expression, table, graph, solve, equation, variable, isolate, coefficient, distributive property, lowest common denominator, identity, formula

Prerequisite Skills

- Solve and check two-step linear equations.
- Simplify algebraic expressions, substitute numbers for variables in expressions, and graph and analyze the relation.
- Write and evaluate expressions.
- Perform operations with real numbers.

Lesson Description

In the problem posed in the **Introduction**, Ben needs $1800 for a trip. He develops an equation he can use to find how many years it will take to have $1800 if he has $1500 now and doesn't plan to add to the account. The equation derives from the simple interest formula, $A = P + Prt$, although the formula is not developed in this lesson. For an interest rate of 6% per year, the development of the formula is:

$$A = P + Prt$$
$$1800 = 1500 + 1500 \left(\frac{0.06}{12} \right) t, \text{ where } t \text{ is number of months}$$
$$1800 = 1500 + 7.5t$$

At this point, students do not have the skills needed to solve the equation. Instead, they set up a table of values to estimate the number of months it will take for $1500 to grow to $1800. In the **Summary**, students use equation-solving strategies they learned in the **Tutorial** and **Examples** to find the exact number of months.

The **Tutorial** and **Examples** develop students' ability to solve equations in which the variable can appear on one side or both sides of the equal sign. It is stressed that the operations performed at each step in the solution must result in an equivalent equation with the same balance. Students are encouraged to use the properties of equality to solve the equations. These properties are presented at the beginning of the Tutorial.

The **Tutorial** and **Examples** present three basic types of equations for students to explore and solve:
- $ax + b = c$, where a, b, and c are real numbers
- $a(bx + c) = d$, where a, b, c, and d are real numbers
- $\frac{a}{b}x = c$, where a and b are integers and $b \neq 0$

All three of these forms are useful to know because they are applied in many scientific and business formulas.

In the **Examples**, students solve equations that involve whole numbers, integers, fractions, and decimal numbers. Whenever possible, students can select more than one path to the solution. Students will be required to test all solutions they find by substituting the solutions back into the original equation.

Instructor Intervention

- Before beginning the lesson, you may wish to review the prerequisite skills to make sure these skills have been acquired and can be used effectively. Some students may also need to review how to:
  - simplify expressions by adding and subtracting like terms.
  - set up a table of values.
  - use the table of values to graph a relation.

- As students solve equations, they will need to perform operations with integers and fractions. Make sure students can:
  - add, subtract, multiply, and divide integers.
  - add, subtract, multiply, and divide fractions.
  - find the lowest common denominator for any expression involving the addition and subtraction of fractions.

- It is important to encourage students to write complete solutions as well as a concluding sentence for all equations they solve. Writing a conclusion, or even saying the conclusion out loud, will help students identify solutions that do not make sense and likely contain mathematical errors. For example, a misplaced decimal can result in a conclusion like "It takes $1,000,000 per month, for 25 years, to pay off a $100,000 mortgage."

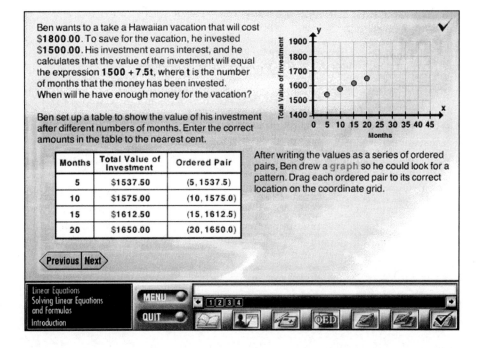

Ben wants to a take a Hawaiian vacation that will cost $1800.00. To save for the vacation, he invested $1500.00. His investment earns interest, and he calculates that the value of the investment will equal the expression $1500 + 7.5t$, where t is the number of months that the money has been invested. When will he have enough money for the vacation?

Ben set up a table to show the value of his investment after different numbers of months. Enter the correct amounts in the table to the nearest cent.

Months	Total Value of Investment	Ordered Pair
5	$1537.50	(5, 1537.5)
10	$1575.00	(10, 1575.0)
15	$1612.50	(15, 1612.5)
20	$1650.00	(20, 1650.0)

After writing the values as a series of ordered pairs, Ben drew a graph so he could look for a pattern. Drag each ordered pair to its correct location on the coordinate grid.

Previous | Next

Linear Equations
Solving Linear Equations
and Formulas
Introduction

MENU
QUIT

Evaluation

- Use questions generated by students for the last problem in the *Student Workbook*. Write each equation on a paper strip and place it in a bag. Then draw out an equation and write it on the board. Students can solve the equation and compare solution methods.

- Observe students as they work through equations and arrive at their solutions.

  - Do they understand the concept of an equation?

  - Do they understand that equivalent equations are formed by performing the same operation on each term on both sides of the equation?

  - Can students explain how they found each equivalent equation as they completed the solution?

  - Are students substituting values back into the original equation to verify their solution? Do they understand why this process is desirable, if not always necessary?

- Understanding how to solve an equation is only part of the lesson. Students must also interpret solutions like 6 = 6 or 6 = 5. Present equations like the ones shown below. Ask students to explain the steps in the solution, and then to tell what the solution means. They should be able to identify when a solution represents a finite set of values (*example*: $x = -4$), the null set (*example*: 6 = 5), or an identity, which means the solution is an infinite number of values (*example*: 6 = 6).

  (a) $-5x + 2x - 1 = -(3x + 1)$
  [Answer: identity]
  (b) $4n - 16n - 5 = -(12n - 10)$
  [Answer: null set]

Remediation

- Visual cues and descriptions may help students who have difficulty applying the **distributive property**. Draw arcs showing how each term inside the parentheses is multiplied by each term outside the parentheses.

  $$5(4a + 3) = (5 \times 4a) + (5 \times 3)$$
  $$= 20a + 15$$

  Emphasize that applying the distributive property is just a way of rewriting factors in expanded form.

- Some students may experience difficulty when working with fractions, and especially with multiplying each term by the lowest common denominator. Review how to find the lowest common multiple of two or more numbers. For example:
  4: 4, 8, 12, 16, 20, **24**, 28, 32, …
  6: 6, 12, 18, **24**, 30, 36, 42, 48, …
  8: 8, 16, **24**, 32, 40, 48, 54, …

  The lowest common multiple of 4, 6, and 8 is 24, because 24 is the least number that is common to all three lists. In this lesson, when eliminating fractions by multiplying by a common denominator, the computer will only accept the lowest common denominator.

- Some answer choices in the lesson are designed to detect common errors. If these choices are selected, a feedback box gives an explanation of the error. One very common error occurs when students try to divide out a factor from only one term in an expression. For example:

  $$\frac{4P + 2Q + 5R}{7Q} = \frac{4P + 2\cancel{Q} + 5R}{7\cancel{Q}}$$
  $$= \frac{4P + 2 + 5R}{7}$$

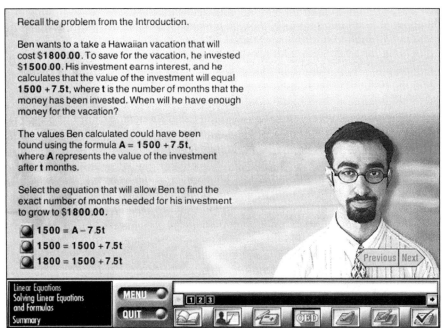

Recall the problem from the Introduction.

Ben wants to a take a Hawaiian vacation that will cost $1800.00. To save for the vacation, he invested $1500.00. His investment earns interest, and he calculates that the value of the investment will equal 1500 + 7.5t, where **t** is the number of months that the money has been invested. When will he have enough money for the vacation?

The values Ben calculated could have been found using the formula **A = 1500 + 7.5t**, where **A** represents the value of the investment after **t** months.

Select the equation that will allow Ben to find the exact number of months needed for his investment to grow to $1800.00.

- 1500 = A − 7.5t
- 1500 = 1500 + 7.5t
- 1800 = 1500 + 7.5t

Linear Equations
Solving Linear Equations and Formulas
Summary

MENU

QUIT

Previous | Next

If students frequently make this mistake, you may wish to conduct a mini-lesson and explain the error using numbers. One such example is shown below.

Simulated Error

$$\frac{3+2+5}{2} \neq \frac{3+\cancel{2}+5}{\cancel{2}}$$

$$\neq \frac{3+1+5}{1}$$

$$\neq 9$$

Correct Answer

$$\frac{3+2+5}{2} = \frac{10}{2}$$
$$= 5$$

- If students make frequent errors, encourage them to record *every* step in the equation-solving process, and taking care not to skip over steps that show an operation being performed on each side. For example:

$$4(n+5) = 36$$
$$4n + 20 = 36$$
$$4n + 20 - 20 = 36 - 20$$
$$4n = 16$$
$$\frac{4n}{4} = \frac{16}{4}$$
$$n = 4$$

Extension

A

Students can translate each sentence from English into algebra and solve the resulting equation.

(a) For what value of m will $3(m+2)$ exceed $2(2m-1)$ by 6? $[m=2]$

(b) The expression $-4(k-7)$ is greater than $2k-2$ by 18. Find the value of k. $[k=2]$

(c) What value of a will make $6(a+2)$ greater than $2(2a+1)$ by 14? $[a=2]$

(d) The sum of $9(b-6)$ and 50 is equal to $3(b+3)$. Find the value of b.

$$\left[b = \frac{13}{6}\right]$$

B

Pose more complex problems such as the following, and ask students to explain how they know each answer is correct.

(a) Is there any value of x for which $2(2x-3)$ equals $4x+1$? [No]

(b) What value of x will make $2(-2x+10y-15)$ subtracted from $5(3x+4y-1)$ equal to

6? $[x=-1]$

(c) For what value of k is 3 a solution of the equation $3(y-2) = 2(y+5) + k$? $[k=-13]$

(d) Find the value of k if the solution of this equation is 4:

$$\frac{2}{3}(m-1) = \frac{1}{2}(m-5) + k.$$

$$\left[k = \frac{5}{2}\right]$$

Enrichment

A

Ask students to find the solution set for each of the following. Remind them to use the distributive property to expand each expression before they solve the equation.

(a) $(y+3)(y-2) = y(y+4)$ $[y=-2]$

(b) $y(y+8) - (y+2)^2 = 4(2y+1) - 8y$ $[y=2]$

(c) $(y+3)^2 = (y-1)^2 + 40$ $[y=4]$

(d) $(m+3)^2 + (2m-1)^2 = 5m^2 + 8$ $[m=-4]$

(e) $(3x+1)^2 - 6x^2 = 3(x^2+1) - 2$ $[x=0]$

(f) $(2h+3)^2 - 4h(h+1) = 5$

$$\left[h = -\frac{1}{2}\right]$$

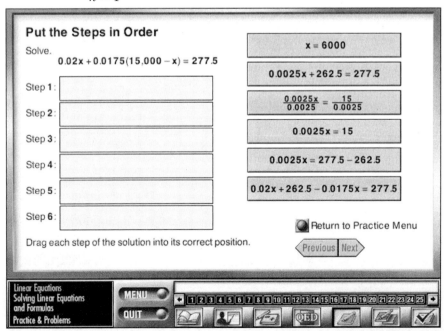

Cross-References

Linear Equations

Student Workbook: pages 42–45

Key Objectives

The student will:

- use a problem-solving strategy to solve problems involving diagrams, percents, mixtures, and formulas.

Key Terms

base angles, vertex angle, complement, supplement, isosceles, parallel, vertical angles, perimeter, percent, mean, median, mode, interest, principal, rate, markdown, discount, distance, rate, time, mixture, solution

Prerequisite Skills

- Solve and check two-step linear equations.
- Simplify algebraic expressions, substitute numbers for variables in expressions, and graph and analyze the relation.
- Translate between an oral and written expression and an equivalent algebraic expression.
- Perform operations with real numbers.

Lesson Description

In this lesson, students develop an organized strategy for solving various problems.

In the **Introduction**, Winnie wants to know the length of each part of the Ironman Triathlon in Hawaii. Students develop a table of data using the appropriate formulas, find a range of possible values using a guess-and-test strategy, and then determine the approximate outcome using a sliding scale. The **Summary** shows how to use an equation to solve the problem more directly.

The **Tutorial** begins by reviewing the five-step problem-solving strategy. Students apply this strategy by working through three problems. In the first problem, students use information about the number of people who worked for the top two U.S. employers in 1998 to determine the number of United States Postal Service employees. The second problem involves using a diagram to find the height of the Statue of Liberty and its pedestal. In the third problem, students find the dimensions of a kennel, given both a diagram and some supporting information. The **Tutorial** presents various verification techniques and emphasizes the importance of checking solutions.

In the **Examples**, students solve various problems using the problem-solving strategy, including problems involving mixtures and percents.

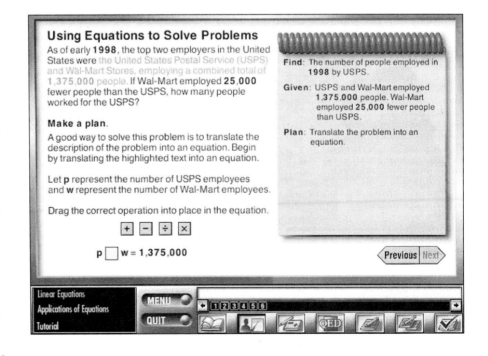

Instructor Intervention

- Make sure that students have the following skills prior to starting the lesson:
  - translating English phrases into algebraic expressions
  - using basic geometry properties related to the angles of a triangle, parallel lines, complementary and supplementary angles, and perimeter and area (for rectangles, circles, and triangles)
  - converting percents to decimal and fraction forms
  - using estimation and mental arithmetic to predict and check calculated answers

- The lesson assumes that students have a solid understanding of solving equations. You may want to review these processes:
  - applying the distributive principle to remove parentheses
  - multiplying both sides of an equation by an appropriate power of 10 to remove decimals
  - multiplying both sides of an equation by the lowest common multiple of the denominators to remove the fractions
  - combining like terms
  - isolating the variable

- Discuss situations occurring in everyday life that involve mixing quantities, finding the relationship between moving objects, or calculating simple interest. This could help students understand the logic of these problems.

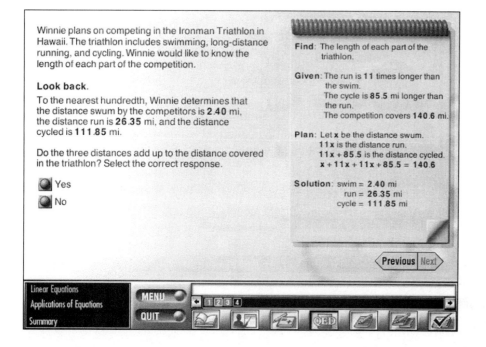

Winnie plans on competing in the Ironman Triathlon in Hawaii. The triathlon includes swimming, long-distance running, and cycling. Winnie would like to know the length of each part of the competition.

Look back.

To the nearest hundredth, Winnie determines that the distance swum by the competitors is **2.40** mi, the distance run is **26.35** mi, and the distance cycled is **111.85** mi.

Do the three distances add up to the distance covered in the triathlon? Select the correct response.

- Yes
- No

Find: The length of each part of the triathlon.

Given: The run is 11 times longer than the swim.
The cycle is 85.5 mi longer than the run.
The competition covers 140.6 mi.

Plan: Let x be the distance swum.
11x is the distance run.
11x + 85.5 is the distance cycled.
x + 11x + 11x + 85.5 = 140.6

Solution: swim = 2.40 mi
run = 26.35 mi
cycle = 111.85 mi

‹ Previous | Next ›

Linear Equations
Applications of Equations
Summary

MENU
QUIT

Evaluation

- Students could create new problems by changing the information in a question from the lesson. They may also want to create their own problems. Have students exchange problems and present complete solutions.

- Observe students as they solve problems. Do they apply the five-step plan? Do they understand the purpose of each step in the solution process? Do they understand the vocabulary? Can they effectively separate needed information from extraneous information? Can they suggest more than one strategy for solving a problem? Do they check their solutions to see if their calculations are correct? if the answer makes sense? if they have answered the question that was asked?

Remediation

- Interpreting word problems relies heavily on language skills. Some students may have difficulty identifying given information and replacing variables in a formula with the correct values. You could set up peer mentors to work with these students.

- Problem solving involves the integration of many different skills. Use the following problems to address areas of possible difficulty:

Diagrams

- Examine the diagram of the flute.

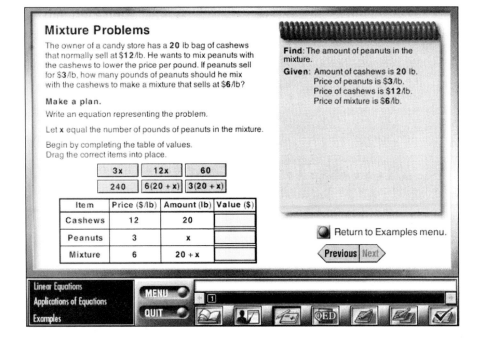

(a) What is the length of the shortest piece? $\left[\dfrac{2}{3}x\right]$

(b) What is the length of the longest piece? $[2x]$

(c) Write an algebraic expression to represent the length of the flute.

$$\left[length = x + 2x + \dfrac{2}{3}x\right]$$

(d) If the flute is 21 in. long, how long is each piece?

$$\left[\dfrac{63}{11}\text{ in.}, \ \dfrac{126}{11}\text{ in.}, \ \dfrac{42}{11}\text{ in.}\right]$$

Interest

- Determine the interest in each situation.
    - (a) $1500 at 6% [$90]
    - (b) x at 5.65% [$0.0565x$]
    - (c) $(850 - x)$ at 7% [$(59.5 - 0.07x)$]

Percent

- Find each number:
    - (a) What number is 5% of 10.56? [0.528]
    - (b) 32.486 is 74% of what number? [43.9]
    - (c) 16 is what percent of 55? [about 29%]

Mixture Problems

The owner of a candy store has a **20 lb** bag of cashews that normally sell at **$12/lb**. He wants to mix peanuts with the cashews to lower the price per pound. If peanuts sell for **$3/lb**, how many pounds of peanuts should he mix with the cashews to make a mixture that sells at **$6/lb**?

Make a plan.

Write an equation representing the problem.

Let **x** equal the number of pounds of peanuts in the mixture.

Begin by completing the table of values.
Drag the correct items into place.

3x	12x	60

240	6(20 + x)	3(20 + x)

Item	Price ($/lb)	Amount (lb)	Value ($)
Cashews	12	20	
Peanuts	3	x	
Mixture	6	20 + x	

Find: The amount of peanuts in the mixture.

Given: Amount of cashews is 20 lb.
Price of peanuts is $3/lb.
Price of cashews is $12/lb.
Price of mixture is $6/lb.

Return to Examples menu.

‹ Previous | Next ›

Linear Equations
Applications of Equations
Examples

MENU
QUIT

Extension

A

Pose this problem and invite students to suggest possible strategies for solving it:

A storekeeper bought a blanket for $50 and tried to sell it for 30% more. The blanket did not sell, so he reduced the selling price by 25%. If the blanket sold at this price, would the storekeeper make money, lose money, or break even on the transaction? [loses $1.25]

B

Ask students to model the following problem using coins and then using an equation. Have them compare the time taken to solve the problem using each method.

Jackson has 95 coins, consisting of quarters and nickels. If the total value of the coins is $8.75, how many of each type of coin does he have? [80 dimes, 15 nickels]

C

Invite students to solve this problem, then create other problems based on the same data:

Sonia won $10,000 in a lottery. She invested part of her winnings at 10% per year and the rest at 11% per year. If the total interest earned after 1 year was $1060, how much was invested at each rate? [$6000 at 11%, $4000 at 10%]

Enrichment

A

Challenge students to write detailed solutions to the following problems and then compare their solution methods.

(a) Tina's total return on her investment was $4200. Part of her investment earned a return of 4% and the rest earned 5%. If the return from the 4% part exceeded the return from the 5% part by $51, how much did she invest at each rate? [$53,137.80 at 4%, $41,490 at 5%]

(b) Two trains 750 mi apart left the station at the same time and started heading toward each other. One train traveled 24 mph slower than the other. If the trains passed each other after 3 h, what was the speed of each train? [faster train traveling at 137 mph, slower train traveling at 113 mph]

(c) Joaquin invested a total of $10,000 in three different investments and earned $1390. The rates of return were 10%, 12%, and 15%. The income from the amount invested at 15% was $710 more than the combined income from the other two investments. How much was invested at each rate? [$1000 at 10%, $2000 at 12%, $7000 at 15%]

(d) A boat takes 5 h to reach a dock 85 mi downstream. It takes 1 h to travel 10 mi upstream. What is the speed of the boat in still water? [13.5 mph] What is the speed of the current? [3.5 mph]

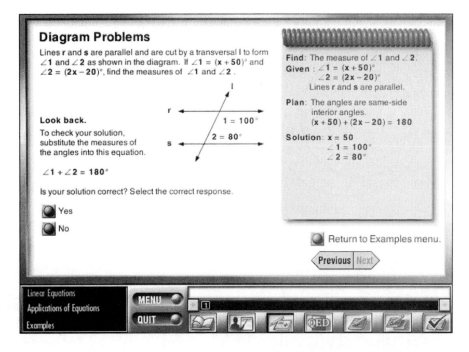

3.4 The Rectangular Coordinate System

Cross-References

Linear Equations

Student Workbook: pages 46–49

Key Objectives

The student will:
- use the rectangular coordinate system to plot and describe points.
- graph mathematical relationships and interpret graphs.

Key Terms

coordinate plane, *x*-axis, *y*-axis, origin, quadrant, coordinates, ordered pairs, *x*-coordinate, *y*-coordinate, variable, independent variable, dependent variable, step function

Prerequisite Skills

- Compare and order integers.
- Create, read, and interpret a table of values.

Lesson Description

In this lesson, students learn about the rectangular coordinate system. They learn to plot points on a coordinate system and to graph mathematical relationships and interpret graphs.

In the **Introduction**, Steve wants to rent a minivan for a trip. He has price formulas from two car-rental companies, EZ Rentals and Getaway Autos. Each formula consists of a flat rate plus a cost per mile driven. The students use a table of values to determine that Getaway Autos is cheaper for a low number of miles driven, but for longer distances, EZ Rentals is the less expensive option. In the **Summary**, the students plot the ordered pairs from their table of values to obtain a visual representation of the data.

The **Tutorial** describes the coordinate plane and explains how to locate and plot points on the plane. In the last section, these skills are used to graph a mathematical relationship. The first three sections in the **Examples** reinforce learning acquired in the **Tutorial**, and the last section introduces step graphs.

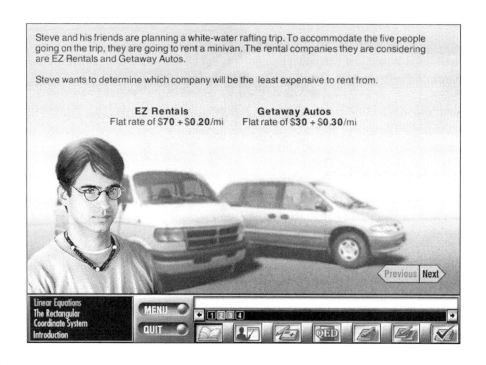

Steve and his friends are planning a white-water rafting trip. To accommodate the five people going on the trip, they are going to rent a minivan. The rental companies they are considering are EZ Rentals and Getaway Autos.

Steve wants to determine which company will be the least expensive to rent from.

EZ Rentals
Flat rate of $70 + $0.20/mi

Getaway Autos
Flat rate of $30 + $0.30/mi

Previous | Next

Linear Equations
The Rectangular Coordinate System
Introduction

MENU
QUIT

Instructor Intervention

- Emphasize that points are plotted by moving across the *x*-axis first and then up or down in line with the *y*-axis. It may help to use the analogy of traveling across a sidewalk, then up or down a ladder.

- In the **Summary**, explain how the points (0, 70) and (0, 30) were derived. [They represent the flat rate for each company.]

- On the Postage Rates graph in the **Practice and Problems** section, point out the break-in-data symbol (the double slash) on the *y*-axis. The scale starts at 0, but since there are no points with *y*-values between 0 and 32, this interval is not shown. The break-in-data symbol can be used on either axis, and can also be shown as a zigzag.

Steve wants to determine which company will be the least expensive to rent from.

EZ Rentals
Flat rate of **$70** + **$0.20**/mi

Getaway Autos
Flat rate of **$30** + **$0.30**/mi

Steve decides to graph of the data. He begins by writing ordered pairs for the data.

EZ Rentals

Distance (mi)	Cost ($)	(x, y)
100	90	(100, 90)
300	130	(☐ , 130)
500	170	(500, ☐)

Getaway Autos

Distance (mi)	Cost ($)	(x, y)
100	60	(☐ , ☐)
300	120	(300, ☐)
500	180	(500, ☐)

Drag each value to its correct position in the table.

| 60 | 100 | 120 | 170 | 180 | 300 |

〈Previous │ Next〉

Linear Equations
The Rectangular
Coordinate System
Summary

MENU

QUIT

[1][2][3][4]

Evaluation

- Students should have worksheets of blank coordinate grids. Ask them to add the following labels to their grids: *x*-axis, *y*-axis, origin, quadrant I, quadrant II, quadrant III, quadrant IV, (x, y), $(-x, -y)$, $(-x, y)$, $(x, -y)$. Then place a transparency on an overhead projector, and have students provide the correct answers.

- In groups, have the students use a coordinate plane to answer the following question:

  Bart's rectangular backyard measures 10 yd wide by 60 yd long. He wants to put a fence around a rectangular garden. The garden will be 10 yd wide, but the length has not yet been determined.

  (a) Fencing costs $20/yd. Complete the chart to calculate the cost of fencing if the length is 10 yd, 15 yd, 20 yd, 25 yd, and 30 yd.

Length (yd)	Total Fencing (yd)	Cost ($)
10	$2(L + W) = 40$	$800
15		
20		
25		
30		

  (b) Graph the relationship between the length of the garden and the cost of the fence.
    (i) What are the length options if Bart wants to spend $1200 or less?
    (ii) How much would it cost to fence the entire backyard?

- Observe students as they graph the data and interpret the results. Can they label the axes and quadrants correctly? Can they convert the data from a chart into ordered pairs? Can they plot ordered pairs correctly? Can they interpret a graph to answer specific questions?

Remediation

- Review the **Key Terms** listed at the beginning of these teaching notes. You might make a bulletin board display to show the names of the axes, the origin, the quadrant numbers, and the signs of the coordinates for points in each quadrant.

- If students are mislocating points because of sign errors, draw a coordinate plane without grid lines or numbers. Name a point, such as $(-4, 2)$, and ask students to locate the quadrant where this point would be found.

- If students are plotting points in the wrong order, have them trace their path along the grid with a fingertip. Remind them to move across first and then up or down.

Extension

A

Create a worksheet with two coordinate grids. On the first grid, locate several points along the line $y = x$. On the second, locate points along $y = -x$. Invite students to name the coordinates of each point and to explain the patterns they see. Then have them join points on each grid and look for other points that belong on the same lines.

Students may wish to draw some oblique lines on their own grids and look for patterns in the coordinates of points along each line.

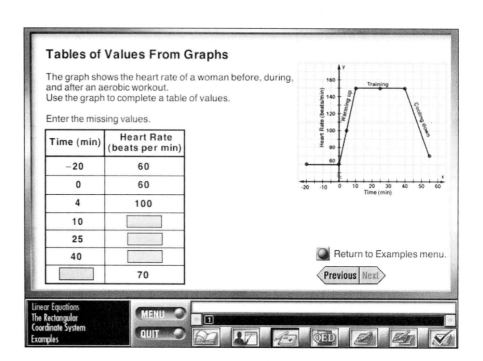

B

Students could analyze the coordinates of the midpoint of a horizontal line and the coordinates of the midpoint of a vertical line. Challenge them to develop a rule for using the coordinates of the endpoints to find the midpoint of each type of line.

Answer: midpoint of a horizontal line

$$= \left(\frac{x_1 + x_2}{2}, y \right);$$

midpoint of a vertical line

$$= \left(x, \frac{y_1 + y_2}{2} \right)$$

Enrichment

A

Students might research and compare these methods for locating points:
(a) the alphanumeric system used on city or road maps
(b) the lines of latitude and longitude used on a globe or world map
(c) the sections, townships, or ranges used on a municipal map
(d) the azimuth or equator systems used with star maps

B

Arrange for guest speakers to talk to the class about relevant topics. For example:
• A natural resources officer or police officer could explain the use of search-and-rescue grids.
• A dentist or dental assistant could explain the chart numbering system for teeth.
• An airplane design engineer could explain how ordered triples (x, y, z) are used.

C

Provide students with the given graphs from physics and chemistry and have them answer the following questions:

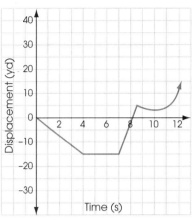

Displacement–Time Graph for a Car

(a) If north is positive and south is negative, in what direction was the car traveling from 0 to 4 seconds? [south]
(b) For how many seconds was the car stopped? [3 seconds]
(c) After how many seconds did the car return to its starting position? [after about 8 seconds]
(d) What does the slope of a displacement-time graph measure? [velocity]

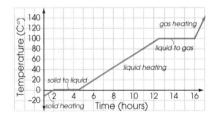

Warming Curve for a Particular Volume of Water

(a) What is happening to the water at the first plateau? the second plateau?
(b) What is happening to the water at the first rise in the graph? second rise in the graph? third rise in the graph?

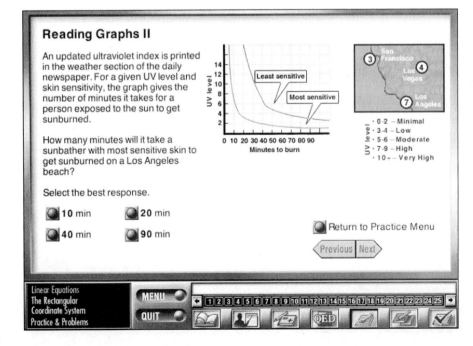

Reading Graphs II

An updated ultraviolet index is printed in the weather section of the daily newspaper. For a given UV level and skin sensitivity, the graph gives the number of minutes it takes for a person exposed to the sun to get sunburned.

How many minutes will it take a sunbather with most sensitive skin to get sunburned on a Los Angeles beach?

Select the best response.

10 min   20 min
40 min   90 min

Return to Practice Menu
Previous | Next

Least sensitive
Most sensitive
UV level
Minutes to burn

San Francisco
Las Vegas
Los Angeles

· 0-2 – Minimal
· 3-4 – Low
· 5-6 – Moderate
· 7-9 – High
· 10+ – Very High

UV level

Linear Equations
The Rectangular Coordinate System
Practice & Problems

MENU
QUIT

1 2 3 4 5 6 7 8 9 10 11 12 13 14 15 16 17 18 19 20 21 22 23 24 25

4 POLYNOMIALS AND FACTORING

4.1 Multiplying Polynomials

Cross-References

Polynomials and Factoring

Student Workbook: pages 50–53

Key Objectives

The student will:
- multiply a trinomial by a binomial.
- multiply two trinomials.
- find powers of polynomials.
- multiply three polynomials where one is a monomial, one is a binomial, and the third is a trinomial.

Key Terms

partial product, numerical coefficient, commutative property, distributive property, like terms, simplify, expand, factor, descending order

Prerequisite Skills

- Identify constant terms, coefficients, and variables in polynomial expressions.
- Represent multiplication, division, and factoring of monomials, binomials, and trinomials of the form $x^2 + bx + c$.
- Find the product of two monomials, a monomial and a binomial, and two binomials.

Lesson Description

This lesson extends the students' understanding of polynomial products to situations where:
(a) at least one factor has more than two terms.
(b) there are more than two factors.

In the **Introduction**, an editorial assistant must arrange a group of drawings whose dimensions are expressed algebraically. Students create an expression to show the area of the page covered by drawings. In the **Summary**, students simplify this expression and then substitute a value for x to find the area.

The **Tutorial** establishes the following steps for multiplying two polynomials:
- Predict the number of partial products.
- Multiply each term of the first polynomial by each term of the second polynomial.
- Simplify the expanded polynomial by collecting like terms.
- Arrange the terms of the expanded polynomial in descending order.

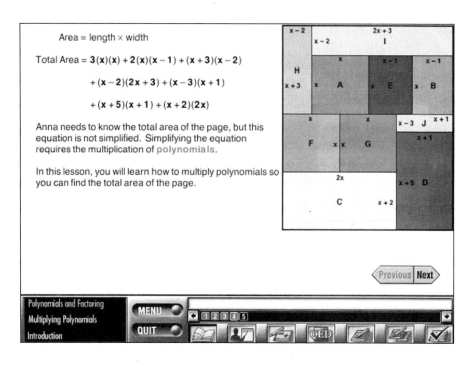

In the **Examples**, students review these steps and learn to apply them in situations involving three or more factors, including some situations with polynomial powers.

Instructor Intervention

- Early in the lesson, students may find it helpful to use grid diagrams to find and check partial products. Remind them that they can access the *Binomial Grid Explorer* through the pull-down menu.

- Before students begin the lesson, review the key terms listed on the preceding page in this manual. Make sure students know how to recognize like terms. For example, point out that $4a^2$ and $2a^2$ are like terms but $4a^2$ and $2a^2b$ are not.

- Review the exponent laws. Students could make and display large colorful posters for the laws that apply in multiplication situations. If possible, you might enlist support from your school's art department, so students can use art time or art resources to work on their posters.

  When the posters are finished, display them in the classroom for the students' reference.

Lesson Components

Examples

Expanding Polynomials (1)
Collecting Like Terms (1)
Three or More Factors (1)
Polynomials as Powers (1)
Problem Situations(1)

Practice and Problems

Partial Products
Collecting Like Terms
Three Factors
Error Analysis
Problem Situations

Extra Practice

Partial Products
Collecting Like Terms
Three Factors
Error Analysis
Problem Situations

Self-Check

Partial Products (2)
Collecting Like Terms (2)
Three Factors (2)
Error Analysis (2)
Problem Situations (2)

Minimum score: 7 out of 10

Area = length × width

Total Area = $3(x)(x) + 2(x)(x - 1) + (x + 3)(x - 2)$

$\qquad + (2x + 3)(x - 2) + (x + 1)(x - 3)$

$\qquad + (x + 5)(x + 1) + (2x)(x + 2)$

Anna needs to know the total area of the page, but this equation is not simplified. Simplifying the equation requires the multiplication of polynomials.

In this lesson, you will learn how to multiply polynomials so you can find the total area of the page.

Previous   Next

Polynomials and Factoring
Multiplying Polynomials
Introduction

MENU
QUIT
1 2 3 4 5

Evaluation

- Choose a selection of problems from the **Practice and Problems** or **Extra Practice** sections, or from the *Student Workbook*, and ask students to hand in complete written solutions. Evaluate the solutions to determine whether students are:
  - (a) checking to see whether they have found all the partial products.
  - (b) multiplying terms correctly.
  - (c) correctly identifying and combining like terms.
  - (d) avoiding sign errors.
  - (e) recording terms in the expanded polynomials in descending order.

- Describe a problem situation similar to one from the lesson or *Student Workbook*. Have students work in small groups to solve the problem and then present and compare solutions.

  You may wish to assign group grades or have the students grade themselves after they have listened to the presentations of other groups.

Remediation

- Ask students to use the *Binomial Grid Explorer* to help them create grid models that illustrate the product of two terms, such as $x \times 4x$ or $3 \times 2x^2$. Once they have mastered the multiplication of terms, they can create models to show products of two polynomial factors. (Choose factors that will produce a product with no exponent greater than 2.) Have students record the polynomial that represents each product.

- Pose several multiplication problems that can be modeled with algebra manipulatives. With the aid of the overhead projector, use manipulatives on a four-quadrant grid to model each partial product as students work at their desks. Encourage questions and discussion and invite volunteers to model some examples.

- If students are having difficulty, you may wish to focus on some specific problem types. Choose practice examples from each of these categories:
  - (a) binomial × trinomial
  - (b) trinomial × trinomial
  - (c) monomial × binomial × binomial
  - (d) monomial × binomial × trinomial

- If students are finding it difficult to distinguish between terms and polynomials (i.e., multiplying terms such as $4x^2y \times 2xy$ incorrectly to get products such as $8 + x^3 + y^2$), it may help them to rewrite the terms with multiplication symbols (i.e., $4x^2y \times 2xy$ becomes $4 \times x^2 \times y \times 2 \times x \times y$).

- If students are making frequent sign errors, it may help them to express all polynomials as addition expressions before they multiply. For example, they could restate $4x^2 - 2x - 8$ as $4x^2 + (-2x) + (-8)$.

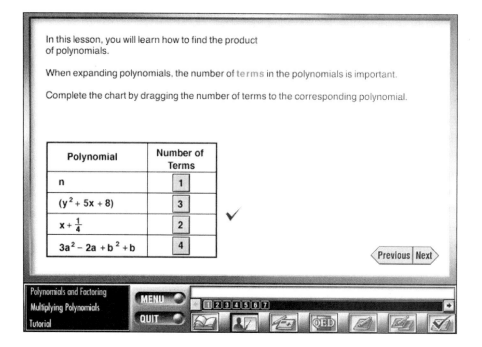

Extension

A

Invite individual students or small groups to present a detailed account of how they solved one of the problems from the lesson or *Student Workbook*. Students could use audiotapes, videotapes, cartoons, computer animation, overhead transparencies, slides, or other media to make the presentation as appealing as possible.

B

Ask individuals or small groups to create and solve multiplication problems similar to those in the lesson. Students can write each solution on a separate piece of paper and then exchange problems. When the problems are solved, students can compare solutions to check accuracy and contrast the methods they used.

Enrichment

A

Students who are proficient in this area could talk with students who feel less secure and then design some activities that might help. Encourage them to make the activities fun as well as informative. For example, they might:
- create a game.
- investigate a real-world problem situation.
- draw cartoons that deal with problem areas.

B

Have students use the compound interest formula detailed in the **Examples** section to calculate the cost of a $1000 loan at several different rates of interest.

Some students may wish to investigate current rates on a specific type of loan or investment and then develop and solve a problem based on this information.

C

Challenge students to suggest alternative or more efficient ways to solve problems from the lesson. You may wish to offer extra credit for valid suggestions.

D

Present problems that involve the product of:
(a) a trinomial and a four-term polynomial.
(b) two four-term polynomials.

E

Students could search books about mathematics or use the Internet to find information about the Binomial Theorem, which can be used to find powers of binomials.

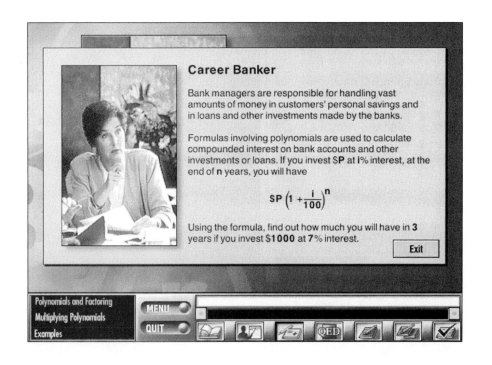

Career Banker

Bank managers are responsible for handling vast amounts of money in customers' personal savings and in loans and other investments made by the banks.

Formulas involving polynomials are used to calculate compounded interest on bank accounts and other investments or loans. If you invest P at $i\%$ interest, at the end of n years, you will have

$$\$P \left(1 + \frac{i}{100}\right)^n$$

Using the formula, find out how much you will have in **3** years if you invest **$1000** at **7%** interest.

Exit

Polynomials and Factoring
Multiplying Polynomials
Examples

MENU
QUIT

Cross-References

Polynomials and Factoring

Student Workbook: pages 54–57

Key Objectives

The student will:
- learn how to factor out the greatest common factor from polynomials.
- factor polynomials by grouping.

Key Terms

factor, natural number, prime factor, prime factorization, ascending, prime-factored form, factor stack, greatest common factor (GCF), coefficient, monomial, binomial, trinomial, term, power, base, exponent, distributive property, prime polynomial, divisor

Prerequisite Skills

- Explain and apply the exponent laws for powers with integral exponents.
- Determine equivalent forms of algebraic expressions by identifying common factors and factoring trinomials of the form $ax^2 + bx + c$.
- Find the quotient when a polynomial is divided by a monomial.

Lesson Description

In this lesson, students learn how to factor out the greatest common factor and how to factor polynomials by grouping the terms first.

The **Introduction** presents a problem about environmental contamination. Students calculate the amount of soil that needs to be cleaned by adding together the volumes of several different-sized cylinders. Although students obtain the correct answer, their procedure is time-consuming, requires many steps, and is prone to error. In the **Summary**, students use their newly-acquired factoring skills to simplify the volume calculations and find the volume of soil more efficiently.

In the **Tutorial**, students use the prime-factored forms of 60, 84, and 180 to find their GCF. They extend the concept of finding the GCF using prime factors to monomials and polynomials.

The **Examples** investigate specific cases involving factoring out the GCF and factoring by grouping terms:
- recognizing prime polynomials, where the GCF is 1
- factoring out the negative of the GCF
- factoring by grouping
- multi-step factoring, which involves factoring out the GCF first, then factoring by grouping
- factoring formulas

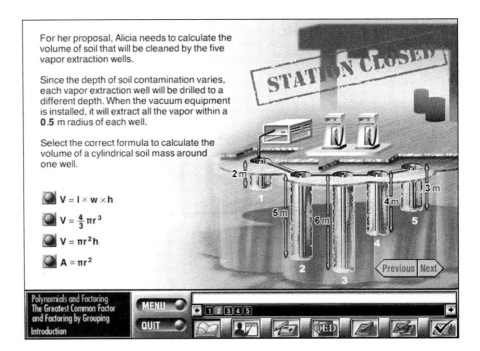

For her proposal, Alicia needs to calculate the volume of soil that will be cleaned by the five vapor extraction wells.

Since the depth of soil contamination varies, each vapor extraction well will be drilled to a different depth. When the vacuum equipment is installed, it will extract all the vapor within a **0.5 m** radius of each well.

Select the correct formula to calculate the volume of a cylindrical soil mass around one well.

- $V = l \times w \times h$
- $V = \frac{4}{3} \pi r^3$
- $V = \pi r^2 h$
- $A = \pi r^2$

Polynomials and Factoring
The Greatest Common Factor
and Factoring by Grouping
Introduction

MENU
QUIT

Instructor Intervention

- Before starting the lesson, review the exponent laws and the rules for multiplying and dividing integers.

- Students will need to use pencil and paper for some exercises in the **Practice**, **Extra Practice**, and **Self-Check** sections.

- When students use pencil and paper to factor by grouping, encourage them to show the groups by drawing an arc below the terms. Discourage using parentheses to group terms, as this could be confused with multiplication.

- Explain that, when prime-factoring, writing each factor in ascending and alphabetical order will make the similarities between factor lists more readily apparent.

- Illustrate that the operation signs in polynomials can be thought of as leading signs of separate terms. For example, $3xy - 14x + xyz$ can be thought of as three terms: $+3xy$, $-14x$, and $+xyz$. Thinking of the terms in this way may help students factor out a negative GCF.

- Emphasize the importance of checking factorizations. Review how to expand polynomials using the distributive property and the FOIL method.

- Students should always check to make sure they have factored completely. Each factor of a completely factored expression will be prime.

Lesson Components

 Examples

Factoring Out the GCF (1)
Prime Polynomials (1)
Factoring Out the Negative of the GCF (1)
Factoring by Grouping (2)
Multi-Step Factoring (1)
Factoring Formulas (1)

 Practice and Problems

Finding the GCF
Factoring Out the GCF
Factoring by Grouping
Multi-Step Factoring
Factoring Formulas

 Extra Practice

Factoring Out the GCF
Prime Polynomials
Factoring Out the Negative GCF
Factoring by Grouping
Multi-Step Factoring
Factoring Formulas

 Self-Check

Factoring Out the GCF (2)
Prime Polynomials (1)
Factoring Out the Negative GCF (2)
Factoring by Grouping (2)
Multi-Step Factoring (2)
Factoring Formulas (1)

Minimum score: 7 out of 10

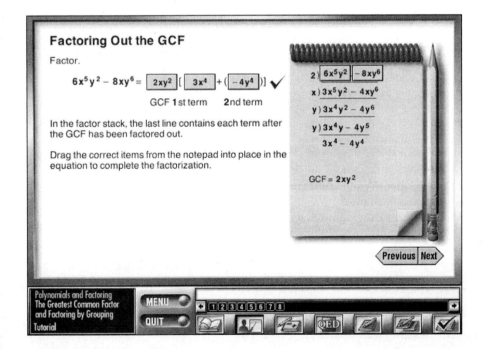

Evaluation

- Have students complete this quiz individually, then compare and discuss their answers in small groups.
  1. Use prime factorization to find the GCF of 12, 52, and 64. Show your work.
  2. Factor the polynomial $10x^3y - 30x^2y^2 + 5x^2y$. Expand the final answer to check your solution.
  3. Factor $4mn - 9st$. State what kind of polynomial this is and the value of the GCF.
  4. Factor $-5y^3 - 10y^2 + 15y$ by factoring out the GCF. Repeat by factoring out the negative of the GCF. Discuss which answer would be easier to work with for subsequent factoring.
  5. Factor $7u + v^2 - 7v - uv$ by grouping. Then group the terms in a different way and factor again.
  6. Completely factor the polynomial $12m^2n - 6mn^2 + 12mn - 6n^2$.
  7. Solve the equation for y.
     $$xy - xz = yz$$

- Observe students as they work through the activities. Do they understand the process of prime factorization? Can they find the GCF? Can they factor out the GCF? Can they factor by grouping? Do they recognize when they need to factor out the negative of the GCF?

Remediation

- Provide practice on how to change signs when factoring out the negative of a GCF. Start by having students separate the terms for several polynomials (as discussed in the **Instructor Intervention** section) to create a list of signed terms. Then ask students to state the negative of each term in the list before rejoining the new terms as polynomials.

- Some students may have difficulty with the process of prime factorization because of poor multiplication and division skills. Encourage these students to review the laws of divisibility and to practice multiplying small numbers.

- Some students may have trouble factoring the GCF out of polynomials. In a polynomial such as $6x^2y^2z + 4xy^2z^2 - 10y^3z$, they could rewrite each term as the product of the GCF and another factor. Demonstrate that it is easy to obtain both factors from the prime factorization.

$$6x^2y^2z = \boxed{2} \times 3 \times x \times x \times \boxed{y} \times \boxed{y} \times \boxed{z}$$
$$4xy^2z^2 = \boxed{2} \times 2 \times x \times \boxed{y} \times \boxed{y} \times \boxed{z} \times z$$
$$-10y^3z = \boxed{2} \times 5 \times \boxed{y} \times \boxed{y} \times y \times \boxed{z}$$

Since the GCF is $2y^2z$, the remaining items make up the other factor:

$$6x^2y^2z = \text{GCF} \times \boxed{3x^2}$$
$$4xy^2z^2 = \text{GCF} \times \boxed{2xz}$$
$$-10y^3z = \text{GCF} \times \boxed{5y}$$

Therefore, the factored form is $2y^2z(3x^2 + 2xz - 5y)$. Note that this method is demonstrated in the **Tutorial** using factor stacks.

Extension

A

Some students may find it difficult or tedious to factor an expression like $3x^2 + 2x - 8$ using the usual trinomial factoring method because it requires guessing and testing to find the factors: $(3x \pm ?)(x \pm ?)$. Suggest that students try other ways of factoring trinomials. For example, have students factor $3x^2 + 2x - 8$ by first replacing $+2x$ with $-4x + 6x$ and then factoring by grouping.

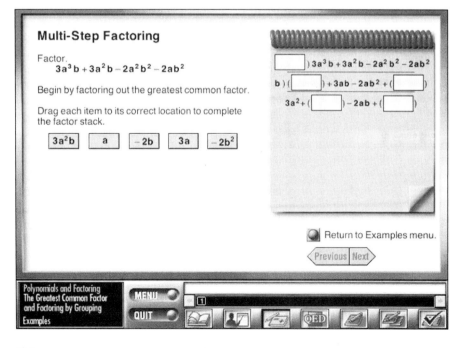

Multi-Step Factoring

Factor.
$$3a^3b + 3a^2b - 2a^2b^2 - 2ab^2$$

Begin by factoring out the greatest common factor.

Drag each item to its correct location to complete the factor stack.

| $3a^2b$ | a | $-2b$ | $3a$ | $-2b^2$ |

$\boxed{}$) $3a^3b + 3a^2b - 2a^2b^2 - 2ab^2$

b) ($\boxed{}$) $+ 3ab - 2ab^2 + ($ $\boxed{}$)

$3a^2 + ($ $\boxed{}$) $- 2ab + ($ $\boxed{}$)

Return to Examples menu.

Previous | Next

Polynomials and Factoring
The Greatest Common Factor
and Factoring by Grouping
Examples

MENU

QUIT

$$3x^2 - 4x + 6x - 8$$
$$= 3x^2 + 6x - 4x - 8$$
$$= 3x(x+2) - 4(x+2)$$
$$= (3x-4)(x+2)$$

Students should notice that $-4x + 6x$ was chosen to replace $+2x$ because $-4x$ and 8 can be grouped and then factored, as can $6x$ and $3x^2$. They could try to apply this factoring method to other problems.

Ask students to explain why $(x+1)$ is a factor of the first polynomial, but *not* a factor of the second polynomial.

1. $x(xy-3)(x+1)$
2. $x + (xy-3)(x+1)$

Enrichment

Present some examples of how factoring is used in real life. Suggest that students solve these problem situations:

1.

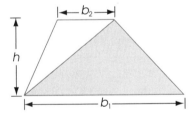

(a) Write an expression that gives the area of the shaded part of the figure.

$$\left[\frac{1}{2}b_1 h\right]$$

(b) Do the same for the unshaded part of the figure.

$$\left[\frac{1}{2}b_2 h\right]$$

(c) Add the results from parts (a) and (b) and then factor that expression. What

important formula from geometry do you obtain?

$$\left[\frac{1}{2}h(b_1 + b_2); \quad \text{the formula}\right]$$

for the area of a trapezoid]

2.

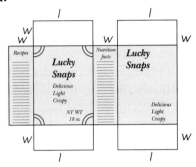

The amount of cardboard needed to make the cereal box can be found by computing the area, A, which is given by the formula $A = 2wh + 4wl + 2lh$ where w is the width, h is the height, and l is the length. Solve the equation for the width.

$$\left[w = \frac{A - 2lh}{2h + 4l}\right]$$

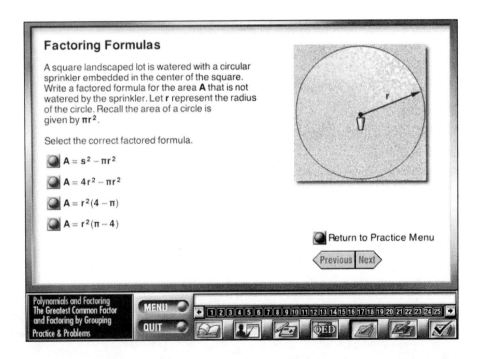

Factoring Formulas

A square landscaped lot is watered with a circular sprinkler embedded in the center of the square. Write a factored formula for the area **A** that is not watered by the sprinkler. Let **r** represent the radius of the circle. Recall the area of a circle is given by πr^2.

Select the correct factored formula.

- $A = s^2 - \pi r^2$
- $A = 4r^2 - \pi r^2$
- $A = r^2(4 - \pi)$
- $A = r^2(\pi - 4)$

Return to Practice Menu

Previous Next

Polynomials and Factoring
The Greatest Common Factor
and Factoring by Grouping
Practice & Problems

MENU   QUIT

Factoring Trinomials and Difference of Squares

Cross-References

Polynomials and Factoring

Student Workbook: pages 58–61

Key Objectives

The student will:

- factor polynomials of the forms $ax^2 + bx + c$ and $a^2x^2 - b^2y^2$.
- solve problems involving factoring.

Key Terms

factor, product, monomial, binomial, trinomial, polynomial, numerical coefficient, term, perfect square trinomial, difference of squares

Prerequisite Skills

- Apply exponent laws for powers with integral exponents.
- Represent multiplication, division, and factoring of monomials, binomials, and trinomials of the form $x^2 + bx + c$, using concrete materials and diagrams.
- Determine equivalent forms of algebraic expressions by identifying common factors and factoring trinomials of the form $x^2 + bx + c$.
- Find the quotient when a polynomial is divided by a monomial.

Lesson Description

This lesson focuses on factoring trinomials of the form $ax^2 + bx + c$ and then extends the factoring process to polynomials of several other types. In the **Introduction**, students use a systematic guess-and-test strategy to find the dimensions of a townhouse courtyard with an area of 1225 yd^2. In the **Summary**, they return to this problem to see how factoring a polynomial can expedite the solution process.

The **Tutorial** reviews factoring $x^2 + bx + c$ trinomials and illustrates each situation with a tile model. Students learn that a similar process can be used to factor $ax^2 + bx + c$ trinomials:

1. Find all possible pairs of first terms with a product of ax^2.
2. Systematically combine the first term pairs with all the possible pairs of factors for c.
3. Look for the combination that results in the correct value for b. (This is the sum of the products of the outside and inside terms of the binomial factors.)
4. Check the result by multiplying the binomial factors to see if the product is the original trinomial.

This process is sometimes long, but a systematic approach will always yield the correct factor pairs.

In the **Examples**, students learn to recognize and factor other types of polynomials, including perfect square trinomials $(4x^2 + 20x + 25)$,

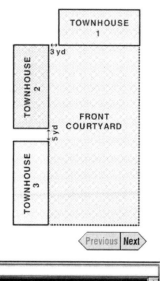

Three years ago, Lorne's company, Lorne's Landscaping, laid the sod in the front courtyard of a townhouse project in his home town. Now his company is being asked to cement backyard patios at the same complex.

Lorne thought he had, on file, all the dimensions required to prepare a cost estimate, but he was only able to find a rough sketch of the project, and a note stating that the front courtyard had required **1225 yd²** of sod.

binomials that represent a difference of squares $(4x^2 - 25)$, and trinomials that can be restated in the form $ax^2 + bx + c$ by substituting a variable for part of an expression (*example:* $6x^4 - x^2 - 2 = 6p^2 - p - 2$, where $p = x^2$). Students also determine all the integral values for b for which a given $ax^2 + bx + c$ trinomial can be factored, and they apply factoring methods to find the dimensions of a rectangle.

Instructor Intervention

- Encourage students to use the *Binomial Grid Explorer* to review how to factor polynomials of the form $x^2 + bx + c$.

- Students may need to review the FOIL method (First, Outside, Inside, Last) for multiplying binomials. This should help students remember to include the middle term when they are squaring a binomial. For example, $(2x-3)(2x-3) = 4x^2 - 12x + 9$, not $4x^2 + 9$.

- Students may need help as they begin using the outside product/inside product method of finding the numerical coefficient of the middle term. (This shortcut is described in the **Tutorial**.)

- When students are checking to see if a trinomial is a perfect square, encourage them to ask themselves:

  Is the middle term equal to double the product of the square roots of the first and last terms?

  For example, in $4x^2 + 20x + 25$, is $+20x$ equal to $2(2x)(5)$?

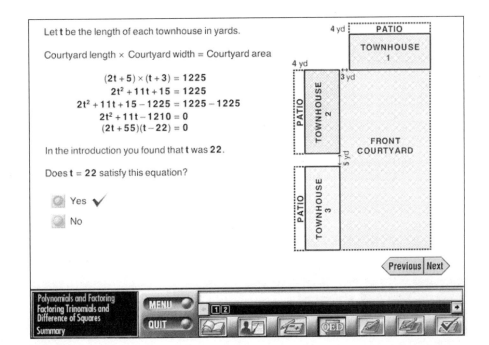

Evaluation

- Have students complete these exercises independently and then form groups to compare and contrast answers and methods. Each group could present one solution.

  1. Factor:
     (a) $x^2 + 6x + 8$
        $[(x+4)(x+2)]$
     (b) $2x^2 + 5x + 3$
        $[(2x+3)(x+1)]$
     (c) $25x^2 - 16$
        $[(5x+4)(5x-4)]$
     (d) $16x^2 - 56x + 49$
        $[(4x-7)^2]$

  2. Determine if $(5x+7)$ is a factor of $5x^2 + 12x + 7$.
     [yes]

  3. Find all possible integral values of b for which $3x^2 + bx - 16$ can be factored.
     [$\pm2, \pm8, \pm13, \pm22, \pm47$]

  4. A rectangle has an area of $3x^2 + 13x - 10$. Find expressions for its length and width.
     $[(3x-2)(x+5)]$

- Observe students as they factor polynomial expressions. Can they recognize the different types of polynomials? Do they use the correct approach for factoring each type? Do they organize their searches for factors in a systematic way?

- Ask students to describe the steps they use to factor a polynomial.

Remediation

- Make sure students understand that a polynomial is in factored form when it is expressed as a product of other polynomials.

- Review these terms.
  (a) factor
  (b) polynomial
  (c) trinomial
  (d) binomial
  (e) term
  (f) numerical coefficient
  (g) perfect square trinomial
  (h) difference of squares

- Class or small-group quizzes with one or two problems can help to pinpoint students who need help. If a student seems to be having difficulty, invite him or her to solve a problem and then explain the solution for you. Arrange time to work with small groups of students who need the same type of assistance, or assign these students to work with partners who can help them.

- Watch for students who overlook potential binomial factor combinations because they are not using an organized approach.

  Invite them to review the **Tutorial** and **Examples** to see how factor combinations are listed in order and then have them apply a similar order in their own lists. Encourage them to look for positive/ negative patterns that will help them find all possible pairs of each type.

- Students may find it helpful to use the *Binomial Grid Explorer* to factor some expressions, since this will help to bring abstract algebraic expressions to a more concrete level.

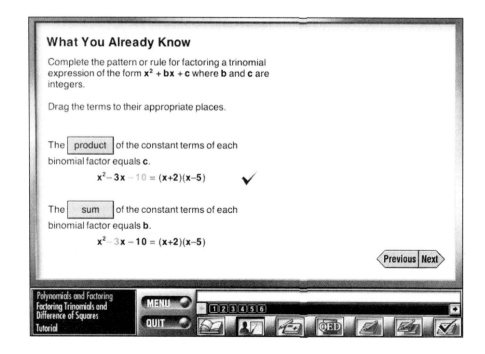

Extension

A

Have small groups generate expressions to be factored, including at least one example of each of these types:

(a) a trinomial of the form
$x^2 + bx + c$

(b) a trinomial of the form
$ax^2 + bx + c$

(c) a perfect square trinomial

(d) a difference of squares

(e) an error analysis problem

Ask each group to provide a page of sample solutions for their problems. Groups can trade problems, solve them, and then use the sample solutions to check their work. You may wish to save examples of some problems for assessment purposes.

B

Have students generate problems that can be factored, if factors are not limited to the integers. For example:
$x^2 - 5 = (x - \sqrt{5})(x + \sqrt{5})$

C

Students could solve these geometry problems and then generate similar problems of their own.

(a)

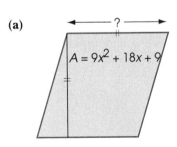

$A = 9x^2 + 18x + 9$

(b)

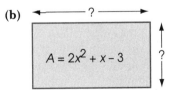

$A = 2x^2 + x - 3$

Enrichment

A

Pose this sequence of problems for students.

Multiply $(x - 1)(x - 2)(x - 3)$. Simplify the product and then substitute each of these values into the result. For which values is the expression equal to 0? Why?
(a) 1 **(b)** 2 **(c)** 3 **(d)** 4 **(e)** 5 **(f)** 6

B

The Factor Theorem states that $(x - a)$ is a factor of a polynomial if the value of the polynomial is 0 when a replaces x throughout. Why is this theorem true? [*example*: When you substitute a for x, the value of $(x - a)$ becomes $(x - x)$ or 0. No matter what the other factors are, the result must be 0, since one of the factors is 0.]

C

Use the Factor Theorem to create an expression that will have $(x - 6)$ for a factor. [*example*: $x^2 + 5x - 66$]

D

After students have discovered the Factor Theorem (see previous activity), challenge them to use the theorem to factor a sum or difference of cubes, such as $x^3 - 2^3$.
$[(x - 2)(x^2 + 2x + 4)]$

Have them generate and factor several other examples. Can they develop a general rule for factoring a difference of cubes?
$[x^3 - a^3 = (x - a)(x^2 + ax + a^2)]$

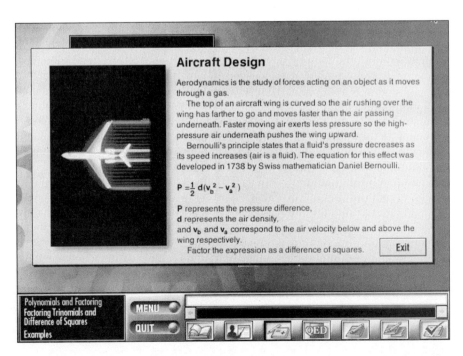

Aircraft Design

Aerodynamics is the study of forces acting on an object as it moves through a gas.

The top of an aircraft wing is curved so the air rushing over the wing has farther to go and moves faster than the air passing underneath. Faster moving air exerts less pressure so the high-pressure air underneath pushes the wing upward.

Bernoulli's principle states that a fluid's pressure decreases as its speed increases (air is a fluid). The equation for this effect was developed in 1738 by Swiss mathematician Daniel Bernoulli.

$P = \frac{1}{2} d(v_b^2 - v_a^2)$

P represents the pressure difference,
d represents the air density,
and **v_b** and **v_a** correspond to the air velocity below and above the wing respectively.

Factor the expression as a difference of squares.

Exit

Polynomials and Factoring
Factoring Trinomials and
Difference of Squares
Examples

MENU

QUIT

4.4 **Sum and Difference of Two Cubes**

Cross-References

Polynomials and Factoring

Student Workbook: pages 62–65

Key Objectives

The student will:

- recognize and factor the sum of two cubes and the difference of two cubes.
- factor the sum of two cubes and the difference of two cubes that contain a common factor.
- factor the difference of two terms of degree 6.

Key Terms

numerator, denominator, difference of squares, distributive property, terms, greatest common factor

Prerequisite Skills

- Find common factors in a polynomial.
- Factor trinomials and differences of squares.

Lesson Description

In the **Introduction**, Ben is reviewing his high-school math textbook to prepare for a math course, but encounters a problem that he doesn't know how to solve quickly. Students simplify $\frac{y^3 + 27}{y + 3}$ by reasoning and using trial and error. They return to the problem in the **Summary** and solve it again, this time using their skills at factoring a sum of two cubes.

The **Tutorial** begins by reviewing how to factor a difference of squares and relates this to factoring a difference of cubes. Students practice finding and recognizing perfect cubes, and then they investigate the formulas for factoring a sum of two cubes and a difference of two cubes. They use these formulas to factor a few expressions.

In the **Examples**, students factor more complicated expressions involving sums and differences of cubes. They factor an expression which requires first factoring out a greatest common factor, and an expression that is a difference of two squares with two cubes, $x^6 - 64$. In the final example, students apply their knowledge to a problem about the velocity of a rocket which uses the formula

$$Velocity = \frac{\frac{1}{2}bt_1{}^3 - \frac{1}{2}bt_0{}^3}{t_1 - t_0}$$

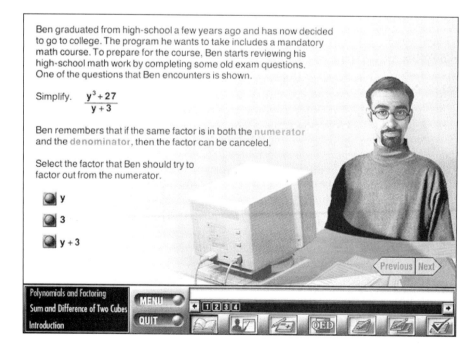

Ben graduated from high-school a few years ago and has now decided to go to college. The program he wants to take includes a mandatory math course. To prepare for the course, Ben starts reviewing his high-school math work by completing some old exam questions. One of the questions that Ben encounters is shown.

Simplify. $\dfrac{y^3 + 27}{y + 3}$

Ben remembers that if the same factor is in both the numerator and the denominator, then the factor can be canceled.

Select the factor that Ben should try to factor out from the numerator.

- y
- 3
- y + 3

Previous | Next

Polynomials and Factoring
Sum and Difference of Two Cubes
Introduction

MENU
QUIT
[1][2][3][4]

Instructor Intervention

- Before starting this lesson, review these factoring skills:
  - finding and factoring out common factors and the greatest common factor
  - factoring trinomials
  - factoring by grouping
  - factoring a difference of two squares

- Have students practice expanding expressions using the distributive property. Stress that students should check answers by multiplying the factors to see if the result is the original expression.

- Students should be familiar with the exponent laws and be able to apply them appropriately. You could set up student mentors or small groups of students to work together to review the exponent laws.

One of the questions that Ben encounters on an old exam is shown.

Simplify.

$$\frac{y^3 + 27}{y + 3} = \frac{y^3 + 3^3}{y + 3}$$

To factor the numerator, Ben uses the first and last pattern for factoring the sum of two cubes. Select the correct result.

$\frac{(y+3)(y^2 + 3y + 9)}{y + 3}$

$\frac{(y+3)(y^2 - 3y + 9)}{y + 3}$ ✓

$\frac{(y+3)(y^2 + 3y - 9)}{y + 3}$

$\frac{(y+3)(y^2 - 3y - 9)}{y + 3}$

The College

ADMISSIONS

Previous | Next

Polynomials and Factoring
Sum and Difference of Two Cubes
Summary

MENU
QUIT

123

Evaluation

- Ask students to describe, in words and in mathematical notation, how to factor a sum of two cubes and a difference of two cubes. Expressing the procedures in two ways may better help students remember the patterns.

- In small groups or partners, have students create questions based on those in the **Examples** section. The students should exchange problems and write complete solutions. Encourage students to add complexity to their questions by including greatest common factors, or using a difference of two squares with two cubes.

- Observe students as they work. Have they memorized the patterns for factoring a sum of two cubes and a difference of two cubes? Do they know how to factor a difference of two squares with two cubes? Do they complete these steps when factoring a sum or difference of two cubes?
  1. Factor out common factors.
  2. Find the cube roots, F and L, of the first and second terms.
  3. Use the appropriate formula to find the factors.
  4. Check the answer by using the distributive property to expand the factored form.

Remediation

- Review radicals, especially square roots and cube roots, and give some problems that involve taking square roots and cube roots.

- Students may require extra help to interpret application problems. Point out the patterns of similarity between word problems of a similar nature.

- Some students may take a long time to factor sums or differences of cubes because they don't readily recognize perfect cubes and their roots. Have students write the first ten perfect cubes in their notebooks and encourage them to memorize them.

Extension

A

Students could try factoring sums or differences of cubes where one or both of the terms involve fractions. For example:

1. $\dfrac{1}{27} + x^{12}$

Answer: $\left(\dfrac{1}{3} + x^4\right)\left(\dfrac{1}{9} - \dfrac{1}{3}x^4\right) + x^8$

2. $z^9 - \dfrac{1}{8}$

Answer: $\left(z^3 - \dfrac{1}{2}\right)\left(z^6 + \dfrac{1}{2}z^3 + \dfrac{1}{4}\right)$

B

Challenge students to factor these expressions:

1. $(x-2)^3 + 64$
   Answer: $[(x-2) + 4][(x-2)^2 - 4(x-2) + 16]$
2. $(x^2 + 1)^3 + (y+2)^3$
   Answer: $[(x^2 + 1) + (y+2)]$ $[(x^2 + 1)^2 - (x^2 + 1)(y+2) + (y+2)^2]$
3. $(x-3)^6 - 729$
   Answer: $[(x-3) + 3][(x-3)^2 - (x-3)(3) + 3^2][(x-3) - 3][(x-3)^2 + (x-3)(3) + 3^2]$

Problem Situations

The formula for the average velocity of a rocket is

$$\text{Velocity} = \frac{\frac{1}{2}bt_1{}^3 - \frac{1}{2}bt_0{}^3}{t_1 - t_0},$$

where t_0 and t_1 are two different points in time after liftoff and **b** is a constant in feet per cubic second. Simplify the formula.

$$V = \frac{\frac{1}{2}bt_1{}^3 - \frac{1}{2}bt_0{}^3}{t_1 - t_0}$$

$$= \frac{\frac{1}{2}b(t_1{}^3 - t_0{}^3)}{t_1 - t_0}$$

The numerator can be further factored. Select the formula that can be used.

 $F^3 - L^3 = (F - L)(F^2 + FL + L^2)$

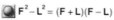 $F^3 + L^3 = (F + L)(F^2 + FL + L^2)$

$F^2 - L^2 = (F + L)(F - L)$

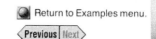 Return to Examples menu.

Previous | Next

Polynomials and Factoring
Sum and Difference of Two Cubes
Examples

MENU
QUIT
[1]

Suggest that students simplify the algebra by using variables to represent parts of each expression and then substituting the original value into the answer. For example, in the third problem, they could use a to represent $(x-3)$ and b to represent 3.

C

Present problems involving negative exponents. For example:

1. $(2x)^{-3} - 125y^{-9}$
   Answer: $[(2x)^{-1} - 5y^{-3})][(2x)^{-2} + (2x)^{-1}(5y^{-3}) + 25y^{-6}]$

2. $64x^{-12} - (3y)^{-6}$
   Answer: $[4x^{-4} - (3y)^{-2}]$
   $\times [(4x^{-4})^2 + (4x^{-4})(3y)^{-2} + (3y)^{-4}]$

3. $a^3 b^{-12} + c^{-6}$
   Answer: $(ab^{-4} + c^{-2})[(ac^{-4})^2 - (ab^{-4})(c^{-2}) + (c^{-2})^2]$

Enrichment

A

Ask: Given the patterns for factoring a sum of two cubes and a sum of two fifth powers, develop the pattern for factoring a sum of two seventh powers.

$a^3 + b^3 = (a + b)(a^2 - ab + b^2)$
$a^5 + b^5 = (a + b)(a^4 - a^3 b + a^2 b^2 - ab^3 + b^4)$

Answer: $a^7 + b^7 = (a + b)(a^6 - a^5 b + a^4 b^2 - a^3 b^3 + a^2 b^4 - ab^5 + b^6)$

B

After students complete **Enrichment** activity A, ask them to describe, in their own words, the factors for a sum of any two like powers, $a^n + b^n$, where n is an odd integer.

C

Have students look for or create application problems involving a sum or difference of two cubes. For example, they could create a problem involving the sum or difference of the volumes of two similarly shaped objects.

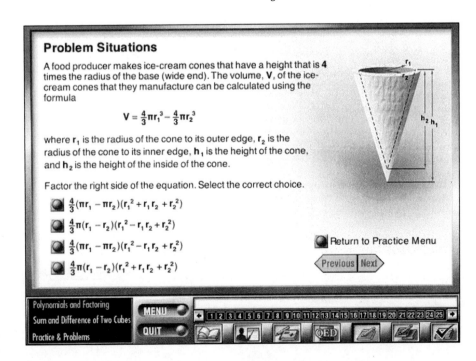

Problem Situations

A food producer makes ice-cream cones that have a height that is **4** times the radius of the base (wide end). The volume, **V**, of the ice-cream cones that they manufacture can be calculated using the formula

$$V = \tfrac{4}{3}\pi r_1^3 - \tfrac{4}{3}\pi r_2^3$$

where r_1 is the radius of the cone to its outer edge, r_2 is the radius of the cone to its inner edge, h_1 is the height of the cone, and h_2 is the height of the inside of the cone.

Factor the right side of the equation. Select the correct choice.

○ $\tfrac{4}{3}(\pi r_1 - \pi r_2)(r_1^2 + r_1 r_2 + r_2^2)$

○ $\tfrac{4}{3}\pi(r_1 - r_2)(r_1^2 - r_1 r_2 + r_2^2)$

○ $\tfrac{4}{3}(\pi r_1 - \pi r_2)(r_1^2 - r_1 r_2 + r_2^2)$

○ $\tfrac{4}{3}\pi(r_1 - r_2)(r_1^2 + r_1 r_2 + r_2^2)$

○ Return to Practice Menu

‹Previous | Next›

Polynomials and Factoring
Sum and Difference of Two Cubes
Practice & Problems

MENU
QUIT

1 2 3 4 5 6 7 8 9 10 11 12 13 14 15 16 17 18 19 20 21 22 23 24 25

Dividing Polynomials by Binomials

Key Objectives
The student will:
- divide a polynomial by a binomial.
- express the results of polynomial division in a variety of forms.
- solve problems involving division of polynomials.

Key Terms
dividend, divisor, quotient, degree, cubic, quadratic

Prerequisite Skills
- Divide real numbers using long division.
- Divide monomials.
- Multiply polynomials.

Lesson Description

This lesson extends the division concepts from the previous lesson. In the **Introduction**, students learn that algebra can be used to analyze sales data and to predict market trends. The following equation is developed to compare snowboard sales with ski sales over the years 1988 to 1996:

$$\frac{snowboard\ sales}{ski\ sales} = \frac{1000(t^2+1)}{1000(t+19)}$$

In the **Summary**, students use division to simplify the expression and then determine the ratios for given years.

The **Tutorial** demonstrates these four repeated steps for long division: divide, multiply, subtract, and bring down. Students see how the steps are applied when 1269 is divided by 57 and then follow similar steps to divide $x^2 + 6x - 9$ by $x + 1$. Students learn that they can express the result in a way that allows them to check the quotient:

$$dividend = (divisor)(quotient) + remainder$$

They also learn that this equation can be reorganized to express the division situation as a rational expression:

$$\frac{dividend}{divisor} = quotient + \frac{remainder}{divisor}$$

In the **Examples**, students practice division in different situations, including some involving cubic polynomials. Some problems illustrate that terms in the dividend and divisor must be arranged in order of degree (or exponent of the variable). Others deal with missing terms in the dividend and divisor and the need to replace them with place holders such as $+\ 0x^2$ or $+\ 0x$.

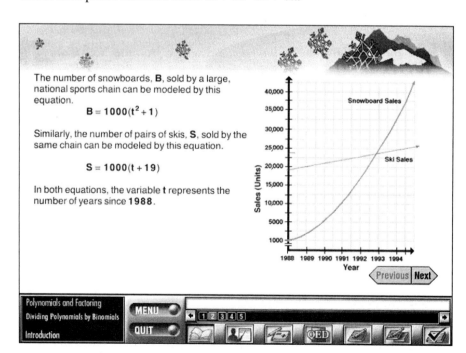

The number of snowboards, **B**, sold by a large, national sports chain can be modeled by this equation.

$$B = 1000(t^2 + 1)$$

Similarly, the number of pairs of skis, **S**, sold by the same chain can be modeled by this equation.

$$S = 1000(t + 19)$$

In both equations, the variable **t** represents the number of years since **1988**.

Instructor Intervention

- In the **Introduction**, students may need help to interpret the two graphs used to represent ski sales and snowboard sales. The graph of the linear relation $(t + 19)$ demonstrates ski sale growth, while the graph of the quadratic relation $(t^2 + 1)$ represents growth in snowboard sales.

- The subtraction step in the division process may be difficult, particularly where negative coefficients are involved. It may help students to record the subtraction in conventional linear form and then eliminate the brackets. For example:
$$(2x^2 - 5x) - (2x^2 - 3x) = 2x^2 - 5x - 2x^2 + 3x$$
$$= -2x$$

- Encourage students to complete all the **Examples**, since these introduce new learning. In the final problem, students encounter the possibility of an algebraic remainder.

- Before students begin the **Summary**, review the graphs shown in the **Introduction** to reinforce the relationship between snowboard sales and ski sales and the change in that relationship over time. This should help students to interpret the ratios in this section.

- Encourage student discussion about the meaning of a zero remainder. Ask students to identify problems from the lesson or *Student Workbook* that could have been solved using factoring.

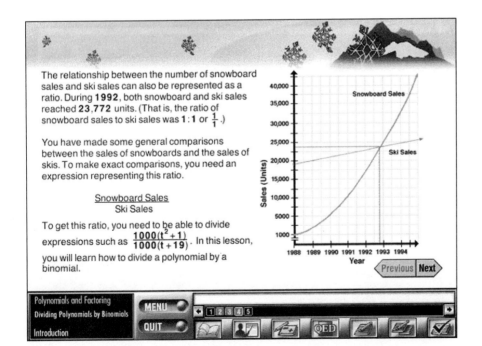

The relationship between the number of snowboard sales and ski sales can also be represented as a ratio. During **1992**, both snowboard and ski sales reached **23,772** units. (That is, the ratio of snowboard sales to ski sales was **1 : 1** or $\frac{1}{1}$.)

You have made some general comparisons between the sales of snowboards and the sales of skis. To make exact comparisons, you need an expression representing this ratio.

$$\frac{\text{Snowboard Sales}}{\text{Ski Sales}}$$

To get this ratio, you need to be able to divide expressions such as $\frac{1000(t^2 + 1)}{1000(t + 19)}$. In this lesson, you will learn how to divide a polynomial by a binomial.

Polynomials and Factoring
Dividing Polynomials by Binomials
Introduction

MENU
QUIT
1 2 3 4 5

Evaluation

- Write the following division problem on the board or on an overhead transparency.

$$\frac{9x^2 + 6x^3 + 4}{3x - 1}$$

  Ask the students to identify the dividend, divisor, quotient, and remainder and then construct a long division statement and label the parts.

  Have the students divide and then number the lines in the solution. Ask them to write a brief explanation of what was done in each line.

  Finally, have the students record the results in two different ways and verify the quotient.

- Observe students as they are working and check the results. Do the students record the division correctly? Do they arrange the terms in the dividend in descending order? Do they see the need to use a place holder in the dividend? Are they aligning like terms vertically in the solution? Can they multiply and subtract terms correctly?

- Have students complete an arithmetic long division and an algebraic long division (perhaps one from the **Extra Practice** section or the *Student Workbook*) and show the connections between the steps. Can students explain why the second term in the divisor is ignored during the division step?

- Ask why a place holder is needed when a term is missing from the dividend. Is this the same reason why a place holder is used when a term is missing from the divisor?

Remediation

- A thorough review of long division with integers will ensure that students have a clear understanding of the algorithm before they proceed to algebraic long division.

- A review of division of monomials may help students who are experiencing difficulty with the "divide" step.

- Students who are having difficulty may want to do work on paper for the "divide," "multiply," and "subtract" steps before entering responses. Some may need to record each operation separately in a linear format.

- It may be helpful to post a worked example with notes and guidelines for student reference as students proceed through the **Examples** and the **Practice** and **Extra Practice** sections.

- Students with weak algebraic skills may have difficulty with complex problems because of the many algebraic steps involved in a solution. Working with a partner may help these students achieve success.

Extension

A

Long division can help in factoring polynomials for which there is no specific factoring technique. Given a polynomial and one known factor, students can use a combination of long division and factoring to break down a polynomial into a product of factors.

Have students multiply binomial and trinomial factors to create polynomial products and then use the results to write problems similar to Problem 17 in the *Student Workbook*. Students can exchange problems and try combining long division with factoring to find solutions.

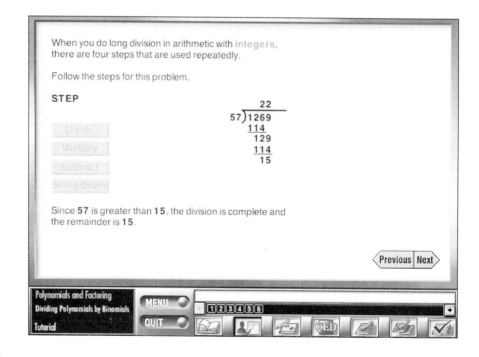

Ask the students to record the factors they used to create the problems, since these will be needed to check results.

B

Challenge students to divide a polynomial in two variables by a binomial in two variables. For example:

$$\frac{10m^3 + 5m^2n + 15mn^2 + 25n^3}{m - n}$$

$[10m^2 + 15mn + 30n^2,\ \text{R}\ 55n^3]$

Enrichment

A

Synthetic division can be taught as a shorthand for the long division process where the divisor is $x \pm n$ and n is an integer. This is a method of bypassing the variables and making calculations from the coefficients alone. (As with long division, place holders must be substituted if there are missing terms.)

Long Division:

$$
\begin{array}{r}
2x^2 + 7x - 1 \\
x - 3\ \overline{\smash{\big)}\ 2x^3 + x^2 - 22x + 3} \\
\underline{2x^3 - 6x^2} \\
7x^2 - 22x \\
\underline{7x^2 - 21x} \\
-x + 3 \\
\underline{-x + 3} \\
0
\end{array}
$$

Synthetic Division:

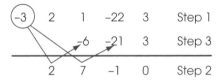

Result is $2x^2 + 7x - 1$ $R0$

Step 1: Write the constant from the divisor (circled). Then write all the coefficients from the dividend in order.

Step 2: Carry down the first coefficient from the dividend.

Step 3: Multiply the constant from the divisor by the carried-down coefficient to get the first number in Step 3. Subtract the

Step 3 number from the Step 1 number. Then multiply the constant by the result to get the next Step 3 number. Continue until you have filled all the spaces in Step 2. Restore the variables, in order, to the Step 2 numbers to find the quotient and remainder.

B

An **asymptote** is a straight line that a curve continually approaches but does not meet. Students can use long division to find asymptotes of rational functions. For example, the rational function $y_1 = \dfrac{2x}{x + 5}$ can be divided to give $\dfrac{2x}{x + 5} = 2 - \dfrac{10}{x + 5}$. The graphs of $y_1 = \dfrac{2x}{x + 5}$ and $y_2 = 2$ show that y_2 is an asymptote of y_1. Because the value of the remainder fraction $\dfrac{10}{x + 5}$ becomes very small as x becomes very large, the difference between y_1 and y_2 diminishes as x increases.

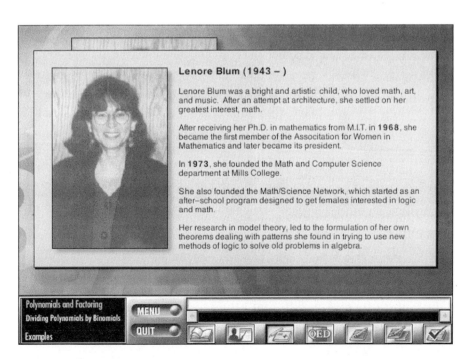

Lenore Blum (1943 –)

Lenore Blum was a bright and artistic child, who loved math, art, and music. After an attempt at architecture, she settled on her greatest interest, math.

After receiving her Ph.D. in mathematics from M.I.T. in **1968**, she became the first member of the Association for Women in Mathematics and later became its president.

In **1973**, she founded the Math and Computer Science department at Mills College.

She also founded the Math/Science Network, which started as an after–school program designed to get females interested in logic and math.

Her research in model theory, led to the formulation of her own theorems dealing with patterns she found in trying to use new methods of logic to solve old problems in algebra.

Polynomials and Factoring
Dividing Polynomials by Binomials
Examples

MENU

QUIT

5 RATIONAL EXPRESSIONS

Rational Expressions: Finding Equivalent Forms

Key Objectives
The student will:
- write rational expressions in their simplest equivalent form.
- solve problems involving rational expressions.

Key Terms
factor, numerator, denominator, simplify, simplest form, ratio, equivalent

Prerequisite Skills
- Factor polynomials by common factoring, trinomial factoring, and finding a difference of squares.
- Convert fractions to decimals.
- Translate word problems into variable expressions.

Lesson Description

This lesson deals with simplifying rational expressions. The numerators in these expressions are polynomials, and the denominators are factorable monomials, binomials, or trinomials.

In the **Introduction**, students are faced with the problem of deciding whether different-sized cartons have a volume ratio that meets marketing specifications. Students initially solve the problem by calculating each volume independently. In the **Summary**, students solve the carton problem more efficiently by applying algebraic methods developed in the lesson.

The **Tutorial** begins with the familiar idea of expressing fractions in simplest terms and then shows how similar methods can be used to simplify ratios involving algebraic terms.

In the **Examples**, students focus on strategies they can use in specific situations: using the greatest common factor, factoring trinomials, and factoring out –1. Students also solve problems involving two variables, use multiple calculations to simplify complex expressions, and solve word problems.

Instructor Intervention

- Before students begin the lesson, review the processes of common factoring, trinomial factoring, and factoring differences of squares.
- A review of numerical simplifications might help some students. For example:
$$\frac{4}{6} = \frac{(2)(2)}{(2)(3)} = \frac{2}{3} \qquad \frac{27}{36} = \frac{(9)(3)}{(9)(4)} = \frac{3}{4}$$
- Demonstrate how multiplication by –1 changes a factor. For example:
$$-1(x - 4) = (4 - x)$$
To help students simplify the process of factoring out –1, pose the following set of problems:
(a) Substitute several different values for x into the expression

$\dfrac{x-3}{3-x}$. What do you notice?

(b) How could you simplify $\dfrac{x-n}{n-x}$? Explain.

(c) Give an example of a rational expression you could simplify using the information you found in parts (a) and (b). Show how to simplify your expression.

- Watch for errors that show a lack of understanding of the factoring process. For example:

$$\frac{8a^2-4a}{6a^2-4a}=\frac{8a^2}{6a^2}=\frac{8}{6}=\frac{4}{3} \qquad\qquad \frac{4a+b^2}{2}=2a+b^2$$

Encourage students who make these errors to write complete solutions, showing multiplication expressions for factored terms. It may also help to provide some error analysis problems similar to those shown.•

- To help students eliminate common factors from the numerator and the denominator, relate variable problems to numerical examples with a similar structure. For example, students could examine these steps for simplifying the expression.

$$\frac{x^4-1}{x^2-3x+2}$$

$\dfrac{x^4-1}{x^2-3x+2}$ is similar to $\dfrac{30}{14}$

$\dfrac{(x^2+1)(x^2-1)}{(x-2)(x-1)}$ is similar to $\dfrac{(5)(6)}{(7)(2)}$

$\dfrac{(x^2+1)(x+1)(x-1)}{(x-2)(x-1)}$ is similar to $\dfrac{(5)(3)(2)}{(7)(2)}$

$\dfrac{(x^2+1)(x+1)}{(x-2)}$ is similar to $\dfrac{(5)(3)}{(7)}$

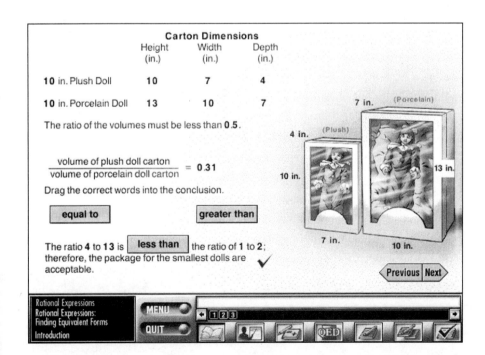

Evaluation

- Choose a selection of problems from the **Practice** or **Extra Practice** section, or from the *Student Workbook*, and ask students to hand in complete written solutions. Evaluate the solutions to determine whether students are:
  - **(a)** completely factoring the numerator and denominator in rational expressions.
  - **(b)** identifying common factors of terms and expressions.
  - **(c)** identifying differences of squares, factorable trinomials, and situations where it is helpful to factor out −1.
  - **(d)** eliminating common factors in the numerator and the denominator.
  - **(e)** reordering terms as necessary to identify common factors.

- As students are working, invite them to explain the process they are using to factor a rational expression. Do they understand the term **factor**? Can they explain why it is possible to eliminate common factors from the numerator and denominator without changing the value of the expression? What aspects of the process do they find easy or difficult?

- Have students work in pairs. Each partner creates four examples of factorable rational expressions similar to those presented in the lessons. Then students exchange problems and simplify the expressions.

  Have the students analyze each other's work for errors and then discuss the results.

  This activity will provide practice not only with simplifying rational expressions, but also with multiplying binomial and trinomial terms.

- Ask students to discuss the similarities of simplifying numerical and algebraic expressions. Explain the concept of a factor in a numerical and algebraic sense.

Remediation

- Review these terms.
  - **(a)** ratio
  - **(b)** factor
  - **(c)** numerator
  - **(d)** denominator
  - **(e)** simplest form

- Review these factoring methods.
  - **(a)** common factoring
  - **(b)** trinomial factoring
  - **(c)** factoring a difference of squares
  - **(d)** dividing an expression by −1

- Using algebra manipulatives to model simple factoring situations might be helpful for visual/tactile learners. Demonstrate using an overhead projector.

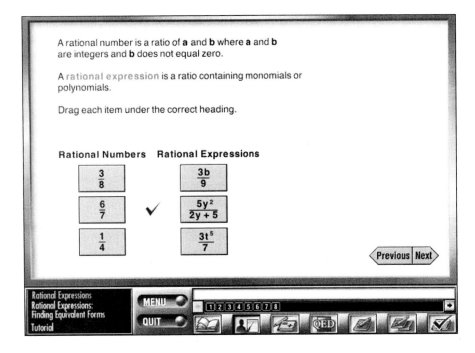

A rational number is a ratio of **a** and **b** where **a** and **b** are integers and **b** does not equal zero.

A rational expression is a ratio containing monomials or polynomials.

Drag each item under the correct heading.

Rational Numbers   **Rational Expressions**

$\dfrac{3}{8}$ $\dfrac{3b}{9}$

$\dfrac{6}{7}$ ✓ $\dfrac{5y^2}{2y+5}$

$\dfrac{1}{4}$ $\dfrac{3t^5}{7}$

Previous | Next

Rational Expressions
Rational Expressions:
Finding Equivalent Forms
Tutorial

MENU
QUIT

1 2 3 4 5 6 7 8

Extension

A

Pose this geometry problem for the students and then invite them to create and solve other problems about geometric shapes and solids.

A regular-sized cup of popcorn has a radius of x cm and a height of $(x + 5)$ cm. For a super-sized cup, each dimension increases by 5 cm.

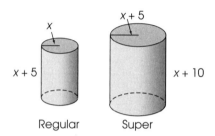

Regular   Super

(a) Write a ratio to express the relationship between the volume of a regular-sized cup and the volume of a super-sized cup. Then simplify the ratio.

$$\left[\frac{x^2}{(x+5)(x+10)}\right]$$

(b) If the radius of the regular-sized cup is 4 cm, evaluate the ratio you found in part (a).

$$\left[\frac{8}{63}\right]$$

(c) If a regular-sized cup costs 50¢, about how much should a super-sized cup cost? Why? [about $4, since it is about 8 times as large]

B

Ask why this expression cannot be simplified as shown:

$$\frac{x^2 + x - 2}{x^2 - 1} = \frac{x - 2}{-1} = -x + 1$$

Pairs of students can create and solve other error analysis problems. Have each student create a problem and then write a solution containing an error. Partners can trade problems and identify the errors.

C

Have students ask science instructors to suggest practical situations where reduction of variable expressions is useful. Some may wish to develop science demonstrations based on information they find.

D

Ask students to use algebra manipulatives or the *Binomial Grid Explorer* to model factoring situations from the lesson. Students could demonstrate their solutions for the class using an overhead projector.

Enrichment

A

Introduce trigonometric expressions, such as:

$$\frac{\cos^2 x - \sin^2 x}{\cos^2 x + \cos x \sin x + \sin^2 x}$$

B

Students could use a graphing calculator or other technology to see how the graph of

$y = \dfrac{x^2 - 9}{x - 3}$ differs from the graph of $y = x + 3$.

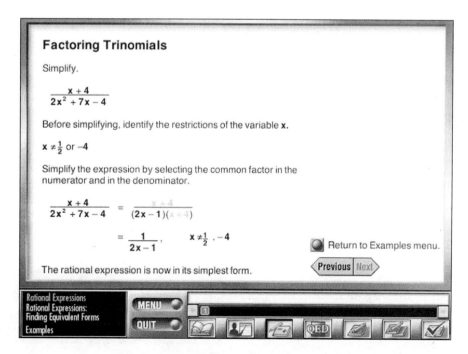

Factoring Trinomials

Simplify.

$$\frac{x + 4}{2x^2 + 7x - 4}$$

Before simplifying, identify the restrictions of the variable **x**.

$x \neq \frac{1}{2}$ or -4

Simplify the expression by selecting the common factor in the numerator and in the denominator.

$$\frac{x + 4}{2x^2 + 7x - 4} = \frac{x + 4}{(2x - 1)(x + 4)}$$

$$= \frac{1}{2x - 1}, \qquad x \neq \frac{1}{2}, -4$$

The rational expression is now in its simplest form.

○ Return to Examples menu.

⟨ Previous | Next ⟩

Rational Expressions
Rational Expressions:
Finding Equivalent Forms
Examples

MENU
QUIT

Cross-References

Rational Expressions

Student Workbook: pages 74–77

Key Objectives
The student will:
- determine nonpermissible values of a rational expression by inspection and by factoring the denominator.

Key Terms
nonpermissible, numerator, denominator, factor, undefined

Prerequisite Skills
- Solve and verify linear equations and inequalities in one variable.
- Factor polynomial expressions of the form $ax^2 + bx + c$ and $a^2x^2 - b^2y^2$.

Lesson Description

In previous lessons, students encountered many situations in which values for variables were limited in some way. Here, they examine limits placed on variables in the denominators of rational expressions. A variable is **nonpermissible** in the denominator if it gives the denominator a value of 0, since division by 0 is undefined.

In the **Introduction**, students examine a mathematical proof that shows $1 = 2$. While this makes no intuitive sense, the proof initially seems correct. However, when students learn that variables in the denominator are not permitted to give the denominator a value of 0, they identify the flaw in the proof. This idea is developed in more detail in the **Summary**.

The **Tutorial** uses a real-life situation to show why division by zero is not possible. Students see that while it is possible to share \$0 among different numbers of people $\left(\dfrac{0}{n}\right)$, it is not possible to share a number of dollars among 0 people $\left(\dfrac{0}{n}\right)$. They conclude that in a rational expression, the denominator cannot equal 0.

In the **Examples**, students explore various situations involving rational expressions. In some, students can identify nonpermissible values simply by inspection. In others, they need to factor the denominators first and then set each factor equal to 0. The point is also made that, in some situations, there are no nonpermissible values for a given expression.

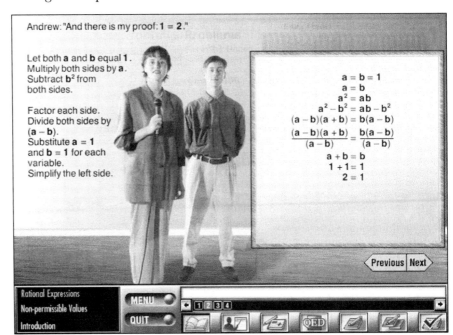

Andrew: "And there is my proof: **1 = 2**."

Let both **a** and **b** equal **1**.
Multiply both sides by **a**.
Subtract **b²** from both sides.

Factor each side.
Divide both sides by
(**a** – **b**).
Substitute **a** = **1**
and **b** = **1** for each
variable.
Simplify the left side.

$$a = b = 1$$
$$a = b$$
$$a^2 = ab$$
$$a^2 - b^2 = ab - b^2$$
$$(a - b)(a + b) = b(a - b)$$
$$\frac{(a - b)(a + b)}{(a - b)} = \frac{b(a - b)}{(a - b)}$$
$$a + b = b$$
$$1 + 1 = 1$$
$$2 = 1$$

Previous | Next

Rational Expressions
Non-permissible Values
Introduction

MENU
QUIT
◄ 1 2 3 4 ►

Instructor Intervention

- Review factoring methods for trinomials, differences of squares, and expressions involving two variables.

- Make sure students realize that there is no need to factor the numerator of an expression to find nonpermissible values, since these values are determined only by the denominator.

  Some students may wonder what would happen in a situation where a common factor was eliminated from both the numerator and the denominator. Use an example such as the following to show that nonpermissible values must be found before the common factors are eliminated, since the nonpermissible values for the simplified expression will differ from those of the original.

$$\frac{4a^2 - 1}{4a^2 - 8a - 5} = \frac{(2a+1)(2a-1)}{(2a+1)(2a-5)}$$
$$= \frac{2a-1}{2a-5}$$

  Both $\frac{5}{2}$ and $-\frac{1}{2}$ are nonpermissible values for a in the initial expression, while only $\frac{5}{2}$ is nonpermissible for the simplified expression.

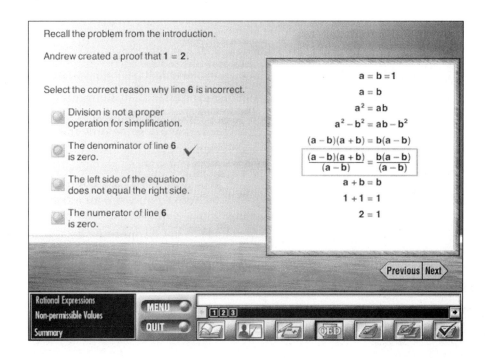

Recall the problem from the introduction.

Andrew created a proof that **1 = 2**.

Select the correct reason why line **6** is incorrect.

- Division is not a proper operation for simplification.
- The denominator of line **6** is zero.
- The left side of the equation does not equal the right side.
- The numerator of line **6** is zero.

$$a = b = 1$$
$$a = b$$
$$a^2 = ab$$
$$a^2 - b^2 = ab - b^2$$
$$(a - b)(a + b) = b(a - b)$$
$$\frac{(a - b)(a + b)}{(a - b)} = \frac{b(a - b)}{(a - b)}$$
$$a + b = b$$
$$1 + 1 = 1$$
$$2 = 1$$

Previous | Next

Rational Expressions
Non-permissible Values
Summary

MENU
QUIT
1 2 3

Evaluation

- Arrange the students in pairs. Have each pair create four rational expressions so that there is one problem of each of these types:
  - (a) an expression whose non-permissible values can be found by inspection
  - (b) a factorable trinomial in the denominator
  - (c) a difference of squares in the denominator
  - (d) a problem and solution where the solution contains an error

  Students can write solutions for the problems and then trade with another pair. When both pairs have solved their problems, have them compare results.

- Present several of the problems created for the previous activity. Students can solve each problem independently while one student works at the overhead projector. After students have completed each problem, they can compare their work with the overhead solution and then discuss alternative problem-solving methods.

- Observe the students as they search for nonpermissible values. Do they realize that they need to consider only the denominator in an expression? Can they factor expressions as necessary? Can they identify nonpermissible values from the factors, either by inspection or by setting the factor equal to 0?

- Ask how students can check nonpermissible values. [by substitution] How can they make sure they have found all the nonpermissible values? [Compare the number of values with the number of factors in the denominator.]

- Ask students to write rational expressions for a given set of nonpermissible values.

Remediation

- Watch for students who have difficulty with problems that involve factorable denominators. For a review of factoring, use ideas listed in the **Remediation** section of "Factoring Trinomials and Difference of Squares."

- If students are able to factor denominators but still have difficulty identifying nonpermissible values, they may need to review the steps involved in solving an equation for x. To identify specific difficulties, ask students to write out the equations they use and to show each step in the solution process. For example:
$$2x - 3 = 0$$
$$2x - 3 + 3 = 0 + 3$$
$$2x = 3$$
$$\frac{2x}{2} = \frac{3}{2}$$
$$x = \frac{3}{2}$$

- Make sure students determine nonpermissible values before they simplify expressions. See the **Instructor Intervention** section for a solution you can use to show why this is necessary.

  Emphasize that the numerator does not need to be factored at all, since only the denominator is involved.

- Ask students to use counters to help them write an answer to each question.
  - (a) What happens if you try to divide a set of 10 counters into groups of 0?
  - (b) What happens if you try to share a set of 10 counters among 0 groups?

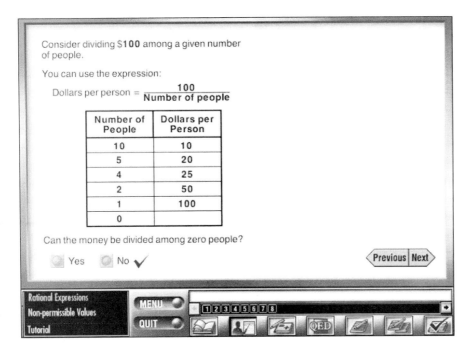

Consider dividing $100 among a given number of people.

You can use the expression:

$$\text{Dollars per person} = \frac{100}{\text{Number of people}}$$

Number of People	Dollars per Person
10	10
5	20
4	25
2	50
1	100
0	

Can the money be divided among zero people?

Yes   No ✓

Previous | Next

Rational Expressions
Non-permissible Values
Tutorial

MENU
QUIT

1 2 3 4 5 6 7 8

(c) Why do you think mathematicians say that dividing by 0 gives you a result that cannot be defined?

Extension

A

Students could use a graphing calculator to graph a function based on one of the expressions from the lesson. How are the nonpermissible values represented by the graph?

Students could also graph functions in order to determine nonpermissible values.

B

Ask students to suggest practical situations where the only permissible values are:
(a) positive
(b) negative
(c) greater than 1000
(d) less than or equal to 1 [e.g., probabilities]
(e) decimal numbers in hundredths [e.g., prices]

What other situations can students suggest where there are limits on values?

C

Review the quadratic formula: invite students to create rational expressions with denominators that can be factored using the quadratic formula. Students can trade problems and find the nonpermissible values.

$$x = \frac{-b \pm \sqrt{b^2 - 4ac}}{2a}$$

Enrichment

A

Challenge students to create a rational expression where the number of nonpermissible values is
(a) 0
(b) 1
(c) 2
(d) 3
(e) 4 or more

B

Students could simplify these expressions and find the nonpermissible values.

(a) $\dfrac{3y^2 + y - 4}{3xy - 12 + 4x - 9y}$

(b) $\dfrac{y^3 + y^2 - y - 1}{y^2 + 2y + 1}$

(c) $\dfrac{(2x - 7)^2 - 49}{4x^3 - 24x^2 - 28x}$

(d) $\dfrac{xy - 9 + 3x - 3y}{x^2 y - 27 + 3x^2 - 9y}$

(e) $\dfrac{x^2 + 15y - 3xy - 5x}{2x^2 - 3y - 6xy + x}$

(f) $\dfrac{x^3 - 4y^3 - 4xy^2 + x^2 y}{x^3 - x^2 y - 2xy^2}$

Answers:

(a) $\dfrac{y-1}{x-3}, x \neq 3, y \neq -\dfrac{4}{3}$

(b) $y - 1; y \neq -1$

(c) $\dfrac{1}{x+1}, x \neq -1, 0, 7$

(d) $\dfrac{1}{x+3}, x \neq -3, 3; y \neq -3$

(e) $\dfrac{x-5}{2x+1}, x \neq -\dfrac{1}{2}, 3y$

(f) $\dfrac{x+2y}{x}, x \neq -y, 2y, 0$

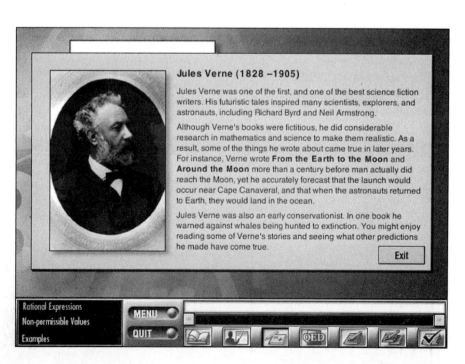

Jules Verne (1828 –1905)

Jules Verne was one of the first, and one of the best science fiction writers. His futuristic tales inspired many scientists, explorers, and astronauts, including Richard Byrd and Neil Armstrong.

Although Verne's books were fictitious, he did considerable research in mathematics and science to make them realistic. As a result, some of the things he wrote about came true in later years. For instance, Verne wrote **From the Earth to the Moon** and **Around the Moon** more than a century before man actually did reach the Moon, yet he accurately forecast that the launch would occur near Cape Canaveral, and that when the astronauts returned to Earth, they would land in the ocean.

Jules Verne was also an early conservationist. In one book he warned against whales being hunted to extinction. You might enjoy reading some of Verne's stories and seeing what other predictions he made have come true.

Exit

Rational Expressions
Non-permissible Values
Examples

MENU
QUIT

5.3 Multiplying and Dividing Rational Expressions

Cross-References
Rational Expressions

Student Workbook: pages 78–81

Key Objectives
The student will:
- perform the operations of multiplication and division on rational expressions.

Key Terms
rational number, rational expression, reciprocal, factor, divisor, dividend, numerator, denominator, polynomial, numerical coefficient, nonpermissible value

Prerequisite Skills
- Factor polynomial expressions of the form $ax^2 + bx + c$ and $a^2x^2 - b^2y^2$.
- Define a rational expression and determine equivalent forms of simple rational expressions, including those with factorable denominators.
- Determine the nonpermissible values for the variable in rational expressions.

Lesson Description

In this lesson, students learn how to multiply and divide rational expressions using the same basic methods they use to multiply and divide fractions.

The **Introduction** presents a problem in which students divide two fractions to find the diameter of an electrical wire. In the **Summary**, students use a formula involving rational expressions to find the same information.

The **Tutorial** begins with fraction multiplication and then moves through multiplication of several pairs of rational expressions, increasing the level of difficulty each time. In each case, students find the nonpermissible values, look for common factors, and then find the product.

The latter part of the **Tutorial** deals with division, again moving from division of fractions through division with increasingly difficult pairs of rational expressions. As with fractions, students divide rational expressions by multiplying the dividend by the reciprocal of the divisor.

In the **Examples**, students practice multiplication and division with factorable rational expressions and then move on to exercises with multiple operations and complex expressions. The final example demonstrates that some problem situations impose nonpermissible values that cannot be determined from the expressions alone.

Jim is building a computer. The power supply kit needs a connection wire that has a resistance, **R**, of $\frac{8}{15}$ Ω/cm (ohms per centimeter). If the resistance constant, **K**, of the wire material is $\frac{3}{10}$ Ω-cm (ohm-centimeters), what is the diameter of the wire Jim needs for his power supply kit?

This is the formula for the diameter of the wire in centimeters.

$$d = \sqrt{\frac{K}{R}}$$

Instructor Intervention

- Draw a connection between fraction operations and work with rational expressions. Many students may need to review fraction multiplication and division before they begin this lesson.

- To prepare students for the factoring they will encounter in this lesson, review how to use common factors in the numerator and denominator to reduce a fraction such as $\frac{12}{24}$ to simplest terms.

  Show how prime factoring can be used to make sure all common factors have been eliminated from the numerator and denominator:
  $$\frac{12}{24} = \frac{2 \times 2 \times 3}{2 \times 2 \times 2 \times 3} = \frac{1}{2}$$

- If the greatest common factor of two integers is 1, the two numbers are called "relative primes." Ask:

  (a) What is an example of a fraction formed by relative primes? $\left[\text{e.g., } \frac{8}{9}\right]$

  (b) How do relative primes relate to fractions in simplest terms? [If a fraction is in simplest terms, the numerator and denominator are relative primes.]

- Review how to factor polynomials, where:

  (a) the numerical coefficients of the terms have a common factor (e.g., $2x^2 + 4x + 2$).

  (b) the polynomial is a factorable trinomial (e.g., $x^2 + 4x + 3$).

  (c) the polynomial is a difference of squares (e.g., $x^2 - 36$).

- In a division exercise with rational expressions, students will need to look at the numerator of the divisor as well as the denominator in order to identify nonpermissible values. Ask why this is necessary. [You can't divide by the reciprocal of the divisor, so the numerator of the divisor becomes the denominator, which cannot equal 0.]

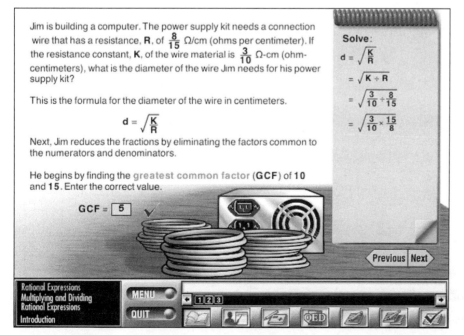

Evaluation

- Choose a selection of problems from the **Practice** or **Extra Practice** sections, or from the *Student Workbook* and ask students to hand in complete written solutions. Evaluate the solutions to determine whether students are:

  (a) completely factoring the numerator and denominator in each rational expression.

  (b) identifying common factors.

  (c) identifying differences of squares, factorable trinomials, and situations where it is helpful to factor out −1.

  (d) successfully multiplying polynomial numerators and denominators.

- To see whether students are connecting rational operations with fraction operations, have them list the general steps needed to simplify a problem. If the connection needs to be reinforced, demonstrate with two parallel problems – one with simple fractions and one with rational expressions. For example:

$$\frac{2}{3} \times \frac{3}{4} \text{ and } \frac{2x}{3y} \times \frac{3y^2}{4x}$$

- Have students solve a problem and number each step in the solution. Record several different solutions on the board and discuss variations in approach.

Remediation

- Assess each student's ability to perform these tasks and provide practice as necessary:

  (a) Multiply two fractions.

  (b) Divide two fractions.

  (c) Factor the numerator and denominator of a fraction and reduce to simplest terms.

  (d) Factor a polynomial. (See "Factoring Trinomials and Difference of Squares.")

  (e) Multiply polynomials. (See "Multiplying Polynomials.")

  (f) Identify and eliminate common factors in the numerator and denominator of a rational expression. (See "Rational Expressions: Finding Equivalent Forms.")

  (g) Find nonpermissible values (See "Nonpermissible Values.")

- Many students know how to divide fractions by multiplying by the reciprocal of the divisor, but do not understand why this method works. Use an example such as $\frac{3}{4} \div \frac{2}{3}$ to demonstrate these points:

  (a) $\frac{3}{4} \div \frac{2}{3}$ means "How many sets of $\frac{2}{3}$ can you make from $\frac{3}{4}$?"

  (b) To find the number of sets of $\frac{2}{3}$ you can make from $\frac{3}{4}$, first find the number of sets of $\frac{2}{3}$ you can make from 1 whole. $\frac{2}{3} \times$ its reciprocal $\left(\frac{3}{2}\right) = 1$, so you can make $\frac{3}{2}$ sets of $\frac{2}{3}$ from 1 whole.

  (c) You can make $\frac{3}{2}$ sets of $\frac{2}{3}$ from 1 whole, so you can make $\frac{3}{4}$ as many sets from $\frac{3}{4}$.

  $$\frac{3}{4} \times \frac{3}{2} = \frac{9}{8}$$

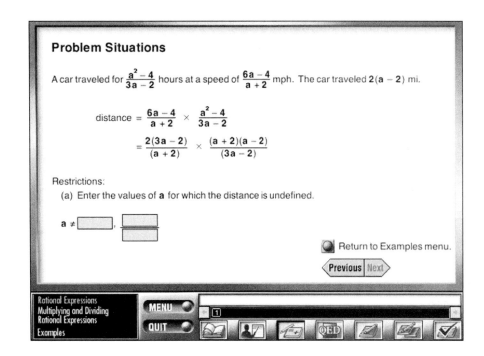

Problem Situations

A car traveled for $\frac{a^2 - 4}{3a - 2}$ hours at a speed of $\frac{6a - 4}{a + 2}$ mph. The car traveled $2(a - 2)$ mi.

$$\text{distance} = \frac{6a - 4}{a + 2} \times \frac{a^2 - 4}{3a - 2}$$

$$= \frac{2(3a - 2)}{(a + 2)} \times \frac{(a + 2)(a - 2)}{(3a - 2)}$$

Restrictions:

(a) Enter the values of **a** for which the distance is undefined.

a ≠ [   ] , [   ]

Return to Examples menu.

Previous | Next

Rational Expressions
Multiplying and Dividing
Rational Expressions
Examples

MENU
QUIT

- Discuss why it is possible to eliminate common factors from the numerator and denominator of a fraction. Ask:
  - (a) Why is it easier to multiply and divide fractions when they are in simplest terms?
  - (b) How can you use common factors to simplify $\frac{2}{3} \times \frac{3}{4}$ before you multiply? Why is it helpful to do so?
  - (c) Why is it important to look for common factors in rational expressions before you multiply or divide?

Extension

A

Invite students to generate factorable trinomials from factor pairs, then use these trinomials to create multiplication and division exercises for classmates to complete. Challenge students to structure these exercises so common factors can be eliminated from the factored expressions.

B

Pose problems that involve more complex factoring, such as grouping. For example:
$$z^4 + 4z^3 - 2z - 8$$
$$= z^3(z+4) - 2(z+4)$$
$$= (z+4)(z^3 - 2)$$

Enrichment

A

Problems 8 and 9 in the *Student Workbook* deal with geometry situations in which some values are nonpermissible because they yield negative lengths and areas.

Have students determine the range of nonpermissible values for each problem and then create similar geometry problems for other students to solve.

B

Pose problems that involve sums and differences of cubes. For example:
$$z^4 + 4z^3 - 8z - 32$$
$$= z^3(z+4) - 8(z+4)$$
$$= (z+4)(z^3 - 8)$$
$$= (z+4)(z-2)(z^2 + 2z + 4)$$

C

Pose problems involving the multiplication or division of complex fractions. For example:

$$\dfrac{\dfrac{x^2 + x - 6}{6x^2 + 7x - 5}}{\dfrac{12x^2 - 5x - 2}{2x^2 + 7x - 4}} \div \dfrac{\dfrac{2x^2 + 7x + 3}{4x^2 - 23x - 6}}{\dfrac{6x^2 - x - 2}{x^2 + 2x - 8}}$$

$$\left[= \frac{x - 6}{3x + 5} \right]$$

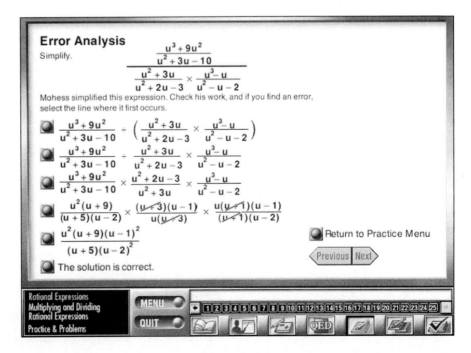

Multiplying and Dividing Rational Expressions **81**

5.4 Adding and Subtracting Rational Expressions

Cross-References

Rational Expressions

Student Workbook: pages 82–85

Key Objectives

The student will:
- perform the operations of addition and subtraction on rational expressions.

Key Terms

rational expression, equivalent, numerator, denominator, lowest common denominator, factor, simplify, nonpermissible value

Prerequisite Skills

- Factor polynomial expressions of the form $ax^2 + bx + c$ and $a^2x^2 - b^2y^2$.
- Define a rational expression and determine equivalent forms of simple rational expressions, including those with factorable denominators.
- Determine the nonpermissible values for the variable in rational expressions.

Lesson Description

In this lesson, students learn to use common denominators to add and subtract rational expressions. The **Introduction** begins with the formula that determines the resistance of a circuit when two resistors are connected in parallel:

$$\frac{1}{R_I} = \frac{1}{R_1} + \frac{1}{R_2}$$

Students review how to use a common denominator to add two fractions as they substitute values for R_1 and R_2 into the formula. They repeat with several pairs of values, and examine the results in table form to see that the sum of the two fractions is always equal to $\frac{R_1 + R_2}{R_1 \times R_2}$. In the **Summary**, students connect this version of the formula to the procedures they developed during the lesson.

Like the **Introduction**, the **Tutorial** begins with fraction operations. Students develop a three-step process for adding and subtracting rational expressions:
- Find the lowest common denominator. (If necessary, factor the denominators and simplify each expression.)
- Write the equivalent expressions using the LCD.
- Add or subtract the expressions.

In the **Examples**, students perform addition and subtraction with

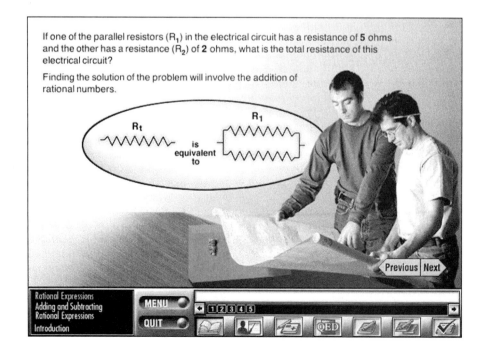

If one of the parallel resistors (R_1) in the electrical circuit has a resistance of **5** ohms and the other has a resistance (R_2) of **2** ohms, what is the total resistance of this electrical circuit?

Finding the solution of the problem will involve the addition of rational numbers.

problems at increasing levels of difficulty, beginning with like denominators and ending with unlike denominators that require both factoring and simplifying. In the last example, students add expressions to generate an algebraic description of a boat trip.

In the next lesson, students will apply their understanding of operations with rational expressions as they solve rational equations.

Instructor Intervention

- The problem in the **Introduction** involves the formula for determining the resistance of an electrical circuit when two resistors are joined in parallel. Resistance is the property of an electrical circuit that opposes or resists the flow of current. In this formula, R_t represents the total resistance to the flow of current (I), R_1 is the resistance of the first resistor, and R_2 is the resistance of the second resistor.

- Observe students at work to make sure they are using factoring to simplify expressions before they add. Eliminating common factors makes it possible to solve problems more quickly and also helps students avoid calculation errors.

- Although the product of two denominators is always a common denominator, it is not always the *lowest* common denominator. Demonstrate with a fraction example such as $\frac{5}{6} + \frac{3}{4}$, where the LCD is 12, not 24.

- Many problems in this lesson specify nonpermissible values for variables in the denominators. Discuss how these values were identified.

The relationship between the sum of R_1 and R_2 and the product of R_1 and R_2 was then explored.

This table shows the result of your investigation.

R_1	R_2	$R_1 + R_2$	$R_1 R_2$	$\frac{1}{R_t} = ?$	R_t
5	2	5+2	(5)(2)	$\frac{7}{10}$	$\frac{10}{7}$
4	5	4+5	(4)(5)	$\frac{9}{20}$	$\frac{20}{9}$
10	30	10+30	(10)(30)	$\frac{40}{300}$ or $\frac{2}{15}$	$\frac{15}{2}$
100	25	100+25	(100)(25)	$\frac{125}{2500}$ or $\frac{1}{20}$	20
100	50	100+50	(100)(50)	$\frac{150}{5000}$ or $\frac{3}{100}$	$\frac{100}{3}$

Select the correct heading for the fifth column.

$\frac{1}{R_t} = \frac{R_1 + R_2}{R_1 R_2}$ $\frac{1}{R_t} = \frac{R_1 - R_2}{R_1 R_2}$ $\frac{1}{R_t} = \frac{R_1 R_2}{R_1 + R_2}$ ⟨Previous | Next⟩

Rational Expressions
Adding and Subtracting
Rational Expressions
Summary

MENU
QUIT

 Lesson Components

 Examples

Like Denominators (2)
Unlike Denominators (no factoring) (2)
Unlike Denominators (factoring) (2)
Unlike Denominators (factoring and simplifying) (2)
Problem Situations (1)

 Practice and Problems

Finding the LCD and Writing Equivalent Rational Expressions
Addition
Subtraction
Error Analysis
Problem Situations

 Extra Practice

Like Denominators
Unlike Denominators
Factoring Unlike Denominators
Factoring and Simplifying Unlike Denominators
Problem Situations

Self-Check

Like Denominators (1)
Unlike Denominators (4)
Factoring Unlike Denominators (2)
Factoring and Simplifying Unlike Denominators (2)
Problem Situations (1)

Minimum score: 7 out of 10

Evaluation

- Ask pairs of students to generate six pairs of rational expressions, then find the LCD for each pair. To check their work, students could exchange with another pair.

- Have students generate a problem of each type listed below and copy it onto one side of an index card. On the other side of the card, students can write the complete solution.
  (a) Add two expressions with like denominators.
  (b) Subtract two expressions with unlike denominators where the denominators cannot be factored.
  (c) Add two expressions with unlike denominators where the denominators can be factored.
  (d) Subtract two expressions with unlike denominators where the denominators can be factored.
  Save the index cards so students can use them for additional practice.

- Observe how students add and subtract rational expressions. Can they find the lowest common denominator? Can they restate expressions with common denominators? Can they identify factorable expressions and factor them correctly? Do they check sums and differences to make sure they are in simplest form?

- Ask students to write a paragraph to answer each question.
  (a) How can you add or subtract two rational expressions?

  (b) How can you determine the LCD of two rational expressions?

- Have students check one another's solutions to determine if there are any errors and to assist in making corrections.

Remediation

- Review how to add and subtract polynomials and provide practice exercises if necessary. Pay special attention to subtraction, since students do not always realize that the minus sign applies to all the terms in the subtrahend. For example, in $(x + 2) - (x - 5)$, the 5 is added, not subtracted.

  Some students may find it less confusing to rewrite all subtraction sentences in terms of addition.
  $(x + 2) - (x - 5)$
  $= (x + 2) + (-x + 5)$

- Success with this lesson depends on an ability to factor and multiply polynomials. It may be useful to refer to suggested remediation activities from the lessons "Factoring Trinomials and Differences of Squares" and "Multiplying and Dividing Rational Expressions."

- Practice with adding and subtracting fractions may be helpful for some students. Focus on how to find the LCD and how to restate each fraction with the common denominator.

  Help students avoid common errors, such as adding the denominators as well as the numerators. For example:
  $$\frac{4}{9} + \frac{2}{9} \neq \frac{6}{18}$$

  Once students are secure with fraction operations, move on to simple rational expressions with like and unlike denominators, such as those in sections 1 and 2 of the **Examples**.

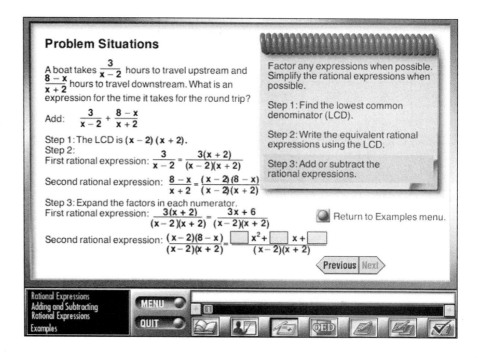

Extension

A

Ask students if the LCD of two numbers or polynomials is always the same as the LCM (lowest common multiple). Have them give examples to support their conclusions.

B

Students might create and solve problems that involve multiple operations with rational expressions, including multiplication and division as well as addition and subtraction. Review the rules for order of operations in these situations.

C

Have students create and solve problems that involve the areas and perimeters of geometric shapes, where side lengths are rational expressions.

Enrichment

A

Have students solve the following problem, then develop related problems based on the lens formula. Some students may wish to research the topic of lenses in more detail and prepare a class presentation.

The lens formula, $\dfrac{1}{d_o} + \dfrac{1}{d_i} = \dfrac{1}{f}$, expresses the distance relationships formed around a lens. The variable d_o represents the distance from the lens to an object, d_i is the distance from the lens to the image, and f is the focal length of the lens.

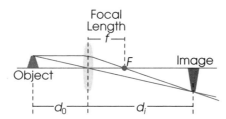

(a) Solve the lens equation for d_i.

(b) If the focal length of the lens in your eye is approximately 0.64 in., and you look at an object 50 ft away, find d_i. (Note that f, when substituted into the lens formula, is –0.64 in. since the focus of the eye is located on the opposite side of the lens from the object.)

(c) If the object is moved so that it is only 30 ft away, find d_i.

B

Pose problems that require students to solve complex rational expressions. For example:

$$\dfrac{\dfrac{1}{p} - \dfrac{3}{q}}{\dfrac{11}{2q}}$$

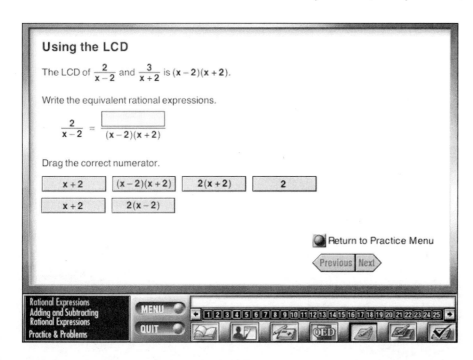

5.5 Solving Rational Equations

Cross-References

Rational Expressions

Student Workbook: pages 86–89

Key Objectives

The student will:
- find and verify the solutions of rational equations.

Key Terms

rational expression, rational equation, lowest common denominator, root, solution, polynomial

Prerequisite Skills

- Factor polynomial expressions of the form $ax^2 + bx + c$ and $a^2x^2 - b^2y^2$.
- Solve and verify first-degree, single-variable equations.
- Write mathematical expressions that arise from problem-solving contexts.

Lesson Description

In this lesson, students learn to solve rational equations by eliminating the denominators. Problems have been chosen so that rational equations will simplify to linear, not quadratic, equations.

The **Tutorial** leads students through three straightforward equations, focusing on the procedure rather than on computational details. As students move from number denominators to polynomial denominators, they learn to find the LCD, and use it to simplify the equations. They also check solutions by substitution.

The **Examples** section provides an examination of the different forms of rational equations, including those with monomial denominators, binomial denominators, and factorable denominators. In the final section, students develop an equation to solve a problem.

Denise sets up a table to help her solve the problem.

Method of Transportation	Distance Traveled (mi)	Speed (mph)	Time (h)
Train	250	x	$\dfrac{250}{x}$
Plane	250	$5x$	$\dfrac{250}{5x}$

Let **x** be the speed of the train. According to the paragraph, the plane is five times faster than the train, so the speed of the plane is **5x**.

The paragraph says the train takes four hours longer than the plane to travel **250** mi. This relationship can be used to create an equation between the train and plane times.

Select the equation that correctly relates the train and plane times.

$\dfrac{250}{x} + 4 = \dfrac{250}{5x}$

$\dfrac{250}{x} = \dfrac{250}{5x} + 4$

$\dfrac{250}{x} = \dfrac{250}{5x} - 4$

$\dfrac{250}{x} = \dfrac{250}{5x}$

"Planes travel at ... means a plane travels five times as fast as a passenger train ... to travel 250 mi, the train requires four more hours than the plane, which makes the plane a much more efficient means of transportation for the business traveler ... "

Previous | Next

Rational Expressions
Solving Rational Equations
Introduction

MENU
QUIT

1 2 3

Instructor Intervention

- Before students begin this lesson, review how to solve a first-degree, single-variable equation, such as $3x + 1 = 4x - 5$, by balancing the left and right sides.

- Review how to solve equations of the form $\frac{a}{b} = c$, such as $-\frac{x}{5} = 3$.

  Students should see that by multiplying both sides by b, they can eliminate the denominator without changing the value of the equation.

- To review the concept of the lowest common denominator, ask:
  - What is a lowest common denominator?
  - How can you find the LCD of two rational expressions, such as

    $\dfrac{5}{2x + 6}$ and $\dfrac{3}{x^2 + 3x}$?

- In this lesson, students will discover that some solutions to equations are nonpermissible because they result in denominators that simplify to 0. Discuss why this occurs.

- The **Examples**, **Practice**, and **Extra Practice** sections all include problems that involve factorable denominators. Before students begin these sections, review how to factor polynomials such as $3x + 9$, $x^2 + 5x + 6$, and $x^2 - 9$.

Lesson Components

Examples
Monomial Denominators (1)
Binomial Denominators (1)
Denominators with Factors (1)
Problem Solving (1)

Practice and Problems
Solving Equations with One
   Denominator
Solving Equations with Two
   Denominators
Solving Equations with
   Binomial Denominators
Error Analysis
Problem Situations

Extra Practice
Monomial Denominators
Binomial Denominators
Factoring
Denominators with Factors
Verifying
Problem Solving

Self-Check
Monomial Denominators (2)
Binomial Denominators (2)
Factoring (2)
Denominators with Factors (2)
Verifying (1)
Problem Solving (1)

Minimum score: 7 out of 10

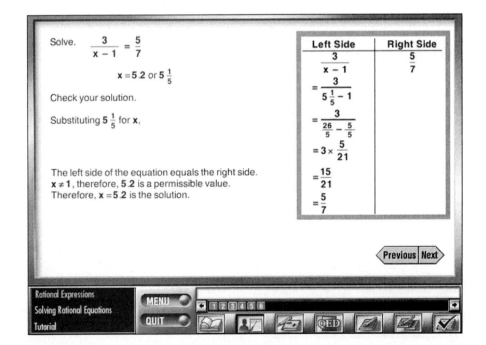

Solve. $\dfrac{3}{x-1} = \dfrac{5}{7}$

$x = 5.2$ or $5\frac{1}{5}$

Check your solution.

Substituting $5\frac{1}{5}$ for **x**,

The left side of the equation equals the right side.
x ≠ 1, therefore, **5.2** is a permissible value.
Therefore, **x** = **5.2** is the solution.

Left Side	Right Side
$\dfrac{3}{x-1}$	$\dfrac{5}{7}$
$= \dfrac{3}{5\frac{1}{5} - 1}$	
$= \dfrac{3}{\frac{26}{5} - \frac{5}{5}}$	
$= 3 \times \dfrac{5}{21}$	
$= \dfrac{15}{21}$	
$= \dfrac{5}{7}$	

Previous | Next

Rational Expressions
Solving Rational Equations
Tutorial

MENU
QUIT

Evaluation

- Have students identify the nonpermissible values for these equations, then solve and verify. Ask volunteers to present their solutions for the class.

  (a) $\dfrac{d+3}{6} = \dfrac{1}{2} + \dfrac{d}{3}$

  (b) $\dfrac{5}{3x} + 1 = \dfrac{23}{3x}$

  (c) $\dfrac{y}{y+3} - \dfrac{2}{3} + \dfrac{3}{y+3} = 0$

  (d) $\dfrac{5}{x^2-9} + \dfrac{6}{x+3} = \dfrac{11}{x+3}$

  [Answers: (a) no nonpermissible values, $d = 0$ (b) $x \neq 0$, $x = 6$ (c) $y \neq -3$, $y = -3$ is nonpermissible, so no solution (d) $x \neq \pm 3$, $x = 4$]

- Observe how students solve rational equations. Can they identify the LCD? Can they multiply two polynomials? Can they eliminate common factors from the numerator and denominator of a rational expression? Do they remember to multiply the entire expression on each side of the equal sign by the LCD? Can they identify nonpermissible values?

- Ask:
  (a) Why does multiplying both sides of an equation by the LCD eliminate the denominators?
  (b) Why is a $\dfrac{1}{0}$ form considered to be undefined?

- Observe how students verify solutions, since their approach can indicate their level of understanding of rational operations. Do they check to see if a solution is undefined before they begin the verification process? Can they add, subtract, multiply, and divide rational numbers? Do they correctly apply the rules for order of operations? Do they use estimation or perform some operations mentally?

Remediation

- Review these processes:
  (a) identifying the LCD for two or more rational expressions
  (b) multiplying and dividing fractions
  (c) multiplying two monomials, a monomial by a binomial, and two binomials
  (d) eliminating common factors from the numerator and denominator of a rational expression
  (e) factoring binomials and differences of squares
  (f) solving a rational equation

- Students may sometimes try to solve equations before they eliminate the denominators. Point out that in most cases, it is more effective to eliminate the denominators first, since this simplifies the terms of the equation.

- Students should be fluent in solving problems of the form $a = \dfrac{b}{c}$, since this form is often fundamental to mathematical formulas. Invite students to look for examples in the problem-solving sections of the lesson.

  Make sure students recognize that wherever $a = \dfrac{b}{c}$, these related factor/product relationships must also exist:

  $$c = \dfrac{b}{a} \qquad ac = b$$

Monomial Denominators

Solve.

$$\dfrac{4}{x} + \dfrac{3}{2x} = \dfrac{11}{4}, \ x \neq 0$$

$$4x\left(\dfrac{4}{x} + \dfrac{3}{2x}\right) = 4x\left(\dfrac{11}{4}\right)$$

$$4x\left(\dfrac{4}{x}\right) + 4x\left(\dfrac{3}{2x}\right) = 4x\left(\dfrac{11}{4}\right)$$

Simplify.

| 16 | + | 6 | = | 11x | ✓ |

Drag the terms to complete the simplified equation.
Match the order of the terms.

| 16x² | | 6x |

| 12x² |

Return to Examples menu.

⟨ Previous | Next ⟩

Rational Expressions
Solving Rational Equations
Examples

MENU

QUIT

1

Extension

A

Encourage students to look for patterns of variables and numbers in rational equations that will help them predict solutions. For example, they should be able to identify a factorable polynomial or a difference of squares by sight.

To build understanding, invite students to try to estimate solutions before they calculate.

B

So far, students have always solved equations by isolating a variable on one side and a number on the other. You may wish to introduce the idea that equations can also be solved by isolating 0 on one side. For example:

$$3x + 14 = 35$$
$$3x - 21 = 0$$
$$(3x - 21) \div 3 = 0 \div 3$$
$$x - 7 = 0$$

Therefore, $x = 7$.

C

If students create their own problems with rational expressions, or use alternative approaches to solving problems in the lesson, they may find that their calculations yield factorable quadratic equations. If this happens, explain how to isolate 0 on one side in order to solve these equations. For example:

$$x^2 + 2 = 3x$$
$$x^2 - 3x + 2 = 0$$
$$(x - 2)(x - 1) = 0$$

If two factors have a product of 0, then one or both factors must be equal to 0.

If $(x - 2) = 0$, then $x = 2$.
If $(x - 1) = 0$, then $x = 1$.

Both $x = 2$ and $x = 1$ are solutions to this equation.

D

Students could adapt formulas from the problem situations in the lesson in order to create rational equations to exchange and solve.

Enrichment

A

Review how to graph ordered pairs on a coordinate grid. Then introduce a rational equation such as $y = \dfrac{3}{x}$.

Demonstrate how to substitute different values for x in order to generate ordered pairs. Record the ordered pairs in a table. For example:

x	y
1	3
2	1.5
3	1
4	0.75

Have students generate and graph other equations where y is equal to a rational expression. Ask:

What do you notice about the graphs of equations of the form

$y = \dfrac{k}{x}$? [The graph has two parts; each is a 180° rotation of the other about the origin.]

Can you find any rational equations that generate other types of graphs? [yes, since some rational equations are equivalent to simpler equations]

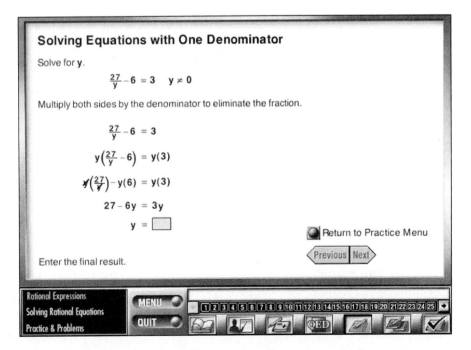

Solving Equations with One Denominator

Solve for **y**.

$$\frac{27}{y} - 6 = 3 \quad y \neq 0$$

Multiply both sides by the denominator to eliminate the fraction.

$$\frac{27}{y} - 6 = 3$$

$$y\left(\frac{27}{y} - 6\right) = y(3)$$

$$\cancel{y}\left(\frac{27}{\cancel{y}}\right) - y(6) = y(3)$$

$$27 - 6y = 3y$$

$$y = \boxed{}$$

Enter the final result.

Return to Practice Menu

Previous Next

Rational Expressions
Solving Rational Equations
Practice & Problems

MENU

QUIT

1 2 3 4 5 6 7 8 9 10 11 12 13 14 15 16 17 18 19 20 21 22 23 24 25

6 RELATIONS AND FUNCTIONS

6.1 Differences Between Relations and Functions

Cross-References
Relations and Functions

Student Workbook: pages 90–93

Key Objectives
The student will:
- learn to define relations and functions.
- learn to differentiate between relations that are functions and relations that are not.

Key Terms
ordered pair, relation, function, element, binary relation, map, one-to-one mapping, one-to-many mapping, many-to-one mapping

Prerequisite Skills
- Construct a table of values for a relation given a rule, and plot the corresponding ordered pairs on a coordinate grid.
- Identify the two values $+\sqrt{a}$ and $-\sqrt{a}$ that are solutions of the equation $y^2 = a$.
- Recognize some common types of relations given the graphs, and graph relations.

Lesson Description

In this lesson, students learn to define relations and to differentiate between relations that are functions and relations that are not.

The **Introduction** begins with a logic problem students can solve using a grid diagram. Three sisters, Maria, Gloria, and Angela, are the mothers of three children, Alicia, Marcos, and Juan. Students use given clues to determine which sister is Marcos's mother. In the **Summary**, students apply a mapping strategy based on the relation "*y* is the aunt of *x*" to solve the same problem.

The **Tutorial** explains that a mathematical relation is a property that connects two or more sets of numbers or elements and that the elements that satisfy a relation are often written as ordered pairs. Students use mapping to see that a value for *x* (or input value) can have one or more connections to the set of values for *y* (or output values). Students also learn that a function is a relation if each value of *x* maps to one and only one value of *y*.

In the **Examples** section, students identify the functions by mapping elements, by applying the Vertical Line Test to graphs, and by analyzing values shown in a table. They use the shapes of graphs to draw inferences about the types of relations that the graphs represent.

Instructor Intervention

- Before students begin this lesson, introduce the symbols used in set notation. Elements within a set are enclosed in set brackets. The ∈ symbol is used to designate an element of a given set. (*example*: $x \in \{1, 2, 3, 4\}$ means "*x* is an element of the set 1, 2, 3, 4.")

- It is important that students understand the concepts in this lesson. For instance, it is not enough to be able to use the Vertical Line Test. Students must also be able to explain that this test works because each point on the line has the same *x*-value and that a graph where there is more than one *y*-value for a given *x*-value cannot represent a function.

- Use everyday examples to help students understand the terms **relation** and **function**. For example, the set {hot dog, hamburger, ham sandwich} is related to the set {ketchup, mustard, relish}, but the relation is not a function since more than one condiment can be used on each sandwich. Ask students to suggest related situations that represent:

  (a) one-to-one mapping [*example*: {hot dog, hamburger, ham sandwich} {wiener, beef patty, ham}]

  (b) many-to-one mapping [*example*: {hot dog, hamburger, pencil, eraser} and {bun, pencil case}]

  Encourage students to look for other real-life examples of relations and to identify characteristics that show whether they are functions or non-functions.

- Students may have trouble identifying many-to-one mappings from equations and graphs. Just as a vertical line is used to identify functions, a horizontal line can be used to identify graphs of relations with many-to-one mappings. If the horizontal line touches the graph at more than one point, then there is more than one *x*-value for a given *y*-value.

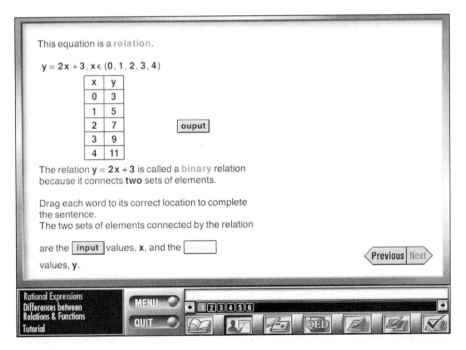

This equation is a relation.

$y = 2x + 3$, $x \in (0, 1, 2, 3, 4)$

x	y
0	3
1	5
2	7
3	9
4	11

ouput

The relation **y = 2x + 3** is called a binary relation because it connects **two** sets of elements.

Drag each word to its correct location to complete the sentence.
The two sets of elements connected by the relation

are the input values, **x**, and the _____

values, **y**.

Previous Next

Rational Expressions
Differences between
Relations & Functions
Tutorial

MENU
QUIT

1 2 3 4 5 6

Evaluation

- Ask small groups to identify:
  - **(a)** an everyday relation that is a function.
  - **(b)** an everyday relation that is not a function.
  - **(c)** an equation that represents a relation that is a function.
  - **(d)** an equation that represents a relation that is not a function.
  - **(e)** a graph that represents a relation that is a function.
  - **(f)** a graph that represents a relation that is not a function.

  Students should prepare a summary of each relation, including a mapping diagram and any assumptions or restrictions that affect the sets. You may wish to use the students' scenarios to help you develop questions for a quiz or exam.

- Observe the students as they complete the lesson and the *Student Workbook*. Can they explain each term listed in the **Key Terms** section at the beginning of the lesson? Can they list several different ways in which a relation can be represented? Can they explain how to identify a function by mapping? by analyzing a graph? by looking at a table of values?

Remediation

- Encourage students to use mapping to confirm conclusions they have made about relations between sets of values. Make sure they consistently record x-values (input values) on the left and y-values (output values) on the right.

  Some students will likely find many-to-one mappings more difficult to classify than the other two types. It may help to display diagrams with the three possible mapping situations (one-to-one, many-to-one, and one-to-many), labeled to show that one-to-one and many-to-one relations represent functions, and one-to-many relations do not.

- In order to find elements of related sets, students will sometimes need to solve equations. Review how to solve quadratic equations, such as $y^2 = x$, where $x = 4$.

  Make students aware that these equations have restricted values because x must always be positive. Elicit that there are two possible values for y for each value of x. Having students verify the positive and the negative values can help them remember this property.

- Review the use of a graphing calculator or computer graphing utility. Students should be able to identify graphs associated with common algebraic relations. Note that graphing calculators are not useful in situations where the relation is not a function.

- Students may become confused as they try to map relations such as "y is the father of x" because the order in the sentence differs from the (x, y) order. It might help to have students identify the ordered pair as (x, y is the father of x).

- Invite students to use computer spreadsheet applications to generate ordered pairs from a given equation. Some spreadsheets have graphing components that will allow students to graph the results.

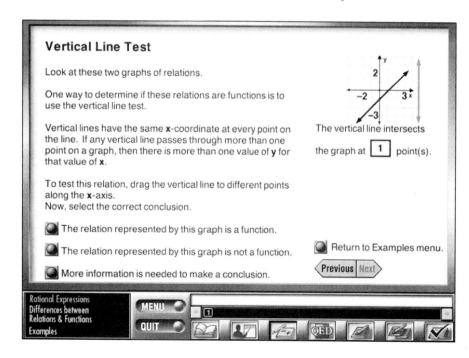

Extension

A

Students might investigate common relations for assumptions and restrictions. For example, the Pythagorean relation is commonly used as a function by students at this level.

$$x^2 + y^2 = a^2$$

If a is a constant, this relation gives just one positive value of y for each value of x. Under the restriction $y \geq 0$, the relation behaves like a function. However, it is not a function. This becomes important as students extend their work with right triangles in trigonometry to angles outside the first quadrant.

B

Students can search the media for everyday examples of relations. Sports, politics, and economics all provide relations between elements of two or more sets. In each case, ask:
(a) Is the relation a function?
(b) What assumptions or restrictions are being applied?

C

Invite students to work with spreadsheets to make a table of values for a relation that is not a function then graph the relation. This requires students to split equations such as $x^2 + y^2 = 25$ into two functions: $x = a$ *positive value* and $y = a$ *negative value*.

Use this concept to discuss the relationship between the graphs of $y = x$ and $y^2 = x$.

Enrichment

A

In this lesson, mappings involve only finite sets. Students should be aware that mappings can also be used with infinite sets. Mapping some elements of a set can help students predict whether the relation is also a function. In later lessons, mapping will give students a visual anchor for concepts such as inverse functions.

B

Use technology to investigate relations that are represented by recursive definitions. For example, students could investigate $x_{n+1} = ax_n(1 - x_n)$ for different values of a and using different values of x_1 between 0 and 1.

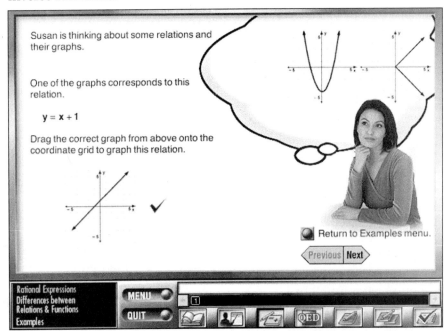

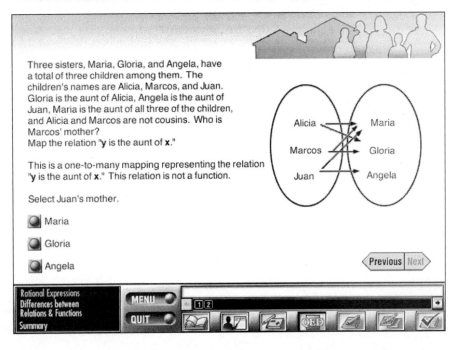

Cross-References

Relations and Functions

Student Workbook: pages 94–97

Key Objectives

The student will:

- represent a function using a table of values, a set of ordered pairs, a rule in word or equation form, and a graph.
- convert one form of function representation to another.
- represent and use step functions.

Key Terms

relation, function, dependent variable, independent variable, constant, table of values, ordered pair, cubic function, linear function, quadratic function, rational function, square root function, step function

Prerequisite Skills

- Recognize and define a relation and a function.
- Use mathematical expressions and equations to generalize a pattern.
- Draw a graph of a function from its equation.

Lesson Description

A function can be represented as a set of ordered pairs (or table of values), as a rule in word or equation form, or as a graph. In this lesson, students explore aspects of these different forms of function representation.

The **Introduction** describes a situation in which interpreters are to be hired to translate for diplomats who speak 25 different languages. Students use a combination of strategies to find out how many interpreters will be necessary. They develop a table of values, draw diagrams, and look for number patterns.

In the **Summary**, students develop an equation from the table of values created in the **Introduction**. When they substitute the value 25 into the equation, they find that they can quickly and efficiently calculate the number of interpreters that will be necessary. In fact, they can easily use the same equation to calculate the number of interpreters that will be necessary for any number of languages. This helps to highlight the advantages algebra offers over other problem-solving strategies.

The **Tutorial** is built around a geometry problem. As students explore the relations they can use to find the sum of the interior angles in any polygon, they review these skills:

- creating a table of values
- identifying and plotting independent and dependent variables
- distinguishing between discrete and continuous data
- identifying a graph of a linear function
- extrapolating an equation from a table of ordered pairs

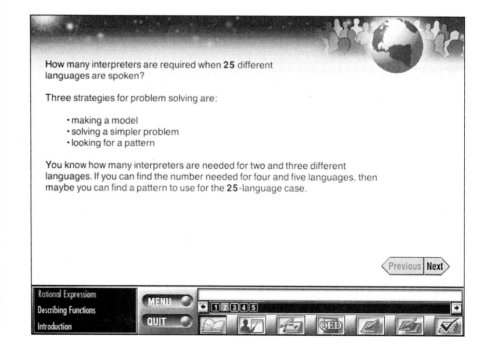

How many interpreters are required when **25** different languages are spoken?

Three strategies for problem solving are:

- making a model
- solving a simpler problem
- looking for a pattern

You know how many interpreters are needed for two and three different languages. If you can find the number needed for four and five languages, then maybe you can find a pattern to use for the **25**-language case.

Previous | Next

Rational Expressions
Describing Functions
Introduction

MENU
QUIT
1 2 3 4 5

In the **Examples**, students practice converting functions from one form to another. They also investigate the relationships between different types of equations and their graphs. One situation involves a step function.

By the end of the lesson, students should be able to recognize and use functions in any of these forms:
- a set of ordered pairs (or a table of values)
- an equation (or verbal rule)
- a graph

Instructor Intervention

- This lesson reviews and consolidates a number of previously taught skills:
  (a) plotting ordered pairs
  (b) interpreting graphs
  (c) writing expressions to describe number patterns
  Watch for students who may need additional practice.

- In the **Introduction**, students find the number of interpreters who will be needed for 25 diplomats who all speak different languages. You can use role-playing to help students better understand the situation.

  Ask volunteers to represent two diplomats who speak different languages. When students determine that two diplomats will need one interpreter, extend the group to three diplomats, then four, and finally five.

- Observe how students use calculators to evaluate expressions. Students in need of assistance could work with partners.

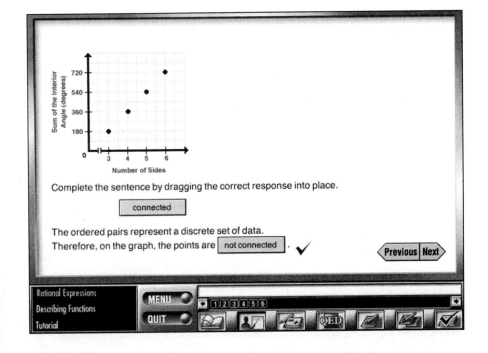

Evaluation

- Observe students as they complete the lesson. Can they give verbal descriptions of rules they have found for functions? Are they using appropriate terminology? Can they explain how they arrived at each rule?

- Have small groups create a series of diagrams where the number of items in each diagram is a function of the diagram number. (See Problem 25 in **Practice and Problems**.) Each group should represent the function with a set of ordered pairs, a graph, and an equation.

  The groups can present their diagrams and invite the class to write an equation for each function. After a few minutes, students in the class can compare their results with the groups.

- Invite small groups to describe a practical situation for each of these function types:
  (a) linear
  (b) quadratic
  (c) cubic
  (d) exponential
  (e) square root
  (f) rational
  (g) step

  Ask students to represent each function with a set of ordered pairs, a graph, and an equation. Some groups may wish to present their work in the form of a poster.

Remediation

- Review the shapes of graphs of linear, quadratic, cubic, exponential, rational, and square root functions as well as the characteristics of the corresponding equations.

- Review these skills.
  (a) graphing ordered pairs
  (b) using ordered pairs to name points on a graph
  (c) identifying dependent and independent variables
  (d) evaluating an expression by substituting values for variables

- Students often find it difficult to write an equation for a graph or a table of values. Invite students to make a list of questions and suggestions that they have found helpful as they guess and test equations. For example:
  (a) Is there a rapid growth in the *y*-coordinates? (If so, the function may be exponential.)
  (b) Are there sudden jumps in the *y*-values? (It may be a step function.)
  (c) In each ordered pair, is one value close to the square or square root of the other?

For additional practice, provide a set of simple tables of values and ask students to identify an equation for each. Have the students write the rule in words first and then rewrite it as an equation. Some students may need assistance in translating the rule into algebraic form.

Extension

A

In the **Tutorial**, students use algebra to find sums of interior angles in polygons. Use this activity to help students understand why the sum of the interior angles is a function of the number of sides.
(a) Draw five different triangles. Find the sum of the angles in each triangle. Compare results with another pair.

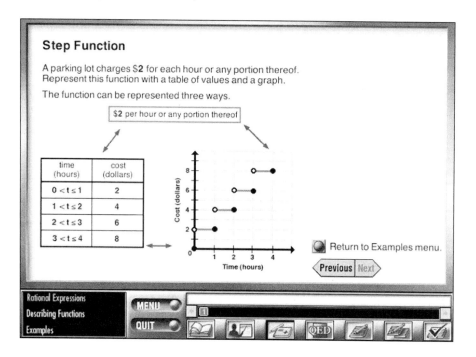

(b) What is the sum of the interior angles in any triangle?

(c) Draw five different quadrilaterals. Draw a diagonal to divide each quadrilateral into two triangles. What do you think will be the sum of the angles in each quadrilateral? Check by measuring and adding.

(d) Repeat part (c) for a set of pentagons and then for a set of hexagons. (You will need to draw more than one diagonal to divide each figure into triangles.) Why does the number of sides determine the number of triangles you can make? Why does the number of triangles determine the sum of the interior angles?

B

Invite students to create a game where players match representations of the same function. Encourage students to try to make the game both easy to learn and fun to play. Games that involve strategy or problem solving are usually more fun to play than games based solely on chance.

C

Provide equations based on familiar mathematical or scientific formulas. Ask students to identify the practical application for each equation. For example, $y = \pi x^2$ describes the area of a circle as a function of the radius, and $y = 1000x$ can be used to convert meters to kilometers.

Students could create a set of ordered pairs or draw a graph to represent each formula.

Enrichment

A

In the **Introduction**, the interpreter problem involved the sum of the natural numbers $1 + 2 + 3 + \ldots + 23 + 24$. Have students research the life of Carl Friedrich Gauss to find the shortcut used by Gauss as a boy to determine the sum of the first 100 natural numbers. Some students may wish to do further research about the sums of arithmetic series.

B

Another pattern students used in the interpreter problem was the set of triangular numbers: 1, 3, 6, 10, … . This is one set of numbers that can be derived from Pascal's Triangle. Students may wish to investigate the origins and uses of this triangle.

C

Having determined a formula for finding the sum of the interior angles in any polygon, students should be able to draw a regular polygon for any given number of sides. Invite students to find regular polygons that will tessellate and then create a tessellation.

D

Students can explore the *Tower of Hanoi* problem and describe the *minimum* number of moves needed to complete the puzzle as a function of the number of objects in a stack. To solve the puzzle, a stack of rings must be moved from one peg to another, one at a time, so no larger ring is ever placed on top of a smaller one. Students may find it helpful to research the *Tower of Hanoi* on the Internet.

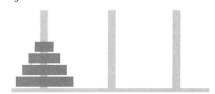

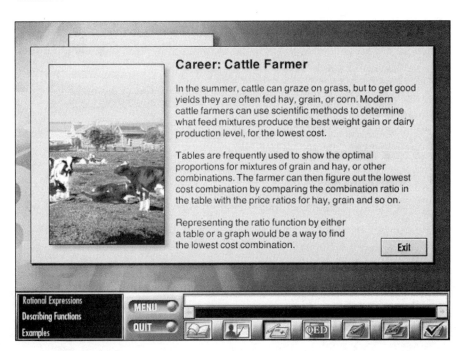

Career: Cattle Farmer

In the summer, cattle can graze on grass, but to get good yields they are often fed hay, grain, or corn. Modern cattle farmers can use scientific methods to determine what feed mixtures produce the best weight gain or dairy production level, for the lowest cost.

Tables are frequently used to show the optimal proportions for mixtures of grain and hay, or other combinations. The farmer can then figure out the lowest cost combination by comparing the combination ratio in the table with the price ratios for hay, grain and so on.

Representing the ratio function by either a table or a graph would be a way to find the lowest cost combination.

Exit

Rational Expressions
Describing Functions
Examples

MENU
QUIT

6.3 Function Notation

Cross-References

Relations and Functions

Student Workbook: pages 98–101

Key Objectives

The student will:
- express functions using function notation.
- evaluate functions using function notation.

Key Terms

function, notation, input, output, independent variable, dependent variable

Prerequisite Skills

- Evaluate expressions by substitution.
- Solve first-degree, single-variable equations.
- Describe a function in terms of ordered pairs, a rule, or a graph.

Lesson Description

This lesson introduces function notation and demonstrates how to use this notation to evaluate functions.

The **Introduction** uses the context of a gumball-making machine. Students select a radius and then use the formula for finding the volume of a sphere to determine the volume of the gumball the machine will produce. Students see that choosing a greater radius produces a gumball with a greater volume, since volume is a function of the radius. In the **Summary**, students return to the gumball machine problem to review concepts from the lesson. They rewrite the formula for the volume of a sphere using function notation and then calculate the volume for a radius of 5 cm.

The **Tutorial** examines the need in mathematics for different notations. By the time students complete this section, they should be able not only to record functions with appropriate notation, but also to evaluate functions by substituting numerical values for variables.

In the **Examples**, students evaluate functions for both numerical values and expressions. They discover that functions can also be evaluated by locating corresponding values on a graph. In the final section, students solve problems in which two functions are added or multiplied.

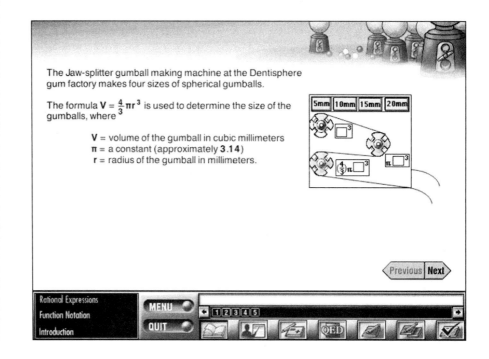

The Jaw-splitter gumball making machine at the Dentisphere gum factory makes four sizes of spherical gumballs.

The formula $V = \frac{4}{3}\pi r^3$ is used to determine the size of the gumballs, where

V = volume of the gumball in cubic millimeters
π = a constant (approximately **3.14**)
r = radius of the gumball in millimeters.

Instructor Intervention

- Review the rules for order of operations before students begin the lesson:

  Brackets
  Exponents
  Division and
  Multiplication
  Addition and
  Subtraction

- Review how to locate points on graphs and name coordinates of points.

- Provide practice with evaluating expressions by substituting values for variables. Include examples that involve exponents. For example, ask: What is the value of $a^3 - 3a^2$ if $a = -2$?

- Encourage students to avoid sign errors by placing brackets around substituted values. For example, using the problem cited above:

What is the value of $a^3 - 3a^2$ if $a = -2$?

Incorrect
$$-2^3 - (3 \times -2^2) = -8 - (3 \times -4)$$
$$= -8 - (-12)$$
$$= 4$$

Correct
$$(-2)^3 - 3(-2)^2 = -8 - 3(4)$$
$$= -8 - 12$$
$$= -20$$

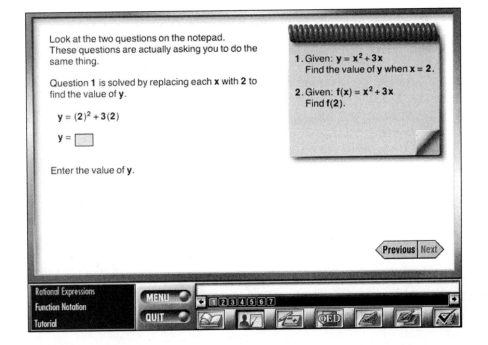

Look at the two questions on the notepad. These questions are actually asking you to do the same thing.

Question **1** is solved by replacing each **x** with **2** to find the value of **y**.

$$y = (2)^2 + 3(2)$$

$y = \boxed{}$

Enter the value of **y**.

1. Given: $y = x^2 + 3x$
   Find the value of y when x = 2.

2. Given: $f(x) = x^2 + 3x$
   Find f(2).

⟨Previous | Next⟩

Rational Expressions
Function Notation
Tutorial

MENU
QUIT

Lesson Components

 Examples

Substituting a Numerical
  Value (1)
Substituting an Expression (2)
Evaluating a Function
  Graphically (2)
Combining Functions (2)

 Practice and Problems

The First Step
Real-Life Functions
Working Backwards
Error Analysis
More Than One Function

 Extra Practice

Substituting a Numerical
  Value
Substituting an Expression
Real-Life Functions
Evaluating Functions
  Graphically
More Than One Function

 Self-Check

Substituting a Numerical
  Value (2)
Substituting an Expression (2)
Real-Life Functions (2)
Evaluating Functions
  Graphically (2)
More Than One Function (2)

Minimum score: 7 out of 10

Evaluation

- Divide the class into pairs. Each person creates an equation that is a function and then exchanges functions with his or her partner. Each partner must then rewrite the equation using function notation and decide on three values to be used to evaluate the function. (One of the three values should be an expression.)

  The function is then returned to the original writer to be evaluated for these three values. Pairs can exchange with other pairs to correct their work.

- Create several problems similar to those in the **Extra Practice** section or the *Student Workbook*. Write two or more solutions for each problem so one is correct and the others contain errors. (Use errors that reflect those made by students during their work with the lesson.)

Have students identify the incorrect solution and give a detailed description of the errors. For example:

(a) Which student found the correct value for $f(x + 3)$ if $f(x) = -7x^2 + 1$? Explain where the others went wrong.

John
$$\begin{aligned} f(x+3) &= -7(x+3)^2 + 1 \\ &= -7(x^2 + 6x + 9) + 1 \\ &= -7x^2 - 42x - 63 + 1 \\ &= -7x^2 - 42x - 62 \end{aligned}$$

Julio
$$\begin{aligned} f(x+3) &= -7(x+3)^2 + 1 \\ &= -7(x^2 + 9) + 1 \\ &= -7x^2 - 63 + 1 \\ &= -7x^2 - 62 \end{aligned}$$

Jacob
$$\begin{aligned} f(x+3) &= (x+3)(-7x^2 + 1) \\ &= -7x^3 - 21x^2 + x + 3 \end{aligned}$$

(b) Which student found the correct value for $2g\left(\sqrt{2}\right)$ if $g(x) = \dfrac{4}{x^2} - 2$? Explain where the others went wrong.

Marla
$$\begin{aligned} 2g\left(\sqrt{2}\right) &= \frac{4}{\sqrt{2}^2} - 2 \\ &= \frac{4}{4} - 2 \\ &= 1 - 2 \\ &= -1 \end{aligned}$$

Mira
$$\begin{aligned} 2g\left(\sqrt{2}\right) &= 2\left(\frac{4}{\sqrt{2}^2} - 2\right) \\ &= 2\left(\frac{4}{2} - 2\right) \\ &= 2(2 - 2) \\ &= 0 \end{aligned}$$

Matilda
$$\begin{aligned} 2g\left(\sqrt{2}\right) &= 2\left(\frac{4}{\sqrt{2}^2} - 2\right) \\ &= 2\left(\frac{4}{4} - 2\right) \\ &= 2(1 - 2) \\ &= -2 \end{aligned}$$

Remediation

- To alleviate the apprehension students often feel when they encounter new types of mathematical notation, show several examples of equations both with and without function notation. Explain that the two questions in each part are just different ways of stating the same information.

  (a) For $y = \sqrt{x+2}$, find y when $x = 7$.
  For $f(x) = \sqrt{x+2}$, find $f(7)$.

  (b) For $y = \dfrac{x}{x^2 - 1}$, find y when $x = 5$. For $g(x) = \dfrac{x}{x^2 - 1}$, find $g(5)$.

  (c) For $y = x^3 - 2x + 1$, find y when $x = -3$. For $h(x) = x^3 - 2x + 1$, find $h(-3)$.

Substituting a Numerical Value

Evaluate $g(x) = 3x(x + 4) - 1$ for $x = 0$, $x = -3$, and $x = \frac{1}{10}$.

Select the method you would like to use.

⬤ Simplify the function by removing the brackets and then substitute the input value.

⬤ Substitute the input value and then simplify.

⬤ Return to Examples menu.

‹ Previous | Next ›

Rational Expressions
Function Notation
Examples

MENU
QUIT
[1]

- If students have problems substituting values into equations written in function notation, have them work through a problem such as the following:

If $f(x) = x^2 - x + 1$, find $f(4)$, $f(a)$, $f(\pi)$, $f(\spadesuit)$, $f(x^2 - 2)$, and $f(math)$.

$f(4) = (4)^2 - (4) + 1 = 13$
$f(a) = (a)^2 - (a) + 1 = a^2 - a + 1$
$f(\pi) = (\pi)^2 - (\pi) + 1 \doteq 17.728$
$f(\spadesuit) = (\spadesuit)^2 - (\spadesuit) + 1 = \spadesuit^2 - \spadesuit + 1$
$f(x^2 - 2) = (x^2 - 2)^2 - (x^2 - 2) + 1$
$\qquad = x^4 - 4x^2 + 4 - x^2 + 2 + 1$
$\qquad = x^4 - 5x^2 + 7$
$f(math) = (math)^2 - (math) + 1$

Extension

A

Explain that there are several different types of function notation. Students can try writing and evaluating other functions using each type of notation shown.

$y = 3x - 2$
$f(x) = 3x - 2$
$(x, 3x - 2)$
$f: x \to 3x - 2$
$\{(x, f(x)) \mid f(x) = 3x - 2\}$
$f: \{(x, y) \mid y = 3x - 2\}$

You may wish to provide sample problems. For example: Find $f(-5)$ for the following functions:

(a) $f(x) = x^3 - 7$

(b) $f: x \to \sqrt{-5x}$

(c) $\left\{(x, f(x)) \mid f(x) = -\dfrac{1}{x}\right\}$

(d) $f: \left\{(x, y) \mid y = \dfrac{3}{5}x^2 - 1\right\}$

Enrichment

A

Have pairs of students develop function notation problems to exchange with another pair. For example:

(a) Graph a function and then use function notation to name the graph. Choose three different values for which your classmates will evaluate the function.

(b) Use function notation to represent a real situation. Choose three different values for which your classmates will evaluate the function.

B

Students could find examples of functions in their science textbooks and rewrite each one using function notation.

C

The hidden screen at the beginning of the **Examples** section raises the topic of validating ISBN numbers on published material. Ask if an ISBN number could also be validated by multiplying the first digit by 1, the second by 2, and so on to the ninth digit, which is multiplied by 9. With this method, the check number (the last digit of the ISBN) is subtracted from the sum of the products and the result is divided by 11. Students can test several ISBN numbers found on published materials to confirm that this method also works.

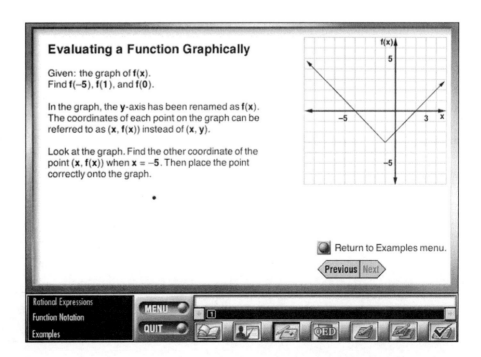

Evaluating a Function Graphically

Given: the graph of **f(x)**.
Find **f(−5)**, **f(1)**, and **f(0)**.

In the graph, the **y**-axis has been renamed as **f(x)**. The coordinates of each point on the graph can be referred to as (**x**, **f(x)**) instead of (**x**, **y**).

Look at the graph. Find the other coordinate of the point (**x**, **f(x)**) when **x** = −5. Then place the point correctly onto the graph.

Return to Examples menu.

Previous Next

Rational Expressions
Function Notation
Examples

MENU
QUIT

Cross-References

Relations and Functions

Student Workbook: pages 102–105

Key Objectives

The student will:

- determine the domain and range of a relation by examining the graph of the relation.
- express the domain and range in set notation.

Key Terms

domain, range, continuous, discontinuous, discrete

Prerequisite Skills

- Plot linear and nonlinear data, using appropriate scales.
- Classify numbers as natural, whole, integer, rational, or irrational.

Lesson Description

This lesson deals with the domain and range of relations. The students will learn to determine the domain and range of a relation by examining the graph.

In the **Introduction**, students examine hot tub designs to determine which ones meet the specifications of the builder. To meet these specifications, a tub must touch all four sides of a rectangular hole 3 yd long and 2 yd wide. In the **Summary**, students examine graphs of the designs to see that all four share a common domain and range.

The **Tutorial** begins with a review of the ways to express relations (words, equations, ordered pairs, and graphs) and then introduces the terms **domain** (set of all *x*-values for a relation) and **range** (set of all *y*-values). Students examine a graph of $y = 2x$ for a finite number of integer values and then see how the domain and range change as the graph is extended in each direction. The graph also changes to reflect real-number values. The **Tutorial** ends with a vocabulary check that helps students consolidate their understanding of new terms.

The **Examples** focus on different types of relations: first graphs of integer-ordered pairs, then linear relations (with and without restrictions on the domain) and then common nonlinear relations, such as ellipses and sinusoids. The final section of the **Examples** deals with graphs involving discontinuities.

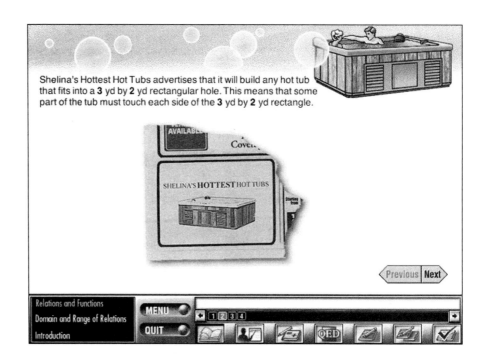

Shelina's Hottest Hot Tubs advertises that it will build any hot tub that fits into a **3** yd by **2** yd rectangular hole. This means that some part of the tub must touch each side of the **3** yd by **2** yd rectangle.

Previous | Next

Relations and Functions
Domain and Range of Relations
Introduction

MENU
QUIT

1 2 3 4

QED

Instructor Intervention

- As students move from integer graphs to solid line graphs, it may be helpful to review the number systems. Make sure students understand that the set of real numbers encompasses natural numbers, whole numbers, integers, rational numbers, and irrational numbers. A solid line is also used to represent the set of rational numbers (Q), since there is always a rational number between any two others.

- Set notation is used in this lesson to record the domain and range of a relation. To ensure that students understand the symbols, have them read several examples aloud and then explain the meaning. For example:
  $\{x \mid x \geq 12, x \in R\}$ is read: "the set of all values for x, such that x is greater than or equal to 12, and x is an element of the set of real numbers."
  This means that x can be any real number from 12 onward, including 12.

- Discuss the graphical significance of the symbols $>$, $<$, $\geq$, and $\leq$. Ask questions such as:
  (a) How are these domains shown differently on a graph: $\{x \mid x > 12, x \in R\}$ and $\{x \mid x \geq 12, x \in R\}$?
  (b) What does it mean if there is an open circle around a point on a graph? a closed circle?

- Vocabulary is very important in this lesson. Make sure that students can explain the concepts of continuity and discontinuity.

- The concepts of input and output are at the heart of a lesson on domain and range, since restrictions on the input (domain) affect the output (range). Some restrictions result in a graph that continues to approach a value indefinitely, but never quite reaches it. Use examples to show how this is possible, and why $>$ or $<$ is used to describe the situation.

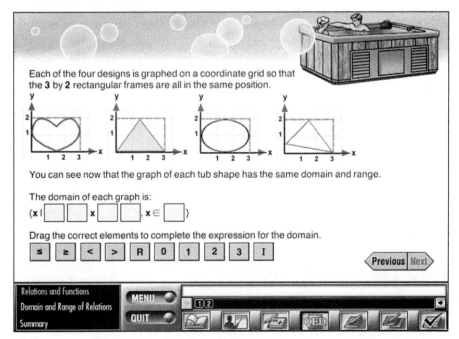

Previous | Next

Relations and Functions
Domain and Range of Relations
Summary

MENU
QUIT

Lesson Components

Examples
Integer Graphs (1)
Linear Graphs (2)
Nonlinear Graphs (3)
Graphs with
   Discontinuities (3)

Practice and Problems
Determining the Domain
Determining the Range
Error Analysis
Comparing Graphs
Applications

Extra Practice
Integer Graphs
Linear Graphs
Nonlinear Graphs
Graphs with Discontinuities

Self-Check
Integer Graphs (2)
Linear Graphs (2)
Nonlinear Graphs (3)
Graphs with
   Discontinuities (3)

Minimum score: 7 out of 10

Evaluation

- Show a selection of graphs from various sources, including magazine or newspaper articles and previous lessons. Ask students to write their observations about the domain and range for each graph and then express this information in set notation.

- Invite students to suggest everyday situations that involve relations and then to describe the domain and range for each situation. For example, car rentals involve a relation between cost (y) and distance driven (x). Suppose you pay a $20 flat rate plus 30¢ per mile. The graph would be a straight line sloping up to the right from an open dot around $20 on the y-axis. The distance must be a real number greater than 0, so the domain is continuous for $x > 0$ mi. In practice, the cost will be rounded to the nearest hundredth of a dollar, but the exact cost can be any amount greater than $20, so the range is continuous for $y > \$20$. If a person traveled 50 mi, for a total cost of $35, the domain would be $\{x \mid 0 < x \leq 50, x \in R\}$. The range would be $\{y \mid 20 < y \leq 35, y \in R\}$.

- Observe students as they interpret graphs. Do they have a solid understanding of number systems? Can they interpret statements written in set notation? Are they using mathematical terms such as **continuous**, **discontinuous**, and **discrete**? Can they use set notation to describe the domain and range of a relation?

Remediation

- Some students may lack the necessary understanding of number systems and how to represent them graphically.

  Provide examples of number lines that show only domains. Invite students to write a sentence to describe each domain and then write the set notation. For example:

  This is the set of real numbers greater than 0.
  $\{x \mid x > 0, x \in R\}$

  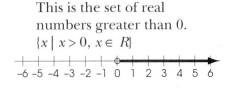

  This is the set of integers greater than or equal to –2.
  $\{x \mid x \geq -2, x \in I\}$

- Some students may need to review new vocabulary. They might revisit the **Tutorial** to list and define all the terms that are new to them. The final frame in the **Tutorial** provides a vocabulary check that could be used to confirm definitions.

- If students become frustrated with set notation, they could record their answers in word form instead.

- Students may ask why it is useful for them to study this topic. Use a situation from their own experience to help them see applications. For example, suppose the cost of producing the school newspaper depends on two items: a $50 fixed cost plus a variable cost of 10¢ per paper. Ask students to identify the input value (the number of papers needed) and the output value

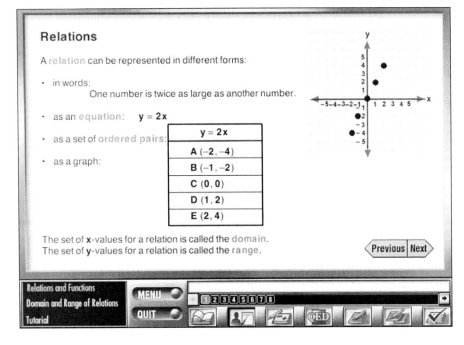

(the cost). Point out that by limiting the range, they also impose limits on the domain that can help them decide how many papers they can afford to produce for a given amount of money.

Extension

A
Pose the following problem and then invite students to create similar problems of their own.

The equation is $y = 4x + 3$.
The domain is $x \in \{1, 2, 6, 12\}$.
What is the range?

(Students can substitute the x-values into the equation to find all possible values for y.)

B
To learn about asymptotes, students could graph $y = \dfrac{10}{x}$.
They should see that the graph approaches $x = 0$, but it can never reach this point because $\dfrac{10}{0}$ is undefined.

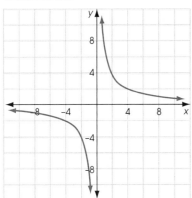

The two axes are asymptotes, straight lines that approach the curve but never touch it.

C
Some students could choose an everyday situation that involves a relation and then graph it, and describe the domain and range.

Enrichment

A
Ask students to look for everyday relations that generate unusual-looking graphs or that have unusual domains and ranges.

B
Students who have completed the **Extension** activity about asymptotes could look for other equations that yield graphs with asymptotes.

C
Students could try to determine an equation or a set of ordered pairs that corresponds to a given domain and range.
For example:

The domain is $\{x \mid x \in R\}$.
The range is $\{y \mid y = 2, y \in R\}$.

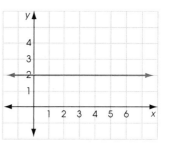

In some cases, the relation is not unique. For example:

The domain is $\{x \mid 1 \le x \le 5, x \in R\}$.
The range is $\{y \mid 0 \le y \le 4, y \in R\}$.

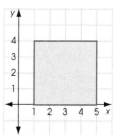

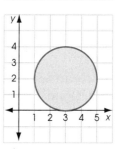

(One possible relation is $y = x$, where $x \in \{1, 2, 3, 4, \text{or } 5\}$.)

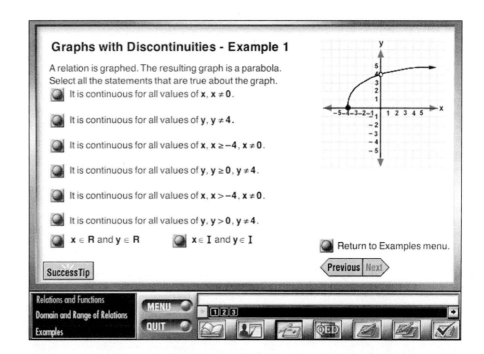

Graphs with Discontinuities - Example 1

A relation is graphed. The resulting graph is a parabola. Select all the statements that are true about the graph.

○ It is continuous for all values of **x, x ≠ 0**.

○ It is continuous for all values of **y, y ≠ 4**.

○ It is continuous for all values of **x, x ≥ −4, x ≠ 0**.

○ It is continuous for all values of **y, y ≥ 0, y ≠ 4**.

○ It is continuous for all values of **x, x > −4, x ≠ 0**.

○ It is continuous for all values of **y, y > 0, y ≠ 4**.

○ **x ∈ R and y ∈ R**   ○ **x ∈ I and y ∈ I**

○ Return to Examples menu.

SuccessTip   Previous | Next

Relations and Functions
Domain and Range of Relations
Examples
MENU
QUIT

7 LINEAR FUNCTIONS

7.1 Linear Functions

Key Objectives
The student will:
- determine the intercepts, slope, domain, and range of a given linear function.

Key Terms
linear function, *x*-intercept, *y*-intercept, slope, rise, run, domain, range

Prerequisite Skills
- Solve problems involving rise, run, and slope of line segments.
- Draw the graph of a function from its equation.
- Represent functions as a set of ordered pairs, as an equation, or as a graph.
- Determine the domain and range of a function from its graph.

Lesson Description

In this lesson, students learn to use the equation $y = mx + b$ to find the intercepts, slope, domain, and range of a linear function. In the **Introduction**, students examine the concept of slope as they compare roof designs for a house with walls 670 cm high. They use a triangle with a rise of 1 and a run of 4 (the minimum slope permitted by the building code) to determine that a roof with this slope would add 115 cm to the height of the house. In the **Summary**, students see how a linear function $\left(y = \frac{1}{4}x + 670 \right)$ can be used to find the height of the roof for the given slope. They also determine the domain and range of the function and explore the graphs of other functions sharing the same *y*-intercept.

The **Tutorial** uses the context of an experiment with springs and weights to develop these concepts:
- The slope of a straight line is defined by $\frac{rise}{run}$ or $\frac{y_2 - y_1}{x_2 - x_1}$. In $y = mx + b$, m represents the slope.
- The *y*-intercept is where a graph meets the *y*-axis. In $y = mx + b$, b represents the *y*-intercept.
- The *x*-intercept is where a graph meets the *x*-axis.
- The domain of a relation is the set of all *x*-values, and the range is the set of all *y*-values.

A series of problems in the **Examples** reinforces and extends the learning initiated in the **Tutorial**. Students discover that they can find the *x*-intercept of a linear function by substituting 0 for *y* in $y = mx + b$

and then solving for x. In one of the **Examples**, they graph a relation using the slope and y-intercept. In another, they find the domain and range for a vertical line ($x = 3$) and then discover that the slope for such a relation is undefined. In the final example, students apply their knowledge to solve a problem involving a car's deceleration.

The next lesson will extend these concepts as students explore relations representing direct and partial variations.

Instructor Intervention

- Before students begin this lesson, review the concept of slope. Demonstrate how the slope of a line on a coordinate grid can be calculated by finding $\frac{rise}{run}$ or $\frac{y_2 - y_1}{x_2 - x_1}$. You could use ideas from the **Introduction** to demonstrate **rise** and **run** and to outline one practical application for finding the slope of a line.

- Review the meaning of the terms **domain** and **range**. Talk with students about how they would solve a selection of problems similar to the ones in the lesson "Domain and Range of Relations."

- Whenever students calculate the slope of a line on a graph, they should compare the result with the graph to make sure it makes sense. Remind them that a line sloping up to the right has a positive slope because the x- and y-coordinates increase or decrease together. A line sloping down to the right has a negative slope because one coordinate increases as the other decreases.

- Encourage students to work through all the **Examples** to gain exposure to a range of different situations.

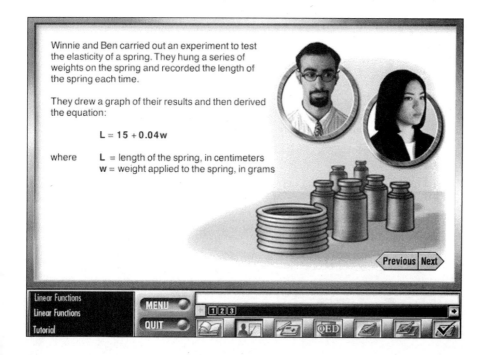

Lesson Components

Examples
Example 1 (1)
Example 2 (1)
Example 3 (1)
Example 4 (1)
Example 5 (1)
Example 6 (1)

Practice and Problems
Matching Graph Features
Error Analysis
Using $y = mx + b$ (with Graphs)
Using $y = mx + b$
Problem Situations

Extra Practice
Matching Graph Features
Error Analysis
Using $y = mx + b$ (with Graphs)
Using $y = mx + b$
Problem Situations

Self-Check
Matching Graph Features (2)
Error Analysis (2)
Using $y = mx + b$ (with Graphs) (2)
Using $y = mx + b$ (2)
Problem Situations (2)

Minimum score: 7 out of 10

Evaluation

- Have small groups each create a problem similar to one from the **Practice and Problems** section of the lesson. They should write the problem on one overhead transparency and a full solution on another.

  Each group can present its problem for the rest of the class to solve. Then students can compare their solutions with the one generated by the group who created the problem.

- Observe the class as they solve problems from the lesson. Can they explain the terms **slope, x-intercept, y-intercept, domain**, and **range**? Can they explain how to determine each feature from an equation? from a graph?

- Ask students to write a paragraph to explain how they would obtain the slope of a line from:
  (a) a graph.
  (b) an equation.
  (c) a table of values.

- On a coordinate grid, ask students to draw a line that fits each description.
  (a) The slope is negative.
  (b) The domain is positive. Remember: The graph would have an open point at $(0, 0)$ since 0 is neither positive nor negative.
  (c) The slope is undefined.
  (d) The x- and y-intercepts are both positive.

Remediation

- Some students may not have had previous experience with the concept of slope. Explain that the slope of a line is a ratio between the vertical distance covered and the horizontal distance covered. Draw an oblique line (sloping up and right) on a sheet of paper. Have a student draw in a vertical line to show the rise and a horizontal line to show the run. The result will be a right triangle.

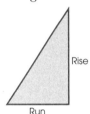

The students can measure the rise and the run and then find $\frac{rise}{run}$ to calculate the slope.

Repeat with a similar line drawn on a coordinate grid. Show how to use the scales on the axes to determine the rise and run. Finally, repeat with a line on a coordinate grid that has a negative slope.

Students may need to work with graphs that show only one line before they attempt the more complex problems in the lesson.

- To consolidate understanding, students could copy each completed solution in their notebooks and then create and solve a similar problem.

- If students are having difficulty generating information from the equation $y = mx + b$, they might find it helpful to graph the function.

- Review the problems in the **Practice and Problems** section and help students choose the ones that seem best suited to their ability.

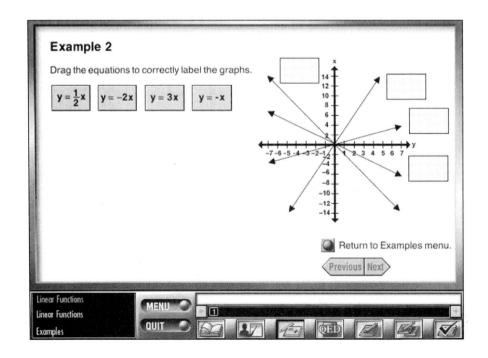

Extension

A

Students might investigate non-linear relations, such as $y = x^2$ or $y = \frac{1}{x}$. Have them graph several points in each relation to determine the general shape of the curve and then identify the domain and range in each case. Ask why these equations result in curved graphs rather than straight lines.

Graphing calculators can make it easier for students to experiment independently with equations and graphs as they look for other nonlinear relations.

B

Have students interview retail sales persons to find out whether and how they use linear equations at work. Some students may wish to develop a presentation based on information they find.

C

Invite students to look for examples of everyday situations involving relations that:
(a) have a negative slope.
(b) have a positive slope.
(c) have limits on the domain.
(d) have limits on the range.
(e) have a y-intercept less than 0.
(f) have an x-intercept greater than 0.

Enrichment

A

Students who completed the **Extension** activity on nonlinear relationships could form pairs to discuss ways to describe the slope of a nonlinear relation.

B

Students could investigate the slopes of wheelchair ramps, driveways, or staircases. Have them prepare a poster or presentation based on their discoveries.

C

Pose this problem:

Eddie ran 10 mi at a steady speed of 10 mph.

Draw a graph with time, t, on the horizontal axis and speed, v, on the vertical axis.

Give the slope, domain, and range of the function. Explain the meaning of each.

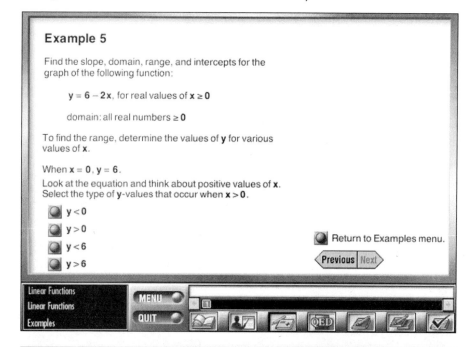

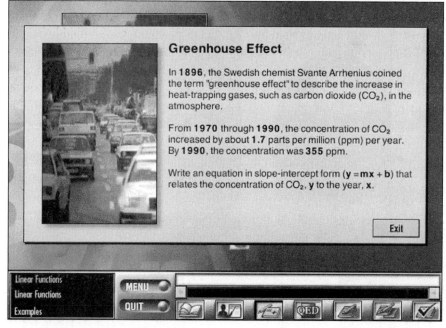

7.2 Direct and Partial Variation

Cross-References

Linear Functions

Student Workbook: pages 110–113

Key Objectives

The student will:
- explain and model linear relationships involving direct and partial variations.

Key Terms

direct variation, partial variation, constant of variation, slope, constant of proportionality, dependent variable, independent variable

Prerequisite Skills

- Determine the equation of a line when given information that uniquely determines the line.
- Represent data using function models.
- Determine the intercepts, slope, domain, and range of a linear function when given its equation.

Lesson Description

This lesson helps students learn to differentiate between direct and partial variations represented by linear relations. A practical example of this difference is profiled in the **Introduction**, where a house painter weighs the merits of two billing systems. Should he charge $10 for every hour worked, or should he charge a flat rate of $200 plus $6 per hour? Students examine tables of values, graphs, and equations to determine that the partial variation ($P = \$200 + \$6t$) is better for jobs that last up to 50 h, but the direct variation ($P = \$10t$) is better for longer jobs. In the **Summary**, students use strategies from the lesson to compare the two billing systems without using tables of values or graphs.

The **Tutorial** develops the concept of direct variation in several problem contexts. Students see that when one variable increases or decreases, the other does the same at a proportional rate. This produces a linear graph that passes through the origin.

The **Tutorial** reviews the equation for a linear graph, $y = mx + b$, where m is the slope of the line and b is the y-intercept. Students learn that the slope of the line is also called the **constant of variation** (k), because the slope represents a constant relationship between the dependent variable and the independent variable. Since the y-intercept for a direct variation is at the origin, the relation can be described with the equation $y = kx$.

In the **Examples**, students find equations and identify the constant of variation in situations involving both positive and negative direct variations. They also investigate partial variations and represent these relations with equations. Finally, students apply concepts from the lesson in problem situations.

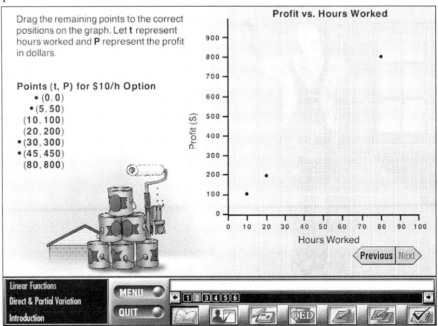

Drag the remaining points to the correct positions on the graph. Let **t** represent hours worked and **P** represent the profit in dollars.

Points (t, P) for $10/h Option
- (0, 0)
- (5, 50)
- (10, 100)
- (20, 200)
- (30, 300)
- (45, 450)
- (80, 800)

Profit vs. Hours Worked

Profit ($)

Hours Worked

Previous Next

Linear Functions
Direct & Partial Variation
Introduction

MENU
QUIT

1 2 3 4 5 6

Instructor Intervention

- Students will need calculators for some problems in this lesson.

- Proportions are discussed as a solution method for direct variation problems. Review the different methods that can be used to solve proportions. For example, to solve $\frac{25}{16} = \frac{100}{y}$ students could:

  (a) determine that $25 \times 4 = 100$ in the numerator, so $16 \times 4 = y$ in the denominator.
  (b) change $\frac{25}{16}$ to 1.5625 and then solve for y.
  (c) multiply both sides of the proportion by $16y$ to eliminate the denominators and then solve for y.
  (d) use cross-multiplication: $25y = 16 \times 100$.
  Explain that this method is a short-cut version of the method described in part (c).

- When students are setting up proportions, encourage them to be consistent about placing the y-values in the numerators. This will help to reinforce the equation used to find slope, and also help students to avoid mismatch errors.

- Some students initially may need help in distinguishing the independent variables (y-values) from the dependent ones (x-values).

- This lesson relies on the students' ability to determine the slope and the y-intercept of a line. Review the definition of slope, the concepts of rise and run, and the location of x- and y- intercepts

- Students will use the formula $y = mx + b$ to find the equation of a line. Review the roles of m and b in determining a linear equation. As students complete the **Tutorial** and **Examples**, help them see that $y = kx + 0$ or $y = kx$ (for a direct variation) and $y = b + kx$ (for a partial variation) are simply different ways of expressing $y = kx + b$.

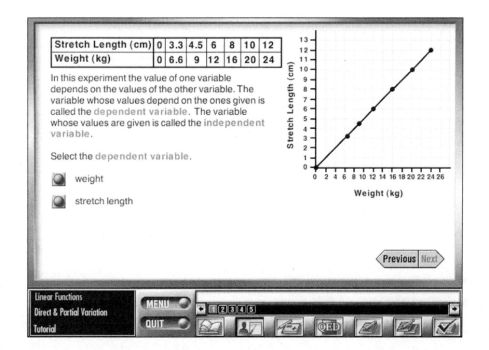

Lesson Components

 Examples

Direct Variation: Finding the Equation (1)
Direct Variation: The Constant of Variation (1)
Direct Variation: Applications (1)
Partial Variation: Defining the Equation (1)
Partial Variation: Finding the Equation (1)
Partial Variation: Applications (1)

Practice and Problems

Identification
Finding the Equation
Direct Variation Problems
Partial Variation Problems: Working Backwards
Linear Applications

Extra Practice

Direct Variation: Finding the Equation
Direct Variation: The Constant of Variation
Direct Variation: Applications
Partial Variation: Finding the Equation
Partial Variation: Equations from Graphs
Partial Variation: Applications

Self-Check

Direct Variation: Finding the Equation (1)
Direct Variation: The Constant of Variation (2)
Direct Variation: Applications (2)
Partial Variation: Finding the Equation (2)
Partial Variation: Equations from Graphs (1)
Partial Variation: Applications (2)

Minimum score: 7 out of 10

Evaluation

- Invite small groups to create two example problems, one involving a direct variation and the other a partial variation. Ask each group to solve their problems on a separate piece of paper, taking care to use the proper format and mathematical notation. Representatives from each group can then use an overhead projector to present their problems for the rest of the class.

  Allow time for the class to write a complete solution for the first problem and then have the representatives present their solution for comparison. Repeat with the remaining problems.

- Observe how students create and solve problems based on direct and partial variations. Can they articulate the difference between the two variation types? Can they explain the role of the constant of variation in a direct variation? Can they describe the relationship between the fixed amount and the variable amount in a partial variation? Can they develop equations to solve problems? Can they solve the equations?

Remediation

- Review the vocabulary outlined in the **Key Terms** section at the beginning of this lesson.

- Review these processes:
  (a) solving an equation with one variable
  (b) determining the slope of a line from a graph
  (c) determining the slope of a line from two points
  (d) determining the y-intercept from a graph
  (e) determining the y-intercept from a table of values
  (f) using the slope and the y-intercept to determine the equation of a line

Extension

A

Students might research and report on the concept of inverse variation. They should consider the following questions:
(a) How are two quantities related in an inverse relationship? Give an example.
(b) What does the graph of an inverse relationship look like?
(c) Does an inverse relationship have a constant of variation? If so, how is it determined?
(d) What is the inverse equation? [$x_1y_1 = x_2y_2$]

B

Once students have had a chance to explore inverse relationships in the previous activity, pose problems such as the following:

1. If x varies inversely as y, and $x = 5$ when $y = 3$, what is y when $x = 15$? [9]
2. If x varies inversely as y, find the effect on x for each condition:
   (a) y is doubled [halved]
   (b) y is halved [doubled]
   (c) y is tripled [reduced by one-third]
3. Traveling time varies inversely as the speed at which one travels. If a journey takes 3 h at 60 mph, how long will it take at 80 mph?

C

Have students look for other types of direct variation relationships and use them to create problems. Ask how each equation could be expressed in more than one way. For example:

Partial Variation: Defining the Equation

The partial variation equation looks like this:

C = F + kd

In this equation, **C** is the total cost, **F** is the fixed cost, and **kd** is the variable part of the cost. Within the variable part, **kd**, **k** is the constant of variation and **d** is the independent variable.

Rena hired an electrician who charged a flat service charge of $30 plus $35/h for each hour worked. **C** represents the total cost in dollars and t represents the time in hours.

Select the partial variation equation that represents her total cost.

- **C = 35 + 30t**
- **t = 35 + 30C**
- **C = 30 + 35t**
- **C = 30 − 35t**

Return to Examples menu.

Previous | Next

Linear Functions
Direct & Partial Variation
Examples

MENU
QUIT

(a) The value of a diamond (V) varies directly with the square of its mass (M).

$$V = kM^2 \text{ or } \frac{V}{M^2} = k \text{ or } M^2 = \frac{V}{k}$$

(b) The time (t) it takes a pendulum to complete one full swing varies directly with the square root of its length, L.

$$t = k\sqrt{L} \text{ or } k = \frac{t}{\sqrt{L}}$$

D

Invite students to trade and solve problems created for the previous activity. You may also wish to include problems such as the following:

1. The distance a hockey puck travels on ice varies directly with the square of the speed of the puck. A puck, moving at a speed of 4 ft/s, travels 220 ft before stopping. How fast is a puck moving if it travels 495 ft before stopping? [6 ft/s]

2. The volume of a sphere varies directly with the cube of its radius. When the radius is 3 units, the volume is $36p$ cubic units. Find the radius of a sphere having a volume of $\frac{9}{2p}$ cubic units.

$$\left[\sqrt[3]{\frac{9}{8p^2}} \right]$$

3. The time it takes a pendulum to complete one full swing varies directly with the square root of its length. A pendulum that is 1 yd long swings once every 2 s. If a pendulum is 72 yd long, how long will it take to complete one full swing? Evaluate to the nearest whole second. [17 s]

Enrichment

A

Pose this geometry problem:

The shaded portion of the diagram is equal in area to the inner circle.

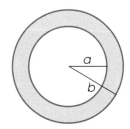

(a) Prove that the area of the small circle varies directly with the area of the large circle.

(b) Does a vary directly as b? Explain.

B

Pose this problem:

Three car-rental companies are competing for the weekend market.

Company	Fixed Rate	Additional Cost ($/mi)
A	50	0.10
B	30	0.15
C	25	0.25

(a) For each company, find an equation that relates total cost, C, to distance traveled, d.

(b) On the same grid, graph the relation that each equation represents.

(c) Discuss the circumstances under which it is to your advantage to rent from each company.

Partial Variation: Finding the Equation

Snowmobile Rentals

Braheem rented a snowmobile from Sleds R Us. The terms were $21 per day plus $0.15/mi. The table shows a breakdown of the relation between cost and distance for one day's rental.

Complete the graph by dragging the three missing points to the grid.

Distance (mi)	Cost ($)	Points (Distance, Cost)
0	21.00	•(0, 21.00)
10	22.50	(10, 22.50)
20	24.00	•(20, 24.00)
30	25.50	(30, 25.50)
40	27.00	(40, 27.00)
50	28.50	•(50, 28.50)
70	31.50	(70, 31.50)
160	45.00	(160, 45.00)
200	51.00	(200, 51.50)

Return to Examples menu.

Previous | Next

Linear Functions
Direct & Partial Variation
Examples

MENU
QUIT
[1]

Rate of Change and Slope of a Line

Cross-References

Linear Functions

Student Workbook: pages 114–117

Key Objectives

The student will:
- solve problems involving rise, run, and slope of line segments.

Key Terms

slope, rise, run, *x*-coordinate, *y*-coordinate, coefficient, general equation, collinear points, vertical, horizontal

Prerequisite Skills

- Use concrete materials and diagrams to develop the Pythagorean relationship.
- Use the Pythagorean relationship to calculate the measure of the third side of a right triangle.
- Solve problems involving distances between points in the coordinate plane.
- Solve problems involving midpoints of line segments.

Lesson Description

This lesson introduces the concepts of rise and run and explains how these are used to calculate slope and to locate points on a line with a given slope.

In the **Introduction**, a company provides Internet access at a flat cost of $11.95 for 15 h, plus $1.40 for each additional hour. Students make a table to determine the number of hours that can be purchased for $20. In the **Summary**, students plot two points that represent (*cost, hours*) and then use these points to determine the slope of the line. From the slope, they calculate the *x*-coordinate of the point (*k*, 20), which represents the number of hours obtainable for $20.

As the **Tutorial** begins, students rank three ski runs according to steepness. When the runs are represented on a coordinate plane, a relationship emerges between the equations and the coordinates of points on each line. Students discover that the equation with the greatest coefficient describes the steepest run.

As the **Tutorial** proceeds, students learn the following:
- In the general equation $y = mx$, the letter *m* represents the slope of the line.
- The slope of a line is equal to $\frac{rise}{run}$.
- To find the slope of a line segment from the coordinates of two known points, you can use the equation $m = \frac{y_2 - y_1}{x_2 - x_1}$.

Jim is working part-time in the Internet department at E-Biz Communications. He receives a call from Mr. Shek who wants to purchase a **$20.00** Internet Premium Plan gift certificate for his granddaughter Alyssa. He asks Jim how much Internet time that will give Alyssa.

Linear Functions
Rate of Change and Slope of a Line
Introduction

MENU
QUIT

- If a line segment rises from left to right, the slope is positive. If a line segment falls from left to right, the slope is negative.
- If the slope of *AB* is equal to the slope of *BC*, then *A*, *B*, and *C* are collinear.

The **Examples** deal with various related concepts, including the slopes of horizontal and vertical lines, and the classification of line segments by slope. Students find one coordinate of a point where the other is known and look for additional points along a given line segment. In the final problem, slope is used to determine the original height of a tree that has been partially felled by a lightning strike.

Instructor Intervention

- Review the Distance Formula, the Midpoint Formula and sine, cosine, and tangent ratios, since these will be used during the course of the lesson.

- Students may find it helpful to think of slope in terms of stepping up and across from one point on a line to the next. For example, a slope of $\frac{2}{3}$ means that you can plot the line by plotting one point, then stepping (up 2, right 3) to reach the next. (Negative numbers represent steps down or to the left.)

- The **Remediation** section includes an activity that may help students better understand the relationship between slope and the tangent ratio.

- The next lesson will build on concepts developed here as students learn how to determine the equation of a line from its slope.

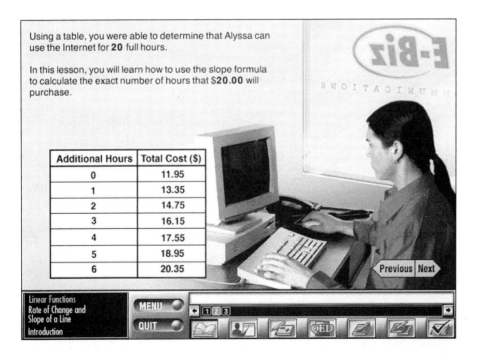

Using a table, you were able to determine that Alyssa can use the Internet for **20** full hours.

In this lesson, you will learn how to use the slope formula to calculate the exact number of hours that **$20.00** will purchase.

Additional Hours	Total Cost ($)
0	11.95
1	13.35
2	14.75
3	16.15
4	17.55
5	18.95
6	20.35

Previous | Next

Linear Functions
Rate of Change and
Slope of a Line
Introduction

MENU

QUIT

Evaluation

- Have pairs or small groups create a problem that fits one of these categories and write a solution. Choose one problem of each type to use for a review quiz. Use the results of the quiz to identify areas that need reinforcement.

  1. Use the formula $m = \dfrac{rise}{run}$ to find the slope of a line shown in a diagram.

  2. Use the formula $m = \dfrac{y_2 - y_1}{x_2 - x_1}$ to find the slope of a line from its endpoints alone.

  3. You are given the slope of the line, the coordinates of one point, and one coordinate of another point. Find the unknown coordinate.

  4. Find another point on a line segment where you know either two points or one point and the slope of the line.

  5. Create a word problem about an everyday situation where the solution uses the formula $m = \dfrac{rise}{run}$.

  6. Create a word problem about an everyday situation where the solution uses the formula $m = \dfrac{y_2 - y_1}{x_2 - x_1}$.

- Observe the students as they create and solve slope problems. Can they substitute values into the slope formulas? Do they understand how to use slope to locate other points? Can they apply slope formulas in problem situations?

Remediation

- Some students may have difficulty determining if a slope answer is logical. Post these formulas and guidelines for reference:

  $$m = \frac{rise}{run} \qquad m = \frac{y_2 - y_1}{x_2 - x_1}$$

  - If $m > 0$, the line segment is oblique and rises to the right.
  - If $m = 0$, the line segment is horizontal.
  - If $m < 0$, the line segment is oblique and falls to the right.
  - If m is undefined, the line segment is vertical.

- Have students complete the table below to develop an understanding of the relationship between slope and the tangent ratio. (Answers are shown in parentheses.) Ask why the slope of AB is always equal to the tangent of $\angle A$.

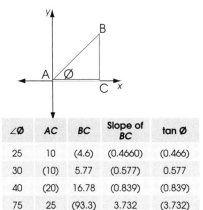

$\angle\emptyset$	AC	BC	Slope of BC	$\tan\emptyset$
25	10	(4.6)	(0.4660)	(0.466)
30	(10)	5.77	(0.577)	0.577
40	(20)	16.78	(0.839)	(0.839)
75	25	(93.3)	3.732	(3.732)

Extension

A

Students with graphing calculators could explore features that would help them work with slope. For example, they could use a TI-83 calculator to create a line segment that joins $A(1, 2)$ to $B(4, 5)$:

1. Select [2ndF] [MODE].
2. Select [2ndF] [PRGM] to access the draw menu.
3. Select 2: Line(.
4. The calculator will display Line(. Enter the coordinates of the two points in the form (x_1, x_2, y_1, y_2) and close the brackets. The result should appear as: Line (1, 2, 4, 5).
5. Press [ENTER] to see the graph.

B

Students could experiment with changing the scales on graphs to see how this affects the appearance of the slope. Emphasize that the $\dfrac{rise}{run}$ method for finding slope must take into account the distance represented by each vertical and horizontal unit along the scale. If the slope is to be accurately portrayed by a graph, the x- and y-scales should be the same.

C

Pose problems that involve trigonometry. For example:

Find the slope of AB.

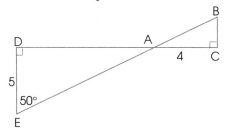

[Answer: 0.84]

Enrichment

A

Have students plot an oblique rectangle on a coordinate grid first and then compare the slopes of the sides to look for relationships among the slopes of parallel and perpendicular lines.

B

Pose this problem:

Gene has cut out a right triangle where the legs are 3 and 4 units long. He places the triangle on a coordinate grid so the legs lie along the x- and y-axes and the hypotenuse has a slope of $\frac{3}{4}$.

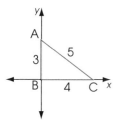

Show how Gene could place the cardboard triangle in a different way so one vertex is at the origin and the slope is:

(a) $-\frac{3}{4}$ **(b)** $\frac{4}{3}$

(c) $-\frac{4}{3}$ **(d)** $\frac{3}{4}$

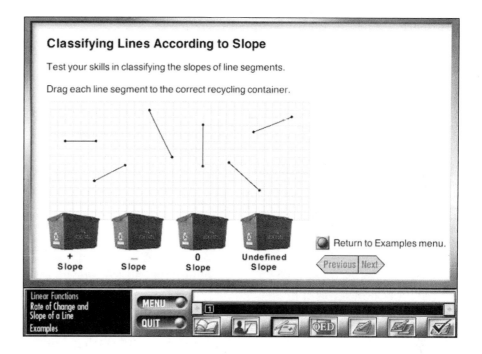

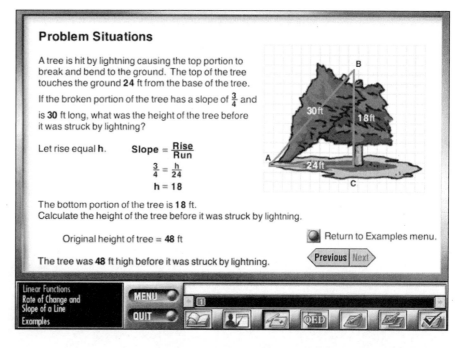

7.4 Determining the Equation of a Line

Cross-References

Linear Functions

Student Workbook: pages 118–121

Key Objectives

The student will:
- determine the equation of a line, given information that uniquely determines the line.

Key Terms

x-axis, *y*-axis, *x*-intercept, *y*-intercept, origin, slope, rise, run, linear equation, slope-intercept form, standard form

Prerequisite Skills

- Solve problems involving midpoints of line segments.
- Solve problems involving rise, run, and slope of line segments.

Lesson Description

This lesson demonstrates how to determine the equation of a line from:
- the slope and the coordinates of one point on the line.
- the coordinates of two points on the line.
- the graph of the line.

In the **Introduction**, students try to determine the cost of carpet installation by guessing and testing. They know that the installer charges a flat rate, plus an amount per square yard, and that a customer paid $120 for 40 yd^2 and $145 for 90 yd^2. In the **Summary**, students apply concepts from the lesson as they use the coordinates of the two known points to generate the equation that represents this relationship.

The **Tutorial** introduces the terms **x-intercept** and **y-intercept**, and demonstrates how to use the slope and *y*-intercept of a line to determine its equation. Students learn to express equations in two different forms:
- $y = mx + b$ (slope-intercept form), where m is the slope and b is the *y*-intercept
- $Ax + By + C = 0$ (standard form), where fractions have been eliminated and A is positive.

In the **Examples**, students generate linear equations from various combinations of given information. They also examine the equations of horizontal and vertical lines and generate linear equations from problem situations.

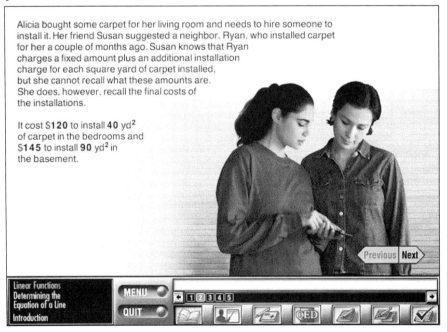

Alicia bought some carpet for her living room and needs to hire someone to install it. Her friend Susan suggested a neighbor, Ryan, who installed carpet for her a couple of months ago. Susan knows that Ryan charges a fixed amount plus an additional installation charge for each square yard of carpet installed, but she cannot recall what these amounts are. She does, however, recall the final costs of the installations.

It cost **$120** to install **40** yd^2 of carpet in the bedrooms and **$145** to install **90** yd^2 in the basement.

Linear Functions
Determining the
Equation of a Line
Introduction

MENU
QUIT

Previous | Next

Instructor Intervention

- Review how to solve rational equations, such as $\frac{4}{3} = \frac{9-1}{x-2}$. Point out that even though some equations, like this one, can be solved by looking for equivalent fractions, it is usually more efficient to eliminate the denominators by multiplying.

- Invite students to explain why they can multiply an equation such as $-5x - y - 6 = 0$ by -1 to create a positive coefficient for x. They should see that they are actually multiplying both sides of the equation, but that the 0 does not change because $-1 \times 0 = 0$.

- A Success Tip in the **Tutorial** suggests that students use a graphing calculator to graph several lines to see how the value of b affects the position of the line. Make sure students know how to use a graphing calculator to plot a line. For example, on the TI-83 calculator:

  Press $Y=$ and enter the first equation as $Y_1 = 2x$, using the [X,T,Ø,n] key to enter the variable x. To see the graph, press [GRAPH]. To adjust the scales, use [WINDOW].

  Students might also experiment with using the [ZOOM] and [TRACE] features. When students press TRACE, they will be able to use the arrow keys to move a cursor left or right along the line and the coordinates will be displayed at the bottom of the graph. If the cursor is not immediately visible, it is likely beyond the range of the screen. Select ZOOM OUT to extend this range.

  Point out that students can enter all four equations at once in order to see all four graphs displayed on the same coordinate plane.

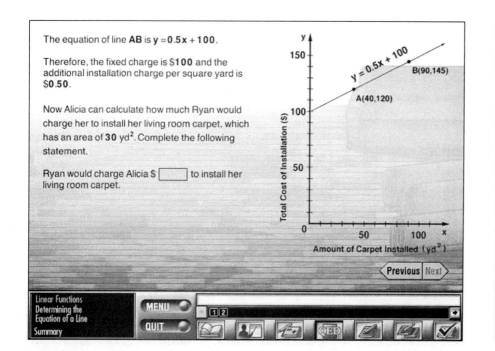

Determining the Equation of a Line **119**

Evaluation

- Pose problems such as the following. In each case, students are to give the equation of the line in the form of their choice.

  (a) A line with slope $\frac{3}{4}$ passes through $A(-3, 6)$.

  (b) A line passes through $B(4, 9)$ and $C(5, 3)$.

  (c) The x-intercept is -2. The y-intercept is 7.

  (d)

  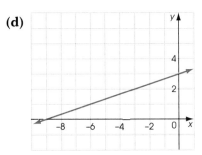

  [Answer: $y = \frac{1}{3}x + 3$ or $x - 3y + 9 = 0$]

  (e) A spring with no weights attached is 10 in. long. For each 1 oz weight attached to the spring, the spring's length increases by 0.25 in. Find the equation and graph the relationship.

- Observe the students as they determine linear equations. Can they calculate the slope of a line? Can they define the terms **x-intercept** and **y-intercept**? Do they recognize that there is more than one way to generate the equation? Can they express an equation in both forms and explain the advantages of each?

Remediation

- Some students may have difficulty understanding the relationship between the slope-intercept form and the standard form of a linear equation. Emphasize that both equations describe the same line and show how an equation can be transformed from one form to another. For example:

$$y = -\frac{1}{3}x + 4$$
$$3y = -1x + 12 \quad \text{①}$$
$$0 = -1x - 3y + 12 \quad \text{②}$$
$$0 = x + 3y - 12 \quad \text{③}$$
$$x - 3y + 12 = 0 \quad \text{④}$$

  ① Multiply both sides by 3 to eliminate the fraction.

  ② Subtract $3y$ from both sides.

  ③ Multiply both sides by -1 to make the Ax term positive.

  ④ Invert the equation to match the form $Ax + By + C = 0$

- Review the terms **x-intercept** and **y-intercept**. Explain that even though an intercept can be expressed as a single number, a point is implied. For example, if the y-intercept is 2, the line crosses the y-axis at $(0, 2)$.

Demonstrate how to use the equation to find the x-intercept. For example:

$$y = -\frac{1}{3}x + 4 \quad \text{①}$$
$$0 = -\frac{1}{3}x + 4 \quad \text{②}$$
$$-4 = -\frac{1}{3}x \quad \text{③}$$
$$-12 = -x \quad \text{④}$$
$$12 = x \quad \text{⑤}$$

① At the x-intercept, the y-coordinate is 0.

② Substitute 0 for y.

③ Subtract 4 from both sides.

④ Multiply both sides by 3.

⑤ The x-intercept is 12 or $(12, 0)$.

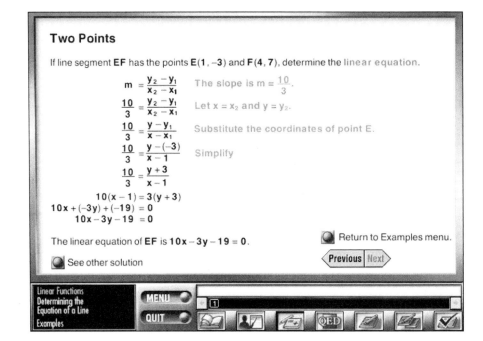

Extension

A

Students could use the relationship between $y = mx + b$ and $Ax + By + C = 0$ to determine the rules that connect A, B, and C to the slope and the y-intercept. Have them generate example equations to test their ideas.

If the slope is expressed in fraction form as $\dfrac{m_1}{m_2}$, then:

$$y = \frac{m_1}{m_2}x + b \rightarrow 0 = m_1 x - m_2 y + m_2 b$$

In the form $Ax + By + C = 0$, students can determine the slope by finding $\dfrac{A}{-B}$, and the y-intercept by finding $\dfrac{C}{-B}$.

B

Once students understand the relationships in the previous activity, they can develop formulas for finding the x-intercept from each form of the equation. For example:

For $y = mx + b$, the x-intercept $= -\dfrac{b}{m}$ since:

$$y = mx + b$$
$$0 = mx + b$$
$$-b = mx$$
$$-\frac{b}{m} = x$$

For $Ax + By + C$, the x-intercept $= -\dfrac{C}{A}$ since:

$$Ax + By + C = 0$$
$$Ax + B(0) + C = 0$$
$$Ax + C = 0$$
$$x = -\frac{C}{A}$$

C

Invite students to find and compare families of lines that have a common slope or intercept. For example, these lines have the same y-intercept:

$$y = 2x + 4 \qquad y = 3x + 4$$

D

Challenge students to use linear equations to solve geometry problems such as the following.

Find:
(a) the length of the altitude.
(b) the area of $\triangle ABC$.
(c) the midpoint of line AC.

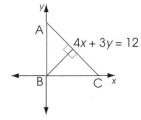

Enrichment

A

Students could analyze graphs of direct and partial variations and suggest practical situations that might be represented by each graph.

B

Ask how students could use the equations of two lines to find the coordinates of the point at which they meet. For example:

Where $y = 2x + 8$ meets $y = 3x + 6$, the x- and y-coordinates are the same. Since the y-coordinates are the same:

$$2x + 8 = 3x + 6$$
$$2 = x$$

If $2 = x$, then
$$y = 2(2) + 8$$
$$y = 12$$

The lines meet at $(2, 12)$.

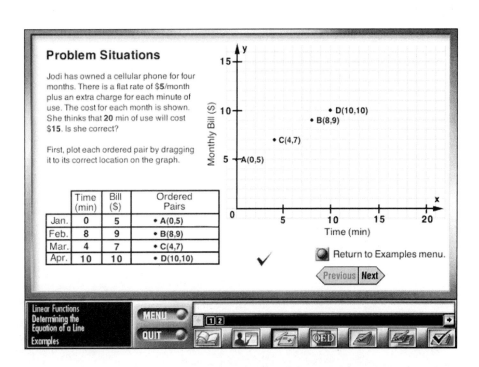

8 LINEAR SYSTEMS

8.1 Solving Linear Systems by Graphing

Cross-References

Linear Systems

Student Workbook: pages 122–125

Key Objectives

The student will:
- find the solution to a pair of linear equations by finding the point of intersection of their graphs.

Key Terms

linear system, independent, collinear, inconsistent, slope, *y*-intercept, *x*-intercept

Prerequisite Skills

- Solve linear equations.
- Graph linear functions.

Lesson Description

This lesson and the next deal with solving systems of linear equations. Here, students graph equations to find the intersection point of the graphs. In the next lesson, students will learn to solve systems algebraically.

In the **Introduction**, students plot stars in the Big Dipper by locating the intersection points for lines that are graphed by the computer. In the **Summary**, students graph equations themselves by identifying and joining *x*- and *y*-intercepts. This time, the intersection points represent stars in the Little Dipper.

The **Tutorial** reviews the nature of linear equations and illustrates that two or more equations graphed together are called a system. Students build a table of values to identify five points on each line and then they plot the lines and find the intersection point. Since this point satisfies both equations, it is a solution to the system. Since there is only one intersection point, there is only one solution.

The **Examples** introduce two other methods that can be used to graph equations:
1. Write each equation in the form $y = mx + b$. Plot the *y*-intercept (b) for one equation and then use the slope (m) to identify another point on the line. Repeat with the other equation.
2. Identify the *x*- and *y*-intercepts of each line. To find the *x*-intercept, let $y = 0$ in the equation. To find the *y*-intercept, let $x = 0$. Plot each line by joining the *x*- and *y*-intercepts.

The **Examples** also demonstrate how to classify systems as independent (one solution), inconsistent (no solution, since the lines are parallel), or dependent (number of solutions is infinite, since the lines are collinear).

In the final section of the **Examples**, students apply their understanding of linear systems as they solve a problem involving money invested at two different rates of interest.

Instructor Intervention

- Before they begin this lesson, students may need to practice isolating linear equations for *y* in terms of *x*. Graphing calculators require that equations be expressed in this form.

- Encourage students to experiment with several different methods of graphing equations, including making a table of values, finding the *y*-intercept and the slope, and finding the *x*- and *y*-intercepts. (These methods are developed in the **Examples**.) Ask: "In what circumstances does each method work well? not so well?"

  Explain that understanding the advantages and disadvantages of these methods makes it possible to solve problems more efficiently.

- Remind students to verify solutions by substituting the coordinates of intersection points into the original equations.

- It is important for students to complete the section "Classifying Systems" in the **Examples**, since this section introduces the three different types of systems (independent, inconsistent, and dependent).

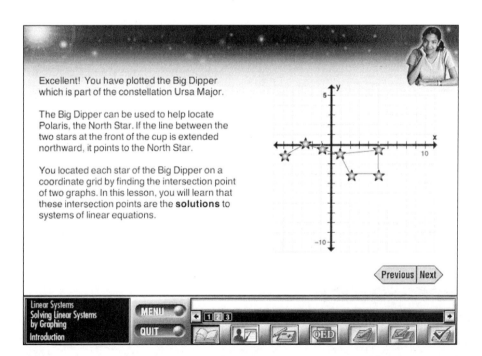

Excellent! You have plotted the Big Dipper which is part of the constellation Ursa Major.

The Big Dipper can be used to help locate Polaris, the North Star. If the line between the two stars at the front of the cup is extended northward, it points to the North Star.

You located each star of the Big Dipper on a coordinate grid by finding the intersection point of two graphs. In this lesson, you will learn that these intersection points are the **solutions** to systems of linear equations.

Previous | Next

Linear Systems
Solving Linear Systems
by Graphing
Introduction

MENU
QUIT

1 2 3

Lesson Components

 Examples

The Slope *y*-Intercept
  Method (1)
Using Intercepts (1)
Verifying Solutions (1)
Classifying Systems (1)
Problem Situations (1)

 Practice and Problems

Identifying Solutions
Number of Solutions
Working Backwards
Error Analysis
Problems

 Extra Practice

Using a Table of Values
Using the Slope *y*-Intercept
  Method
Using Intercepts
Verifying Solutions
Classifying Systems
Problem Situations

✓ **Self-Check**

Using a Table of Values (1)
Using the Slope *y*-Intercept
  Method (2)
Using Intercepts (2)
Verifying Solutions (1)
Classifying Systems (2)
Problem Situations (1)

Minimum score: 7 out of 9

Evaluation

- Have each student generate a system of equations by drawing two intersecting, parallel, or collinear lines on a coordinate grid so each line meets the y-axis at a lattice point. Students can use the slope and y-intercept of each line to write the equation in the form $y = mx + b$.

  Use several of these systems for a class evaluation activity. (You may wish to rewrite some of the equations in different forms.)

  Display the systems you have chosen. Have students solve each system by graphing the equations (without using a graphing calculator) and then have students identify the system as independent, inconsistent, or dependent.

  You may wish to have the students work in pairs, so they can consult with another pair if they cannot agree on a solution.

- Observe the students at work. Can they express an equation in different forms? Can they evaluate equations by substituting values for variables? Do they choose efficient methods for graphing equations? Do they verify each solution by substituting the coordinates into the original equations?

- Write one linear equation on the board and ask the class to supply a second equation so the system will have a single solution, no solution, or an infinite number of solutions. Have students explain their reasoning.

- Hand out cards labeled with linear equations so each student has a different equation. Then write a single linear equation on the board. Have each student determine the solution to the system involving your line and the one described on his or her card. Graphing calculators could be used to verify solutions.

Remediation

- Review these processes.
  (a) Graphing points listed in a table of values.
  (b) Finding the slope and the x- and y-intercepts from an equation in the form $y = mx + b$.

- Point out that in order to graph a straight line, it is only necessary to identify two points. The simplest way to do this is to create a table of values with two different values for x, substitute each value into the equation, and record the resulting value for y each time.

  Students may prefer to use this method not only because it is easier, but also because it can be used in all circumstances.

- Some students may have difficulty substituting values into equations to verify solutions. Some types of graphing calculators remove the need for this step, since they allow students to refer to the "Table" list to scroll down the x-values and find the matching y-values. Encourage students to use this calculator capability to confirm the solutions they read off the graphs on the calculator screen.

- Provide pictures of the three different types of systems, independent, inconsistent, and dependent, for the students to refer to as necessary.

Verifying Solutions

Verify that the solution to the system is $(-3, -2)$.

$$4x - 3y + 6 = 0$$
$$y + 2 = 0$$

Since $(-3, -2)$ **satisfies** both equations, it is the solution to the system.

Left Side	Right Side
$4x - 3y + 6$	0
$= 4(-3) - 3(-2) + 6$	
$= -12 + 6 + 6$	
$= 0$	

Left Side	Right Side
$y + 2$	0
$= -2 + 2$	
$= 0$	

Return to Examples menu.

‹ Previous Next ›

Linear Systems
Solving Linear Systems
by Graphing
Examples

MENU

QUIT

QED

Extension

A

Have students graph two lines on a coordinate grid so they have no solution, one solution, or an infinite number of solutions. Then invite students to use the slope and *y*-intercept of each line to generate the system of equations.

B

Students could create or solve systems that involve three linear equations. What minimum requirements are necessary in order for a three-equation system to be independent?

C

An interest in systems involving three or more linear equations or inequalities could lead to careers in operations research, computer or communications networks, manufacturing systems, or artificial intelligence development.

Students could interview someone who does this type of work or contact a college or university that offers a training course in this area. Searching the topic of "operations research" on the Internet might be a helpful starting point.

D

Inside a computer, simple on/off circuits are used to identify the presence or absence of information. Students could investigate the design of computer systems to find out how graphs and solutions to systems of linear equations might be involved in this process.

Enrichment

A

Students may wish to research the Global Positioning System, which uses satellite radio signals to determine locations on the earth's surface. Ask how this system is related to solving systems of linear equations.

B

Small groups can use multiple copies of a city, regional, or provincial map to play Checkpoint.

1. Label the grid lines on the map to approximate quadrant 1 of a coordinate grid. Number the lines along both axes by 1s, starting at the origin. (The numbers on most maps are between lines, not on them.)

2. Choose a mystery location to be your group's checkpoint. Mark it on a coordinate grid you have drawn on grid paper. (The labels on the axes of your coordinate grid should match the ones on the map.)

3. Identify two lines that pass through your checkpoint so each line meets the *y*-axis exactly at a lattice point and passes through one other lattice point. Use these points to find the slope and *y*-intercept for your lines. Write an equation for each line in the form $y = mx + b$.

4. Check your equations by graphing them with a graphing calculator to make sure they pass through or very close to your checkpoint. If you wish, you can change each equation to a different form.

5. Trade systems with another group. Graph the equations to identify the other group's checkpoint. (Since even a small error can divert a line from the checkpoint, it's best to use a graphing calculator for this part.) Once you have the approximate coordinates of the checkpoint, you can return to the map to identify places in that region.

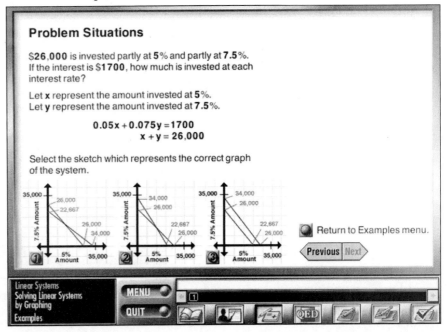

Problem Situations

$26,000 is invested partly at **5%** and partly at **7.5%**. If the interest is **$1700**, how much is invested at each interest rate?

Let **x** represent the amount invested at **5%**.
Let **y** represent the amount invested at **7.5%**.

$$0.05x + 0.075y = 1700$$
$$x + y = 26,000$$

Select the sketch which represents the correct graph of the system.

Return to Examples menu.

Previous | Next

Linear Systems
Solving Linear Systems
by Graphing
Examples

MENU
QUIT

8.2 Solving Linear Systems by Elimination

Cross-References

Linear Systems

Student Workbook: pages 126–129

Key Objectives

The student will:

- solve systems of two linear equations using the algebraic techniques of elimination and substitution.
- solve problem situations that can be modeled algebraically using a system of linear equations.

Key Terms

elimination, substitution, dependent, independent, inconsistent, coefficient, variables, system, linear equations

Prerequisite Skills

- Identify constant terms, coefficients, and variables in polynomial expressions.
- Add and subtract polynomial expressions.
- Solve and verify first-degree, single-variable linear equations.
- Model situations that can be represented by first-degree equations.
- Represent data using linear models.
- Determine the equation of a line.
- Determine the slope and intercepts of the graph of a line.
- Use graphs to solve systems of linear equations.

Lesson Description

This lesson involves solving a system of two linear equations using the algebraic methods of substitution and elimination. A typical system might be: $\begin{cases} 2x - y = 4 \\ 3x + 2y = 6 \end{cases}$

In the **Introduction**, students try to find optimum ticket prices for a concert. Students are guided through the creation of a system of equations whose solution will provide an answer to the problem. Using estimation and a graph of the system, an approximate solution is obtained. The **Introduction** uses a spreadsheet computer model to estimate the ticket prices. In the **Summary**, students return to the problem and solve it algebraically using methods learned in the **Tutorial** and the **Examples**.

In the **Tutorial**, students are presented with systems of equations that vary in difficulty. They are shown both the method of substitution and the method of elimination as algebraic techniques leading to the solution of systems of two linear equations. The problems and solutions in the **Tutorial** also teach the students which of the two methods may be more efficient.

In the **Examples**, students are exposed to systems that are inconsistent and systems that are dependent. They can examine what happens in the algebraic solution of such systems. Graphical solutions of the systems are shown in conjunction with the algebraic solution. The importance of verifying solutions is emphasized in the **Examples**. The last example illustrates how to create and solve a word problem using a system of two equations with two unknowns.

Jim is a promoter for the entertainment firm Best Time Promotions. He is setting the ticket prices for an upcoming rock show that is expected to sell out. It is going to be held in a concert hall that has **2100** seats on the main floor and **2900** seats in the balcony. From experience, Jim knows that the main floor tickets should be **$10.00** more than the balcony tickets. He needs to set the ticket prices so the total revenues will be **$80,000**.

Instructor Intervention

- Review the terms **inconsistent**, **dependent**, and **independent** as they apply to systems of equations (graphical solutions).

- Because systems of linear equations are often used in problem solving, the algebraic modeling of problems may require considerable review.

- Students may benefit from practice in translating word equations to algebraic equations.

- Review the writing of equivalent forms of an algebraic equation.

- In the elimination method, students can either add or subtract equations. More capable students may be comfortable with either addition or subtraction, but weaker students may prefer just one method. Have weaker students practice writing the subtrahend as a statement of opposite terms and then add the two equations.

- Students may at times be unclear about whether to use elimination or substitution. Reassure them that either method is valid. If the equations are arranged so that the same variable in each equation is lined up in the same column, elimination may be the better choice:
  For example: $4x - 5y = 8$
  $\qquad\qquad\quad 3x + y = 1$

- Review the addition and subtraction of like terms so that when the elimination method is used, students will be proficient.

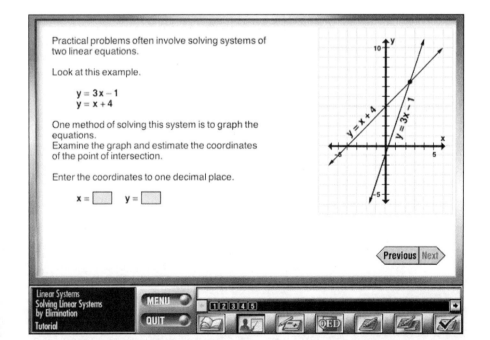

Evaluation

- Have small groups of students find practical problems that can be modeled using a system of equations. Ask each group to post the problems on a bulletin board and challenge the other groups to solve them. Doing a couple of problems a week throughout the year may help in cumulative review.

- Add some mental math exercises.
  - **(a)** Present a complete solution to a system and have students identify where the error occurs.
  - **(b)** Present a system and several ordered pairs of points and have students choose which ordered pair is the solution.
  - **(c)** Present systems that are inconsistent, dependent, or independent and have students identify the type.
  - **(d)** Give one equation in a system and ask students to create a second equation that will produce a system that is inconsistent, dependent, or independent.
  - **(e)** Give one equation in a system along with a point that satisfies the equation and ask students to generate a second equation that will pass through the same point.
  - **(f)** For example, give:
  $$\begin{cases} 3x + 4y = 2 \\ 5x + y = A \end{cases}$$

  Both lines pass through the same point, whose x-coordinate is 2. Find A.

Remediation

- Review the terms **coefficient**, **variable**, and **constant term** as they relate to linear equations such as $4x - 3y = 8$.

- Students need to be efficient at various algebraic substitution techniques. For example:
  Solve for x in the equation $2x + 3y = 7$, if y is 3.

- Students also need to be proficient in working with equations with two variables and solving for one of the variables in terms of the other. For example:
  Solve $3x - 2y = 4$ for y in terms of x.

  If $y = x - 3$, write the expression $3x - 4y$ in terms of x.

- The rearrangement of equations is an important skill in this topic, especially if the method of elimination is to be used efficiently. Have students practice writing equations in forms such as $Ax + By = C$. For example:
  Rearrange $\dfrac{2x - 3}{3} + \dfrac{y + 3}{2} = 1$
  in the form $Ax + By = C$.

- Have students practice simplifying some equations where a common factor exists. For example:
  The expression $3x + 6y = 12$ is the same as $x + 2y = 4$.

- Have students practice multiplying equations by a constant. For example:
  Multiply $2x - 3y = 5$ by -3.

Extension

A

Have students add or subtract two linear equations with two variables creating a third equation in which neither variable is eliminated. Then ask them to graph all three lines. For example:

$$\text{add} \quad \begin{array}{r} 2x + 3y = 8 \\ 4x - 2y = 1 \\ \hline 6x + y = 9 \end{array}$$

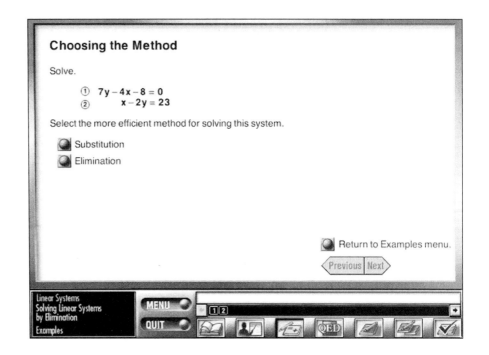

Choosing the Method

Solve.

① $7y - 4x - 8 = 0$
② $x - 2y = 23$

Select the more efficient method for solving this system.

⦿ Substitution
⦿ Elimination

⦿ Return to Examples menu.

‹Previous | Next›

Linear Systems
Solving Linear Systems
by Elimination
Examples

MENU

QUIT

①②

Have students first create "families" of lines that intersect at a common point in this manner and then graph and write the equations of the horizontal and vertical lines that pass through this common point. Ask them to compare the solution of the original system with the equations of the vertical and horizontal lines.

B

Have students investigate cases of systems with three linear equations in two variables. Students should list all the graphical solutions possible with the three equations (for example, having two lines parallel and one line intersecting the other two, or having all three lines parallel). Then ask the students to create algebraic equations that will satisfy each possibility. For example:

$$\begin{cases} 2x - 3y = 7 \\ 2x - 3y = 9 \\ 3x + 4y = 0 \end{cases}$$

Give students two systems that look almost identical, but where only one coefficient is changed.

$$\begin{cases} 7x + 8y = -8 \\ 7x + 8y = -8 \end{cases}$$

$$\begin{cases} 8x + 9y = 18 \\ 8x + 10y = 18 \end{cases}$$

Ask them to solve each one algebraically and explain why the solutions are so vastly different. If graphing calculators are available, students may wish to examine their solutions and compare the systems.

Enrichment

A

Have students solve systems of equations with literal coefficients. Challenge them to create a general formula to solve for either variable. For example:

Solve this system for x.
$$\begin{cases} Ax + By = M \\ Cx + Dy = N \end{cases}$$

Have students apply their formula to some of their previous systems.

If some students have access to a graphing/programmable calcu-

lator, they may wish to try to create a program that will solve a system in this manner. Have them investigate determinants and their connection with linear systems.

Present students with systems such as the following and ask them to find values of A and B that will produce independent, inconsistent, or dependent systems.

$$\begin{cases} 3x + 4y = 5 \\ 2x + Ay = B \end{cases}$$

B

Have students investigate linear systems of three equations and three unknowns and determine whether the algebraic methods of elimination or substitution can be applied.

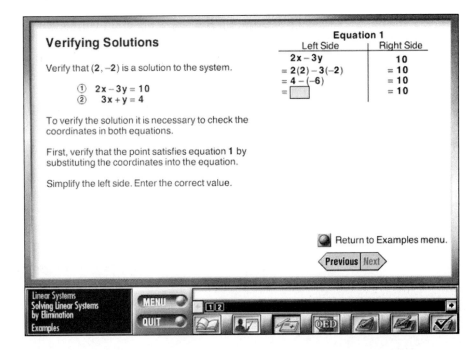

8.3 Solving Three Equations in Three Variables

Cross-References
Linear Systems

Student Workbook: pages 130–133

Key Objectives
The student will:
- solve a system of three linear equations in three variables.

Key Terms
linear equation, solve, slope-intercept form, substitute, system, variable, coefficient, absolute value, common factor, difference of squares, dimension, eliminate, FOIL method, graph, lowest common multiple (LCM), ordered triple, plane

Prerequisite Skills
- Solve and verify linear, single-variable equations.
- Solve systems of linear equations in two variables.

Lesson Description

In this lesson, students learn how to solve a system of three linear equations in three variables using algebraic techniques.

The **Introduction** poses a problem about concert attendance. A promotion company wants to break down a typical audience by age so it can increase profits from sales of concert tickets and T-shirts. Students choose variables to represent three age-group categories and develop three equations based on total attendance, ticket sales, and T-shirt sales. In the **Summary**, students simplify the equations to eliminate decimal values and common factors, and then solve the system using algebraic techniques introduced in the **Tutorial** and **Examples**.

The **Tutorial** begins with two linear equations in two variables. Students consider three ways to solve the system—graphing, elimination, and substitution—and then explore how to use the same methods to solve a system of three linear equations in three variables.

Students learn that an equation with three variables defines a plane in three-dimensional space. The solution of the system is represented by the point(s) of intersection, (x, y, z), of three planes.

The last part of the **Tutorial** shows how to solve a system of three equations algebraically:
- Add or subtract two of the equations in order to eliminate one variable. The result is a new equation.
- Use a similar procedure to eliminate the same variable from a different pair of equations.
- Solve the two new equations as a system of two linear equations in two variables.
- Substitute the values of the two known variables into any of the original equations, then solve for the third variable. Write the solution as an ordered triple.

In the **Examples**, students learn to verify solutions by substitution, and to eliminate one variable by restating it in terms of another. They also explore systems with no solution, systems with an infinite number of solutions, and systems in which one of the three equations has only two variables.

Instructor Intervention

- Reassure students that there are many different ways to find the solution to a system of three linear equations. Point out that equations can be paired in different ways, and that different variables can be targeted for elimination.

  Students should recognize that some paths to the solution will be simpler than others, and that they can simplify the process by choosing to eliminate a variable that has small coefficients in all three equations.

- As students solve systems, they should check to make sure equations are in simplest form. Eliminating common factors may result in easier calculations and fewer errors.

- There are two ways to write solutions. For example, the ordered triple $(3, -5, 6)$ may also be written as $x = 3$, $y = -5$, and $z = 6$. Encourage students to conclude each solution with a sentence that gives the value for each variable. This will help them avoid mismatches as they verify solutions by substitution. Remind them that, in an ordered triple, the variables are usually stated in alphabetical order.

Lesson Components

Examples

Checking Solutions (2)
Substitution Method (1)
No Solution (1)
Infinite Number of Solutions (1)
Missing Variables (1)
Problem Situations (1)

Practice and Problems

First Steps
Eliminating One Variable
Solutions
Error Analysis
Problem Situations

Extra Practice

Select the Solution
First Step
Complete the Question
Solve the System
Problem Situations

Self-Check

Select the Solution (3)
First Step (2)
Complete the Question (2)
Solve the System (2)
Problem Situations (1)

Minimum score: 7 out of 10

A concert promotion company wants to increase its profits from the sale of concert tickets and T-shirts. The promoters believe that by understanding the age breakdown of the audience, they can adjust prices and do a better job of targeting the sale of tickets. In addition, they can order a combination of T-shirt sizes that will match the buying patterns of the audience.

The promoters already have some information about sales at the concerts. They would like to use that information to determine the age characteristics of the audience.

Linear Systems
Solving Three Equations in Three Variables
Introduction

MENU
QUIT

Previous Next

Evaluation

- Present this system of three equations:

  ① $6x + 3y - z = 2$

  ② $4x + 2y + 2z = 4$

  ③ $10x + 3y + 4z = -1$

  Ask:

  (a) Are all three equations in simplest form? If not, how could you simplify them?

  (b) Would you start by eliminating the x-terms, the y-terms, or the z-terms? Explain.

  (c) Suppose you decided to eliminate the y-terms from equations ① and ②. What is the LCM of the two y-coefficients? Are there any other values you could use? Why is it easier to use the LCM than to use these other values?

  (d) Write equations ① and ②. Show how you would eliminate the y-terms from these equations. Then complete the rest of the solution to find the values for x, y, and z. [$x = -2$, $y = 5$, $z = 1$]

  Invite a volunteer to present one possible solution for the class. Discuss variations used by other students. Ask why there are so many different paths to the solution.

- Present some step-by-step solutions that contain errors. Create these solutions yourself or use incorrect solutions taken from previous years' tests or exams. In each case, students are to identify and explain the errors, then correct the solutions.

Remediation

- Students may not remember how to find the lowest common multiple (LCM) for two numbers. Demonstrate with several examples, then present some practice exercises. Remind students that the LCM is always a positive number. For example, the LCM of -8 and 12 is 24, not -24.

- When a student gets the wrong answer, the cause can usually be traced to an algebraic error, rather than to an error in method. Encourage students to review incorrect solutions carefully to look for algebraic errors, and especially for sign errors, rather than simply starting over from the beginning.

- Sign errors are common, especially when students subtract an equation that contains negative terms. For example:

  ①　　　$3x + 2y - z = 25$

  ②　$-\ 3x - 3y + 6z = \ 9$

  　　　　$\boxed{-y}\ - 7z = 16$

The student has inadvertently added the y-terms instead of subtracting.

Encourage the students to avoid subtraction by multiplying the second equation by -1 first, and then adding.

①　　　　　$3x + 2y - z = 25$

② $\times -1\ \underline{+\ -3x + 3y - 6z = \ 9}$

　　　　　　　$5y - 7z = 16$

- Use an open book to show how two planes (facing pages) meet at a line of intersection (the binding). This will help student visualize how two planes could meet and intersect.

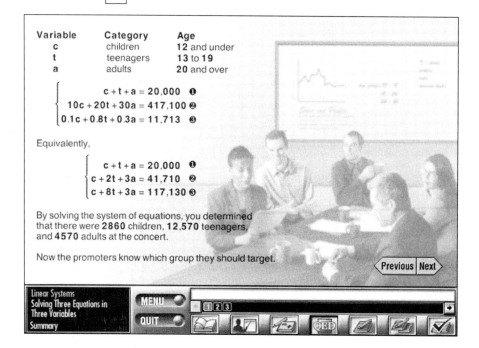

Variable	Category	Age
c	children	12 and under
t	teenagers	13 to 19
a	adults	20 and over

$$\begin{cases} c + t + a = 20{,}000 & ① \\ 10c + 20t + 30a = 417{,}100 & ② \\ 0.1c + 0.8t + 0.3a = 11{,}713 & ③ \end{cases}$$

Equivalently,

$$\begin{cases} c + t + a = 20{,}000 & ① \\ c + 2t + 3a = 41{,}710 & ② \\ c + 8t + 3a = 117{,}130 & ③ \end{cases}$$

By solving the system of equations, you determined that there were **2860** children, **12,570** teenagers, and **4570** adults at the concert.

Now the promoters know which group they should target.

⟨Previous | Next⟩

Linear Systems
Solving Three Equations in Three Variables
Summary

MENU

QUIT

[1][2][3]

Extension

A

Most of the problems in this lesson have integral coefficients and yield integral solutions. Present some systems with rational solutions and invite students to solve them. For example:

(a) $\begin{cases} 2a + 3b + 2c = 1 \\ 3a + 2c = 10 \\ a + b = 1 \end{cases}$

$[a = 3,\ b = -2,\ c = \frac{1}{9}]$

(b) $\begin{cases} 3a + 4b + c = -2 \\ 2a - c = -10 \\ 4b - 4a = 15 \end{cases}$

$[a = -3,\ b = \frac{3}{4},\ c = 4]$

You may also wish to pose problems with rational coefficients or rational terms that have variable denominators.

B

Small groups can conduct an experiment to examine the probability that a set of three equations will have a unique solution. Invite each group to create five systems of random equations, each with three equations in three variables. Have students solve each system to see whether there is one solution, no solution, or an infinite number of solutions.

Groups can combine their data to find out what percent of the systems had a single solution. To show why it is so unlikely that three random equations will have a single solution, use a model like the one shown in the **Tutorial**.

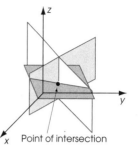

x   Point of intersection

Place three yardsticks to represent the three axes. One way to do this is to lay two of them along the edges of a rectangular table so they cross at the corner, and then hold the third upright so it meets the others. Use a sheet of paper to review the idea that an equation represents the length, width, and height of a plane in three-dimensional space.

Ask three volunteers to hold sheets of paper in various positions within the cubic area bounded by the axes. Discuss why it is much more likely that the planes will not intersect than that they will.

Enrichment

A

Show students how to set up a matrix using a system of three linear equations in three variables. Then, show them how to use a graphing calculator to solve the system.

For more information on matrices, see "Solving Linear Systems by Matrices" and "Solving Linear Systems by Determinants."

B

Students may be interested in learning how to use the determinant to verify that equations represented in a matrix have a unique solution.

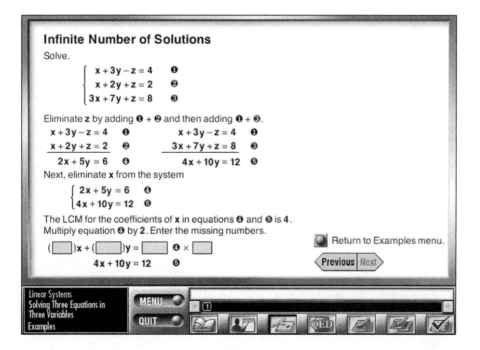

Infinite Number of Solutions

Solve.

$\begin{cases} x + 3y - z = 4 & \text{❶} \\ x + 2y + z = 2 & \text{❷} \\ 3x + 7y + z = 8 & \text{❸} \end{cases}$

Eliminate **z** by adding ❶ + ❷ and then adding ❶ + ❸.

$\begin{array}{ll} x + 3y - z = 4 & \text{❶} \\ \underline{x + 2y + z = 2} & \text{❷} \\ 2x + 5y = 6 & \text{❹} \end{array}$ $\begin{array}{ll} x + 3y - z = 4 & \text{❶} \\ \underline{3x + 7y + z = 8} & \text{❸} \\ 4x + 10y = 12 & \text{❺} \end{array}$

Next, eliminate **x** from the system

$\begin{cases} 2x + 5y = 6 & \text{❹} \\ 4x + 10y = 12 & \text{❺} \end{cases}$

The LCM for the coefficients of **x** in equations ❹ and ❺ is **4**.
Multiply equation ❹ by **2**. Enter the missing numbers.

$(\boxed{})x + (\boxed{})y = \boxed{}$ ❹ × $\boxed{}$

$4x + 10y = 12$ ❺

 Return to Examples menu.

⟨ Previous | Next ⟩

Linear Systems
Solving Three Equations in
Three Variables
Examples

MENU

QUIT

①

8.4 Solving Linear Systems by Matrices

Cross-References

Linear Systems

Student Workbook: pages 134–137

Key Objectives

The student will:

- learn to use matrices to solve systems of linear equations.

Key Terms

extrapolate, array, matrix, row, column, element, augmented matrix, row-echelon form, Gaussian elimination, inconsistent systems, dependent systems

Prerequisite Skills

- Solve linear systems of equations by graphing and by elimination.
- Solve three equations in three variables.

Lesson Description

In the **Introduction**, Jim needs to find the cost of printing 75 programs for the theater club. He knows the cost of printing 20 and 40 programs, and uses this information to make a graph and extrapolate the cost for 75 programs. He is also able to use the graph to estimate the initial cost of setting the type. In the **Summary**, students write expressions to represent the total cost in terms of the number of programs, the cost of printing each program, and the initial type-setting cost. They write a system of two equations in two variables to represent the problem, and solve it using matrices to obtain an exact answer.

The **Tutorial** begins by introducing the various characteristics and components of a matrix. Students learn how matrices can be used to represent systems of equations, and how to apply elementary row operations. The **Tutorial** also shows how to solve systems of equations using Gaussian elimination.

In the **Examples**, students practice and extend what they learned in the **Tutorial**. They solve systems of three equations, and learn about independent and inconsistent systems.

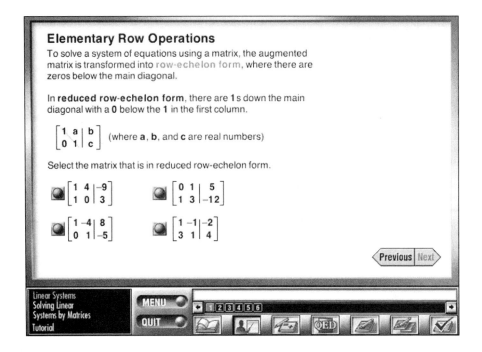

Instructor Intervention

- Post the three elementary row operations for students' reference.

- Working with matrices requires a high level of skill at performing operations with integers. Students should also be proficient at finding the reciprocal of a number.

- Although it is important that students recognize the value of obtaining matrices in row-echelon form, allow them to judge for themselves whether this is the most efficient way to solve a system. Stress that Gaussian elimination is only one of many possible ways of solving systems of equations. An equally valid method is to use matrices to simplify the system, then solve it using substitution.

- The elementary row operations can become complex, and students may forget which operation they are performing. Recording row operations at each step will help keep students on track, and will make it easier to retrace the sequence of steps when checking work.

- Remind students of the meaning of **inconsistent** and **dependent** systems.

  - An inconsistent system has no solution. For example:
    $$\begin{cases} x + y = 1 \\ x + y = 3 \end{cases}$$
    There is no ordered pair (x, y) that will make both equations true. Graphically, inconsistent equations represent parallel lines or parallel planes that never intersect.

  - A dependent system has an infinite number of solutions. For example:
    $$\begin{cases} 2x + 3y = 2 \\ x - y = 5 \end{cases}$$
    Any ordered pair (x, y) that satisfies one equation will be a solution to the system. Graphically, dependent equations represent the same line or plane.

Evaluation

- Now that students know several ways to solve systems of equations, encourage them to analyze systems before solving them to determine the best solution method, rather than relying exclusively on one method. Divide the class into three groups, and present the quiz below. Have each group solve two problems using substitution, two using elimination, and two using Gaussian elimination, so that each problem is solved three ways. Since some questions are very difficult to solve with all methods, allow students to stop their solutions to these problems at a preliminary stage.

1. $\begin{cases} x - 8y = -15 \\ x + 3y = -4 \end{cases}$

2. $\begin{cases} 2x + 3y = 25 \\ x - y = 5 \end{cases}$

3. $\begin{cases} 13x - 17y = 14 \\ 15{,}600x - 20{,}400y \\ = 16{,}800 \end{cases}$

4. $\begin{cases} x = 6 \\ x + y + z = 7 \\ 3x + z = 24 \end{cases}$

5. $\begin{cases} 7x + 14y - 21z = 16 \\ 9x + 40y + 16z = 40 \\ x + 2y - 3z = 12 \end{cases}$

6. $\begin{cases} 9y + \frac{1}{4}x + 3z = 12 \\ 2x - 2y + 2z = -3 \\ x + 3y + \frac{1}{12}z = 4 \end{cases}$

When the groups have completed the quiz, discuss with the class which method was best for each question and why they think so.

Remediation

- Some students may find matrices intimidating because they seem like abstract blocks of numbers. Emphasize the direct connection between a system of equations and its augmented matrix. Work through two parallel solutions of the same system, one solution using the elimination method and the other using an augmented matrix and Gaussian elimination. Point out that the numbers involved in the solutions are identical, but that matrices are simply a cleaner and more efficient way of arriving at the same solution.

- Students with weak numeracy and computation skills may find it easier to choose sequences of row operations that do not introduce fractions. Point out that avoiding fractions will usually produce a simplified system rather than a matrix in row-echelon form.

- Students may have difficulty reducing a row such as [6 3 | 12], which requires multiplying by a fraction. Ask: What number can this row be *divided* by? Then multiply the row by the reciprocal of that number. Similarly, if students have difficulty adding the negative of a row, encourage them to think of the operation as a subtraction first.

Extension

A

Introduce students to a matrix in reduced row-echelon form that has 1s in the main diagonal and 0s as every other element (except those in the constants column). For example, in the system worked in the **Tutorial**, the initial augmented matrix is

$$\begin{bmatrix} 2 & 1 & 5 \\ 1 & -1 & 4 \end{bmatrix}$$

The reduced row-echelon form of the matrix is

$$\begin{bmatrix} 1 & -1 & 4 \\ 0 & 1 & -1 \end{bmatrix}$$

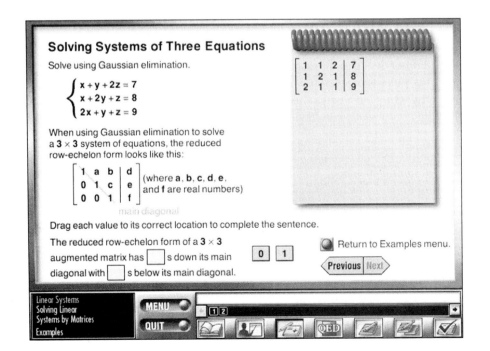

Solving Systems of Three Equations

Solve using Gaussian elimination.

$\begin{cases} x + y + 2z = 7 \\ x + 2y + z = 8 \\ 2x + y + z = 9 \end{cases}$

$\begin{bmatrix} 1 & 1 & 2 & 7 \\ 1 & 2 & 1 & 8 \\ 2 & 1 & 1 & 9 \end{bmatrix}$

When using Gaussian elimination to solve a 3 × 3 system of equations, the reduced row-echelon form looks like this:

$\begin{bmatrix} 1 & a & b & d \\ 0 & 1 & c & e \\ 0 & 0 & 1 & f \end{bmatrix}$ (where a, b, c, d, e, and f are real numbers)

main diagonal

Drag each value to its correct location to complete the sentence.

The reduced row-echelon form of a 3 × 3 augmented matrix has ☐ s down its main diagonal with ☐ s below its main diagonal.

0   1

Return to Examples menu.

Previous Next

Linear Systems
Solving Linear
Systems by Matrices
Examples

MENU
QUIT

Using row operations, the matrix can be further simplified to

$$\begin{bmatrix} 1 & 0 & 3 \\ 0 & 1 & -1 \end{bmatrix}$$

This special version of the reduced row-echelon form directly gives the solution $x = 3$ and $y = -1$ without requiring substitution.

B

In the lesson, students select the equations that represent problem situations from among several choices. Now challenge students to create the equations themselves. Present these problems.

(a) A strawberry grower picked a total of 87 quarts of strawberries in 3 days. On Friday, she picked 15 more quarts than on Thursday. On Saturday, she picked 3 quarts fewer than on Friday. How many quarts of strawberries did she pick each day? [Thursday = 20 quarts, Friday = 35 quarts, Saturday = 32 quarts]

(b) A veterinarian wants to make a food mix for hamsters that contains 18.5 g of protein, 4.9 g of fat, and 13 g of moisture. She has three mixes available. The table shows the amount of protein, fat, and moisture in each mix as a percent of the total weight (in grams) of each mix. How many grams of each mix should she use to get the desired new mix? [50 grams of mix A, 40 grams of mix B, 30 grams of mix C]

Mix	Protein (%)	Fat (%)	Moisture (%)
A	20	2	15
B	10	6	10
C	15	5	5

Enrichment

A

Encourage students to identify patterns in the matrices that indicate whether a system is independent, dependent, or inconsistent. They should notice that:

1. If one row is a multiple of another row, then row operations will result in a row of 0s, indicating a dependent system.
2. If the coefficients in one row are multiples of those in another row, but the constants are not related in the same way, the row operations will give a row of 0s followed by a constant, indicating an inconsistent system.

Students could express the solution to dependent systems graphically. For example, if the final matrix is

$$\begin{bmatrix} 2 & 1 & 4 \\ 0 & 0 & 0 \end{bmatrix}.$$

the system represented is

$$\begin{cases} 2x + y = 4 \\ 0x + 0y = 0 \end{cases}.$$

Therefore, the solution can be represented by the line $2x + y = 4$.

B

Invite students to research the contribution of Arthur Cayley to the development of matrix theory.

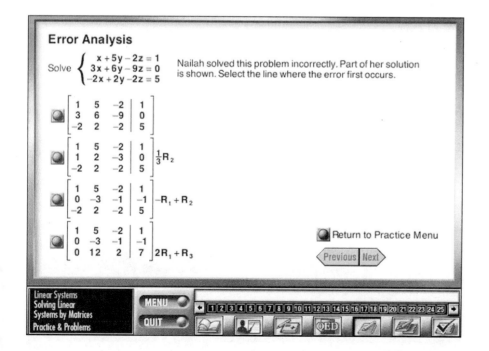

Error Analysis

Solve $\begin{cases} x + 5y - 2z = 1 \\ 3x + 6y - 9z = 0 \\ -2x + 2y - 2z = 5 \end{cases}$

Nailah solved this problem incorrectly. Part of her solution is shown. Select the line where the error first occurs.

$\begin{bmatrix} 1 & 5 & -2 & 1 \\ 3 & 6 & -9 & 0 \\ -2 & 2 & -2 & 5 \end{bmatrix}$

$\begin{bmatrix} 1 & 5 & -2 & 1 \\ 1 & 2 & -3 & 0 \\ -2 & 2 & -2 & 5 \end{bmatrix} \frac{1}{3}R_2$

$\begin{bmatrix} 1 & 5 & -2 & 1 \\ 0 & -3 & -1 & -1 \\ -2 & 2 & -2 & 5 \end{bmatrix} -R_1 + R_2$

$\begin{bmatrix} 1 & 5 & -2 & 1 \\ 0 & -3 & -1 & -1 \\ 0 & 12 & 2 & 7 \end{bmatrix} 2R_1 + R_3$

Return to Practice Menu

Previous | Next

Linear Systems
Solving Linear
Systems by Matrices
Practice & Problems

MENU
QUIT

1 2 3 4 5 6 7 8 9 10 11 12 13 14 15 16 17 18 19 20 21 22 23 24 25

Solving Linear Systems by Determinants

Cross-References

Linear Systems

Student Workbook: pages 138–141

Key Objectives

The student will:

- learn about a mathematical structure called a determinant.
- calculate determinants and use them to solve systems of equations.

Key Terms

array, row, column, coefficient, constant, matrix, square matrix, augmented matrix, coefficient matrix, determinant, minor, elimination, Gaussian elimination, Cramer's rule, inconsistent, dependent, diagonals

Prerequisite Skills

- Solve systems of equations by elimination.
- Solve systems of equations by Gaussian elimination.
- Identify inconsistent systems and dependent systems.
- Understand the terminology of matrices.

Lesson Description

This lesson introduces the concept of a determinant for a square matrix. The students learn how to evaluate a 2×2 and a 3×3 determinant, and they develop and use Cramer's rule to solve systems of equations with two or three unknowns.

In the **Introduction**, a dietitian must mix foods to form a meal that has a prescribed amount of fat, carbohydrates, and protein. The students model the problem with a system of three equations in three unknowns. Although the system could be solved using Gaussian elimination, this method is prone to error because of the numerous operations involved. The motivation for the lesson is to find a less tedious method—Cramer's rule.

The **Tutorial** begins by defining determinants and then uses the definition to develop a formula for evaluating a 2×2 determinant. In the second part of the **Tutorial**, the students learn about minors: the definition of a minor, how to recognize minors, and how to evaluate 3×3 determinants by expanding the minors. In the last part of the **Tutorial**, students develop Cramer's rule and use it to solve a system of two equations in two unknowns.

In the first **Examples** section, students apply Cramer's rule to a 2×2 system of equations. The second section shows how determinants can be used to identify dependent or inconsistent systems of equations. In

Anna is a hospital dietitian. Using only the foods listed in the table, she wants to plan a meal that will supply exactly **14** g of fat, **9** g of carbohydrates, and **9** g of protein. The table shows the nutrient content of **1** oz of each of the foods. How many ounces of each food should the meal include?

Food (1 oz)	Fat (g)	Carbohydrates (g)	Protein (g)
A	2	1	2
B	3	2	1
C	1	1	2

Linear Systems
Solving Linear Systems
by Determinants
Introduction

MENU

QUIT

Previous | Next

the third section, Cramer's rule is extended to a 3×3 system of equations, and in the last section, students solve a problem by forming a system of two equations and solving the system using Cramer's rule.

Instructor Intervention

- Before the lesson, talk with students about the difficulties they've had with solving systems of equations using Gaussian elimination or other algebraic methods.

- The **Introduction** requires students to form an equation from information presented in a table. Some students may need help with this process.

- In the **Practice and Problems** section, it is assumed that students will solve the systems of equations using Cramer's rule rather than any other method. Encourage the students to look back to make sure that their solutions make sense. They could check their answers using any other method of solving systems of equations.

Anna is a hospital dietitian. Using only the foods listed in the table, she wants to plan a meal that will supply exactly **14** g of fat, **9** g of carbohydrates, and **9** g of protein. The table shows the nutrient content of **1** oz of each of the foods. How many ounces of each food should the meal include?

Food (1 oz)	Fat (g)	Carbohydrates (g)	Protein (g)
A	2	1	2
B	3	2	1
C	1	1	2

Let **x** represent the number of ounces of food A.
Let **y** represent the number of ounces of food B.
Let **z** represent the number of ounces of food C.

Using Cramer's rule, you were able to solve the system of equations that represents the problem.

$$\begin{cases} 2x + 3y + z = 14 \\ x + 2y + z = 9 \\ 2x + y + 2z = 9 \end{cases}$$ is solved by **x = 2, y = 3, z = 1**

⟨Previous | Next⟩

Anna's meal should contain **2** oz of food **A**, **3** oz of food **B**, and **1** oz of food **C**.

Linear Systems
Solving Linear Systems
by Determinants
Summary

MENU

QUIT

← 1 2 3 4 →

Evaluation

- Arrange students in groups and have them evaluate a 3×3 determinant by expanding the minors about different rows and columns. See if they can all arrive at the same value for the determinant. Ask students to compare the number of steps involved and the potential for error with the different expansions. They should notice that:
  - Expanding a row or column that contains a 0 is easier to evaluate because it eliminates some terms, resulting in fewer steps.
  - Expanding a row or column that contains a 1 is easier because you don't have to multiply the minor after evaluating it.
  - Expanding a row or column that contains a negative number is more likely to result in sign errors.

- Students could create 2×2 matrices so the determinants will evaluate to a number that you provide. Compare the various matrices and look for patterns.

- Observe students as they work.
  - Do they use the correct pattern of plus/minus signs depending on which row or column they expand?
  - Do they choose the best row or column to expand?
  - Do they recognize when they should use Gaussian elimination and when they should use Cramer's rule?

Remediation

- Review the **Key Terms** listed at the beginning of these teaching notes. You might have students create a bulletin board display explaining Cramer's rule and how to evaluate determinants, and then label the different parts. The display could be modeled on the summary given in the *Student Workbook*.

- Some students may make errors because they have difficulties with integers. Present some simple determinants to evaluate, and then slowly increase the difficulty level. For example, for 2×2 determinants, you could work through these problems in order:

  1. $\begin{vmatrix} 0 & 0 \\ 2 & 3 \end{vmatrix}$ 2. $\begin{vmatrix} 0 & 1 \\ -5 & 2 \end{vmatrix}$

  3. $\begin{vmatrix} 1 & 4 \\ 1 & 3 \end{vmatrix}$ 4. $\begin{vmatrix} 3 & -1 \\ 2 & 1 \end{vmatrix}$

  5. $\begin{vmatrix} 5 & 1 \\ 4 & -2 \end{vmatrix}$ 6. $\begin{vmatrix} -3 & -2 \\ 5 & 6 \end{vmatrix}$

- The **Tutorial** uses the elimination method to develop Cramer's rule. Some students may need to review this method of solving systems of equations. Have the students solve one or two systems using the method of elimination.

- For some problems, students will need to form their own systems of equations from given information. Review how to highlight key words and organize given information in chart form.

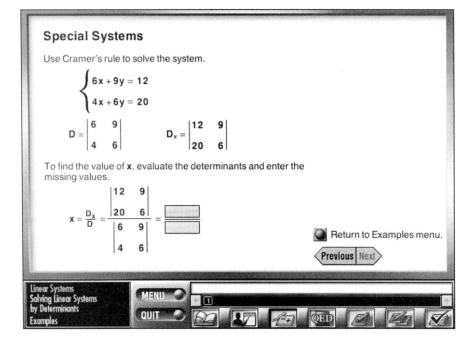

Special Systems

Use Cramer's rule to solve the system.

$$\begin{cases} 6x + 9y = 12 \\ 4x + 6y = 20 \end{cases}$$

$$D = \begin{vmatrix} 6 & 9 \\ 4 & 6 \end{vmatrix} \qquad D_x = \begin{vmatrix} 12 & 9 \\ 20 & 6 \end{vmatrix}$$

To find the value of **x**, evaluate the determinants and enter the missing values.

$$x = \frac{D_x}{D} = \frac{\begin{vmatrix} 12 & 9 \\ 20 & 6 \end{vmatrix}}{\begin{vmatrix} 6 & 9 \\ 4 & 6 \end{vmatrix}} = \boxed{}$$

Return to Examples menu.

Previous | Next

Linear Systems
Solving Linear Systems by Determinants
Examples

MENU

QUIT

Extension

A

Encourage students to extend Cramer's rule to any $n \times n$ system of equations. They could use this information to evaluate 4×4, 5×5, or larger square matrices.

B

Discuss row reduction and ask whether row reduction of a square matrix affects the value of the determinant. Provide a 3×3 determinant for students to evaluate. They could use the elementary row operations to obtain two zeros in any row, and then evaluate by expanding the minors along that row. Then they could try to generalize the results.

C

Present the following information on diagonalized matrices:

- A matrix is in diagonalized form if all the entries not on the main diagonal are zero.

- The rows or columns of determinants that are 3×3 and larger can be row reduced to obtain a diagonalized matrix.

Then ask students to evaluate the determinants.

$$\begin{vmatrix} 2 & 0 & 0 \\ 0 & 3 & 0 \\ 0 & 0 & 4 \end{vmatrix}$$

$$\begin{vmatrix} 1 & 2 & -1 & -2 \\ 2 & 1 & -3 & 0 \\ 2 & -2 & 1 & 1 \\ 1 & -1 & -1 & 2 \end{vmatrix}$$

Ask: Why it is easier to find the determinant of a diagonalized matrix than of a non-diagonalized matrix?

D

Present this system of equations.

$$\begin{cases} x - y = 4 \\ 2x + y = 5 \end{cases}$$

Ask students to solve the system using each of the following methods: graphing, substitution, elimination, matrices (Gaussian elimination), and Cramer's rule. They could list the advantages and disadvantages of each method and try to generalize a pattern for knowing when each method will be most efficient.

Enrichment

A

Give students the opportunity to use a programmable calculator or computer software to enter and evaluate determinants.

B

Invite students to investigate real-life situations involving the evaluation of determinants that arise from large systems of equations. They could ask science and business instructors to help them identify examples from biology, engineering, chemistry, physics, and economics.

C

Students can research and report on the life and research of Gabriel Cramer, developer of Cramer's rule.

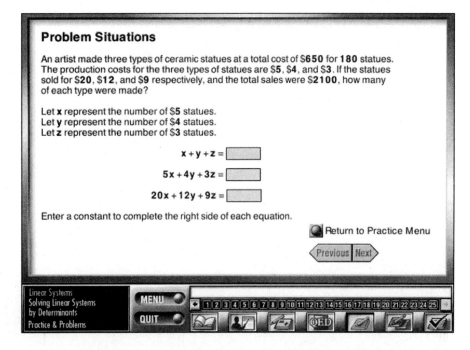

8.6 Solving Systems of Linear Inequalities

Cross-References
Linear Systems

Student Workbook: pages 142–145

Key Objectives
The student will:
- design and solve linear and nonlinear systems of inequalities in two variables.
- model problem situations involving systems of inequalities.

Key Terms
linear inequality, rational inequality, system, hyperbola, quadrant

Prerequisite Skills
- Graph linear inequalities in two variables.
- Solve systems of linear inequalities using technology.

Lesson Description

In this lesson, students will design and solve linear and nonlinear systems of inequalities in two variables. They will also apply these skills to model problem situations.

In the **Introduction**, students investigate an investment problem in which two sums of money are to be invested at different interest rates, with a higher risk associated with the higher rate. Students use tables to look at different combinations of investments. The **Summary** provides a more detailed analysis of the investment possibilities using inequalities and graphs.

The **Tutorial** uses the problem-solving plan to work out a farming problem involving profits for raising chickens and turkeys in which each type of poultry has different selling prices. Students solve such problems involving inequalities by:
1. defining the variable.
2. creating the inequalities to represent the problem.
3. determining the graph of the system.
4. determining the solution by shading the correct intersecting regions of the graph.

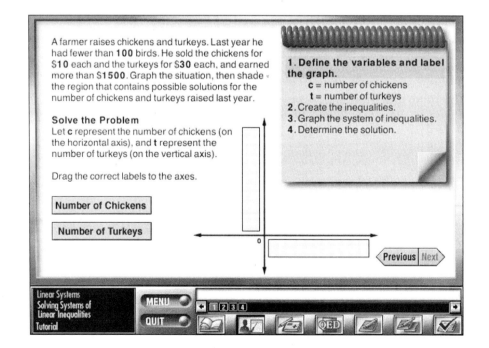

Instructor Intervention

- A review of the steps in the problem-solving strategy may be useful before beginning the lesson:
  Think about the problem: Assemble all the necessary facts.
  Make a plan: Decide on a strategy to solve the problem.
  Solve the problem: Execute your strategy.
  Look back: Check your solution.
  Look ahead: Think about other types of problems that can be solved with the same strategy.

- The **Practice and Problems** section has five problems that are solved in detail by working through the steps from left to right across the board. Remind students of this order, to avoid random selection of questions.

- The **Examples** hidden picture deals with nutrition – a subject that applies inequalities using minimum daily amounts for various nutrients and maximum daily calorie intakes for diet control. Students may be asked to investigate such requirements for a healthy diet and create graphical presentations of their findings.

Lesson Components

Examples
Interpreting Graphs (1)
Graphing Inequalities (1)
Identifying Inequalities (1)

Practice and Problems
Think about the problem.
Make a plan.
Solve the problem.
Look back. Look ahead.

Extra Practice
Determining Boundaries of a System
Determining Inequalities of a System
Determining Solution Points
Graphing Systems

Self-Check
Determining Boundaries of a System (1)
Determining Inequalities of a System (2)
Determining Solution Points (2)
Graphing Systems (1)

Minimum score: 4 out of 6

Interpreting the Graph of a System of Inequalities

Ryan recorded the points he earned in the past hockey season. He obtained a point for scoring a goal or assisting on a goal. The shaded region on Ryan's graph represents all the possible combinations of goals and assists that he could have earned.

Select the true statements. Select **Done** when you have finished.

- Ryan scored less than **50** goals.
- Ryan had less than **30** assists.
- Ryan scored more than **50** goals.
- He had, at most, twice as many goals as assists.
- Ryan had more than **30** assists.
- He had, at most, twice as many assists as goals.

Done

Return to Examples menu.

Previous Next

Linear Systems
Solving Systems of
Linear Inequalities
Examples

MENU
QUIT

Evaluation

- Prepare a transparency of an empty coordinate grid, a transparency covered with red dots, a transparency covered with blue stripes, and a transparency covered with green triangles. Create word problems containing the following types of inequalities and write each word problem on a separate transparency:
  - vertical linear inequality, horizontal linear inequality
  - oblique linear inequality, vertical or horizontal inequality
  - two oblique linear inequalities
  - three oblique linear inequalities
  - nonlinear inequality, oblique linear inequality
  - state the system of the graphed linear inequalities and identify the true statements of the graph's interpretation

Divide the class into groups of three. Display the first problem on the overhead. Student A within the group must attempt to solve the problem for 20 points. Meanwhile, Student B must attempt to solve the problem for 10 points, and Student C must attempt to solve the problem for 5 points.

Using the empty coordinate grid transparency and the colored transparencies (red dots, blue stripes, green triangles) as half-planes, present the solution to the class. Have the students and groups tally their points. Note: If the class does not divide evenly into groups of three, ask the extra students to present the ques-

tions and solutions.

Continue with another question. This time Student B attempts to gain 20 points, Student C attempts to gain 10 points, and Student A attempts to gain 5 points.

After the problems have been solved, survey the total points each student obtained and determine if a specific portion of the lesson should be reviewed.

- Observe the students as they attempt to solve each problem. Can they convert the word problem into the appropriate inequalities? Can they convert each inequality into the appropriate form so it can be graphed? Can the students graph inequalities correctly? Can they determine the system of inequalities that is represented on a graph? Can they interpret the system of inequalities that is represented on a graph?

Remediation

- Review the meaning of the inequality symbols and make a chart of the different word phrases associated with each symbol. For example, >: "is greater than" or "exceeds."

- Some students may have difficulty converting the problem into the appropriate inequalities. Have the students solve word problems involving systems of linear equations. Rewrite the word problems to involve systems of linear inequalities. Discuss how the new problem must be solved differently.

- Some students may have difficulty interpreting a system of inequalities that is represented on a graph. Prepare graphs containing a single linear equation or a single linear inequality, and have the students practice interpreting the information that is represented.

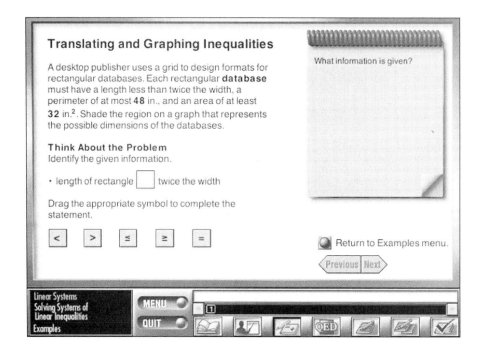

- Determine whether or not any students require assistance in using their graphing calculators to graph linear or nonlinear inequalities.

Extension

A

Challenge students to create graphing questions about real-life events; for example, a time/length graph of the size of a shadow throughout the day or a time/displacement graph of a pendulum or a round-trip flight.

B

Have students research **constraints** and **feasible region** and present how these terms are similar to boundary lines and intersecting regions. Also have them apply these terms to a word problem.

Enrichment

A

Have students describe where systems of linear inequalities are represented in real life: For example, many quilt patterns are based on simple shapes such as squares and triangles.

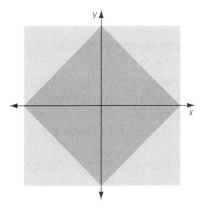

Write the system of inequalities that generate the inner square and each of the triangles on the quilt pattern.

B

Have each student design and color a quilt pattern on a square piece of graph paper and then label each inequality appropriately. These squares could then be displayed on the bulletin board as a class quilt. The designs and corresponding linear inequalities could also reinforce the unique slope features of parallel and perpendicular lines.

C

Have students play a modified version of Battleship by using linear inequalities and the resulting half-planes created to determine the coordinates of the enemy's battleship.

D

Have students role-play a financial advisor/client scenario about possible investment options that are available. (Similar to the **Introduction/Summary** of the lesson.)

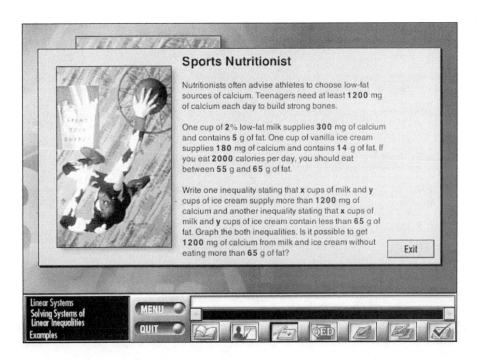

Sports Nutritionist

Nutritionists often advise athletes to choose low-fat sources of calcium. Teenagers need at least **1200** mg of calcium each day to build strong bones.

One cup of **2%** low-fat milk supplies **300** mg of calcium and contains **5** g of fat. One cup of vanilla ice cream supplies **180** mg of calcium and contains **14** g of fat. If you eat **2000** calories per day, you should eat between **55** g and **65** g of fat.

Write one inequality stating that **x** cups of milk and **y** cups of ice cream supply more than **1200** mg of calcium and another inequality stating that **x** cups of milk and **y** cups of ice cream contain less than **65** g of fat. Graph the both inequalities. Is it possible to get **1200** mg of calcium from milk and ice cream without eating more than **65** g of fat?

Exit

Linear Systems
Solving Systems of
Linear Inequalities
Examples

MENU

QUIT

8.7 Linear Programming

Cross-References

Linear Systems

Student Workbook pages 146–149

Key Objectives

The student will:

- solve a linear programming problem.
- use linear programming to answer questions about real-life situations.
- find the best solutions when several conditions have to be met.

Key Terms

constraints, feasible region, corner points, Corner-Point Principle, objective function, optimum solution

Prerequisite Skills

- Graph linear inequalities, in two variables.
- Solve systems of linear equations in two variables.
- Solve, graphically, systems of linear inequalities in two variables using technology.
- Design and solve linear systems, in two variables, to model and solve problem situations.

Lesson Description

In this lesson, students determine optimal solutions to decision-making problems. They learn that they can model many business problems about maximizing profits or minimizing expenses using linear programming.

The **Introduction** presents a problem containing several constraints dealing with radio advertising. Students determine the inequalities expressing two of these constraints, as well as the objective function, and then determine possible solutions. In the **Summary**, students find all six constraints, determine the feasible region of the graph, and find the optimum solution using the Corner-Point Principle.

In the **Tutorial** and the **Examples** students use linear programming. In the **Tutorial** they learn the steps required to solve a problem by using linear programming. They determine two of the constraints, and by inspection, determine the production limits caused by them. Then they write inequalities for all the constraints in the problem. They graph these constraints to determine the feasible region, or all possible solutions to the problem.

Next, they determine the objective function that is to be maximized. They test six points in the feasible region by calculating the value of the objective function for each point. Students observe that the maximum value for the objective function is at a corner point.

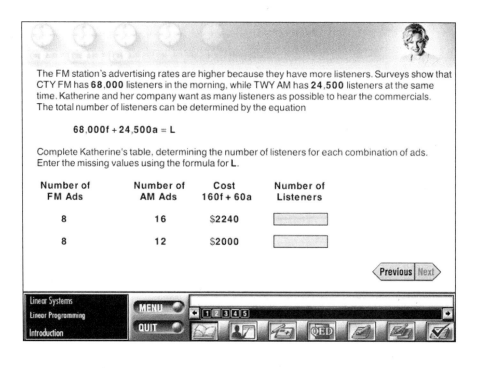

The FM station's advertising rates are higher because they have more listeners. Surveys show that CTY FM has **68,000** listeners in the morning, while TWY AM has **24,500** listeners at the same time. Katherine and her company want as many listeners as possible to hear the commercials. The total number of listeners can be determined by the equation

68,000f + 24,500a = L

Complete Katherine's table, determining the number of listeners for each combination of ads. Enter the missing values using the formula for **L**.

Number of FM Ads	Number of AM Ads	Cost 160f + 60a	Number of Listeners
8	16	$2240	
8	12	$2000	

Previous | Next

Linear Systems
Linear Programming
Introduction

MENU
QUIT

1 2 3 4 5

Instructor Intervention

- If students do not have a graphing calculator, they can use graph paper and a ruler. The lesson provides instructions for manually graphing the systems. Ensure that the students' graphs are correct.

- Students may need help in converting the English phrases in the problem in the **Tutorial** to inequalities, or constraints. Point out that as each constraint is developed, the pertinent phrases in the problem are highlighted. Have students to work in pairs to discuss and develop these constraints.

- Discuss with the students why usually only the first quadrant is used in linear programming. Explain that while, in theory, the origin may be a corner point, in real-life problems, it may not be a feasible solution.

- Before beginning Example 3, engage the class in a discussion regarding the fact that not all corner points may occur at integral values, as shown on the graph. Determine a method to find these corner points. Discuss what to do when fractional values are not realistic solutions (e.g., you can't sell a part of a bicycle).

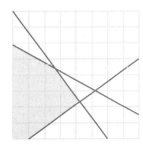

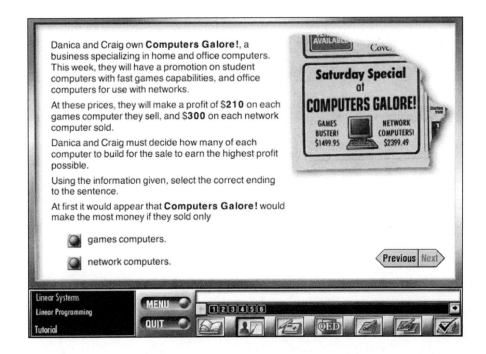

Danica and Craig own **Computers Galore!**, a business specializing in home and office computers. This week, they will have a promotion on student computers with fast games capabilities, and office computers for use with networks.

At these prices, they will make a profit of **$210** on each games computer they sell, and **$300** on each network computer sold.

Danica and Craig must decide how many of each computer to build for the sale to earn the highest profit possible.

Using the information given, select the correct ending to the sentence.

At first it would appear that **Computers Galore!** would make the most money if they sold only

- games computers.
- network computers.

Evaluation

- Use problems similar to the ones in the *Student Workbook* to create a worksheet. Work through at least one of the problems with the class.

As a class, decide on the variables to be used and the axis for each variable.

Have students complete the problem in steps:

1. Determine the constraints.
   (a) In the problem, underline each phrase that defines a constraint.
   (b) Decide on the variables to be used and the axis for each variable.
   (c) Write inequalities for each constraint.

2. Find the feasible region.
   (a) Graph the constraints or inequalities.
   (b) Determine the region of intersection of the inequalities. This is the feasible region.

3. Determine feasible solutions.
   (a) Create a table of the corner points.

4. Find the optimum solution.
   (a) Write an equation for the objective function.
   (b) Evaluate the objective function for each corner point.
   (c) Answer the problem, stating the maximum or minimum value of the objective function and the respective values of the variables.

Students should be given at least one problem where the corner points are not integral values as well as a problem where they must examine points near the corner point to determine solutions.

Check the students' constraints before they graph the feasible region. Check to ensure that their graphs are correct. If students are drawing the graphs, check for accuracy.

Students may work in groups to discuss their answers, agreeing upon one answer before having it checked by the instructor.

Remediation

- Encourage students to use meaningful variables and to label their axes. Discuss with students an appropriate scale to use for each problem, if they are graphing the feasible region manually.

- Students who are having difficulty with setting up the constraints should work with a partner. Have students read aloud the problem to each other, discuss each constraint, and then write the constraint in words before translating it to an inequality. Ask them to check each other's constraints. Before graphing, you may want to verify that the constraints are correct. Using a table to organize the information may help students write the constraints.

- Students who are still experiencing difficulty can refer to the previous lessons on designing and solving linear and non-linear systems.

- Students may wish to use a spreadsheet to evaluate quickly the corner points for the objective function.

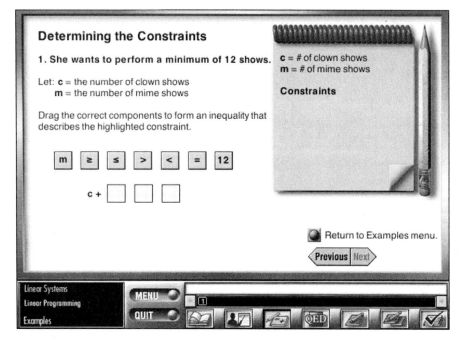

Extension

A

Have students manually graph Problem 2 from the *Student Workbook*:

Determine the feasible region, given the constraints.

Determine the corner points of the feasible region.

Then give the students the following instructions:

1. Complete the table.

2. Graph each objective function using the same grid as the feasible region.

3. For each line, construct two parallel lines—one that is tangent above the feasible region and the other below the feasible region. Each line must pass through a corner point. Evaluate the objective functions for each corner point.

4. Construct two more parallel lines—one that intersects the feasible region and one that does not. Select a point on each line and evaluate the objective function.

5. Compare the values of the objective function for Steps 3 and 4. Ask students: What does it mean when the graph of an objective function does not intersect the feasible region?

Objective Function	Objective Function Value	Objective Function	Slope Intercept Form
$S = x + 2y$	10	$10 = x + 2y$	$y = -\frac{1}{2}x + 5$
$Q = x - 2y$	2	$2 = x - 2y$	$y = \frac{1}{2}x - 1$

B

Have students go back to Problem 1 from the *Student Workbook* (or give them a similar question):

Given the constraints: $x \geq 0$; $y \geq 0$; $x + 5y \leq 45$; $3x + 5y \leq 55$; $3x + 2y \leq 40$, what is the maximum value for the objective function $C = 3x + 5y$?

Students will notice that the solution is a complete line segment between two corner points $(5, 8)$ and $(10, 5)$. The maximum value is 55 for each point on the line segment.

For each of the five problems in the *Student Workbook*, after students have arrived at an answer, ask them to modify one of the constraints, change the objective function, or add more information as in the Look Ahead problems in the **Practice** section. Have students provide answers to these new problems.

Alternatively, have students modify the problem as above, and present the new problem to the class to solve.

Enrichment

A

Have students research a business, industry, or any other area where linear programming could help with business decisions. Challenge them to make up two questions using information they have learned. The students should pose their questions clearly, giving pertinent and interesting information about the company. The objective functions should be realistic.

Ask the students to provide clear and complete solutions to each of their questions on a separate sheet of paper. The axes should be labeled, and the scale appropriate to the problem.

Some students may wish to extend their questions, simulating a look into the future of the business, where one or more constraints or the objective function will change. Alternatively, they may wish to interpret the solutions and add additional information, similar to the last problem in **Practice and Problems**.

The students can exchange questions. Either the solution can be made available for them to check their own work or the student who created the question can check other students' solutions.

9 FUNCTIONS

9.1 Functions and Operations

Cross-References
Functions

Student Workbook: pages 150–153

Key Objectives
The student will:
- add, subtract, multiply, and compose functions.

Key Terms
dependent variable, independent variable, equation, function, relation, domain, range, ordered pair, table, graph, Vertical Line Test, function notation, coefficient, like terms, composition of functions, commutative

Prerequisite Skills
- Describe a function in terms of ordered pairs, a rule, and a graph.
- Use function notation to evaluate and represent functions.

Lesson Description

In the **Introduction**, the surface temperature of Mars, 208 K, is converted to degrees Fahrenheit. Students first convert from kelvins to degrees Celsius, and then from degrees Celsius to degrees Fahrenheit. In the **Summary**, students compose the two conversion formulas to create a single formula for converting directly from kelvins to degrees Fahrenheit.

The **Tutorial** reviews function notation and the various ways to represent a function: as an equation, a set of ordered pairs, a table, and a graph. Students then learn how to add and subtract functions, first using a graphical method, then algebraically. The **Tutorial** also discusses methods for multiplying and composing functions.

The first three **Examples** sections provide practice with the skills learned in the **Tutorial**. Students then use their knowledge to perform combinations of operations on functions. The last section explores some practical situations that require these operations.

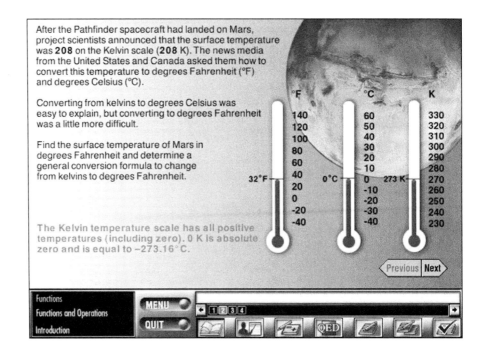

After the Pathfinder spacecraft had landed on Mars, project scientists announced that the surface temperature was **208** on the Kelvin scale (**208** K). The news media from the United States and Canada asked them how to convert this temperature to degrees Fahrenheit (°F) and degrees Celsius (°C).

Converting from kelvins to degrees Celsius was easy to explain, but converting to degrees Fahrenheit was a little more difficult.

Find the surface temperature of Mars in degrees Fahrenheit and determine a general conversion formula to change from kelvins to degrees Fahrenheit.

The Kelvin temperature scale has all positive temperatures (including zero). 0 K is absolute zero and is equal to −273.16°C.

Instructor Intervention

- Discuss the differences between a function and a non-function. (See the lessons "Differences Between Relations and Functions" and "Describing Functions.")

- Demonstrate how to evaluate functions using function notation. (See the lesson "Function Notation.")

- Demonstrate how composing functions involves finding a function of a function. Make sure students understand the order in which the functions are evaluated in a composition, and relate this order to the notation $f(g(x))$ or $g(f(x))$.

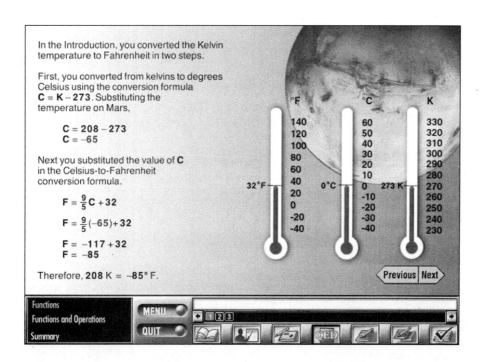

In the Introduction, you converted the Kelvin temperature to Fahrenheit in two steps.

First, you converted from kelvins to degrees Celsius using the conversion formula **C = K − 273**. Substituting the temperature on Mars,

C = 208 − 273
C = −65

Next you substituted the value of **C** in the Celsius-to-Fahrenheit conversion formula.

$F = \frac{9}{5}C + 32$

$F = \frac{9}{5}(-65) + 32$

F = −117 + 32
F = −85

Therefore, **208** K = **−85°** F.

Functions
Functions and Operations
Summary

MENU
QUIT

Previous | Next

Evaluation

- Ask students to graph linear functions and simple quadratic functions. On the graphs, have them draw vertical lines representing the height of the graph (i.e., the value of the function) at specific x-values. The functions can be added, subtracted, and multiplied by adding, subtracting, or multiplying the lengths of the lines and graphing the results on a new grid. Students could compare the graphs of the sum, difference, and product to the graphs of the original functions.

- Present various real-life situations that involve composition of functions. You could refer to the example from the **Introduction**, or one of the problems in the *Student Workbook*. Discuss with students how to compose functions so the resulting function correctly expresses the desired relationship.

Remediation

- Some students may need to review how the concepts of domain and range relate to a function graph before they are able to undertake the graphical manipulations in the lesson.

- Evaluating functions requires skill in combining functions using specific values of x and in substituting expressions into a function. Allow students to practice their arithmetic and algebra skills by providing functions to evaluate.

Extension

A

Challenge students to develop a model for graphing the division of functions. What special care must be taken with the domain and range? [divisor cannot equal 0] Can any two functions be divided? [cannot divide by a function that is equal to 0] What would happen to the quotient when the denominator function equals 0? [the value of the quotient is undefined] How could this situation be represented on a graph of the quotient? [a point of discontinuity or an asymptote]

B

Students could explore how they might use the vertical lines mentioned in the **Evaluation** section to compose functions. Discuss how the range value

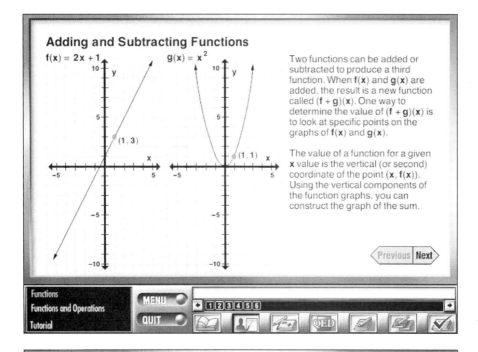

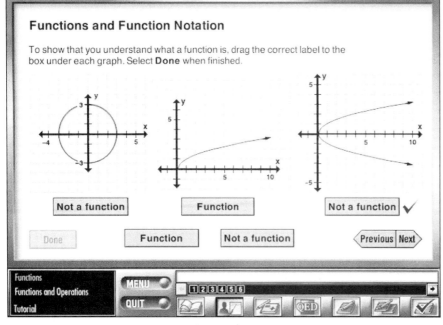

(the *y*-value) of the "inner" function becomes the domain value (the *x*-value) of the "outer" function. How can they show this on a graph of the composition? Use limited domains and ranges and then ask students to compare the domains and ranges of the graphs.

C

Use graphing calculators or computer graphing software to investigate all types of function operations. For a pair of functions, students should graph each one individually and then graph their sum, difference, product, quotient, and composition (both ways), to contrast and compare.

D

Ask students to search for pairs of functions that can be composed so that $f(g(x)) = x$. Relate this to simple inverse operations such as multiplication by 2 followed by division by 2, squaring a square root, and so on.

Enrichment

A

Explore the types of functions that result from certain combinations. For example, what type of function results from the sum or difference of two linear functions? [linear function] the product of two linear functions? [quadratic function] What results when a linear function and a quadratic function are composed? [quadratic function] How does the order of composition affect the result? [degree of function will not be affected; coefficients and constants will be different] Students

could create a table of their results and predict the degree of the resulting polynomial function.

B

Students can research the history of functions in mathematics. Why are functions an important concept? How did function notation develop? Who were the major contributors to the development of function theory?

C

Students can explore other types of functions, such as absolute value functions, greatest integer functions, and step functions. How can these types of functions be added, multiplied, or composed? What does the result look like? Students may not know how to analyze these functions algebraically, so a graphical analysis may be necessary.

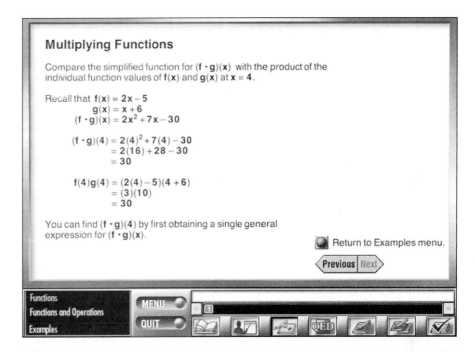

Multiplying Functions

Compare the simplified function for $(f \cdot g)(x)$ with the product of the individual function values of $f(x)$ and $g(x)$ at $x = 4$.

Recall that
$$f(x) = 2x - 5$$
$$g(x) = x + 6$$
$$(f \cdot g)(x) = 2x^2 + 7x - 30$$

$$(f \cdot g)(4) = 2(4)^2 + 7(4) - 30$$
$$= 2(16) + 28 - 30$$
$$= 30$$

$$f(4)g(4) = (2(4) - 5)(4 + 6)$$
$$= (3)(10)$$
$$= 30$$

You can find $(f \cdot g)(4)$ by first obtaining a single general expression for $(f \cdot g)(x)$.

Return to Examples menu.

Previous Next

Functions
Functions and Operations
Examples

MENU
QUIT

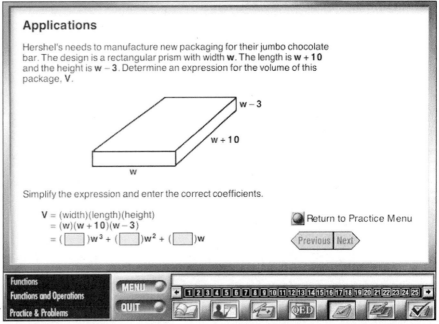

Applications

Hershel's needs to manufacture new packaging for their jumbo chocolate bar. The design is a rectangular prism with width **w**. The length is **w + 10** and the height is **w − 3**. Determine an expression for the volume of this package, **V**.

Simplify the expression and enter the correct coefficients.

$$V = (\text{width})(\text{length})(\text{height})$$
$$= (w)(w + 10)(w - 3)$$
$$= (\boxed{})w^3 + (\boxed{})w^2 + (\boxed{})w$$

Return to Practice Menu

Previous Next

Functions
Functions and Operations
Practice & Problems

MENU
QUIT

9.2 Inverse Functions

Cross-References
Functions

Student Workbook: pages 154–157

Key Objectives
The student will:
- find the inverse of a function algebraically.
- find the inverse of a function graphically.
- show that two functions are inverses of each other.
- determine whether the inverse of a function is a function.
- evaluate an inverse for a value.

Key Terms
function, inverse, domain, range, Vertical Line Test, Horizontal Line Test, one-to-one correspondence

Prerequisite Skills
- Describe a function in terms of ordered pairs, a rule, and a graph.
- Recognize differences between relations and functions.
- Use function notation to evaluate and represent functions.
- Determine the domain and range of a relation from its graph.
- Perform operations on functions and compose functions.
- Solve literal equations.
- Recognize when an answer should include only the positive (principal) square root and when it should include both positive and negative square roots of a number.

Lesson Description

In this lesson, students learn about inverse functions. They learn how to find and evaluate inverses.

In the **Introduction**, students restate the temperature equation $F = \frac{9}{5}C + 32$ in terms of C to convert 86°F to degrees Celsius. Once they have the inverse equation, $C = \frac{5}{9}(F - 32)$, they can make the conversion simply by substituting 86° for F and solving for C. In the **Summary**, students replace F and C in the two equations with function notation. By composing the functions both ways, they discover that the two functions are inverses of each other.

The **Tutorial** begins with a brief review of the concept of inverse operations. Students explore the concept of the inverse of a relation by interchanging the x- and y-values in a table of ordered pairs, and then finding the inverse of a linear function algebraically (by interchanging x and y and solving for y). By examining the graph of a function and its inverse, students learn how to determine whether the inverse is also a function.

In the **Examples**, students practice finding inverses algebraically and graphically and also examine other characteristics of inverses. They determine whether two functions are inverses of each other, and discover that the domain of a function becomes the range of the inverse. They also learn how to evaluate an inverse for a particular value.

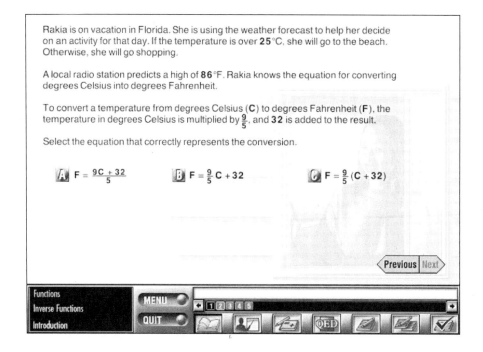

Rakia is on vacation in Florida. She is using the weather forecast to help her decide on an activity for that day. If the temperature is over **25°C**, she will go to the beach. Otherwise, she will go shopping.

A local radio station predicts a high of **86°F**. Rakia knows the equation for converting degrees Celsius into degrees Fahrenheit.

To convert a temperature from degrees Celsius (**C**) to degrees Fahrenheit (**F**), the temperature in degrees Celsius is multiplied by $\frac{9}{5}$, and **32** is added to the result.

Select the equation that correctly represents the conversion.

A $\quad F = \frac{9C + 32}{5}$ $\qquad$ B $\quad F = \frac{9}{5}C + 32$ $\qquad$ C $\quad F = \frac{9}{5}(C + 32)$

Previous | Next

Functions
Inverse Functions
Introduction

MENU
QUIT

Instructor Intervention

- Before starting the lesson, introduce students to the concept of inverse functions by having them do this exercise in pairs:

  Ask one partner to make a list of ordered pairs for the function $f(x) = 2x + 12$, while the other partner makes a list of ordered pairs for the function $g(x) = \dfrac{x - 12}{2}$. Ask students what they notice about the two lists. Students could graph each function and examine how the lines are related.

- Students may need additional explanation for the example "Evaluate an Inverse." Explain that since $f(2)$ means "find the value of y when $x = 2$," $f^{-1}(2)$ means "find the value of x when $y = 2$." This is why, to find $f^{-1}(2)$, you can set $f(x)$ equal to 2 and solve for x.

- Make sure that students don't interpret $f^{-1}(x)$ as $\dfrac{1}{f(x)}$. Explain that $f^{-1}(x)$ is a symbol that represents the inverse of the function $f(x)$.

- Only set notation is used in this lesson. Interval notation could also be demonstrated for the students. For example, $[-2, 3)$.

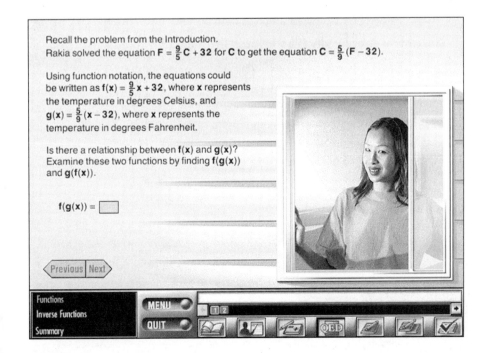

Recall the problem from the Introduction.
Rakia solved the equation $F = \frac{9}{5}C + 32$ for C to get the equation $C = \frac{5}{9}(F - 32)$.

Using function notation, the equations could be written as $f(x) = \frac{9}{5}x + 32$, where x represents the temperature in degrees Celsius, and $g(x) = \frac{5}{9}(x - 32)$, where x represents the temperature in degrees Fahrenheit.

Is there a relationship between $f(x)$ and $g(x)$? Examine these two functions by finding $f(g(x))$ and $g(f(x))$.

$f(g(x)) = \boxed{}$

Previous | Next

Functions
Inverse Functions
Summary

MENU
QUIT

Evaluation

- Students could play Guess that Number. One partner thinks of a secret number, n, applies several operations to it, and tells the other partner the operations that were used and the result. The other partner uses this information to try to find the secret number. The pair should find an equation to represent the problem, a function to represent the operations, and the inverse of the function. They could also graph each equation and its inverse. For example one student could start with:

"I have a secret number. If you add 5, take the square root of the result, and then subtract 4, the result is –2. What is my secret number?" Then the equation would be

$-2 = \sqrt{n+5} - 4, \quad n = -1$, the function would be

$f(n) = \sqrt{n+5} - 4$, and the inverse function would be

$f^{-1}(x) = (x+4)^2 - 5, \quad x \geq -4$.

Observe students as they play the game. Can they accurately translate from English to algebra and vice versa? Are they isolating the unknown correctly? Are they using the correct notation for the original function and its inverse? Are students trying to plot some inverse points from the original graph first? How many students graph the inverse using the algebraic form and a table of values, and how many try to reflect the original function over the line $y = x$?

Remediation

- Students may have difficulty finding the inverse of a rational function such as

$f(x) = \dfrac{x+1}{x-3}$. Provide a step-by-step solution with explanatory notes. For example, to find the inverse of the given function:

$$y = \frac{x+1}{x-3} \qquad \text{①}$$

$$x = \frac{y+1}{y-3} \qquad \text{②}$$

$$x(y-3) = (y+1) \qquad \text{③}$$

$$xy - 3x = y + 1 \qquad \text{④}$$

$$xy - y = 3x + 1 \qquad \text{⑤}$$

$$y(x-1) = 3x + 1 \qquad \text{⑥}$$

$$y = \frac{3x+1}{x-1} \qquad \text{⑦}$$

① Change the function notation to y.
② Interchange x and y.
③ Multiply to remove the fraction.
④ Expand.
⑤ Collect the terms containing y on one side.
⑥ Factor out y.
⑦ Isolate y.

- Some students may have difficulty composing two functions to show that they are inverses. Review composition of functions.

- Students who have trouble reflecting over the line $y = x$ could create a design on a coordinate grid and then sketch the inverse by:

  (a) using a MIRA on the line $y = x$ to see the reflection.

  (b) folding the paper over the line $y = x$ and tracing the design on the other side of the paper. When the students unfold the paper, a copy of the design will have been reflected over the line $y = x$.

They could also use either method to sketch the inverse of linear functions that they create.

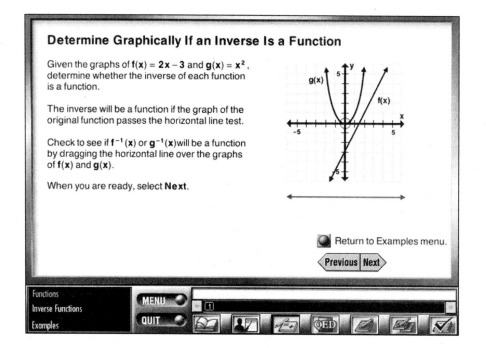

Determine Graphically If an Inverse Is a Function

Given the graphs of $f(x) = 2x - 3$ and $g(x) = x^2$, determine whether the inverse of each function is a function.

The inverse will be a function if the graph of the original function passes the horizontal line test.

Check to see if $f^{-1}(x)$ or $g^{-1}(x)$ will be a function by dragging the horizontal line over the graphs of $f(x)$ and $g(x)$.

When you are ready, select **Next**.

Return to Examples menu.

Previous | Next

Functions
Inverse Functions
Examples

MENU
QUIT

Extension

A

Go back to the Guess that Number game (see **Evaluation**) and ask students if inverses can be used to find the secret number more quickly. Students should see that substituting the result from the first equation into the inverse function gives the secret number.

B

Students have learned that a function is a one-to-one correspondence if there is only one y-value for each value of x. If a function is a one-to-one correspondence, then its inverse will also be a function. Ask: For a function that is not one-to-one, how can you restrict the domain so that its inverse will be a function? [For any y-value that corresponds to more than one x-value, exclude from the domain all but one of those x-values.]

C

Ask students to find examples of relations whose inverses map onto themselves. [For example,

$y = x$, $y = \dfrac{1}{x}$, $y = -x$, and

$y = -x + 3$.]

Enrichment

A

Students could research how functions are used in any application that interests them. They should state the original function, explain how it is used, find the inverse, and determine whether it is also a function. For example, the formula that is used when matter is converted into energy is $E = mc^2$, where E is the energy in joules, m is the mass of the matter in kilograms, and c is the speed of light (2.998×10^8 m/sec). The inverse is

$E = \dfrac{m}{c^2}$,   which is also a

function.

B

Challenge students to find where a relation and its inverse intersect. They could do this for several relations, then ask: Is it possible to know, without drawing the inverse, where a relation and its inverse will intersect? Students should notice that a graph and its inverse always intersect at points where the x- and y-coordinates are the same; that is, the points of intersection are always along the line $y = x$.

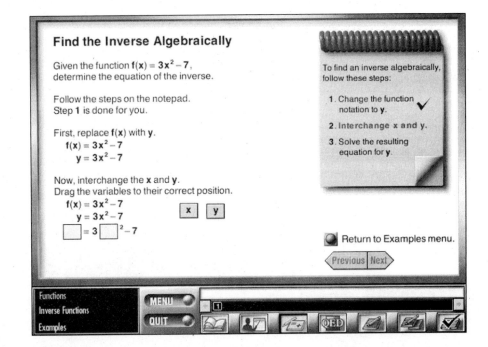

Find the Inverse Algebraically

Given the function $f(x) = 3x^2 - 7$, determine the equation of the inverse.

Follow the steps on the notepad. Step 1 is done for you.

First, replace $f(x)$ with y.
  $f(x) = 3x^2 - 7$
    $y = 3x^2 - 7$

Now, interchange the x and y. Drag the variables to their correct position.
  $f(x) = 3x^2 - 7$
    $y = 3x^2 - 7$ $\boxed{x}$ $\boxed{y}$
  $\boxed{} = 3\boxed{}^2 - 7$

To find an inverse algebraically, follow these steps:

1. Change the function notation to **y**. ✓

2. Interchange **x** and **y**.

3. Solve the resulting equation for **y**.

Return to Examples menu.

⟨Previous⟩ ⟨Next⟩

Functions
Inverse Functions
Examples
MENU
QUIT
1

Graphs of Quadratic Functions

Cross-References
Functions

Student Workbook: pages 158–161

Key Objectives
The student will:
- identify characteristics of graphs of quadratic functions.
- use these characteristics to solve problems.

Key Terms
parabola, quadratic function, degree, vertex, symmetry, maximum, x-intercept, y-intercept, domain, range, set builder notation, concavity

Prerequisite Skills
- Describe a function in terms of ordered pairs, a rule, and a graph.
- Determine the domain and range of a relation.

Lesson Description

In this lesson, students learn how to identify the characteristics of the graph of a quadratic function and use these characteristics to solve problems.

In the **Introduction**, Henry learns that the NASA Sojourner's initial bounce as it landed on Mars followed a parabolic path defined by the function $y = -0.0015x^2 + 0.3x$. He graphs the function and notices that the range of the graph must be limited in order for the graph to accurately represent the problem, since the bounce height can't be negative. Then he labels the initial point, the highest point, and the final point on the curve, but he does not know how to continue analyzing the graph. In the **Summary**, he completes his analysis using the correct terminology.

In the first part of the **Tutorial**, students learn about the connection between parabolas and quadratic functions, and practice identifying quadratic functions. Then they graph a quadratic function using a table of values, and examine each characteristic of the graph, including the vertex (and direction of opening), the axis of symmetry, the intercepts, and the domain and range.

The **Examples** expand on knowledge gained in the **Tutorial**, and then synthesize the information in two problem situations involving quadratic functions. The first problem is about a trampolinist whose path in the air is defined by the function $y = -16x^2 + 32x + 2$. The students need to determine her maximum height, the time it took to

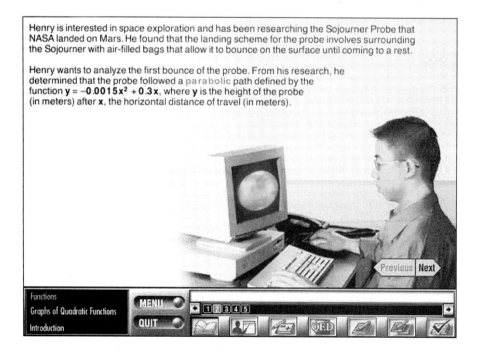

Henry is interested in space exploration and has been researching the Sojourner Probe that NASA landed on Mars. He found that the landing scheme for the probe involves surrounding the Sojourner with air-filled bags that allow it to bounce on the surface until coming to a rest.

Henry wants to analyze the first bounce of the probe. From his research, he determined that the probe followed a parabolic path defined by the function **y = –0.0015x² + 0.3x**, where **y** is the height of the probe (in meters) after **x**, the horizontal distance of travel (in meters).

Previous | Next

Functions
Graphs of Quadratic Functions
Introduction

MENU
QUIT

1 2 3 4 5

reach the maximum height, and the total time she was in the air. The second problem involves finding two numbers with a given difference and a minimum product.

Instructor Intervention

- Before students begin this lesson, make sure they can all plot functions using a graphing tool such as a graphing calculator. They should be able to change the domain and range, zoom in/out, and use the trace buttons to identify the coordinates of various points on the graph.

- Make sure students can develop graphs from quadratic functions given in these forms:
  (a) $y = a(x - h)^2 + k$
  (b) $y = ax^2 + bx + c$
  (c) $y = (x - g)(x - h)$ or $x(x - g)$

- Encourage students to work in pairs while using graphing tools. By working together, students can pool their knowledge to suggest better domain and range changes to find the vertex and intercepts of the functions. The partners can also help each other avoid typing mistakes when entering the different parameters and forms of the equation.

- It may be useful to model the different types of maximum/minimum problems that students will face. Reinforce that students should follow the problem-solving model, and that if they are stuck on a particular step of the model, they should seek help before continuing to the next step.

Lesson Components

🗇 Examples
Maximum/Minimum (1)
Axis of Symmetry (1)
Intercepts (1)
Domain and Range (1)
Problem Situations (2)

📓 Practice and Problems
Identifying Characteristics
Communication
Error Analysis
Function Comparisons
Problem Situations

🖻 Extra Practice
Exploring the Quadratic
The Intercepts
Domain/Range
Problem Situations

☑ Self-Check
Exploring the Quadratic (2)
The Intercepts (2)
Domain/Range (2)
Problem Situations (2)

Minimum score: 6 out of 8

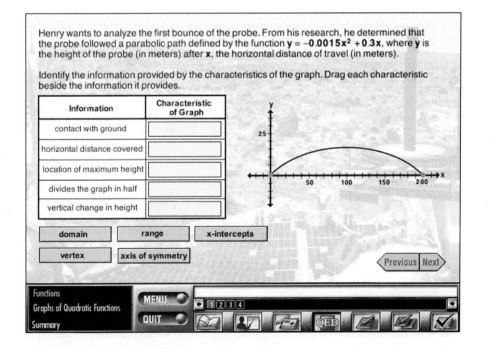

Henry wants to analyze the first bounce of the probe. From his research, he determined that the probe followed a parabolic path defined by the function **y = –0.0015x² + 0.3x**, where **y** is the height of the probe (in meters) after **x**, the horizontal distance of travel (in meters).

Identify the information provided by the characteristics of the graph. Drag each characteristic beside the information it provides.

Information	Characteristic of Graph
contact with ground	
horizontal distance covered	
location of maximum height	
divides the graph in half	
vertical change in height	

domain range x-intercepts
vertex axis of symmetry

Previous | Next

Functions
Graphs of Quadratic Functions
Summary

MENU
QUIT
1 2 3 4

Evaluation

- Divide the class into pairs. Ask each pair to graph a quadratic function and identify these characteristics:
  - ◆ direction of opening
  - ◆ maximum/minimum value
  - ◆ vertex
  - ◆ equation of the axis of symmetry
  - ◆ x- and y-intercepts
  - ◆ domain and range

  Each pair could present their graph and its characteristics to the class.

- Observe students as they complete the lesson activities. Can they understand the relationship between the graph, the equations, and the characteristics? Can they create graphs from quadratic functions given in various forms? Can they use a problem-solving model to solve word problems that involve maximum/minimum or intercept answers?

Remediation

- Review how to expand different forms of quadratic functions (listed in **Instructor Intervention**) to put them into general form, $y = ax^2 + bx + c$.

- Review graphing linear and nonlinear functions with a graphing tool, as well as with a table of values. Some students may have difficulty finding the vertex on a graphing tool. Provide practice with working with the zoom out/zoom in feature and the trace feature.

- Students may have difficulty writing the equations of vertical lines. Draw a vertical line on a coordinate grid and have students create a table of values for points on this line. Point out that the x-coordinate is the same for every point on that line, so the equation is $x =$ "x-coordinate of each point." Link this to the fact that knowing only one point on a vertical line allows you to write the equation of the line. Since the axis of symmetry is a vertical line passing through the vertex, knowing the coordinates of the vertex makes it easy to write the equation of the axis of symmetry.

Extension

A

Students could create a web showing the relationships

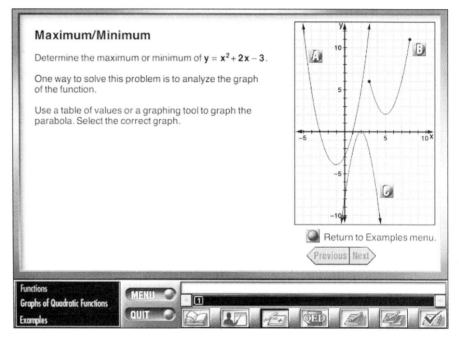

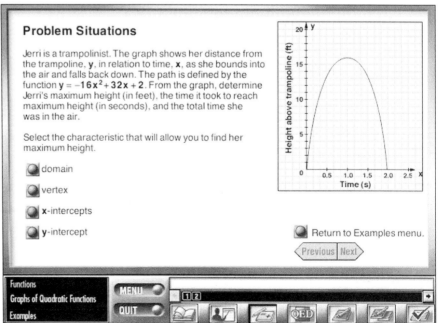

between characteristics of quadratics and identify when they can find other characteristics if given only a few. For example, ask: If you are given only the direction of opening and the vertex, what else can you find?

B

Ask students to sketch parabolas that meet certain restrictions. Start by having only one restriction, for example, by asking for any parabola with a vertex in quadrant I. You could keep adding more specific restrictions until the result is one particular graph. Encourage students to combine restrictions in various ways to find which restrictions can occur together and which cannot. For example:

- The restrictions "opens down" and "has a minimum value" cannot both be true for the same graph.

- If a parabola has a vertex above the x-axis and an unrestricted domain, it must have two x-intercepts if it opens down, but it cannot have any x-intercepts if it opens up.

Challenge students to describe as many characteristics as possible from a quadratic equation without looking at the graph. Can they identify the direction of opening, the maximum/minimum value, the vertex, the domain and range, and so on?

Enrichment

A

Ask how the general form, $y = ax^2 + bx + c$, could be used to find:

(a) the y-intercept.
(b) the direction in which the parabola opens.

For (a), students simply need to substitute 0 for x to see that c represents the y-intercept. For (b), they may need to analyze several graphs, including $y = x^2$ and $y = -x^2$, before they see that the parabola opens up if a is positive and down if a is negative.

B

Present an equation written in the standard form of the quadratic function, $y = a(x - h)^2 + k$, and graph it. Challenge students to find the translational effects of modifying a, h, and k. Establish a link between a in standard form and in general form, and between the coordinates of the vertex and (h, k).

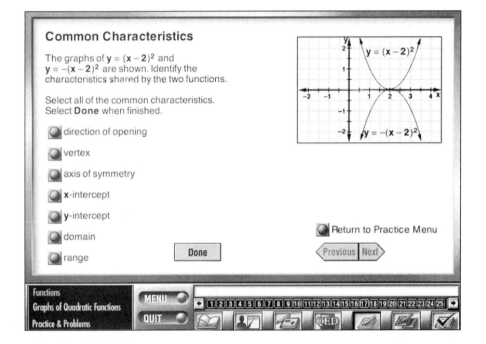

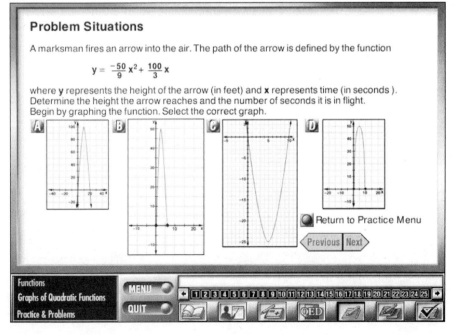

Completing the Square

Cross-References

Functions

Student Workbook: pages 162–165

Key Objectives

The student will:

- learn how to factor a quadratic function of the general form $y = ax^2 + bx + c$ and rewrite it in standard form, $y = a(x - h)^2 + k$, by completing the square.

Key Terms

perfect square trinomial, binomial squared, complete the square

Prerequisite Skills

- Substitute numbers for variables in expressions, and graph and analyze the relation.
- Identify constant terms, coefficients, and variables in polynomial expressions.
- Evaluate polynomial expressions, given the value(s) of the variable(s).
- Determine the following characteristics of the graph of a quadratic function:
  - vertex
  - domain and range
  - axis of symmetry
  - intercepts
- Factor polynomial expressions of the forms $ax^2 + bx + c$ and $a^2x^2 - b^2y^2$.

Lesson Description

In this lesson, students rewrite quadratic equations in standard form, $y = a(x - h)^2 + k$, by completing the square, and learn about the effect of a on the graphs of quadratic functions.

The **Introduction** involves finding the number of orange trees per acre that will maximize the yield of oranges at an orchard. Initially, students use a guess-and-test method, but stop after a few trials because the method is too inefficient. In the **Summary**, completing the square of the quadratic function $y = -10x^2 + 100x + 6000$ immediately gives the number of orange trees that will produce the maximum yield.

In the **Tutorial**, students review the characteristics of graphs of quadratic functions, then compare the graph of the basic parabola, $y = x^2$, to the graph of $y = -x^2$ to see how the negative value of a affects the graph. Next, they complete separate tables of values for $y = 2x^2$ and $y = \frac{1}{2}x^2$, graph these functions, and compare the parabolas to the graph of $y = x^2$, again noting the effect of a. Up until this point, all parabolas have had their vertices at $(0, 0)$, so in the next example, students study a parabola with a different vertex. In the final example, they complete the square for the quadratic function $y = x^2 - 6x + 5$ and then select the corresponding graph.

The first two **Examples** involve writing the equation of a parabola by comparing it to the basic $y = x^2$ graph. Then students change equations from the general form, $y = ax^2 + bx + c$, to the standard form,

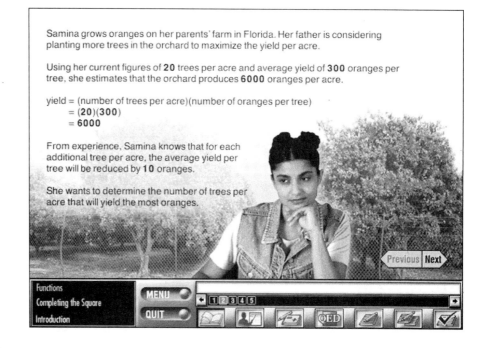

Samina grows oranges on her parents' farm in Florida. Her father is considering planting more trees in the orchard to maximize the yield per acre.

Using her current figures of **20** trees per acre and average yield of **300** oranges per tree, she estimates that the orchard produces **6000** oranges per acre.

yield = (number of trees per acre)(number of oranges per tree)
      = **(20)(300)**
      = **6000**

From experience, Samina knows that for each additional tree per acre, the average yield per tree will be reduced by **10** oranges.

She wants to determine the number of trees per acre that will yield the most oranges.

$y = a(x - h)^2 + k$, by completing the square, and sketch and graph the functions. In the last example, the students identify characteristics of the graph of a quadratic function without graphing.

Instructor Intervention

- Review how the following terms relate to the graph of a quadratic function: **vertex**, **domain**, **range**, **axis of symmetry**, **intercepts**

- Before students begin the **Tutorial**, you may wish to review absolute value. In both the general form, $y = ax^2 + bx + c$, and the standard form, $y = a(x - h)^2 + k$, the absolute value of a is important. For $|a| > 1$ ($a \leq -1$ or $a > 1$), the parabola will be narrower than the basic $y = x^2$ parabola, and for $0 < |a| < 1$, the parabola will be wider than the basic $y = x^2$ parabola.

- Before students begin the **Summary**, return to the equation that was presented in the **Introduction**, *new yield* = $(20 + x)(300 - 10x)$. Have them multiply the two binomials and ask how this equation might be used to solve the orchard problem. Then direct the students to the **Summary** for the solution to the orchard problem.

- You can use the problem presented in the **Introduction** and **Summary** to help students see how completing the square can be used to solve problems about maximum and minimum more quickly and more accurately than substituting numbers in a trial-and-error manner.

- Emphasize the importance of checking results. Ask students to calculate the y-intercept for each question and check for this point on the graph. A graphing calculator could also be used to check the coordinates of the vertex, the direction of opening, and the shape of the parabola.

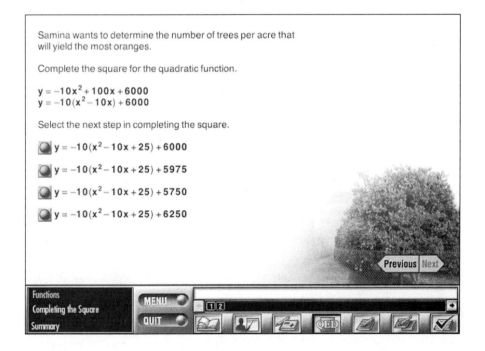

Samina wants to determine the number of trees per acre that will yield the most oranges.

Complete the square for the quadratic function.

$y = -10x^2 + 100x + 6000$
$y = -10(x^2 - 10x) + 6000$

Select the next step in completing the square.

- $y = -10(x^2 - 10x + 25) + 6000$
- $y = -10(x^2 - 10x + 25) + 5975$
- $y = -10(x^2 - 10x + 25) + 5750$
- $y = -10(x^2 - 10x + 25) + 6250$

Previous | Next

Functions
Completing the Square
Summary

MENU
QUIT

Evaluation

- Invite students to create quadratic equations of the form $y = ax^2 + bx + c$ that have the following criteria:
  - **(a)** $a = 1$, b is an even number, c is any number
  - **(b)** a is an even number, b is an even number, c is any number
  - **(c)** $a = 1$, b is an odd number, c is any number
  - **(d)** a is a whole number not equal to 1, b is any number not divisible by a, c is any number
  - **(e)** a is a fraction, b is a whole number, c is any number
  - **(f)** a is a fraction, b is a fraction, c is any number

  Then ask students to complete the square for their own equations. They should check their answers by multiplying out the new standard forms to see if they expand to the original general forms. By examining the standard forms, students should be able to describe the graph of each parabola (its vertex, direction of opening, shape, etc.), as compared to the basic $y = x^2$ graph.

- Observe students as they complete the activities. Do they know when to complete the square and when this method is not necessary? Do they know what steps to follow? Are they consistent? Can they explain what they are doing? Once they have completed the square, can they describe the graph of the parabola?

- Ask students to explain the terms **perfect square trinomial** and **binomial squared** and give examples.

Remediation

- Review the terms factor, greatest common factor, and numerical coefficient.

- Some students may have difficulty remembering the steps to complete the square. They could write a summary of the steps. For example:
  1. Group the x^2- and x-terms together inside parentheses.
  2. Factor out a, the coefficient of the x^2-term. Adjust the coefficient of the x-term.
  3. Create a perfect square trinomial. Subtract the same value that was added for the trinomial.
  4. Simplify, and express the trinomial as a squared binomial.

Students should keep this summary in front of them as they solve each question. Stress consistency in their steps.

- For students who have trouble completing the square, work through the different types of functions given in the **Evaluation** section step-by-step. Begin with examples where $a = 1$ and b is an even number. When they have success with this type of quadratic function, discuss how the next type has only one thing different. Progress in this manner through all the types listed.

- For the **Evaluation** activity, it may be helpful to have students work in pairs. Each person could create their own functions independently, and then the partners could switch for checking.

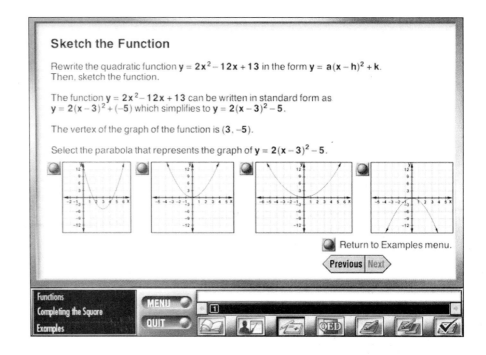

- When the value of a isn't 1, students often add or subtract the wrong amount to complete the square because they forget to multiply this amount by the value outside the parentheses. Present this problem and ask the students to identify and correct the error. Have them carefully follow the steps given above to help them find the error.

Complete the square.
$y = 2x^2 + 8x + 14$
$y = (2x^2 + 8x) + 14$
$y = 2(x^2 + 4x) + 14$
$y = 2(x^2 + 4x + 4) + 14 - 4$
$y = 2(x + 2)^2 + 10$

[error in second last line; $2(4) = 8$ should be subtracted]

Extension

A

Ask whether students prefer to find the vertex of a quadratic function by completing the square or by using the

$V_x = -\dfrac{b}{2a}$ formula to find x and

then substituting to find y. Discuss the advantages and disadvantages of each technique.

B

Explain that when an equation is in the form $y = ax^2 + bx + c$, students can use the quadratic formula to find the x-intercepts of the corresponding graph.

Quadratic formula:

$\dfrac{-b \pm \sqrt{b^2 - 4ac}}{2a}$

Have the students apply the formula to find the x-intercepts for several quadratic equations with two real roots. Then challenge

students to derive the quadratic formula by using the completing the square method on $ax^2 + bx + c = 0$. If they aren't sure about how to begin, suggest that they return to the section of the **Tutorial** that shows how the vertex formula was derived.

Enrichment

A

Writings of the ninth-century Persian scholar, al-Kwarismi, contain a geometric demonstration of completing the square. Students could research these writings and give a presentation to the class illustrating this geometric demonstration.

B

Students could research some applications of parabolic shapes, for example, in automobile headlights, telescopes, and cellular phone antennas. Ask how the shape helps to focus light or radio waves at a central point.

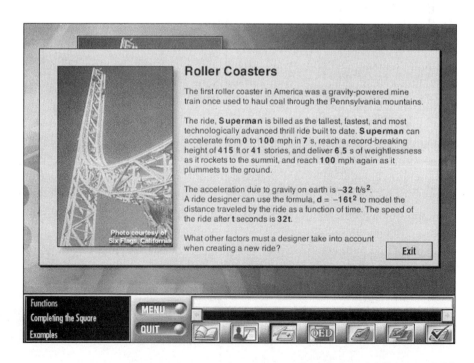

Translations of Quadratic Functions

Cross-References

Functions

Student Workbook: pages 166–169

Key Objectives

The student will:
- learn about graphs and transformations of quadratic functions.

Key Terms

parabola, quadratic, vertex, completing the square, axis of symmetry, y-intercept, transformation, translation, congruent, standard form, general form

Prerequisite Skills

- Identify the vertex and axis of symmetry of a parabola from a graph.
- Rewrite the equation $f(x) = ax^2 + bx + c$ in the form $f(x) = a(x - h)^2 + k$ using the process of completing the square.

Lesson Description

In the **Introduction**, students need to move a floodlight from its current position so that it illuminates as much of a restaurant's entrance as possible. Since the light casts a parabolic shape on the building, quadratic functions can be used to describe the original and new locations of the illuminated area. Students note that the parabola representing the new location is a translation of the original parabola. They complete the square of the new quadratic function to write it in standard form. In the **Summary**, students interpret the standard form of the parabola to identify the direction and size of the translation, and they locate the light at the point represented by the vertex.

In the **Tutorial**, students compare tables of values for three quadratic functions, $y = x^2$, $y = \frac{1}{2}x^2$, and $y = 2x^2$, and review how the coefficient, a, affects the shape of the parabola. They compare the basic quadratic function, $y = x^2$, with various transformations of $y = x^2$ using tables of values, and note how each transformation affects the graph of the function. The general expressions for vertical and horizontal translations of $y = x^2$ are presented, and students use these expressions to predict characteristics of translated functions without graphing them. Finally, they learn how to graph functions given in either general or standard form, and then graph a function, finding all its important characteristics.

The **Examples** expand on knowledge gained in the **Tutorial**. In the first example, students predict the shape and direction of several graphs by comparing their equations to $y = x^2$. The next two examples involve sketching graphs that are given in either general or standard form. In the final section, students develop the equations for transformed graphs given their original equations and a description of the transformation.

Instructor Intervention

- Before starting this lesson, review the vocabulary outlined in the **Key Terms** section.

- Students should be proficient at using their graphing calculators.

- Graph paper should be available for students to sketch the functions.

- Make sure that students recognize the difference between the general and standard forms of a quadratic function.

- Students should be comfortable with completing the square. Briefly review the process and post the steps for students' reference. (See the lesson "Completing the Square.")

- Encourage students to use a table of values for the first few translations. Seeing a list of the coordinates can make the pattern of changes more apparent. A table of values also reinforces the meaning of the axis of symmetry by showing how points are mirrored on a graph.

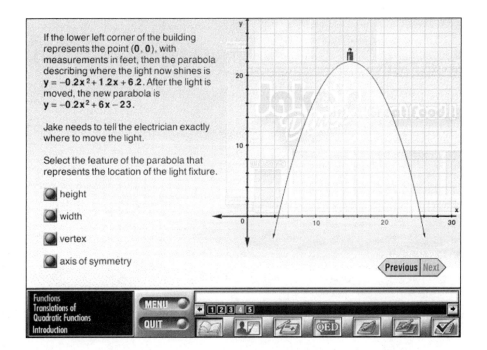

If the lower left corner of the building represents the point (**0, 0**), with measurements in feet, then the parabola describing where the light now shines is $y = -0.2x^2 + 1.2x + 6.2$. After the light is moved, the new parabola is $y = -0.2x^2 + 6x - 23$.

Jake needs to tell the electrician exactly where to move the light.

Select the feature of the parabola that represents the location of the light fixture.

- height
- width
- vertex
- axis of symmetry

Previous Next

Functions
Translations of
Quadratic Functions
Introduction

MENU
QUIT

1 2 3 4 5

Evaluation

- Ask students to write the following quiz individually. For each question, students should describe the graph, and then sketch it. Have them find all the applicable characteristics: direction of opening, vertex, and axis of symmetry.
  - **(a)** $y = x^2 + 2$ [upward, $(0, 2)$, $x = 0$]
  - **(b)** $y = (x + 3)^2$ [upward, $(-3, 0)$, $x = -3$]
  - **(c)** $y = x^2 - 4$ [upward, $(0, -4)$, $x = 0$]
  - **(d)** $y = (x - 5)^2$ [upward, $(5, 0)$, $x = 5$]
  - **(e)** $y = -(x + 3)^2$ [downward, $(-3, 0)$, $x = -3$]
  - **(f)** $y = 2(x - 5)^2$ [upward, $(5, 0)$, $x = 5$]
  - **(g)** $y = -0.5(x + 4)^2$ [downward, $(-4, 0)$, $x = -4$]
  - **(h)** $y = 3(x - 3)^2 - 2$ [upward, $(3, -2)$, $x = 3$]
  - **(i)** $y = 4x^2 - 1$ [upward, $(0, -1)$, $x = 0$]
  - **(j)** $y = -2(x + 1)^2 + 3$ [downward, $(-1, 3)$, $x = -1$]

  When they have completed the quiz, have students check their answers in groups and ask each group to present a solution to the class.

- Describe a series of transformations performed on a graph and challenge groups to race to see who can be the first to find the equation of the final graph. For example:
  1. Start with $y = x^2 + 4$.
  2. Translate to the left 3 units.
  3. Reflect in the x-axis.
  4. Translate up 7 units.

  [Final graph: $y = -(x + 3)^2 + 3$]

Remediation

- Some students may have difficulty working with the standard form of a quadratic. Show how $y = x^2$ can be rewritten as $y = a(x - h)^2 + k$, where $a = 1$, $h = 0$, and $k = 0$.

- Students may mistakenly think that the vertex of $3(x + 2)^2 + 5$ is at (h, k), or $(2, 5)$. Remind them that since the standard form is $y = a(x - h)^2 + k$, the vertex is actually at $(-2, 5)$.

- Students may become confused about how various transformations affect the equation of a graph and vice versa. Work through examples of each type of transformation: translations left and right, translations up and down, vertical and horizontal stretching, and reflections in the x-axis. Make sure that students see how changes to h, k, and a relate to changes in the graph. Post a summary of the examples as a reference.

- Students may have difficulty drawing graphs of transformed quadratic equations, especially when two or more transformations are combined. Encourage students to sketch the graph at each stage to help them keep track of the correct directions and magnitudes of the translations.

Extension

A

Challenge students to find a method for reflecting a quadratic function over any line. They should begin by reviewing how to reflect a quadratic function over the x-axis, the y-axis, and the line $y = x$. They should note the following at each step:

1. To reflect a graph over the x-axis, replace y with $-y$, and solve for y. For example, when $y = x^2 + 2$ is reflected over the x-axis, the equation of the reflection is:
$$-y = x^2 + 2$$
$$y = -x^2 - 2$$

2. To reflect a graph over the y-axis, replace x with $-x$. For

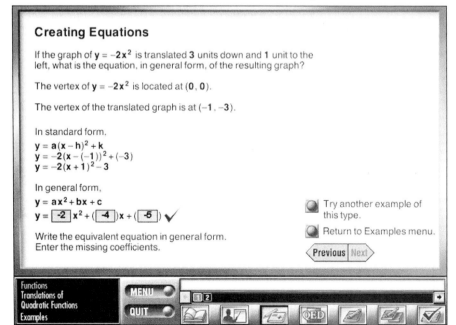

Creating Equations

If the graph of $y = -2x^2$ is translated **3** units down and **1** unit to the left, what is the equation, in general form, of the resulting graph?

The vertex of $y = -2x^2$ is located at $(0, 0)$.

The vertex of the translated graph is at $(-1, -3)$.

In standard form,
$y = a(x - h)^2 + k$
$y = -2(x - (-1))^2 + (-3)$
$y = -2(x + 1)^2 - 3$

In general form,
$y = ax^2 + bx + c$
$y = \boxed{-2} x^2 + (\boxed{-4})x + (\boxed{-5})$ ✓

Write the equivalent equation in general form. Enter the missing coefficients.

⊙ Try another example of this type.

⊙ Return to Examples menu.

‹Previous | Next›

Functions
Translations of
Quadratic Functions
Examples

MENU

QUIT

example, when $y = (x - 5)^2 + 2$ is reflected over the y-axis, the equation of the reflection is:
$$y = (-x - 5)^2 + 2$$

3. To reflect a graph over the line $y = x$, replace x with y and replace y with x, and solve for y. (Students should remember this from their work on inverse functions.) For example, when $y = 2x^2$ is reflected over the line $y = x$, the equation of the reflection is:
$$x = 2y^2$$
$$\frac{1}{2}x = y^2$$
$$y = \pm\sqrt{\frac{1}{2}x}$$

4. To reflect $y = x^2$ over the line $y = 2x$, replace y with $2x$ and replace x with $\frac{1}{2}y$ obtained by solving the equation of the line for x). The equation of the reflection is:
$$2x = \left(\frac{1}{2}y\right)^2$$
$$2x = \frac{1}{4}y^2$$
$$y^2 = 8x$$
$$y = \pm 2\sqrt{2x}$$

B

Have the students sketch functions where the y-values are large enough to justify using different scales on the x- and y-axes, e.g., $y = x^2 - 40$.

Enrichment

A

Students could investigate how parabolas are related to conic sections. They should discover that a parabola is created when a cone intersects a plane that is parallel to a side of the cone. From this starting point, encourage students to investigate the other conic sections.

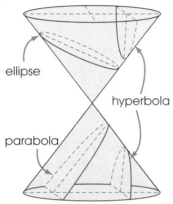

B

Have students research the development of quadratic equations. They could start by looking at the quadratic equations history page at the website http://www-history.mcs.st-and.ac.uk/.

C

Challenge students to use the graph to find the mirror point of any point (p, q), given that the axis of symmetry is $x = h$.

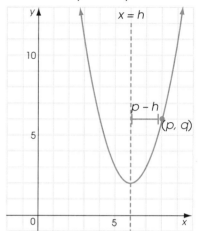

Students should discover these conclusions:

• The y-coordinate, q, will be the same for the mirror point as for the original point.

• The distance from p to the axis of symmetry is $p - h$. Subtract twice this distance from p to obtain the x-coordinate of the mirror point.
$$p - 2(p - h) = p - 2p + 2h$$
$$= 2h - p$$

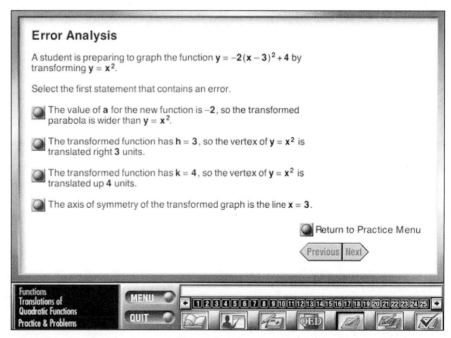

Error Analysis

A student is preparing to graph the function $y = -2(x - 3)^2 + 4$ by transforming $y = x^2$.

Select the first statement that contains an error.

○ The value of **a** for the new function is **−2**, so the transformed parabola is wider than $y = x^2$.

○ The transformed function has **h = 3**, so the vertex of $y = x^2$ is translated right **3** units.

○ The transformed function has **k = 4**, so the vertex of $y = x^2$ is translated up **4** units.

○ The axis of symmetry of the transformed graph is the line **x = 3**.

○ Return to Practice Menu

⟨ Previous | Next ⟩

Functions
Translations of
Quadratic Functions
Practice & Problems

MENU
QUIT

1 2 3 4 5 6 7 8 9 10 11 12 13 14 15 16 17 18 19 20 21 22 23 24 25

10 QUADRATIC EQUATIONS

10.1 Solving Quadratics by Graphing

Cross-References
Quadratic Equations

Student Workbook: pages 170–173

Key Objectives
The student will:
- solve quadratic equations by graphing.
- relate the solutions of quadratic equations to the zeros of their corresponding quadratic functions.

Key Terms
quadratic equation, linear equation, quadratic function, linear function, zero, solution, *x*-intercept

Prerequisite Skills
- Solve nonlinear equations.
- Distinguish between relations that are functions and relations that are not.
- Perform graphical transformations of quadratic functions.
- Complete the square.
- Identify the characteristics of quadratic functions.

Lesson Description

In this lesson, students use graphing to find the zeros of quadratic functions. Most students will need graphing calculators to draw the graphs, although an alternate method of graphing is described in the lesson.

In the **Introduction**, students solve a problem relating the price of a helicopter tour to the number of customers who will take the tour. The number of customers is expected to decrease by 40 for each \$5 increase in the price. Students create a table of values to see the range of prices that will allow the tour organizers to earn \$2000 or more. In the **Summary**, students generate a quadratic equation to describe the situation and then use a graph to find the roots. These roots represent the least and greatest prices that will enable the organizers to earn the \$2000 they need.

The **Tutorial** begins by defining quadratic equations and introducing key terms. Students learn this process for identifying the roots of a quadratic equation:
- Write the quadratic equation in the general form $ax^2 + bx + c = 0$.
- Write the corresponding quadratic function.
- Graph the function.
- Locate the *x*-intercepts on the graph.
- Verify that these are the roots of the equation by substituting them into the original quadratic equation.

Later, the **Tutorial** introduces the standard form of a quadratic equation: $a(x - h)^2 + k$. Students discover that *a* is an indicator of whether the function opens up or down (up if a is positive and down if it is negative) and that the vertex of the function is at (h, k).

The **Examples** section reviews and extends the work done in the **Tutorial**. Students read roots shown on given graphs, estimate roots not located on lattice points, determine characteristics of a graph from the standard form equation, and solve problems involving quadratic functions.

Instructor Intervention

- Students will need graphing utilities to complete the problems in the *Student Workbook*.

- This lesson shows how to graph quadratic functions by transforming graphs of $y = x^2$. With a graphing calculator, these transformations will not be necessary.

  Some students may need assistance with entering equations in various forms. This may be a good opportunity to introduce the key as a way of entering exponents.

- In the **Tutorial**, students will encounter the idea that you can state an equation in standard form $[a(x - h)^2 + k]$ by following these steps for completing the square of a trinomial:
  Step 1: $x^2 - 2x - 8 = 0$
  Step 2: $(x^2 - 2x + 1) - 9 = 0$
  Step 3: $(x - 1)^2 - 9 = 0$

  Help students see that the h term in the standard form is always half of the b term in the general form, $ax^2 + bx + c = 0$. Knowing this will help them better understand how to generate the trinomial square in Step 2.

Last year the helicopter service charged **$30** for the ride and had **200** customers. Susan estimates that for every **$5** increase in the ride price there will be **40** fewer customers. The total cost to run the service is **$2000**.

Select the price in the table that will allow the company to break even.

Price ($)	Number of Customers	Revenue ($)
30	200	6000
25	240	6000
20	280	5600
15	320	4800
10	360	3600
5	400	2000

Previous Next

Quadratic Equations
Solving Quadratics by Graphing
Introduction
MENU
QUIT

Lesson Components

Examples

Reading Roots from Graphs (1)
Estimating Roots from Graphs (1)
Graphing from Standard Form (1)
Number of Solutions (1)
Problem Situations (1)

Practice and Problems

Number of Solutions
Graphing from Standard Form
Reading Roots from Graphs
Error Analysis
Problem Situations

Extra Practice

Estimation of Roots
Number of Roots
Verification
Solving Quadratic Equations
Problem Situations

Self-Check

Estimation of Roots (2)
Number of Roots (2)
Verification (2)
Solving Quadratic Equations (3)
Problem Situations (1)

Minimum score: 7 out of 10

Evaluation

- Have students work independently to solve each of these problems and then form small groups to compare and contrast answers and methods. Provide graphing calculators for students to use to graph functions as necessary. Each group could present one solution to the class.

  1. Is –0.5 is a root of $6x^2 - x - 2 = 0$? Justify your answer. [yes]
  2. Is $x = 2$ a good estimate for the zero of $f(x) = 4x^2 - 10x - 24$? Explain.
  3. Make a graph to estimate the roots of $2x^2 + 9x + 10 = 0$. [–2.5 and –2]
  4. Make a graph to estimate the zeros of $f(x) = -x^2 + 2x + 15$. [5 and –3]
  5. How are roots, zeros, and x-intercepts similar? How are they different?
  6. Are there three consecutive integers whose squares have a sum of 1331? [no]

- Observe how students solve quadratic equations by graphing. Can they change equations from one form to another? Can they enter equations correctly into a graphing utility? Can they use features such as Zoom and Trace to help them identify the x-intercepts? Do they verify the intercepts by substituting them back into the original equation? Do they use logical reasoning to check graphs and x-intercepts?

Remediation

- Students may be confused by the terms "root," "solution," "zero," and "x-intercept." Help students see that the x-intercepts on the graph are values for x that make y equal to 0. This is why they represent the roots of the equation and the zeros of the function. If the terms present difficulty, students may find it helpful to substitute mentally the term "x-intercept" each time they see the word "root" or "zero" in a problem.

- Most of the problems in this lesson involve the analysis of computer- or calculator-generated graphs. Students may need help with calculator features that will help them find the x-intercepts.

- In order to verify solutions, students will need to make calculations such as $2(3)^2 - 7(3) + 5$. Help students explore calculator features such as parentheses keys and order of operations signs to find an efficient way to enter such calculations. For some calculators, it will be necessary to enter = several times during the process.

- Algebraic errors made while students are changing an equation from one form to another will result in inaccurate graphs and incorrect solutions. Observe the students at work to identify algebra concepts and skills that may need review. For example:
  (a) eliminating a quantity from one side by adding or subtracting on both sides
  (b) dividing a polynomial by a monomial
  (c) moving terms inside and outside parentheses
  (d) squaring a binomial

- Students will be able to use the general form of an equation ($ax^2 + bx + c = 0$) to solve most of the problems in this lesson. If some have difficulty with the form $a(x-h)^2 + k$, you might suggest that they bypass sections in the **Examples** and **Practice** sections that make reference to the standard form.

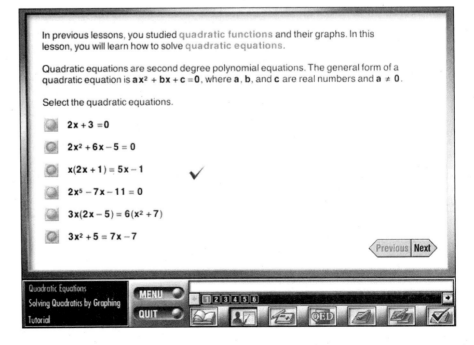

Extension

A

Once students have expressed an equation in the form $a(x-h)^2 + k = 0$, they can find the roots simply by solving for x. Invite them to choose several problems from the unit, express the equations in standard form, and then find the roots algebraically. For example:

$$2(x+3)^2 - 8 = 0$$
$$(x+3)^2 - 4 = 0$$
$$(x+3)^2 = 4$$
$$x + 3 = 2 \text{ or } x + 3 = -2$$
$$x = -1 \text{ or } x = -5$$

B

Students may wish to investigate satellite dishes to see how the parabolic shape efficiently captures electromagnetic waves.

C

If students have programmable calculators, they should be able to write a simple program using the following to complete the square for a quadratic function written in the general form.

$$f(x) = ax^2 + bx + c$$
$$f(x) = a\left(x + \frac{b}{2a}\right)^2 + \frac{4ac - b^2}{4a}$$

Where the vertex is:

$$\left(-\frac{b}{2a}, \frac{4ac - b^2}{4a}\right)$$

Challenge students to write another program they can use to evaluate a quadratic equation for a given root.

D

Small groups might explore the range of abilities among different types of graphing calculators. (Provide manuals if possible.)

Almost all calculators will trace along the graph and show the x- and y-values for different locations. Most will also zoom into areas of the graph for a more precise solution. Some will show a table of values where students can select a value for x and then see the corresponding value for y. A few varieties may even be able to solve for the x-intercepts.

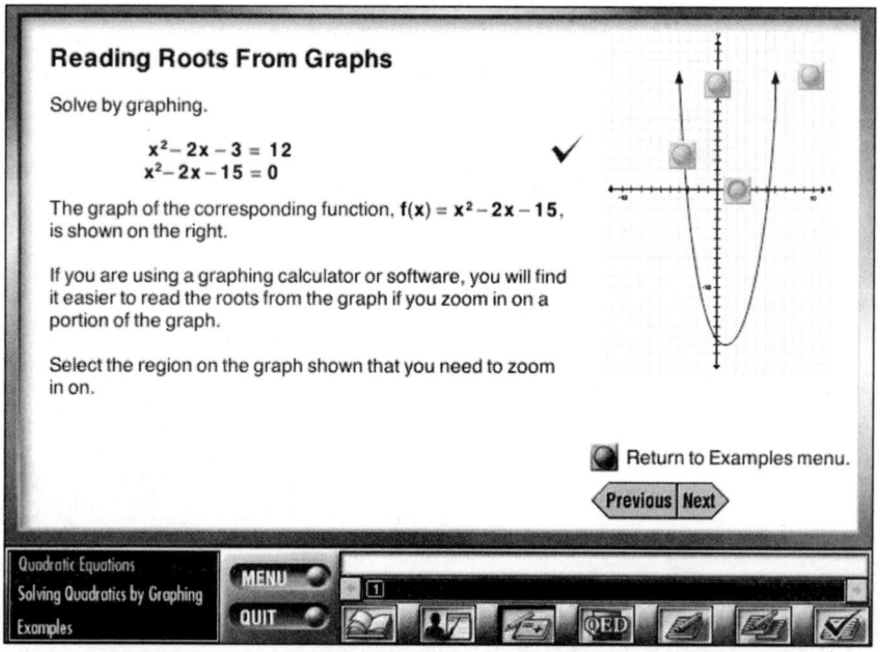

Enrichment

A

Ask students to describe how the graph of $y = x^2$ is related to each of the following graphs. Encourage them to experiment with different graphs of each form to help them identify the relationships.

(a) $y = ax^2$
(b) $y = x^2 + k$
(c) $y = (x - h)^2$
(d) $y = a(x - h)^2 + k$

Can they explain why the sign of a indicates whether the graph opens up or down? Can they explain why the vertex of a graph is located at (h, k)?

B

Students may be interested to know that a parabola is the shape that is formed when a cone is sliced on a plane parallel to a side of the cone.

Invite the students to research conic sections to find out how each of these shapes is produced
(a) hyperbola
(b) ellipse
(c) frustum

Some students may be interested in studying other aspects of conic sections, including applications (such as the study of planetary orbits) and relationships to algebra.

Reading Roots From Graphs

Solve by graphing.

$$x^2 - 2x - 3 = 12$$
$$x^2 - 2x - 15 = 0$$

The graph of the corresponding function, $f(x) = x^2 - 2x - 15$, is shown on the right.

If you are using a graphing calculator or software, you will find it easier to read the roots from the graph if you zoom in on a portion of the graph.

Select the region on the graph shown that you need to zoom in on.

Return to Examples menu.

Previous Next

Quadratic Equations
Solving Quadratics by Graphing
Examples

MENU
QUIT

10.2 Solving Quadratics by Factoring

Cross-References
Quadratic Equations

Student Workbook: pages 174–177

Key Objectives
The student will:
- solve quadratic equations using factoring methods.
- relate solutions to quadratic equations to the zeros of corresponding quadratic functions.
- generate quadratic functions for given zeros.

Key Terms
quadratic equation, quadratic function, quadratic graph, verify, root, zero, *x*-intercept

Prerequisite Skills
- Factor polynomials.
- Solve nonlinear equations.
- Make graphical transformations of quadratic functions.

Lesson Description

In the previous lesson, students learned how to solve quadratic equations by graphing them. Here, they use factoring to determine the roots of equations and the zeros of functions.

In the **Introduction**, students graph a quadratic function in order to solve a problem involving a baseball game. They use the graph to determine that a runner will reach home plate ahead of a ball being thrown from center field. In the **Summary**, students return to the same problem, this time using factoring to find the solution.

The **Tutorial** reviews quadratic functions and illustrates how to use factoring to find the zeros of a function, where a zero is defined as a value of *x* that makes the function equal to zero. These are the steps students use to find the zeros of a function:
1. Set the function equal to zero.
2. Factor the function.
3. Set each factor equal to zero.
4. Solve for *x*.

The **Examples** explore the relationship between quadratics and their factors in more depth. In addition to finding zeros and roots, students:
- substitute values into quadratic equations to verify whether given numbers are roots.
- generate equations from given roots.
- apply factoring to find zeros and roots in problem situations.

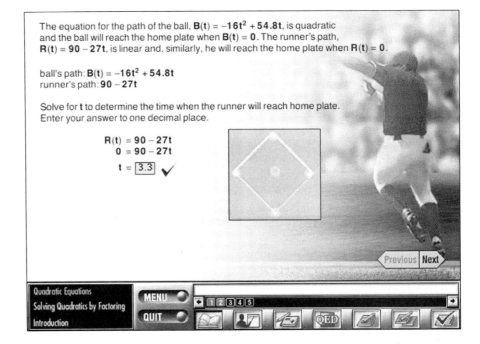

The equation for the path of the ball, $B(t) = -16t^2 + 54.8t$, is quadratic and the ball will reach the home plate when $B(t) = 0$. The runner's path, $R(t) = 90 - 27t$, is linear and, similarly, he will reach the home plate when $R(t) = 0$.

ball's path: $B(t) = -16t^2 + 54.8t$
runner's path: $90 - 27t$

Solve for **t** to determine the time when the runner will reach home plate. Enter your answer to one decimal place.

$$R(t) = 90 - 27t$$
$$0 = 90 - 27t$$
$$t = \boxed{3.3} \checkmark$$

Quadratic Equations
Solving Quadratics by Factoring
Introduction

MENU
QUIT

Instructor Intervention

- Before students begin the lesson, review how to multiply binomial factors. The acronym FOIL (First, Outside, Inside, Last) may help students recall that they need to multiply four different pairs of terms.

- Students may find it confusing that some problems require them to find roots of equations while others ask for zeros of functions. Emphasize that the procedure for finding roots and zeros is the same, since the roots of the equation indicate the points at which the graph of the function will cross the *x*-axis.

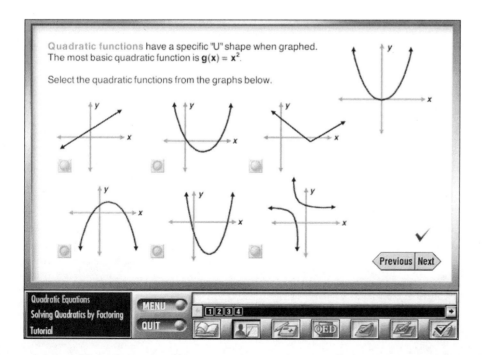

Evaluation

- Have students complete these exercises independently and then form groups to compare and contrast answers and methods. Each group could present one solution.

1. Verify that -3 is a root of $2x^2 + 7x + 3 = 0$.

2. Show that $-\frac{2}{3}$ is not a zero of $f(x) = 2x^2 + 7x + 3$.

3. Determine if 2.5 is a root of $2x^2 - 7x - 5$. [no]

4. Find the roots of $50 - 2x^2 = 0$. [5 and –5]

5. Find the roots of $-10x + 2x^2 - 28 = 0$. [7 and –2]

6. Find the roots of $6x^2 = 11x + 10$. [$\frac{5}{2}$ and $-\frac{2}{3}$]

7. Give an equation that has roots 4 and $-\frac{7}{3}$. [$x^2 - \frac{5}{3}x - \frac{28}{3}$ or a multiple]

8. Give an equation with roots $-\frac{3}{5}$ and $\frac{5}{8}$. [$x^2 - \frac{1}{40}x - \frac{3}{8}$ or a multiple]

Remediation

- Review these terms.
  (a) quadratic equation
  (b) quadratic function
  (c) graph of a quadratic
  (d) verify
  (e) root
  (f) zero
  (g) x-intercept

- Students may need to review factoring methods for trinomials. Use trinomials of the form $ax^2 + bx + c$. Choose some examples where a is a factor of b and c and others where a is not.

To factor $3x^2 - 7x - 6$:

Step 1: Find two terms whose product is the first term in the trinomial ($3x^2$). Place these terms first in each binomial factor.
$(3x \qquad)(x \qquad)$

Step 2: Find all the pairs of factors whose product is the third term in the trinomial, -6.
Factor pairs for -6 include 1 and -6, 2 and -3, 3 and -2, and 6 and -1.

Step 3: Combine first terms from Step 1 with second terms from Step 2 to create possible binomial factors. Look for a combination that results in the "target" numerical coefficient of the middle term ($-7x$) in the trinomial.
$(3x + 2)(x - 3)$

- In some instances, students will need to reorganize equations into the form $ax^2 + bx + c = 0$. Review this process with several practice problems. Include examples of each of these types:
  (a) There are terms on both sides of the equation. (e.g., $x^2 + 4x = 32$)
  (b) Terms are in a different order. (e.g., $28 + x^2 - 11x = 0$)
  (c) A number can be factored out of the trinomial. (e.g., $2x^2 - 22x - 120 = 0$)
  (d) One of the terms appears to be missing. (e.g., $3x^2 - 15x = 0$)
  (e) The polynomial represents a difference of squares. (e.g., $x^2 - 36 = 0$)

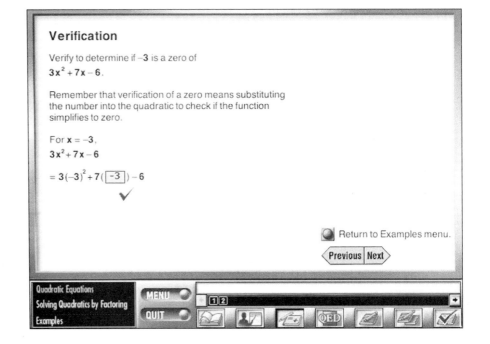

Verification

Verify to determine if **-3** is a zero of $3x^2 + 7x - 6$.

Remember that verification of a zero means substituting the number into the quadratic to check if the function simplifies to zero.

For $x = -3$,
$3x^2 + 7x - 6$
$= 3(-3)^2 + 7(\boxed{-3}) - 6$
✓

Return to Examples menu.

‹ Previous | Next ›

Quadratic Equations
Solving Quadratics by Factoring
Examples

MENU

QUIT

Extension

A

Students could explore how the zeros of a quadratic function can help them visualize its graph. For example, $f(x) = x^2 - 6x + 8$ has zeros 2 and 4. This indicates that the graph intersects the *x*-axis at 2 and 4. The coefficient of the x^2 term is positive so the graph will be shaped like a U, not an arch. The *x*-coordinate of the vertex will be located at the mean of 2 and 4, or $x = 3$. Since $f(3) = 3^2 - 6(3) + 8 = -1$, the vertex is $(3, -1)$.

B

Have students explore this alternative method for finding binomial factors of a trinomial of the form $ax^2 + bx + c$. Ask them to follow these steps to factor $6x^2 + x - 2$.

Step 1: Find *ac*.
$6(-2) = -12$

Step 2: Write *ac* as the product of two factors whose sum is *b*.
$4(-3) = -12$, and $-3 + 4 = 1$.

Step 3: Use the two factors to rewrite the *bx* term in the trinomial.
$6x^2 + x - 2 = 6x^2 + 4x + (-3x) - 2$

Step 4: Group the first two terms and the second two terms. Then factor out the common factor in each group.
$(6x^2 + 4x) + [(-3x) - 2]$
$= 2x(3x + 2) - 1(3x + 2)$

Step 5: Rearrange the terms to form two binomials.
$2x(3x + 2) - 1(3x + 2)$
$= (2x - 1)(3x + 2)$

Have students use this method to factor $4x^2 + 5x - 6$.
[$(4x - 3)$ and $(x + 2)$.]

C

Students with graphing calculators can explore the $\boxed{\text{SOLVE}}$ function on their calculators. Since each type of calculator functions somewhat differently, encourage students to bring in operating manuals.

Enrichment

A

Students may wish to investigate professional ball sports such as golf, baseball, or soccer to find information about the initial velocities at which the balls travel and the paths they take. Information of this type can be obtained from the Internet. Useful search terms might include:
• golf ball speeds
• soccer ball speeds
• baseball speeds
• ball velocity
• acceleration
Students might also investigate the laws of motion to see how these influence the paths of the balls.

B

Review the Pythagorean theorem, and then pose these geometry problems:

1. Find the side lengths of a right triangle whose longest side is 2 in. more than one side and 9 in. more than the other side. [8 in., 15 in., 17 in.]

2. If the length of a square is extended by 10 ft, and the width is extended by 12 ft, the resulting rectangle has an area three times as large as that of the original square. What is the side length of the original square? [15 ft]

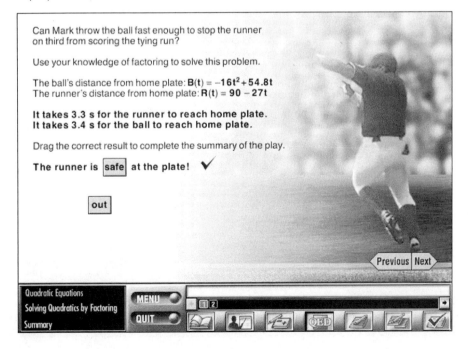

Can Mark throw the ball fast enough to stop the runner on third from scoring the tying run?

Use your knowledge of factoring to solve this problem.

The ball's distance from home plate: $B(t) = -16t^2 + 54.8t$
The runner's distance from home plate: $R(t) = 90 - 27t$

It takes 3.3 s for the runner to reach home plate.
It takes 3.4 s for the ball to reach home plate.

Drag the correct result to complete the summary of the play.

The runner is $\boxed{\text{safe}}$ at the plate! ✓

$\boxed{\text{out}}$

Previous | Next

Quadratic Equations
Solving Quadratics by Factoring
Summary

MENU
QUIT

Cross-References

Quadratic Equations

Student Workbook: pages 178–181

Key Objectives

The student will:
- explore imaginary and complex numbers.
- perform operations involving these numbers.

Key Terms

real numbers, imaginary numbers, product property of radicals, perfect square, natural number, complex number, Venn diagram, distributive property, complex conjugates, rationalize, common factor, quadratic equation, quadratic formula, FOIL

Prerequisite Skills

- Give examples of numbers that satisfy the conditions of natural, whole, integral, and rational numbers, and show that these numbers comprise the rational number system.
- Find and verify the solutions of rational equations.
- Perform operations on irrational numbers of monomial and binomial form, using exact values.

Lesson Description

In this lesson, students explore imaginary and complex numbers and perform operations involving these numbers.

The **Introduction** presents a problem involving direct current (DC) electric circuits and Ohm's Law ($V = IR$, where V is electric potential, I is current, and R is resistance). Students use Ohm's Law to find the electric potential of a battery given the current and resistance. Since each quantity used in the equation is a real number, the answer is a real number. The **Summary** uses an alternating current (AC) circuit example, where students must determine the electric potential of an outlet. Impedance takes the place of resistance in Ohm's Law, giving the equation $V = IZ$, where Z is impedance. Students must multiply complex numbers to find the answer, which is also a complex number.

The **Tutorial** defines imaginary numbers, and the students learn how to express negative square roots in terms of i. Next, they examine powers of i and discover a pattern relating all powers of i to i, -1, $-i$, and 1. Then complex numbers are defined in terms of real and imaginary parts, and students add and subtract two complex numbers.

The **Examples** build on learning gained in the **Tutorial**. Students learn how to simplify, multiply, and divide imaginary and complex numbers. The last example involves solving a quadratic equation that has complex numbers as roots.

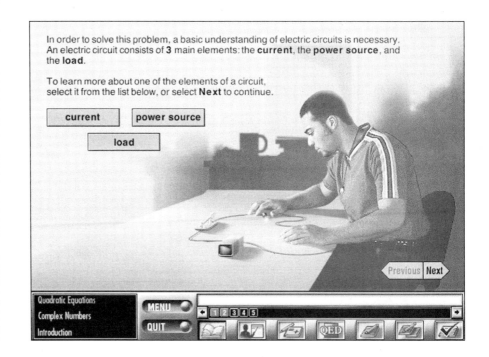

In order to solve this problem, a basic understanding of electric circuits is necessary. An electric circuit consists of **3** main elements: the **current**, the **power source**, and the **load**.

To learn more about one of the elements of a circuit, select it from the list below, or select **Next** to continue.

current   power source

load

Quadratic Equations
Complex Numbers
Introduction

Instructor Intervention

- As students perform operations on complex and imaginary numbers, they will need to use many previously acquired skills. Make sure students can:
  - perform operations with radicals, polynomials, and irrational numbers.
  - apply the FOIL method.
  - use the exponent laws.
  - determine the roots of a quadratic equation.

- Although the lesson on the quadratic formula occurs after this one, students should remember the formula from previous grades. Review the formula and post it as reference.

$$x = \frac{-b \pm \sqrt{4ac}}{2a}$$

- Point out that the product and quotient properties of radicals only hold true for real numbers. For example, if the product property were applied to $\sqrt{-3} \times \sqrt{-12}$, the result would be $\sqrt{36} = 6$, which is incorrect. The product property can only be applied to imaginary numbers after i is factored out.

$$\sqrt{-3} \times \sqrt{-12} = \sqrt{3}i \times \sqrt{12}i$$
$$= \sqrt{36i^2}$$
$$= 6i^2$$
$$= -6$$

- Make clear how complex and imaginary numbers relate to the other number systems. You could explain why each new number system was created, for example:

"At first, people used only whole numbers. When the concepts of fractions and numbers less than zero began to make sense, rational numbers and negative numbers were introduced. Then, in the sixth century B.C., Pythagoreans recognized the need for irrational numbers. Finally, in the 16th century, mathematicians created imaginary numbers to enable them to solve equations such as $x^2 = -3$."

Evaluation

- Divide students into groups. Each group should come up with one question of each of the following types:
  - basic knowledge and definitions
  - converting negative square roots to i form
  - determining equivalent powers of i (*example*: $i^{51} = -i$)

- adding complex numbers
- multiplying complex numbers
- dividing complex numbers
- error analysis of a worked solution

The groups could rotate the questions and solve them, and then rotate the completed solutions for checking by a third group.

- Observe students as they work. Can they convert to and from i form? Can they recognize equivalent powers of i? Do they use the exponent laws and the properties of radicals correctly? Can they identify complex conjugates?

Remediation

- It may take time for students to become comfortable with the idea of negative square roots, so emphasis on definitions is important.

- Review the prerequisite skills listed in **Instructor Intervention**.

- Some students may have difficulty performing operations on complex numbers. Compare these questions with examples that use binomial expressions so students can see how the processes compare. For example:

$$(2 + 3x)(2 + 4x)$$
$$= 4 + 8x + 6x + 12x^2$$
$$= 12x^2 + 14x + 4$$

$$(2 + 3i)(2 + 4i)$$
$$= 4 + 8i + 6i + 12i^2$$
$$= 4 + 14i + 12(-1)$$
$$= 14i - 8$$

Extension

A

Create problems similar to those given in the **Extra Practice** section, but increase the level of difficulty. Examples:

1. Instead of simply adding two complex numbers, use questions such as $(3 + 7i^{23}) + (6 - 5i) - i^{68}$. [Answer: $8 - 12i$]

2. Instead of multiplying only two complex numbers, ask

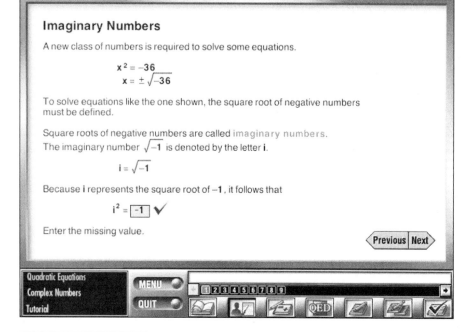

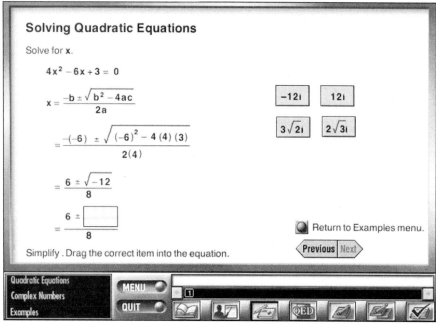

students to multiply three or more complex numbers:
$(7 + 3i)(2 - 4i)[(i + 2)^2]$
[Answer: $122 + 38i$]

3. Present complex numbers in different ways.
For example, express
$\dfrac{3+2i}{7-4i}$ as $\dfrac{3+\sqrt{-4}}{7-\sqrt{-16}}$.

4. Create questions that require a series of operations (e.g., finding the LCD, factoring) before the complex number is found. For example, instead of asking students to solve $3x^2 - x + 1 = 0$, have them solve $(2x + 1)(3x + 1)$ or
$$\dfrac{5}{3x+1} + \dfrac{x-4}{2x+1} = 0.$$

B

You could also create challenging problems that involve thinking in different ways. For example:

1. Changing a question: Change the question so that the next step is $20 + 5i - 24i - 6i^2$.
$(5 - 6i)(2 + i)$

2. Working backwards: Enter the missing numbers that satisfy the following statement of equivalence.
$$\dfrac{\blacksquare}{200 - 300i} = \dfrac{42 + 6i}{50}$$
[Answer: 52]

Enrichment

A

Invite students to learn about rectangular, polar, and exponential forms of complex numbers and how to convert between the forms. They could research Euler's formula on this topic, and could try to perform operations on complex numbers in polar form.

B

Ask students to investigate graphing complex numbers on the complex plane.

C

Encourage students to research applications of complex numbers in the real world (in electrical engineering, in fractal geometry) or to research the history of complex numbers.

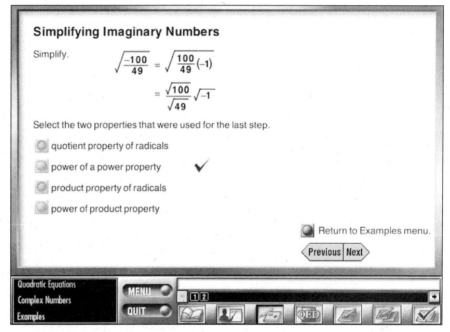

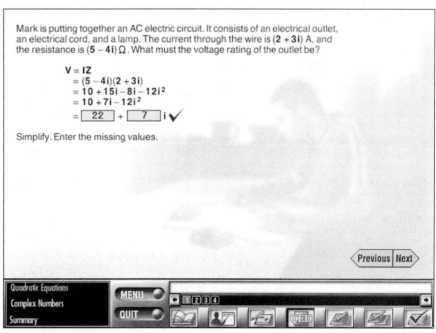

The Quadratic Formula

Cross-References

Quadratic Equations

Student Workbook: pages 182-185

Key Objectives

The student will:

- use the quadratic formula to solve quadratic equations.
- use the determinant to identify the number of solutions to a quadratic equation.
- apply the quadratic formula in problem situations.

Key Terms

quadratic equation, quadratic function, quadratic graph, quadratic formula, verify, root, solution, zero, x-intercept, square root

Prerequisite Skills

- Solve nonlinear equations.
- Connect algebraic and graphical transformations of quadratic functions using completing the square as required.
- Perform operations with irrational numbers.

Lesson Description

Now that students have learned to solve equations by graphing and factoring, they are ready to begin using the quadratic formula. The **Introduction** presents a situation in which a photograph is to be framed so the area of the frame is equal to 40% of the area of the photograph. Students generate an equation and then use a sliding indicator to determine the value for *x* that results in the correct frame area. In the **Summary**, students see how the same problem can be solved by substituting values from their equation into the quadratic formula:

$$x = \frac{-b \pm \sqrt{b^2 - 4ac}}{2a}$$

In the **Tutorial**, students learn that they can find the roots of any polynomial by restating it so a perfect square trinomial is isolated on one side (completing the square). This is especially useful in situations where the polynomial cannot be factored. By reorganizing the trinomial $ax^2 + bx + c$ in this way, they generalize the quadratic formula.

The final section of the **Tutorial** identifies the part of the quadratic formula called the determinant ($b^2 - 4ac$) and demonstrates how the determinant is used to predict the number of roots for a quadratic equation:

- If $b^2 - 4ac > 0$, the equation has two roots.
- If $b^2 - 4ac = 0$, the equation has one root.
- If $b^2 - 4ac < 0$, the equation has no roots.

The **Examples** reinforce and extend the ideas presented in the **Tutorial**. As well as finding roots and using the discriminant to predict the number of roots, students generate quadratic equations from given roots and apply the quadratic formula in problem situations.

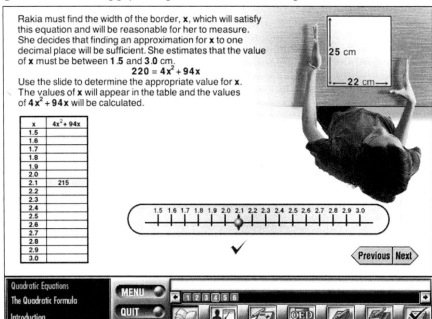

Rakia must find the width of the border, **x**, which will satisfy this equation and will be reasonable for her to measure. She decides that finding an approximation for **x** to one decimal place will be sufficient. She estimates that the value of **x** must be between **1.5** and **3.0** cm.

$$220 = 4x^2 + 94x$$

Use the slide to determine the appropriate value for **x**. The values of **x** will appear in the table and the values of $4x^2 + 94x$ will be calculated.

x	4x²+ 94x
1.5	
1.6	
1.7	
1.8	
1.9	
2.0	
2.1	215
2.2	
2.3	
2.4	
2.5	
2.6	
2.7	
2.8	
2.9	
3.0	

1.5 1.6 1.7 1.8 1.9 2.0 2.1 2.2 2.3 2.4 2.5 2.6 2.7 2.8 2.9 3.0

Previous | Next

Quadratic Equations
The Quadratic Formula
Introduction

MENU

QUIT

1 2 3 4 5 6

Instructor Intervention

- Review the ± and ≐ symbols. Students should understand that 3 ± 4 represents both 3 + 4 and 3 − 4, or 7 and −1. The ≐ symbol means "is approximately equal to." A number that follows this sign is an approximate value, not an exact value.

- A calculator with a square root key is essential to this lesson. It would also be useful to provide a graphing calculator for students to use as they experiment with the quadratic formula.

- Encourage students to use calculator memory keys to store calculated values, rather than keying them in again for each new calculation. This will improve accuracy. (Even using this method, students will sometimes find that correct values for x produce equations with a value slightly more or less than 0, because of approximations.)

For example, to verify this root students could begin by storing the value of x in the calculator memory.

For $4x^2 - 7x + 2 = 0$, $x = \dfrac{7 + \sqrt{17}}{8} \doteq 1.390\,388\,203$

Here is one possible key sequence for verifying this value for x:

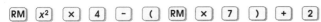

If the calculator has an x button and the value of the root is stored in x, the student can simply ask for the value of $4x^2 - 7x + 2$. In this case, the calculator will often give a value such as 3 E − 12. Explain that this means 3×10^{-12}, which is so small as to be approximately equal to 0, since the value for x was approximated.

Lesson Components

Examples
The Discriminant (2)
Finding Roots of Quadratic
   Equations (1)
Finding a Quadratic Equation
   from Its Roots (1)
Problem Situations (1)

Practice and Problems
Identifying a, b, and c
The Discriminant
Solving for Roots
Error Analysis
Problem Situations

Extra Practice
Identify a, b, and c
The Discriminant
Finding Roots
Find an Equation from Its
   Roots
Problem Situations

Self-Check
Identify a, b, and c (2)
The Discriminant (2)
Finding Roots (2)
Find an Equation from Its
   Roots (2)
Problem Situations (2)

Minimum score: 7 out of 10

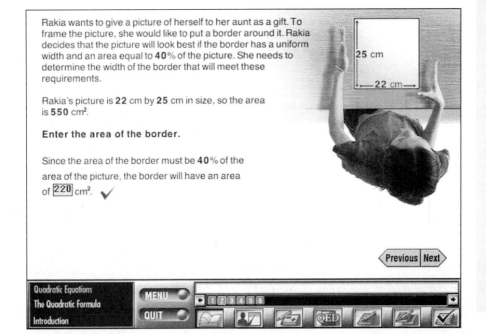

Rakia wants to give a picture of herself to her aunt as a gift. To frame the picture, she would like to put a border around it. Rakia decides that the picture will look best if the border has a uniform width and an area equal to **40**% of the picture. She needs to determine the width of the border that will meet these requirements.

Rakia's picture is **22** cm by **25** cm in size, so the area is **550** cm².

Enter the area of the border.

Since the area of the border must be **40**% of the area of the picture, the border will have an area of 220 cm². ✓

Previous | Next

Quadratic Equations
The Quadratic Formula
Introduction

MENU

QUIT

The Quadratic Formula **183**

Evaluation

- Have students complete these exercises independently and then form groups to compare and contrast answers and methods. Each group could present one solution.

1. Write the equation $2(x + 1) = 3x(2 - 5x)$ in the form $ax^2 + bx + c = 0$. $[15x^2 - 4x + 2 = 0]$

2. Give the values of a, b, and c for $2x^2 + 6 = 7x$. $[a = 2, b = -7, c = 6]$

3. When the quadratic formula is applied, an equation has a discriminant greater than 0. How many roots will the equation have? [2]

4. The graph of a quadratic function has one x-intercept. What can you tell about the value of the discriminant for this function? [discriminant = 0]

5. Determine whether $\dfrac{5 + \sqrt{13}}{2}$ is a root of $5x^2 - 15x + 9 = 0$. [no]

6. Determine whether $3 - \sqrt{5}$ is a root of $2x^2 + 3x + 15 = 0$. [no]

7. Find the roots.
   (a) $3x^2 - 11x - 14 = 0$ $[\dfrac{11 \pm 17}{6}$, so $x \doteq 4.7$ or $x = -1]$
   (b) $3x^2 - 6x + 1 = 0$ $[\dfrac{6 \pm \sqrt{24}}{6}$, so $x \doteq 1.8$ or $x \doteq 0.2]$
   (c) $2x(x + 1) = 3x(2 - x) + 7$ $[\dfrac{4 \pm \sqrt{156}}{10}$, so $x \doteq 1.6$ or $x \doteq -0.85]$

8. Give an equation that has roots $2 \pm \sqrt{5}$. [*example*: $0.5x^2 - 2x - 0.5$]

9. Give two equations that have roots $\dfrac{5 \pm \sqrt{2}}{5}$. [*example*: $2.5x^2 - 5x + 2.3$; $25x^2 - 50x + 23$]

The Quadratic Formula

For any quadratic equation $ax^2 + bx + c = 0$,

the solution is $x = \dfrac{-b \pm \sqrt{b^2 - 4ac}}{2a}$.

Some quadratic equations cannot be solved by factoring. Therefore, the quadratic formula must be used.

Find the roots of the quadratic equation using the quadratic formula.
$2x^2 + 5x - 11 = 0$

Identify **a**, **b**, and **c**.

$a = \boxed{2}$ $b = \boxed{5}$ $c = \boxed{-11}$ ✔

⟨Previous | Next⟩

Quadratic Equations
The Quadratic Formula
Tutorial

MENU QUIT 1 2 3 4 5 6 7

Remediation

- Before students begin the lesson, review these skills. Provide additional practice as needed.
  (a) finding the square root of a number
  (b) applying rules for order of operations when substituting values into equations
  (c) reorganizing an equation into the form $ax^2 + bx + c = 0$

- Post a copy of the quadratic formula in the classroom, since students will need to refer to it often.

- Have students establish keystroke sequences they can use with their calculators to perform each of the following operations. Ask students to record the sequences so they can refer to them as needed.
  (a) find a square root
  (b) square a number
  (c) enter a calculation in parentheses
  (d) store a value in memory
  (e) recall a value from memory
  (f) add the square root of a number to a positive or negative number and then divide by a third number
  (g) substitute a value for x into an expression such as $2x^2 + 6x - 5$

- Since different types of calculators operate in different ways, these keystroke sequences may vary quite widely. You may wish to discuss these coping strategies with students who are having difficulty:

(a) calculate with positive numbers and then change the signs as needed

(b) change the order of the terms in an expression

(c) calculate values separately, write down the results, and then use a calculator to combine the values (results obtained this way will be slightly less accurate)

- Emphasize that results among students may differ quite widely because of differences in calculators and how they are used. Make sure students understand that when they are verifying approximated roots, they should aim for equation values that are close to 0, rather than exactly 0.

Extension

A

Challenge students to relate the roots to the position of the vertex of the graph of the corresponding quadratic function. [The vertex is located at the mean of the roots.]

B

Students with graphing calculators could use a simple program to verify values of x for quadratic functions. Have them enter the quadratic function in the $y =$ portion and then enter values of x to be verified.

C

Students who have access to a programmable calculator (e.g., a TI-82) might enter a program that uses the quadratic formula to calculate values for x. When run, it asks for the values of a, b, and c. Then it calculates the dis-

criminant for the students.

Enrichment

A

Invite students to design a rectangular quilt 3 yd wide and 4 yd long so it consists of a uniform border surrounding a smaller rectangle inside. Ask them to use the quadratic formula to generate border measurements that will result in an inner rectangle that represents:

(a) $\frac{1}{2}$ of the area of the quilt
[0.5 yd]

(b) $\frac{1}{3}$ of the area of the quilt
[0.7 yd]

(c) $\frac{1}{4}$ of the area of the quilt
[0.8 yd]

If students are having difficulty getting started, suggest that they begin by drawing a diagram and then generating an equation to describe the area of the inside rectangle.

Note that in this problem, the quadratic formula will generate some values for x that are impossible widths for the quilt border because they are too large. Encourage students to use a diagram to check the reasonableness of their answers.

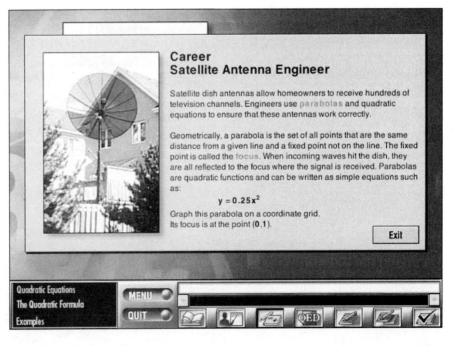

Career
Satellite Antenna Engineer

Satellite dish antennas allow homeowners to receive hundreds of television channels. Engineers use parabolas and quadratic equations to ensure that these antennas work correctly.

Geometrically, a parabola is the set of all points that are the same distance from a given line and a fixed point not on the line. The fixed point is called the focus. When incoming waves hit the dish, they are all reflected to the focus where the signal is received. Parabolas are quadratic functions and can be written as simple equations such as:

$$y = 0.25x^2$$

Graph this parabola on a coordinate grid. Its focus is at the point (0,1).

Exit

Quadratic Equations
The Quadratic Formula
Examples

MENU
QUIT

Using Discriminants and Graphs

Key Objectives
The student will:
- determine the nature of the roots of a quadratic equation.

Key Terms
quadratic, parabola, quadratic formula, discriminant, inequality, *x*-intercept

Prerequisite Skills
- Factor polynomial expressions of the form $ax^2 + bx + c = 0$.
- Determine the vertex and intercepts of the graph of a quadratic function.
- Connect algebraic and graphical transformations of quadratic functions by completing the square as required.
- Solve quadratic equations and relate the solutions to the zeros of a corresponding quadratic function by factoring, the quadratic formula, and graphing.

Lesson Description

In this lesson, students learn how to determine the nature of the roots of a quadratic equation by using the discriminant. The discriminant is the expression $b^2 - 4ac$, which is found under the radical in the quadratic formula.

The **Introduction** demonstrates how to use a given equation to determine the selling price of a new book. After making some trial-and-error calculations, the publisher decides to use a graph to find the range of selling prices that will yield a profit. In the **Summary**, the publisher uses the discriminant to determine if it is possible for the company to earn a specific profit.

In the **Tutorial**, students use factoring, graphing, and the quadratic formula to find the two distinct roots of a quadratic equation. Graphing the parabola allows students to see the two *x*-intercepts of the parabola. Factoring and the quadratic formula help the students find the exact values of the two roots. Through further examples, students discover how the expression within the radical of the quadratic formula (the discriminant) will allow them to decide if there are two, one, or no real roots for a quadratic equation.

The **Examples** show how to use the properties of the discriminant to solve various problems. In the first and second problems, students learn that a quadratic equation can be factored only if the discriminant is greater than or equal to zero. In the third problem, they examine the sum and product of the roots of a quadratic equation to

see that the sum of the roots is $-\frac{b}{a}$, and the product is $\frac{c}{a}$. In the final problem, students use this relationship to determine an unknown coefficient in an equation where one root is twice the other.

Instructor Intervention

- Students may be confused by the terms **roots**, **zeros**, and **x-intercepts**, and may not recognize, at first, that all three represent the same value. Explain that even though the values are the same for the roots of an equation ($x^2 + 5x + 6 = 0$), the zeros of a function ($y = x^2 + 5x + 6$), and the x-intercepts of the graph of this function, different terms are used to indicate which form is being discussed.

- The classifications "two real roots," "one real root," and "no real roots" used in this lesson are linked to $b^2 - 4ac > 0$, $b^2 - 4ac = 0$, and $b^2 - 4ac < 0$, respectively. A more precise description of these classifications is "two unique or distinct roots," "two identical roots," and "two non-real or imaginary roots." Some students may be confused about the meaning of "one real root" because they do not understand how a quadratic equation can be created with only one factor. Using the description "two identical real roots" lets students know that there are still two identical factors that are used to create the quadratic equation.

- The **Introduction** and **Summary** show how algebra can be used to predict the profit for the sales of a book. Ask how the equation and the corresponding graph could be used to make other predictions. For example, students might recall that the maximum profit can be found by finding the vertex of the graph.

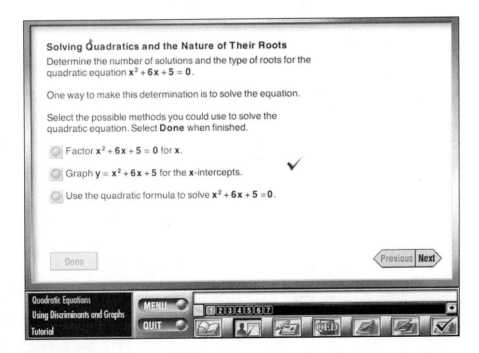

Solving Quadratics and the Nature of Their Roots
Determine the number of solutions and the type of roots for the quadratic equation $x^2 + 6x + 5 = 0$.

One way to make this determination is to solve the equation.

Select the possible methods you could use to solve the quadratic equation. Select **Done** when finished.

○ Factor $x^2 + 6x + 5 = 0$ for x.

○ Graph $y = x^2 + 6x + 5$ for the x-intercepts. ✓

○ Use the quadratic formula to solve $x^2 + 6x + 5 = 0$.

Done   ‹Previous | Next›

Quadratic Equations
Using Discriminants and Graphs   MENU
Tutorial   QUIT   1 2 3 4 5 6 7

Evaluation

- The final problem in the *Student Workbook* asks students to create quadratic equations with two real roots, one real root, and no real roots. Present some of the resulting equations to the class and ask students to use $b^2 - 4ac > 0$, $b^2 - 4ac = 0$, and $b^2 - 4ac < 0$ to check the number of roots for each one.

- Give students the sum and product of the roots of a quadratic equation and ask them to write the equation in $ax^2 + bx + c = 0$ form. (The goal for students is to identify the values of a, b, and c from the formulas $sum = -\dfrac{b}{a}$ and $product = \dfrac{c}{a}$.)

  Start with simple fractions that have common denominators. Then increase the difficulty of the examples by using fractions that require students to find a common denominator. You can also use whole numbers in conjunction with fractions.

Remediation

- Many students have trouble relating mathematical statements such as $x > 0$ or $b^2 - 4ac < 0$ to their connection with positive and negative numbers. Use an integer line to review how each inequality relates to 0.

  ```
       <              >
  ←--+--+--+--+--+--+--+--→
    -3 -2 -1  0  1  2  3
  ```

  Show that all values less than 0 are negative numbers and that all values greater than 0 are positive.

- Many students may initially have difficulty identifying the correct sign for b because of the negative sign in the sum formula, especially when the value of b is already negative. A common error for students is not maintaining the sign of the coefficient. For example: $x^2 - 5x + 11 = 0$, where $a = 1$, $b = -5$, $c = 11$

$$sum = -\frac{b}{a}$$
$$= -\frac{(-5)}{1}$$
$$= -(-5)$$
$$= 5$$

Encourage students who have trouble with this sign change to show the substitution step.

Extension

A

In the **Examples**, the formulas

$$sum = -\frac{b}{a} \quad \text{and} \quad product = \frac{c}{a}$$

are found by comparing roots with equations. Some students might be interested in discovering how to use the quadratic formula to determine the sum and product formulas.

The quadratic formula

$$x = \frac{-b \pm \sqrt{b^2 - 4ac}}{2a} \quad \text{includes a}$$

$\pm$ sign, so there are two possible roots:

$$\frac{-b + \sqrt{b^2 - 4ac}}{2a} \quad \text{and}$$

$$\frac{-b - \sqrt{b^2 - 4ac}}{2a}$$

The sum of these two roots is:

$$\frac{-b + \sqrt{b^2 - 4ac}}{2a} + \frac{-b - \sqrt{b^2 - 4ac}}{2a}$$
$$= \frac{-2b}{2a}$$
$$= \frac{-b}{a}$$

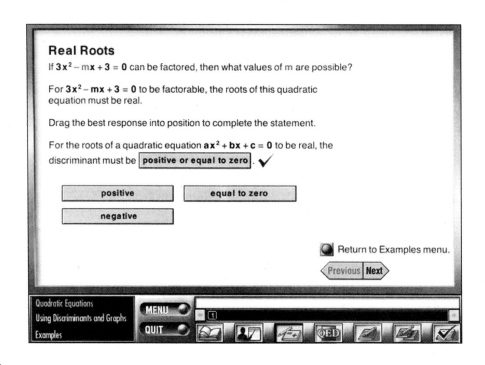

Real Roots

If $3x^2 - mx + 3 = 0$ can be factored, then what values of m are possible?

For $3x^2 - mx + 3 = 0$ to be factorable, the roots of this quadratic equation must be real.

Drag the best response into position to complete the statement.

For the roots of a quadratic equation $ax^2 + bx + c = 0$ to be real, the discriminant must be positive or equal to zero . ✓

| positive | equal to zero |
| negative |

🔘 Return to Examples menu.

‹Previous | Next›

Quadratic Equations
Using Discriminants and Graphs
Examples

MENU
QUIT

The product of these two roots is:

$$\frac{-b+\sqrt{b^2-4ac}}{2a}\times\frac{-b-\sqrt{b^2-4ac}}{2a}$$

$$=\frac{b^2-(b^2-4ac)}{4a^2}$$

$$=\frac{4ac}{4a^2}$$

$$=\frac{c}{a}$$

B

Introduce the following equation as a method for finding the quadratic equation that will produce two given roots: $x^2-(sum)x+(product)=0$. Start with simple examples (e.g., roots = –6 and 2) and have students multiply the two factors, $(x+6)(x-2)$, to confirm that the resulting equation is correct.

Once students are comfortable with this equation form, introduce irrational roots:

Example 1: roots $=2\pm\sqrt{3}$

$$sum=\left(2+\sqrt{3}\right)+\left(2-\sqrt{3}\right)$$
$$=4$$

$$product=\left(2+\sqrt{3}\right)\times\left(2-\sqrt{3}\right)$$
$$=4-3$$
$$=1$$

Therefore, the quadratic equation with the roots $2\pm\sqrt{3}$ is $x^2-4x+1=0$.

This equation form is especially useful for finding the equation when the roots are imaginary or complex.

Enrichment

A

In this lesson, the quadratic inequalities are of the form $x^2>k$ and critical values are found by solving the equation $x^2=k$.

$$x^2=k$$
$$x=\pm\sqrt{k}$$

Critical values of $x^2>k$ are $\pm\sqrt{k}$.

To increase the difficulty of possible questions, show students that the critical values may also be found by factoring.
$$x^2<a^2$$
$$x^2-a^2<0$$
$$(x+a)(x-a)<0$$
Critical values $=\pm a$

Using factoring will enable students to find the critical values for quadratic inequalities of each of these forms:
$$x^2-bx<0$$
$$x^2+bx+c>0$$
$$ax^2+bx+c\le0$$

B

The discriminant may also be used to identify conic sections. For a second-degree equation in the general form $ax^2+bxy+cy^2+dx+ey+f=0$, if at least one of the coefficients is non-zero, the values of these coefficients will allow you to determine which conic section the equation represents:
- If $b^2-4ac>0$, the conic section is a hyperbola.
- If $b^2-4ac=0$, the conic section is a parabola.
- If $b^2-4ac<0$, the conic section is an ellipse (or a circle if $a=c$).

If a, b, and c all equal zero, the equation will not be a second-degree equation. This use of the discriminant may be referred to as the discriminant theorem for conic sections.

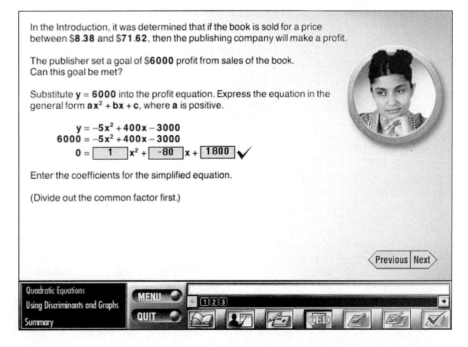

In the Introduction, it was determined that if the book is sold for a price between **$8.38** and **$71.62**, then the publishing company will make a profit.

The publisher set a goal of **$6000** profit from sales of the book. Can this goal be met?

Substitute **y = 6000** into the profit equation. Express the equation in the general form **ax² + bx + c**, where **a** is positive.

$$y=-5x^2+400x-3000$$
$$6000=-5x^2+400x-3000$$
$$0=\boxed{1}x^2+\boxed{-80}x+\boxed{1800}\;\checkmark$$

Enter the coefficients for the simplified equation.

(Divide out the common factor first.)

Previous | Next

Quadratic Equations
Using Discriminants and Graphs
Summary

MENU
QUIT

Cross-References

Quadratic Equations

Student Workbook: pages 190–193

Key Objectives

The student will:

- describe, graph, and analyze polynomial functions.

Key Terms

polynomial, degree, leading coefficient, constant, zero, multiplicity, constant function

Prerequisite Skills

- Demonstrate a general knowledge of polynomials.
- Describe a function and use function notation to evaluate and represent functions.
- Determine the domain, range, and intercepts of a function from its graph.
- Solve quadratic equations and determine the character of their real and non-real roots.

Lesson Description

In the **Introduction**, the owner of an amusement park hires a demographer to find out what percentage of the population will be between the ages of 18 and 24 in the year 2012. This data will help the park owner decide whether to make improvements or sell the property when his mortgage comes due that year. Students try to find the percentage by examining a table of values, but they realize that this method is not accurate enough. In the **Summary**, they analyze a graph of the data to solve the problem.

The **Tutorial** introduces the general polynomial form, $f(x) = a_n x^n + a_{n-1} x^{n-1} + a_{n-2} x^{n-2} + ... + a_1 x^1 + a_0$, where $a_n \neq 0$, and reviews characteristics of this form, such as the leading coefficient, degree, constant term, and y-intercept. Students examine linear functions (including constant functions), quadratic functions, and cubic functions, and then use their understanding of the relationship between degree, leading coefficient, and shape to analyze higher degree polynomial functions. They also analyze the graphs of several functions, using zeros to assist them.

In the **Examples**, students examine the multiplicity of zeros and work through a complete analysis of cubic functions. They estimate zeros of functions from tables of values or graphs. The **Examples** conclude with an analysis of higher-degree functions.

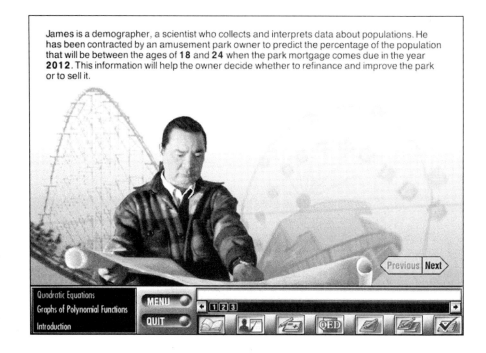

James is a demographer, a scientist who collects and interprets data about populations. He has been contracted by an amusement park owner to predict the percentage of the population that will be between the ages of **18** and **24** when the park mortgage comes due in the year **2012**. This information will help the owner decide whether to refinance and improve the park or to sell it.

Quadratic Equations
Graphs of Polynomial Functions
Introduction

MENU
QUIT

Previous | Next

Instructor Intervention

- Make sure students understand that, for most of their purposes, the notations y and $f(x)$ are interchangeable.

- You may wish to introduce the synthetic substitution method for evaluating polynomial functions. Although the method seems complicated at first, once students have learned it, they will find it easier and faster than using a calculator for evaluating some expressions. The technique is demonstrated below.

To evaluate $3x^3 - 2x^2 + 7x + 6$ for $x = 15$, first rewrite the polynomial so that all terms have a degree of one:

$$3x^3 - 2x^2 + 7x + 6 = (3x^2 - 2x + 7)x + 6$$
$$= [(3x - 2)x + 7]x + 6$$

To evaluate the polynomial for any value of x:

$$[(3x - 2)x + 7]x + 6$$

Step 1: Multiply 3 by x.
Step 2: Subtract 2.
Step 3: Multiply by x.
Step 4: Add 7.
Step 5: Multiply by x.
Step 6: Add 6.

The procedure below shows a simple way to perform the steps. Remember to include a 0 in the first line of numbers for any "missing" terms (e.g., if a polynomial is missing an x^2-term, include a 0 to take its place).

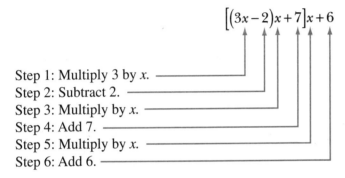

Ask: If the calculated answer is 0, what is the significance of the value of x?

Lesson Components

Examples
Multiplicity (2)
Analysis of Cubic Functions (1)
Estimating Zeros (2)
Graphs of Higher Order Functions (2)
Analysis of Higher Order Functions (1)

Practice and Problems
Describing Polynomial Functions
Graphs of Polynomial Functions
Analyzing Polynomial Functions
Error Analysis

Extra Practice
Multiplicity
Analysis of Cubics
Estimating Zeros
Graphs of Higher Order Functions
Analysis of Higher Order Functions

Self-Check
Multiplicity (3)
Analysis of Cubics (2)
Estimating Zeros (1)
Graphs of Higher Order Functions (2)
Analysis of Higher Order Functions (2)

Minimum score: 7 out of 10

Evaluation

- Invite students to play a game in pairs where one student states a degree for a polynomial function and the other responds by sketching an appropriate curve, or vice versa. A similar matching activity could be played with domain/range, sign of the leading coefficient, multiplicities, and so on.

- Suggest that students create a "directory" of graphs and their equations. They should include examples of the types of graphs encountered in the lesson. This directory could then be used to generate questions for a short quiz.

- Ask students to create functions that have certain characteristics and then predict such things as domain, range, shape, y-intercept, direction of opening, and so on. Then have the students check their answers with a graphing tool.

- Write various functions on an overhead or on the board. Invite students to race to see who can be the first to evaluate the functions for various values of x. Encourage them to think first about which evaluation method would be the most efficient for each function and for each value of x.

Remediation

- Students may have difficulty with this lesson because they are not proficient at using a graphing calculator. Provide help with these skills:

  - setting the tool windows to default settings
  - adjusting the settings to display most of the critical portions of graphs on-screen
  - obtaining a table of values
  - using the trace and zoom features

- Some students may need help with factoring techniques, especially grouping.

- Ensure that students understand the relationship of the terms *linear*, *quadratic*, *cubic*, *quartic*, and *quintic* to the degree.

- Some students may become confused by the concepts of multiplicity, total zeros, total different zeros, and total different real zeros. Present several functions and work through the graphing process step-by-step. At each step, allow students to see the connections between the number of factors, the number of zeros, and the multiplicity.

Extension

A

Students could use a graphing tool to investigate the changes in the graphs of polynomial functions as the leading coefficient and/or the constant term changes in magnitude. You could present the following problem.

Graph the function $f(x) = x^3 + x^2 - 8x - 12$ on a graphing calculator:

(a) What happens to the graph when the leading coefficient increases? [The graph becomes narrower and the value of the zeros change, but the basic shape and the y-intercept remain the same.]

(b) What happens to the graph when the constant term increases or decreases? [The graph moves up or down. It has the same shape, but the zeros and the y-intercept change.]

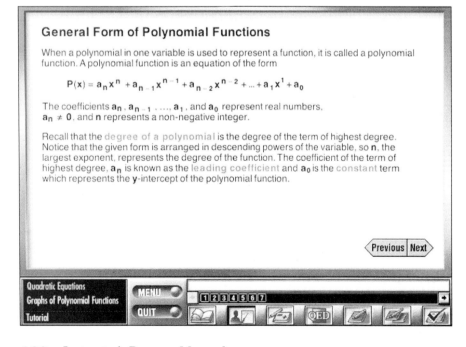

General Form of Polynomial Functions

When a polynomial in one variable is used to represent a function, it is called a polynomial function. A polynomial function is an equation of the form

$$P(x) = a_n x^n + a_{n-1} x^{n-1} + a_{n-2} x^{n-2} + \dots + a_1 x^1 + a_0$$

The coefficients a_n, a_{n-1}, ..., a_1, and a_0 represent real numbers, $a_n \neq 0$, and n represents a non-negative integer.

Recall that the degree of a polynomial is the degree of the term of highest degree. Notice that the given form is arranged in descending powers of the variable, so n, the largest exponent, represents the degree of the function. The coefficient of the term of highest degree, a_n is known as the leading coefficient and a_0 is the constant term which represents the y-intercept of the polynomial function.

Previous | Next

Quadratic Equations
Graphs of Polynomial Functions
Tutorial
MENU
QUIT
1 2 3 4 5 6 7

(c) What happens to the graph when the entire polynomial is multiplied by a positive constant? [The shape of the graph remains basically the same, as do the zeros, but the y-intercept changes.]

(d) What happens to the graph when the entire polynomial is multiplied by –1? [The graph is reflected in the x-axis.]

B

Provide some information about a polynomial function, and ask students to find the simplest function that this information could represent. For example:

Real Zeros	Multiplicity
–2	1
–1	1
2	2

The simplest function that could have these characteristics is $f(x) = x^4 - x^3 - 6x^2 + 4x + 8$. Have students graph the function to verify the zeros.

Enrichment

A

Invite students to investigate Descartes' Rule of Signs, a rule that determines an upper bound to the number of positive zeros and to the number of negative zeros of a polynomial. Have them use the law to predict the number of zeros for various functions and then graph the functions to check.

A

Supply students with a function and its derivative (e.g., $2x^3 + 4x^2 - 5x - 1$ and $6x^2 + 8x - 5$). Ask students to investigate the relationship between the sign value of the derivative and the intervals in which the function increases or decreases. Next, ask students to determine what happens to the graph at the point where the function changes from increasing to decreasing and vice versa.

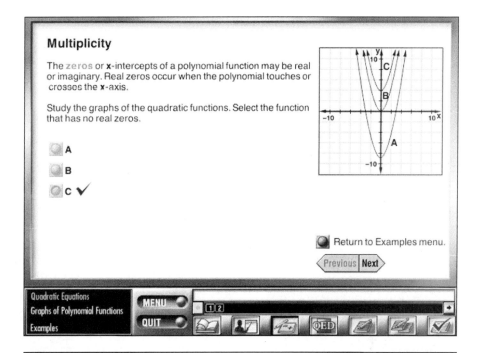

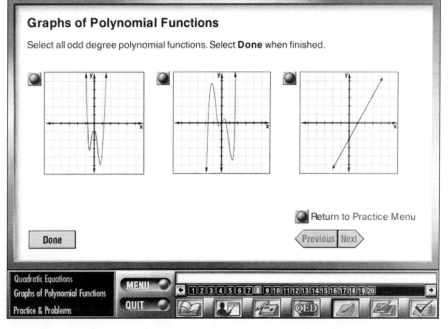

Cross-References

Quadratic Equations

Student Workbook: pages 194–197

Key Objectives

The student will:

- describe, graph, and analyze rational functions.

Key Terms

rational function, rational expression, polynomial, discontinuous, continuous, asymptote, domain, range, degree, symmetry

Prerequisite Skills

- Describe, graph, and analyze polynomial functions using technology.
- Determine nonpermissible values for a variable in rational expressions.
- Use a graphing tool to draw the graph of a function from its equation.
- Use function notation to evaluate and represent functions.
- Determine the domain and range of a relation from its graph.

Lesson Description

The **Introduction** presents a problem about Winnie and Rakia's bracelet-making business. They need to find whether the average cost of making a bracelet can be $8.50 if the equation for the average cost is $A(x) = \dfrac{8.50x + 325}{x}$. By guessing and testing several numbers, students conclude that the average cost of making one bracelet will never be exactly $8.50. They verify this conclusion in the **Summary** by graphing the function. The graph shows that there is a horizontal asymptote at $y = 8.50$, so the average cost will approach, but never reach, $8.50.

The **Tutorial** begins by reviewing the definition of a rational function and how to identify rational functions in written and graphical form. Then students graph $y = \dfrac{1}{x}$ and $y = \dfrac{3x}{2x - 1}$ and study the characteristics of these graphs to see that there are horizontal and vertical asymptotes that each graph approaches but does not touch. Students use the intercepts and asymptotes of the graph for $y = \dfrac{3x}{2x - 1}$ to determine the domain and range of the function.

The **Examples** lead students through problems involving points of discontinuity and horizontal asymptotes. The "Horizontal Asymptotes" example gives rules that students can use to quickly identify horizontal asymptotes without using a table of values. In the first "Predicting Graphs" example, students use the graph, the zero, and the domain and range of $y = x^2 - 1$ to predict these characteristics for

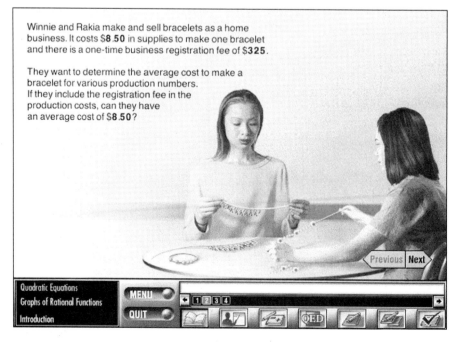

Winnie and Rakia make and sell bracelets as a home business. It costs **$8.50** in supplies to make one bracelet and there is a one-time business registration fee of **$325**.

They want to determine the average cost to make a bracelet for various production numbers. If they include the registration fee in the production costs, can they have an average cost of **$8.50**?

Quadratic Equations
Graphs of Rational Functions
Introduction

MENU
QUIT
[1] [2] [3] [4]

QED

$y = \dfrac{1}{x^2 - 1}$. In the last example, students learn how to determine a graph's lines of symmetry, and how these lines of symmetry can help in drawing a graph more quickly.

Instructor Intervention

- An understanding of the reciprocal function is a solid foundation on which to build. Start with monomial reciprocal functions, and then show how the graph is affected as the polynomials that make up the function become more complex.

- Before starting the lesson, review techniques for factoring polynomials. Proficiency at factoring will be very helpful in identifying asymptotes.

- On a graphing calculator, demonstrate how to use parentheses or other advanced features to enter the rational function as two separate polynomial functions.

- Students need to be able to identify the degree of a function in order to find horizontal asymptotes. Review these points:

  - The degree of a polynomial is the highest degree of any of its terms.

  - If the function is a constant, the degree is 0. For example, $3 = 3x^0$ has a degree of 0.

  - If there is no exponent, the degree is 1. For example, $3x + 6 = 3x^1 + 6$ has a degree of 1.

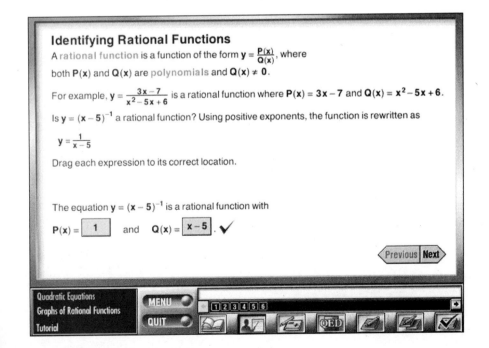

Identifying Rational Functions

A rational function is a function of the form $y = \dfrac{P(x)}{Q(x)}$, where both $P(x)$ and $Q(x)$ are polynomials and $Q(x) \neq 0$.

For example, $y = \dfrac{3x - 7}{x^2 - 5x + 6}$ is a rational function where $P(x) = 3x - 7$ and $Q(x) = x^2 - 5x + 6$.

Is $y = (x - 5)^{-1}$ a rational function? Using positive exponents, the function is rewritten as

$y = \dfrac{1}{x - 5}$

Drag each expression to its correct location.

The equation $y = (x - 5)^{-1}$ is a rational function with

$P(x) = \boxed{1}$ and $Q(x) = \boxed{x - 5}$. ✔

⟨ Previous | Next ⟩

Quadratic Equations
Graphs of Rational Functions
Tutorial

MENU
QUIT
⟨ 1 2 3 4 5 6 ⟩

Evaluation

- Ask pairs to graph various functions. One partner uses a graphing calculator, and one uses pencil and paper. They graph functions with these characteristics and compare their results.
  - one vertical asymptote, numerator is a constant (*example*: $\dfrac{5}{x-1}$)
  - two vertical asymptotes, numerator is a constant (*example*: $\dfrac{6}{x^2-9}$)
  - one vertical asymptote, numerator is of degree one (*example*: $\dfrac{x+1}{x-5}$)
  - two vertical asymptotes, numerator is of degree one (*example*: $\dfrac{x-2}{x^2+5x+6}$)
  - one vertical asymptote, numerator is negative (*example*: $\dfrac{-4}{x+3}$)
  - two vertical asymptotes, numerator is negative (*example*: $\dfrac{-8}{x^2-3x-4}$)
  - a function that has a point of discontinuity (*example*: $\dfrac{x^2-1}{x+1}$)

- Observe the students as they work. Watch for errors in calculator entry. Do they understand the effect of restrictions? Do they understand the effect of a negative sign? Do they understand how the graph is affected when the numerator is a constant?

Remediation

- Review the vocabulary outlined in the **Key Terms** section of this lesson.

- Show students how to use tables of values to sketch graphs, first using the simpler functions, then moving on to more complex functions. Point out the trend in the values as an asymptote is approached.

- Some students may need additional help with these processes: factoring polynomials, isolating a variable, solving equations, and entering an equation into a graphing calculator.

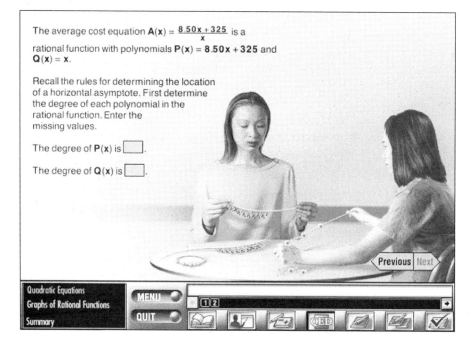

The average cost equation $A(x) = \dfrac{8.50x + 325}{x}$ is a rational function with polynomials $P(x) = 8.50x + 325$ and $Q(x) = x$.

Recall the rules for determining the location of a horizontal asymptote. First determine the degree of each polynomial in the rational function. Enter the missing values.

The degree of $P(x)$ is [ ].

The degree of $Q(x)$ is [ ].

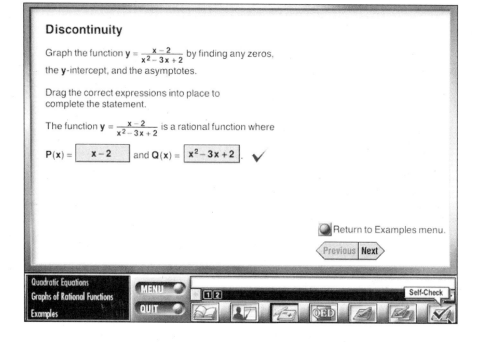

Discontinuity

Graph the function $y = \dfrac{x-2}{x^2-3x+2}$ by finding any zeros, the y-intercept, and the asymptotes.

Drag the correct expressions into place to complete the statement.

The function $y = \dfrac{x-2}{x^2-3x+2}$ is a rational function where

$P(x) = \boxed{x-2}$ and $Q(x) = \boxed{x^2-3x+2}$. ✓

Return to Examples menu.

Extension

A

Ask students to create a table of values for each function using very small and very large values of x (both positive and negative).

$$y = \frac{7}{x^2 + 2x + 4}$$

$$y = \frac{3x^2}{x^2 - 5x + 6}$$

$$y = \frac{x^2}{x - 4}$$

Discuss limits to infinity. Point out that the rules students learned for finding horizontal asymptotes are derived from analyzing limits in this way.

B

Invite the students to accurately draw the graph of a certain function, then have others try to determine the equation.

Enrichment

A

Challenge students to discover what happens to the asymptotes when the degree of either $P(x)$ or $Q(x)$ is greater than 0, 1, or 2.

B

Students could investigate how rational functions are used in scientific applications such as light intensity, electrical current, radio transmission, Boyle's Law of Gases, and problems involving physical work energy. Invite students to develop a mini-presentation on their chosen topic to give to the class.

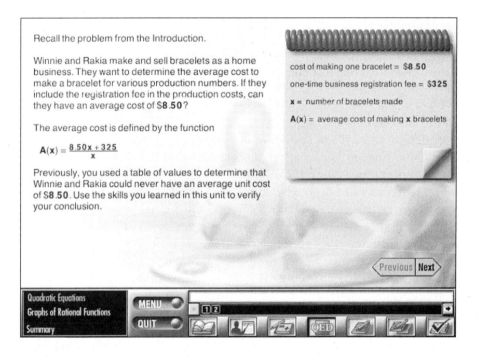

Recall the problem from the Introduction.

Winnie and Rakia make and sell bracelets as a home business. They want to determine the average cost to make a bracelet for various production numbers. If they include the registration fee in the production costs, can they have an average cost of $8.50?

The average cost is defined by the function

$$A(x) = \frac{8.50x + 325}{x}$$

Previously, you used a table of values to determine that Winnie and Rakia could never have an average unit cost of $8.50. Use the skills you learned in this unit to verify your conclusion.

cost of making one bracelet = **$8.50**

one-time business registration fee = **$325**

x = number of bracelets made

A(x) = average cost of making **x** bracelets

Previous | Next

Quadratic Equations
Graphs of Rational Functions
Summary

MENU
QUIT

1 2

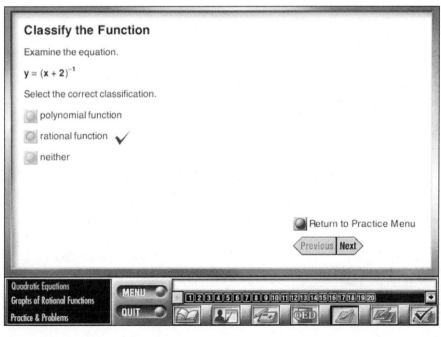

Classify the Function

Examine the equation.

$$y = (x + 2)^{-1}$$

Select the correct classification.

- ○ polynomial function
- ◉ rational function ✓
- ○ neither

○ Return to Practice Menu

Previous | Next

Quadratic Equations
Graphs of Rational Functions
Practice & Problems

MENU
QUIT

1 2 3 4 5 6 7 8 9 10 11 12 13 14 15 16 17 18 19 20

11 SOLVING EQUATIONS

11.1 Absolute Value Equations

Cross-References

Solving Equations

Student Workbook: pages 198–201

Key Objectives

The student will:

- learn how to formulate and apply strategies to solve absolute value equations.

Key Terms

absolute value, solve, root, extraneous root, verify, positive, negative, functions, intersection

Prerequisite Skills

- Solve and verify first-degree, single-variable equations.

Lesson Description

In this lesson, students learn the definition of absolute value and use various techniques to solve different types of absolute value equations. They also learn the importance of verifying solutions of absolute value equations.

In the **Introduction**, Winnie finds an absolute value function in her friend Samina's college textbook, but doesn't know how to solve it. Samina begins her explanation of absolute value by referring to the distance between two cities: If Colorado Springs is 144 miles north of the New Mexico/Colorado border, and Denver is 212 miles north of the same border, the distance from Colorado Springs to Denver is 68 miles and the distance from Denver to Colorado Springs is –68 miles. However, distance is always a positive value, so absolute value notation can be used to ensure a positive result. Samina uses this idea to explain the general rules for absolute value. In the **Summary**, Winnie solves the absolute value function from the textbook using what she has learned.

In the **Tutorial**, students learn two techniques for solving absolute value equations. The first technique is to consider each case separate-

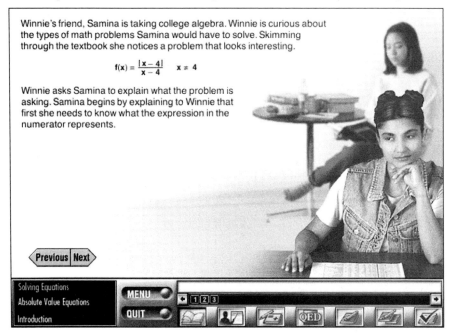

Winnie's friend, Samina is taking college algebra. Winnie is curious about the types of math problems Samina would have to solve. Skimming through the textbook she notices a problem that looks interesting.

$$f(x) = \frac{|x-4|}{x-4} \qquad x \ne 4$$

Winnie asks Samina to explain what the problem is asking. Samina begins by explaining to Winnie that first she needs to know what the expression in the numerator represents.

Previous | Next

Solving Equations
Absolute Value Equations
Introduction

MENU
QUIT
1 2 3

ly – replace the absolute value equation with two equations not containing absolute value (one which assumes that the absolute value expression is positive and one which assumes it is negative). The second technique is to graph $y = $ *right side* and $y = $ *left side* to find the points of intersection of the two graphs. The x-coordinates of these points are the solutions of the original equation.

The **Examples** pose problems where students simplify absolute value equations, encounter extraneous roots, and solve equations containing more than one absolute value expression.

Instructor Intervention

- Remind students that solutions of absolute value equations resulting from algebraic techniques (non-graphical techniques) must be verified to identify any extraneous roots.

- As students work through the lesson, they will need to use several previously learned skills:
  - isolating a variable or an expression
  - verifying solutions
  - graphing functions

- Students may be confused by the solution process for absolute value equations. They may not understand why the solution for one absolute value equation requires solving two separate equations not containing absolute value, and they may be unsure about what these two new equations should be. Because the method for solving an absolute value equation derives from the definition of absolute value, it may be helpful to write the definition on a bulletin board display for students' reference. Work through one solution with the class, and encourage students to add a list of solution steps to the display.

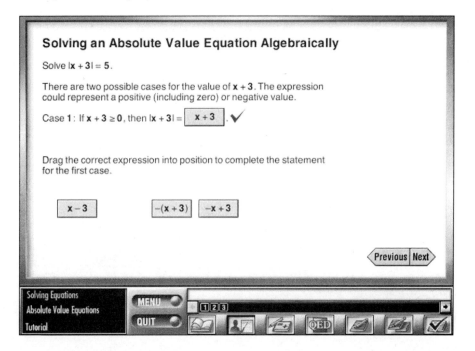

Evaluation

- Give a true/false quiz with statements such as the following. Ask students to explain why each statement is true or false.

1. The absolute value of a number is always the number. [F]
2. $|2| - |-3| = 5$ [F]
3. $|-3| + |5| + |-8| - |-4| = -2$ [F]
4. $|x + 5| + |7 - x| = 14$ if $x = -6$ [T]
5. $|x - 5| = -(x - 5)$ if $x < 5$ [T]
6. $3|x - 3| + |x + 5| - |2x + 4|$ $= -12$ if $x = -2$ [F]
7. $|12x - 3| = 3|4x - 1|$ [T]

- Graph $y = |x + 5|$ and $y = -3$ on the same grid, and ask students to find the solution of the system. Ask: For what values of x does $|x + 5| = -3$? [Since the graphs don't intersect, there is no solution.]

- Graph $y = |x - 4|$ and $y = 3$ on the same grid, and ask students to find the solution of the system. Ask: For what values of x does $|x - 4| = 3$? [The solution can be determined from the graph; the solutions are $x = 1$ or $x = 7$.]

Remediation

- Review techniques for solving equations. Solving absolute value equations requires isolating the absolute value expression, writing the two separate cases, and then isolating the variable. Make sure that students can isolate an expression as well as a variable.

- Students who make many sign errors should work with the most basic absolute value problems. When they can substitute into absolute value expressions successfully, they should be able to proceed to solving equations.

- For students who have difficulty understanding the concept of absolute value, review the definition of absolute value, using simple examples, or consider the graph of the absolute value function. The true/false quiz in the **Evaluation** section could be used to check understanding of absolute value.

Extension

A
Encourage students to graph more complicated problems such as $|x + 5| = |x - 7|$. This could be done using graphing calculators.

B
Familiarize students with the graph of $y = |x|$ and use the standard transformations to discuss the graphs of:

1. $y = |x| + 3$
2. $y = |x - 5|$
3. $y = |2x|$
4. $y = -|x|$
5. $y = 3|x|$
6. $y = -2|x + 4| - 3$

C
Students could create absolute value equations that have two solutions, one solution, and no solution.

Enrichment

A
Students could consider the graph of $|y| = x$ and discuss whether it is a function. Ask: Under what conditions is an absolute value equation a function? not a function?

B
Have students investigate inequalities containing absolute value. They could try to find the solutions to the inequalities $|x - 3| < 5$ and $|x + 4| > 7$.

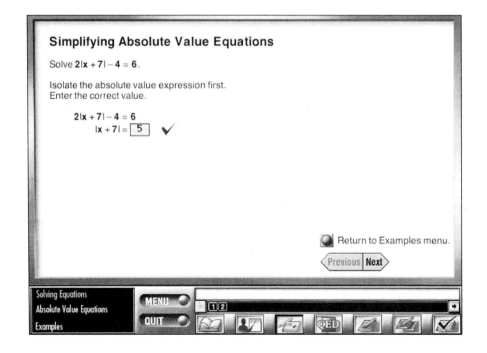

C

Ask students whether $|x| = \sqrt{x^2}$ could also be used as a definition of $|x|$.

D

Have students consider the absolute value equation $|x - 5| + |x + 3| = 14$. For an equation like this, it helps to group possible solutions according to whether they are greater than 5, between −3 and 5, or less than −3.

Case 1: $x \geq 5$

If $x \geq 5$, then $x - 5 \geq 0$, and $|x - 5| = x - 5$.
If $x \geq 5$, then $x + 3 \geq 0$, and $|x + 3| = x + 3$.

$$|x - 5| + |x + 3| = 14$$
$$x - 5 + x + 3 = 14$$
$$x = 8$$

By substituting 8 for x into the original equation, it is verified that $x = 8$ is a solution.

Case 2: $-3 \leq x < 5$

If $x < 5$, then $x - 5 < 0$, and $|x - 5| = -(x - 5)$.
If $x \geq -3$, then $x + 3 \geq 0$, and $|x + 3| = x + 3$.

$$|x - 5| + |x + 3| = 14$$
$$-(x - 5) + x + 3 = 14$$
$$-x + 5 + x + 3 = 14$$
$$8 = 14$$

This statement is false. There is no solution to the equation $|x - 5| + |x + 3| = 14$ in the interval $-3 \leq x < 5$.

Case 3: $x < -3$

If $x < -3$, then $x - 5 < 0$, and $|x - 5| = -(x - 5)$.
If $x < -3$, then $x + 3 < 0$, and $|x + 3| = -(x + 3)$.

$$|x - 5| + |x + 3| = 14$$
$$-(x - 5) - (x + 3) = 14$$
$$-x + 5 - x - 3 = 14$$
$$-2x + 2 = 14$$
$$-2x = 12$$
$$x = -6$$

By substituting −6 for x into the original equation, it is verified that $x = -6$ is a solution.

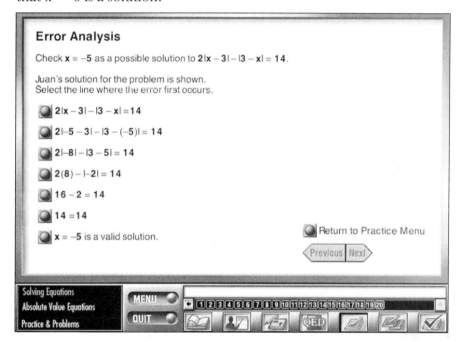

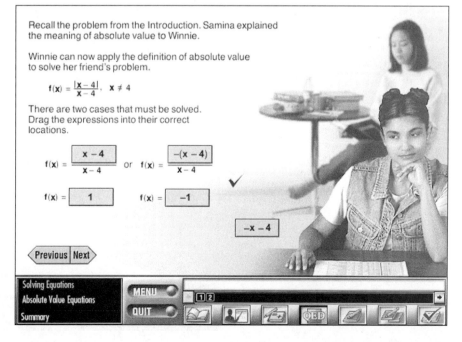

11.2 **Radical Equations**

Cross-References
Solving Equations

Student Workbook: pages 202–205

Key Objectives
The student will:
- solve simple radical equations involving a single radical.
- solve radical equations containing two radicals.
- solve word problems involving radical equations.

Key Terms
radical, square root, principle square root, extraneous root, FOIL, solve, isolate

Prerequisite Skills
- Solve and verify linear equations.
- Translate phrases into mathematical expressions.
- Factor polynomials of the type $ax^2 + bx + c = 0$.
- Solve quadratic equations.
- Add and subtract polynomial expressions.
- Find the product of polynomials.
- Evaluate polynomial expressions by substituting values for variables.
- Square binomials with and without radicals.

Lesson Description

In the **Introduction**, a police officer tries to determine the speed a car was traveling at before an accident. He knows that the speed can be determined using the length of the skid marks and the equation $s = \sqrt{30df}$, where s is the speed of the vehicle, d is the length of the skid marks, and f is the coefficient of friction. The officer tries solving the problem using a guess-and-test method, but finds it too inefficient. The students quickly solve the problem in the **Summary** by applying their knowledge of solving radical equations.

In the **Tutorial**, students review the concept of a square root and then learn the technique of squaring both sides of an equation to remove radicals, giving access to the variable under the square root. They also learn about the concept of extraneous roots as they apply to radical equations.

The **Examples** provide practice in solving various types of radical equations. The questions include equations where factoring must occur, equations that have more than one radical, equations that have nested radicals $(e.g., \sqrt{\sqrt{x}})$, and word problems involving radicals.

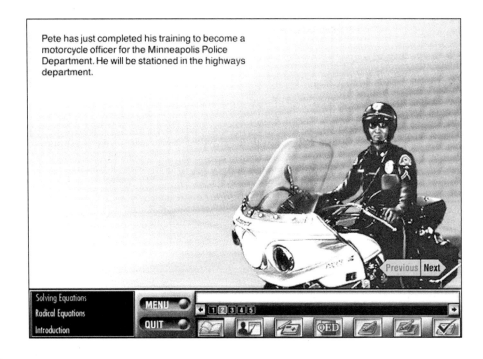

Pete has just completed his training to become a motorcycle officer for the Minneapolis Police Department. He will be stationed in the highways department.

Instructor Intervention

- The problems in this lesson build on many previously-acquired skills. You may want to review:
  - ◆ solving equations.
  - ◆ squaring binomials, especially binomials that include radicals.
  - ◆ calculating square roots; emphasize that a positive square root cannot equal a negative number.
  - ◆ verifying solutions; roots should be checked to determine if they are extraneous.

- Discuss what students can do when the root does not give the expected result.

  - ◆ Check the solution again.
  - ◆ Check the work.
  - ◆ Have another student check the work.
  - ◆ Check to see if the question was copied correctly.
  - ◆ Compare solutions with other students.

- Students could use graphing technology to solve radical equations.

- When students don't immediately recognize the correct choice in an on-screen exercise, encourage them to solve the problem on paper rather than simply guess at answers.

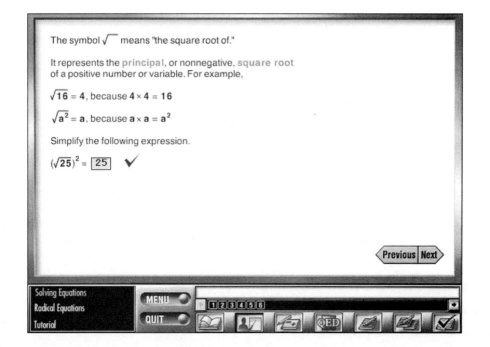

The symbol $\sqrt{}$ means "the square root of."

It represents the principal, or nonnegative, square root of a positive number or variable. For example,

$\sqrt{16} = 4$, because $4 \times 4 = 16$

$\sqrt{a^2} = a$, because $a \times a = a^2$

Simplify the following expression.

$(\sqrt{25})^2 = \boxed{25}$ ✔

Previous | Next

Solving Equations
Radical Equations
Tutorial

MENU
QUIT

1 2 3 4 5 6

Evaluation

- Divide the class into teams. Have each team create a ten-question quiz that includes at least one problem from each of these categories:
  - **(a)** definitions of terms and symbols
  - **(b)** equations with one radical
  - **(c)** equations with two radicals
  - **(d)** equations with a nested radical
  - **(e)** radical equations that require factoring
  - **(f)** practical applications of radical equations (geometry formulas are a good start: Pythagorean relationship, Distance Formula, etc.)

  For each problem, students should write the question, the solution steps, and the final answer on separate sheets of paper. Students can either write these in mixed-up order or cut them apart to separate them. The groups could then exchange quizzes and race to see which group can be the first to correctly match all the parts for all ten questions.

- Observe students as they solve radical equations. Do they isolate the radical before squaring? Can they square binomials that contain radicals? Do they recognize when they need to square twice? Can they factor? simplify? Do they check for extraneous roots?

Remediation

- Review the vocabulary in the **Key Terms** section at the beginning of the lesson.

- Students may have difficulty squaring expressions such as $\sqrt{2x+3}-1$. Begin by reviewing the FOIL technique using simple binomials, like $(n-1)^2$. Then show how $(\sqrt{2x+3}-1)^2$ is like $(n-1)^2$ by letting n replace $\sqrt{2x+3}$ in the first expression. For example:

$$(\sqrt{2x+3}-1)^2 \Rightarrow (n-1)^2 \qquad ①$$
$$= n^2 - 2n + 1 \qquad ②$$
$$= (\sqrt{2x+3})^2 - 2(\sqrt{2x+3}) + 1 \quad ③$$
$$= 2x + 3 - 2\sqrt{2x+3} + 1 \qquad ④$$
$$= 2x + 4 - 2\sqrt{2x+3}$$

① Replace $\sqrt{2x+3}$ with n.
② Square the expression.
③ Replace n with $\sqrt{2x+3}$.
④ Simplify.

- Assign exercises on evaluating expressions for given values.

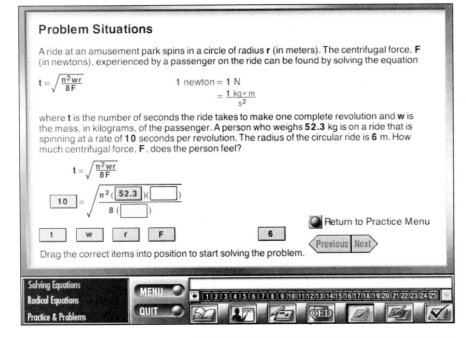

Problem Situations

A ride at an amusement park spins in a circle of radius **r** (in meters). The centrifugal force, **F** (in newtons), experienced by a passenger on the ride can be found by solving the equation

$$t = \sqrt{\frac{\pi^2 w r}{8F}}$$

1 newton = 1 N
$$= \frac{1 \text{ kg} \times \text{m}}{\text{s}^2}$$

where **t** is the number of seconds the ride takes to make one complete revolution and **w** is the mass, in kilograms, of the passenger. A person who weighs **52.3** kg is on a ride that is spinning at a rate of **10** seconds per revolution. The radius of the circular ride is **6** m. How much centrifugal force, **F**, does the person feel?

$$t = \sqrt{\frac{\pi^2 w r}{8F}}$$

$$10 = \sqrt{\frac{\pi^2 (\boxed{52.3})(\ \ )}{8(\ \ )}}$$

| t | w | r | F | | 6 |

Return to Practice Menu
Previous | Next

Drag the correct items into position to start solving the problem.

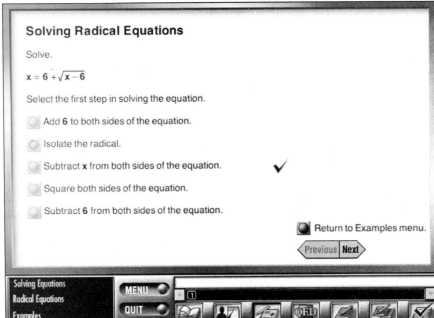

Solving Radical Equations

Solve.

$$x = 6 + \sqrt{x-6}$$

Select the first step in solving the equation.

- Add **6** to both sides of the equation.
- Isolate the radical.
- Subtract **x** from both sides of the equation. ✓
- Square both sides of the equation.
- Subtract **6** from both sides of the equation.

Return to Examples menu.
Previous | Next

Extension

A

Challenge students to solve radical equations involving root indices other than 2, including variable root indices. Students can use graphing technology to solve for these roots.

B

Invite students to investigate radical inequalities. They could try to find the solutions to the inequalities $\sqrt{x+4} > 9$ and $\sqrt{4-x} - \sqrt{x+6} \le 2$.

Enrichment

A

Ask students to graph some of the radical equations from the lesson and look for common characteristics among the graphs.

B

Students could research different subject areas to find where radical equations are used, and then create problems for classmates to solve. Some possible equations:

- $R = \sqrt{F_1^2 + F_2^2}$ a formula for the resultant or effective force, R, if F_1 and F_2 are forces pulling at right angles to each other

- $d = \sqrt{\dfrac{3h}{2}}$ distance in miles from a spacecraft to Earth's horizon, where h is the height of the spacecraft in feet

- $f = \sqrt{\dfrac{\pi F^2}{4A}}$ a formula for the f-stop of a camera, where F is the focal length and A is the aperture

- $d = \sqrt{(x_2 - x_1)^2 + (y_2 - y_1)^2}$ the distance in the coordinate plane from (x_1, y_1) to (x_2, y_2)

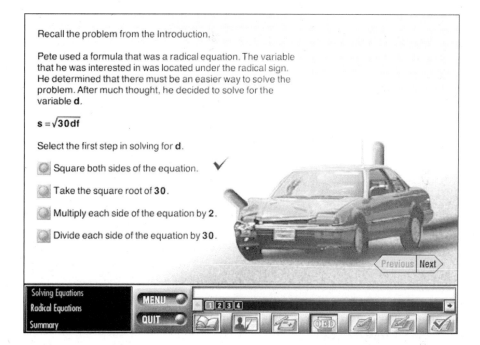

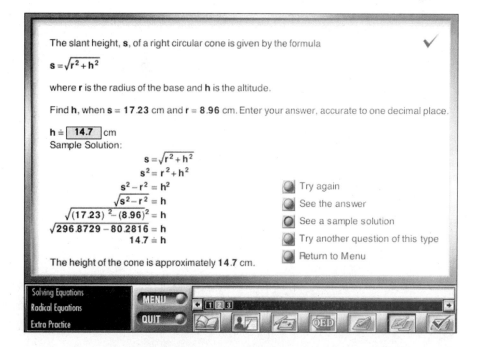

11.3 Rational Equations

Cross-References
Solving Equations

Student Workbook: pages 206–209

Key Objectives
The student will:
- learn how to solve equations with terms containing the unknown in the denominator.

Key Terms
rational equation, term, denominator, nonpermissible value, lowest common denominator, radical equation, polynomial, factor, distributive property, FOIL

Prerequisite Skills
- Factor polynomial expressions of the forms $ax^2 + bx + c$ and $a^2x^2 - b^2y^2$.
- Find the product of polynomials.
- Determine the nonpermissible values for the variable in rational expressions.
- Find and verify the solutions of rational expressions.
- Solve quadratic equations using factoring, the quadratic formula, and graphing.
- Solve absolute value and radical equations.

Lesson Description

In this lesson, students solve rational equations that simplify to quadratics.

In the **Introduction**, students need to calculate an airplane's average flight speed on the round trip between New York and South America. Due to prevailing northerly winds, an airplane can fly south faster than it can fly north. The students create an expression for the traveling time at each speed, where the second expression is derived from the first, and then add the two expressions to create a rational equation representing the total traveling time. In the **Summary**, students use strategies they learned in the **Tutorial** and **Examples** to solve the equation.

The first part of the **Tutorial** reviews how to recognize a rational equation. Then students learn how to determine the nonpermissible values and the LCD for rational equations, and how to solve rational equations.

In the **Examples** and **Practice** sections, students practice what they learned in the **Tutorial**. They begin by solving rational equations that have factored denominators, then progress to equations that require factoring and equations that involve absolute value or radical expressions.

Jim is flying from New York City to a remote location in South America, a distance of **4200** mi. His jet plane can make the round trip in **13** h. Because of the prevailing northerly winds, the plane is able to fly south about **100** mph faster than it flies north.

What is the speed of the plane when Jim is traveling from New York City to his southern destination?

Previous | Next

Solving Equations
Rational Equations
Introduction

MENU
QUIT

Instructor Intervention

- This lesson builds on knowledge acquired in previous lessons. Review the lessons in the "Rational Expressions" section.

- You may want to review different factoring techniques prior to starting this lesson. Invite the students to create a bulletin board display summarizing common factoring, factoring differences of squares, and trinomial factoring. For trinomial factoring, they could organize their information in a table:

| If the last term is positive: | $ax^2 + bx + c$ | Look for factors of ac with a sum of b. | Example: To factor $2x^2 - 15x + 7$, find factors of 14 with a sum of -15. The numbers are -1 and -14, so the factors are: $(2x - 1)(x - 7)$ |
| If the last term is negative: | $ax^2 + bx - c$ | Look for factors of ac with a difference of b. | Example: To factor $x^2 - 5x - 24$, find factors of -24 with a difference of -5. The numbers are 8 and 3, so the factors are: $(x + 3)(x - 8)$ |

- To prepare, work through a few examples of simple rational equations (i.e., equations that simplify to linear equations, as in the lesson "Solving Rational Equations"). Show students that complicated equations follow the same solution process as simple ones, but have an additional factoring step.

- Review how to find the lowest common multiple of three numbers, and then use the same steps to find the lowest common denominator for a rational expression. For example:

Numbers
$$\frac{1}{15} + \frac{3}{5} - \frac{1}{6}$$
$$\frac{1}{(3)(5)} + \frac{3}{5} - \frac{1}{(2)(3)}$$
$$\text{LCD} = (3)(5)(2)$$

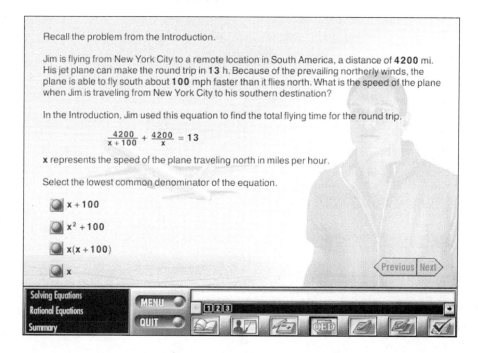

Recall the problem from the Introduction.

Jim is flying from New York City to a remote location in South America, a distance of **4200** mi. His jet plane can make the round trip in **13** h. Because of the prevailing northerly winds, the plane is able to fly south about **100** mph faster than it flies north. What is the speed of the plane when Jim is traveling from New York City to his southern destination?

In the Introduction, Jim used this equation to find the total flying time for the round trip.

$$\frac{4200}{x + 100} + \frac{4200}{x} = 13$$

x represents the speed of the plane traveling north in miles per hour.

Select the lowest common denominator of the equation.

- $x + 100$
- $x^2 + 100$
- $x(x + 100)$
- x

⟨Previous | Next⟩

Solving Equations
Rational Equations
Summary

MENU

QUIT

Evaluation

- In groups of three or four, have students create rational equations that simplify to quadratics, and that meet these conditions:
  - must have two real solutions
  - must have two integer solutions
  - must have one real solution and one extraneous solution

The students should create complete solutions. Groups can exchange their problems, or you can collect them and use them on tests or quizzes.

Students should see that the easiest way to create the equations is to work backward. You could present these tips:

- Start by writing factors from the solutions. For example, if a solution is $x = 8$, one factor will be $(x - 8)$.

- Remember to include extraneous solutions in the denominator. For example, if an extraneous solution is $x = -3$, the factor $(x + 3)$ must be in the denominator.

- To make the questions complex and interesting, include other factors that eventually cancel out.

- Ask students to write in their journals the steps involved in solving rational equations and any special cases they encountered while working through this lesson.

- Give students an incorrect solution to a rational equation and ask them to identify

the error(s), speculate how the error may have occurred, and then correct the mistake. Common errors could include:

- neglecting to find nonpermissible values before solving an equation.
- multiplying only fractional terms of the rational equation by the LCD, overlooking the monomial non-fractional term(s).
- applying the distributive property incorrectly.
- incorrect factoring.

Your students' work will be a good source of errors. When grading assignments, quizzes, and tests, take note of critical errors that your students make for later use.

- Observe students as they solve rational equations. Can they identify nonpermissible values? Do they routinely use the *lowest* common denominator? Do they multiply all terms by the LCD correctly? Can they factor? simplify? Do they check for extraneous solutions?

Remediation

- Review the distributive property of multiplication, including some examples involving negative signs, for example, $-3(x + 2) = -3x - 6$ and $-(x - 2) = -x + 2$.

- Review how to find the lowest common multiple of three numbers, and then use the same steps to find the lowest common denominator for a rational expression.

Rational Expressions

$$\frac{2x}{x^2 - 9} + 2 - \frac{x - 3}{x^2 + 7x + 12}$$

$$\frac{2x}{(x + 3)(x - 3)} + \frac{2}{1} - \frac{x - 3}{(x + 3)(x + 4)}$$

$$LCD = (x + 3)(x - 3)(x + 4)$$

Steps for Finding LCD

Factor the denominator.

Multiply the factors, without repeating any factors in the multiplication.

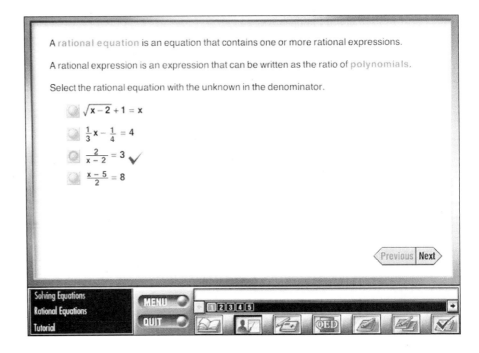

- Students often have difficulty multiplying monomials by trinomials and binomials by binomials. Concentrate on the algebra skills needed for this lesson, especially on using the distributive property and FOIL.

- Some students may not understand *why* they multiply each term in an equation by the LCD. Explain that this step is essential because it cancels out the denominators.

Extension

A

Problems that simplify to cubic and higher-degree expressions make a natural extension to this lesson. For example:

$$\frac{x^2 - 4}{x + 1} - \frac{x}{x - 1} = \frac{-2}{x^2 - 1}$$

Solution set = {–2, 3}, since 1 and –1 are nonpermissible values.]

B

Present some rational equations which can't be solved by factoring, but require using the quadratic formula. For example:

$$\frac{3x}{x^2 - 4} + \frac{2}{x - 2} = \frac{2x - 1}{x^2 + 5x + 6}$$

[Answer: $x = \dfrac{-24 \pm 2\sqrt{114}}{6}$, so $x = -0.44$ or $x = -5.09$]

Enrichment

A

Invite students to create word problems involving rational equations. They could use the distance-speed-time relationship, modeling their problem on the one from the **Introduction**. (Note: For a problem similar to that in the **Introduction**, if one speed is *x*, a quadratic rational equation will result only if the other speed is a binomial linear expression in terms of *x*. A monomial relationship, such as $2x$, will result in a linear rational equation.) Students could use realistic figures for their word problems by referring to air/train/bus schedules.

B

Introduce questions that require factoring polynomials with a degree of 3 or higher. Show students how to group an expression to make it factorable.

$$\begin{aligned}
\text{e.g., } & x^3 + 2x^2 - x - 2 \\
&= x^2(x + 2) - 1(x + 2) \\
&= (x + 2)(x^2 - 1) \\
&= (x + 2)(x + 1)(x - 1)
\end{aligned}$$

Then present some rational equations where the numerator or denominator requires using this factoring method. Proceed to questions that require the use of the remainder and factor theorems. Remainder theorem: If a polynomial $F(x)$ is divided by $x - r$, then the remainder is equal to $F(r)$.
Factor theorem: A polynomial $F(x)$ has a factor $x - r$ if and only if $F(r) = 0$.

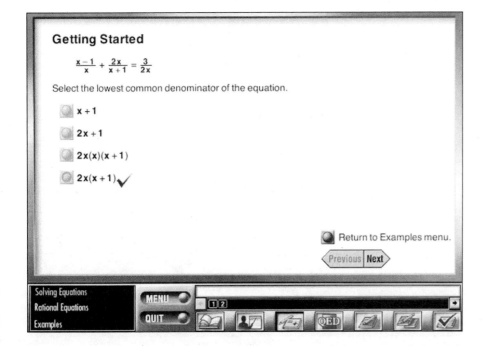

Getting Started

$$\frac{x - 1}{x} + \frac{2x}{x + 1} = \frac{3}{2x}$$

Select the lowest common denominator of the equation.

- x + 1
- 2x + 1
- 2x(x)(x + 1)
- 2x(x + 1) ✓

Return to Examples menu.

Previous Next

Solving Equations
Rational Equations
Examples

MENU
QUIT
1 2

11.4 Rational Inequalities 1

Cross-References
Solving Equations

Student Workbook: pages 210–213

Key Objectives
The student will:
- learn how to find the solution to quadratic, polynomial, and rational inequalities in one variable.
- graph quadratic inequalities in two variables.

Key Terms
factor, critical value, sign chart, zero property, set builder notation, interval notation, rational inequality, root, ascending order

Prerequisite Skills
- Evaluate polynomial expressions given the value of the variables.
- Determine the roots of quadratic equations.
- Solve and graph inequalities.

Lesson Description

In the **Introduction**, Jim's basketball team plans to raise money for a team trip by selling chocolates.

Using a price vs. profit formula, the students test randomly chosen prices to find the associated profit, but find it difficult to identify a range of prices that will yield a profit. This problem is solved in the **Summary** using inequalities.

The **Tutorial** begins by reviewing the graph of the parabola $y = x^2$ and relates this to the inequality $y < x^2$. Students learn how to solve and graph quadratic inequalities in two variables and how to solve quadratic, polynomial, and rational inequalities in one variable. Since an inequality with only one variable cannot be graphed, the students find the critical values that make the expression equal to 0 and then use a number line to test numbers in the regions created by these values. The result of their analysis determines the solution, which can be expressed in either set or interval notation.

In the **Examples**, students practice the skills they learned in the **Tutorial**. Further examples introduce inequalities with three or more factors or with exponents greater than 2, and inequalities that require simplification before they can be solved.

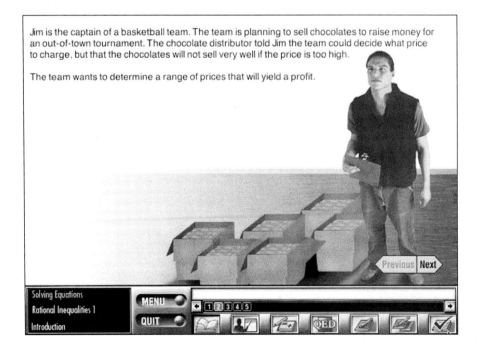

Jim is the captain of a basketball team. The team is planning to sell chocolates to raise money for an out-of-town tournament. The chocolate distributor told Jim the team could decide what price to charge, but that the chocolates will not sell very well if the price is too high.

The team wants to determine a range of prices that will yield a profit.

Previous | Next

Solving Equations
Rational Inequalities 1
Introduction

MENU
QUIT

◄ 1 2 3 4 5 ►

Instructor Intervention

- Make sure students understand when to use a number line and when to use a coordinate grid. Make the connection that an inequality can only be graphed if it has values for both x and y.

- Students may not understand how to determine the sign for a region. Explain that testing any number in a region and finding the sign of the resulting value will indicate the sign of all the points in the region. For example,
  For $(x + 4)(x - 5) < 0$, if $x = -5$:

  $$((-5) + 4)((-5) - 5)$$
  $$= (-1)(-10)$$
  $$= 10$$

  Explain that it is not the value, 10, that is important, but the fact that it is positive. The positive sign indicates that all numbers in that region will yield positive values when tested. To confirm, test more numbers within that region.

- Review the mathematical meanings of "and" and "or." Connect this with how the solution of an inequality is written. Also, emphasize that, when writing solutions, values must be written in ascending order (e.g., $-2 < x < 8$, not $8 > x > -2$), and nonpermissible values should not be included.

- Discussing the concepts of $-\infty$ and ∞ may help students understand why these values are never included in the solutions for inequalities.

- Explain that even though nonpermissible values give an undefined result, they can still serve as an indicator of a change of sign in the values of the inequality.

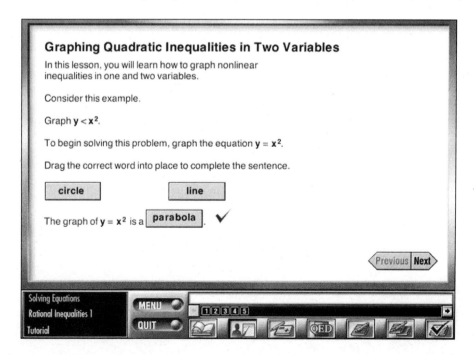

Lesson Components

 Examples

Quadratic Regions (1)
Polynomial Inequalities (1)
Higher Order Polynomials (1)
Rational Inequalities (1)
Simplifying Inequalities (1)

 Practice and Problems

Sign Charts
Graphing Inequalities
Interval Notation
Quadratic Regions
Error Analysis

 Extra Practice

Quadratic Inequalities in 2 Variables
Testing Regions
Quadratic Inequalities in 1 Variable
Polynomial Inequalities
Rational Inequalities

 Self-Check

Quadratic Inequalities in 2 Variables (2)
Testing Regions (2)
Quadratic Inequalities in 1 Variable (2)
Polynomial Inequalities (2)
Rational Inequalities (2)

Minimum score: 7 out of 10

Evaluation

- Sketch sample quadratic regions that represent inequalities. (You could use examples from the lesson.) Have students determine the relational operator ($<$, $\leq$, $=$, $\geq$, or $>$) for the quadratic region drawn.

- Students could construct an inequality from a given solution (e.g., $(-\infty, 2] \cup (6, \infty)$). Allow for various solutions. Ask students to explain the logic used to arrive at each inequality.

- Ask groups of students to write a ten-question quiz, using each of the five operators ($<$, $\leq$, $=$, $\geq$, $>$), and including a question from each of these categories:
  - quadratic inequality in one variable
  - polynomial inequality in one variable
  - rational inequality in one variable
  - graphing a quadratic inequality in two variables

To ensure that the equations they develop will be factorable, the students should start with the factors (e.g., $(x-2)(x+7)$) and then use these to develop a question. The groups should switch questions, provide complete solutions, and tell how the solution would be different if each of the other four operators were used.

- Observe students as they work with inequalities. Can they identify the different kinds of inequalities (quadratic, polynomial, or rational)? Can they find critical values? Do they understand how to determine sign values for a region? Do they know when to use a number line and when to use a grid? Can they graph quadratic inequalities?

Remediation

- Encourage students who have difficulty graphing parabolas to review the lesson "Solving Quadratics by Graphing."

- Review factoring techniques. Students may miss critical values because they neglect to remove common factors or to factor differences of squares and sums/differences of cubes.

- Some students may mistakenly state that an inequality like $-7(x+2) < 0$ has critical values of 0 or +7 (since $-7 + 7 = 0$). Emphasize that critical values are found by equating factors to 0. This will help them realize that $-7 \neq 0$ and thus is not a critical value.

- Students might determine the sign values of quadratic functions by simply memorizing the $+ - +$ pattern when a is positive, and the $- + -$ pattern when a is negative. Work through a few higher order polynomial inequalities to ensure they understand the process behind finding sign values.

Extension

A

Provide questions with unfactorable quadratics so that students can practice using the quadratic formula. This will provide practice with estimating the values of square roots, and evaluating the unfactorable quadratic for its sign value(s). Include examples that result in non-real roots and null solutions.

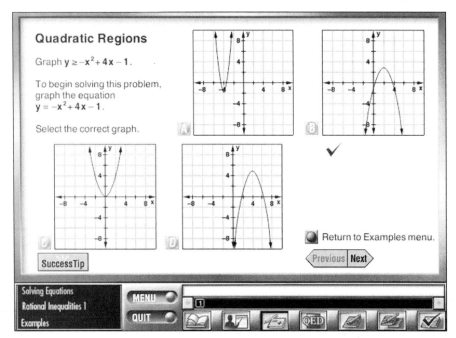

B

Ask students to examine the graphs of $y_1 = x^2 - x - 6$ and $y_2 = x^2 + 2x - 3$.

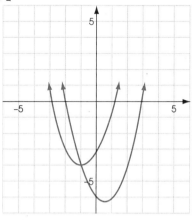

Ask:

(a) Over what interval is $y_1 < y_2$?
(b) Over what interval is $y_1 > y_2$?
(c) Over what interval is $y_1 \leq y_2$?
(d) Over what interval is $y_1 \geq y_2$?

Enrichment

A

Challenge students to graph and solve systems of inequalities in two variables. Questions may involve a combination of linear and quadratic inequalities or two quadratic inequalities. Show students how to indicate solutions using solid/broken lines for the boundaries, different colors or patterns for the regions, and open/closed dots for the solution points.

B

Explain that inequalities can be used to determine the domain of certain functions. For example, in $f(x) = \sqrt{x}$, the radicand must be positive ($x \geq 0$), so the domain is all values greater than or equal to 0 (i.e., $[0, \infty)$). Thus,

for the function $f(x) = \sqrt{x+5}$,

the domain will be all values in which $x + 5 \geq 0$ (or $x \geq -5$, which is $[-5, \infty)$). Ask students to find the domain for more complex radicands such as quadratics

$\left(e.g., f(x) = \sqrt{x^2 - 5x - 14} \right).$

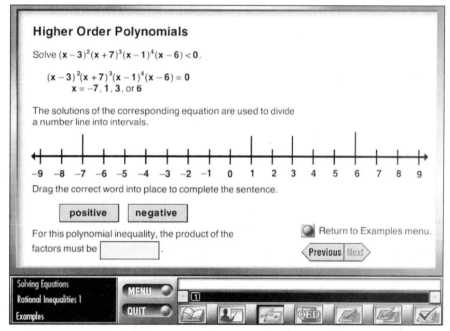

Cross-References
Solving Equations

Student Workbook: pages 214–217

Key Objectives
The student will:
- learn how to solve absolute value and radical inequalities.

Key Terms
rational inequality, absolute value, radical, factor, sign chart, zero product property, compound inequality, conjunction, disjunction, interval notation, set builder notation, root, extraneous root, ascending order

Prerequisite Skills
- Graph linear inequalities, in two variables.
- Add, subtract, multiply, and divide radical expressions.
- Graph and solve absolute value functions.

Lesson Description

In this lesson, students learn how to solve absolute value and radical inequalities both algebraically and graphically.

In the **Introduction**, the foreman of a paper company needs to calibrate a paper-cutting machine. International standards allow only a certain amount of variance in paper dimensions, so the machine must be set to always cut paper within the range of acceptable values for length and width. This range is determined in the **Summary** using absolute value inequalities.

In the **Tutorial**, students learn how to solve absolute value and radical inequalities. They practice their skills in the **Examples**, and also learn how to quickly recognize "special case" inequalities without having to completely solve the inequality. The last example involves solving $\sqrt{x+2} < x^2$ by graphing the corresponding functions on the same coordinate grid, finding the points of intersection, and determining when the graph of $\sqrt{x+2}$ is less than the graph of x^2.

Ben works as a foreman at a paper company. He has an order for sheets of paper that are **84.1** cm in length and **59.4** cm in width. He needs to calibrate the machinery so that it will cut the paper to meet the standards set by the International Standards for paper size.

Instructor Intervention

- Familiarize students with the meaning of these special symbols: $\emptyset$ represents "no solution," "undefined," or the empty set, and R refers to the set of all real numbers.

- Encourage students to recognize the special cases for absolute value and radical inequalities. Since it is not possible for either a radical or an absolute value expression to result in a negative value, the inequalities $\sqrt{n} < 0$, $\sqrt{n} \leq$ *a negative number*, $|n| < 0$, and $|n| \leq$ *a negative number* (where n is any expression), will always have a solution that is the empty set ($\emptyset$). By the same logic, since $|n|$ is always greater than a negative number, the solution to $|n| > 0$ and $|n| \geq 0$ will always be the set of all real numbers. Stress that students must isolate the absolute value or radical expression before looking for special cases.

- Clarify how the restriction for a radical is found, and explain why it is a restriction. Students may find it confusing that radical inequality questions in this lesson determine the restriction in terms of what values are not valid for the radical. For example, for $\sqrt{x+6} > 10$, the restriction on x is:

$$x + 6 < 0$$
$$x < -6$$

This statement means "x cannot be less than –6," but students may think it means "x must be less than –6." It may be helpful to solve for the values that satisfy the radical, and then reverse the relation for the restriction.

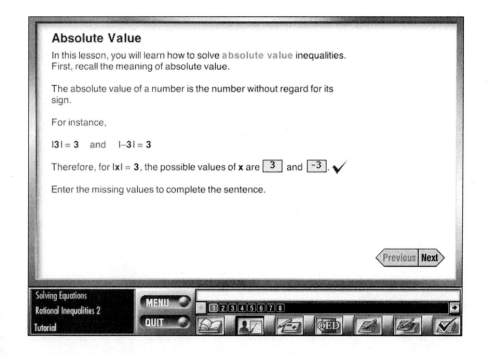

Evaluation

- Present questions in which part of the solution is already provided. By having students concentrate on various stages of the solution process, you will be able to identify which skills are causing difficulties.

- Ask several students to write the solution to the same question on the board so that alternative solution sequences can be observed. Discuss these variations and have students indicate the pros and cons of each. Also, see if students can point out any mathematical inconsistencies or incorrect statements.

- Observe students as they solve problems from the lesson and note where difficulties occur. Address these problems when reviewing the solution. Encourage students to help each other understand how to solve a difficult part of a question.

Remediation

- Some students may mistakenly reverse the inequality sign in all situations involving a negative value, for example, when the operation is subtraction or when the negative is a constant (e.g., in $2x > -4$). Emphasize that the inequality sign should be reversed only when multiplying or dividing by a negative number. Use concrete examples to clarify. For example, students could work through this exercise:
  1. Relate 3 and 6. (i.e., use $<, \leq, >, \geq,$ or $=$ between

the numbers)
  2. Multiply 3 and 6 by 2 and relate the new values.
  3. Multiply 3 and 6 by -2 and relate the new values.
  4. Continue applying all the operations (division, addition, and subtraction) on 3 and 6, using both positive and negative numbers. Relate the new values at each step.
  5. Repeat the exercise starting with two negative numbers, or with one positive and one negative number.

Record the information in a table and allow the students to discover the pattern.

- You may need to review joining inequalities using "and" and "or." Explain that for $|x| < 5$, the two cases are separated with an "and," and are represented by a number line graph like

because values of x are *included* within the boundaries -5 and 5. In contrast, for $|x| > 5$,

the two cases are separated with "or," and are represented with two graphs like

because the values of x are *excluded* outside the boundaries of -5 and 5.

- It may help students to think in terms of "distance from zero" when working with absolute values. $|x| > 3$ means "any value more than three units away from 0," while $|x| < 3$ means "any value less than three units away from 0."

- Review graphing techniques. Familiarize students with the basic shapes of various functions and walk through the steps to produce the graph of each function.

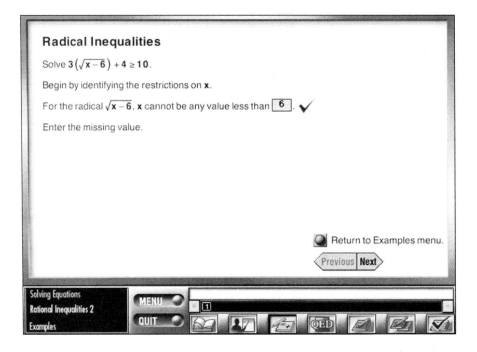

Extension

A

Ask students to graph the square root function contained within a radical inequality. They should notice that in finding the restriction of square roots, they are also finding the domain of the square root function.

B

Encourage students to solve inequalities such as $|x + 6| < |2x - 3|$ by graphing. They could use the graphs to guide them when finding the solution algebraically. For example:

To solve $|x + 6| < |2x - 3|$, ask students to first graph $y = |x + 6|$ and $y = |2x - 3|$ and label the "branches" (the labels refer to x-values):

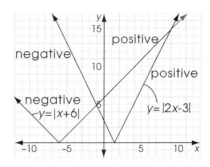

Point out that the graph shows the inequality is true when:
- The positive branch of $y = |x + 6|$ is less than the negative branch of $y = |2x - 3|$ $\Rightarrow x + 6 < -(2x - 3)$.
- The positive branch of $y = |x + 6|$ is less than the positive branch of $y = |2x - 3| \Rightarrow x + 6 < 2x - 3$.

Have students solve each of the inequalities and then use a number line to find the solution of $|x + 6| < |2x - 3|$. They should also notice that the solution can be determined by inspecting the graph and noting the points of intersection.

As an additional challenge, ask students to solve inequalities such as $|x - 3| + |x + 2| \geq 7$. The first step in this case is to isolate one of the absolute value statements before graphing. For example, rewrite the inequality as $|x - 3| \geq -|x + 2| + 7$, and then graph $y = |x - 3|$ and $y = -|x + 2| + 7$.

Enrichment

A

Challenge students to create several radical or absolute value inequalities in two variables which, when graphed on the same grid, produce geometric shapes. For example, if the inequalities $y \leq |x + 6|$ and $y \geq |2x - 3|$ were plotted on the same grid, the solution area would be the triangle shown **Extension** part B.

B

Invite students to find real-life situations in which absolute value inequalities are used. They could start by looking at the design specifications for almost any mass-produced product, searching for phrases like "tolerance," "margin of error," "give or take," and "plus or minus."

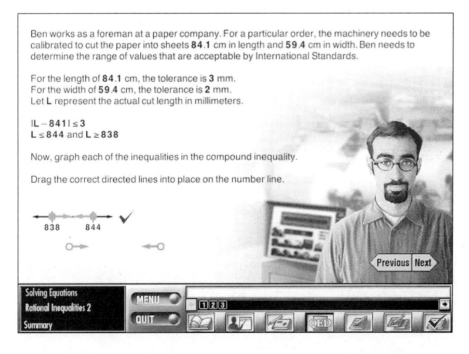

Ben works as a foreman at a paper company. For a particular order, the machinery needs to be calibrated to cut the paper into sheets **84.1** cm in length and **59.4** cm in width. Ben needs to determine the range of values that are acceptable by International Standards.

For the length of **84.1** cm, the tolerance is **3** mm.
For the width of **59.4** cm, the tolerance is **2** mm.
Let **L** represent the actual cut length in millimeters.

|L − 841| ≤ 3
L ≤ 844 and L ≥ 838

Now, graph each of the inequalities in the compound inequality.

Drag the correct directed lines into place on the number line.

Cross-References

Solving Equations

Student Workbook: pages 218–219

Key Objectives

The student will:

- simplify fractions that have fractions or negative exponents in the numerator and/or denominator.

Key Terms

complex fraction, numerator, denominator, lowest common denominator (LCD), distributive property

Prerequisite Skills

- Add, subtract, multiply, and divide rational numbers.
- Express an integer in exponential form.
- Evaluate powers that have positive and/or negative exponents.

Lesson Description

A complex fraction is one that has a fraction in the numerator and/or denominator, or that contains a power with a negative exponent. In this lesson students learn how to use two different methods – the LCD method and the Division method – to simplify numeric and variable complex fractions.

The **Introduction** demonstrates how to calculate the resistance in an electric circuit using this formula:

$$Total\ resistance = \frac{1}{\dfrac{1}{R_1} + \dfrac{1}{R_2}}$$

When students substitute the given values 2 and 3 for R_1 and R_2 the result is the complex fraction $\dfrac{1}{\dfrac{1}{2} + \dfrac{1}{3}}$.

At first, students simplify the fraction by converting $\frac{1}{2}$ and $\frac{1}{3}$ to decimal form. Then, in the **Summary**, they find the resistance more accurately by using the LCD method introduced in the **Tutorial**.

There, students examine these two methods for simplifying complex fractions:

- *LCD method*: Multiply the numerator and denominator of a complex fraction by the LCD of all the individual fractions that make up the complex fraction.

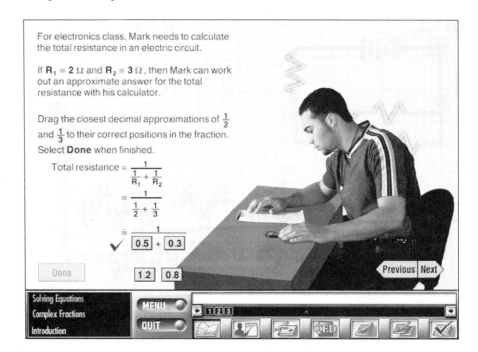

- *Division method*: Simplify the numerator and denominator so they are simple fractions, and then divide the numerator by the denominator.

The **Examples** review the approaches introduced in the **Tutorial** and extend them to complex fractions with variables and negative exponents.

Instructor Intervention

- Review that a fraction is in simplest terms when the numerator and denominator have no common factors. Have students practice simplifying some fractions, such as $\dfrac{12}{16}$, as well as some rational expressions, such as $\dfrac{a}{3a}$ or $\dfrac{b+1}{4b+4}$.

- It is important for students to understand that they can eliminate common factors, but not necessarily common terms. For example, many students make errors of this type:

$$\frac{a^2 + a}{a^2} = \frac{\cancel{a^2} + a}{\cancel{a^2}}$$
$$= \frac{a}{1}$$
$$= a$$

Help them see that a is a factor of both the numerator and the denominator, but that a^2 is not.

$$\frac{a^2 + a}{a^2} = \frac{a(a+1)}{a^2}$$
$$= \frac{a+1}{a}$$

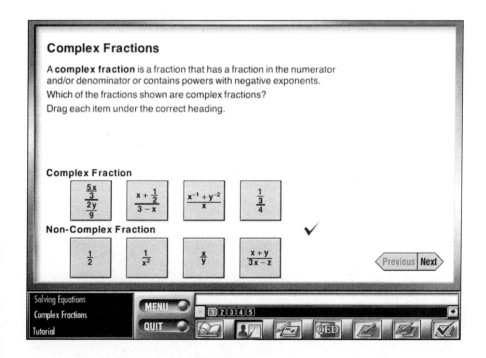

Complex Fractions

A **complex fraction** is a fraction that has a fraction in the numerator and/or denominator or contains powers with negative exponents.

Which of the fractions shown are complex fractions?

Drag each item under the correct heading.

Complex Fraction

| $\dfrac{\frac{5x}{3}}{\frac{2y}{9}}$ | $\dfrac{x + \frac{1}{2}}{3 - x}$ | $\dfrac{x^{-1} + y^{-2}}{x}$ | $\dfrac{\frac{1}{3}}{4}$ |

Non-Complex Fraction

| $\dfrac{1}{2}$ | $\dfrac{1}{x^2}$ | $\dfrac{x}{y}$ | $\dfrac{x+y}{3x-z}$ |

Previous | Next

Solving Equations
Complex Fractions
Tutorial

MENU
QUIT
1 2 3 4 5

Evaluation

- Present one of the complex fractions generated by students for the final problem in the *Student Workbook*. Ask the students to demonstrate how to simplify the fraction using both the LCD method and the Division method. Note whether the students look for common factors in the numerator and denominator before they apply the LCD method.

- Have students use the LCD method to simplify the complex fraction shown here. Ask them to write a verbal explanation of what they did in each step in the solution.

$$\frac{\dfrac{2x}{2x^2 - 5x - 3}}{\dfrac{2}{(x-3)(3x+2)}}$$

[Answer: $\dfrac{x(3x+2)}{2x+1}$]

- Present the following problem to determine whether students recognize that a complex fraction has not been simplified until the numerator and denominator have both been factored, and any common factors have been eliminated.

$$\frac{\dfrac{3x^2 - x - 4}{x+4}}{\dfrac{2x^2 + 5x + 3}{x-1}}$$

[Answer: $\dfrac{(3x-4)(x-1)}{(x+4)(2x+3)}$]

- Observe students as they simplify complex fractions with algebraic terms. Can they factor polynomials? Can they multiply them? When a minus sign is applied to an expression in brackets, do the students properly distribute the sign as they eliminate the brackets?

Remediation

- Review how to factor trinomials of the form $ax^2 + bx + c$. Begin with examples where $a = 1$, and then proceed to other coefficients.

- Review these processes:
  (a) identifying and factoring a sum or difference of squares
  (b) factoring out (-1)

- The simplest way to find the lowest common denominator for two or more numbers is to list multiples of each number until you find a multiple common to all the lists. For example:
  2: 2, 4, 6, 8, 10, 12, 14, 16, 18, **20**
  4: 4, 8, 12, 16, **20**
  5: 5, 10, 15, **20**, 25

  However, some students may prefer to identify a common denominator by simply multiplying the numbers.

  $2 \times 4 \times 5 = \mathbf{40}$

  The multiplication method will always result in a common denominator, but not necessarily in the lowest comment denominator. This may make the calculations more complex, but should still result in the correct answer.

Numerical Complex Fractions

Simplify the fraction using the division method.

$$\frac{\frac{2}{3} + 1}{\frac{1}{3} + 1}$$

Select the first step.

- ○ Write the numerator and denominator as single fractions. ✓
- ○ Rewrite as division.
- ○ Rewrite as multiplication.
- ○ Factor.

○ Return to Examples menu.

‹Previous | Next›

Solving Equations
Complex Fractions
Examples

MENU
QUIT

Extension

A

Invite students to develop calculator sequences they can use to simplify numerical complex fractions, such as

$$\frac{\frac{3}{4}+2}{\frac{1}{8}+1}$$

Encourage students to make use of the parentheses keys and calculator memory. If they record the key sequences they use, they can compare with classmates to see whether more than one method is possible. Ask why calculator results may not always be as accurate as results obtained on paper.

B

Any number can be expressed as a complex fraction made up entirely of whole numbers and unit fractions. Fractions like these are called continued fractions.

To express a number as a continued fraction, start by extracting any wholes. Then express the remaining fraction as

$$\frac{1}{reciprocal}$$. Continue the

process with each successive numerator until there are no fractions left with denominators other than 1. For example:

$$\frac{48}{17} = 2 + \frac{14}{17}$$

$$= 2 + \frac{1}{\frac{17}{14}}$$

$$= 2 + \frac{1}{1 + \frac{3}{14}}$$

$$= 2 + \frac{1}{1 + \frac{1}{\frac{14}{3}}}$$

$$= 2 + \frac{1}{1 + \frac{1}{4 + \frac{2}{3}}}$$

$$= 2 + \frac{1}{1 + \frac{1}{4 + \frac{1}{\frac{3}{2}}}}$$

$$= 2 + \frac{1}{1 + \frac{1}{4 + \frac{1}{1 + \frac{1}{2}}}}$$

Have students choose several improper fractions to convert to continued fraction form. Then have them choose one continued fraction and show how to use methods from the lesson to return it to its original form. Encourage them to begin at the bottom and to simplify one fraction at a time.

Enrichment

A

Complex fractions can sometimes be used to display formulas in simpler ways. Have students look for examples of formulas in physics or engineering that could be or have been simplified in this way.

For example, a formula using

an expression like $\frac{1}{\frac{1}{a}+\frac{1}{b}}$ is easi-

er to use than the equivalent

formula $\frac{ab}{a+b}$ because if you

substitute numbers for a and b, you need to do only one substitution for each variable in the first formula, but two in the second.

B

After students have completed the Extension activity about continued fractions, they could do research to find out which early mathematicians used continued fractions, and how they used them.

12 EXPONENTIAL AND LOGARITHMIC FUNCTIONS

12.1 Exponential Equations

Cross-References

Exponential and Logarithmic Functions

Student Workbook: pages 222–225

Key Objectives

The student will:

- learn how to solve equations where the variable is found in the exponent of one or more terms.

Key Terms

decimal notation, number system, place value, binary, exponent, term, base, power, product law, quotient law, hexadecimal number system

Prerequisite Skills

- Explain and use the exponent laws to simplify expressions with variable bases and to evaluate expressions with numerical bases.
- Determine the value of powers with integer exponents, using the exponent laws.
- Solve nonlinear equations by factoring.
- Solve and verify first-degree, single-variable equations.

Lesson Description

In this lesson, students learn to solve exponential equations where the bases are powers of one another. In this type of equation, the sides can be written as powers with a common base.

The **Introduction** asks students to determine the number of digits in a binary number given the following conditions: In both its binary and its hexadecimal (base-16) representations, the number is a 1 followed by a string of 0s; and the hexadecimal representation is nine digits shorter than the binary representation. Students solve the problem using a chart to compare binary, decimal, and hexadecimal representations of equivalent numbers. In the **Summary**, students discover that, since 16 is a power of 2, it is possible to solve the problem using exponential equations.

In the **Tutorial**, students learn that when there is one power on each side of the equation and the bases are equal, the exponents are also equal. They also learn how to rewrite one side of an exponential equation to obtain a common base.

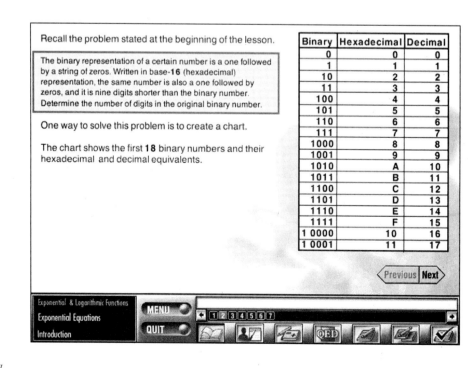

The **Examples** provide increasingly difficult exponential equations for practice. Students must employ a number of different techniques to solve the equations, including rewriting both sides of the equation, using negative exponents, using the power laws, and solving quadratic equations.

Instructor Intervention

- You may want to review the power laws before students begin the lesson.

- Make sure that students are familiar with common powers (powers of 2, 3, 4, 5, 6, 10). For example, students should know that both 27 and 81 are powers of 3.

- Review how to solve first-degree, single-variable equations, and factoring techniques for solving quadratic equations.

- One of the equations given in the **Tutorial** is $3^x = 9$. Students solve this equation in two ways: using a base of 3 and using a base of 9. Review both solutions with the students and explain that using the smaller base helps them avoid rational exponents.

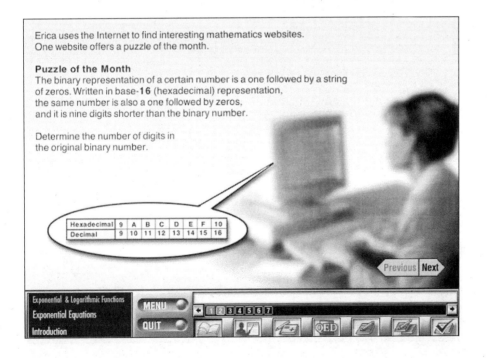

Erica uses the Internet to find interesting mathematics websites. One website offers a puzzle of the month.

Puzzle of the Month
The binary representation of a certain number is a one followed by a string of zeros. Written in base-**16** (hexadecimal) representation, the same number is also a one followed by zeros, and it is nine digits shorter than the binary number.

Determine the number of digits in the original binary number.

Hexadecimal	9	A	B	C	D	E	F	10
Decimal	9	10	11	12	13	14	15	16

Previous | Next

Exponential & Logarithmic Functions
Exponential Equations
Introduction

MENU
QUIT

1 2 3 4 5 6 7

Evaluation

- Suggest that students create their own exponential equations and solutions that have various parts missing. For example:

$$6^{(x-3)} = \frac{1}{\blacksquare} \quad [36]$$
$$6^{(x-3)} = 6^{-2}$$
$$\blacksquare = -2$$
$$x = 1 \quad [x-3]$$

Work through the problems with the class, and show the students how to determine the missing values by examining the previous and/or following steps. Encourage students to try to identify when there is and when there isn't enough information to solve the problem.

- Each student could create an exponential equation and have a partner solve it. Observe the equations that are created. Do students use numbers that are powers of one another? Is the variable part of the exponent?

- Observe students as they solve exponential equations. Can they express numbers as powers of other numbers? Do they use the power laws correctly? Do they understand negative exponents? Do they recognize when they have to factor an expression?

Remediation

- Students who are having difficulty solving exponential equations could write a list of steps to follow.
  1. Examine the equation and try to identify the common base of the powers.
  2. Write each side of the equation as a power with that base. Remember to apply the power laws correctly.
  3. Once the bases are equal, the exponents are equal. Write an equation setting the two exponents equal.
  4. Solve the equation. If necessary, use factoring techniques.

- Students may have trouble if they are not familiar with powers of small numbers. Encourage them to memorize these powers:

$2^2 = 4$	$4^2 = 2^4 = 16$
$2^3 = 8$	$4^3 = 64$
$2^4 = 4^2 = 16$	$4^4 = 2^8 = 256$
$2^5 = 32$	$5^2 = 25$
$2^6 = 8^2 = 64$	$5^3 = 125$
$2^7 = 128$	$6^2 = 36$
$2^8 = 4^4 = 256$	$6^3 = 216$
$3^2 = 9$	$7^2 = 49$
$3^3 = 27$	$8^2 = 64$
$3^4 = 9^2 = 81$	$9^2 = 81$
$3^5 = 243$	and powers of 10

Extension

A

Students could solve the exponential equations given in the "Write the Equation" section of the **Practice and Problems**.

B

Invite students to solve more complex exponential equations with fractional bases. For example:

$$\left(\frac{3}{4}\right)^{(x+5)} = \frac{16}{9}$$
$$\left(\frac{3}{4}\right)^{(x+5)} = \left(\frac{4}{3}\right)^{2}$$
$$\left(\frac{3}{4}\right)^{(x+5)} = \left(\frac{3}{4}\right)^{-2}$$
$$x + 5 = -2$$
$$x = -7$$

C

Provide some exponential equations with more than one variable in the exponent and ask students to solve for one of the variables in terms of the other. For example, have them solve for x in $2^{x+6} = 8^{x+y}$.

$$[\text{Answer: } \frac{6-3y}{2}]$$

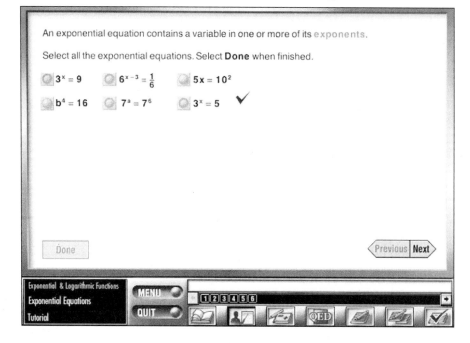

An exponential equation contains a variable in one or more of its exponents.

Select all the exponential equations. Select **Done** when finished.

- $3^x = 9$
- $6^{x-3} = \frac{1}{6}$
- $5x = 10^2$
- $b^4 = 16$
- $7^a = 7^6$
- $3^x = 5$ ✔

Done   ◁Previous | Next▷

Exponential & Logarithmic Functions
Exponential Equations
Tutorial

MENU
QUIT
1 2 3 4 5 6

Enrichment

A

In the lesson, quadratic equations were always solvable by factoring. Ask students to solve an exponential equation resulting in a quadratic equation that cannot be factored. Encourage them to use another method, such as the quadratic formula, to complete the solution. For example, ask students to solve:

$$4(2^{x^2}) = 8^{3x}$$

[Answer: $x \doteq 8.77$ or 0.23]

B

Challenge students to estimate the solution to an equation where a common base cannot be used. Students could use their calculators to guess and check values. Challenge them to find the solution to three decimal places.

C

Students could graph exponential equations using a graphing calculator. For example:

$$2^{x^{2+2x}} = \frac{1}{2}$$
$$2^{x^{2+2x}} - \frac{1}{2} = 0 \qquad ①$$
$$y = 2^{x^{2+2x}} - \frac{1}{2} \quad ②$$

① Subtract $\frac{1}{2}$ from both sides.

② Then graph the corresponding function.

Students could also use the graphing calculator to solve the equations in parts A and B.

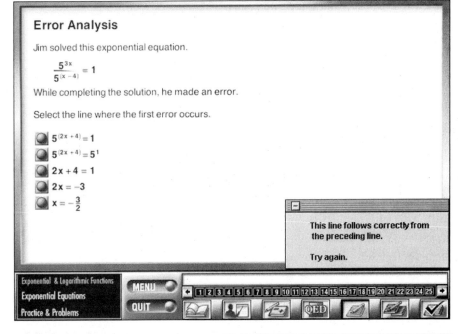

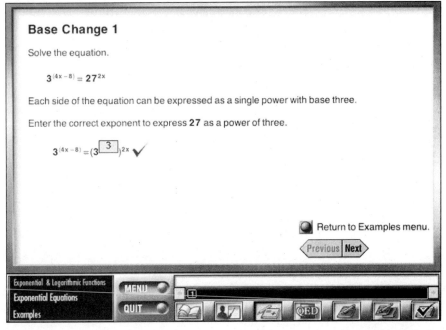

Graphing Exponential Functions

Cross-References
Exponential and Logarithmic Functions

Student Workbook: pages 226–229

Key Objectives
The student will:
- learn to graph and analyze an exponential function, both with and without technology.

Key Terms
exponential function, base, domain, range, horizontal asymptote, intercepts, increasing, decreasing, reflection, translation, interval notation

Prerequisite Skills
- Use a graphing tool to draw the graph of a function from its equation.
- Determine the domain and range of a function from its graph.
- Describe and plot data representing exponential relationships, with appropriate scales.
- Solve exponential equations where one base is a power of the other base.

Lesson Description

The **Introduction** presents a puzzle found in a math textbook: A king promises to give an inventor grains of wheat, where the number of grains doubles with each successive square of a chessboard. Students set up a table of values to estimate at which square the number of grains will exceed one million, then one billion. They notice the exponential pattern: The number of grains of wheat is a power of 2, where the exponent is one less than the number of the square. In the **Summary**, students determine an exponential function for the chessboard problem. They graph the function and read the solutions to the problem from the graph.

The **Tutorial** begins by reviewing how to recognize exponential functions. Students use tables of values to graph the exponential functions $y = 2^x$ and $y = \left(\dfrac{1}{2}\right)^x$. For each function they determine the domain and range, the horizontal asymptote, and whether the function is increasing or decreasing.

In the **Examples**, students graph exponential functions using a graphing calculator or a table of values. They analyze each graph to determine the function's domain, range, asymptotes, intercepts, and whether it is increasing or decreasing. The general form of a translated exponential function, $y = a^{(x+k)} + p$, is presented, and students examine how translating a graph affects its characteristics. In the last example, students practice reading information from exponential graphs.

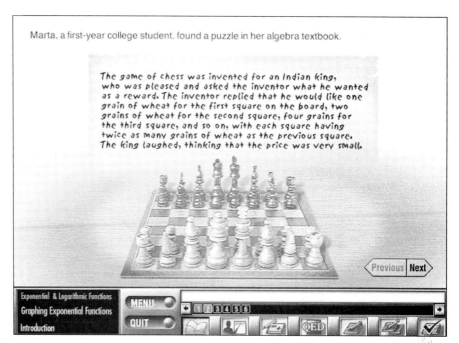

Marta, a first-year college student. found a puzzle in her algebra textbook.

The game of chess was invented for an Indian king, who was pleased and asked the inventor what he wanted as a reward. The inventor replied that he would like one grain of wheat for the first square on the board, two grains of wheat for the second square, four grains for the third square, and so on, with each square having twice as many grains of wheat as the previous square. The king laughed, thinking that the price was very small.

Exponential & Logarithmic Functions
Graphing Exponential Functions
Introduction

MENU
QUIT

1 2 3 4 5 6

Previous | Next

Instructor Intervention

- Ensure that students are comfortable using their calculators. Have students evaluate some exponential functions on their calculators to practice. Discuss the places where parentheses are necessary.

- Students should also be familiar with their graphing calculators. Review the trace and zoom features and how to set appropriate windows on their calculators. Suggest using different line thicknesses when graphing two functions to make comparison easier, and, if a table feature is available, encourage students to use it to determine values on the graphs.

- Review how to write domains and ranges using both interval and set notation.

- When students are working through the first "Analyzing Graphs" **Example**, point out that $y = 3^x$ is the mirror image of both $y = \left(\frac{1}{3}\right)^x$ and $y = 3^{-x}$. Ask students to explain why the graphs of $y = \left(\frac{1}{3}\right)^x$ and $y = 3^{-x}$ are the same.

- Make sure that students don't mistakenly call $y = \left(\frac{1}{2}\right)^x$ and $y = 2^x$ inverses. Point out that the bases are reciprocals of each other. Encourage students to graph a few more reciprocal pairs to discover that these types of functions are always reflections of each other in the y-axis.

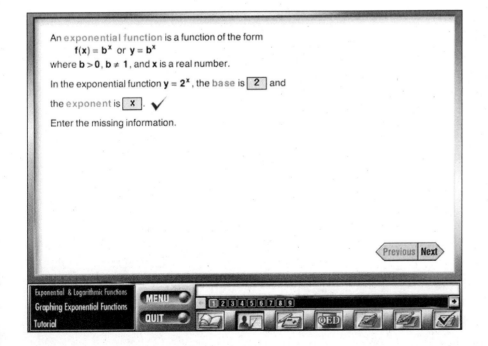

An exponential function is a function of the form
   $f(x) = b^x$ or $y = b^x$
where $b > 0$, $b \neq 1$, and x is a real number.

In the exponential function $y = 2^x$, the base is $\boxed{2}$ and the exponent is $\boxed{x}$. ✓

Enter the missing information.

⟨Previous | Next⟩

Exponential & Logarithmic Functions
Graphing Exponential Functions
Tutorial

MENU
QUIT
1 2 3 4 5 6 7 8 9

Evaluation

- Divide the class into several groups. Ask each group to create a problem that requires graphing exponential functions and identifying relevant characteristics (domain, range, asymptotes, intercepts, reflections, translations, etc.). Have each group solve their problem to ensure it works the way they intend, then collect the problems and compile them into a worksheet to distribute to the entire class. When students have completed the worksheet, have each group present a solution.

- Ask the groups to exchange the functions they created for the previous activity, and then to change the function in one way: change the exponent, the constant, or the base. (Restrict the changes to adding or subtracting a constant.) They should write the new function in the form $y = a^{(x + k)} + p$, graph it on the same grid as the original one, and perform the same analysis as for the first activity. Have each group present their two graphs to the class, explaining how the change in the function changed the characteristics of the graph. Students should note that changing the exponent or the constant results in a translation, while changing the base stretches the graph either vertically (*new base > original base*) or horizontally (*new base < original base*).

- Observe students as they work. Can they graph exponential functions using a table of values or a graphing tool? Do they understand how to find the various characteristics of an exponential function? Can they evaluate exponential functions for specific values? Can they work with the general form of a translated exponential function?

Remediation

- Review evaluating exponential expressions with students. Show students why $2^0 = 1$, $2^{-1} = \frac{1}{2}$, and $\left(\frac{1}{2}\right)^{-2} = 4$.

- Some students may have difficulty with the concept of reflections. To help them understand reflections over the *y*-axis, have them graph a function on graph paper, fold the paper along the *y*-axis, and trace the function on the other side of the paper. When the students unfold the paper, a copy of the design will have been reflected over the *y*-axis. Perform a similar exercise for the *x*-axis.

- Help students understand the meaning of asymptotes. For example, present the equation $y = 2^x$, and help students see that as *x* gets smaller and smaller, the corresponding value of *y* approaches 0; similarly, for $y = \left(\frac{1}{2}\right)^x$, students should notice that as *x* gets larger and larger, the corresponding value of *y* approaches 0.

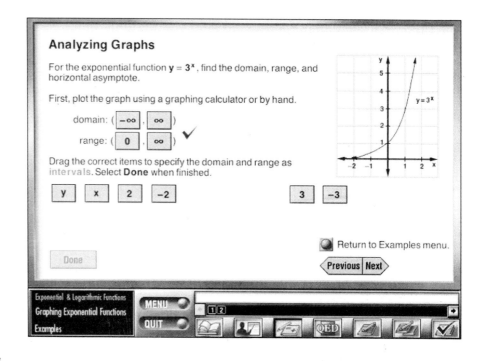

Extension

A

Have students graph the exponential function $y = 3^x$. Next, ask them to examine the related exponential functions $y = -(3^x)$, $y = 3^{-x}$, and $y = -(3^{-x})$, and to predict the effect of the negative signs on each graph. They should sketch each function using as guides their predictions and the graph of $y = 3x$. Then have them graph the functions using a table of values or a graphing tool and compare them to their predicted graphs. Ask students to write a concluding statement describing the graph of each function with respect to $f(x)$ if

$G(x) = f(-x)$
$H(x) = -f(x)$
$J(x) = -f(-x)$

B

Invite students to explore why the definition of an exponential function, $y = b^x$ (where $b > 0$, $b \ne 1$), contains the restriction $b > 0$. Ask them to explore the relation $y = (-2)^x$. They should make a table of values for integral values of x from -4 to 4, and then plot the points. Next, ask them to rewrite the expression $y = (-2)^{\frac{1}{2}}$ as a radical, and comment on its solution. Finally, ask them to make a concluding statement about why a relation of the form $y = b^x$, where $b < 0$, is not an exponential function.

C

Invite students to explore why the definition of an exponential function, $y = b^x$ (where $b > 0$, $b \ne 1$), contains the restriction $b \ne 1$. Ask them to explore the relation $y = 1^x$. They should make a table of values for integral values of x from -4 to 4, and then plot the points. Ask students to use the graph to explain why this relation is not an exponential function.

Enrichment

A

Graph the function without using a calculator:
$f(x) = 2^{x-3} + 4$

Next, have students graph the following functions, using the conclusions they made in **Extension** activity A:

$G(x) = f(-x)$ [reflected over y-axis]
$H(x) = -f(x)$ [reflected over x-axis]
$J(x) = -f(-x)$ [reflected over x-axis, then over y-axis]

B

Challenge students to find the equation of the reflection of $y = b^x$ over

(a) the y-axis $\left[y = \left(\dfrac{1}{b} \right)^x \right]$

(b) the x-axis $[y = -b^x]$

(c) the y-axis and then x-axis

$\left[y = -\left(\dfrac{1}{b} \right)^x \right]$

Marta's instructor challenged the class to find the first square with more than one million grains of wheat, and the first with more than one billion grains, and the number of grains on the last square.

Marta set up a table to examine several of the squares on the chessboard.

She found that, in general, square **x** contains $2^{(x-1)}$ grains of wheat.

Square	Grains of Wheat
8	$128 = 2^7 = 2^{(8-1)}$
16	$32,768 = 2^{15} = 2^{(16-1)}$
24	$8,388,608 = 2^{23} = 2^{(24-1)}$
32	$2,147,483,648 = 2^{31} = 2^{(32-1)}$

Previous | Next

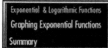

Exponential & Logarithmic Functions
Graphing Exponential Functions
Summary

MENU
QUIT
1 2 3 4

12.3 Exponential Functions

Cross-References
Exponential and Logarithmic Functions

Student Workbook: pages 230–233

Key Objectives
The student will:
- use exponential equations and graphs of exponential functions to solve problems.

Key Terms
exponential function, base, principal, rate, annual, semiannual, quarterly, exponential growth, radioactive decay, depreciation

Prerequisite Skills
- Solve exponential equations having bases that are powers of one another.
- Graph and analyze an exponential function, using technology.

Lesson Description

In this lesson, students solve problems using exponential functions and graphs.

In the **Introduction**, students use a guess-and-test method to try to determine the principal amount that will produce a compound amount of $16,000 in five years at a given rate of interest. They start with an opening balance of $10,000 and calculate the closing balance for each of the five years. Since the final closing balance is too small, they repeat the exercise with a principal of $12,000. This results in a closing balance that is too large. In the **Summary**, students quickly and efficiently determine the exact principal required by using the

exponential formula for compound interest: $A = P(1 + \frac{r}{k})kt$, where A

is the compound amount, P is the principal, r is the annual interest rate, k is the number of compounding periods each year, and t is the time in years.

The **Tutorial** develops the formula for compound interest. Students use this formula to solve problems that require finding compound amounts or the principal required to produce a compound amount. They examine the graph of the formula to determine the time required for an amount to double.

In the **Examples**, students:
- determine the rate of growth of a population by solving the population growth formula, $A = A_0(1 + r)^t$, for r.
- use a table to develop the exponential formula for a population of bacteria that doubles every five hours.
- find how long it will take for a quantity of yeast cells to triple.
- graph an exponential decay function and using it to solve a problem about half-lives.
- compare the nominal and effective interest rates for four investments to help them choose the most profitable option.

Instructor Intervention

- Ensure that students are comfortable using their calculators, especially the exponent keys. Work through a problem from the lesson together, discussing where parentheses are necessary and which keystroke sequences are possible.

- Students should be able to use a graphing calculator. Review the trace and zoom functions and how to set appropriate windows. If the students' calculators have a table capability, show how to read values from the table to verify points on their graphs.

- Review how to convert percents to decimals. When percent values such as interest or growth rates are substituted into an equation, the decimal form is required.

- In the first example, students determine the rate of growth of a population by solving the formula $38,500 = 22,500(1 + r)^{10}$ for r. They could verify their solution by graphing the function $P = 22,500(1 + r)^{10}$ on a graphing calculator. Zooming in to find the x-value corresponding to a y-value close to 38,500 will give the rate, r. If students don't have access to a graphing calculator, discuss what a reasonable rate of growth might be. Have students calculate the value of P when $r = 10\%$ [$P \doteq 58,359$] and again when $r = 5\%$ [$P \doteq 36,650$]. Point out that the rate is much closer to 5% than 10%. Continue guessing and testing values for r until a value of about 38,500 is reached [at $r = 5.5\%$, $P \doteq 38,433$].

- Clarify why the solution process for the first example requires two steps. Explain that students must first use the given values to find the growth rate and then use this value to find the final answer. They should note that they need to solve twice because both the rate and the time are unknowns.

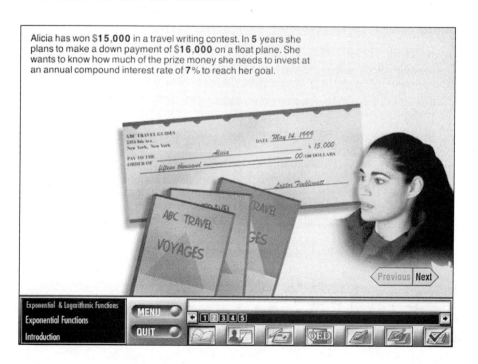

Alicia has won **$15,000** in a travel writing contest. In **5** years she plans to make a down payment of **$16,000** on a float plane. She wants to know how much of the prize money she needs to invest at an annual compound interest rate of **7**% to reach her goal.

Evaluation

- Present graphs of both exponential growth and exponential decay. Ask students to explain, in words, the similarities and differences between the graphs, the similarities and differences between their corresponding equations, and how they can tell whether an equation represents exponential growth or exponential decay.

Exponential Growth

$$y = 100(1 + 0.1)^x$$

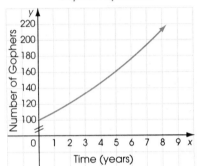
Gopher Population

Exponential Decay

$$y = \left(\frac{1}{2}\right)^{\frac{x}{5760}}$$

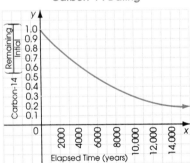
Carbon-14 Dating

- Ask students to graph $A = \$5000(1 + 0.07)^t$, and then complete the following problems:
  (a) How long will it take for the principal amount to double? to triple? [about 11 years, about 16 years]
  (b) What will the compound amount be in two years? [\$5724.50]

(c) When will the compound amount be \$8000? [about 7 years]

Engage the students in a discussion of the different steps they used to answer each problem. Ask how they determined an appropriate window to use, and have them explain how they arrived at their answer.

Remediation

- Some students may have difficulty identifying when a relationship is exponential. As they work through the problems, have them develop a list of key words to watch for: **compound interest**, **doubling**, **tripling**, **radioactive decay**, **half-life**

Emphasize that if something is being repeatedly multiplied or divided by the same amount, then its growth or decrease is exponential. Relate this to data that are related recursively. (See "Data in Tables 2.")

- Students often find it difficult to develop their own exponential equations from problem information. Work through various types of growth and decay problems step-by-step, and show how the given information is translated into mathematical notation. Help them see these patterns:
  - the general form of the growth equation is $A = P(1 + r)^t$
  - the time variable is in the exponent: t
  - the rate at which something grows/decreases is in the base: r
  - the power, $(1 + r)^t$, is multiplied by the initial amount, P
  - the final/present/future amount is on the left side: A

They could show this information on a diagram of the different parts of an exponential function.

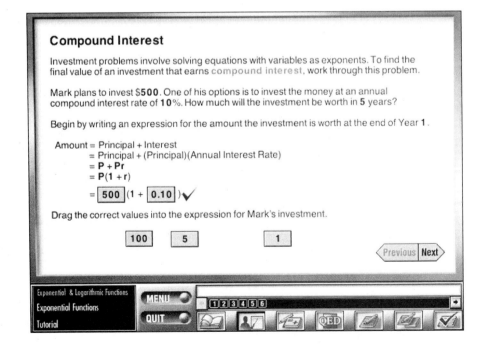

Extension

A

In Example 1 in the *Student Workbook*, students calculate the effective interest rate for different compounding periods if the annual rate is 10%. Ask students to graph the results on one graph, and comment on the increase in the effective interest rate as the compounding period becomes smaller and smaller. They should notice that as the length of the compounding period decreases, the effective interest rate increases, but the increase is less and less.

B

Explain that you can sometimes use spreadsheet software to solve problems about exponential growth. For example, the students could set up a spreadsheet to model the problem described in the **Tutorial**.

	A	B	C	D
1	Year	Opening Balance	Interest	Closing Balance
2	1	$10,000	=B2*10%	=B2+C2
3	2	=D2	=B3*10%	=B3+C3
4	3	=D3	=B4*10%	=B4+C4

	A	B	C	D
1	Year	Opening Balance	Interest	Closing Balance
2	1	$10,000	$1,000	$11,000
3	2	$11,000	$1,100	$12,100
4	3	$12,100	$1,210	$13,310

Students may wish to set up their own spreadsheets to model other problems from the lesson.

Enrichment

A

Students may select one of several topics to research.

1. Research the population of the world. At what rate is it growing? Calculate the population density on Earth by comparing the number of people to the amount of land on Earth. At the current rate of growth, in how many years will there be a density of one person per square yard of land? Do you think this will actually happen? What factors might prevent this from happening?

2. Research leases for several different motor vehicles. Why might vehicles with the same list price have different lease prices? Prepare a table of the list prices of several different vehicles, their lease prices for various terms (two-year, three-year, four-year, etc.), and their residual value (the guaranteed value of the vehicle at the end of the lease). Why are the payments for a two-year lease greater than the payments for a three-year lease? Calculate the rate of depreciation for each vehicle.

3. Research the growth of various epidemics throughout history (*examples*: the bubonic plague, AIDS). Do they grow exponentially in the short run? What factors may prevent these epidemics from continuing to grow at an exponential rate?

4. Research the Chernobyl disaster. What radioactive substances were emitted? What is the radioactive half-life of these substances? In how many years will it be considered safe for people to inhabit the area again?

5. Why do medications have a shelf life? What are the dangers of taking a medication that has expired?

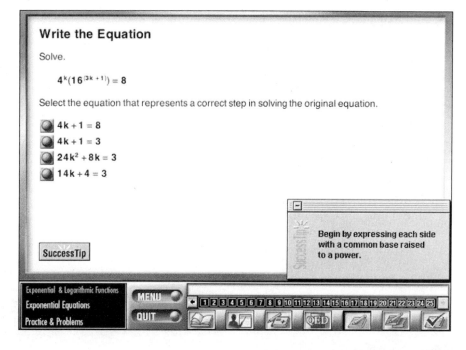

Write the Equation

Solve.

$$4^k(16^{(3k+1)}) = 8$$

Select the equation that represents a correct step in solving the original equation.

- $4k + 1 = 8$
- $4k + 1 = 3$
- $24k^2 + 8k = 3$
- $14k + 4 = 3$

Begin by expressing each side with a common base raised to a power.

SuccessTip

Exponential & Logarithmic Functions
Exponential Equations
Practice & Problems

MENU
QUIT

1 2 3 4 5 6 7 8 9 10 11 12 13 14 15 16 17 18 19 20 21 22 23 24 25

Properties of Logarithms

Cross-References

Exponential and Logarithmic
Functions

Student Workbook: pages 234–237

Key Objectives

The student will:
- learn the properties of
  logarithms.
- learn how logarithmic
  functions relate to
  exponential functions and
  write equivalent
  exponential and
  logarithmic equations.
- use the change-of-base
  formula to rewrite
  logarithmic expressions.
- solve problems involving
  the pH of a solution using
  logarithms.

Key Terms

compound interest, guess and
test, exponential function,
inverse function, domain,
range, product law, distributive property, order of operations, scientific notation

Prerequisite Skills

- Solve and verify
  exponential equations and
  identities.
- Solve exponential
  equations with bases that
  are powers of one another.
- Graph exponential
  functions.
- Model and solve problems
  involving exponential
  functions.

Lesson Description

In this lesson, students learn about logarithmic functions and how
they relate to exponential functions. They explore the properties of
logarithms, and learn how to solve for an exponent variable algebraically.

The **Introduction** presents the formula for compound interest: $A = P(1 + i)^n$, where P is the starting principal, A is the final amount, i is
the interest rate, and n is the number of compounding periods.
Students need to find how long it will take for money to double at different interest rates, but since they don't know how to solve for an
exponent variable, they guess and test values for n. In the **Summary**,
students solve the problem again, this time using the properties of
logarithms to find n algebraically.

The **Tutorial** develops the relationship between exponential and logarithmic functions and then explains the properties of logarithms
and the laws that govern operations with logarithms.

In the **Examples**, students convert between exponential and logarithmic form, expand and condense logarithmic expressions, and use
logic and given information to evaluate a logarithm without using a
calculator. In "Logarithmic Change-of-Base," students take the logarithm of both sides of an equation as a step towards solving the equation. The last example is a problem situation, in which students apply
their knowledge to a real-life problem about pH.

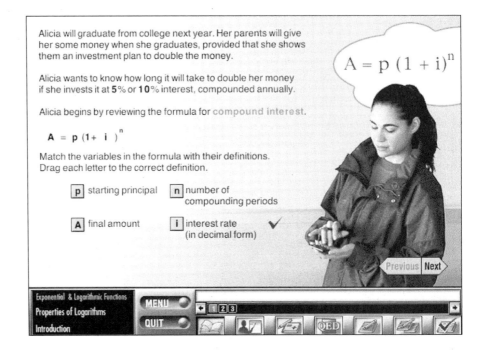

Instructor Intervention

- Before starting the lesson, have pairs or groups of students review the exponent laws and properties. They could create a bulletin board display of the laws for their reference as they work through the lesson. Students may remember the logarithm laws more easily if they always keep in mind the exponent laws and the relationship between exponents and logarithms.

- You may want to work through a few examples with students to familiarize them with using the $\boxed{\log}$ key on their calculators. Students with the same type of calculator could be grouped together so they can help one another learn the appropriate keystroke sequences.

- After completing the **Tutorial**, summarize the properties of logarithms with students by having them describe the laws of logarithms in sentence form as well as using mathematical notation. Add this summary to the bulletin board display, relating the properties of logarithms to the properties of exponents.

- Explain the meaning of logarithm notation in words and using a diagram.

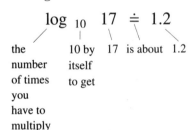

$\log_{10} 17 \doteq 1.2$ means "The number of times you have to multiply 10 by itself to get 17 is about 1.2."

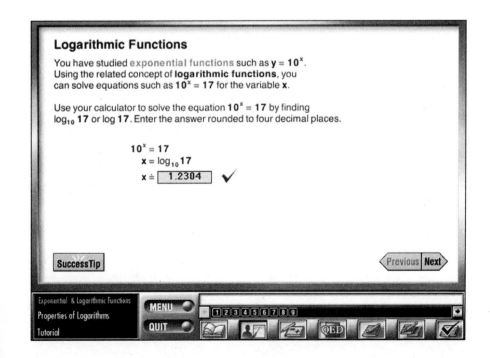

Logarithmic Functions

You have studied exponential functions such as $y = 10^x$.
Using the related concept of **logarithmic functions**, you can solve equations such as $10^x = 17$ for the variable **x**.

Use your calculator to solve the equation $10^x = 17$ by finding $\log_{10} 17$ or $\log 17$. Enter the answer rounded to four decimal places.

$$10^x = 17$$
$$x = \log_{10} 17$$
$$x \doteq \boxed{1.2304} \quad \checkmark$$

SuccessTip

◁ Previous | Next ▷

Exponential & Logarithmic Functions
Properties of Logarithms
Tutorial

MENU
QUIT

1 2 3 4 5 6 7 8 9

Evaluation

- Have students work in small groups to create five problems, modeled on each of the first five **Examples**. Circulate the problems among other groups. The students should justify their solutions using the laws of logarithms.

- Use class discussion to check the students' understanding of the laws and properties of logarithms. One student could describe a law in words using appropriate terminology, then a different student could write the law using mathematical notation, and a third could identify the related exponent law. Work through all the logarithm laws and properties in this way.

- Observe students as they work. Have they memorized the laws and do they use them correctly? Do they understand the connection between exponents and logarithms? Can they evaluate a logarithm using a calculator?

Can they convert between exponential and logarithmic forms? Can they both condense and expand logarithms? Do they recognize when a logarithm requires a change of base?

Remediation

- Some students may know the exponent and logarithm laws, but still have difficulty understanding when to apply them to solve and simplify equations. Review how to use the exponent laws to solve exponential equations, then progress to logarithm laws.

- Review key terms such as **exponent**, **power**, **base**, and **logarithm**. Help students develop a diagram to show how these words relate to logarithmic and to exponential expressions.

- When expanding or condensing logarithmic expressions, students may not know when they should stop. Encourage

them to check their lists of properties to make sure there are no more ways to expand or simplify.

- Some students may require extra help interpreting the questions in practical application problems. Point out the similarities among the questions encountered in the lesson, and encourage students to make connections between the information in the problem and the resulting mathematical expression. It may be helpful to write the four problem-solving steps on the board.

Extension

A

The logarithmic equations in the lesson could all be solved by simply applying the exponent and logarithm laws. Ask students to solve some equations which require the additional step of working with quadratic or rational equations. For example:

(a) $\log_2 x + \log_2 (x + 4) = 5$
$[x = 4]$

(b) $\log_4 (x + 8) - \log_4 (x - 1)$
$= 2 \left[x = \dfrac{8}{5} \right]$

(c) $\log_3 (2x + 5) - \log_3 (x - 3)$
$= 1 \ [x = 14]$

Students could create more problems of the same type and exchange them with classmates. Note that, in order for the equations to be solvable using known techniques, the logarithms must have the same base. Also inform students that you cannot take the logarithm of an expression equal to zero (e.g., in (b), neither $(x + 8)$ nor $(x - 1)$ can equal 0).

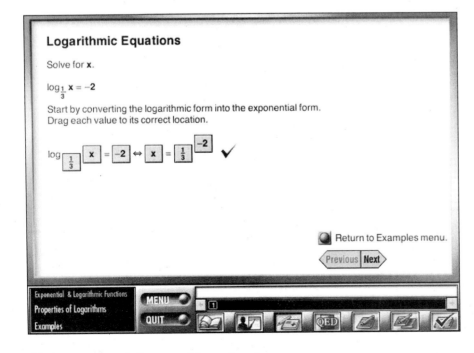

Logarithmic Equations

Solve for **x**.

$\log_{\frac{1}{3}} x = -2$

Start by converting the logarithmic form into the exponential form.
Drag each value to its correct location.

$\log_{\frac{1}{3}} \boxed{x} = \boxed{-2} \leftrightarrow \boxed{x} = \boxed{\tfrac{1}{3}}^{\boxed{-2}} \checkmark$

Return to Examples menu.
⟨Previous | Next⟩

Exponential & Logarithmic Functions
Properties of Logarithms
Examples
MENU
QUIT

B

There are many practical application problems for logarithms. Have students consider the following examples.

(a) The total cost of maintaining inventory on a specific food item is minimized when the size, x, of each order is $x = \sqrt{\dfrac{2cd}{e}}$, where c is the cost of placing an order, d is the monthly demand, and e is the monthly carrying cost. Express $\log x$ in expanded form.

$[\log x = \frac{1}{2}(\log 2 + \log c$
$+ \log d - \log e)]$

(b) The average velocity, v, of a gas particle can be calculated using $v = k\sqrt{PV}$, where P is the pressure of the gas, v is its volume, and k is a constant. Express $\log V$ in expanded form.

$[\log v = \log k$
$+ \frac{1}{2}(\log P + \log V)]$

(c) The period of simple harmonic motion, p, can be calculated using $p = 2\pi\sqrt{\dfrac{m}{k}}$, where m is the mass and k is the proportionality constant between stress and strain. Express $\log p$ in expanded form.

$[\log x = \log 2\pi$
$+ \frac{1}{2}(\log m - \log k)]$

C

To reinforce the laws of logarithms, have students copy and complete the following table using calculators, and then use the values in the table to complete the activities.

x	2	3	4	5	8	10	15
$\log x$							

(a) Determine each sum.
  (i) $\log 2 + \log 5$ [1]
  (ii) $\log 2 + \log 4$ [0.90309]
  (iii) $\log 3 + \log 5$ [1.17609]
Compare the sums you found to the logarithms in the table. What pattern do you notice?

(b) Determine each difference.
  (i) $\log 8 - \log 4$ [0.30103]
  (ii) $\log 10 - \log 2$ [0.69897]
  (iii) $\log 15 - \log 5$ [0.47712]
Compare the differences you found to the logarithms in the table. What pattern do you notice?

(c) Determine each product.
  (i) $2 \times \log 2$ [0.60206]
  (ii) $3 \times \log 2$ [0.90309]
Compare the products you found to the logarithms in the table. What pattern do you notice?

Enrichment

A

Ask students to research practical applications of logarithms. Some possible topics are: Richter scale, population growth, radioactive decay. The research could integrate the mathematics and science curriculum.

B

Have students research the life and contributions of John Napier (1550–1617), who invented logarithms.

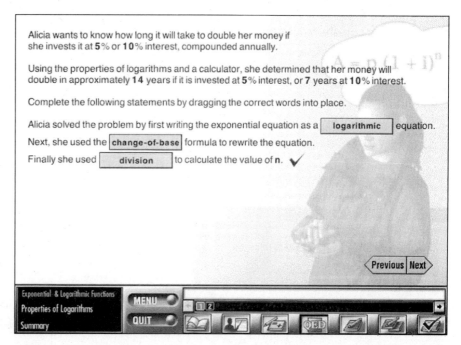

Alicia wants to know how long it will take to double her money if she invests it at **5**% or **10**% interest, compounded annually.

Using the properties of logarithms and a calculator, she determined that her money will double in approximately **14** years if it is invested at **5**% interest, or **7** years at **10**% interest.

Complete the following statements by dragging the correct words into place.

Alicia solved the problem by first writing the exponential equation as a [**logarithmic**] equation.

Next, she used the [**change-of-base**] formula to rewrite the equation.

Finally she used [**division**] to calculate the value of **n**. ✓

Previous | Next

Exponential & Logarithmic Functions
Properties of Logarithms
Summary

MENU
QUIT

Logarithmic Equations

Cross-References

Exponential and Logarithmic Functions

Student Workbook: pages 238–241

Key Objectives

The student will:

- solve and verify exponential and logarithmic equations and identities.

Key Terms

exponent, base, logarithm, common logarithm, exponential equation, logarithmic equation, identity

Prerequisite Skills

- Explain the relationship between the laws of logarithms and the laws of exponents.
- Change functions from exponential form to logarithmic form and vice versa.
- Solve exponential equations having bases that are powers of one another.
- Solve nonlinear equations by factoring.
- Explain and apply the exponent laws for powers with integral exponents.

Lesson Description

In this lesson, students learn how to solve and verify logarithmic equations and identities. They also learn how to solve exponential equations using logarithms.

The **Introduction** explains how the carbon dating method is used to determine the age of organic materials such as fossils. Since carbon-14 (C-14) has a half-life of about 5700 years, the approximate age of a fossil can be determined using the formula $A = A_0 \left(2^{-\frac{t}{5700}} \right)$

where 5700 represents the half-life of C-14, A is the amount of C-14 present at time t, and A_0 is the original amount of C-14 (i.e., at $t = 0$). To find the age of a fossil, students substitute given values into the equation and solve the resulting exponential equation by writing each side as a power with the same base. However, they are not able to determine the age of another fossil because the resulting exponential equation cannot be written with common bases. In the **Summary**, students determine the age of the second fossil by solving the exponential equation using logarithms.

The **Tutorial** begins by reviewing how to solve simple exponential equations using a common base. Students then apply their knowledge of the properties of logarithms to solve an exponential equation where a common base is not possible. The **Tutorial** presents other methods for solving logarithmic equations, including using the properties of logarithms to express each side of the equation as a single logarithm, and changing the equation to exponential form.

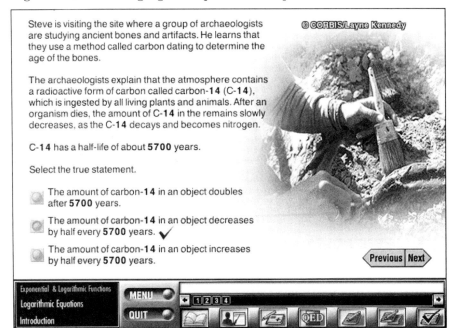

Steve is visiting the site where a group of archaeologists are studying ancient bones and artifacts. He learns that they use a method called carbon dating to determine the age of the bones.

© CORBIS/Layne Kennedy

The archaeologists explain that the atmosphere contains a radioactive form of carbon called carbon-**14** (C-**14**), which is ingested by all living plants and animals. After an organism dies, the amount of C-**14** in the remains slowly decreases, as the C-**14** decays and becomes nitrogen.

C-**14** has a half-life of about **5700** years.

Select the true statement.

- The amount of carbon-**14** in an object doubles after **5700** years.
- The amount of carbon-**14** in an object decreases by half every **5700** years. ✔
- The amount of carbon-**14** in an object increases by half every **5700** years.

Previous | Next

Exponential & Logarithmic Functions
Logarithmic Equations
Introduction

MENU
QUIT
1 2 3 4

In the **Examples**, students practice these techniques for solving exponential equations using logarithms, and for solving logarithmic equations:
- using the product property of logarithms
- using the quotient property of logarithms
- writing the coefficient as an exponent
- changing a constant to a logarithm
- changing to exponential form
- taking the common logarithm of both sides of an exponential expression

They also learn ways to verify solutions, and they apply their knowledge to help them verify an identity.

Instructor Intervention

- Make sure students understand the logarithm properties and can convert from exponential to logarithmic form and vice versa.

- Review the meaning of an identity. Point out that students should work on each side of an identity separately rather than apply the same operation to both sides (as they would do with an equation).

- Students should understand how to use their calculators to evaluate logarithmic expressions such as $\dfrac{\log 5}{2 \log 3 - \log 5}$. Discourage students from recording and re-entering rounded logarithm values – this method is inefficient and less accurate than inputting an expression directly using the parentheses and memory keys.

- The first two **Examples** show two different ways of solving logarithmic equations that contain a constant. The two techniques are:
  1. Isolate the constant (this step was done for the students in the first example), write the other side as a single logarithm, and change the equation to exponential form.
  2. Change the constant to a logarithm, express each side as a single logarithm, and then rewrite the equation without logarithms.

  Make sure that students recognize the two different ways, and encourage them to analyze a problem to decide which way would be better before solving the problem.

- Remind students that it's not possible to take the logarithm of a negative number because $\log_b x$ only exists if $b > 1$ and $x > 0$. Students know that $\log_b x$ means "how many times you have to multiply b by itself to get x." This knowledge should show them that $\log_{10}(-100)$ does not have a solution because you cannot multiply 10 by itself to get -100. Therefore, it is important to always verify that solutions are valid.

Evaluation

- Divide the class into groups and have each one create a ten-question quiz on exponential and logarithmic equations. They should write a complete solution for each problem, and then remove parts of the solution to be filled in by another group. Encourage students to include at least one identity in their quiz. The quizzes should have problems which require using these techniques:
  - solving a simple exponential equation that uses common bases
  - taking the common logarithm of both sides of an exponential expression
  - using the properties of logarithms to express each side of an equation as a single logarithm
  - writing a coefficient as an exponent or vice versa
  - changing a constant to a logarithm
  - changing logarithmic form to exponential form

  As students fill in the blanks on the quizzes, they should check to see whether enough information was given to complete the solutions, and whether the quiz incorporated all the techniques listed.

- Observe students as they complete the activities. Do they know the logarithm properties, and do they apply them correctly? Do they analyze an equation before starting the solution to decide the best method to use? Do they recognize when to take the common logarithm of both sides, and when there is a coefficient that must be written as an exponent? Can they change from logarithmic to exponential form and vice versa? Do they know what to do when there is a constant in the equation? Do they remember to verify their solutions?

Remediation

- If students have trouble deciding how to solve logarithmic equations, help them analyze the equation first to decide on the best method to use. Some questions they can ask are:
  - Are there coefficients that need to be written as exponents?
  - Are there constants in the equation?
  - Can each side be written as a single logarithm?
  - Would it help to convert a logarithmic equation to exponential form? an exponential equation to logarithmic form?

Extension

A

Challenge students to solve exponential equations that involve more complicated algebra.

For example, these exponential equations have more than one variable in the exponent:

(a) $4^{6x-a} = 3^{a-5x}$

Find a in terms of x.

[Answer: $\dfrac{x(6 \log 4 + 5 \log 3)}{\log 12}$
$\doteq 5.55789x$]

(b) $6^{3x-a} = 5^{a-2x}$

Find x in terms of a.

[Answer: $\dfrac{a(\log 30)}{3 \log 6 + 2 \log 5}$
$\doteq 0.39576a$]

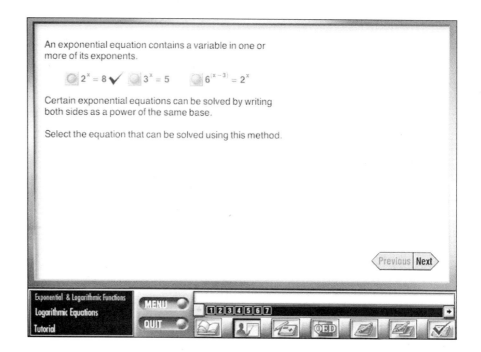

An exponential equation contains a variable in one or more of its exponents.

$2^x = 8$ ✓ $3^x = 5$ $6^{(x-3)} = 2^x$

Certain exponential equations can be solved by writing both sides as a power of the same base.

Select the equation that can be solved using this method.

Previous | Next

Exponential & Logarithmic Functions
Logarithmic Equations
Tutorial

MENU
QUIT
1 2 3 4 5 6 7

B

The second question in the "First Steps" **Practice** section, $\left(\log_x 2 = \frac{1}{3}\right)$, can be solved in two ways: After changing the equation to exponential form, raise both sides to another power; or, take the common logarithm of both sides. The lesson shows the first method. Have students solve the equation using the second method, and look for other equations that can be solved both ways. Then encourage students to identify situations where one method is easier than another. For example, it is easier to solve $x^{0.57} = 2$ by taking the logarithm of both sides than by raising to another power.

Enrichment

A

Have students solve logarithmic equations that involve complicated applications of the properties of logarithms. For example, they could solve $\log_3 x = \log_4 5$.

$$\left[x = (3^{\log 5})^{\frac{1}{\log 4}} \right]$$

B

Have students demonstrate how to use a graphing calculator to approximate the solutions to logarithmic equations. For example:

$\log x + \log (x - 3) = 1$
① $\log x + \log (x - 3) - 1 = 0$
② $\log x + \log (x - 3) - 1 = y$

① Subtract 1 from both sides.
② Graph the corresponding function.

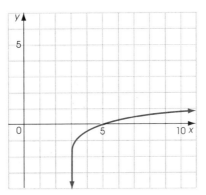

The solution is the *x*-intercept of the function.

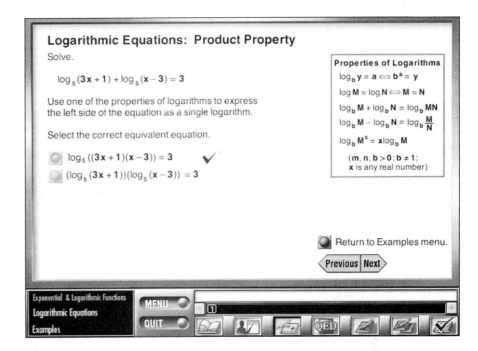

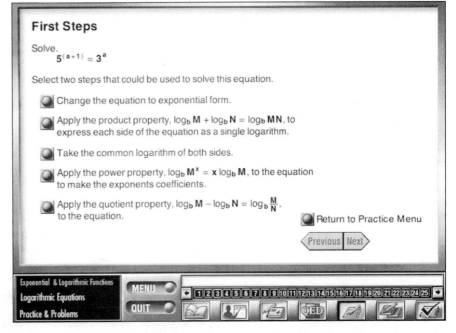

Cross-References

Exponential and Logarithmic Functions

Student Workbook: pages 242–245

Key Objectives

The student will:
- graph logarithmic functions and their inverses.
- analyze the graphs of logarithmic functions.
- translate graphs of logarithmic functions.
- predict the shape of a logarithmic function.
- use the graph of a logarithmic function to predict values.

Key Terms

graph, logarithmic function, exponential function, increasing function, decreasing function, domain, range, asymptote, intercept, inverse, symmetry, translation

Prerequisite Skills

- Graph points and curves on a Cartesian plane.
- Use the definition of logarithm to convert exponential expressions to logarithms and vice versa.
- Construct a table of values with two variables.
- Apply the properties of logarithms.

Lesson Description

In the **Introduction**, students learn about the Richter scale, which is used to measure the magnitude of earthquakes. A simplified version of the formula is $R = \log \frac{A}{P}$ where R is the magnitude and A and P are the amplitude and period. Students use the Richter scale formula and their knowledge of the properties of logarithms to complete a table showing the value of $\frac{A}{P}$ for different magnitudes. From the table, they conclude that an earthquake of magnitude 8.5 was about 300 times more severe than an earthquake of magnitude 6. Students find a more accurate answer in the **Summary** by graphing the logarithmic function and estimating the values from the graph.

The **Tutorial** begins by reviewing the definition of a logarithm and relating it to its exponential form. Students use the exponential form to create tables of values for $y = \log_2 x$ and $y = \log_{\frac{1}{2}} x$, and then they analyze the graphs of the functions to find similarities and differences in their characteristics: whether the graph is increasing or decreasing, the domain and range, the equation of the asymptote, and the x-intercept. They graph the inverse of $y = \log_2 x$ by exchanging x and y in the equation to get $x = \log_2 y$ and rewriting $x = \log_2 y$ in exponential form so that it can be solved for y. After graphing the inverse, students note that the graphs of $y = \log_2 x$ and its inverse are symmetric (they are reflections of each other over the line $y = x$.) Finally, students create tables of values for a function and its translation and

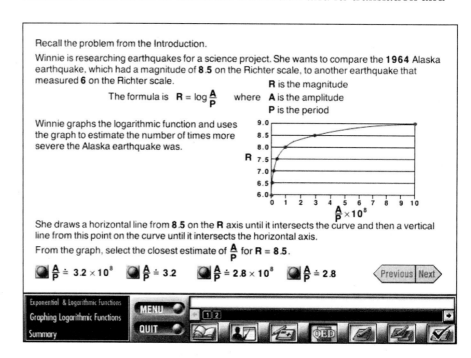

examine the resulting graphs to develop the general formula for the vertical translation of a logarithmic function.

In the **Examples**, students graph logarithmic functions, predict the shape of a logarithmic function from related graphs, and learn about horizontal translations. They also analyze a graph for its important characteristics.

Instructor Intervention

- Before starting the lesson, review the **Key Terms**.

- Review the concept of the inverse of a function and the algebraic and graphical relationship between a function and its inverse.

- Students should be able to express domains and ranges using both interval and set notation.

- Make sure that students are proficient at using graphing tools, especially the zoom and trace features. If graphing calculators are not available, students could work in pairs and alternate drawing the graphs by hand. Graph paper should be provided for this purpose.

- Post the change-of-base formula so that students can use the graphing calculator for bases other than 10.

$$y = \log_b x = \frac{\log x}{\log b}$$

- When graphing a function like $y = \log_2 x$, the lesson recommends first writing the logarithm in exponential form ($2^y = x$), then substituting values for y to find values for x. Point out that the more conventional way of finding ordered pairs is to substitute values for x to find values for y, but that it is much easier with logarithmic functions to follow the process in reverse.

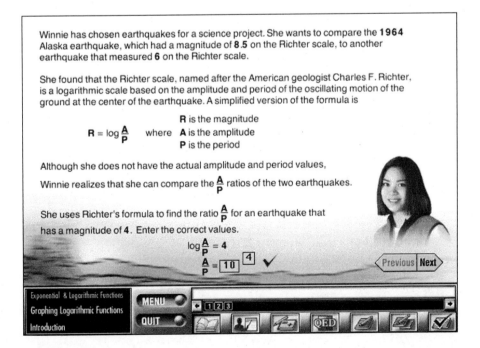

Evaluation

- Pose graphing problems such as the following.
  - **(a)** How is the graph of $y = \log_b x$, where $b > 1$, related to the graph of $y = b^x$, where $b > 1$? Sketch graphs to illustrate the relationship.
  - **(b)** How is the graph of $y = \log_b x$, where $0 < b < 1$, related to the graph of $y = b^x$, where $0 < b < 1$? Sketch graphs to illustrate the relationship.
  - **(c)** What do these graphs show about the relationship between a logarithmic function and its inverse?

  Ask students to choose values of b that fit each pattern in order to make the graphs.

- Have pairs explain the following to each other, using example graphs to check their answers.
  - **(a)** How is the graph of $y = \log_b (x - h)$ obtained from the graph of $y = \log_b x$? [Move the graph h units to the right.]
  - **(b)** How is the graph of $y = \log_b x + k$ obtained from the graph of $y = \log_b x$? [Move the graph k units upward.]
  - **(c)** How is the graph of $y = \log_b (x - h) + k$ obtained from the graph of $y = \log_b x$? [Move the graph h units to the right and k units upward.]
  - **(d)** How is the graph of $y = \log_2 (x + 4) - 3$ obtained from the graph of $y = \log_2 x$? [Move the graph 4 units to the left and 3 units down.]

- Observe students as they graph logarithmic functions. Do they know how to find values of x and y using a table of values? Do they find values using the exponential form of the logarithmic function? Can they identify the characteristics of various logarithmic functions? Can they find inverses of functions and translations of functions?

Remediation

- Some students may have difficulty determining the shape of the graph for different values of b in $y = \log_b x$. Post graphs of $y = \log_{\frac{1}{2}} x$ and $y = \log_2 x$ for reference:

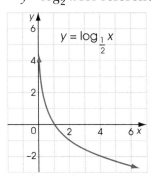

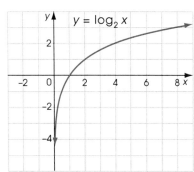

- Remind students that when they graph a function they should include the following steps.
  - **(a)** Label the axes x and y.
  - **(b)** Put numbers on the axes. Use a scale that will allow the graph to fit; this may mean using a different scale on the vertical and horizontal axes.
  - **(c)** Label the graphs.
  - **(d)** Show that the graphs continue by putting arrows on the endpoints.
  - **(e)** Label important features in the graph such as asymptotes and intercepts.

Extension

A

Present graphing problems that involve using function notation to combine logarithmic functions. For example:

- **(a)** Graph the function $f(x) = 10^x$. Find the domain and range. [domain: $\{x \mid x \in R\}$, range: $\{y \mid y > 0, y \in R\}$]
- **(b)** Graph the function $g(x) = \log x$. Find the domain and range. [domain: $\{x \mid x > 0, x \in R\}$, range: $\{y \mid y \in R\}$]
- **(c)** Graph the function $h(x) = g(f(x)) = \log (10^x)$. Find the domain and range. [domain: $\{x \mid x \in R\}$, range: $\{y \mid y \in R\}$]
- **(d)** Graph the function $k(x) = f(g(x)) = 10^{\log x}$. Find the domain and range. [domain: $\{x \mid x > 0, x \in R\}$, range: $\{y \mid y > 0, y \in R\}$]
- **(e)** What simple function has the same graph as $h(x)$ and $k(x)$? [The function $y = x$ has the same graph as $h(x)$; the function $y = x$, $\{x \mid x > 0, x \in R\}$, has the same graph as $k(x)$.
- **(f)** How are $f(x)$ and $g(x)$ related? [They are inverses.]

The students know how to perform vertical and horizontal translations using two basic graphs, one for $y = \log_b x$ where $b > 1$ and one for $y = \log_b x$ where $0 < b < 1$. However, students only need to remember one graph to be able to perform all translations because logarithmic functions where $0 < b < 1$ can be converted into reflections of functions where $b > 1$. Ask students to explore this idea using an example:

$$y = \log_{\frac{1}{2}} x$$

$$y = \frac{\log x}{\log \frac{1}{2}} \quad \text{Use the change-of-base formula.}$$

$$y = \frac{\log x}{\log 1 - \log 2} \quad \text{Use the quotient property of logarithms.}$$

$$y = \frac{\log x}{0 - \log 2} \quad \log 1 = 0$$

$$y = \frac{\log x}{-\log 2}$$

$$y = -\frac{\log x}{\log 2} \quad \text{Use the definition of a logarithm.}$$

$$y = -\log_2 x$$

Therefore, the graph $y = \log_{\frac{1}{2}} x$

is the same as the graph of $y = -\log_2 x$, which is a reflection of $y = \log_2 x$ over the y-axis.

Enrichment

Have students graph these functions to prove the properties of logarithms:

$$y = \log_2 \frac{x}{3}$$

$$y = \log_2 x - \log_2 3$$

Ask: What do you notice about these graphs? Based on your observations, what can you conclude about the two functions? Once students have determined the properties of logarithms from the graphs, have them graph these functions:

$$y = \log_2 x^2$$

$$y = 2 \log_2 x$$

Ask students to explain why the two graphs are different.

Challenge students to solve these translation problems.

(a) How do the graphs of $y = \log_2 3x$ and $y = \log_2 x$ compare? Is it possible to draw the graph of $y = \log_2 3x$ using a translation of $y = \log_2 x$? [Yes; move $y = \log_2 x$ upward by $\log_2 3$ units to get $y = \log_2 3x$.]

(b) How do the graphs of $y = 3 \log_2 x$ and $y = \log_2 x$ compare? Is it possible to draw the graph of $y = 3 \log_2 x$ using a translation of $y = \log_2 x$? [No.]

(c) How would you sketch the graph of $y = \log_2 (3x + 2)$ using the properties in (a) and (b)?

Hint: Begin by changing $y = \log_2 (3x + 2)$ to the form

$$y = \log_2 3\left(x - \left(-\frac{2}{3}\right)\right).$$

[$y = \log_2 (3x + 2)$ can be drawn by moving the graph of $y = \log_2 x$ to the left by $\frac{2}{3}$ units and upward by $\log_2 3$ units.]

(d) How could you reflect a graph in the x-axis? [Keep the x-coordinate and change the sign of the y-coordinate.]

(e) How could you reflect a graph in the y-axis? [Keep the y-coordinate and change the sign of the x-coordinate.]

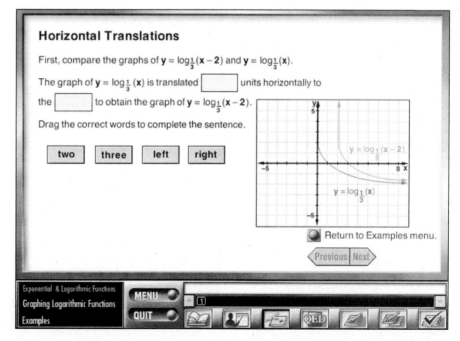

Horizontal Translations

First, compare the graphs of $y = \log_{\frac{1}{3}}(x - 2)$ and $y = \log_{\frac{1}{3}}(x)$.

The graph of $y = \log_{\frac{1}{3}}(x)$ is translated [ ] units horizontally to the [ ] to obtain the graph of $y = \log_{\frac{1}{3}}(x - 2)$.

Drag the correct words to complete the sentence.

| two | three | left | right |

$y = \log_{\frac{1}{3}}(x - 2)$

$y = \log_{\frac{1}{3}}(x)$

Return to Examples menu.

Previous | Next

Exponential & Logarithmic Functions
Graphing Logarithmic Functions
Examples

MENU
QUIT

Exponential and Logarithmic Functions

Student Workbook: pages 246–249

Key Objectives

The student will:

- learn how to solve problems involving exponents and logarithms.

Key Terms

interest, compound interest, logarithm, exponential equation, exponent, half-life, scientific notation, rule of seventy

Prerequisite Skills

- Solve and verify exponential and logarithmic equations and identities.
- Model, graph, and apply exponential functions to solve problems.
- Change functions from exponential form to logarithmic form and vice versa.

Lesson Description

The **Introduction** explains the rule of 70: The number of years needed to double an investment equals 70 divided by the annual interest rate. Students start checking this rule using the formula for compound interest, $A = P(1 + i)^n$, but are unable to complete the check because they don't know how to solve for a variable exponent. They solve the problem in the **Summary** using logarithms.

The **Tutorial** presents the population growth formula, $P = P_0 \times 2^{kt}$. Students use rules of logarithms to determine the population constant if the population triples every 20 years. Then they use the population constant to find how long it would take for the population to grow to 100,000 if it is currently 20,000.

In the **Examples**, students solve a problem about radioactive decay and the half-life of carbon-14. They follow the problem-solving steps to find the age of a bone fragment that contains 60% of the carbon-14 it initially had. The **Practice and Problems** section introduces other formulas involving logarithms, including the Richter scale formula and the decibel gain formula.

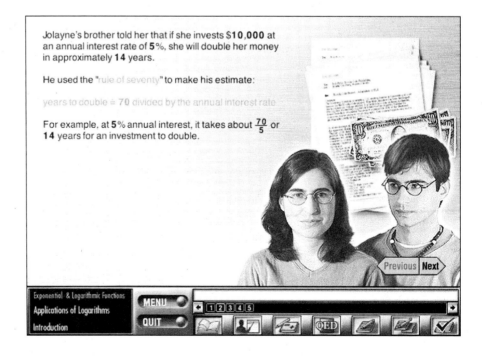

Jolayne's brother told her that if she invests **$10,000** at an annual interest rate of **5%**, she will double her money in approximately **14** years.

He used the "rule of seventy" to make his estimate:

years to double ÷ 70 divided by the annual interest rate

For example, at **5%** annual interest, it takes about $\frac{70}{5}$ or **14** years for an investment to double.

Exponential & Logarithmic Functions
Applications of Logarithms
Introduction

MENU
QUIT
1 2 3 4 5

Previous Next

Instructor Intervention

- In compound interest problems where the period of compounding is not a year (e.g., monthly, semiannually, etc.), make sure that students understand the difference between the number of compounding periods and the number of years.

- Students may be confused by the solution process for population problems, where they must first solve for the constant k, and then solve for the other unknown. Explain that multiple steps are needed because there are two unknowns.

- Emphasize that students should avoid rounding answers until the last step. You may need to review how to use the calculator memory keys.

- Remind students that for some types of problems, such as $2 = 2^{12k}$, there are two solution methods, one involving logarithms, as shown in the lesson, and one that doesn't use logarithms:

$$2^1 = 2^{12k}$$
$$12k = 1$$
$$k = \frac{1}{12}$$

Assure students that both methods are correct, and allow them to use their preferred method.

Lesson Components

Examples

Think about the problem.
Make a plan.
Solve the problem.
Look back.
Look ahead.

Practice and Problems

Think about the problem.
Make a plan.
Solve the problem.
Look back.
Look ahead.

Extra Practice

One-Step Solutions
Comparing Earthquakes
Money Matters
Radioactive Decay
Population Growth

Self-Check

One-Step Solutions (2)
Comparing Earthquakes (2)
Money Matters (2)
Radioactive Decay (2)
Population Growth (2)

Minimum score: 7 out of 10

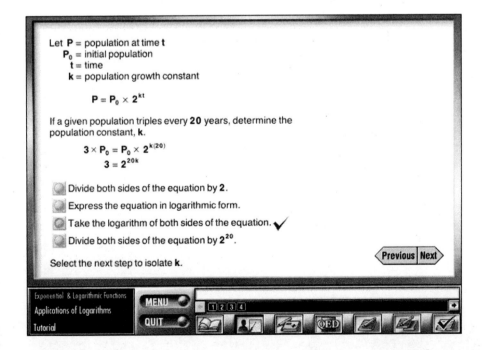

Let P = population at time t
  P_0 = initial population
  t = time
  k = population growth constant

$$P = P_0 \times 2^{kt}$$

If a given population triples every **20** years, determine the population constant, **k**.

$$3 \times P_0 = P_0 \times 2^{k(20)}$$
$$3 = 2^{20k}$$

- Divide both sides of the equation by **2**.
- Express the equation in logarithmic form.
- Take the logarithm of both sides of the equation. ✓
- Divide both sides of the equation by 2^{20}.

Select the next step to isolate **k**.

‹ Previous | Next ›

Exponential & Logarithmic Functions
Applications of Logarithms
Tutorial

MENU
QUIT

1 2 3 4

Evaluation

- Ask students to research the intensities of recent earthquakes and then use the Richter scale formula from the **Practice** section to solve the following problems:
  - **(a)** Assume the period is 0.5 seconds for all earthquakes, and find the amplitude of each.
  - **(b)** Assume the amplitude is 500,000 micrometers for all earthquakes, and find the period of each.
  - **(c)** Identify any patterns or trends in the data.

  This could be worked into a cross-curricular assignment with the addition of problems from a geography class.

- Students could create their own problems modeled on those in the **Practice** section. You could collect the problems and compile them into quizzes, or have students exchange the problems and write complete solutions.

- Observe students as they complete the activities. Can they correctly translate from English into mathematical notation? Do they know which formula to use? Do they understand the solution process behind solving all the types of problems in the lesson?

Remediation

- Review the relationship between exponents and logarithms. Make sure that students can explain this relationship in their own words.

- Review the rules of logarithms. While working through this lesson, the program assumes that students need only the occasional reminder of these rules.

- Students may be familiar with a compound interest formula that differs from the one used in this lesson. Explain that i is the interest rate per compounding period.

$$i = \frac{annual\ interest\ rate}{number\ of\ compounding\ periods\ per\ year}$$

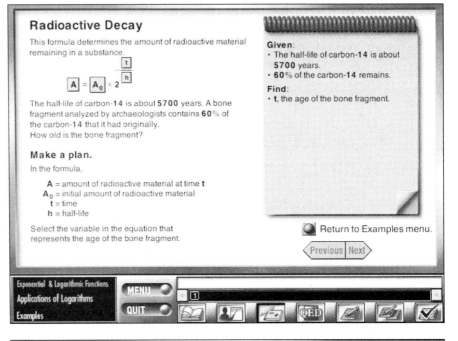

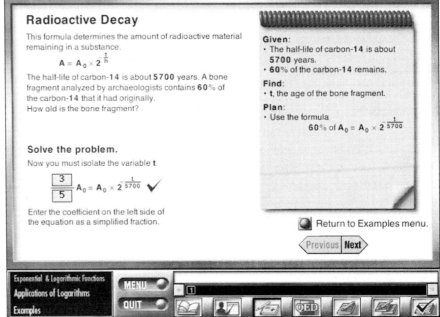

Extension

A

Ask students to investigate Newton's Law of Cooling, another application of logarithms. Have the students explain how police use this formula.

B

Students could research how logarithms are used in oceanography to help measure light intensity.

Enrichment

A

Students may want to study the area closest to them that has earthquake activity. Local data could be compared to data from other areas to better understand how severe local earthquakes have been.

B

Have students research the current rates on bank accounts, mutual funds, and so on. They could then make up some investment problems to use in a group activity where each group solves problems from another group.

C

Invite students to look into local population data and discuss whether the population growth formula can be applied to their data.

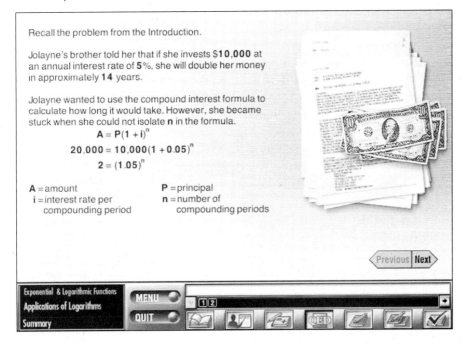

Recall the problem from the Introduction.

Jolayne's brother told her that if she invests $10,000 at an annual interest rate of 5%, she will double her money in approximately 14 years.

Jolayne wanted to use the compound interest formula to calculate how long it would take. However, she became stuck when she could not isolate n in the formula.

$$A = P(1 + i)^n$$
$$20{,}000 = 10{,}000(1 + 0.05)^n$$
$$2 = (1.05)^n$$

A = amount
i = interest rate per compounding period

P = principal
n = number of compounding periods

Previous | Next

Exponential & Logarithmic Functions
Applications of Logarithms
Summary

MENU
QUIT
1 2

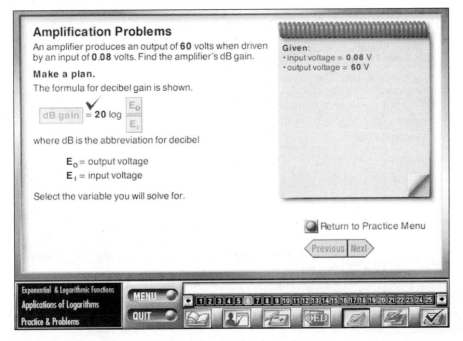

Amplification Problems

An amplifier produces an output of **60** volts when driven by an input of **0.08** volts. Find the amplifier's dB gain.

Make a plan.

The formula for decibel gain is shown.

$$\text{dB gain} = 20 \log \frac{E_o}{E_i}$$

where dB is the abbreviation for decibel

E_o = output voltage
E_i = input voltage

Select the variable you will solve for.

Given:
• input voltage = 0.08 V
• output voltage = 60 V

Return to Practice Menu

Previous | Next

Exponential & Logarithmic Functions
Applications of Logarithms
Practice & Problems

MENU
QUIT
1 2 3 4 5 6 7 8 9 10 11 12 13 14 15 16 17 18 19 20 21 22 23 24 25

Cross-References

Exponential and Logarithmic Functions

Student Workbook: pages 250–253

Key Objectives

The student will:

- use the natural exponential function, $y = e^x$, to investigate problems that involve continuous growth or decay.

Key Terms

compound interest, irrational number, domain, range, asymptote, translation, reflection, dilatation, scientific notation, continuous exponential growth, compound interest formula, decreasing function, increasing function

Prerequisite Skills

- Graph and analyze an exponential function, on paper and using a graphing calculator or program.
- Model, graph, and apply exponential functions to solve problems.
- Solve and verify exponential and logarithmic equations and identities.

Lesson Description

This lesson introduces students to the natural exponential function and its applications to problems about continuous growth.

In the **Introduction**, students need to decide between two investment options. They calculate the value of the first option using the formula $A = P\left(1 + \dfrac{r}{k}\right)^{kt}$ (where A is the amount of money after t years, P is the original investment, and r is the annual interest rate compounded k times a year). The second option presents a problem, however, because it offers continuous compounding, which denotes a k-value of infinity. Since the value of the formula cannot be calculated for $k = \infty$, students test larger and larger values of k to see if there is a pattern in the resulting values. Students return to the problem in the **Summary** and use their knowledge of the natural exponential function to verify that the calculations are correct.

In the **Tutorial**, students calculate the value of A for various interest rates, compounded continuously. They graph their results and identify that the relationship between r and the value of $\left(1 + \dfrac{r}{k}\right)^k$ as k increases toward ∞ can be represented by the natural exponential function, $f(r) = e^r$. This function is also written as $f(x) = e^x$.

The **Examples** develop students' understanding of the natural exponential function, its graph, and transformations of its graph. Students also learn about continuous exponential decay.

Instructor Intervention

- Emphasize that, since the natural exponential function is $f(r) = e^r$, the points on the natural logarithm graph are of the form (r, e^r). Some students may prefer to use x instead of r, to correspond with the notation used on their calculators.

- Encourage students to try to explain the significance of constants in practical application problems. For example, in the equation $F = 70 + 210e^{-0.025t}$ (from **Practice** problem 15), the constant 70 represents the room temperature in degrees Fahrenheit.

- Students could program a spreadsheet to evaluate a function and then enter progressively larger growth rates to investigate what happens to the function as the growth rate approaches ∞. This would allow students to easily see the pattern in the function, and would also help them find points to plot.

- Make sure students understand that, when something is "compounded continuously," its interest is continuously added to its principal.

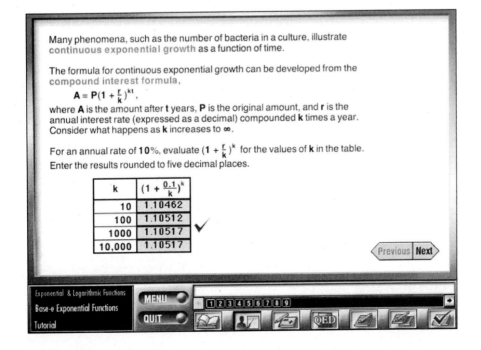

Many phenomena, such as the number of bacteria in a culture, illustrate continuous exponential growth as a function of time.

The formula for continuous exponential growth can be developed from the compound interest formula,

$$A = P\left(1 + \frac{r}{k}\right)^{kt},$$

where **A** is the amount after **t** years, **P** is the original amount, and **r** is the annual interest rate (expressed as a decimal) compounded **k** times a year. Consider what happens as **k** increases to ∞.

For an annual rate of **10**%, evaluate $\left(1 + \frac{r}{k}\right)^k$ for the values of **k** in the table. Enter the results rounded to five decimal places.

k	$\left(1 + \frac{0.1}{k}\right)^k$
10	1.10462
100	1.10512
1000	1.10517
10,000	1.10517

Previous | Next

Exponential & Logarithmic Functions
Base-e Exponential Functions
Tutorial

MENU
QUIT
1 2 3 4 5 6 7 8 9

Evaluation

- Have students write this quiz individually and then check their answers in groups.
  1. If $f(x) = e^x$, evaluate the following to five decimal places.
     (a) $f(-3)$ [0.04979]
     (b) $f(0.2)$ [1.22140]
  2. Describe the transformation of the graph of $y = e^x$ that would give the graph of $y = e^{-x} + 1$. [reflection in the y-axis followed by a vertical translation 1 unit up]
  3. $5000 is invested at 6.5% annual interest, compounded continuously. Determine the amount of the investment after 8 years. [$8410.14]
  4. The population of a country is modeled by $A = Pe^{rt}$. Because of economic conditions, the population has been steadily declining at the rate of 3% per year for 10 years. If the current population is 1.4 million, determine the population 10 years ago. [1.9 million]
  5. If $T(t) = 23 + 105e^{-0.2t}$ gives the temperature of a cake in degrees Celsius t minutes after it is removed from the oven, determine the temperature of the cake after 15 minutes. [28°C]

- Observe students as they complete the activity. Can they evaluate e^x for different values of x? Can they perform transformations on graphs of $y = e^x$? Can they correctly interpret word problems about exponential growth or decay?

Remediation

- Remind students how to enter percents into their calculators. For example, when entering 2% into an exponential growth equation, they need to replace r with 0.02, not 2.

- Students may make mistakes with horizontal translations of $f(x) = e^x$ because they are different than would be expected. Remind students that in the equation $f(x) = e^{(x + c)}$, if c is positive, the translation is to the *left*, and if c is negative, the translation is to the *right*.

- Some students may find the notation used with base-e exponential functions intimidating. Remind them that e is just a number equal to

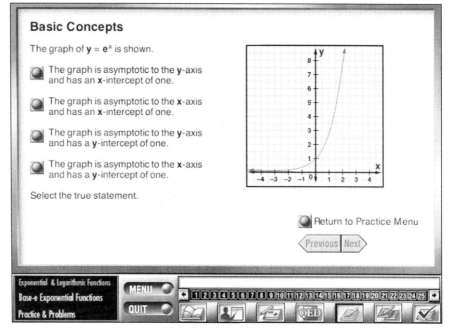

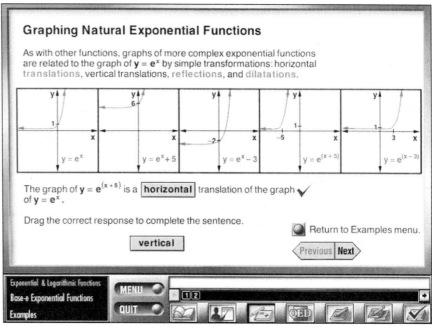

2.7182.... Point out where e is located on a number line, and then show that the graph of $y = e^x$ is between the graphs of $y = 2^x$ and $y = 3^x$.

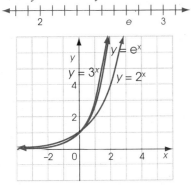

Extension

A

Students could research the history of the natural exponential function. Ask: Why is the function called the "natural" exponential function, and when was e introduced to represent the base of this function? Students could use this website as a starting point: http://www.maths.tcd.ie/pub/HistMath/People/Euler/RouseBall/RB_Euler.html

B

Invite students to use a graphing calculator to study the effects of multiplying the base or exponent in $y = e^x$ by a constant. For example, have students graph:

(a) $y = 2e^x$, $y = 5e^x$, $y = 10e^x$

(b) $y = e^{2x}$, $y = e^{5x}$, $y = e^{10x}$

Then encourage students to include these types of transformations in problems that they create involving combinations of transformations.

Enrichment

A

Challenge students to investigate De Moivre's Theorem and how it connects trigonometry, sequences and series, and the exponential function.

B

Pose the following problems:

(a) Graph the following:
$(x) = \ln x$, $g(x) = \log x$,
$$h(x) = \frac{\ln x}{\ln 10}, \text{ and}$$
$$i(x) = \frac{\log x}{\log e}.$$

(b) Compare the graphs. What property of logarithms does this suggest?

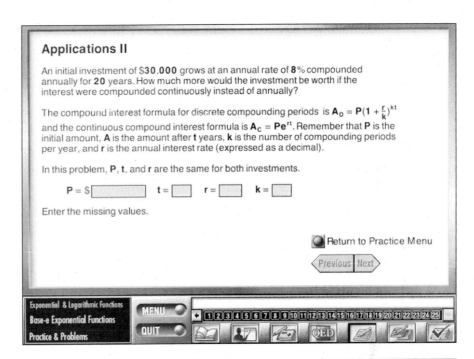

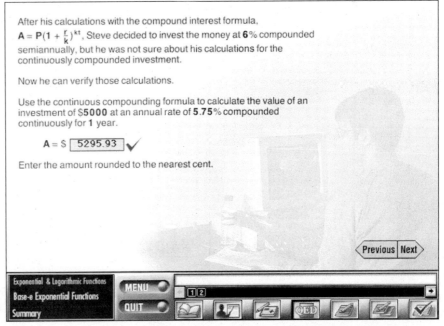

12.9 Base-e Logarithms

Key Objectives

The student will:

- study the relationship between the natural exponential function and its inverse function, the natural logarithm.

Key Terms

irrational number, domain, range, natural logarithm, intercept, asymptote, exponential function, inverse, logarithmic function, symmetry, translation

Prerequisite Skills

- Determine the inverse of a function.
- Solve and verify exponential and logarithmic equations and identities.
- Evaluate and graph base-*e* exponential functions.

Lesson Description

In this lesson, students study the relationship between the natural exponential function and its inverse function, the natural logarithm.

The **Introduction** presents the exponential function $A = 4e^{-0.17t}$, where A represents the concentration of a drug in a patient's bloodstream and t represents time. Students need to determine when a certain concentration will be reached, but since they don't know how to solve base-*e* logarithmic functions, they find the time by graphing the function. In the **Summary**, students solve the problem algebraically by solving for t.

The **Tutorial** notes that the value of *e* is between 2 and 3 and connects this to the fact that the graph of $y = \log_e x = \ln x$ is between $y = \log_2 x$ and $y = \log_3 x$. Students identify the domain, range, *x*-intercept, and asymptote of the graph of $y = \ln x$, and note that all logarithmic functions have graphs with an *x*-intercept of 1 and a vertical asymptote of $x = 0$. They also learn that $y = e^x$ and $y = \ln x$ are inverse functions, so their graphs are symmetric with respect to the line $y = x$. The last section of the **Tutorial** deals with evaluating natural logarithm expressions and solving exponential and logarithmic equations.

In the **Examples**, students learn about formulas that use ln *x*, with particular reference to the doubling time formula, $t = \dfrac{\ln 2}{r}$. Students apply the laws of logarithms and switch between logarithmic and exponential forms to solve equations.

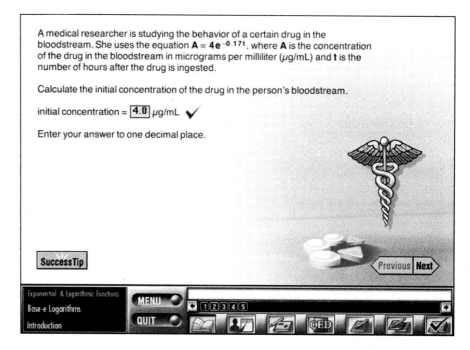

A medical researcher is studying the behavior of a certain drug in the bloodstream. She uses the equation $\mathbf{A} = \mathbf{4e}^{-0.17t}$, where $\mathbf{A}$ is the concentration of the drug in the bloodstream in micrograms per milliliter (µg/mL) and $\mathbf{t}$ is the number of hours after the drug is ingested.

Calculate the initial concentration of the drug in the person's bloodstream.

initial concentration = 4.0 µg/mL ✓

Enter your answer to one decimal place.

SuccessTip

Previous Next

Exponential & Logarithmic Functions
Base-e Logarithms
Introduction

MENU
QUIT
1 2 3 4 5

Instructor Intervention

- Point out that all the properties of natural logarithms can be derived from the fact that the natural logarithm is the inverse of the exponential function $y = e^x$. Show the inverse operations involved in other inverse functions, and then link this to the inverse operation that connects $y = e^x$ and $y = \ln x$.

$$x^2 = y \leftrightarrow \sqrt{y} = x \qquad\qquad e^x = y \leftrightarrow \ln y = x$$
$$5^2 = 25 \leftrightarrow \sqrt{25} = 5 \qquad e^{2.85} \doteq 17.29 \leftrightarrow \ln 17.29 \doteq 2.8!$$

- Make sure that students understand how and when to switch between equivalent forms of logarithmic and exponential equations. For the equations below, have the students try to switch forms at each step. They should notice that they must simplify the equations before switching to equivalent forms.

  (a) $32 = 2 \ln (x - 5) + 4$
  $28 = 2 \ln (x - 5)$
  $14 = \ln (x - 5)$

  (b) $15 = 3e^{x-2} - 6$
  $21 = 3e^{x-2}$
  $7 = e^{x-2}$

- Students should be familiar with the $\boxed{e^x}$ and $\boxed{\ln}$ keys on their calculators. Group students with similar calculators and have them practice using these keys before starting the lesson. Also encourage students to use the parentheses keys on their calculators when evaluating complex expressions involving logarithms, such as

$$\ln \left(10 - \frac{2}{3} \right).$$

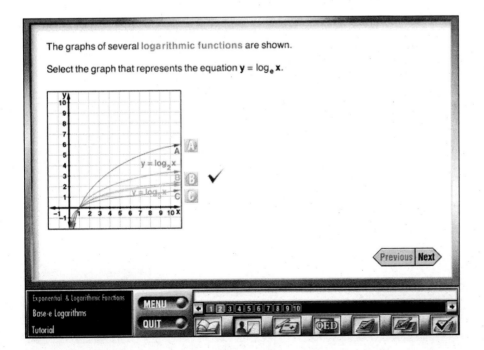

The graphs of several logarithmic functions are shown.

Select the graph that represents the equation $y = \log_e x$.

Evaluation

- Ask students to write in their journals an explanation of what *inverse function* mcans and to explain how it applies to base-*e* logarithms.

- Divide the class into three groups. Ask each group to complete one of these activities:
  - **(a)** Write three problems that require using the properties of ln *x*; include each property at least once.
  - **(b)** Write three problems involving transformations of ln *x*; be sure to include both vertical and horizontal translations.
  - **(c)** Write three problems about solving exponential and logarithmic equations; use different formulas for each problem.

  A different group could answer the problems and then give a mini-presentation to the class on the topic.

- Observe the students as they complete the activities. Do they understand that $e^x = y$ and $y = \ln x$ are inverses? Can they explain the significance of this relationship? Can they identify transformations of $y = \ln x$, both graphically and algebraically? Are they proficient at applying the logarithm properties? Can they switch between logarithmic and exponential forms easily?

Remediation

- Students may become confused by exponential and logarithmic equations that have no solutions. Emphasizing that the range of the exponential function ($y > 0$) becomes the domain of the logarithmic function ($x > 0$) may help students understand why certain values are invalid. Use a graph showing both $y = \ln x$ and $y = e^x$ to demonstrate.

- Some students may have difficulty identifying translations of the graph of $y = \ln x$ because they don't understand the difference between $\ln (x + 4)$ and $\ln x + 4$. Have students evaluate each expression for different values of x to demonstrate that the functions are different. You could also work through a few other examples with students showing the difference between these functions and their graphs.

- Students may have difficulty determining vertical translations of the graph of $y = \ln x$. Ask them to focus on the *y*-value of the point where $x = 1$, and to compare it to the graph of $y = \ln x$, where $y = 0$ when $x = 1$. The *y*-value gives the vertical translation. For example, a graph that passes through the point $(1, 3)$ has been translated 3 units up and has the equation $y = \ln x + 3$.

- If students have trouble identifying horizontal transformations of the graph $y = \ln x$, have them focus on the vertical asymptote, and compare it to the graph of $y = \ln x$, which has a vertical asymptote at the *y*-axis, or $x = 0$. The vertical asymptote of a graph gives the horizontal translation. For example, a graph with a vertical asymptote at $x = 4$ has been translated 4 units to the right and has the equation $y = \ln (x - 4)$.

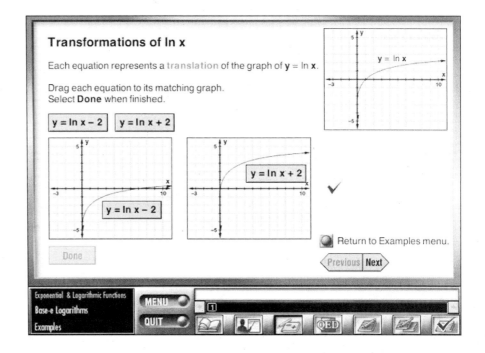

Extension

A

Invite students to try this exercise:

(a) Write $y = 3^{x-2}$ as a function that uses base e.

$$[y = (e^{\ln 3})^{x-2}]$$

(b) Write $y = \log_7 (x - 2)$ as a function that uses the natural logarithm.

$$\left[y = \left(\frac{1}{\ln 7} \right) \ln (x - 2) \right]$$

Have them repeat this exercise with other exponential and logarithmic functions. They should notice that any exponential function can be written as a base-e function, and any logarithmic function can be written as a natural logarithmic function. Discuss how rewriting functions might help solve some types of equations.

B

Ask students to derive the doubling time formula, $t = \dfrac{\ln 2}{r}$, given the formula $A = Pe^{rt}$. They should obtain this derivation:

When the population has doubled, $A = 2P$. Therefore,

$$2P = Pe^{rt}$$
$$2 = e^{rt}$$
$$\ln 2 = rt$$
$$t = \frac{\ln 2}{r}$$

As an additional challenge, students could derive formulas for tripling and quadrupling times.

Enrichment

A

Ask students to investigate how the expressions $y = a + \ln x$ and $y = ae^{bx}$ are used in regression equations. Students could be asked to find data that has a nonlinear trendline and then write the equation of the trendline in logarithmic and exponential form.

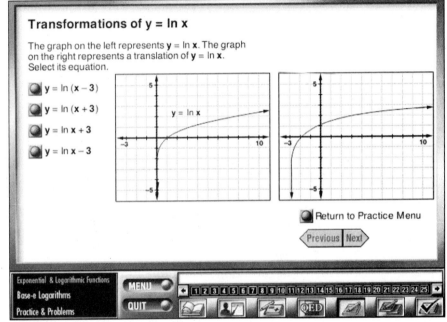

Transformations of y = ln x

The graph on the left represents **y = ln x**. The graph on the right represents a translation of **y = ln x**. Select its equation.

- y = ln (x − 3)
- y = ln (x + 3)
- y = ln x + 3
- y = ln x − 3

Return to Practice Menu

Previous | Next

Exponential & Logarithmic Functions
Base-e Logarithms
Practice & Problems

MENU   QUIT

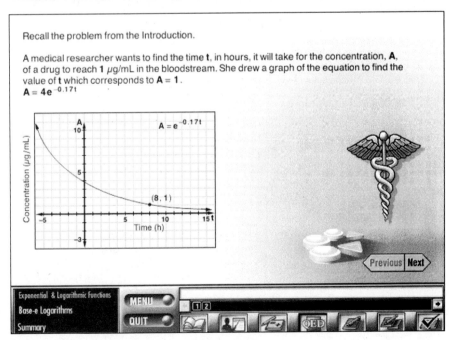

Recall the problem from the Introduction.

A medical researcher wants to find the time **t**, in hours, it will take for the concentration, **A**, of a drug to reach **1** μg/mL in the bloodstream. She drew a graph of the equation to find the value of **t** which corresponds to **A = 1**.

$A = 4e^{-0.17t}$

Previous | Next

Exponential & Logarithmic Functions
Base-e Logarithms
Summary

MENU   QUIT

Answers

1.1 Data in Tables I

1. A trend is a pattern in data that you can use to compare the present to the past or to make a prediction for the future.

3. (a) *examples:* (i) No one store is cheapest for everything. (ii) The price of tomato sauce is between 20¢ and 25¢ at every store. (iii) Price Way and Food Plus have higher prices for more items than the other two stores.

   (b) Snack Mart for milk, ABC for the complete list

   (c) $P = 3g + 2t + 4b$

   (d) ABC, at $9.68

4. (a) *example:* steep rise to 1979, followed by slow fall-off

   (b) increase from $56.50 to $69.40 took place over one year, but increase from $39.30 to $56.50 took place over 3 years

   (c) 1979

   (d) 1975; 1970

   (e) *example:* $52.17, based on a repeat of the average annual percent decrease from 1980–83

5. (a) Brooks 41, Clark 35, Jao 45, Nichols 51, Pierce 45, Tyler 47

   (b) 44

   (c) $P = wh + 0.5w(h - 40)$, where P is gross pay, w is the employee's hourly wage, and h is the total number of hours worked

6. Calgary and Los Angeles would change places, but the other teams would remain in the same order.

1.2 Data in Tables II

1. If the table is recursive, information in one row depends on information in a previous row.

2. (a) the amount to be repaid, excluding interest

   (b) the percent of the principal charged at intervals for the loan

   (c) length of time it will take to pay off the loan

3. $interest\ rate = \dfrac{interest}{principal}$. Round the result to a decimal in hundredths, then express the number of hundredths as a percent.

4. (a) Sunday

   (b) 5%, since $\dfrac{14}{279.95} = 0.05$

   (c) Friday's price is 90% of Thursday's price.

   (d) $P_2 = 0.9 \times P_1$ (e) $185.15 (f) $176.88

5. (a) 0.5%   (b) $55.76

   (c) *Interest Earned* $= 0.005 \times (O + 400)$

   (d) $5430.45

6. $17,121.52

7. (a) After the first row of data, the opening balance is equal to the year-end balance from the year before.

1.3 The Real Number System

1. natural, whole, integer, rational, real

2. *example:* $1.121231234..., \sqrt{2}, \pi$

3.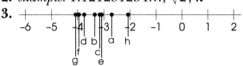

4. R

5. (a) (ii)   (b) (iv)   (c) (vi)

   (d) (v)   (e) (i)   (f) (iii)

6. (a) 7.0   (b) 19.0   (c) −11.0

   (d) 2.6457513   (e) 6.4807407

   (f) not possible

7. *examples:*

   (a) rational, because the number is natural

   (b) irrational, because $\sqrt{5}$ is a nonterminating, nonrepeating decimal

   (c) irrational, because π is irrational, so 2π must also be irrational

   (d) rational, because 1 is a natural number

   (e) rational, because 0.1875 terminates

   (f) rational, because $15.125 = 15\frac{1}{8}$ or $\frac{121}{8}$

   (g) irrational, because the number is a nonterminating, nonrepeating decimal

   (h) rational, because the decimal has a repeating period

   (i) irrational, because the number is a nonterminating, nonrepeating decimal

8.

Number	Square Root
1	1
2	1.414213562...
3	1.732050808...
4	2
5	2.236067978...
6	2.449489743...

7	2.645751311...
8	2.828427125...
9	3
10	3.16227766...

Note: Although $\sqrt{10}$ appears to terminate after 8 decimal places, this only occurs because the next digit is a 0.

(a) 1, 4, 9

(b) 2, 3, 5, 6, 7, 8, 10

9.

Number	Square Root
0.01	0.1
0.02	0.141421356...
0.03	0.17320508...
0.04	0.2
0.05	0.223606797...
0.06	0.244948974...
0.07	0.264575131...
0.08	0.282842712...
0.09	0.3
0.10	0.316227766...

Note: Although $\sqrt{0.03}$ may appear to terminate after 8 digits, this only happens because the next digit is a 0. Relate $\sqrt{\dfrac{3}{100}}$ to $\sqrt{3}$. There is at least one more digit, 8, after the 0.

(a) 0.01, 0.04, 0.09

(b) 0.02, 0.03, 0.05, 0.06, 0.07, 0.08, 0.1

10.

Number	Square Root
0.1	0.316227766...
0.2	0.447213595...
0.3	0.547722557...
0.4	0.632455532...
0.5	0.707106781...
0.6	0.774596669...
0.7	0.836660026...
0.8	0.894427191...
0.9	0.948683298...
1.0	1

(a) 1.0

(b) 0.1, 0.2, 0.3, 0.4, 0.5, 0.6, 0.7, 0.8, 0.9

(c) The natural numbers in Problem 8 had 1 in the denominator, so those with perfect square numerators were perfect squares, and in Problem 9 the numbers had 100, a perfect square, in the denominator, so those with perfect square numerators were perfect squares. The fraction forms of the numbers in Problem 10 had 10 in the denominator. Since 10 is not a perfect square, the only perfect square number was $\dfrac{10}{10}$ which simplifies to $\dfrac{1}{1}$.

11. (d) $\sqrt{2}$

(e) Measure the diagonal with a string or paper strip and mark a distance exactly that far from 0 along the number line.

(f) $\sqrt{3} = 1.732050808$, $\sqrt{5} = 2.236067978$, $\sqrt{7} = 2.645751311$

1.4 Solving Problems

1. *examples:* +: sum, added to, plus, more than, increased by; −: difference, subtracted from, minus, less than, decreased by; ×: multiplied by, increased, of, squared; ÷: divided by, quotient, shared into, groups of, ratio

2. (a) (iv) (b) (v) (c) (ii)
   (d) (vi) (e) (i) (f) (iii)

3. (d) and (f) are both equal to $\dfrac{6^3}{4}$ or 54

4. *examples:* (a) four subtracted from the sum of two and three
   (b) eight more than five groups of six
   (c) the square root of thirty-seven
   (d) one fourth of the product of twenty-two and four squared
   (e) the sum of the square root of five and the square root of seven
   (f) the product of nine times four and three times five
   (g) the quotient of six cubed and six squared
   (h) the square of four minus twelve
   (i) half of the difference of seventy-five and negative two to the fifth power
   (j) the cube root of one hundred sixteen to the fourth power

5. (a) $\sqrt{6} \approx 2.45$ (b) $10 - 6 = 4$
   (c) $12^2 = 144$ (d) $17 + 13 = 30$
   (e) $\dfrac{1}{4}$ (f) $1 + 2 + 3 + 4 + 5 + 6 = 21$
   (g) $\sqrt{243} = 15.59$ (h) $9^2 + 26 = 107$
   (i) $\dfrac{62 + 73}{2} = 67.5$ (j) $0.2 \times 600 = 120$
   (k) $\dfrac{1}{6} + \dfrac{1}{9} + \dfrac{1}{12} = \dfrac{13}{36}$

6. (a) −45,435,388 (b) 125,000
   (c) −2396 (d) 351
   (e) 770,943,744 (f) 0.006937075
   (g) 3125 (h) 1.587401052

7. Sachi multiplied before subtracting, but the problem says to subtract first, then find a percent of the result. Also, the decimal form of 40% is 0.4, not 40.

Corrected solution:

$(12^3 - 5^2) \times 40\% = (1728 - 25) \times 0.4$
$\qquad\qquad\qquad = 1703 \times 0.4$
$\qquad\qquad\qquad = 681.2$

8. *examples:* **(a)** Find the sum of one and two, then divide the result by three. **(b)** Multiply nine by four, divide the product by three, and multiply the quotient by five. **(c)** Multiply forty thousand two hundred by five hundredths. **(d)** Find the sum of the square of twelve and the cube of eighteen. **(e)** Find the square root of twenty-seven to the fourth power.

9. To find the reciprocal of the square root of twenty-five, enter: $\boxed{1}\,\boxed{\div}\,\boxed{2}\,\boxed{5}\,\boxed{\checkmark}$

10. **(a)** 2^5 **(b)** 56

1.5 Operations with Real Numbers

1. *example:* To find $\sqrt{12}$:
   Number Line: $\sqrt{12}$ is between perfect squares $\sqrt{9}$ and $\sqrt{16}$, so it is between 3 and 4. Since 12 is a bit less than halfway between 9 and 16, estimate about 3.4.
   Fractions: $\sqrt{12}$ is between perfect squares $\sqrt{9}$ and $\sqrt{16}$, so it is between 3 and 4. The distance from 9 to 16 is 7 units, and the distance from 9 to 12 is 3 units, so $\sqrt{12}$ must be $\frac{3}{7}$ more than $\sqrt{9}$. $\sqrt{12}$ is about $3\frac{3}{7}$ or 3.428571428.
   A calculator gives 3.464101615 as an approximation for $\sqrt{12}$, so using fractions gives a much more accurate result.

2. *example:* $\boxed{1}\,\boxed{5}\,\boxed{\checkmark}\,\boxed{=}$

3. *examples:*
   (i) Calculator shows $\sqrt{15}$ is about 3.8729833346.
   (ii) Since you need to round to three decimal places, look at the number in the fourth decimal place, 9.
   (iii) Since 9 is greater than 4, round the third decimal place up from 2 to 3. The rounded value is 3.873.

4. *examples:*
   (a) 2.45   **(b)** 4.58   **(c)** 6.56
   (d) 12.17   **(e)** 54.08   **(f)** 25.63

5. *example:* $\boxed{3}\,\boxed{\text{2ndF}}\,\boxed{\checkmark}\,\boxed{1}\,\boxed{5}\,\boxed{=}$

6. **(a)** 3.650   **(b)** 1.414   **(c)** 30.000
   (d) 2.876   **(e)** −709.930   **(f)** 10.535
   (g) 36.661   **(h)** 1.764   **(i)** 2.000
   (j) 7.581   **(k)** −10.000   **(l)** 56.569

7. *examples:*
   (i) $2 \times \sqrt{3} \times 4 \times \sqrt{3} =$ **(ii)** $+(3 \times \sqrt{5}) =$

(iii) $-(2 \times \sqrt{2}) =$ **(iv)** $\div(5 \times \sqrt{2}) =$
(v) Round to two decimal places. Result is 3.94.

8. **(a)** 2.739   **(b)** 0.530
   (c) 144.000 **(d)** 12.369

9. **(i)** Dane's initial quotient has a digit missing. It should be 2.2̲24859546.
   (ii) In the second step, Dane should have multiplied before he added. The correct solution is:

$$\frac{3\sqrt{11}}{2\sqrt{5}} \doteq \frac{9.949874371}{4.472135955}$$
$$\doteq 2.224859546$$
$$2.224859546 \times \sqrt{6} \doteq 5.449770637$$
$$5.449770637 + 4\sqrt{2} \doteq 11.10662489$$
$$\doteq 11.11$$

10. $518.36
11. 56.55 m
12. 16.971 m

2.1 Rational Exponents

1. root index is 7; radicand is 9^3
2. 3: 9, 27; 4: 16, 64; 5: 25, 125
3. **(a)** $x^{\frac{1}{3}}$ **(b)** $3^{-\frac{2}{5}}$ **(c)** $94^{\frac{17}{6}}$
   (d) $\dfrac{1}{52^{\frac{7}{2}}}$ **(e)** $(13x)^{\frac{2}{3}}$

4. **(a)** $\sqrt[4]{n}$ **(b)** $\dfrac{1}{\sqrt{11}}$ **(c)** $\sqrt[3]{w^8}$
   (d) $\sqrt[5]{45^4}$ or $\sqrt[10]{45^8}$ **(e)** $\sqrt[5]{3b^2}$

5. $x \geq 0$, since a negative number cannot be multiplied by itself an even number of times to give a negative result. (*example:* $\sqrt{9}$ is a real number, but $\sqrt{-9}$ is not.)

6. **(a)** 9
   (b) $\sqrt[3]{(-27)^2}$ is not a real number because the root index is even, so a calculator may display an error message; $\sqrt[3]{-27}$ is a real number.

7. **(a)** −9   **(b)** 125   **(c)** 16   **(d)** 1024   **(e)** 4

8. **(a)** x^2 **(b)** $k^{\frac{1}{27}}$

9. $\sqrt[3]{\dfrac{1}{x^2}} \times \sqrt{x^3} = \sqrt[3]{x^{-2}} \times \sqrt{x^3}$

$$= x^{-\frac{2}{3}} \times x^{\frac{3}{2}}$$
$$= x^{-\frac{4}{6}} \times x^{\frac{9}{6}}$$
$$= x^{\frac{5}{6}}$$
$$= \sqrt[6]{x^5}$$

$\sqrt[6]{64^5} = \left(\sqrt[6]{64}\right)^5$
$$= 2^5$$
$$= 32$$

2.2 Simplifying Radical Expressions

1. **(a)** the quantity under the radical sign, e.g., $25x^2$ in $\sqrt{25x^2}$

   (b) a number expressing a power, e.g., 2 in $4x^2$, 3 in $\sqrt[3]{27}$

   (c) expressions involving roots with different indexes and/or bases

2. **(a)** simplify
   (b) factor
   (c) squares, cubes

3. **(a)** $\sqrt{4 \times 5}$
   (b) $\sqrt{4} \times \sqrt{5}$
   (c) $\sqrt{4 \times 5} = \sqrt{4} \times \sqrt{5}$

4. *examples:*
   (a) The multiplication property is used to combine under one radical sign radicals that are multiplied together, or to separate into parts one radical with a radicand that is a product, e.g.,

   $\sqrt[3]{24x}\sqrt[3]{2x^3} = \sqrt[3]{24x \times 2x^3}$,

   $\sqrt[4]{512a^5} = \sqrt[4]{256a^4}\left(\sqrt[4]{2a}\right)$

   (b) The division property is used to combine under one radical sign radicals that are divided, or to separate into parts one radical with a radicand that is a quotient,

   e.g., $\dfrac{\sqrt{55p^2}}{\sqrt{11p}} = \sqrt{\dfrac{55p^2}{11p}}$, $\dfrac{\sqrt[3]{64x^5}}{\sqrt[3]{8x^2}} = \sqrt[3]{\dfrac{64x^5}{8x^2}}$

5. Like radicals have the same root index and the same radicand. $\sqrt[4]{3x^3}$ and $5\sqrt[4]{3x^3}$ are like radicals; $\sqrt{5x^3}$ and $5x\sqrt[3]{3x^3}$ are not.

6. *examples:*
   (a) $\sqrt{5}$, $\sqrt[3]{5}$ **(b)** $\sqrt{5}$, $\sqrt{6}$

7. no; no

8. The correct solution is:

   $\sqrt[3]{250} = \sqrt[3]{(125)(2)}$
   $$= \sqrt[3]{125}\sqrt[3]{2}$$
   $$= 5\sqrt[3]{2}$$

9. **(a)** $4\sqrt{15}$ **(b)** $2\sqrt[4]{2}$ **(c)** $3\sqrt[3]{10}$
   (d) $-3\sqrt[3]{3}$ **(e)** $4\sqrt[5]{3}$ **(f)** $\dfrac{3}{10}\sqrt{2}$
   (g) $\dfrac{-2}{3}\sqrt[3]{2}$

10. **(a)** $2x\sqrt[2]{2x}$ **(b)** $r^5\sqrt[3]{r2}$ **(c)** $2xy\sqrt[3]{2x^2y}$
    (d) $9j^2\sqrt[3]{jk}$ **(e)** $\dfrac{1}{8a^2}\sqrt{17xy}$ **(f)** $\dfrac{3}{5}x\sqrt{2}$
    (g) $\dfrac{10}{7x}\sqrt{2y}$

11. **(a)** 11 **(b)** $7x$ **(c)** $2x$
    (d) 2 **(e)** 2 **(f)** $3x$

12. **(a)** $\sqrt{2}$ **(b)** $5\sqrt{5}+5$ **(c)** $2\sqrt{2}$
    (d) $-8\sqrt[3]{10}$ **(e)** $16\sqrt[4]{2}$ **(f)** $10\sqrt[4]{3}$
    (g) $-4\sqrt{2}$ **(h)** $3\sqrt{5}$ **(i)** $6x\sqrt{2x}$
    (j) $5x\sqrt[3]{2x}$ **(k)** $\sqrt{2x}$ **(l)** $y\sqrt{z}$

13. 24 yd^2

2.3 Multiplying and Dividing Radical Expressions

1. **(a)** 5, $\sqrt{7}$ **(b)** distributive **(c)** $\sqrt{3}$
2. **(a)** 48 **(b)** $6\sqrt{6}$
   (c) cannot be simplified **(d)** $6\sqrt{6}$
3. **(a)** $5 \times 6\sqrt[3]{6}$ simplifies to $30\sqrt[3]{6}$
   (b) $\dfrac{30\sqrt[3]{15}}{5}$ simplifies to $6\sqrt[3]{15}$
4. *example:* On the right side, $\dfrac{\sqrt{3}}{\sqrt{7}}$ has been multiplied by $\dfrac{\sqrt{7}}{\sqrt{7}}$, which equals 1. When you multiply an expression by 1, the value does not change, so the left side is equal to the

right side.

5. This expression contains a radical, $\sqrt[3]{5}$, in the denominator.

6. *example:* When you multiply $\sqrt[3]{m} \times \sqrt[3]{m}$, the result is $\sqrt[3]{m^2}$, not $\sqrt[3]{m^3}$.

You need to multiply a cube root by itself three times in order to eliminate the radical:
$m = \sqrt[3]{m} \times \sqrt[3]{m} \times \sqrt[3]{m}$

7. *example:* To rationalize the denominator, you want to make the denominator equal to $\sqrt[4]{3^4}$, or 3. If you multiply the fraction by $\dfrac{\sqrt[4]{3}}{\sqrt[4]{3}}$, the denominator becomes $\sqrt[4]{3^2}$. To get 3^4 under the radical sign, you need to multiply the fraction by $\dfrac{\sqrt[4]{3} \times \sqrt[4]{3} \times \sqrt[4]{3}}{\sqrt[4]{3} \times \sqrt[4]{3} \times \sqrt[4]{3}}$ or $\dfrac{\sqrt[4]{3^3}}{\sqrt[4]{3^3}}$.

8. There is a fraction under the radical sign.

9. **(a)**
$$\begin{aligned}
5\sqrt{8} \times 7\sqrt{6} &= 5(7)\sqrt{8}\sqrt{6} \\
&= 35\sqrt{48} \\
&= 35\sqrt{2 \times 2 \times 2 \times 2 \times 3} \\
&= 35(4)\sqrt{3} \\
&= 140\sqrt{3}
\end{aligned}$$

(b)
$$\begin{aligned}
\dfrac{9}{\sqrt[3]{4a^2}} &= \dfrac{9 \times \sqrt[3]{2a}}{\sqrt[3]{4a^2} \times \sqrt[3]{2a}} \\
&= \dfrac{9\sqrt[3]{2a}}{\sqrt[3]{8a^3}} \\
&= \dfrac{9\sqrt[3]{2a}}{2a}
\end{aligned}$$

10. **(a)** $4\sqrt[3]{2}$ **(b)** $6x^2y\sqrt{5}$

   (c) $10\sqrt{3}$ **(d)** $5b\sqrt{2b} - 40b\sqrt{b}$

11. *example:* When you apply the FOIL rule to $(\sqrt{m}+3)(\sqrt{m}-3)$, you get

$(m - 3\sqrt{m} + 3\sqrt{m} - 9$ or $m - 9$. The product of the outside terms cancels out the product of the inside terms, and mutiplying a radical first term by itself eliminates the radical sign.

12. **(a)** $2 - \sqrt{6}$ **(b)** $3\sqrt{11} + 8\sqrt{16}$

   (c) $-\sqrt{35} - 5$ **(d)** $7 + \sqrt{21x}$

13. **(a)** $\dfrac{\sqrt{30}}{6}$

   (b) $\dfrac{(8 - \sqrt{10})(\sqrt{7} + 3\sqrt{3})}{-20}$ or

$\dfrac{8\sqrt{7} + 24\sqrt{3} - \sqrt{70} - 3\sqrt{30}}{-20}$

   (c) $\dfrac{5\sqrt[3]{12n}(\sqrt[3]{100n^{10}})}{140n^5}$ or $\dfrac{\sqrt[3]{150n^2}}{14n^5}$

   (d) $\dfrac{\sqrt[4]{x^2}}{x^2}$

14. $\dfrac{\sqrt[3]{2\pi GM^2}}{2\pi}$

3.1 Simplifying Algebraic Expressions

2. *examples:*
   (a) You use the **associative property** when you are adding or multiplying three or more terms, and you want to perform one part of the calculation before the other part. For example:
   $(26p \times 2) \times 5 = 26p \times (2 \times 5)$

   (b) You use the **commutative property** when you are adding or multiplying two or more numbers, and you want to change the order of the terms. This helps when you are grouping like terms.
   For example:
   $3a + 2b^2 + 5a = 3a + 5a + 2a^2$

   (c) You use the **distributive property** when you want to multiply an addition or subtraction expression by another term. There are usually parentheses around the terms that are added or subtracted.
   For example:
   $4p(3 - 5y) = (4p \times 3) + (4p \times -5y)$

3. **(a)** associative:
   $$\begin{aligned}
   (11 - 7) - 14 &= 4 - 14 \\
   &= -10 \\
   11 - (7 - 14) &= 11 - (-7) \\
   &= 18
   \end{aligned}$$
   Therefore, $(11 - 7) - 14 \neq 11 - (7 - 14)$

   (b) commutative:
   $15 - 7 = 8$ $7 - 15 = -8$
   Therefore, $15 - 7 \neq 7 - 15$

4. Like terms are terms that have exactly the same variables and exponents.
   Examples of Like Terms
   $4x, 5x, 20x$
   $15a^2, a^2, -a^2$
   $17ab, 6ab, ba$
   Examples of Unlike Terms

5x, 8x²,

$5x$, $8x^2$,

$10b^2$, $8c^2$, $5d^2$

$7ab$, $5cb$, $6a^2b$

5. *example:* $2 \times b$ is the same as $2b$, so it is really only one term. The distributive property only applies when an expression in parentheses contains two or more terms that are connected by addition or subtraction.

6. (a) 3   (b) $2x^2$, x, 6
   (c) 2 is the coefficient of x^2, -1 is the coefficient of x
   (d) no like terms

7. (a) like   (b) unlike   (c) like
   (d) like   (e) unlike

8. (a) $-72q$ (b) $8cd$ (c) $-12b$
   (d) $21st$ (e) $-24abc$

9. (a) The negative sign means that the amount in parentheses is to be multiplied by -1. Another way to write the expression would be $-1(2x - 4)$.
   (b) $-2x + 4$ or $4 - 2x$

10. (a) $3a + 6$ (b) $-18x - 9y$
    (c) $15 - 3a$ (d) $4 - z$
    (e) $4x + 7y - 2$

11. (a) $6a$ (b) $11ab$ (c) $10a - 6$
    (d) $15a^2 - 12a$ (e) 12

12. (a) $4x + 30$ (b) $18p + 4$
    (c) $-3a + 7$ or $7 - 3a$ (d) $9x^2 - 2x$
    (e) $-p - k$

13. (a) $15(30 + x)$ ft²
    (b) $(15 \times 30) + (15 \times x)$ ft² $= 450 + 15x$ ft²
    (c) $15(30 + x) = 450 + 15x$
    (d) distributive property

3.2 Solving Linear Equations and Formulas

1. (a) If a, b, and c are real numbers and $a = b$, then $a + c = b + c$ and $a - c = b - c$.
   (b) If a, b, and c are real numbers and $a = b$, then $ca = cb$ and $\dfrac{a}{c} = \dfrac{b}{c}$, $c \neq 0$.

2. (a) subtract 3
   (b) divide by -5
   (c) 15 is the greatest common factor of all three denominators.

3. (a) -6 is a solution to the equation.
   (b) -6 is not a solution to the equation.

4. (a) $x = -225$ (b) $t = 7.9$
   (c) $g = 0.014$ (d) $x = -4$
   (e) $x = 28$ (f) $x = -48$
   (g) $a = 2.52$ (h) $y = 10.4$

5. (a) $x = x$, identity   (b) $x = -9$

(c) $y = 12$ (d) $k = 0.06$
(e) $p = -8$ (f) $s = -20$
(g) $s = \dfrac{8}{3}$

(h) $8 = 12$, null set   (i) $k = \dfrac{15}{8}$

(j) $a = \dfrac{15}{4}$ (k) $a = \dfrac{21}{5}$

6. (a) $x = 13$ (b) $x = -40$ (c) $a = 4$
   (d) $x = -14$ (e) $x = -3$ (f) $y = 8$

7. (a) $m = \dfrac{E}{c^2}$
   (b) $w = T - ma$
   (c) $C = \dfrac{5}{9}(F - 32)$
   (d) $I = \dfrac{2K - Mv^2}{w^2}$

8. In the third line, A cannot be canceled out of the fraction on the left side. The solution is $\dfrac{K - Ax}{A} = B$.

9. 621

10. $4.94

3.3 Applications of Equations

1. (a) complementary
   (b) isosceles
   (c) principle
   (d) average
   (e) markdown

2.

Source of Noise	Decibels (d)	Compared to Conversation
Conversation	d	
Vacuum cleaner	$d + 15$	15 decibels more
Circular saw	$2d - 10$	10 decibels less than twice
Jet takeoff	$2d + 20$	20 decibels more than twice
Whispering	$0.5d - 10$	10 decibels less than half
Rock band	$2d$	twice

3. (a)

Type of Question	Number	Value of Each Question	Total Value
Multiple choice	x	5	$5x$
True/false	$3x$	2	$6x$
Essay	$x - 2$	10	$10x - 20$
Fill-in	x	5	$5x$

   (b) true/false
   (c) $26x - 20$

4. $30,000 - x$

5. (a)
$$0.09x + 0.08(2000 - x) = 400$$
$$100(0.09x + 0.08(2000 - x)) = 100(400)$$
$$9x + 8(2000 - x) = 40,000$$
$$9x + 16,000 - 8x = 40,000$$
$$x = 24,000$$

(b) $\quad 0.2(5) + 0.6x = 0.4(5 + x)$

$$10(0.2(5) + 0.6x) = 10(0.4(5 + x))$$
$$2(5) + 6x = 4(5 + x)$$
$$10 + 6x = 20 + 4x$$
$$2x = 10$$
$$x = 5$$

7. 30 mi

8. No. When the solutions are added together, the 12% solution will "weaken" the 30% solution, and at the same time the 30% solution will "strengthen" the 12% solution, so the combined solution will be between 12% and 30%.

9. Jakob is 16 years old and David is 18 years old.

10. 40 gal of the 40% mixture and 10 gal of the 30% mixture

11. 3 min from the time the officer leaves

12. $8500 in NewTekniks, $1500 in the CD

13. 2 ft

3.4 The Rectangular Coordinate System

2. $A(2, 4)$, $B(-3, 3)$, $C(-2.5, -1.5)$, $D(4.5, -4.5)$, $E(3, 0)$, $F(-4, -3)$, $G(0, 0)$, $H(0, -4)$

3.

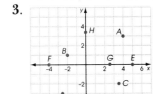

4.

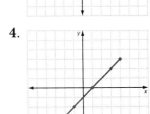

5. (a) 1990–1991, 1994–1995
   (b) 1990–1991
   (c) 1993
   (d) approximately 1,100,000 barrels

6. *examples:*
   (a) $(90^0, 30^0)$ **(b)** $(80.5^0, 26^0)$
   (c) $91.5^0, 29.5^0)$

7. (a) $(2, -1)$ **(b)** no   **(c)** yes

8. *examples:*
   (a) $(50, 3000)$, $(128, 3800)$, $(80, 11,000)$
   (b) between 10,000 and 11,000 ft

9.

Thawing Guidelines

10. (b) between Chelan and Doremy
   (c) between Biggar and Chelan

4.1 Multiplying Polynomials

3. All have 6 partial products.
   (a) $x^3 + 7x^2 + 9x - 9$
   (b) $y^3 + 2y^2 - 23y - 40$
   (c) $p^3 - 3p^2 - 11p - 2$
   (d) $x^3 + \dfrac{5}{4}x^2 - \dfrac{1}{16}$
   (e) $b^4 - 2b^2 - 16a^2c^2 + 8ac$
   (f) $a^2 - b^2 + ac - bc$

4. (a) $x^3 - 6x^2 + 12x - 8$
   (b) $x^3 - 12x^2 + 48x - 64$
   (c) $x^3 + 6x^2 - x - 30$
   (d) $27x^3 + 135x^2 + 225x + 125$
   (e) $x^6 - 12x^4 + 48x^2 - 64$

5. All have 9 partial products.
   (a) $x^4 + 2x^3 + 4x^2 + 3x + 2$
   (b) $x^4 + 2x^3 + 3x^2 + 2x + 1$
   (c) $4x^4 + 8x^3 + 12x^2 + 8x + 4$

6. (a) $2x^6 + 6x^5 + 14x^4 + 18x^3 + 18x^2 + 10x + 4$
   (b) $x^6 + 3x^5 + 6x^4 + 7x^3 + 6x^2 + 3x + 1$

7. (a) $8x^2 + 24x + 16$ **(b)** $-2a^2 - 2a + 60$
   (c) $4x^2 + 32x + 48$ **(d)** $-2m^2 + 9m - 9$
   (e) $8x^2 + 2y^2 - 8xy$ **(f)** $27x^2 + 18x + 3$
   (g) $4x^3 + 28x^2 + 36x - 36$
   (h) $-2a^2 + 2b^2 - 2ac + 2bc$
   (i) $4y^3 + 8y^2 - 92y - 160$
   (j) $-x^4 + 2x^3 - x$

8. (a) $4x^4 + 8x^3 - 32x^2 + 72x - 36$
   (b) $-3x^4 + 12x^3 - 36x^2 + 48x - 48$

9. $A = P(r^3 + 3r^2 + 3r + 1)$

10. $SA = 6x^2 + 24x + 24$; $V = x^3 + 6x^2 + 12x + 8$

11. $A = 2x^2 - 4x + 2$

12. $V = \dfrac{4}{3}\pi(27x^6 + 27x^5 + 9x^4 + x^3)$

If $\pi = 3.14$, then
$$V = 4.19(27x^6 + 27x^5 + 9x^4 + x^3)$$

4.2 The Greatest Common Factor and Factoring by Grouping

1. prime-factored
2. prime
3. **(a)** $6 - 4t$ can be further factored to $2(3 - 2t)$.
   (b) $3t - 2t^2$ can be further factored to $t(3 - 2t)$.
4. If you apply the distributive property to a number you have factored, you will get the original statement you started with.
5. **(a)** 2×7^2
   (b) 13×5^2
   (c) $2^5 \times 3^2$
6. **(a)** 4
   (b) $3x^2yz$
   (c) $5m$
7. **(a)** $2(x + 4)$ **(b)** $2x(x - 3)$
   (c) $3y^2(y + 1)$ **(d)** not possible
   (e) $13ab^2c(c^2 - 2a^2)$ **(f)** not possible
   (g) $5t^2(5t^4 - 2t + 1)$
   (h) $9x^7y^3(5x^3 - 7y^4 + 9x^3y^7)$
   (i) $u^4v^3(48u^2v^3 - 16v - 3u^2)$
8. **(a)** $-3(a + 2)$ **(b)** $-6(b - 2)$
   (c) $-6ab(3a + 2b)$ **(d)** $-7t^3(3t^2 - 4)$
   (e) $-7u^2v^3z^2(9uv^3z^7 - 4v^4 + 3uz^2)$
9. **(a)** $(x + y)(4 + t)$ **(b)** $(a - b)(r - s)$
   (c) $(m + n)(m + n + 1)$ **(d)** $-x(a - b)(b + c)$
10. **(a)** $(a - b)(r + s)$ **(b)** $(x - 4)(x - y)$
    (c) $(a + b)(x - 1)$ **(d)** $(x + y)(x + y + z)$
11. **(a)** $2b(2 - d)(c + d)$
    (b) $x(x - y)(x - 2y + z)$
12. **(a)** $h = \dfrac{A - 2wl}{2(w + 3l)}$

    (b) $m_2 = \dfrac{mm_1}{m_1 - m}$

4.3 Factoring Trinomials and Difference of Squares

1. **(a)** a whole number that exactly divides another whole number. If polynomials are multiplied together, then each polynomial is a factor of the product.
   (b) an algebraic expression consisting of two or more terms
   (c) a polynomial consisting of three terms
   (d) a polynomial consisting of two terms
   (e) a part of a polynomial that is separated from the rest by a plus or minus sign. In $x + 10$, x and 10 are both terms.
   (f) a numerical multiplier of the variables in an algebraic term. In $3x - 2y$, 3 and 2 are coefficients.

(g) a trinomial that is the product of two equal factors; e.g., $x^2 - 2x - 1$ is a perfect square trinomial because it equals $(x - 1)(x - 1)$.
(h) in algebra, an expression of the form $a^2 - b^2$. It can be factored to be $(a - b)(a + b)$.

2. **(a)** $2p \times 2p = 4p^2$, not $2p^2$; $2(2p) - 3(2p) = -2p$, not $-p$; $(2p + 3)(p - 2)$
   (b) middle term is negative, but there are no negative terms in factors; $(3r - 5)(r - 5)$
   (c) sum of outside product + inside product is $5s$, not $7s$; $(3s + 1)(s + 2)$
   (d) product of two negative terms should be positive, not negative; no middle term in product; $(2p + 3)(2p - 3)$
3. **(a)** $(2m + 5)(2m - 3)$ **(b)** $(3n - 5)^2$
   (c) $(5v - 4)^2$ **(d)** $(6a + 11)(6a - 11)$
   (e) $(3c + 7d)(3c - 7d)$ **(f)** $(2h + 5)(h - 4)$
   (g) $(2k - 5)(3k - 4)$ **(h)** $2(x^2 + 2)(x^2 + 5)$
4. ± 4
5. 11, 29, 16
6. $2x - 3$ and $x + 4$
7. $3x + 5$ and $x + 11$
8.
$$\frac{1}{2}(4800) = (80 - 2x)(60 - 2x)$$
$$2400 = 4800 - 160x - 120x + 4x^2$$
$$4x^2 - 280x + 2400 = 0$$
$$4(x^2 - 70x + 600) = 0$$
$$4(x - 60)(x - 10) = 0$$
$x = 60$ or $x = 10$
$x = 60$ is not a possible solution, so when $x = 10$, Mira mows a 40 yd by 60 yd area.
9. **(a)** difference of squares; $(3p + 2)(3p - 2)$
   (b) neither; expression cannot be factored
   (c) perfect square; $(5r + 1)^2$
   (d) neither; the expression cannot be factored
10. **(a)** True; the last term represents the square of the second term in the binomial factor, and the square of any integer is always positive.
    (b) False; the middle term is only negative if the second term of the binomial factor is negative.
12. $(p + \sqrt{2})(p - \sqrt{2})$

13. $\left(2x + \dfrac{1}{2}\right)^2$

14. $(9x^2 - 6x + 1) - (25y^2 + 40y + 16)$
    $= (3x - 1)^2 - (5y + 4)^2$
    $= [(3x - 1) + (5y + 4)][(3x - 1) - (5y + 4)]$
    (difference of squares)
    $= (3x + 5y + 3)(3x - 5y - 5)$

4.4 Sum and Difference of Two Cubes

1. 1, 8, 27, 64, 125, 216, 343, 512, 729, 1000
2. *examples:*
   (a) a whole number that exactly divides another whole number
   (b) to write an expression in extended but equivalent form
   (c) an algebraic expression consisting of one or more terms
   (d) an algebraic expression consisting of two terms
   (e) an algebraic expression consisting of three terms
   (f) an element of a sequence or series
   (g) in algebra, an expression of the form $a^3 - b^3$
   (h) in algebra, an expression of the form $a^3 + b^3$

3. *examples:*
   Similarities: involves finding roots; factored result has two terms
   Differences: can only factor a difference of squares, but can factor a sum and a difference of cubes; factored result for difference of squares is two binomials, but for difference of cubes it is a binomial and a trinomial

4. (a) still need to factor out the greatest common factor
   (b) the two remaining factors are sums or differences of cubes which need to be factored

5. (a) $(x + y)(x^2 - xy + y^2)$
   (b) $(x - 2)(x^2 + 2x + 4)$
   (c) $(3x + 4y)(9x^2 - 12xy + 16y^2)$
   (d) $(3a - b)(9a^2 + 3ab + b^2)$
   (e) $(x + 3)(x^2 - 3x + 9)$
   (f) $(t - 4)(t^2 + 4t + 16)$
   (g) $(4x + 5y)(16x^2 - 20xy + 25y^2)$

6. (a) $3(x + 3)(x^2 - 3x + 9)$
   (b) $2x(1 + 2x)(1 - 2x + 4x^2)$
   (c) $4(x - 3)(x^2 + 3x + 9)$
   (d) $4x(2 - x)(4 + 2x + x^2)$

7. (a) $2(2 + x)(4 - 2x + x^2)(2 - x)(4 + 2x + x^2)$
   (b) $(a - b)(a^2 + ab + b^2)(a + b)(a^2 - ab + b^2)$
   (c) $(2x^2 - 5y)(4x^4 + 10x^2y + 25y^2)$
   (d) $(5xy^2 - 6z^3)(25x^2y^4 + 30xy^2z^3 + 36z^6)$
   (e) $(3x - y)(9x^2 + 3xy + y^2)(3x + y)$ $(9x^2 - 3xy + y^2)$
   (f) $(4x^2 + 5y)(16x^4 - 20x^2y + 25y^2)$
   (g) $(a - 3b)(a^2 + 3ab + 9b^2)(a + 3b)$ $(a^2 - 3ab + 9b^2)$

   (h) $(2x - 5y^2)(4x^2 + 10xy^2 + 25y^4)$
   (i) $6a(2x^2 - y)(4x^4 + 2x^2y + y^2)$
   (j) $3(a - 3b)(a^2 + 3ab + 9b^2)(a + 3b)$ $(a^2 - 3ab + 9b^2)$
   (k) $(x - a^2y)(x^2 + a^2xy + a^4y^2)$

8. (a) $(x + y + z)(x^2 - x(y + z) + (y + z)^2)$
   (b) $(a - b)a^3 + 27$
   (c) $(x - y - 5)((x - y)^2 + 5(x - y) + 25)$
   (d) $(m + n)(2 - x)(4 + 2x + x^2)$
   (e) $y(x - y)(x + y)^2(x^2 - xy + y^2)$

9. (a) $2x^3(4 - x)(16 + 4x + x^2)$
   (b) $(3x - 1)(9x^2 + 3x + 1)$
   (c) $5(a - 3b)(a^2 + 3ab + 9b^2)$
   (d) $(x - y)(a + z)(a^2 - az + z^2)$
   (e) $(xy^2 + 5ab^2)(x^2y^4 - 5ab^2xy^2 + 25a^2b^4)$
   (f) $(4x + 1)(16x^2 - 4x + 1)$

10. $2, x + 3, x^2 - 3x + 9$

11. (a) $V = \frac{4}{3}\pi r_1^3 - \frac{4}{3}\pi r_2^3$

    (b) $\frac{4}{3}\pi(r_1 - r_2)(r_1^2 + r_1r_2 + r_2^2)$

    (c) 165.46 in.^{3}

4.5 Dividing Polynomials by Binomials

1. dividend is $x^2 + 10$; divisor is $x - 4$; quotient is $x + 4$; remainder is 26
3. (a) $(3p^3 - 2p^2 + 6p - 8) \div (p - 2)$
   (b) statement is correct
4. (a) three subtraction errors are shown in boxes

$$\begin{array}{r} 3p^2 - 8p + 10 \\ p-2\overline{\smash{\big)}\,3p^2 - 2p^2 + 6p - 8} \\ \underline{3p^3 - 6p^2} \\ \boxed{-8p^2} + 6p \\ \underline{-8p^2 + 16p} \\ \boxed{10p} - 8 \\ \underline{10p - 20} \\ \boxed{-28} \end{array}$$

Corrected solution:

$$\begin{array}{r} 3p^2 + 4p + 14 \\ p-2\overline{\smash{\big)}\,3p^2 - 2p^2 + 6p - 8} \\ \underline{3p^3 - 6p^2} \\ 4p^2 + 6p \\ \underline{4p^2 - 8p} \\ 14p - 8 \\ \underline{14p - 28} \\ 20 \end{array}$$

5. $b^2 + 6b - 18 = (b + 8)(b - 2) - 2$
6. $4m^2 - 6m - 5 = (m - 4)(4m + 10) + 35$
7. $3q^3 + 5q^2 + 4q - 3 = (3q - 1)(q^2 + 2q + 2) - 1$
8. $4x^4 + 0x^3 + 8x^2 + 0x + 16$
$= (x - 4)(4x^3 + 16x^2 + 72x + 288) + 1168$
9. $12x^3 + 0x^2 + 1x + 1 = (2x + 1)(6x^2 - 3x + 2) - 1$
10. $m^4 - m^3 + m^2 - m = (m^2 - m)(m^2 + 1)$
11. $6x^2 - 24 = (2x + 4)(3x - 6)$;
length $= (3x - 6)$ cm
12. $P = 6x^2 + 4x + 10$
13. $336r^3 + 1008r^2 + 1008r + 336$
14. 472
15. 700
16. *example*: The divisor is a factor of the dividend.
17. yes
18. *example*: $c = -6$

5.1 Rational Expressions: Finding Equivalent Forms

1. Similar: still eliminate common factors from the numerator and denominator
Different: the expression has variable terms
2. (a) $\dfrac{4xy^2}{3}$ (b) $2p - 5$ (c) $\dfrac{5t^2 - 2}{3t}$
(d) $\dfrac{2(2a - 1)}{3a - 2}$ (e) 2 (f) $5c - 3d$
(g) $\dfrac{4a + b^2}{2}$ (h) $\dfrac{2y - 1}{4}$ (i) $\dfrac{y - 3}{y + 4}$
(j) $\dfrac{(-1)(x + r)}{3x + 2r}$ (k) $\dfrac{(-1)(e + 2)}{e + 4}$
(l) $\dfrac{(x^2 + 9)(x + 3)}{x + 1}$
3. (a) $\dfrac{(x + 3)(x + 1)}{(x - 3)(x + 2)}$ (b) $\dfrac{-4(y + 1)}{3(y + 3)}$ (c) $\dfrac{(3a - 1)}{2}$
(d) $-9 - r^2$ (e) -1
4. (a), (d), and (f) are not always true.
(a) $4x - 3y = -3y + 4x$, not $3y - 4x$
(d) $7 - 4x = (-1)(-7 + 4x)$ or $(-1)(4x - 7)$, but not $(-1)(7 - 4x)$
(f) $(3 + a) = (a + 3)$, but $(3 - a) \neq (a - 3)$
5. (a) Solution 4
(b) Solution 1: denominator in line 2 should be $(2x - 3)(3x - 1)$
Solution 2: line 4 is incorrect, since $\dfrac{2x + 3}{2x - 3}$ cannot be simplified by adding unlike terms Solution 3: line 4 is incorrect, since $\dfrac{2x + 3}{2x - 3}$ cannot be simplified by factoring out $2x$

6. (a) $\dfrac{x(x + 3)}{(x + 3)(x + 6)}$; $\dfrac{x}{x + 6}$ (b) $\dfrac{1}{2}$

5.2 Nonpermissible Values

1. Because the value of the expression would be undefined
2. *example*:
For *rate* × *time* = *distance*.
Determine the time it takes a car to travel 100 mi when time is 0 hours.
$R = \dfrac{d}{t} = \dfrac{100 \text{ mi}}{0 \text{ h}} =$ undefined
3. (a) yes
(b) -2: yes; 2: no
(c) yes
(d) -4: yes; 8: no
4. (a) 0 (b) 0 (c) 2
(d) $3, -\dfrac{1}{4}$ (e) $y, -y$ (f) $\dfrac{4}{3}, -\dfrac{4}{3}$
(g) 2 (h) $4, -4$ (i) -2
(j) $3, -4$
5. $k = 4$
6. (a) $x = \dfrac{3}{2}$
(b) *example*: No; the original version has $x = \dfrac{1}{3}$ and $\dfrac{3}{2}$, but the simplified version only has $x = \dfrac{3}{2}$. This happens because a common factor was factored out of the original expression. If the value of this factor were 0, it couldn't be factored out, because you can't divide by 0.
7. (a) $\dfrac{x - 4}{x - 3}$, $x = 3, -3$ (b) $\dfrac{2}{t + 5}$, $t = 3, -5$
(c) $\dfrac{x - 5}{x - 2}$, $x = 2, -5$ (d) $\dfrac{4b - 1}{b + 9}$, $b = 9, -9$
(e) $\dfrac{11 - x}{x + 6}$, $x = -6, -1$
(f) $\dfrac{x - y}{2x - y}$, $x = \dfrac{y}{2}$, $y = 2x$, $x = -\dfrac{5}{3}y$, $y = -\dfrac{3}{5}x$
8. (a) w cannot be equal to 0
(b) w cannot be negative
(c) L must be greater than 0
9. (a) *example*: as velocity decreases, time increases
(b) *example*: if velocity is 0, then time is undefined
(c) *example*: In general, velocity is not given a negative value. In physics, velocity is assigned a negative value if the object is traveling away from a destination.

5.3 Multiplying and Dividing Rational Expressions

1. **(a)** A common factor is a quantity that divides evenly into two numbers.
   (b) When you multiply a number by its reciprocal, the product is 1.
   (c) The divisor is the amount you divide by.
   (d) The dividend is the amount you divide into parts.

2. Similarities:
   You multiply and divide the same way. For multiplication, you multiply the numerators and the denominators. For division, you multiply by the reciprocal of the divisor. To simplify the factors and the product, you eliminate common factors by dividing the numerator and the denominator by the same amount.
   Differences:
   With rational expressions, you have to consider nonpermissible values. Also, it's more important to factor out common factors before you multiply rational expressions, because the multiplication can get very complicated if the expressions are long or if there are a lot of them.

3. **(a)** $\dfrac{b^2}{3a^2}$, $a \neq 0$, $b \neq 0$

   (b) $\dfrac{(c+5)(2c+3)}{c}$, $x \neq 0$, $\dfrac{3}{2}$, 7

   (c) $-\dfrac{x+2}{x-6}$, $x \neq 6$, 7, $-\dfrac{1}{2}$, 3

   (d) $\dfrac{4m-1}{2m-1}$, $m \neq -\dfrac{2}{3}$, $\dfrac{1}{2}$, $\dfrac{1}{5}$, -4

4. **(a)** $\dfrac{8x^2z^4}{15y^6}$, x, y, $z \neq 0$

   (b) $\dfrac{x+1}{(x+4)(x+5)}$, $x \neq -1$, 1, -5, -3, -4

   (c) $\dfrac{2y+1}{3y+2}$, $y \neq -\dfrac{2}{3}$, 4, -3, 3

   (d) $\dfrac{c-2d}{c+2d}$, $c \neq -d$, $-2d$, $-3d$, $2d$

5. **(a)** $\dfrac{bx}{5c^3}$, a, b, c, x, $y \neq 0$
   (b) $y+3$, $y \neq 0$, 4, -3, 7, -1
   (c) x, $x \neq 3a$, $-3a$, a, $-a$
   (d) 1, $x \neq -\dfrac{4}{3}$, $\dfrac{1}{2}$, $-\dfrac{3}{2}$, 4, $\dfrac{2}{3}$, $-\dfrac{1}{2}$

(e) $\dfrac{3n-2}{n+4}$, $n \neq -\dfrac{1}{5}$, 5, $-\dfrac{1}{2}$, $-\dfrac{3}{2}$, -4, $\dfrac{2}{3}$, -3,

6. **(a)** $\dfrac{3a^2}{b}$, x, y, a, $b \neq 0$

   (b) $\dfrac{2(x-2)}{x}$, $x \neq 0$, -2

   (c) $\dfrac{2}{x+5}$, $x \neq -4$, -5, -3, 2

   (d) $\dfrac{2a-1}{a+2}$, $a \neq -\dfrac{3}{2}$, 1, $\dfrac{1}{2}$, $-\dfrac{1}{7}$, -2

7. Caitlin forgot to list the nonpermissible values.
   $s \neq -\dfrac{5}{2}$, 4, $\dfrac{3}{8}$, $\dfrac{2}{3}$, $\dfrac{8}{3}$
   She could also have factored out opposites to simplify the expression further.
   $\dfrac{\cancel{(3s-2)}(-1)(8s-3)}{(-1)\cancel{(3s-2)}(3s-8)} = \dfrac{8s-3}{3s-8}$

8. **(a)** $\pi \times \dfrac{(x+3)(x+3)}{(2x-5)(2x-5)}$, $x \neq \dfrac{5}{2}$, $\dfrac{1}{2}$
   (b) 36π or 113.1
   (c) This would make the denominator equal to 0 in the expression for the length of the radius.

9. **(a)** $-\dfrac{x+3}{2x-5}$, $x \neq -\dfrac{4}{3}$, -3, $\dfrac{5}{2}$, $-\dfrac{7}{3}$
   (b) 5
   (c) This would make the width negative.

5.4 Adding and Subtracting Rational Expressions

1. **(a)** the simplest expression that has both denominators as factors
   (b) an algebraic expression that represents the ratio of two expressions
   (c) a value for a variable that makes the denominator equal to 0

2. Similarities:
   To add or subtract, you need to restate both expressions in terms of a common denominator. You do this by multiplying both expressions by another expression that is equal to 1. Sometimes it helps to simplify the expressions by eliminating common factors from the numerator and the denominator.
   Differences:
   Adding and subtracting rational expressions is more difficult because the operations are more complicated and it is harder to identify common factors.

3. **(a)** 40   **(b)** a^2 **(c)** $6y$

(d) $x^2 - 1$ **(e)** $15(x+3)$

4. (a) $\dfrac{10}{5x}, \dfrac{7x^2}{5x}$ **(b)** $\dfrac{xy+y}{xy^2}, \dfrac{5x}{xy^2}$

(c) $\dfrac{3x+6}{6(x+1)}, \dfrac{2x-6}{6(x+1)}$ **(d)** $\dfrac{x^2+x-6}{x^2-4}, \dfrac{x^2+2x}{x^2-4}$

5. (a) $\dfrac{5a-3}{(a+6)(a-5)}$ **(b)** $\dfrac{a-48}{(a+7)(a-4)}$

(c) $\dfrac{3t-4}{6(t+3)}$ **(d)** $\dfrac{2q^2-12q-1}{(9+q)(9-q)}$

(e) $\dfrac{8y}{(y-4)(y+4)}$ **(f)** $\dfrac{9a^2+16a+1}{(6a+1)(a+2)(a+3)}$

(g) $\dfrac{3(d-14)}{d-6}$ **(h)** $\dfrac{x^2+4x-2}{4(x+3)(x-2)}$

(i) $\dfrac{k^2}{k-1}$ **(j)** $\dfrac{2x+9}{x+3}$

(k) $\dfrac{-x^2+5x-2}{(x-1)(2x-1)}$

6. Simplifying the expression sometimes helps you eliminate common factors from the numerator and denominator. This results in a simpler LCD and easier calculations. For example, in Problem 5(f), not simplifying the expression gives the LCD $(6a^2 + 13a + 2)(a^2 + 5a + 6)$ and the sum $\dfrac{9a^3+24a^2+23a+2}{(6a^2+13a+2)(a^2+5a+6)}$. If you factor the denominators, you find that $(a+2)$ is common to both, so you can use a simpler LCD, $(6a+1)(a+2)(a+3)$, resulting in a simpler sum, $\dfrac{9a^2+16a+1}{(6a+1)(a+2)(a+3)}$.

7. $\dfrac{x^3+17x^2+7x-4}{x(x+2)(3x-1)}$

8. $\dfrac{t^2+10t+19}{(t+2)(t+3)}$

9. Tabor could have simplified both of the original expressions before he added. His answer is correct, but it is not in simplest form.

$\dfrac{5x+25}{(x+5)(x-2)} = \dfrac{5(x+5)}{(x+5)(x-2)} = \dfrac{5}{x-2}$

$\dfrac{2(x-4)}{(x-4)(x+3)} = \dfrac{2}{x+3}$

$\dfrac{5}{x-2} - \dfrac{2}{x+3} = \dfrac{3x+19}{(x-2)(x+3)}$

5.5 Solving Rational Equations

1. When you multiply the numerator by a multiple of the denominator, the numerator itself becomes a multiple of the denominator. When you eliminate common factors from the expression, the denominator becomes 1.

2. The balance between the left and right sides will be lost if a change is made to one side but not the other.

4. Substitute the calculated value for the variable into the original equation and simplify. If the left side equals the right side, the solution is correct.

5. 6: **(a)** none   **(b)** $x \neq 0$
    (c) $x \neq 0$ **(d)** $x \neq 0$
   7: **(a)** $x \neq -1$ **(b)** $y \neq 3$
    (c) $x \neq \dfrac{3}{2}$ **(d)** $n \neq 7, 25$
   8: **(a)** $x \neq \pm 1$ **(b)** $y \neq \pm 3$
    (c) $t \neq 0, 5$ **(d)** $x \neq 0, \pm 1$

6. (a) $x = 4$ **(b)** $x = -\dfrac{1}{2}$

   (c) $x = \dfrac{8}{3}$ **(d)** $x = 15$

7. (a) $x = 5$ **(b)** $y = 13$
   (c) $x = 6$ **(d)** $n = -20$

8. (a) no solution, since $x = 1$ is nonpermissible
   (b) $y = 1$ **(c)** $t = -\dfrac{4}{3}$
   (d) $x = 2$

9. 20,000 rolls

10. $\dfrac{5}{8+n} = \dfrac{1}{3}$, so $n = 7$

11. Jamilla forgot to multiply the -2 on the left side of the equation by the LCD.

$-2 \times 3(x+1) = -6(x+1)$
$ = -6x - 6$

Now the simplified equation becomes:
$9 - 6x - 6 = 5$
$3 - 6x = 5$
$-6x = 2$
$x = -\dfrac{1}{3}$

12. 600 ft/min, 300 ft/min

13. $\dfrac{5x+10}{x^2-4} \times 2 = \dfrac{15}{12}$, so $x = 10$

14. $\dfrac{15}{0.5h} = \dfrac{24}{0.5(h+3)}$, so $b = 6$ cm

6.1 Differences Between Relations and Functions

2. one-to-one mapping: where each element in the first set maps to only one element in the

second set

many-to-one mapping: where there is more than one *x*-value for a given *y*-value

one-to-many mapping: where an element in the first set maps to many elements in the second set.

3. **(a)** (0, 5) (1, 4) (2, 3) (3, 2) (4, 1)
   (b) yes, since this is a one-to-one mapping

4. **(a)**   **(b)**

   (c)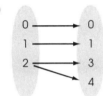

5. *example*: same: all are binary relations; different:
   (a) is one-to-one
   (b) is many-to-one
   (c) is one-to-many

6. **(a)** because it's one-to-one
   (b) because it's many-to-one

7. **(a)** 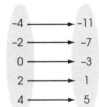   **(b)**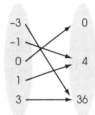

8. **(a)** because it's one-to-one
   (b) because it's many-to-one

9. **(a)** (3, 1)   **(b)** (3, 4)
   (c) (2, 2)   **(d)** (3, 4) and (4, 3)

10. functions are (b) and (c)

11. **(a)** A (−7, 2) B (7, 2)
    (b) many-to-one; *example*: there are 2 possible values for *x* when *y* = 2

12. **(a)** one-to-one   **(b)** one-to-one

6.2 Describing Functions

1. **(a)** distance traveled depends on time
   (b) volume depends on pressure
   (c) area depends on length

2. **(a)** In a two-column table, the independent variable is usually placed in the first column in a set of points. The independent variable is the first relative

value of each point.
   (b) The independent variable is graphed along the *x*-axis.
   (c) The independent variable is isolated on one side of the equation.

3. **(a)** $\left(-1, -\dfrac{17}{3}\right) \left(\dfrac{45}{2}, 10\right)$ **(b)** (−4, 44) (3, 23)
   (c) (4, 7) (12, 11)   **(d)** (2, 8) (4, 80)
   (e) (−2, −15) (1, 0)   **(f)** (1, −4) (−3, −6)

4. (a), (b), (c), (d)

5. 9

6. **(a)** $y = 2x + 1$ **(b)** $y = \dfrac{24}{x}$

   (c) $y = x^2 - 5$ **(d)** $y = 2\sqrt{x}$

7. **(a)** $y = \sqrt{x} - 2$ **(b)** $y = 3^x$
   (c) $2 per hour or any portion thereof

8. ordered pairs are (1, 1), (2, 3), (3, 6), (4, 10);

$$number\ of\ dots = \frac{figure\ number\ (figure\ number + 1)}{2}$$

9. 15

6.3 Function Notation

1. *example*: to help understand the relationship between an independent and dependent variable; a consistent way to represent that relationship

2. input: the domain of a function
   output: the range of a function

3. **(a)** $f(x) = \sqrt{x} - 3$ **(b)** $f(x) = \dfrac{x^3}{x-1}$

4. **(a)** Find the square of *x* and then multiply by −1.
   (b) Divide *n* by 4 and then subtract n^3.
   (c) Multiply *p* by (*p* − 2).
   (d) Find the square root of *g*.

5.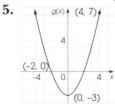

6. **(a)** 4   **(b)** −2   **(c)** −0.6
   (d) $-\dfrac{1}{4}$ **(e)** *x* − 3   **(f)** $a^2 - 2$

7. **(a)** −3   **(b)** 2, −8   **(c)** 4

8. 3, −3

9. $d(1) = 12.5$; $d(7) = 612.5$; $d(12) = 1800$

10. **(a)** $f(g(2)) = 2$; $g(f(2)) = 2$ **(b)** yes
    (c) $f(g(0)) = 4$; $g(f(0)) = 4$ **(d)** no

11. 4, −4

12. **(a)** 1.76 m   **(b)** 50 s

13. **(a)** -6 **(b)** 6 **(c)** -11
   (d) $2h$ **(e)** -5 **(f)** -1
   (g) -1 **(h)** 47 **(i)** $2a + h$
   (j) 1

14. **(a)** 2 **(b)** 4 **(c)** 2 **(d)** -2 **(e)** 6

6.4 Domain and Range of Relations

1. the set of first coordinates of the ordered pairs
2. the set of x-values on the x-axis
3. the set of second coordinates of the ordered pairs
4. the set of y-values on the y-axis
5. The graph is a dotted line without bounds. There is an open point at $x = 5$, since there is no corresponding y-value. The other points are located at all possible integer values for x and are closed points.
6. The graph is a solid line extending without bounds. There is an open point at $y = 0$, since there is no corresponding x-value.
7. The graph is a solid, horizontal line extending without bounds. The y-intercept is at $(0, 7)$.
8. The graph is a dotted vertical line extending without bounds through the x-intercept $(5, 0)$. The points are located at all possible integer values of y.
9. **(a)** $\{x \mid x \in R\}; \{y \mid y \in R\}$
   (b) $\{x \mid x \in R\}; \{y \mid y \leq 3, y \in R\}$
   (c) $\{x \mid 0 \leq x \leq 4, x \in R\}; \{y \mid 1 \leq y \leq 5, y \in R\}$
   (d) $\{x \mid x \neq 0, x \in R\}; \{y \mid y > 0, y \in R\}$
10. **(a)** $x \in \{3, 4, 5\}; y \in \{1, 2, 3, 4\}$
   (b) $\{x \mid -4 \leq x < 4, x \in R\}; \{y \mid -2 \leq y < 5, y \in R\}$
   (c) $\{x \mid x \leq -1, x > 1, x \in R\}; y \in \{-4, 2\}$
   (d) $\{x \mid -4 \leq x \leq 4, x \in R\}; \{y \mid -4 \leq y \leq 4, y \in R\}$

11.

12. $\{x \mid x > 0, x \in R\}$;
$y = 20, 30, 40, 50, 60, 70, 80, 90$
The cost is \$20 for the first hour and \$10 for each additional hour or portion thereof. If you finish exactly at the end of an hour, you are charged for the hour just completed, but not the next hour.

7.1 Linear Functions

1. When a graph crosses the x-axis, the value of y is zero. By substituting zero for y and using the value for the slope and y-intercept, you can solve for x.
2. Slope is defined as rise over run. $y_2 - y_1$ defines rise, or the change in the y-axis, and $x_2 - x_1$ defines run, or the change in the x-axis.
3. **(a)** domain: x is a real number ≥ 0; range: y is a real number ≥ 1
   (b) domain: x is a real number; range: $y = 2$
   (c) domain: $x = -4, -2, 0, 2$; range: $y = 0, -1, -2, -3$
4. **(a)** y-intercept: -2, x-intercept: 4, slope: $\frac{1}{2}$
   (b) y-intercept: 2, x-intercept: -3, slope: $\frac{2}{3}$
   (c) y-intercept: 5, x-intercept: 4, slope: $-\frac{5}{4}$
   (d) y-intercept: 0, x-intercept: 0, slope: -1
5. **(a)** $y = \frac{1}{2}x - 2$ **(b)** $y = \frac{2}{3}x + 2$
   (c) $y = -\frac{5}{4}x + 5$ **(d)** $y = -x$
6. **(a)** y-intercept: -5, x-intercept: 2
   (b) y-intercept: 2, x-intercept: -3
   (c) y-intercept: 4, x-intercept: 2
7. **(a)**

   (b)
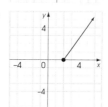

   (c)
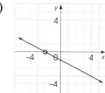

8. **(a)** y-intercept: 4, slope: -2
   (b) y-intercept: -6, slope: $\frac{3}{2}$
9. **(a)** domain: $x = 0, 1, 2, 3, 4$
      range: $y = 6, 2, -2, -6, -10$
   (b) domain: $x = 1, 2, 3, 4, 5$
      range: $y = 1.5, 2, 2.5, 3, 3.5$
   (c) domain: x is a real number
      range: y is a real number
   (d) domain: x is a real number ≥ 0

range: y is a real number ≥ 1

10. all pass through $(4, 3)$

11. (a) -1 (b) 0 (c) 1.5

12. (a) slope: 2, y-intercept: 5, x-intercept: -2.5

    (b) slope: $\frac{2}{3}$, y-intercept: -4, x-intercept: 6

    (c) slope: $-\frac{1}{2}$, y-intercept: -3, x-intercept: -6

    (d) slope: -1.5, y-intercept: 6, x-intercept: 4

13. (a) yes

    (b) no; if x and y are positive, then
$\frac{y-0}{0-x} = \frac{positive}{negative}$, which must result in a
negative slope

14. (b) and (e)

15. (a) and (d)

16. AB: x is a real number where $-2 \leq x \leq 5$, y is a
real number where $0 \leq y \leq 5$, $\frac{5}{7}$; BC: x is a real
number where $5 \leq x \leq 7$, y is a real number
where $-3 \leq y \leq 5$, -4; CA: x is a real number
where $-2 \leq x \leq 7$, y is a real number where
$-3 \leq y \leq 0$, $\frac{3}{7}$

7.2 Direct and Partial Variation

1. (a) where y varies directly with x, and the
y-intercept is at the origin: $y = kx$

    (b) where y varies partially with x, but the
y-intercept is not at the origin: $y = kx + b$

    (c) the constant k in the equation for direct
variation $y = kx$; the slope

    (d) the output or y-values of a relation

    (e) the input or x-values of a relation

    (f) the unchanging cost for a given situation

    (g) cost which depends on another variable

2. For a direct variation, the y-intercept is at zero
and for partial variation, the y-intercept is not
at zero; $y = kx$, and $y = kx + b$, respectively.
example:

Direct Variation: Partial Variation:

$y = 3x$ $y = 2x + 1$

$(0, 0); (1, 3); (2, 6)$ $(0, 1); (1, 3); (2, 5)$

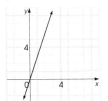

3. (a) $k = 2$ (b) $k = 12$ (c) $k = 5$

4. (a) $y = kx$ (b) $y = 64$

5. (a) $y = 50$ (b) $y = 3.6$

6. (a) 90   (b) 168   (c) 234   (d) 19.5

7. (a) 12   (b) 32   (c) 17   (d) 59

8. (a) $C = 6 + 0.75n$ (b)

n	C
1	6.75
2	7.50
3	8.25
4	9.00
5	9.75
6	10.50
7	11.25
8	12.00

(c)

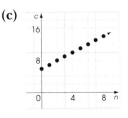

9. (a) $M = kV$ (b) 480 g

10. $3.50

11. $6625

12. (a) $6.75   (b) 15 minutes

13. 0.96 m or 96 cm

14. 25 min

15. *example:* Since the fixed cost is in dollars, the
agent should have used 0.10 for the variable
cost, not 10. Actual cost is $40 + 3260¢ or
$40 + $32.60 or $72.60.

7.3 Rate of Change and Slope of a Line

1. *example:* The slope is the distance a line rises
for each unit of horizontal distance it travels.
You calculate it by dividing the vertical
distance a line travels between two points by
the horizontal distance. Use the formula $\frac{rise}{run}$
if you can count squares, or the formula
$\frac{y_1 - y_2}{x_1 - x_2}$ if you can't. The slope of the line $y = x$
is 1. If a line rises more steeply than $y = x$, the
slope is more than 1. If the line rises less
steeply than $y = x$, the slope is between 0 and
1. If the line is horizontal, the slope is 0. If the
line falls to the right, the slope is negative.

2. *example:* If the *rise* decreases and the *run* stays
the same, a line segment's *slope* becomes *less.*

3. (a) $\frac{3}{5}$ (b) $-\frac{5}{3}$ (c) $-\frac{1}{6}$

    (d) $-\frac{4}{8} = -\frac{1}{2}$ (e) $\frac{8}{4} = 2$ (f) $\frac{4}{2} = 2$

    (g) $\frac{3}{6} = \frac{1}{2}$ (h) $\frac{4}{2} = 2$

4. (a) rise = 2, run = 4, slope = $\frac{1}{2}$

(b) rise = –5, run = 0, slope is undefined

(c) rise = 0, run = 5, slope = 0

5. *example:* Horizontal lines don't rise, so the rise is always $\frac{0}{run}$. Vertical lines have no run, so the slope is $\frac{rise}{0}$, and division by 0 is undefined.

6. (a) no, since slope AB is $\frac{4}{5}$ and slope BC is $-\frac{4}{5}$

(b) no, since slope DE is $\frac{3}{8}$ and slope EF is $-\frac{1}{4}$

(c) yes, since slope GH = slope $HI = -\frac{1}{6}$

7. (a) $y = \frac{2}{3}x + \frac{11}{3}$ **(b)** $y = -\frac{4}{3}x + \frac{17}{3}$

(c) $y = -\frac{3}{2}x + \frac{13}{2}$ **(d)** $y = -4x - 9$

8.   (a)   –

(c) –15

9. *example:* Expressing the slope as an improper fraction shows the relationship between rise (in the numerator) and run (in the denominator).

10. *example:* $\left(5, \frac{8}{3}\right)$ is lower and $\left(1, \frac{16}{3}\right)$ is higher

11. *example:* points are collinear because slope AB = slope $BC = \frac{2}{3}$; points are collinear because all three sets of coordinates satisfy the equation of the line, which is $2x - 3y + 14 = 0$

12. coordinates must satisfy the equation $y = \frac{1}{2}x + 1$, so $4 < x < 6$ and $3 < y < 4$
One example is $(5.25, 3.625)$.

7.4 Determining the Equation of a Line

1. *example:* The x-coordinate of the y-intercept is always 0.

2. (a) a vertical line through 4 on the x-axis

(b) a horizontal line through –1 on the y-axis

(c) an oblique line through $(-1, -1)$, $(0, 0)$, $(1, 1)$, $(2, 2)$, etc., so the x-coordinate = the y-coordinate for each point on the line

3. (a) slope = 3, y-intercept = 6

(b) slope = $-\frac{3}{2}$, y-intercept = 3

4. *example:*

Method 1	Method 2
$3x + y = 8$	If $x = 0$, then
$y = -3x + 8$,	$0 + y = 8$
so y-intercept is 8	so $y = 8$ when $x = 0$

5. (a) $2x - y - 5 = 0$ **(b)** $2x + 3y - 7 = 0$

(c) $x - 2y + 5 = 0$ **(d)** $3x + y + 4 = 0$

6. (a) $x + 5y - 14 = 0$ **(b)** $4x - 3y - 5 = 0$

(c) $x + y - 7 = 0$ **(d)** $4x - 3y - 1 = 0$

7. (a) $y = x + 1$ **(b)** $y = 3$

(c) $x = 4$ **(d)** $y = -x - 2$

8. (a) $y = \frac{1}{2}x - \frac{5}{2}$ **(b)** $y = \frac{1}{3}x - 2$

(c) $y = -\frac{1}{4}x - \frac{1}{4}$ **(d)** $y = 2x - 7$

9. (a) $5x + 4y + 12 = 0$ **(b)** $x + 4y - 4 = 0$

(c) $4x - 3y - 12 = 0$

10. $11x - 3y - 82 = 0$ **11.** $\frac{32}{3}$ or $10\frac{2}{3}$

12. weekly flat rate is \$10; hourly fee is \$4/h

13. (b) $y = \frac{13}{2}x$ or $y = 6.5x$

(c) *example:* The y-intercept is $(0, 0)$, so Kara is paid by the hour, with no flat rate. The slope is 6.5, so Kara is paid \$6.50/h.

8.1 Solving Linear Systems by Graphing

1. (a) two or more linear equations that are considered together

(b) the solution is the intersection of the graphs of the linear equations

(c) Substitute the coordinates of the solution into each linear equation to verify it holds true.

2.

independent	inconsistent	dependent
$y = 1$	$y = 1$	$x = 2$
$y = -x$	$y = -1$	$x = 2$

3. (a) $(2, -10)$ **(b)** $(-5, 4)$ **(c)** $(-1, -1)$

4. (a) $(3, 6)$ **(b)** $(-4, 1)$ **(c)** no solution

5. (a) Line 1: slope: 1; y-intercept: –2
Line 2: slope: $\frac{8}{9}$; y-intercept: –1
solution: $(9, 7)$

(b) Line 1: slope is undefined; no y-intercept
Line 2: slope: 0; y-intercept: 7
solution: $(4, 7)$

(c) Line 1: slope: $-\frac{5}{8}$; y-intercept: 6
Line 2: slope: $-\frac{5}{8}$; y-intercept: 6
number of solutions is infinite because the system is dependent

6. (a) Both lines: x-intercept: 9; y-intercept: 7
number of solutions is infinite

(b) Line 1: x-intercept: 4; y-intercept: 2
Line 2: x-intercept: 7; y-intercept: –7
solution: $(6, -1)$

(c) Line 1: x-intercept: $\frac{8}{3}$; y-intercept: 4

Line 2: x-intercept: 5; y-intercept: 5
solution: $(-2, 7)$

(d) Line 1: x-intercept: $\frac{3}{2}$; y-intercept: $-\frac{3}{4}$

Line 2: x-intercept: 1; y-intercept: -1

solution: $\left(\frac{1}{2}, -\frac{1}{2}\right)$

7. (a) $(3, 4)$ **(b)** $(5, -2)$

8. (a) $\left(-2, -\frac{1}{2}\right)$ **(b)** $\left(\frac{1}{3}, -4\right)$

These solutions do not lie on the lattice points of the grid, so you need to use a combination of estimation and verification to identify them accurately.

9. (a) yes   **(b)** yes

10. Isolate y in each equation. If the equations have unique slopes, the system will have one solution. If the equations have identical slopes but unique y-intercepts, the system will have no solution. If the equations have identical slopes and identical y-intercepts, the equations describe the same line and the system has an infinite number of solutions.

11. (a) m: anything except $\frac{3}{4}$; b: anything

(b) $m = \frac{3}{4}$; b: anything except -2

(c) $m = \frac{3}{4}$; $b = -2$

12. (a) not possible

(b) anything except $d = \frac{8}{3}$

(c) $d = \frac{8}{3}$

13. $(2, -8)$

14. The equations describe the same flight paths. If they fly at different times and/or at different speeds, there will be no intersection.

15. any ordered pairs where $x = y$, and x and y are real numbers

8.2 Solving Linear Systems by Elimination

1. (a) $x = 3$, $y = 2$ **(b)** $x = 4$, $y = 1$
(c) $x = 7$, $y = 15$

2. (a) $a = 2\frac{1}{20}$, $b = -\frac{1}{10}$ **(b)** no solution

(c) $x = \frac{-17}{11}$, $y = \frac{97}{11}$

3. $a = -1$, $b = 1$

4. $A = \frac{8}{5}$

5. $A = 3$, $B = 5$

6. $A = \frac{9}{4}$, $B = \frac{15}{4}$

7. $(3, 6)$, $(5, -2)$, $(-5, 3)$

8. Let x represent the funds, in dollars, invested at 9%. Let y represent the funds, in dollars, invested at 13.5%.

$$\begin{cases} 0.09x + 0.135y = 531 \\ x + y = 5000 \end{cases}$$

$x = \$3200$, $y = \$1800$

9. Let y represent the number of tickets sold at \$4.50. Let s represent the number of tickets sold at \$6.00.

$$\begin{cases} 4.5y + 6s = 792 \\ y + s = 152 \end{cases}$$

$y = 80$, $s = 72$

8.3 Solving Three Equations in Three Variables

1. *example:*

$$\begin{aligned} 10a + 8b - 2c &= 20 \\ + \; 3a - 6b + 2c &= 15 \\ \hline 13a + 2b &= 35 \end{aligned}$$

Multiply the first equation by 2 to make the last term $-2c$. Add the two equations to eliminate the $2c$'s.

2. To find the value of a variable, you need to simplify an equation so there is a variable on one side and a numerical value on the other. To do this, you need to start by eliminating the other variables. After you've found the value for one variable, you can use substitution to find values for the rest.

3. (a) $(2, -1, 3)$ is not a solution
(b) $(4, 2, 0)$ is not a solution
(c) $(-10, -9, 5)$ is not a solution
(d) $(-2, 5, 3)$ is a solution

4. The c-terms were added instead of subtracted, and the numerical term in equation 2 was not subtracted from 0. Equation ④ should be $2a - 7c - 7 = 17$ or $2a - 7c = 24$. The correct solution is $a = 5$, $b = -1$, and $c = -2$.

5. (a) $(2, 1, -1)$ **(b)** no solution
(c) $(-5, -2, 4)$ **(d)** $(3, -2, -4)$
(e) infinite number of solutions
(f) $(2, 4, -3)$

6. Sam has fourteen \$5 bills, eleven \$10 bills, and thirteen \$20 bills.

7. 10 h in class, 30 h studying, 20 h at work

8. 4 g of carbohydrates, 22 g of fat, 2 g of protein

9. \$15,000 at 5%, \$22,000 at 7%, and \$13,000 at 4%.

8.4 Solving Linear Systems by Matrices

1. (a) matrix
   (b) elements
   (c) 3, 4
   (d) row
   (e) augmented
   (f) main diagonal
2. both processes involve eliminating terms to solve the system of equations; elimination uses the variables while matrices don't
3. (a) 2 rows, 3 columns
   (b) 3 rows, 4 columns
4. (a) $x + 6y = 7$; $y = 4$
   (b) $2x - 2y + 9z = 1$; $3x + y + z = 0$; $2x - 6y + 8z = -7$
5. (a) $x - y = -10$; $y = 6$; solution: $x = -4$, $y = 6$
   (b) $x - 2y + z = -16$; $y + 2z = 8$; $z = 4$; solution: $x - -20$, $y = 0$, $z = 4$
6. (a) system has no solution
   (b) system has infinite solutions
7. (a) exchange the first and second rows;

$$\begin{bmatrix} 1 & -4 & | & 4 \\ -3 & 1 & | & -6 \end{bmatrix}$$

   (b) add three times the first row to the second row; $\begin{bmatrix} 1 & -4 & | & 4 \\ 0 & -11 & | & 6 \end{bmatrix}$

8. (a) $x = 1$, $y = 1$
   (b) $x = 1$, $y = 2$
   (c) $x = 2$, $y = -3$
   (d) $x = 2$, $y = 0$
   (e) $x = -1$, $y = -1$
   (f) $x = 1$, $y = 2$
   (g) $x = 0$, $y = -3$
   (h) $x = 5$, $y = -2$
   (i) $x = 1$, $y = 2$, $z = 3$
   (j) $x = 3$, $y = 2$, $z = 1$
   (k) $x = 4$, $y = 5$, $z = 4$
   (l) $x = 1$, $y = 3$, $z = 2$
   (m) $x = 2$, $y = 1$, $z = 0$
   (n) $a = 2$, $b = 0$, $c = 2$
9. (a) inconsistent
   (b) inconsistent
   (c) dependent
   (d) dependent
   (e) $x = 0$, $y = 1$, $z = 3$
   (f) $x = 8$, $y = 4$, $z = 5$
   (g) inconsistent
   (h) dependent
   (i) $x = -4$, $y = 8$, $z = 5$
   (j) $x = -1$, $y = 2$, $z = -2$
   (k) dependent
   (l) inconsistent
10. 25 $5-bills and 15 $2-bills
11. *example:* founder's circle: 100, box seats: 300, promenade: 400

8.5 Solving Linear Systems by Determinants

1. *examples:*
   (a) the entries along a horizontal line in a matrix
   (b) the entries along a vertical line in a matrix
   (c) a matrix of the coefficients with an added column containing the constants
   (d) a matrix where the number of rows equals the number of columns
   (e) the determinant of a sub-matrix obtained by striking out the row and the column in which a chosen element lies
2. Eliminate the row and the column in which the chosen element lies. The resulting determinant is the minor of the chosen element.
3. Form the augmented matrix. Find D_x by substituting the constant values for the x-values. Evaluate the determinant. By Cramer's rule, $x = \dfrac{D_x}{D}$.
4. (a) 8
   (b) 8
   (c) 14
   (d) 0
5. $D = -3(4 - 1) + 0 + 2(-1 - 6)$
   $= -3(3) + 2(-7)$
   $= -9 - 14$
   $= -23$
6. (a) -6
   (b) -48
   (c) -48
7. (a) $x = -1$, $y = 3$
   (b) $x = -3$, $y = -1$
   (c) $x = 3$, $y = 4$
   (d) $x = 1$, $y = 1$, $z = 2$
   (e) $x = 0$, $y = 2$, $z = 2$
   (f) inconsistent system
   (g) dependent system
   (h) $x = -2$, $y = 3$, $z = 1$
8. $x = 50°$, $y = 80°$
9. $8000 in SaveTel, $7000 in OilCo, and $5000 in HiTech
10. $D_x = -36$, $D_y = 24$

11. a zero entry will result in a zero when multiplied by its minor

8.6 Solving Systems of Linear Inequalities

1. **(a)** true   **(b)** false
    (c) false   **(d)** false

2. Let d represent the number of compact discs.
Let t represent the number of tapes.
$d + t > 250$, $10d + 5t \leq 1750$

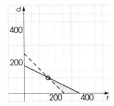

3. not possible

4. Let m represent the number of magazines.
Let n represent the number of newspapers.
$n \geq 2m$, $3m + n > 500$

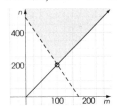

5. Let L represent the length in yards.
Let W represent the width in yards.
$L > W$, $2L + 2W \geq 20$, $LW \geq 30$

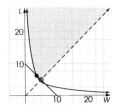

not possible

6. Let d represent the number of dimes.
Let q represent the number of quarters.
$d + q \leq 100$, $10d + 25q \geq 2000$

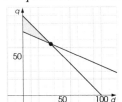

8.7 Linear Programming

1. 55

2. **(a)** maximum value of 39 at (3, 9)
       minimum value of 15 at (3, 3)
   (b) maximum value of –9 at (3, 3)

minimum value of –33 at (3, 9)
   (c) For $S = x + 4y$, the corner point yielding a maximum value gives a minimum value for $Q = x - 4y$, and the corner point yielding a minimum value for S gives a maximum value for Q.

3. **(a)** corner points are: (0, 3) (0, 2) $(4, \frac{2}{3})$ $(\frac{9}{7}, \frac{30}{7})$

        maximum value is $\frac{204}{7}$ at $(\frac{9}{7}, \frac{30}{7})$

   (b) The solution set is {(1, 2) (1, 3) (1, 4) (2, 2) (2, 3) (3, 1) (3, 2)}
        maximum value is 28 at (3, 2)

4. Let c = number of jean jackets
Let p = number of jeans
Let R = profits in dollars

Constraints:	Objective Function
$4c + 2p \leq 440$	$R = 65c + 45p$
$5c + 6p \leq 780$	
$6c + 4p \leq 680$	

corner points (c, p) are: (0, 130) (60, 80) (100, 20) (110, 0)
maximum value is \$7500 at (60, 80)

5. Let g = hours spent golfing
Let b = hours spent cycling
Let C = calories burned in a week

Constraints:	Objective Function
$g + b \leq 30$	$C = 300g + 420b$
$g + b \geq 15$	
$g \geq 2b$	
$b \geq 3$	

corner points (g, b) are: (10, 5) (12, 3) (27, 3) (20, 10)
maximum number of calories burned is 10,200 at (20, 10)
minimum number of calories burned is 4860 at (12, 3)

6. Let l = number of loveseats
Let s = number of sofas
Let P = profit for furniture production in dollars

Constraints:	Objective Functions
$l + s \leq 18$	a) $P = 550l + 800s$
$750l + 1000s \leq 14,000$	b) $P = 450l + 700s$
$l \geq 6$	c) $P = 500l + 500s$
$4l + 6s \leq 78$	

corner points (l, s) are: (6, 9) (6, 0) (12, 5) (16, 2) (18, 0)
   (a) maximum value is \$10,600 at (12, 5)
   (b) maximum value is \$9000 at (6, 9)
   (c) maximum value is \$9000 at (16, 2), (17, 1), or (18, 0)

7. Let a = number of adult bikes
Let c = number of child's bikes

Let P = profit in dollars

Constraints:

Objective Function

$a + c \leq 48$

$P = 75a + 45c$

$210a + 90c \leq 7350$

$a \leq 2c$

maximum value is $2910 at $(a, c) = (25, 23)$

8. Limiting constraint is 8 rock tickets.
   Possible combination of A and B is $(6, 2)$.
   Cost is $956 when $A = 6$ and $B = 2$.

9.1 Functions and Operations

1. For each x-value, find the corresponding values of $f(x)$ and $g(x)$, and add these together.

2. For each x-value, find the corresponding values of $f(x)$ and $g(x)$, and multiply these together.

3. (a) $-3x + 2$ (b) $9x + 2$
   (c) $18x^2 + 12x$ (d) $3x - 2$

4. (a) $5x^2 + 20x$ (b) $-4x^2 - 20x$
   (c) $4x^2 + 20x$ (d) $x^8 + 4x^2 + 5$
   (e) $4x^3 - 4x^2$

5. (a) $12x + 3$ (b) $12x + 1$
   (c) $16x^2 + 8x + 1$ (d) $4x^2 + 1$
   (e) $-x^2 + 1$ (f) $16x + 5$
   (g) $9x$ (h) $12x^2$

6. $f(x) = 2x - 2$ $g(x) = x + 1$

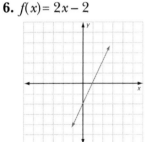 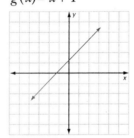

$(f \bullet g)(x) = (2x - 2)(x + 1)$

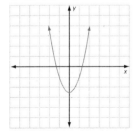

7. $f(x) = 3x$ $g(x) = x - 2$

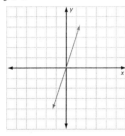 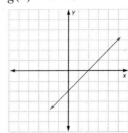

$(f - g)(x) = 2x + 2$

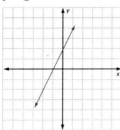

8. $f(x) = x + 2$ $g(x) = x^2$

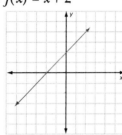 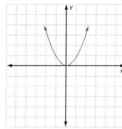

$g(f(x)) = (x + 2)^2$

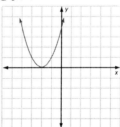

9. $16w + 104$

10. $f(x) = 0.80x$ (20% reduction)
         $g(x) = 1.07x$ (7% sales tax)
    $g(f(x)) = 1.07(0.80x)$
    $g(f(C)) = 0.856C$

11. $K(t) = K(v(t))$
          $= K(30 - 9.8t)$
          $= 0.4(30 - 9.8t)^2$
          $\doteq 360 - 235t + 38t^2$

12. $(f + g)(x) = -x + 1$

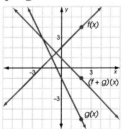

13. (a) $3\frac{3}{4}$ yards
    (b) The amount of fabric depends on the pattern size which depends on the child's chest size.

14. The functions should have been composed, not multiplied.
$$f(g(3)) = (15)^2 + 2(15) + 1$$
$$= 225 + 30 + 1$$

9.2 Inverse Functions

1. $f^{-1}(x) = \sqrt[3]{3(x+1)}$

2. If any horizontal line passes through more than one point, the inverse will not be a function.

3. The inverse is not a function. This notation is reserved for functions.

5. (a) $f^{-1}(x) = \{(2, -1), (4, 3), (-7, 0), (-6, 11)\}$

 (b) $f^{-1}(x) = \dfrac{x+2}{4}$

 (c) $f^{-1}(x) = \dfrac{1}{x-4}$

 (d) $f^{-1}(x) = \sqrt[3]{x-2}$

6. (a)

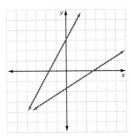

 (b)

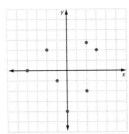

 (c)

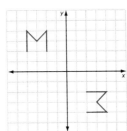

 (d)

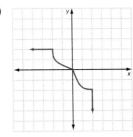

7. The remaining steps are:
$$xy - 2x = 3y$$
$$xy - 3y = 2x$$
$$y(x - 3) = 2x$$
$$g^{-1}(x) = \frac{2x}{x - 3}$$

8. (a) $x = -12$

 (b) $y = \pm\sqrt{x+1} - 3$

 (c) $\{(-2, 3), (3, 2), (0, 2)\}$

9. (a) $x = -12$ is a horizontal line and so passes through more than one point. Therefore, the inverse is not a function.

 (b) The inverse is symmetric, and a horizontal line would pass through more than one point. Therefore, the inverse is not a function.

 (c) (3, 2) and (0, 2) have the same y-value, so a horizontal line would pass through two points. Therefore, the inverse is not a function.

10. $h(k(x)) = \dfrac{1}{3}k(x) - 4$
$$= \frac{1}{3}(3x + 12) - 4$$
$$= x + 4 - 4$$
$$= x$$
Follow the same procedure for $k(h(x))$.

11. (a) and (d)

12. (a) for $f(x)$: domain: $\{x \mid x \le 3\}$, range: $\{y \mid y \le 2\}$
for $f^{-1}(x)$: domain: $\{x \mid x \le 2\}$, range: $\{y \mid y \le 3\}$

 (b) domain and range have switched because x- and y-values have been interchanged

13. (a) $f^{-1}(x) = 2x + 6$, $f^{-1}(0) = 6$, $f^{-1}(-2) = 2$

 (b) $f^{-1}(x) = \dfrac{4}{x} - 1$, $f^{-1}(0)$ is undefined, $f^{-1}(-2) = -3$

 (c) $f^{-1}(x) = \sqrt[3]{-x + 8}$, $f^{-1}(0) = 2$, $f^{-1}(-2) = \sqrt[3]{10}$

 (d) $f^{-1}(x) = \{(-2, 0), (4, -2), (0, 3)\}$, $f^{-1}(0) = 3$, $f^{-1}(-2) = 0$

 (e) $f^{-1}(x) = \dfrac{3x + 4}{2}$, $f^{-1}(0) = 2$, $f^{-1}(-2) = -1$

14. Substitute 0 for $f(x)$ in the equation $f(x) = \dfrac{1}{2}x - 3$ and solve for x.

15. domain: $\{x \mid x \ge -1\}$, range: $\{y \mid y \ge 0\}$ $h^{-1}(x) = x^2 - 1$, $x \ge 0$

9.3 Graphs of Quadratic Functions

1. If the graph opens up, it has a minimum value; if the graph opens down, it has a maximum value.
2. opens down; maximum of 1
3. opens up; minimum of 0
4. (a) The y-coordinate of the vertex is the maximum or minimum value.
   (b) The axis of symmetry is a vertical line through the vertex; therefore, the equation of the axis of symmetry is $x =$ "x-coordinate of vertex."
5. vertex = $(1, -3)$; minimum of -3; equation of axis of symmetry is $x = 1$
6. x-intercepts at $(-1, 0)$ and $(-3, 0)$; y-intercept at $(0, 3)$
7. no x-intercepts; y-intercept at $(0, -1)$
8. domain: $\{x \mid x \in \mathrm{R}\}$
   range: $\{y \mid y \geq -1, y \in \mathrm{R}\}$
9. domain: $\{x \mid x \leq 0, x \in \mathrm{R}\}$
   range: $\{y \mid y \leq 4, y \in \mathrm{R}\}$

9.4 Completing the Square

2. test the graph with a vertical line; examine a table of values to see if the correspondence is one-to-one or many-to-one
3. a represents the shape of the graph relative to the graph of $y = x$, h represents the x-coordinate of the vertex, k represents the y-coordinate of the vertex
4. (a) If a is positive, the graph opens up; if a is negative, the graph opens down.
   (b) For $|a| > 1$, the parabola will be narrower than the basic $y = x^2$ parabola, and for $0 < |a| < 1$, the parabola will be wider than the basic $y = x^2$ parabola.
5. (a) True
   (b) False; this parabola opens upward and is wider than the basic $y = x^2$ graph.
   (c) False; this parabola opens upward and is narrower than the basic $y = x^2$ graph.
   (d) True
6. (a) (iv)
   (b) (ii)
   (c) (ii)
   (d) (i)
7. (a) $y = -7(x^2 - 2x) + 9$
   (b) $f(x) = -2.3(x^2 - 4x) - 5.4$
   (c) $y = 4\left(x^2 - \frac{1}{2}x\right) + 5$
   (d) $y = 15\left(x^2 - \frac{1}{3}x\right) + 2$
   (e) $y = \frac{1}{3}\left(x^2 + \frac{3}{5}x\right) - \frac{4}{9}$
   (f) $f(x) = \frac{3}{8}\left(x^2 + \frac{2}{3}x\right) + \frac{1}{2}$
8. (a) fourth line; $y = (x - 12)^2 - 44$
   (b) fourth line; $y = 5(x - 2)^2 - 16$
   (c) second line; $y = 12\left(x^2 + \frac{1}{2}x\right) - 11$
   (d) third line; $f(x) = -4(x^2 + 8x + 16) + 3 + 64$
   $= -4(x + 4)^2 + 67$
9. (a) $y = (x + 5)^2 + 3$
   (b) $f(x) = 2(x + 2)^2 - 1$
   (c) $y = 3(x - 3)^2 - 26$
   (d) $y = \left(x - \frac{3}{2}\right)^2 + 4\frac{3}{4}$
10. (a) $y = -2(x - 3)^2 + 1$
    vertex = $(3, 1)$; y-intercept = $(0, -17)$
    (b) $y = \frac{1}{2}(x + 2)^2 - 5$
    vertex = $(-2, -5)$; y-intercept = $(0, -3)$
    (c) $f(x) = \frac{1}{4}(x - 4)^2 - 10$
    vertex = $(4, -10)$; y-intercept = $(0, -6)$
    (d) $y = -\frac{3}{2}(x - 2)^2 - 25$
    vertex = $(2, -25)$; y-intercept = $(0, -31)$
11. (a) vertex = $(1, -2)$; y-intercept = $(0, 1)$
    (b) vertex = $(-4, 10)$; y-intercept = $(0, 6)$
    (c) vertex = $(-3, -7)$; y-intercept = $(0, -1)$
    (d) vertex = $\left(-2, 3\frac{1}{6}\right)$; y-intercept = $\left(0, \frac{1}{2}\right)$
12. (a) vertex = $(5, -15)$; y-intercept = $(0, 10)$
    (b) vertex = $(2, 4)$; y-intercept = $(0, -8)$
    (c) vertex = $(-3, 2)$; y-intercept = $\left(0, -2\frac{1}{2}\right)$
    (d) vertex = $(4, -14)$; y-intercept = $(0, 10)$

9.5 Translations of Quadratic Functions

1. (a) quadratic
   (b) vertex
   (c) axis of symmetry
2. *example:* You can just find the size and direction of the translation, and translate the points correspondingly.

3. (a)

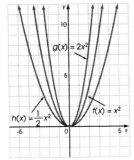

(b)

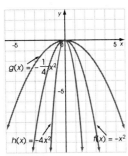

4. $h = -1$

5. (a) to obtain $g(x)$, move $f(x)$ up 3 units; to obtain $h(x)$, move $f(x)$ down 1 unit

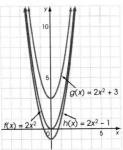

(b) to obtain $g(x)$, move $f(x)$ to the left 2 units; to obtain $h(x)$, move $f(x)$ to the right 3 units

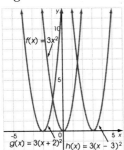

6. (a)

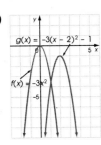

(b)

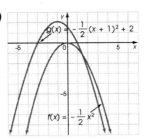

7. (a) $x = 3$, $(6, 18)$
(b) $x = 0$, $(2, 19)$
(c) $x = -2$, $(-8, 15)$
(d) $x = 5$, $(11, 42)$

8. (a) $g(x) = -2(x + 1)^2$, $h(x) = -2(x - 2)^2 + 3$

(b) $g(x) = \frac{1}{2}x^2 - 3$, $h(x) = \frac{1}{2}(x + 4)^2 + 4$

(c) $g(x) = 3(x - 3)^2$, $h(x) = 3(x + 1)^2 - 2$

9. (a) vertex $(1, 2)$, axis of symmetry $x = 1$, opens upward

(b) vertex $(2, -1)$, axis of symmetry $x = 2$, opens downward

(c) vertex $(-3, -4)$, axis of symmetry $x = -3$, opens upward

10.1 Solving Quadratics by Graphing

1. equation/root; function/zero; graph/x-intercept

2. (a) no x-intercepts   **(b)** one x-intercept

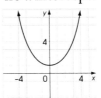   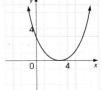

(c) two x-intercepts

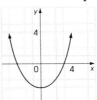

3. no, since a parabola has only two points that can cross the x-axis.

4. (a) yes   **(b)** yes   **(c)** no   **(d)** no
(e) close estimate   **(f)** close estimate
(g) close estimate

5. (a) $2x^2 - 6x + 0 = 0$ or $x^2 - 3x + 0 = 0$; 3 or 0
(b) $x^2 + 5x - 14 = 0$; -7 or 2
(c) $x^2 - 13x + 5 = 0$; (estimated) 12.6 or 0.4
(d) $2x^2 + 5x - 11 = 0$; (estimated) 1.4 or -3.9
(e) $3x^2 + 11x + 4 = 0$ (estimated) -0.4 or -3.3
(f) $x^2 - 2x - 15$; 5 or -3

6. **(a)** –7 or –3
   (b) 2 or 4
   (c) (estimated) –0.54 or –7.5
   (d) –6 or 2
   (e) no zeros
   (f) (estimated) 0.9 or –2.6
   (g) no zeros
7. Leticia made an error when she expanded $(x+2)^2$ and $(x+4)^2$ in line 2 of her solution. From line 2, the solution should be:
$$x^2 + (x^2 + 4x + 4) + (x^2 + 8x + 16) = 155$$
$$3x^2 + 12x - 135 = 0$$
$$f(x) = 3x^2 + 12x - 135$$

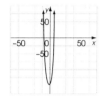

The x-intercepts are at 5 and –9.
If x is 5, then $x+2$ is 7 and $x+4$ is 9.
If x is –9, then $x+2$ is –7 and $x+4$ is –5.
8. 14 and 15 or –14 and –15
9. 23 and 24 or –23 and –24

10.2 Solving Quadratics by Factoring

1. **(a)** a polynomial equation of degree 2 of the general form $ax^2 + bx + c = 0$
   (b) a function that can be written in the form $ax^2 + bx + c$, where a, b, c are real numbers and $a \neq 0$
   (c) The graph of $f(x) = ax^2 + bx + c$ is a parabola. It opens upward for $a > 0$ and downward for $a < 0$.
   (d) substituting the value of x into the original function/equation and seeing if it is true
   (e) the zeros of a quadratic equations
   (f) the values of x for which $f(x)$ or y is zero
   (g) the x-coordinate of a point where the graphed function touches the x-axis
2. **(a)** no   **(b)** no   **(c)** yes
   (d) no   **(e)** no
3. **(a)** 0, 5   **(b)** –2, 5   **(c)** 7, 4
   (d) 3, –1   **(e)** $\frac{5}{3}, -\frac{1}{3}$ **(f)** 6, –1
4. **(a)** –3, –4   **(b)** $-\frac{1}{2}, 2$
   (c) –4, 2   **(d)** $-\frac{9}{10}, -1$
   (e) $-\frac{1}{2}, -2$ **(f)** $-\frac{5}{2}, -\frac{1}{2}$

5. Multiples of these functions are also acceptable answers.
   (a) $f(x) = x^2 - 8x + 15$
   (b) $f(x) = x^2 + \frac{3}{2}x - 1$
   (c) $f(x) = x^2 - \frac{6}{5}x + \frac{9}{25}$
   (d) $f(x) = x^2 + \frac{31}{20}x + \frac{3}{5}$
   (e) $f(x) = x^2 + \frac{6}{7}x$
   (f) $f(x) = x^2 - \frac{25}{4}$
6. Line 7: should be $(2x - 5)(2x + 37) = 0$;
   Lines 11 and 12 should be: If $2x + 37 = 0$, then $2x = -37$, then $x = -\frac{37}{2}$ or –18.5;
   Line 14 should be: If x is –18.5, then $x + 16$ must be –2.5; Line 15 should be: There are two possible solutions to the problem: 2.5 and 18.5 or –2.5 and –18.5.
7. 27 and 28 or –27 and –28
8. 5 ft
9. perimeter is $4(3x - 5)$ or $12x - 20$

10.3 Complex Numbers

2. (a)
3. A complex conjugate has the same real number part as the original number and the opposite complex coefficient part as the original number. It is used to remove the complex number from a denominator by resulting in an addition of squares, $(a + bi)(a - bi) = a^2 + b^2$, which is always a real number.
4. **(a)** true   **(b)** false   **(c)** false
   (d) true   **(e)** false   **(f)** false
5. **(a)** $3i$ **(b)** $\sqrt{11}i$ **(c)** $2\sqrt{6}i$
   (d) $6\sqrt{2}i$ **(e)** $45i$ **(f)** $\frac{5}{3}i$
   (g) –30   **(h)** $-\frac{5}{8}$
6. **(a)** $\pm 5i$ **(b)** $\pm\frac{5\sqrt{2}}{2}i$
   (c) $1 \pm 2\sqrt{3}i$ **(d)** $1 \pm \frac{\sqrt{6}}{2}i$
7. **(a)** $12 - 8i$ **(b)** $2 - 68i$ **(c)** $-2 - 2\sqrt{2}i$
   (d) $-18 + 128i$ **(e)** $22 + 29i$
   (f) $-12 + 28\sqrt{3}i$

8. **(a)** $\frac{12}{5} - \frac{6}{5}i$ **(b)** $\frac{15}{17} + \frac{8}{17}i$

(c) $-\frac{1}{7} + \frac{4\sqrt{3}}{7}i$ **(d)** $0 - \frac{2}{5}i$

9. **(a)** -1 **(b)** $-i$
   (c) i **(d)** 1
10. $9 + 13i$
11. $a = 7, b = 1$
12. possible answers: $\pm 5 \pm 4i$

10.4 The Quadratic Formula

1. **Step 1**: Factor a out of the terms ax^2 and bx. **Step 2**: Determine the value needed to complete the square by dividing the coefficient of x by 2 and squaring. Add and subtract this amount so you do not change the value of the equation. **Step 3**: To complete the square, move the last term from inside the parentheses to the outside by multiplying it by a. **Step 4**: Factor the perfect square trinomial.

   Step 5: Move $-\frac{b^2}{4a}$ and $+ c$ to the right side by using inverse operations. **Step 6**: Divide both sides by a. **Step 7**: Find a common denominator for terms on the right side. **Step 8**: Subtract the terms on the right side. **Step 9**: Find the square root of both sides. **Step 10**: Subtract $\frac{b}{2a}$ from both sides. **Step 11**: Add the terms on the right side.

2. **(a)** $\sqrt{b^2 - 2ac}$
   (b) *example*: discriminant indicates how many roots there will be; simplifies the formula calculation
   (c) roots represent the x-intercepts of the graph of the function
3. **(a)** yes **(b)** no **(c)** no **(d)** no
4. Note: Calculated zeroes may vary slightly, depending on the methods used.

   (a) $x = \frac{-9 \pm \sqrt{21}}{2}$, $x \doteq -6.8$, $x \doteq -2.2$

   (b) $x = \frac{8 \pm \sqrt{124}}{10}$, $x \doteq -0.3$, $x \doteq 1.9$

   (c) $x = \frac{-6 \pm \sqrt{324}}{6}$, $x \doteq 2$, $x \doteq -4$

   (d) $x = \frac{-6 \pm \sqrt{-144}}{10}$, The discriminant is $\sqrt{-144}$; therefore, there are no real roots.

5. **(a)** $\frac{-10 \pm \sqrt{120}}{2}$, $x \doteq 0.5$, $x \doteq -10.5$

   (b) $\frac{-3 \pm \sqrt{57}}{6}$, $x \doteq 0.8$, $x \doteq -1.8$

6. Note: Any multiple of the given equation is also acceptable.
   example: $0.5x^2 - 3x + 2 = 0$; $f(x) = 0.5x^2 - 3x + 2$
   (a) $x^2 - 6x + 4 = 0$; $f(x) = x^2 - 6x + 4$
   (b) $x^2 - 4x - 2 = 0$; $f(x) = x^2 - 4x - 2$
   (c) $9x^2 - 6x - 4 = 0$; $f(x) = 9x^2 - 6x - 4$
   (d) $9x^2 + 24x + 13 = 0$; $f(x) = 9x^2 + 24x + 13$
   (e) $16x^2 - 24x - 14 = 0$; $f(x) = 16x^2 - 24x - 14$
   (f) $49x^2 + 112x + 57 = 0$; $f(x) = 49x^2 + 112x + 57$

7. *example*: To create a new equation with the same roots as a given equation, multiply each term in the given equation by the same amount.
8. **(a)** error message or 0
   (b) Any real number multiplied by itself gives a positive result.
   (c) No square roots are possible for negative numbers under the real number system.
9. 15.2 and 16.2 or –15.2 and –16.2
10. approximately 26.5 in.

10.5 Using Discriminants and Graphs

1. In this form, you can tell whether the equation can be factored. If it can't, it is easier to apply the quadratic formula.
2. Evaluating the discriminant lets you know whether no solutions, one solution, or two solutions are possible. If there are no solutions, you do not need to complete the formula. If there are one or two solutions, you can simplify the formula by substituting the known value for the discriminant.
3. If the discriminant is positive, there are two x-intercepts. If it is 0, the vertex of the graph is on the x-axis. If it is negative, there are no x-intercepts.
4. The value of the square root of a negative number is not a real number, so there are no real solutions to the equation. Since factors must be real numbers, it is not possible to factor the equation.
5. **(a)** no real roots **(b)** two real roots **(c)** one real root
6. **(a)** two real roots **(b)** one real root
   (c) no real roots **(d)** two real roots
   (e) no real roots **(f)** two real roots
7. **(a)** $\{k \mid k = 4\}$ **(b)** $\{k \mid -4\sqrt{14} < k < 4\sqrt{14}\}$

(c) $\left\{k \mid k < -\dfrac{25}{48}\right\}$ (d) $\left\{k \mid k < 3\right\}$

(e) $\left\{k \mid k = \pm 4\right\}$ (f) $\left\{k \mid k < -\dfrac{25}{8}\right\}$

8. (a) sum = 6, product = 13

(b) sum $= -\dfrac{3}{2}$, product $= -\dfrac{7}{4}$

(c) sum $= \dfrac{14}{3}$, product $= -\dfrac{8}{3}$

9. (a) $n = \pm 14$ (b) $n = \pm 9$
10. No, the product of these two numbers cannot be equal to 30.
11. Yes, the rocket can reach a height of 120 m.

10.6 Graphs of Polynomial Functions

1. *examples:*
   (a) the coefficient of the highest-degree term
   (b) the number of times each zero occurs
   (c) a value that makes the polynomial zero
   (d) the highest exponent in the polynomial
   (e) a function having a degree of 4
   (f) a function having a degree of 5
2. A negative leading coefficient produces a graph that falls to the right. A positive leading coefficient produces a graph that rises to the right.
3. Functions of even degree have arms pointing in the same direction, whereas odd degrees produce graphs pointing in opposite directions. The number of changes in direction is at most one less than the degree.
4. (a) $a_n = 1$, $n = 5$, $a_0 = 3$
   (b) $a_n = 7$, $n = 2$, $a_0 = 8$
   (c) $a_n = -2$, $n = 3$, $a_0 = 0$
   (d) $a_n = 1$, $n = 4$, $a_0 = 1$
   (e) $a_n = -1$, $n = 5$, $a_0 = -4$
5. (a) (i)
   (b) (vi)
   (c) (v)
   (d) (iv)
   (e) (iii)
   (f) (ii)
6. 1.8
7. There are 3 different zeros. The one at 0 has a multiplicity of 2 and the other two each have a multiplicity of 1.
8. (a) 16
   (b) 2 and 4
   (c) 2 has a multiplicity of 2 and 4 has a

multiplicity of 1
(d) falls to the right
(e) opposite directions

10.7 Graphs of Rational Functions

3. (a), (d), and (e)
4. (a) $x = 6$ (b) $x = \dfrac{1}{2}$ (c) $x = 0$
   (d) $x = 0$ (e) $x = 0$ (f) $x = 0$
5. (a) $y = 0$ (b) $y = 3$ (c) $y = 1$
   (d) $y = 0$ (e) $y = 0$ (f) $y = 0$

6. (a)

x	y
-10	-0.6
-5	-1.2
-1	-6
0	undefined
1	6
5	1.2
10	0.6

(b)

x	y
-10	1.2
-5	2.4
-1	12
0	undefined
1	-12
5	-2.4
10	-1.2

(c)

x	y
-4	0.13
-2	-0.17
-1	-0.40
0	-0.75
2	-2.5
4	undefined
6	4.5

(d)

x	y
-10	2.5
-6	undefined
-1	-0.20
0	0
1	0.14
4	0.40
6	0.50

7. (a) domain: $\{x \mid x \neq 2, x \in \mathbb{R}\}$, range: $\{y \mid y \neq 1, y \in \mathbb{R}\}$
   (b) domain: $\{x \mid x \neq 0, x \in \mathbb{R}\}$, range: $\{y \mid y \neq 1, y \in \mathbb{R}\}$
   (c) domain: $\{x \mid x \neq -2, 2, x \in \mathbb{R}\}$, range: $\{y \mid y \neq 0, y \in \mathbb{R}\}$, symmetric with respect to y-axis
   (d) domain: $\{x \mid x \neq -1, 4, x \in \mathbb{R}\}$, range: $\{y \mid y \neq 0, y \in \mathbb{R}\}$

8.

vertical asymptote	$x = 2$
horizontal asymptote	$y = 1$
domain	$\{x \mid x \neq 2, x \in \mathbb{R}\}$
range	$\{y \mid y \neq 1, y \in \mathbb{R}\}$
x-intercept	-3
y-intercept	$-\dfrac{3}{2}$

9.

vertical asymptote	$x = 2, -3$
horizontal asymptote	$y = 0$
domain	$\{x \mid x \neq 2, 3 \, x \in \mathbb{R}\}$

range	$\{y \mid y \neq 0,\ y \in \mathbb{R}\}$
x-intercept	none
y-intercept	$-\dfrac{1}{2}$

11.1 Absolute Value Equations

1. *example:* Absolute value means the magnitude of a number, regardless of sign. For example, 6 and –6 both have an absolute value of 6. It is necessary to consider two cases because the expression inside the absolute value signs could be positive or negative.
2. *example:* Absolute value equations are V-shaped because negative values are not possible. Only linear absolute value equations will look like a V.
3. **(a)** 8
   (b) 14
4. **(a)** 9   **(b)** –5   **(c)** 18
5. **(a)** 8   **(b)** 2   **(c)** 9   **(d)** –10
6. $|x| = x$ for $x \geq 0$ $|x| = -x$ for $x < 0$
7. **(a)** 3, –3   **(b)** 7, –11   **(c)** 2, –5
   (d) 13, –3   **(e)** 3, –5   **(f)** 5, –2
8. **(a)** 4   **(b)** –9, –1   **(c)** no solution
   (d) 2, 8   **(e)** –2, 16   **(f)** 1, 3
9. **(a)** $x = -3$ **(b)** $x = 1,\ x = 5$
   (c) $x = -2$ **(d)** no solution
10. Carol forgot to verify her solutions.

$$|x - 8| = 3x \qquad\qquad |x - 8| = 3x$$
$$|-4 - 8| \overset{?}{=} 3(-4) \qquad |2 - 8| \overset{?}{=} 3(2)$$
$$|-12| \overset{?}{=} -12 \qquad\quad |-6| \overset{?}{=} 6$$
$$12 \neq -12 \qquad\qquad\quad 6 = 6$$

False   True
Discard the extraneous root $x = -4$.
Solution set = {2}

11.2 Radical Equations

1. *example:* To isolate a radical means to locate the term containing the variable under the radical sign on one side of the equal sign and have the remaining terms on the other side of the equal sign.
2. *example:* An extraneous root is a root to an equation which will not satisfy the original equation.
3. Roots must be checked to determine if they are extraneous.
4. **(a)** 49   **(b)** 4
   (c) 64   **(d)** no answer

5. **(a)** $\sqrt{4 - x} - \sqrt{x + 6} = 2$
   $$\sqrt{4 - x} = 2 + \sqrt{x + 6}$$
   Isolate a single radical.

   (b) $\sqrt{\sqrt{x^2 - 5}} = 4$ Square both sides.
   $$\sqrt{x^2 - 5} = 16$$

   (c) $\sqrt{x + 2} - 3 = 9$ Isolate the radical.
   $$\sqrt{x + 2} = 12$$

   (d) $5x = 1 + \sqrt{3 - 2x}$ Isolate the radical.
   $$5x - 1 = \sqrt{3 - 2x}$$

   (e) $\dfrac{\sqrt{x + 2}}{3} = 4x$
   $$\sqrt{x + 2} = 12x$$
   Clear the denominator by multiplying by the LCD.

6. **(a)** 9
   (b) 2
7. **(a)** –5   **(b)** –17, 17
   (c) 142   **(d)** $\dfrac{3}{5}$
   (e) 2
8. 3 in. and 6 in.
9. **(a)** The resistance is lower on a wet road.
   (b) Accidents 3, 4, 5, 7, 8, and 9 could have occurred in wet conditions because the coefficient of friction is low. Accidents 1, 2, and 6 could have occurred in dry conditions because the coefficient of friction is higher.

Accident number	Speed of the vehicle (mph)	Length of the skid marks (ft)	Coefficient of friction
1	55	180	0.56
2	61	144	0.87
3	50	172	0.48
4	33	107	0.34
5	64	569	0.24
6	62	215	0.59
7	40	192	0.28
8	32	40	0.85
9	75	815	0.23

   (c) 67 mph, 47 mph
   (d) No. The speed was only $\sqrt{2}$ times as fast. This can be seen by substituting numbers into the formula. Also, the two sets of skid marks could have been made under different weather conditions.
   (e) On dry concrete, the skid marks would be 172 ft, and on wet concrete, the skid marks would be 335 ft.

11.3 Rational Equations

3. (a) 0, 1, and 4

(b) −2, 0, and 2

(c) −1 and $\frac{4}{3}$

(d) −4, −3, and 3

(e) $-\frac{3}{2}, -\frac{1}{3}$, and 1

4. (a) $x(x-1)(4-x)$

(b) $x(x-2)(x+2)$

(c) $(3x-4)(x+1)$

(d) $(x-3)(x+3)(x+4)$

(e) $(x-1)(2x+3)(3x+1)$

5. (a) Solution set $\{\frac{1}{3},\ 2\}$

(b) Solution set = $\{1\}$

(c) Solution set = $\{1\}$

(d) Solution set $\{-4,\ \frac{3}{2}\}$

(e) Solution set = $\{-\frac{1}{2},\ 6\}$

6. 60 mph

7. (a) In the second line, the second term, −2, was not multiplied by the LCD.

(b) In the second line, the first term's denominator does not cancel with the LCD. The term must be changed to $\frac{-1}{x-1}$.

(c) In the third line, $-6x+18$ should be $-6x-18$.

8. $x \le -2$, $x = 1$

11.4 Rational Inequalities 1

1. (a) quadratic

(b) 2

(c) interval

3. (a)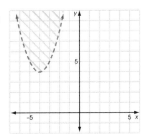

(b)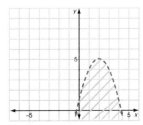

(c)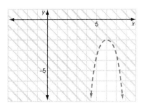

(d)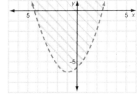

(e)

4. (a) $(-2, 5]$ **(b)** $(-\infty, -6] \cup (7, \infty)$

(c) $[-2, 3) \cup \{11\} \cup (15, \infty)$

5. (a) $(-\infty, -3) \cup (5, \infty)$ **(b)** $(-\infty, -4] \cup [7, \infty)$

(c) $[-6, -4]$ **(d)** $(-\infty, -8) \cup (11, \infty)$

(e) $\left(-\frac{1}{2}, 10\right)$ **(f)** $(-\infty, -10] \cup [4, \infty)$

(g) $\left[-5, \frac{4}{3}\right]$

6. (a) $(-5, -2) \cup (2, \infty)$ **(b)** $(-\infty, -3) \cup (5, 7)$

(c) $[2, 8] \cup [11, \infty)$

(d) $(-\infty, -3) \cup (-3, -1) \cup (6, \infty)$

(e) $[-6, 6]$ **(f)** $(-7, 0) \cup (0, 5)$

(g) $(-\infty, -7] \cup [-2, 8] \cup [10, \infty)$

(h) $(-\infty, -11) \cup (6, 9) \cup (9, \infty)$

7. (a) $(-\infty, 0) \cup (3, \infty)$ **(b)** $[-7, -1]$

(c) $(-\infty, -8) \cup (-5, 2)$

(d) $(-12, -3) \cup [1, \infty)$

(e) $(-8, 2] \cup (3, 4]$

(f) $(-\infty, -6) \cup (-6, 0) \cup (2, 10)$

(g) $(0, 2) \cup (8, \infty)$

(h) $(-\infty, -9) \cup [-3, -1) \cup [3, \infty)$

8. width ≥ 30 in.

9. $10 \le x \le 50$ bracelets per week

10. Emilio found the critical values incorrectly. The critical values are −6, −2, 1, and 4. The solution is $(-6, -2] \cup (1, 4]$.

11.5 Rational Inequalities 2

5. (a) $(-3, 3)$ **(b)** $(-\infty, 1] \cup [11, \infty)$

(c) $[-14, -2]$ **(d)** $(-\infty, -8) \cup (14, \infty)$

(e) R

(f) $\left(-\infty, -\dfrac{3}{2}\right] \cup \left[\dfrac{3}{2}, \infty\right)$

(g) $\varnothing$

(h) $\left[1, \dfrac{11}{3}\right]$

6. (a) $[0, 25)$ **(b)** $[16, \infty)$

(c) $(8, \infty)$ **(d)** $\varnothing$

(e) $(-\infty, -95)$ **(f)** $[-3, 15]$

(g) $(-\infty, 3)$ **(h)** $[28, \infty)$

7. (a) (ii)   **(b)** (iii)   **(c)** (i)

8. (a) $[1, 5]$ **(b)** $(1, \infty)$

(c) $[5, 9]$ **(d)** $(-\infty, 2)$

9. *examples:*

  (a) $|x + 1| \geq 4$ **(b)** $|x - 1| \leq 5$

  (c) $|x| < 4$ **(d)** $|x - 2| > 3$

13. Solution set = $\{-40, 120\}$

11.6 Complex Fractions

1. *example:* A complex fraction has a fraction in the numerator and/or the denominator, or contains a power with a negative exponent.

  examples: $\dfrac{\frac{3}{5}}{\frac{2}{3}}, \dfrac{\frac{3ab}{c}}{4a}, \dfrac{5b^{-1}}{\frac{3b}{4}}$

2. *example:* A complex fraction is in simplest terms when all fractions and negative exponents have been eliminated from the numerator and denominator, and when the numerator and denominator have no common factors. If there are algebraic terms, they should all be in factored form.

3. (a) $\dfrac{71}{57}$ **(b)** $\dfrac{6}{7}$

4. (a) $\dfrac{10(1+x)}{3+4x}$ **(b)** $\dfrac{9}{4}$

(c) $\dfrac{2x+2y-1}{3x+3y-2}$ **(d)** $\dfrac{x+y}{x}$

(e) x **(f)** $\dfrac{-(3y+5)}{2(y+3)}$

(g) $\dfrac{5x-19}{3x-10}$ **(h)** $\dfrac{n-5}{n}$

(i) $\dfrac{2}{2x-5}$ **(j)** $\dfrac{(x+y)(x-2y)}{x}$

(k) $\dfrac{t+4}{t+2}$ **(l)** $\dfrac{5x}{5x-16}$

(m) $\dfrac{(y+9)(y+1)}{(4y+17)(y+3)}$ **(n)** 3

5. Step 3: Factor the numerator and denominator and rewrite the fraction in simplest terms.

$$\dfrac{(3y-1)(y+1)}{2(y^2-1)} = \dfrac{(3y-1)(y+1)}{2(y+1)(y-1)} = \dfrac{(3y-1)}{2(y-1)}$$

6. (a) $\dfrac{y^2+1}{(1-y)(1+y)}$ **(b)** 2

(c) $\dfrac{1}{3}$ **(d)** $\dfrac{a+2}{a-3}$

(e) $\dfrac{-2}{5}$

12.1 Exponential Equations

2. (b) $x = 1$ **(c)** $a = 4$

3. (a) $x = 6$ **(b)** $x = \dfrac{1}{3}$

(c) $a = 5$ **(d)** $x = 4, x = -4$

4. $5^{2(-2)+3} = \dfrac{1}{5}$

  $5^{-4+3} = 5^{-1}$

  $5^{-1} = 5^{-1} \checkmark$

5. (a) $a = \dfrac{3}{2}$ **(b)** $x = 1$

(c) $a = 4$ **(d)** $x = 2$

6. (a) $a = 1$ **(b)** $x = -\dfrac{4}{3}$

(c) $a = 4, a = -1$ **(d)** $h = \dfrac{7}{2}$

(e) $x = -2, x = -1$ **(f)** $x = \dfrac{1}{4}$

(g) $a = \dfrac{4}{3}$ **(h)** $x = 9$

7. $x = 3, x = -3$

8. In the second step, the Quotient Law was used incorrectly. The correct solution is:

$$\dfrac{4^{3x}}{4^{x+1}} = 1 \qquad \text{or} \qquad \dfrac{4^{3x}}{4^{x+1}} = 1$$

$$4^{2x-1} = 1 \qquad\qquad 4^{3x} = 4^{x+1}$$

$$4^{2x-1} = 4^0 \qquad\qquad 3x = x+1$$

$$2x-1 = 0 \qquad\qquad 2x = 1$$

$$2x = 1 \qquad\qquad x = \dfrac{1}{2}$$

$$x = \dfrac{1}{2}$$

9. Using either base, the solution is $x = \dfrac{3}{2}$.

10.(a) $x = -4$ **(b)** $a = \dfrac{3}{7}$

12.2 Graphing Exponential Functions

1. (a) exponential   **(b)** $(-\infty, +\infty)$

(c) $(0, +\infty)$ **(d)** $(0, 1)$

(e) none   **(f)** the x-axis, $y = 0$

(g) increasing   **(h)** 3

2. **(a)** $(0, +\infty)$, $y = 0$, $(0, 1)$, increasing
   (b) $(0, +\infty)$, $y = 0$, $(0, 1)$, decreasing
   (c) $(-2, +\infty)$, $y = -2$, $(0, -1)$, increasing
   (d) $(1, +\infty)$, $y = 1$, $(0, 2)$, increasing
   (e) $(3, +\infty)$, $y = 3$, $(0, 4)$, decreasing
3. **(a)** move 3 left
   (b) move 1 right and 4 up
   (c) move 1 left and 2 down
   (d) move 4 left and 5 down
4. **(a)** increasing   **(b)** decreasing
   (c) increasing
5. **(a)** $y = \left(\dfrac{3}{2}\right)^x$ **(b)** $y = \left(\dfrac{2}{3}\right)^x$

6. **(a)** $y = -\left(\dfrac{2}{3}\right)^x$

7. **(a)** $(0, 5)$, $y = 0$ **(b)** $\left(0, \dfrac{4}{3}\right)$, $y = 0$
   (c) $(0, -3)$, $y = 0$
8. **(a)** $(0, 7)$, $y = 0$ **(b)** $(0, -3)$, $y = 0$
   (c) $(0, 5)$, $y = 4$ **(d)** $(0, -1)$, $y = -2$
   (e) $(0, 5)$, $y = 1$
9. **(a)** 3.43   **(b)** 5,130,000   **(c)** 1.77

12.3 Exponential Functions

1. $9151.43
2. Jamal must invest $4053.39.
3. The effective interest rates are 6.6972%, 6.7126%, and 6.7089%, respectively, so Series B is the best investment.
4. 271,835 people
5. In 1990, there were 5280 subscribers. In 1996, there were 45,150. This growth rate cannot continue indefinitely, because in about 50 years, the number of subscribers would eventually exceed the entire population of the United States.
6. The population is 1.679046×10^8.
7. $\dfrac{32}{243} A_0$

8. 5.0421×10^{-5} coulombs
9. The house will be worth $152,222.05.
10. **(a)** 3 hours
    (b) 5.872×10^9 bacteria
11. 40 bacteria
12. Graph the function $A = 500\dfrac{1}{8}$. The amount, A, will equal 1 in 71 to 72 years.
13. Graph the function $A = \$23,500(1 - 20\%)^t$. Examine the graph to find the point where y is approximately equal to $11,750. The corresponding x-value is approximately 3

years.
14. 10.516%, 10.517%, 10.517%, 10.514%

12.4 Properties of Logarithms

1. *examples:*
   (a) the number of times you have to multiply 10 by itself to get 100 is 2.
   (b) because $\log_b x$ is the exponent to which b is raised to get x
   (c) since the number of times you have to multiply b by itself to get b is 1
2. 10
4. **(a)** $2 + \log_2 5$ **(b)** $3 + \log_3 5$
   (c) $\log_6 x - 2$ **(d)** $\log_8 y - 1$
   (e) $4 \log y$ **(f)** $9 \log z$
   (g) $\dfrac{1}{2} \log 5$ **(h)** $\dfrac{1}{3} \log 7$
5. **(a)** $3 + \log_3 x$ **(b)** $2 - \log x$
   (c) $\dfrac{1}{2} \log_5 27$ **(d)** $1 + \log a + \log b$
6. **(a)** $3 \log x + 2 \log y$
   (b) $\log 4 + \log x + \log z$
   (c) $\log x + \dfrac{1}{2} \log z$
   (d) $\log_3 x - \log_3 y - \log_3 z$
   (e) $2 \log_b x + 3 \log_b y - \log_b z$
   (f) $\dfrac{1}{2} \log_8 x - \dfrac{1}{2} \log_8 y - \log_8 z$
7. **(a)** $\log_2 \dfrac{x+1}{x}$ **(b)** $\log_3 \dfrac{x}{8(x+2)}$
   (c) $\log x^2 \sqrt{y}$ **(d)** $\log_b \dfrac{x}{y}$

   (e) $\log_2 \dfrac{x^3 z^7}{y^5}$ **(f)** $\log_b \dfrac{\sqrt{x+2}}{y^3 z^7}$
8. **(a)** 1.3652   **(b)** 0.8614
   (c) 0.3869   **(d)** 1.3869
   (e) 0.8271   **(f)** 2.2708
   (g) 1.7604   **(h)** 0.5681
9. **(a)** 2.6609   **(b)** 3
   (c) 2.3218   **(d)** 0.3391
   (e) −0.3391   **(f)** −0.8218
10. *example:* The logarithm of a product is equal to the sum of the logarithms of the factors, while this is not necessarily true with the product of logarithms.
11. *example:* The $\boxed{\text{log}}$ key on a calculator applies the logarithmic function with a base of 10, so we can use the change of base formula to find $\log_2$ 7. The key sequence is 7 $\boxed{\text{log}}$ $\boxed{\div}$ 2 $\boxed{\text{log}}$ $\boxed{=}$.
12. **(a)** 10   **(b)** 2   **(c)** 5

(d) 0   **(e)** 7   **(f)** 8

13. **(a)** In the second line, the multiplication should be addition. The expansion is

$$\log x + \frac{1}{5}\log y - \log z.$$

(b) In the first line, the change-of-base formula should have been used to obtain

$$\frac{\log \sqrt{7}}{\log \sqrt{4}}.$$ The final result is 1.4037.

(c) 1.0792 should have been subtracted, not added. The answer is –0.7782.

12.5 Logarithmic Equations

1. **(a)** product   **(b)** quotient
   (c) power   **(d)** base
   (e) exponential   **(f)** logarithmic

2. **(a)** $x = \log_3 7$ **(b)** $x + 1 = \log_2 32$
   $\doteq 1.77$ $= 5$
                              $x = 4$

   (c) $x = \pm 1.08779$

3. **(a)** log; log 2   **(b)** $2x - 3$

4. **(a)** $a = 2$ **(b)** $x = -7$ **(c)** $y = 7$

5. **(a)** No, because log (–1) does not exist.
   (b) Yes, $w = -2$ is a solution.

7. **(a)** $x = 10$ **(b)** $y = 11$
   (c) $a = 4$ **(d)** $b = 625$

8. **(a)** $y = \dfrac{-23}{12}$ **(b)** $x = 3$

9. **(a)** $a = 1.27024$ **(b)** $b = 0$
   (c) $x = 1.80735$ **(d)** $y = -8.21440$
   (e) $x = 0, 2.15338$ **(f)** $a = \pm 1.07385$

10. **(a)** $x = \dfrac{13}{9}$ **(b)** $x = 5$
    (c) $w = 5$ **(d)** $a = 1$
    (e) $x = 3$ **(f)** $w = 9$
    (g) $x = 12, x = 6$ **(h)** $x = \dfrac{8}{7}$
    (i) no solution

11. The error is in the line $x + 2 \log 3 = x \log 6$. The line should be $(x + 2) \log 3 = x \log 6$. The correct answer is $x \doteq 3.16993$.

12.6 Graphing Logarithmic Functions

1. $y = \log x$ and $y = 10^x$ are inverses of one another.

3. **(a)** translate 2 left
   (b) reflect over the x-axis
   (c) translate 2 down

4. **(a)** true   **(b)** (1, 0)   **(c)** true
   (d) false; if $x = 0$, then $y = \log_b x$ is undefined
   (e) true   **(f)** true

5. **(a)** $(0, +\infty)$ **(b)** $(-\infty, +\infty)$

(c) none   **(d)** (1, 0)
(e) increasing   **(f)** $y = 1$

6. **(a)** 0.6   **(b)** 0.9
   (c) $y = \log_{10} x \leftrightarrow 10^y = x$ **(d)** $x \doteq 1.4$
   (e) $x \doteq 5.6$ **(f)** 1.41, 5.62

7. **(a)** $Q(b^a, a)$

8. **(a)** $f(x) = \log_5 x$

x	$f(x)$
$\frac{1}{25}$	–2
$\frac{1}{5}$	–1
1	0
5	1
25	2

(b) $f(x) = \log_6 x$

x	$f(x)$
–6	none
0	none
$\frac{1}{216}$	–3
$\sqrt{6}$	$\frac{1}{2}$
6^8	8

(c) $f(x) = \log_8 x$

x	$f(x)$
–8	none
0	none
$\frac{1}{8}$	–1
$\sqrt{8}$	$\frac{1}{2}$
64	2

9. **(a)**   **(b)**

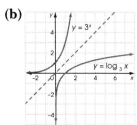

(c)   **(d)**

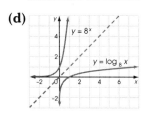

10.

11. **(a)** increasing   **(b)** decreasing

(c) decreasing   **(d)** increasing

12. (a) 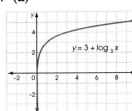   **(b)**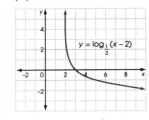

(c) 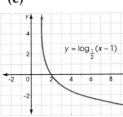   **(d)**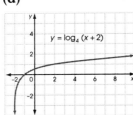

12.7 Applications of Logarithms

1. *example:* The logarithm (with base b) of a number is equal to the exponent to which the base must be raised in order to get the given number.
2. **(a)** 4.6   **(b)** 4   **(c)** 4.5   **(d)** 4.2
3. **(a)** 32   **(b)** 40   **(c)** 46   **(d)** 47
4. 5012 micrometers
5. 50
6. 11,400
7. 8 years
8. 15.4 years
9. 1000
10. 7.23 years
11. 18 years 7 months (223 compounding periods)
12. 3.18 hours

12.8 Base-*e* Exponential Functions

2. **(a)** natural (or base-*e*) exponential function
   (b) There is no *x*-intercept; the *x*-axis is an asymptote.
3. **(a)** 54.60   **(b)** 0.04   **(c)** 20.09
   (d) 1210.29   **(e)** 3250.76
4. decreasing
5.
   $$\frac{\sqrt{3}}{2} \quad \sqrt{2} \quad e \quad \pi$$
   (number line with points between 1, 2, 3)
6. **(a)** vertical translation down 2 units
   (b) horizontal translation left 3 units
   (c) reflection in the *y*-axis, vertical translation down 1 unit
7. $13,375.68

8. annual: $7,636.50, continuous: $7,647.95
9. $2,621.40
10. 10.6 billion
11. 51 cattle
12. 13 years
14. The correct solution is
$$N = 2500e^{(0.025)(90)}$$
$$= 2500e^{2.25}$$
$$= 823{,}719$$
(1.5 hours = 90 minutes)

12.9 Base-*e* Logarithms

3. **(a)** inverse   **(b)** the *y*-axis
   (c) $(0, \infty)$ **(d)** 1
   (e) $e^y = x$ **(f)** undefined
4. $y = \ln x$ and $y = e^x$ are symmetric about the line $y = x$.
5. The inverse of a function f is a function g such that $f(g(x)) = x$. So the statement that $y = \frac{1}{x}$ is an inverse function to itself means that if $y = \frac{1}{x}$ is substituted for x in the equation, then we get $y = x$, the definition of an inverse.
6. **(a)** $y = \ln x - 2$ is a translation of $\ln x$ down 2 units.
   (b) $y = \ln x + 2$ is a translation of $\ln x$ up 2 units.
   (c) $y = \ln(x - 2)$ is a translation of $\ln x$ two units to the right.
   (d) $y = \ln(x + 2)$ is a translation of $\ln x$ two units to the left.
7. 13.9 years
8. 4.6%
9. **(a)** $x = e^3$ **(b)** $x = \ln(1.5) + 1$
10. $\ln\left(\dfrac{s}{fk^3}\right)$
11. $2 \ln x + 3 \ln y - 5 \ln z$
12. 1.58 hours
13. $\ln\left(\dfrac{A}{P}\right) = rt$
14.

r	1%	2%	3%	4%	5%	6%	7%	8%
t	69.3	34.7	23.1	17.3	13.9	11.6	9.9	8.7

At a rate of 7.5%, $t = 9.2$.

15. **(a)** $2158.92   **(b)** $2191.12
    (c) $2219.64   **(d)** $2225.54

Picture Credits

Data in Tables 1: NASA; SSC Programme Ltd.

Data in Tables 2: Tom Dart; First Light © 95 Paul Barton

The Real Number System: CORBIS-BETTMANN; © Imtek Imagineering/Masterfile; *Solving Problems:* Link-Belt/ESS Ltd; Brown Brothers, Sterling, PA

Operations with Real Numbers: CORBIS-BETTMANN; First Light

Rational Exponents: First Folio; Environment Canada

Simplifying Radical Expressions: CORBIS-BETTMANN-UPI; Dick Hemingway

Multiplying and Dividing Radical Expressions: NASA; Particle Data Group, Lawrence Berkeley National Laboratory

Simplifying Algebraic Expressions: CORBIS/Gianni Dagli Orti

Solving Linear Equations and Formulas: Hawai'i Visitors and Convention Bureau/Robert Coello; Mactutor History of Mathematics Archive/University of St. Andrews; Robert Oliver Photography

Applications of Equations: Dick Hemingway; Toronto Sun/Michael Peake

The Rectangular Coordinate System: California Travel and Tourism; NASA

Multiplying Polynomials: Masterfile; CORBIS-BETTMANN

The Greatest Common Factor and Factoring by Grouping: Stock Montage Inc.; CORBIS

Factoring Trinomials and Difference of Squares: Bombardier Inc.; Manitoba Hydro

Sum and Difference of Two Cubes: CORBIS; CORBIS

Dividing Polynomials by Binomials: Lenore Blum/MSRI; CORBIS-BETTMANN

Rational Expressions: Finding Equivalent Forms: Dick Hemingway; Culture Branch, City of Toronto

Nonpermissible Values: CORBIS-BETTMANN

Multiplying and Dividing Rational Expressions: CORBIS-BETTMANN

Solving Rational Equations: Dick Hemingway; Ariel Muller Design

Differences Between Relations and Functions: CORBIS-BETTMANN; CORBIS-BETTMANN

Describing Functions: Dairy Farmers of Ontario; CORBIS-BETTMANN

Function Notation: Dick Hemingway; Dick Hemingway;

Domain and Range of Relations: CORBIS-BETTMANN; CORBIS-BETTMANN

Linear Functions: First Light; Donna McLaughlin/First Light

Direct & Partial Variation: Toronto Sun; Paul Tracy/Toronto Sun

Rate of Change and Slope of a Line: Dick Hemingway; Courtesy of Helena Mitasova, University of Illinois at UrbanaChampaign

Solving Linear Systems by Graphing: Masterfile; First Light

Solving Linear Systems by Elimination: Stark Images Photography; Toronto Sun/Paul Henry

Solving Three Equations in Three Variables: Courtesy of Canadian Wheat Growers

Solving Linear Systems by Matrices: Mactutor History of Mathematics Archive/University of St. Andrews; Dick Hemingway

Solving Linear Systems by Determinants: Mactutor History of Mathematics Archive/University of St. Andrews; Dick Hemingway

Solving Systems of Linear Inequalities: Dairy Farmers of Ontario

Linear Programming: Masterfile; Wild Woods Expeditions

Functions and Operations: NASA; NASA

Inverse Functions: Jackie Lacoursiere; Aracor

Graphs of Quadratic Functions: Marquis by Waterford; Courtesy of Tedmonds Satellite & Cellular

Completing the Square: Mike Addie, Riverside CA; Six Flags, California; First Light

Translations of Quadratic Functions: Adam G. Sylvester/Photo Researchers; David Hamilton

Solving Quadratics by Graphing: Raleigh; Masterfile

Solving Quadratics by Factoring: BC Tourism; CORBIS-BETTMANN

Complex Numbers: Mactutor History of Mathematics Archive/University of St. Andrews

The Quadratic Formula: Dick Hemingway; African Photo Safari

Using Discriminants and Graphs: NASA

Graphs of Polynomial Functions: Dangerless Aerial Sports Club; M.I.T

Graphs of Rational Functions: NASA; Dick Hemingway

Absolute Value Equations: Jackie Lacoursiere; Jackie Lacoursiere

Radical Equations: CORBIS/Lawrence Manning; CORBIS/Comnet Limited; Telesat Canada Satellite; Mactutor History of Mathematics Archive/University of St. Andrews

Rational Equations: Langford Canoe; First Light

Rational Inequalities1: Canadian Home Workshop Magazine; CORBIS/Historical Picture Archive

Rational Inequalities 2: Reuters/Joe Traver/Archive Photos; Lord Egremont, Petworth House Archives

Complex Fractions: Mactutor History of Mathematics Archive/University of St. Andrews

Exponential Equations: CORBIS/Ray Bird, Frank Layne Picture Agency; CORBIS/Layne Kennedy

Graphing Exponential Functions: Intel Corporation; Dick Hemingway

Exponential Functions: Toronto Sun/Michael Peake; CORBIS-BETTMANN

Properties of Logarithms: Mactutor History of Mathematics Archive/University of St. Andrews; Dick Hemingway

Logarithmic Equations: California Institute of Technology; Reuters/Claro Cortes/Archive Photos

Graphing Logarithmic Functions: Mactutor History of Mathematics Archive/University of St. Andrews; Mactutor History of Mathematics Archive/University of St. Andrews

Applications of Logarithms: Archive Photos; Reuters/CORBIS-BETTMANN

Base-e Exponential Functions: Dick Hemingway; Freefall Adventures, Florida School of Accelerated Freefall

Base-e Logarithms: Mactutor History of Mathematics Archive/University of St. Andrews; CORBIS

290 *Instructor's Resource Manual*